Cambridge Essential English Dictionary

SECOND EDITION

CAMBRIDGE
UNIVERSITY PRESS

University Printing House, Cambridge CB2 8BS, United Kingdom

One Liberty Plaza, 20th Floor, New York, NY 10006, USA

477 Williamstown Road, Port Melbourne, VIC 3207, Australia

4843/24, 2nd Floor, Ansari Road, Daryaganj, Delhi – 110002, India

103 Penang Road, #05-06/07, Visioncrest Commercial, Singapore 238467

Cambridge University Press is part of the University of Cambridge.

It furthers the University's mission by disseminating knowledge in the pursuit of education, learning and research at the highest international levels of excellence.

www.cambridge.org
Information on this title: www.cambridge.org/9780521170925

First published 2004
Second edition 2011

20 19

Printed in Poland by Opolgraf

A catalogue record for this publication is available from the British Library

ISBN 978-0-521-17092-5 Paperback

Cambridge Essential English Dictionary

Senior Commissioning Editor
Colin McIntosh

Commissioning Editor for US English
Wendalyn Nichols

Development Editor
Helen Waterhouse

Editorial contributors
Sarah Hilliard
Katherine M. Isaacs
Diane Nicholls
Marina Padakis
Jane Solomon

Global Corpus Manager
Ann Fiddes

Proofreading
Sarah Chatwin
Patrick Phillips

Design
Boag Associates
Claire Parson

Series cover design
Andrew Oliver

Typesetting
Data Standards Limited

Production
Clive Rumble
Chris Williams

Illustrators
Oxford Designers and Illustrators
Corinne Burrows
Ray Burrows
David Shenton

Cover images
Ana Abejon/iStock
MBI/Alamy
Yuri Arcurs/Shutterstock

Contents

Guide to the dictionary

What is an entry?

A dictionary entry tells you what a word means and how to use it. At the beginning of each entry in this dictionary is the main form of the word, in colour. This is the **headword**. A headword can be one word (**light**) or it can be more than one word (**light bulb**).

This guide will help you to use the entries in this dictionary. It will show you how to look for the entry you want and what information you will find in the entry.

Alphabetical order

The English alphabet has 26 letters. The order of the letters is:

Small letters: a b c d e f g h i j k l m n o p q r s t u v w x y z
Capital letters: A B C D E F G H I J K L M N O P Q R S T U V W X Y Z

The entries in the dictionary are in alphabetical order. We ignore spaces and punctuation marks when putting words in alphabetical order. For example, **fairy tale** is found between the words **fairy** and **faith**.

If you are trying to decide the alphabetical order of two words with the same first letter, look at the second letter. Go through each letter of the word from left to right until you find a letter that is different. The first letter that is different shows you what order the words should be in.

To help you remember the alphabetical order of English, the alphabet is shown down the side of each page of the dictionary.

1 Put these words in alphabetical order.

table book light pencil chair sock yacht hair

1 ______ 5 ______
2 ______ 6 ______
3 ______ 7 ______
4 ______ 8 ______

2 Put these words in alphabetical order.

talk take thank teacher tall today Thursday tongue

1 ______ 5 ______
2 ______ 6 ______
3 ______ 7 ______
4 ______ 8 ______

Finding an entry

When you open the dictionary, you will see a word at the top of each page. These help you to find the page that the word you are looking for is on. The word at the top of the left page is the first entry on that page, and the word at the top of the right page is the last entry on that page. If the word you are looking for comes in alphabetical order between these two words, it will be on the two pages you are looking at.

3 Draw a line from the headword to the words that it will appear between.

1 good	port...	...praise
2 police	we'd...	...which
3 early	goal...	...grandchild
4 whale	point...	...population
5 poster	DVD...	...easy

4 Which of these words will you find on the pages that start with mouse and end with must? Draw a line under the words that will be on these two pages.

mouth more much mood

my mug move Mr

mother mustn't music Ms

Variants

Sometimes words can be spelled in more than one way, or another word can be used with exactly the same meaning. These different spellings or different words are shown in brackets at the beginning of the entries:

adviser /əd'vaɪzər/ **noun** (also **advisor**)
someone whose job is to give advice about a subject: *a* ***financial adviser***

bye /baɪ/ **exclamation** (also **bye-bye**)
A1 goodbye: *Bye, see you tomorrow.*

everyone /'evriwʌn/ **pronoun** (also **everybody**)
A2 every person: *I've received a reply from everyone now.* ◦ *Everyone agreed with the decision.*

eyelash /'aɪlæʃ/ **noun** (also **lash**)
one of the short hairs that grow from the edge of your eyelids: *false eyelashes*

There are some differences in spelling between UK and US English. Go to page xvii to find out more.

English Profile levels

In the dictionary entries you will see the numbers and letters A1, A2, B1. These are English Profile levels, and they show you the words or meanings of words that you need to know at different levels. A1 words are the most basic words and should be learned first, followed by A2 words, then B1 words. You can use these levels to decide what are the important words that you need to study. In the entry below you can see that **camera** is an A1 word.

> **camera** /ˈkæmᵊrə/ **noun**
> A1 a piece of equipment used to take photographs

5 Look up these words and write down the English Profile level.

1 bread __________
2 home (noun) __________
3 home (adverb) __________
4 lucky __________
5 fast (adjective) __________
6 fast (adverb) __________

Pronunciations

Pronunciations are shown after the headword. For example, the pronunciation for the word **dog** is shown like this: /dɒg/. The pronunciations are written using the symbols of the International Phonetic Alphabet (IPA). The list on the inside front cover of the dictionary tells you how to read the pronunciation symbols. The most difficult symbols are also shown at the bottom of each page, with an example of a word that contains that sound.

The symbols ˈ and ˌ show you which part of the word to say strongly. The high symbol ˈ shows you the part of the word that you should say in the strongest voice. The low symbol ˌ shows you the part of the word that you should say in a strong voice, but not as strong as ˈ .

The dictionary entries do not show pronunciation for abbreviations used only in writing, such as **cm**, **lb**, **mm**.

6 Look up these words. Draw a line from the word to its pronunciation.

1 fish	/ˈaɪlənd/
2 dictionary	/θruː/
3 island	/saɪn/
4 knee	/niː/
5 through	/fɪʃ/
6 sign	/ˈdɪkʃᵊnᵊri/

7 Put a line under the part of the word that has the strongest stress.

1 doctor
2 incorrect
3 award
4 question
5 record (noun)
6 record (verb)

Parts of speech

A part of speech is one of the grammatical groups into which words are divided, such as noun, verb, and adjective. It shows what job each word does in a sentence. In the dictionary each word has a part of speech label which is shown at the beginning of the entry, after the pronunciation. The names of the parts of speech used in this dictionary are: *noun*, *verb*, *auxiliary verb*, *adjective*, *adverb*, *pronoun*, *preposition*, *conjunction*, *quantifier*, and *exclamation*. *Phrasal verbs* also have a part of speech label.

When two words have the same spelling but different parts of speech, they have separate entries. For example, **bite**[1] and **bite**[2] have the same spelling but are separate because **bite**[1] is a verb and **bite**[2] is a noun.

8 Look up these words. How many parts of speech do they have?

1 light ______3______
2 chat ____________
3 milk ____________
4 hot ____________
5 tax ____________
6 home ____________

9 What part of speech are these words? Look them up in the dictionary to find out.

1 opinion ____noun____
2 curious ____________
3 tent ____________
4 frighten ____________
5 together ____________
6 within ____________

noun

A noun is a word that refers to a person, object, place, event, substance, idea, feeling, or quality. For example, the words **teacher**, **book**, and **beauty** are nouns.

10 Look up these words. Draw a line under the words that are nouns.

hat	happy	actor	between	luck
chair	read	awful	compare	house

Some nouns have only a plural form and cannot be used with **a** or **an**. These nouns are called *plural nouns* and are always used with plural verbs. Nouns such as **scissors** and **glasses** are plural nouns.

scissors /ˈsɪzəz/ **plural noun** A2 a tool for cutting paper, hair, etc. that you hold in your hand and that has two blades: *a pair of scissors*

glasses /ˈglɑːsɪz/ **plural noun** A1 a piece of equipment with two transparent parts that you wear in front of your eyes to help you see better: *a* ***pair of glasses*** ◦ *She was* ***wearing glasses****.*

11 Look up these words to see if they are plural nouns, then draw a circle around the correct verb form in the sentences.

1 Where is/are my **shorts**?
2 The computer **graphics** is/are very good.
3 The **furniture** has/have arrived.
4 My **trousers** is/are dirty.
5 I think **maths** is/are very boring.

Some nouns do not have a plural form and cannot be used with **a** or **an**. These nouns have **[no plural]** after the part of speech label:

knowledge /ˈnɒlɪdʒ/ **noun** [no plural] B1 information and understanding that you have in your mind: *His* ***knowledge of*** *history is amazing.*

12 Look up the words that have a line under them. Are the sentences correct?

		correct	incorrect
1	I need an advice.		✓
2	Can you send me some informations?		
3	They bought some new equipment.		
4	I've got some sand in my shoe.		
5	Someone has stolen my luggages.		
6	I've got a good news for you.		

pronoun
A pronoun is a word that is used instead of a noun that has already been talked about. For example, **she**, **it**, and **mine** are pronouns.

determiner
A determiner is a word that is used before a noun or adjective to show which person or thing you are referring to. For example, **my** in *my old car* and **that** in *that man* are determiners.

adjective
An adjective is a word that describes a noun or pronoun. For example, **small**, **interesting**, and **blue** are all adjectives. In this dictionary adjectives are shown by the abbreviation **adj**.

13 Look up these words. Draw a line under the words that are adjectives.

afraid nibble bag react broken

adventure narrow honest immediately deep

preposition
A preposition is a word that is used before a noun or pronoun to show place, direction, or time. For example, **on** in *Your keys are on the table* is a preposition.

verb, auxiliary verb
A verb is a word that is used to say what someone does or what happens. For example, the words **be**, **arrive**, **make**, and **feel** are verbs. An auxiliary verb is a verb that is used together with another verb to make a new tense or other grammatical form. For example, **have** in *They have arrived* and **be** in *to be called* are auxiliary verbs.

phrasal verb
A phrasal verb is a verb that has two or three words. Together these words have a meaning that is different from each of the separate words. For example, **count on** and **count up** are phrasal verbs.

count on *someone* phrasal verb
to be certain that you can depend on someone: *I can always count on my parents to help me.*

count *someone/something* up phrasal verb
to add together all the people or things in a group

In this dictionary, phrasal verbs are in alphabetical order at the end of the entry for the verb. There is also a list of the most important phrasal verbs on page 468.

14 How many phrasal verbs can you find in the dictionary formed from these verbs?

1 get **2** stand **3** look **4** read

15 Choose a meaning from the box and write it next to the correct phrasal verb.

to start a journey
to argue with someone
to say or write something that is not true
to wait for a short time
to return to a place

1 fall out ____________________
2 make something up ____________________
3 set off ____________________
4 get back ____________________
5 hang on ____________________

adverb

An adverb is a word that gives more information about a verb, adjective, phrase, or other adverb. In the sentence *He ate quickly*, **quickly** is an adverb. In this dictionary adverbs are shown by the abbreviation **adv**.

conjunction

A conjunction is a word that is used to connect phrases or parts of a sentence. For example, the words **and** and **because** are conjunctions.

Irregular forms

Some forms of nouns, verbs, and adjectives have special forms or spellings. These are *irregular* forms. Irregular forms are shown at the beginning of the entry. **Broke** and **broken** are irregular forms of **break**, and **better** and **best** are irregular forms of **good**.

break¹ /breɪk/ **verb** (**broke**, **broken**)
1 A2 to separate into two or more pieces, or to make something separate into two or more pieces: *They had to break a window to get in.*

good¹ /gʊd/ **adj** (**better**, **best**)
1 A1 enjoyable or nice: *a good book* ◦ *Did you have a good time at the party?*

Irregular forms of verbs

Past tenses, past participles, and present participles ('-ing' forms) that are not regular are shown at the entry for the verb. There is also a list of irregular verbs at the back of the book that shows the infinitive form of the verb, its past tense, and the past participle.

Irregular forms have their own entries, which tell you to go to the main form of the word:

went /went/
past tense of go

16 **Write the past tense and past participle of these verbs.**

	past tense	past participle
1 break	____	____
2 make	____	____
3 get	____	____
4 swim	____	____
5 take	____	____

Irregular forms of nouns

To make nouns plural, you normally add **–s**, for example **book**, **books**. Some nouns do not have this regular plural form. If a plural form of a noun is not regular, it is shown in brackets after the headword:

> **shelf** /ʃelf/ **noun** (plural **shelves** /ʃelvz/) A2 a board used to put things on, often attached to a wall: *kitchen shelves*

17 **Look up these nouns. Write down their plural form.**

1 bookshelf bookshelves
2 child ____
3 foot ____
4 man ____
5 mouse ____
6 potato ____
7 sheep ____
8 wife ____

18 **Look up these nouns. Put a line under the correct plural form.**

1 city cities citys cityes
2 life lifes lifs lives
3 fireman firemans firemen firemens
4 tomato tomatoes tomatos tomates

Irregular forms of adjectives

Adjectives can have different forms. The comparative form is used to show that someone or something has more of a particular quality than someone or something else. To make the regular comparative form, you either add **–er** to the end of the adjective or use the word **more** before it.

The superlative form of adjectives is used to show that someone or something has more of a particular quality than anyone or anything else. To make the regular superlative form, you either add **–est** to the end of the adjective, or use the word **most** before it.

Comparative and superlative forms that are not regular are shown at the beginning of the entry:

far[2] /fɑːʳ/ **adj** (**farther** or **further**, **farthest** or **furthest**)
describing the part of something that is most distant from you: *His office is at the far end of the corridor.*

19 Look up these words. Write their comparative and superlative forms.

		comparative	superlative
1	bad	______	______
2	heavy	______	______
3	lazy	______	______
4	good	______	______
5	well	______	______

Definitions

The definition tells you what a word or phrase means. Many words and phrases have more than one meaning. Each different meaning has a number.

All the definitions in this dictionary use simple words. Words that are more difficult than usual are explained in brackets:

camel
/ˈkæməl/ **noun**
B1 a large animal that lives in hot, dry places and has one or two humps (= raised parts on its back)

camel

20 Look up the words in dark letters and answer these questions.

1 How many meanings does the verb **light** have?
2 What is the number of the meaning of **light** that is connected with being able to see?
3 How many meanings does the adjective **bright** have?
4 What is the number of the meaning of **bright** that is connected with being clever?
5 Look at the entry for **present** (noun). How many meanings does the phrase **the present** have?

21 What type of things are the dark words? Look the words up and complete the sentences with a word from the box.

sport tree shoe animal food

1 A **kangaroo** is a type of ____________
2 A **lettuce** is a type of ____________
3 **Boxing** is a type of ____________
4 A **sandal** is a type of ____________
5 An **oak** is a type of ____________

Phrases

A phrase is a group of words that are often used together and have a particular meaning. Phrases are shown in coloured letters.

In the entry for **minute** there are five meanings. Three of them are for phrases:

minute[1] /ˈmɪnɪt/ **noun**
1 A1 a period of time equal to 60 seconds: *It'll take you thirty minutes to get to the airport.* ◦ *She was ten minutes late for her interview.*
2 A2 a very short period of time: *I'll be with you **in a minute**.*
3 wait/just a minute B1 used when asking someone to wait for a short time: *Just a minute – I've left my coat in the restaurant.*
4 at the last minute at the latest time possible: *The concert was cancelled at the last minute.*
5 (at) any minute very soon: *Her train will be arriving any minute.*

If there are brackets around part of a phrase, for example **(at) any minute**, it means that you can leave that part out. So you can say *Her train will arrive at any minute* or *Her train will arrive any minute*.

If there is a slash **/** in a phrase, for example **wait/just a minute**, it means that the phrase can be used with either the part before the slash or the part after the slash. So you can say *wait a minute* or *just a minute*.

Some phrases have **etc.** at the end of them. This means that you can use the phrase with one of the words in the list, or a similar word:

3 save files, work, etc. A2 to store work or information on a computer

Some phrases have **...** after the words. This means that the phrase is the start of a sentence and you can add words to the phrase to make a complete sentence:

3 would you like...? A1 used to offer someone something: *Would you like a drink?* ◦ *Would you like to eat now?*

If you are looking for a phrase in the dictionary, you will usually find it at the entry for the first important word in the phrase. For example, **take it easy** is found at the entry for **easy** (adverb).

22 Look up these phrases. Where did you find them? Write the headword of the entry where you found the phrase.

1 standard of living ___standard___
2 lose your temper (with someone) ______
3 fold your arms ______
4 take the blame ______
5 look like ______
6 let someone know ______
7 for good ______
8 feel bad ______

Example sentences

Example sentences help you to understand a word and show you how to use the word.

Words that are often used together are shown in dark letters in examples:

He has had a lot of ***bad luck*** *in his life.*

Words that are more difficult than usual are explained in brackets:

Did you ***take*** *many* ***pictures*** (= photograph many things) *while you were in Sydney?*

23 Look at the example sentences at the entries for the words in dark letters. Use the example sentences to answer the questions.

1 What type of container do you drink **tea** from?
2 What verb is normally used with the noun **shelter**?
3 What prepositions are used with the verb **reach**?
4 What type of thing can you put in a **stack**?
5 What verb is used with **money** that means 'to use money to buy things'?
6 What do you use with a **needle** to sew?
7 Write the correct word after **need**: *I* ***need*** ___ *leave at five o'clock.*

British and American English

Although English in the UK and English in the US are very similar, there are some differences in vocabulary and spelling.

This dictionary shows you when there are differences. The labels ***UK*** and ***US*** tell you if a word or a meaning of a word is used only in British English or only in American English. If the word you have looked up is used only in British English, and a different word is used in American English, this is shown:

> **tinned** /tɪnd/ **adj** UK (US **canned**)
> Tinned food is sold in metal containers.

This entry shows you that **tinned** is used in British English and **canned** is used in American English.

24 Use the dictionary to find the American English spelling of these words.

	British English	American English
1	colour	color
2	analyse	
3	centre	
4	aluminium	
5	centimetre	
6	defence	
7	humour	
8	pyjamas	
9	scales	
10	towards	

25 Draw a line from the usual British English word to the usual American English word.

	British English	American English
1	jug	stove
2	pavement	elevator
3	trousers	fall
4	cooker	pitcher
5	holiday	vacation
6	lift	sidewalk
7	autumn	pants

Formal and informal

The labels **informal** and **formal** tell you about how a word is used. **Informal** means that a word is used with people you know and is not usually used in serious writing.

> **okay**[2] (also **OK**) /əʊˈkeɪ/ **adj**, **adv** informal
> **1** A1 safe or healthy: *Is your grandmother okay now?*

Formal means that the word is used in serious writing or for communicating with people you do not know well, for example in a shop or in a work situation.

> **madam** /ˈmædəm/ **noun** formal
> **1** B1 used to be polite when you speak or write to a woman who you do not know: *This way, madam.*

Words without a formal or informal label are used in general English.

26 Are these words formal, informal, or general? Use the dictionary to find out.

1 gig ____informal____
2 freezing ____________
3 clean ____________
4 acquire ____________
5 trendy ____________
6 attend ____________
7 terror ____________
8 snooze ____________
9 frequently ____________
10 kin ____________

Related words

Some words which are related to the headword, and which you can easily understand if you know the headword, are shown at the end of entries. Example sentences show you how to use the word:

> **beautiful** /ˈbjuːtɪfəl/ **adj**
> **1** A1 very attractive: *a beautiful woman* ∘ *beautiful scenery*
> **2** A1 very pleasant: *beautiful music* ∘ *It's a beautiful day (= the sun is shining).*
> • **beautifully** **adv** B1 *She sings beautifully.*

Pictures

The dictionary contains pictures to help you understand the meanings of words. There are colour pictures in the middle of the dictionary and black and white pictures at some entries. If there is a colour picture for the entry you are looking at, a note at the bottom of the entry will tell you to look at the colour picture:

> **sunglasses** /ˈsʌnˌglɑːsɪz/ **plural noun**
> A2 dark glasses that you wear to protect your eyes from the sun
> → See **Clothes** on page C5

Opposites

An opposite is a word that is as different as possible from another word. Opposites are given at the end of some entries to give you help in learning vocabulary and to show you the differences between words.

In this entry you can see that the opposite of **tall** is **short**:

> **tall** /tɔːl/ **adj**
> **1** A1 being higher than most other people or things: *He's tall and thin.* ◦ *It's one of the tallest buildings in the city.*
> → Opposite **short** **adj**

27 Look up these words. Write down their opposites.

1 heavy light
2 increase ______
3 friendly ______
4 guilty ______
5 high ______
6 major ______
7 noisy ______
8 rich ______
9 smooth ______
10 weak ______

Common error notes

Throughout the dictionary you will see common learner error notes. These are based on the *Cambridge Learner Corpus*, which is a large collection of students' written work, and give extra information about words that often cause problems for learners. These notes will help you to avoid common mistakes.

28 Look up the words in darker letters and read the common error note at the entry. Now write the correct versions of these sentences.

1. He gave me an **advice**.
2. I did a **mistake** in my exam.
3. He **said** me a story.
4. The house is **quite** when the children go away.
5. What time did you come to **home**?

Cambridge Essential English Dictionary online

You can look up any word in the dictionary online here: **http://dictionary.cambridge.org/essential** . You will find all the words, phrases, definitions, and examples that are in this book, and you will also be able to listen to spoken pronunciations of all the headwords. You can also find more help with learning vocabulary using our vocabulary trainer tool.

Answer key

1 **1** book **2** chair **3** hair **4** light **5** pencil **6** sock **7** table **8** yacht

2 **1** take **2** talk **3** tall **4** teacher **5** thank **6** Thursday **7** today **8** tongue

3 **1** good: goal … grandchild **2** police: point … population **3** early: DVD … easy **4** whale: we'd … which **5** poster: port … praise

4 mouth, more, much, mood, my, mug, move, Mr, mother, mustn't, music, Ms

5 **1** A1 **2** A1 **3** A2 **4** A2 **5** A1 **6** A2

6 **1** fish /fɪʃ/, **2** dictionary /ˈdɪkʃᵊnᵊri/, **3** island /ˈaɪlənd/, **4** knee /niː/, **5** through /θruː/, **6** sign /saɪn/

7 **1** doctor **2** incorrect **3** award **4** question **5** record **6** record

8 **1** 3 **2** 2 **3** 2 **4** 1 **5** 1 **6** 3

9 **1** noun **2** adjective **3** noun **4** verb **5** adverb **6** preposition

10 hat, happy, actor, between, luck, chair, read, awful, compare, house

11 **1** Where are my shorts? **2** The computer graphics are very good. **3** The furniture has arrived. **4** My trousers are dirty. **5** I think politics is very boring.

12 **1** incorrect **2** incorrect **3** correct **4** correct **5** incorrect **6** incorrect

13 afraid, nibble, bag, react, broken, adventure, narrow, honest, immediately, deep

14 **1** 18 **2** 3 **3** 7 **4** 2

15 **1** fall out – to argue with someone **2** make something up – to say or write something that is not true **3** set off – to start a journey **4** get back – to return to a place **5** hang on – to wait for a short time

16 **1** break: broke/broken **2** make: made/made **3** get: got/got **4** swim: swam/swum **5** take: took/taken

17 **1** bookshelves **2** children **3** feet **4** men **5** mice **6** potatoes **7** sheep **8** wives

18 **1** cities **2** lives **3** firemen **4** tomatoes

19 **1** bad: worse/worst **2** heavy: heavier/heaviest **3** lazy: lazier/laziest **4** good: better/best **5** well: better/best

20 **1** 2 **2** 2 **3** 4 **4** 3 **5** 2

21 **1** animal **2** food **3** sport **4** shoe **5** tree

22 **1** standard **2** temper **3** fold **4** blame **5** look **6** know **7** good **8** bad

23 **1** a cup **2** take **3** for, out **4** books **5** spend **6** thread **7** need to

24 **1** colour/color **2** analyse/analyze **3** centre/center **4** aluminium/aluminum **5** centimetre/centimeter **6** defence/defense **7** humour/humor **8** pyjamas/pajamas **9** scales/scale **10** towards/toward

25 **1** jug/pitcher **2** pavement/sidewalk **3** trousers/pants **4** cooker/stove **5** holiday/vacation **6** lift/elevator **7** autumn/fall

26 **1** informal **2** informal **3** general **4** formal **5** informal **6** formal **7** general **8** informal **9** formal **10** formal

27 **1** light **2** decrease **3** unfriendly **4** innocent **5** low **6** minor **7** quiet **8** poor **9** rough **10** strong

28 **1** He gave me some **advice**. **2** I **made** a **mistake** in my exam. **3** He **told** me a story. **4** The house is **quiet** when the children go away. **5** What time did you come **home**?

A, a /eɪ/
the first letter of the alphabet

a (also **an**) weak /ə/ strong /eɪ/ **determiner**
1 A1 used before a noun to mean one thing or person: *I need a car.* ◦ *Can I have an apple?*
2 A1 every or each: *Take one tablet three times a day.*
3 A1 used to say what job someone does: *She's a mechanic.*

> **Common mistake: a or an?**
>
> Remember to use **an** in front of words that begin with a vowel sound. These are words that start with the letters a, e, i, o, or u, or with a sound like those letters.
>
> ***a*** *car,* ***an*** *orange,* ***an*** *hour*

A&E /ˌeɪənd'iː/ **noun** [no plural] UK (US **emergency room**)
the part of a hospital where people go when they need treatment quickly: *She was taken to A&E.*

abandon /ə'bændən/ **verb**
1 to leave someone or something somewhere: *Dad had to abandon the car by the side of the road.*
2 to stop doing something before it is finished: *We abandoned the picnic when it started to rain.*

abbey /'æbi/ **noun**
a group of buildings that includes a large Christian church, where religious men or women once lived: *Westminster Abbey*

abbreviation /əˌbriːvi'eɪʃᵊn/ **noun**
a shorter form of a word or phrase, especially used in writing: *'St' is an abbreviation of the word 'street'.*

ability /ə'bɪləti/ **noun** (plural **abilities**)
B1 the skill or qualities that you need to do something: *He had the* ***ability to*** *explain things clearly.*

able /'eɪbl/ **adj**
A2 If you are able to do something, you can do it: *He'll* ***be able to*** *help you.*

abnormal /æb'nɔːmᵊl/ **adj**
not normal: *abnormal behaviour*

aboard /ə'bɔːd/ **adv**, **preposition**
on or onto a plane, ship, bus, or train: *Welcome aboard flight 109 to Paris.*

abolish /ə'bɒlɪʃ/ **verb**
to end a law or system: *Slavery was abolished in the US in 1865.*

about[1] /ə'baʊt/ **preposition**
1 A1 relating to a particular subject: *What was she talking about?*
2 UK to different parts of a place: *We wandered about the town.*
3 what/how about...? A2 used to suggest something: *How about a coffee?*
4 what/how about...? B1 used to ask for someone's opinion on a particular subject: *What about Ava – is she nice?*

about[2] /ə'baʊt/ **adv**
1 A1 close to a particular number or time, although not exactly that number or time: *It happened about two months ago.*
2 UK to or in different parts of a place: *She just leaves her clothes lying about.*
3 about to do *something* going to do something very soon: *I'm about to leave.*

above /ə'bʌv/ **adv**, **preposition**
1 A1 in a higher position than something else: *Look on the shelf above your head.*
2 A2 more than an amount or level: *This toy is for children aged four and above.*
3 B1 higher on the page: *Please send the articles to the address shown above.*
4 above all B1 most important of everything: *Above all, I'd like to thank my family.*

abroad /ə'brɔːd/ **adv**
B1 in or to a different country: *Are you* ***going abroad*** *this summer?*

abrupt /ə'brʌpt/ **adj**
sudden: *The conversation came to an abrupt end.*

absence /'æbsᵊns/ **noun**
1 a time when you are not in a place: *His absence was noticed.*
2 [no plural] the fact that something does not exist: *the absence of proof*

absent /'æbsᵊnt/ **adj**
B1 not in a place, especially school or

work: *He has been **absent from** school all week.*

absolute /ˈæbsəluːt/ **adj**
complete: *Our trip to Rome was an **absolute disaster**.*

absolutely /ˌæbsəˈluːtli/ **adv**
1 B1 completely: *The food was absolutely delicious.*
2 used to strongly agree with someone: *'Do you agree?' 'Absolutely.'*

absorb /əbˈzɔːb/ **verb**
1 to take in liquid, gas, or heat and hold it: *Cook the rice until all the liquid has been absorbed.*
2 to understand and remember something: *It's hard to absorb so much information.*

abstract /ˈæbstrækt/ **adj**
1 relating to ideas and not real things: *Truth and beauty are abstract concepts.*
2 abstract art involves shapes and colours and not images of real things or people: *abstract paintings*

absurd /əbˈzɜːd/ **adj**
very silly: *Your argument is completely absurd.*

abuse[1] /əˈbjuːs/ **noun**
1 the act of using something for the wrong purpose in a way that is bad: *alcohol abuse*
2 [no plural] the act of being violent or cruel to another person: *child abuse*
3 [no plural] rude words said to someone: *The crowds were shouting abuse at him.*

abuse[2] /əˈbjuːz/ **verb** (**abusing**, **abused**)
1 to be cruel and violent with someone: *Some of the women were abused by their husbands.*
2 to use something for the wrong purpose in a way that is bad: *He abused alcohol all his life.*
3 to say rude words to someone: *The crowd started abusing him.*

abusive /əˈbjuːsɪv/ **adj**
using rude language or violence to be cruel to someone: *an abusive phone call*

academic /ˌækəˈdemɪk/ **adj**
related to education, schools, universities, etc.: *academic standards*

accelerate /əkˈseləreɪt/ **verb**
to start to move or drive faster: *I accelerated to pass the bus.*

accelerator /əkˈseləreɪtəʳ/ **noun**
the part of a car that you push with your foot to make it go faster
→ See **Car** on page C3

accent /ˈæksᵊnt/ **noun**
1 B1 the way that someone speaks, showing where they come from: *an American accent* ◦ *a French accent*
2 a mark written or printed over a letter to show you how to pronounce it: *There's an accent on the 'e' of 'café'.*

accept /əkˈsept/ **verb**
1 B1 to take something that someone offers you: *He accepted the job.* ◦ *He won't accept advice from anyone.*
2 to say that something is true, often something bad: *He refuses to **accept that** he made a mistake.*
3 accept responsibility/blame to admit that you caused something bad that happened: *I accept full responsibility for the accident.*

acceptable /əkˈseptəbl/ **adj**
B1 good enough: *Is her work of an acceptable standard?*

access[1] /ˈækses/ **noun** [no plural]
1 B1 the fact of being able to use or see something: *Do you have **access to** a computer?* ◦ *Internet access*
2 B1 the way that you reach or go into a place: *The only **access to** the island is by boat.*

access[2] /ˈækses/ **verb**
to be able to find and see information, especially using a computer: *You will need a password to access those files.*

accessory /əkˈsesᵊri/ **noun** [usually plural] (plural **accessories**)
something added to something else to make it more attractive or useful: *camera accessories*

accident /ˈæksɪdᵊnt/ **noun**
1 A2 something bad that happens that is not wanted or planned, and that hurts someone or damages some-

thing: *a car accident* ◦ *She* ***had an accident*** *in the kitchen.*
2 by accident B1 without wanting to or planning to: *I deleted the wrong file by accident.*

accidental /ˌæksɪˈdentəl/ **adj**
happening without being wanted or planned: *accidental damage*

accidentally /ˌæksɪˈdentəli/ **adv**
If you do something bad accidentally, you do it without wanting to or planning to: *I accidentally knocked over a glass of water.*

accommodation /əˌkɒməˈdeɪʃən/ **noun** [no plural] UK (US **accommodations** [plural noun])
B1 a place where you live or stay: *rented accommodation*

accompany /əˈkʌmpəni/ **verb** (**accompanying, accompanied**)
1 B1 formal to go to a place with someone: *All children must be accompanied by an adult.*
2 B1 to be sold or supplied with something else: *The book is accompanied by a DVD.*
3 to play a musical instrument with someone else who is playing or singing

accord /əˈkɔːd/ **noun** [no plural]
of your own accord because you decide to, and not because someone tells you to: *She left of her own accord.*

according to /əˈkɔːdɪŋ tuː/ **preposition**
1 B1 as said by someone or as shown by something: *According to Susie, he was alone last night.*
2 based on a particular system or plan: *Students are put in groups according to their ability.*

account[1] /əˈkaʊnt/ **noun**
1 A1 an arrangement with a bank to keep your money there: *I paid the money into my account.*
2 a description of something that happened: *They* ***gave*** *different* ***accounts*** *of the event.*
3 take ***something*** **into account/take account of** ***something*** to think about something when judging a situation: *They took his age into account when judging his performance.* ◦ *A good architect takes account of the building's surroundings.*
4 on no account not for any reason: *On no account must these records be changed.*

account[2] /əˈkaʊnt/ **verb**
account for ***something*** **phrasal verb**
to explain something: *Can she account for the missing money?*

accountancy /əˈkaʊntənsi/ **noun** [no plural] UK (US **accounting** /əˈkaʊntɪŋ/)
the job of being an accountant: *She works in accountancy.*

accountant /əˈkaʊntənt/ **noun**
B1 someone whose job is keeping records of all the money that people or companies spend and earn

accounts /əˈkaʊnts/ **plural noun**
a set of official records of all the money a company spends and earns

accurate /ˈækjərət/ **adj**
B1 correct or exact: *accurate information*
→ Opposite **inaccurate adj**
• **accurately adv**

accusation /ˌækjʊˈzeɪʃən/ **noun**
a statement that you think someone has done something bad: *Her manager* ***made*** *a number of* ***accusations against*** *her.*

accuse /əˈkjuːz/ **verb** (**accusing, accused**)
to say that you think someone has done something bad: *She* ***accused*** *him* ***of*** *stealing from her.*

accustomed /əˈkʌstəmd/ **adj**
be accustomed to ***something*** to have done something so often or have had it so long that it is normal or comfortable for you: *He was accustomed to speaking in public.*

ace /eɪs/ **noun**
a playing card with one symbol on it, which has the highest or lowest value in many card games: *the ace of hearts*

ache[1] /eɪk/ **noun**
B1 pain that continues for a long time: *I've got* ***stomach ache.***

a b c d e f g h i j k l m n o p q r s t u v w x y z

ache² /eɪk/ **verb** (**aching**, **ached**)
to hurt continuously: *My legs are aching after all that exercise.*

achieve /əˈtʃiːv/ **verb** (**achieving**, **achieved**)
B1 to succeed in doing something difficult: *We finally achieved our goal of buying a house.*

achievement /əˈtʃiːvmənt/ **noun**
B1 something good that you have done that was difficult: *This movie is his greatest achievement.*

acid /ˈæsɪd/ **noun**
a liquid that burns or dissolves things: *hydrochloric acid*

acne /ˈækni/ **noun** [no plural]
a skin problem that causes a lot of red spots on the face

acquaintance /əˈkweɪntəns/ **noun**
someone that you have met, but do not know well: *He's a business acquaintance.*

acquainted /əˈkweɪntɪd/ **adj** formal
If you are acquainted with someone, you have met them but do not know them well: *I'd like to get better* ***acquainted with*** *her.*

acquire /əˈkwaɪəʳ/ **verb** (**acquiring**, **acquired**) formal
1 to get something: *My grandfather acquired several valuable paintings.*
2 to learn something: *I've acquired some useful skills in this job.*

acre /ˈeɪkəʳ/ **noun**
a unit for measuring area, equal to 4,047 square metres

across /əˈkrɒs/ **adv**, **preposition**
1 A2 from one side to the other: *I walked across the road.*
2 A2 on the opposite side of: *There's a bank just across the street.* ◦ *The library is* ***across from*** *the school.*

act¹ /ækt/ **verb**
1 B1 to behave in a particular way, usually a bad way: *Stop* ***acting like*** *a child!*
2 B1 to perform in a play or movie
3 to do something to stop a problem: *We have to act now to stop the spread of this disease.*
act as *something* **phrasal verb**
to do a job for a short time: *He acted as an adviser on the project.*

act² /ækt/ **noun**
1 B1 one of the parts in a play
2 something that someone does: *an act of kindness*
3 a law made by a government: *an act of Parliament*
4 a way of behaving in which someone pretends to be or feel something: *She's not really upset – it's just an act.*

acting /ˈæktɪŋ/ **noun** [no plural]
the job of performing in plays and movies

action /ˈækʃən/ **noun**
1 B1 [no plural] exciting or important things that are happening: *He likes movies with a lot of action.*
2 something that you do: *We must* ***take action*** *before the problem gets worse.*
3 out of action damaged or hurt and not able to operate or move: *My car's out of action.*

active /ˈæktɪv/ **adj**
1 B1 busy doing a lot of things: *She's still very active, even at the age of 87.*
2 B1 In an active verb or sentence, the subject of the verb is the person or thing doing the action. For example, 'Andy drove the car' is an active sentence.
3 very involved in an organization or planned activity: *He is an active member of the local drama club.*

actively /ˈæktɪvli/ **adv**
in a way that involves intentional effort: *I've been actively looking for a job for six months.*

activity /ækˈtɪvəti/ **noun**
1 A2 (plural **activities**) something that you do, especially for enjoyment: *Activities on offer include swimming and tennis.*
2 [no plural] the actions of people when they are moving around and doing things: *There was no sign of activity outside.*

actor /ˈæktəʳ/ **noun**
A2 someone who performs in plays, in movies, or on television

actress /ˈæk·trəs/ **noun**
a woman who performs in plays, in movies, or on television

actual /ˈæktʃuəl/ **adj**
1 real, not guessed or imagined: *We were expecting about fifty people, but the actual number was higher.*
2 in actual fact used to show what is really true, or to give more information: *I thought she was Portuguese, but in actual fact she's Brazilian.*

> **Common mistake: actual or current?**
> **Actual** means 'real'. It does not mean 'happening now'.
> *His friends call him Jo-Jo, but his actual name is John.*
> Use **current** to talk about things that are happening or that exist now.
> *She started her current job two years ago.*

actually /ˈæktʃuəli/ **adv**
1 A2 used when you are saying what is true about a situation: *He didn't actually say anything important.* ◦ *So what actually happened?*
2 B1 used when you are emphasizing something surprising: *A friend of mine was actually at the same concert – I hadn't seen her for years!*
3 used when you are disagreeing with someone or saying no to them: *'You never told me.' 'Actually, I did.'*

acute /əˈkjuːt/ **adj**
An acute problem is very bad: *There's an acute shortage of doctors in the area.*

ad /æd/ **noun**
short form of advertisement

AD /ˌeɪˈdiː/
used to show that a particular year came after the birth of Jesus Christ: *1066 AD*

adapt /əˈdæpt/ **verb**
1 to change something to fit a different use or situation: *The original book has been **adapted for** television.*
2 to change the way that you behave or think to fit a new situation: *It took time to **adapt to** my new boss.*

adaptable /əˈdæptəbl/ **adj**
able to change for a different situation or use: *Frogs are **highly adaptable** and live in many environments.*

adapter /əˈdæptəʳ/ **noun** UK
something that is used for connecting two or more pieces of electrical equipment to the same electrical supply

add /æd/ **verb**
1 A2 to put something together with something else, making the whole thing bigger: *Mix the sugar and butter, then add the eggs.* ◦ *Do you have anything to **add to** the list?*
2 A2 to put two or more numbers together to get a total: *Don't forget to add the cost of postage.*
3 B1 to say another thing: *She said she liked him but **added that** he was difficult to work with.*
add *something* up phrasal verb
B1 to put two or more numbers together to get a total: *Have you added up all the figures?*

addict /ˈædɪkt/ **noun**
someone who cannot stop taking a drug or doing something as a habit: *a drug addict*

addicted /əˈdɪktɪd/ **adj**
not able to stop taking a drug or doing something as a habit: *Sam is addicted to computer games.*

addition /əˈdɪʃᵊn/ **noun**
1 in addition (to *something*) B1 added to what already exists, happens, or is true: *In addition to teaching, she works in a restaurant in the summer.*
2 [no plural] the act of adding numbers together to get a total
3 a new or extra thing that is added to something: *Baby Eva is the latest **addition to** the family.*

additional /əˈdɪʃᵊnᵊl/ **adj**
extra: *We need additional information.*
• **additionally** **adv** *Additionally, we request a deposit of £200 in advance.*

address[1] /əˈdres/ **noun**
1 A1 the number of a building and the name of the street, city, etc. where it is
2 A1 a group of letters and signs used to send email to someone or to find information on the Internet: *an **email address*** ◦ *a **Web address***

address[2] /əˈdres/ **verb**
1 to write a name or address on an

a b c d e f g h i j k l m n o p q r s t u v w x y z

envelope or parcel: *A parcel arrived **addressed to** Emma.*
2 to do something in order to stop a problem: *We have to address the problem now.*

address book /əˈdres ˌbʊk/ **noun**
a book or electronic file in which you keep a list of names, addresses, and phone numbers: *She put his new phone number in her address book.*

adequate /ˈædɪkwət/ **adj**
1 enough: *I didn't have adequate time to prepare.*
2 good enough, but not very good: *The sound quality is **adequate for** everyday use.*
• **adequately** **adv**

adjective /ˈædʒɪktɪv/ **noun**
A2 a word that describes a noun or pronoun. The words 'big', 'boring', and 'blue' are all adjectives.

adjust /əˈdʒʌst/ **verb**
1 to change something slightly to make it fit or work better: *You can adjust the heat with this switch.*
2 to change the way you behave or think and become comfortable in a new situation: *They found it difficult to **adjust to** life in a new country.*

adjustment /əˈdʒʌstmənt/ **noun**
a small change that you make to something so that it works better, fits better, or is more suitable: *We've **made** a few adjustments to the **schedule**.*

administration /ədˌmɪnɪˈstreɪʃᵊn/ **noun** [no plural]
the things that you have to do to manage the work of an organization

admiration /ˌædməˈreɪʃᵊn/ **noun** [no plural]
the feeling of liking something or of liking and respecting someone for the good qualities that he, she, or it has: *I have great **admiration for** my teacher.*

admire /ədˈmaɪəʳ/ **verb** (**admiring**, **admired**)
1 B1 to look at something or someone and think that he, she, or it is attractive: *I was just admiring your shirt.*
2 to like something or to like and respect someone for the good qualities that he, she, or it has: *I **admire** him **for** being so determined.*

admission /ədˈmɪʃᵊn/ **noun**
1 B1 [no plural] the money that you pay to enter a place: *The museum doesn't **charge admission** for children.*
2 the act of agreeing that you did something bad: *Her departure was seen by many as an **admission of** guilt.*

admit /ədˈmɪt/ **verb** (**admitting**, **admitted**)
1 B1 to agree that you did something bad, or that something bad is true: *Both men **admitted to** taking illegal drugs.* ◦ *I was wrong – I admit it.*
2 to allow someone to enter a place: *It says on the ticket 'admits 2'.*

adolescence /ˌædᵊlˈesᵊns/ **noun** [no plural]
the period of time in someone's life between being a child and being an adult

adolescent /ˌædᵊlˈesᵊnt/ **noun**
a young person who is between being a child and being an adult

adopt /əˈdɒpt/ **verb**
1 to take someone else's child into your family and legally become the parent of that child: *He was adopted as a baby.*
2 to start doing or using something new: *We've adopted a different approach to solving the problem.*

adopted /əˈdɒptɪd/ **adj**
An adopted child has legally become part of another family: *They have two adopted children.*

adoption /əˈdɒpʃᵊn/ **noun**
the process of legally becoming the parents of someone else's child: *They couldn't have children, so they were considering adoption.*

adore /əˈdɔːʳ/ **verb** (**adoring**, **adored**)
to love someone or something very much: *Sarah adored her father.*

adult[1] /ˈædʌlt/ **noun**
A1 a person or animal that has finished growing and is not now a child

adult[2] /ˈædʌlt/ **adj**
1 having finished growing: *an adult male rat*

2 **A2** for adults or relating to adults: *adult education*

advance¹ /ədˈvɑːns/ **noun**
1 **in advance** **B1** before a particular time: *We booked our tickets in advance.*
2 new discoveries and inventions: *scientific advances*

advance² /ədˈvɑːns/ **verb** (**advancing**, **advanced**)
1 to develop or progress, or to make something develop or progress: *Research has advanced our understanding of the virus.*
2 to move forward, especially while fighting

advanced /ədˈvɑːnst/ **adj**
1 **A2** at a higher, more difficult level: *an advanced English course*
2 **B1** having developed to a more modern stage: *advanced technology*

advantage /ədˈvɑːntɪdʒ/ **noun**
1 **B1** something good that helps you: *One* ***advantage of*** *living in town is having the shops so near.*
2 **take advantage of *something*** **B1** to use the things that are good or that can help you in a situation: *Take advantage of the sports facilities while you're here.*
3 **take advantage of *someone/something*** to treat someone or something badly in order to get what you want: *I think she takes advantage of his generous nature.*

adventure /ədˈventʃəʳ/ **noun**
A2 an exciting and sometimes dangerous experience: *They had quite a few adventures on their travels.*

adventurous /ədˈventʃᵊrəs/ **adj**
An adventurous person likes to try new or difficult things: *I'm going to be more adventurous with my cooking.*

adverb /ˈædvɜːb/ **noun**
A2 a word that gives more information about a verb, adjective, phrase, or other adverb. In the sentence 'He ate quickly', 'quickly' is an adverb.

advert /ˈædvɜːt/ **noun** UK
short form of advertisement

advertise /ˈædvətaɪz/ **verb** (**advertising**, **advertised**)
1 **B1** to tell people about a product or service, on television, on the Internet, in newspapers, etc., so that people will buy it: *Companies are not allowed to advertise cigarettes on television.*
2 **B1** to put information in a newspaper, on the Internet, etc., asking for someone or something that you need: *The school is advertising for teachers.*

advertisement /ədˈvɜːtɪsmənt/ **noun**
A2 a picture, short film, etc. that is designed to persuade people to buy something: *a* ***newspaper/television/online advertisement***

advertising /ˈædvətaɪzɪŋ/ **noun** [no plural]
the business of persuading people to buy products or services: *Sarah works* ***in advertising***.

advice /ədˈvaɪs/ **noun** [no plural]
A2 suggestions about what you think someone should do: *This book* ***gives advice on*** *saving money.* ◦ *I* ***took*** *your* ***advice*** *and went home early.* ◦ *Can I give you a* ***piece of advice***?

Common mistake: advice

Remember that this word is not countable.

I need some advice.

~~*I need an advice.*~~

To make **advice** singular, say **a piece of advice.**

Common mistake: advice or advise?

Be careful not to confuse the noun **advice** with the verb **advise.**

I advise you to see a lawyer.

~~*I advice you to see a lawyer.*~~

advise /ədˈvaɪz/ **verb** (**advising**, **advised**)
B1 to tell someone that they should do something: *I would* ***advise*** *him* ***to*** *see a doctor.*

adviser /ədˈvaɪzəʳ/ **noun** (also **advisor**)
someone whose job is to give advice about a subject: *a* ***financial adviser***

a b c d e f g h i j k l m n o p q r s t u v w x y z

aerial /ˈeəriəl/ **noun** UK (US **antenna**) a piece of metal that is used for receiving television or radio signals

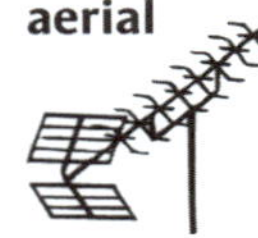

aerobics /eəˈrəʊbɪks/ **noun** [no plural] physical exercises that you do to music, especially in a class

aeroplane /ˈeərəpleɪn/ **noun** UK (US **airplane**) (A2) a vehicle that flies and has an engine and wings
→ See picture at **plane**

aerosol /ˈeərəsɒl/ **noun** a metal container that forces liquid out in small drops when you press a button

affair /əˈfeəʳ/ **noun**
1 a sexual relationship between two people when one or both of them is married to someone else: *He **had an affair** with a woman at work.*
2 a situation, especially a bad one: *The government's handling of the affair has been widely criticized.*

affairs /əˈfeəz/ **plural noun** situations or subjects that involve you: *He refused to discuss his financial affairs.*

affect /əˈfekt/ **verb**
1 to cause a change in someone or something: *How will the new road affect the community?*
2 If an illness affects someone, the person becomes ill: *The disease affects older people.*
3 to cause a strong emotion, especially sadness: *Try not to let her criticism affect you.*

affection /əˈfekʃᵊn/ **noun** [no plural] a feeling of liking or loving someone, or the things you do to show this: *Mum gave us lots of love and affection.*

affectionate /əˈfekʃᵊnət/ **adj** often showing that you like or love someone: *an affectionate little girl*
• **affectionately adv**

afford /əˈfɔːd/ **verb** (B1) to have enough money to buy something or enough time to do something: *Can we afford a new car?* ◦ *I **can't afford to** wait.*

afraid /əˈfreɪd/ **adj**
1 (A2) feeling fear or worry: *I'm **afraid of** big dogs.* ◦ *They were **afraid that** their son would get hurt.*
2 I'm afraid (A2) used to politely tell someone something bad or to politely disagree with someone: *I'm **afraid that** we can't come to your party.*

African American /ˌæfrɪkən əˈmerɪkən/ **noun** an American person whose family came from Africa in the past
• **African-American adj** *the African-American community*

after[1] /ˈɑːftəʳ/ **preposition**
1 (A1) following something that has happened: *We went swimming after lunch.*
2 (A2) following in order: *H comes after G in the alphabet.*
3 (A2) once you have gone past a particular place: *Turn left after the hotel.*
4 (B1) following someone or something: *We ran after him.*
5 despite: *I can't believe he was so rude to you after all the help you've given him!*
6 because of something that happened: *I'll never trust her again after what she did to me.*
7 US used to say how many minutes past the hour it is: *It's five after three.*
8 after all (B1) used to add an explanation to something that you have just said: *You can't expect to be perfect – after all, it was only your first lesson.*
9 day after day, year after year, etc. (B1) happening every day, year, etc. over a long period: *We went to France for our holidays year after year.*
10 be after *something* to be trying to get something: *What type of job are you after?*

after[2] /ˈɑːftəʳ/ **conjunction** (B1) at a later time than something else happens: *We arrived after the game had started.*

after³ /ˈɑːftəʳ/ **adv**
A2 later than someone or something else: *Hilary got here at midday and Matt arrived soon after.*

afternoon /ˌɑːftəˈnuːn/ **noun**
A1 the time between the middle of the day and the evening: *I played tennis on Saturday afternoon.*

> **Common mistake: afternoon**
>
> If you talk about what happens during the afternoon, use the preposition **in**.
>
> *In the afternoon I phoned my girlfriend.*
>
> ~~*At the afternoon I phoned my girlfriend.*~~
>
> If you say a day of the week before **afternoon**, use the preposition **on**.
>
> *I'm going to the dentist on Tuesday afternoon.*

afterwards /ˈɑːftəwədz/ **adv** mainly UK (US usually **afterward**)
A2 at a later time, after something else has happened: *I did my homework and went swimming afterwards.*

again /əˈgen/ **adv**
1 A1 once more: *Ask her again.*
2 A2 as before: *Get some rest and you'll feel better again soon.*
3 again and again B1 many times: *He played the same song again and again.*
4 all over again repeated from the beginning: *I'm not starting my story all over again.*
5 yet again another time after something has happened or been done many times before: *The bus was late yet again.*

against /əˈgenst/ **preposition**
1 A2 competing with someone or something: *Liverpool are playing against AC Milan.*
2 A2 touching something: *Push the bed against the wall.*
3 disagreeing with a plan or activity: *Andrew wants to buy a motorcycle, but I'm against it.*
4 against the law/the rules not allowed by a law or rule: *It's against the law to sell alcohol to teenagers.*

age /eɪdʒ/ **noun**
1 A1 the number of years that someone has lived, or that something has existed: *Mozart died **at the age of** 35.* ◦ *a child **under/over the age of** five* ◦ *Their son is **your age** (= as old as you are).*
2 B1 a period of history: *the Ice Age*
3 [no plural] the state of being old: *Some wines improve **with age**.*

aged /eɪdʒd/ **adj**
A2 having a particular age: *They have one daughter, aged three.*

agency /ˈeɪdʒᵊnsi/ **noun** (plural **agencies**)
B1 a business that provides a service: *an advertising agency*

agenda /əˈdʒendə/ **noun**
a list of subjects that people will discuss at a meeting: *There are several items **on the agenda**.*

agent /ˈeɪdʒᵊnt/ **noun**
1 someone whose job is to deal with business for someone else: *Please contact our agent in Spain for more information.*
2 someone who tries to find out secret information, especially about another country: *a **secret agent***

ages /ˈeɪdʒɪz/ **plural noun** informal
B1 a very long time: *I've been waiting here **for ages**.*

aggressive /əˈgresɪv/ **adj**
angry and violent towards another person: *aggressive behaviour*
• **aggressively** **adv** *These dogs sometimes behave aggressively.*

ago /əˈgəʊ/ **adv**
A2 in the past: *It happened a long time ago.*

agony /ˈægəni/ **noun** (plural **agonies**)
very bad pain: *She was **in agony** after her operation.*

agree /əˈgriː/ **verb** (**agreeing**, **agreed**)
1 A2 to have the same opinion as someone: *I **agree with** you.* ◦ *We all **agreed that** mistakes had been made.* ◦ *They have finally **agreed on** a name for their new dog.*
2 B1 to decide something with someone: *They **agreed to** meet on Sunday.*
3 to say you will do something that someone asks you to do: *She **agreed to** help him.*

agree with *something* **phrasal verb**

to think that something is morally right: *I don't agree with hunting.*

agreement /əˈgriːmənt/ **noun**
1 a promise or decision made between two or more people: *The company and the union* ***reached an agreement****.*
2 [no plural] a situation in which all the people involved in something have the same opinion: *Not everyone was* ***in agreement****.*

agriculture /ˈægrɪkʌltʃəʳ/ **noun** [no plural]
the work of growing plants and taking care of animals that are used for food
• **agricultural** /ˌægrɪˈkʌltʃᵊrᵊl/ **adj** *agricultural machinery*

ahead /əˈhed/ **adj, adv**
1 B1 in front: *She walked* ***ahead of*** *us.*
2 B1 in the future: *He has a difficult time* ***ahead of*** *him.*
3 with more points than someone else in a competition: *Barcelona were ahead after ten minutes.*
4 go ahead informal said to allow someone to do something: *'Can I use your phone?' 'Sure, go ahead.'*

aid /eɪd/ **noun**
1 help, or something such as food or equipment that gives help: *Emergency aid was sent to the flood victims.*
◦ *teaching aids*
2 in aid of *someone/something* UK in order to get money for a group of people who need it: *There's a concert in aid of famine relief.*

AIDS (also **Aids**) /eɪdz/ **noun** [no plural]
a serious illness that stops the body from fighting other illnesses

aim[1] /eɪm/ **noun**
B1 a result that you try to achieve: *The* ***aim of*** *the movie was to make people laugh.*

aim[2] /eɪm/ **verb**
1 B1 to try to do something: *We're* ***aiming for*** *a 10% increase in sales.*
2 to point a weapon towards someone or something: *He* ***aimed*** *the gun* ***at*** *the target.*
3 be aimed at *someone* to be intended to influence a particular person or group: *These advertisements are aimed at young people.*

air /eəʳ/ **noun**
1 A2 [no plural] the mixture of gases around the Earth that we breathe: *I love the smell of the air in the mountains.*
2 A2 [no plural] used especially before another noun about activities that involve planes: *air travel*
3 the air the space above and around things: *He fired his gun into the air.*

air conditioning /ˌeə kᵊnˈdɪʃᵊnɪŋ/ **noun** [no plural]
B1 a system that keeps the air cool in a building or car

aircraft /ˈeəkrɑːft/ **noun** (plural **aircraft**)
a vehicle that can fly

air force /ˈeə ˌfɔːs/ **noun**
B1 the part of a country's military organization that uses planes

airline /ˈeəlaɪn/ **noun**
B1 a company that takes people and things to places in planes

airmail /ˈeəmeɪl/ **noun** [no plural]
the system of sending letters or parcels by plane

airplane /ˈeəpleɪn/ **noun** US (UK **aeroplane**)
a vehicle that flies and has an engine and wings

airport /ˈeəpɔːt/ **noun**
A2 a place where planes take off and land

aisle /aɪl/ **noun**
1 a passage between the lines of seats in a plane, church, theatre, etc.
2 a passage between the shelves in a supermarket

alarm[1] /əˈlɑːm/ **noun**
1 B1 a loud noise that tells you there is danger: *a* ***fire alarm***
2 B1 a clock that makes a noise to wake you: *The* ***alarm went off*** *at 5.30.*
3 [no plural] a sudden feeling of fear that something bad might happen: *There's no need for alarm – we're safe.*

alarm[2] /əˈlɑːm/ **verb**
to worry someone: *I didn't want to alarm him by saying that she was ill.*

aisle

alarm clock /əˈlɑːm ˌklɒk/ **noun**
A2 a clock that makes a noise to wake you

alarm clock

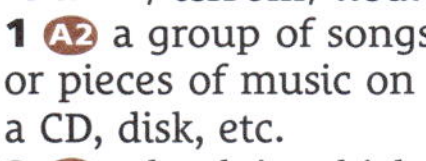

album /ˈælbəm/ **noun**
1 A2 a group of songs or pieces of music on a CD, disk, etc.
2 A2 a book in which you keep photographs, stamps, etc.

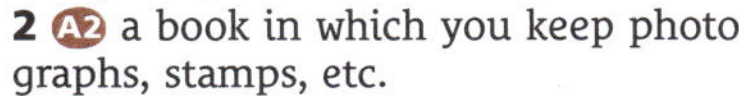

alcohol /ˈælkəhɒl/ **noun** [no plural]
1 A2 drinks such as wine and beer that can make you drunk
2 A2 the substance that can make you drunk that is produced in the process of making wine, beer, etc.

alcoholic /ˌælkəˈhɒlɪk/ **adj**
B1 containing alcohol: *alcoholic drinks*

alert /əˈlɜːt/ **adj**
quick to notice things around you

A level /ˈeɪ ˌlev(ə)l/ **noun**
in the UK, an exam taken at the age of 18, or the qualification itself

algebra /ˈældʒɪbrə/ **noun** [no plural]
a type of mathematics in which numbers are shown by letters and symbols

alien /ˈeɪliən/ **noun**
a creature from another planet

alike /əˈlaɪk/ **adj**, **adv**
B1 similar, or in a similar way: *My mother and I look alike.* ◦ *We think alike.*

alive /əˈlaɪv/ **adj**
B1 living, not dead: *Are your grandparents still alive?*

all[1] /ɔːl/ **pronoun, determiner**
1 A1 every person or thing in a group: *We were all dancing.*
2 A1 for the whole of a period of time: *It's rained all week.*
3 A2 the whole amount of something: *He spends **all of** his money on clothes.*
4 B1 the only thing: *All I want is a new car.*
5 **at all** B1 in any way: *He hasn't changed at all.* ◦ *Can I help you at all?*
6 **in all** used to show the total amount of something: *There were twenty people at the meeting in all.*

Common mistake: all + period of time

You do not say 'the' when you use **all** + a period of time.

all day/morning/week/year/summer
~~*all the day/morning/week/year/summer*~~

all[2] /ɔːl/ **adv**
1 A2 completely or very: *You're all wet!*
2 **all over...** A2 everywhere in a particular place: *He travelled all over the world.*
3 **one, two, etc. all** B1 used to say that two players or teams have the same number of points in a game: *It was three all at half-time.*
4 **all along** from the beginning of a period of time: *I knew all along that it was a mistake.*
5 **all in all** considering everything: *All in all, it was a great holiday.*

allergic /əˈlɜːdʒɪk/ **adj**
having an allergy: *I'm **allergic to** nuts.*

allergy /ˈælədʒi/ **noun** (plural **allergies**)
a medical problem in which you get sick if you eat, breathe, or touch something: *He has an **allergy to** cats.*

alley /ˈæli/ **noun**
a narrow street between buildings

alligator

alligator /ˈælɪgeɪtə(r)/ **noun**
an animal with a long mouth and sharp teeth, that

a b c d e f g h i j k l m n o p q r s t u v w x y z

lives in hot areas with water

allow /əˈlaʊ/ **verb**
B1 to say that someone can do something: *They didn't allow me to finish what I was doing.* ◦ *Smoking is not allowed in the restaurant.* ◦ *You're not allowed to walk on the grass here.*

allowance /əˈlaʊəns/ **noun**
money that you are given regularly to pay for a particular thing: *a clothes allowance*

all right[1] /ˌɔːl ˈraɪt/ **adj**, **adv** (also **alright**)
1 A1 happening successfully or without problems: *Did the interview go all right?*
2 A2 safe or well: *You look pale – are you all right?*
3 A2 used to ask if you can do something or to say that someone can do something: *Is it all right if I put some music on?*
4 B1 good enough, although not excellent: *The hotel wasn't great but it was all right.*
5 that's all right A2 used as an answer when someone thanks you: *'Thanks for cleaning the kitchen.' 'That's all right.'*
6 that's all right A2 something you say when someone says sorry to show that you are not angry: *'I'm sorry, I forgot all about your party.' 'That's all right.'*

all right[2] /ˌɔːl ˈraɪt/ **exclamation** (also **alright**)
A1 used to say yes to a suggestion: *'How about going out for dinner?' 'All right.'*

ally /ˈælaɪ/ **noun** (plural **allies**)
a person or country that helps you when you are arguing or fighting with another person or country

almost /ˈɔːlməʊst/ **adv**
A2 nearly: *I almost missed the bus.* ◦ *We've almost finished.* ◦ *She's almost 18 years old.*

alone /əˈləʊn/ **adj**, **adv**
1 A2 without other people: *She lives alone.* ◦ *I don't like being alone.*
2 without any more or anything else: *Last year alone the company made a million dollars.*
3 leave *someone* alone to stop talking to someone or annoying them: *Leave him alone – he's tired.*
4 leave *something* alone to stop touching something: *Leave your hair alone!*

along[1] /əˈlɒŋ/ **preposition**
1 A2 from one part of a road, river, etc. to another: *a walk along the beach*
2 B1 in a line next to something long: *There is a row of new houses along the river.*

along[2] /əˈlɒŋ/ **adv**
1 B1 forward: *We were just walking along, talking.*
2 come along to arrive somewhere: *Three buses came along at the same time.*
3 bring/take *someone* along B1 to take someone with you to a place: *Can I bring some friends along to the party?*

alongside /əˌlɒŋˈsaɪd/ **adv**, **preposition**
next to someone or something: *A car pulled up alongside ours.*

aloud /əˈlaʊd/ **adv**
B1 in a way that other people can hear: *I laughed aloud.*

alphabet /ˈælfəbet/ **noun**
B1 a set of letters used for writing a language: *The English alphabet starts with A and ends with Z.*

alphabetical /ˌælfəˈbetɪkəl/ **adj**
in the same order as the letters of the alphabet: *Put the names **in alphabetical order**.*
• **alphabetically** **adv** *The books are arranged alphabetically.*

already /ɔːlˈredi/ **adv**
1 A2 before now, or before a time in the past: *I've already told him.*
2 B1 used to say that something has happened earlier than you expected: *I can't believe you've already finished!*

alright /ɔːlˈraɪt/ **adj**, **adv**, **exclamation**
another spelling of all right

also /ˈɔːlsəʊ/ **adv**
A1 in addition: *She speaks French and also a little Spanish.*

alter /ˈɔːltəʳ/ **verb**
to change, or to make someone or something change: *A new haircut can really alter your appearance.*

alteration /ˌɔːltəʳˈeɪʃən/ **noun**
a change: *We've* ***made*** *a few* ***alterations to*** *the kitchen.*

alternate[1] /ɔːlˈtɜːnət/ **adj**
1 one out of every two days, weeks, years, etc.: *I work alternate Saturdays.*
2 US different: *an alternate plan*
• **alternately adv**

alternate[2] /ˈɔːltəneɪt/ **verb** (**alternating, alternated**)
If two things alternate, one thing happens, then the other thing happens, then the first thing happens again: *She easily* ***alternates between*** *Spanish and English.*

alternative[1] /ɔːlˈtɜːnətɪv/ **noun**
one of two or more things that you can choose between: *Olive oil is a healthy* ***alternative to*** *butter.*

alternative[2] /ɔːlˈtɜːnətɪv/ **adj**
1 different: *We can make alternative arrangements if necessary.*
2 different from what is usual or traditional: *an alternative lifestyle*

alternatively /ɔːlˈtɜːnətɪvli/ **adv**
used to give a second possibility: *We could go there by train or, alternatively, I could drive.*

although /ɔːlˈðəʊ/ **conjunction**
1 B1 despite the fact that: *She walked home by herself, although she knew it was dangerous.*
2 B1 but: *He's coming tomorrow, although I don't know what time.*

altogether /ˌɔːltəˈgeðəʳ/ **adv**
1 B1 in total: *There were twenty people there altogether.*
2 completely: *The train slowed down and then stopped altogether.*
3 used to make a statement about several things you have mentioned: *Altogether, I'd say the party was a great success.*

aluminium /ˌæljəˈmɪniəm/ **noun** [no plural] UK (US **aluminum** /əˈluːmɪnəm/)
a light, silver-coloured metal

always /ˈɔːlweɪz/ **adv**
1 A1 every time, or at all times: *I always walk to work.*
2 A2 at all times in the past: *We've always lived here.*
3 forever: *I will always remember you.*
4 B1 used to suggest something: *You can always stay with us if you miss your flight.*

am strong /æm/ weak /əm/, /m/
present simple of be, used with 'I'

a.m. /ˌeɪˈem/
A1 in the morning: *We're open from 9 a.m. to 5 p.m. daily.*

amateur[1] /ˈæmətəʳ/ **adj**
doing something as a hobby: *an amateur photographer*

amateur[2] /ˈæmətəʳ/ **noun**
someone who does something as a hobby

amaze /əˈmeɪz/ **verb** (**amazing, amazed**)
to make someone very surprised: ***It amazes me*** *how much energy you have.*

amazed /əˈmeɪzd/ **adj**
B1 very surprised: *I was* ***amazed at*** *the price.*

amazement /əˈmeɪzmənt/ **noun** [no plural]
the state of being very surprised: *I watched* ***in amazement****.*

amazing /əˈmeɪzɪŋ/ **adj**
1 A2 very good: *My trip to Thailand was really amazing.*
2 B1 very surprising: ***It's amazing that*** *they survived the crash.*
• **amazingly adv** B1 *She played amazingly well.*

ambassador /æmˈbæsədəʳ/ **noun**
an important person who officially represents his or her country in a different country: *the American* ***ambassador to*** *Brazil*

ambition /æmˈbɪʃən/ **noun**
1 B1 something that you want to do in your life: *My ambition is to become a doctor.*
2 [no plural] a strong feeling that you want to be successful or powerful: *He has no ambition.*

a b c d e f g h i j k l m n o p q r s t u v w x y z

ambitious /æmˈbɪʃəs/ **adj**
1 wanting to be successful or powerful: *an ambitious young lawyer*
2 An ambitious plan will need a lot of work and will be difficult to achieve: *This is our most ambitious project so far.*

ambulance

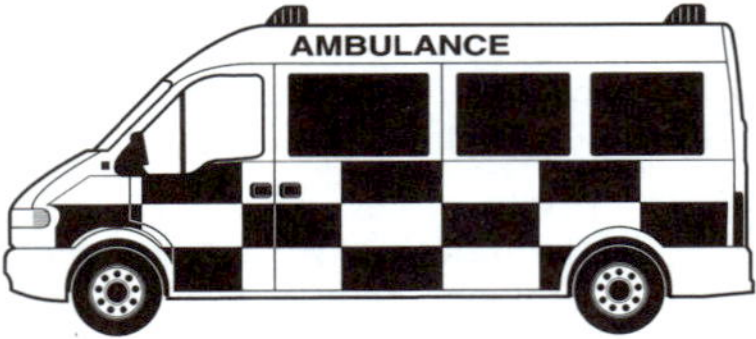

ambulance /ˈæmbjələns/ **noun**
A2 a vehicle that takes people to hospital when they are ill or hurt

American football /əˌmerɪkᵊn ˈfʊt bɔːl/ **noun** [no plural] UK (US **football**)
a game for two teams in which players move a ball along the field by running with it or throwing it
→ See **Sports 2** on page C16

among /əˈmʌŋ/ **preposition** (also **amongst** /əˈmʌŋst/)
1 A2 in the middle of something: *He disappeared among the crowds.*
2 A2 in a particular group: *The decision will be popular among students.*
3 to each one in a group: *She divided the cake among the children.*

amount[1] /əˈmaʊnt/ **noun**
B1 how much there is of something: *He ate a huge* ***amount of*** *food.*

amount[2] /əˈmaʊnt/ **verb**
amount to *something* **phrasal verb**
to have a particular total: *The cost of repairing the roof amounted to £900.*

amuse /əˈmjuːz/ **verb** (**amusing**, **amused**)
1 to make someone smile or laugh: *I thought this article might amuse you.*
2 to keep someone interested and help them to enjoy themselves: *Be sure to pack some games for the children to* ***amuse themselves*** *with.*

amusement /əˈmjuːzmənt/ **noun**
[no plural] the feeling that you have when something makes you smile or laugh: *I watched the performance* ***with*** *great* ***amusement****.*

amusement park /əˈmjuːzmənt ˌpɑːk/ **noun**
a large park where you can ride on machines and have fun

amusing /əˈmjuːzɪŋ/ **adj**
B1 funny: *an amusing letter*

an weak /ᵊn/ strong /æn/ **determiner**
A1 used instead of 'a' when the next word starts with a vowel sound: *an apple* ◦ *an hour*

anaesthetic UK (US **anesthetic**) /ˌænəsˈθetɪk/ **noun**
a drug that stops you from feeling pain during an operation: *The operation is done* ***under anaesthetic*** *(= using anaesthetic).*

analyse (**analysing**, **analysed**) UK (US **analyze**) /ˈænᵊlaɪz/ **verb**
to look at and think about something carefully, in order to understand it: *to analyse information*

analysis /əˈnæləsɪs/ **noun** (plural **analyses** /əˈnæləsiːz/)
the process of analysing something: *A sample of soil was sent* ***for analysis****.*

ancestor /ˈænsestəʳ/ **noun**
a person in your family who lived a long time ago: *My ancestors came from Ireland.*

anchor

anchor /ˈæŋkəʳ/ **noun**
a heavy metal object that is dropped into water to stop a boat from moving

ancient /ˈeɪnʃᵊnt/ **adj**
B1 from a very long time ago: *ancient Greece* ◦ *an ancient statue*

and strong /ænd/ weak /ənd/, /ən/ **conjunction**
1 A1 used to join two words or two parts of a sentence: *tea and coffee* ◦ *We were tired and hungry.*
2 A1 used to say that one thing happens after another thing: *I got dressed and had breakfast.*
3 B1 used between two words that are the same to make their meaning stronger: *We laughed and laughed.*

anesthetic **noun**
the US spelling of anaesthetic

angel /ˈeɪndʒᵊl/ **noun**
B1 a creature like a human with wings, who some people believe lives with God in heaven

angel

anger /ˈæŋgəʳ/ **noun** [no plural]
the feeling that you want to shout at someone or hurt them because they have done something bad

angle /ˈæŋgl/ **noun**
1 a space between two lines or surfaces that meet at one point, which you measure in degrees: *an angle of 90 degrees*
2 the way you think about a situation: *Try looking at the problem* ***from*** *another* ***angle****.*

angle

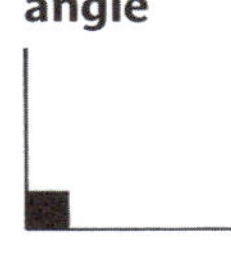

angrily /ˈæŋgrɪli/ **adv**
B1 in a way that shows anger: *He said it angrily.*

angry /ˈæŋgri/ **adj** (**angrier**, **angriest**)
A2 feeling that you want to shout at someone or hurt them because they have done something bad: *He's really* ***angry with*** *me for upsetting Sophie.*

animal /ˈænɪmᵊl/ **noun**
1 A1 something that lives and moves but is not a person, bird, fish, or insect: *a wild animal* ◦ *She supports* ***animal rights*** *(= the idea that animals should be treated well by people).*
2 anything that lives and moves, including people, birds, etc.: *Are humans the only animals that use language?*

ankle /ˈæŋkl/ **noun**
B1 the part of your leg that is just above your foot

ankle

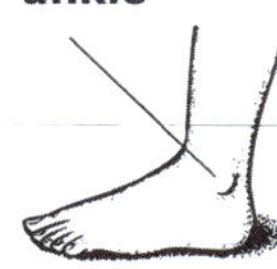

anniversary /ˌænɪˈvɜːsᵊri/ **noun** (plural **anniversaries**)
B1 a day on which you remember or celebrate something that happened on that day in the past: *a wedding anniversary* ◦ *the 50th anniversary of Kennedy's death*

announce /əˈnaʊns/ **verb** (**announcing**, **announced**)
B1 to tell people new information, especially officially: *The company has announced plans to open six new stores.*

announcement /əˈnaʊnsmənt/ **noun**
B1 something that someone says officially, giving new information about something: *The Prime Minister* ***made*** *an unexpected* ***announcement*** *this morning.*

announcer /əˈnaʊnsəʳ/ **noun**
someone who describes what is happening on a live radio or television programme: *a sports announcer*

annoy /əˈnɔɪ/ **verb**
B1 to make someone a little angry: *He's always late and it's starting to annoy me.*

annoyed /əˈnɔɪd/ **adj**
B1 a little angry: *I was* ***annoyed with*** *Jack for being late.*

annoying /əˈnɔɪɪŋ/ **adj**
B1 making you feel a little angry: *He has an* ***annoying habit*** *of interrupting people.*

annual /ˈænjuəl/ **adj**
1 B1 happening once a year: *an annual meeting*
2 B1 measured over a period of one year: *What is your annual income?*
• **annually** **adv** *The festival takes place annually.*

anonymous /əˈnɒnɪməs/ **adj**
from or by someone who does not say or write their name: *an anonymous phone call*
• **anonymously** **adv** *He made the complaint anonymously.*

another /əˈnʌðəʳ/ **pronoun, determiner**
1 A2 one more: *Would you like another drink?* ◦ *They're having another baby.*

a b c d e f g h i j k l m n o p q r s t u v w x y z

2 A2 a different thing or person: *I'm going to look for another job.* ◦ *The disease spreads easily from one person to another.*

> **Common mistake: another or other?**
>
> **Another** means 'one other' and is used with a singular noun. It is written as one word.
>
> *Would you like another cup of coffee?*
>
> ~~*Would you like other cup of coffee?*~~
>
> **Other** is used with a plural noun and means different things or people than the ones you are talking about.
>
> *She had other ambitions.*
>
> ~~*She had another ambitions.*~~

answer[1] /ˈɑːnsəʳ/ **verb**

1 A1 to speak or write back to someone who has asked you a question: *I asked her what time it was, but she didn't answer.* ◦ *I must answer his letter.*

2 A2 to say hello to someone who has telephoned you: *Could someone answer the phone?*

3 B1 to write or say something as a reply to a question in a test

4 to open the door to someone who has arrived: *I knocked several times, but no one answered.*

answer[2] /ˈɑːnsəʳ/ **noun**

1 A1 something that you say or write back to someone who has asked you a question: *I asked him if he was going, but I didn't hear his answer.*

2 A2 the act of picking up a telephone or opening a door: *I rang the bell, but there was no answer.*

3 A2 the correct information given as a reply to a question in a test: *Did you get the answer to question six?*

4 B1 a way of stopping a problem: *It's a big problem, and I don't know what the answer is.*

answering machine /ˈɑːnsərɪŋ məˌʃiːn/ **noun** (also UK **answerphone** /ˈɑːnsəfəʊn/)

a machine that records your message if you telephone someone and they do not answer: *I left a message **on** her **answering machine**.*

ant /ænt/ **noun**

B1 a small insect that lives in groups in the ground

→ See picture at **insect**

antenna /ænˈtenə/ **noun**

1 (plural **antennae**) one of two long, thin parts on the head of an insect or sea creature, used for feeling things

2 (plural **antennas**) mainly US (UK usually **aerial**) a piece of metal that is used for receiving television or radio signals

anti- /ænti-/ **prefix**

1 opposed to or against: *anti-pollution laws* ◦ *anti-American groups*

2 fighting or preventing: *powerful antibiotics* ◦ *an anti-theft device*

antibiotic /ˌæntɪbaɪˈɒtɪk/ **noun**

a medicine that cures infections by destroying bad bacteria: *He is taking antibiotics for an ear infection.*

anti-clockwise /ˌæntiˈklɒkwaɪz/ **adj**, **adv** UK (US **counterclockwise**)

in the opposite direction to the way the hands (= parts that point to the numbers) of a clock move: *Turn the knob anti-clockwise.*

→ See picture at **clockwise**

antique[1] /ænˈtiːk/ **noun**

B1 an object that is old, and often rare or beautiful: *an antique shop*

antique[2] /ænˈtiːk/ **adj**

B1 old and often rare or beautiful: *antique furniture*

antiseptic /ˌæntiˈseptɪk/ **noun**

a substance that you put on an injury to prevent infection: *He put some antiseptic on the cut on his finger.*

• **antiseptic adj** *antiseptic cream*

anxiety /æŋˈzaɪəti/ **noun** (plural **anxieties**)

the feeling of being very worried

anxious /ˈæŋkʃəs/ **adj**

1 B1 worried and very nervous: *She's very **anxious about** her exams.*

2 wanting something to happen soon: *He's **anxious to** get home.*

• **anxiously adv** *We waited anxiously by the phone.*

any[1] /ˈeni/ **determiner**, **pronoun**

1 A1 used in questions and negative

statements to mean 'some': *Is there any cake left?* ◦ *I haven't read* ***any of*** *his books.*
2 A1 used to mean 'one' when it is not important which one: *Any of those shirts would be fine.*

any² /ˈeni/ **adv**
B1 used in questions and negative statements before a comparative adjective to make the sentence stronger: *Do you feel any better?* ◦ *I can't walk any faster.*

anybody /ˈeniˌbɒdi/ **pronoun**
A2 another word for anyone

anyhow /ˈenihaʊ/ **adv**
another word for anyway

any more /ˌeni ˈmɔːʳ/ **adv** (also **anymore**)
A2 used to say that something is different now from what it was in the past: *This coat doesn't fit me any more.*

anyone /ˈeniwʌn/ **pronoun**
1 A2 used in questions and negative statements to mean 'a person or people': *I didn't know anyone at the party.*
2 B1 any person or any people: *Anyone could do that – it's easy.*

anyplace /ˈenipleɪs/ **adv** US
another word for anywhere

anything /ˈeniθɪŋ/ **pronoun**
1 A1 used in questions and negative statements to mean 'something': *I haven't got anything to wear.* ◦ *Was there* ***anything else*** *you wanted to say?*
2 A1 any object, event, or situation: *Tom will eat almost anything.*

anytime /ˈenitaɪm/ **adv** (also UK **any time**)
at a time that is not decided or agreed: *Come round to see me anytime.*

anyway /ˈeniweɪ/ **adv**
1 A2 although something happened or is true: *I hate carrots, but I ate them anyway.*
2 A2 used when you are returning to an earlier subject: *Anyway, as I said, I'll be away next week.*
3 B1 used to give a more important reason for something that you are saying: *I don't need a car, and I can't afford one anyway.*

anywhere /ˈeniweəʳ/ **adv**
1 A2 in or to any place: *Just sit anywhere.* ◦ *I couldn't find a post office anywhere.*
2 A2 used in questions and negative statements to mean 'a place': *He doesn't have anywhere to stay.* ◦ *Is there* ***anywhere else*** *you'd like to go while you're here?*

apart /əˈpɑːt/ **adv**
1 B1 separated by an amount of space or a period of time: *Stand with your feet* ***wide apart.*** ◦ *Our children were born eighteen months apart.*
2 into separate, smaller pieces: *My jacket is so old that it's coming apart.*
3 If two people are apart, they are not in the same place together: *My parents were living apart.*
4 **apart from** B1 except for: *Apart from Jodie, who hurt her leg, all the children were fine.*

apartment /əˈpɑːtmənt/ **noun**
mainly US
A2 a set of rooms for someone to live in on one level of a building or house

apartment block /əˈpɑːtmənt ˌblɒk/ **noun** UK (US **apartment building**)
a large building that is divided into apartments

apologize /əˈpɒlədʒaɪz/ **verb** (**apologizing**, **apologized**)
B1 to say sorry for something bad you have done: *He* ***apologized for*** *being rude.* ◦ *I* ***apologized to*** *her.*

> **apologize to someone**
> Remember to use **to** when you mention the person who receives the apology.
> *I* ***apologized to*** *them immediately.*
> ~~*I apologized them immediately.*~~

apology /əˈpɒlədʒi/ **noun** (plural **apologies**)
B1 something that you say or write to say sorry for something bad you have done: *a letter of apology*

apostrophe /əˈpɒstrəfi/ **noun**
1 a mark (') used to show that letters

or numbers are not there: *I'm (= I am) hungry.*
2 a punctuation mark (') used before the letter 's' to show that something belongs to someone or something: *I drove my brother's car.*

app /æp/ **noun**
short form of application: *a computer app*

apparent /əˈpær^{ə}nt/ **adj**
easy to notice: *It soon became* ***apparent that*** *she had lost interest.*

apparently /əˈpær^{ə}ntli/ **adv**
used to say that you have read or been told something: *Apparently it's going to rain today.*

appeal[1] /əˈpiːl/ **noun**
1 an event in which a lot of people are asked to give money, information, or help: *The appeal raised over £2 million for AIDS research.*
2 [no plural] the quality that makes you like someone or something: *I've never understood the appeal of skiing.*

appeal[2] /əˈpiːl/ **verb**
1 to ask people to give money, information, or help: *The police have* ***appealed for*** *more information.*
2 to attract or interest someone: *Cycling has never* ***appealed to*** *me.*

appear /əˈpɪə^{r}/ **verb**
1 B1 to seem: *He appeared calm and relaxed.*
2 B1 to start to be seen: *She suddenly appeared in the doorway.*
→ Opposite **disappear** **verb**
3 B1 to perform in a movie, play, etc.: *She appears briefly in the new James Bond movie.*
4 to start to exist or become available: *Laptops first appeared in the 1980s.*

appearance /əˈpɪər^{ə}ns/ **noun**
1 B1 the way a person or thing looks: *She's very concerned with her appearance.*
2 an occasion when someone is seen in public: *a public appearance*
3 [no plural] the fact of something starting to exist or becoming available: *The appearance of mobile phones has changed the way people communicate.*

appetite /ˈæpɪtaɪt/ **noun**
the feeling that makes you want to eat: *All that walking has* ***given*** *me an* ***appetite****.*

applaud /əˈplɔːd/ **verb**
to hit your hands together to show that you have enjoyed a performance, speech, etc.: *The audience applauded loudly.*

applause /əˈplɔːz/ **noun** [no plural]
the noise or action of people hitting their hands together to show they have enjoyed something: *There was loud applause at the end of her speech.*

apple /ˈæpl/ **noun**
A1 a hard, round fruit with a green or red skin: *an apple pie*

apple

application /ˌæplɪˈkeɪʃ^{ə}n/ **noun**
1 B1 an official request for something, usually in writing: *an* ***application for*** *a bank loan*
2 a computer program with a particular purpose

application form /ˌæplɪˈkeɪʃ^{ə}n ˌfɔːm/ **noun**
a form that you use to officially ask for something, for example a job

apply /əˈplaɪ/ **verb** (**applying**, **applied**)
1 B1 to officially ask for something: *I've* ***applied for*** *a job.*
2 to affect a particular person or situation: *This law only* ***applies to*** *married people.*
3 to spread something on a surface: *Apply the paint to a clean, dry surface.*

appoint /əˈpɔɪnt/ **verb**
to officially choose someone for a job: *He was* ***appointed as*** *company director last year.*

appointment /əˈpɔɪntmənt/ **noun**
A2 a time you have arranged to see someone: *I've* ***made*** *an* ***appointment*** *with the dentist.*

appreciate /əˈpriːʃieɪt/ **verb** (**appreciating**, **appreciated**)
1 to understand how good something or someone is: *He wouldn't appreciate an expensive wine.*
2 to feel grateful for something: *I really appreciate all your help.*
3 **would appreciate** used when you

a b c d e f g h i j k l m n o p q r s t u v w x y z

are politely requesting something: *I **would appreciate it** if you didn't smoke in the house.*

appreciation /əˌpriːʃiˈeɪʃən/ **noun** [no plural]
1 an understanding of how good something or someone is: *His **appreciation of** art increased as he grew older.*
2 a feeling of being grateful for something: *To show our appreciation, we've bought you a little present.*

approach[1] /əˈprəʊtʃ/ **verb**
1 B1 to come close in distance or time: *The crowd cheered as she approached the finishing line.* ◦ *The new school year is fast approaching.*
2 to deal with something: *I'm not sure how to approach the problem.*

approach[2] /əˈprəʊtʃ/ **noun**
1 a way of doing something: *Neil has a different **approach to** the problem.*
2 [no plural] movement closer to someone or something in distance or time: *the approach of winter*

appropriate /əˈprəʊpriət/ **adj** right for a particular situation or person: *Is this movie **appropriate for** young children?*
→ Opposite **inappropriate** **adj**

approval /əˈpruːvəl/ **noun** [no plural]
1 the belief that something or someone is good or right: *Alan always tries hard to **win** his father's **approval**.*
→ Opposite **disapproval** **noun**
2 official permission: *The project has received approval from the government.*

approve /əˈpruːv/ **verb** (**approving**, **approved**)
1 B1 to allow something: *The council has approved plans for a new library.*
2 to think that something is good or right: *I don't **approve of** smoking.*
→ Opposite **disapprove** **verb**

approximate /əˈprɒksɪmət/ **adj** not completely accurate but close: *What is the approximate cost of a taxi to the airport?*

approximately /əˈprɒksɪmətli/ **adv** B1 close to a particular number or time, but not exactly that number or time: *The college has approximately 700 students.*

April /ˈeɪprəl/ **noun** A1 the fourth month of the year

arch /ɑːtʃ/ **noun** a curved structure that usually supports something, for example a bridge or wall

arch

architect /ˈɑːkɪtekt/ **noun** B1 someone who designs buildings

architecture /ˈɑːkɪtektʃər/ **noun** [no plural]
1 B1 the design and style of buildings: *modern architecture*
2 B1 the skill of designing buildings: *He studied architecture.*

are strong /ɑːr/ weak /ər/ present simple of be, used with 'you', 'we', and 'they'

area /ˈeəriə/ **noun**
1 A2 a part of a country or city: *a poor area*
2 B1 a part of a building or piece of land used for a particular purpose: *a picnic area*
3 a part of a subject or activity: *The university course covers the main areas of engineering.*
4 the size of a flat surface

aren't /ɑːnt/
1 short form of are not: *We aren't going to the party.*
2 **aren't I?** short form of am I not?: *I am invited, aren't I?*

argue /ˈɑːgjuː/ **verb** (**arguing**, **argued**)
1 B1 to speak angrily to someone, telling them that you disagree with them: *My parents are always **arguing about** money.*
2 to give reasons to support or oppose an idea, action, etc.: *She **argued that** it would be cheaper to travel by bus.*

a b c d e f g h i j k l m n o p q r s t u v w x y z

a b c d e f g h i j k l m n o p q r s t u v w x y z

argument /ˈɑːgjəmənt/ **noun**
1 B1 an angry discussion with someone in which you both disagree: *They **had** an **argument** about who should clean the house.*
2 a reason or reasons why you support or oppose an idea, action, etc.: *There are many **arguments against** smoking.*

arise /əˈraɪz/ **verb** (**arising**, **arose**, **arisen**)
If a problem arises, it starts to happen: *The whole problem **arose from** a lack of communication.*

arithmetic /əˈrɪθmətɪk/ **noun** [no plural]
the part of mathematics that deals with the adding, multiplying, etc. of numbers

arm /ɑːm/ **noun**
A1 the long part at each side of the human body, ending in a hand: *She held the baby in her arms.*

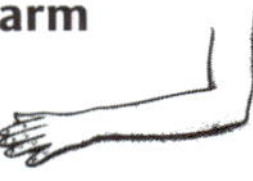
arm

armchair /ˈɑːm ˌtʃeəʳ/ **noun**
A2 a comfortable chair with sides that support your arms

armchair

armed /ɑːmd/ **adj**
carrying or using weapons: *armed guards*

the armed forces /ˌɑːmd ˈfɔːsɪz/ **plural noun**
a country's military forces, for example the army and the navy

armour UK (US **armor**) /ˈɑːməʳ/ **noun** [no plural]
metal clothes that soldiers wore in the past when fighting: *a **suit of armour***

armour

arms /ɑːmz/ **plural noun**
weapons: *the sale of arms*

army /ˈɑːmi/ **noun** (plural **armies**)
B1 a military force that fights wars on the ground: *the British Army*

arose /əˈrəʊz/
past tense of arise

around /əˈraʊnd/ **adv**, **preposition**
1 A2 on all sides of something: *They sat around the table.*
2 A2 in a circular movement: *This lever turns the wheels around.*
3 A2 to or in different parts of a place: *I spent a year travelling around Asia.*
4 A2 here, or near this place: *Is there a supermarket around here?* ◦ *Will you be around next week?*
5 A2 used before a number or amount to mean 'close to, but not exactly': *They will arrive around four o'clock.*
6 B1 to the opposite direction: *He turned around and looked at her.*

arrange /əˈreɪndʒ/ **verb** (**arranging**, **arranged**)
1 B1 to make plans for something to happen: *I've arranged a meeting with him.*
2 to put objects in a particular order or position: *Arrange the books alphabetically by author.*

arrangement /əˈreɪndʒmənt/ **noun**
1 B1 plans for how something will happen: *I've **made arrangements** to go home this weekend.*
2 an agreement between two people or groups: *We have an arrangement that he cleans the house and I do the cooking.*

arrest¹ /əˈrest/ **verb**
B1 If the police arrest someone, they take the person away to ask them about a crime that they might have done: *He was **arrested for** possession of illegal drugs.*

arrest

arrest² /əˈrest/ **noun**
the act of arresting someone: *Police **made** twenty **arrests** at yesterday's demonstration.*

arrival /əˈraɪvəl/ **noun** [no plural]
B1 the act of someone or something

coming to a place: *There was a car waiting for him* ***on his arrival****.*

arrive /ə'raɪv/ **verb** (**arriving**, **arrived**)
A2 to get to a place: *We* ***arrived in*** *Paris at noon.* ◦ *It was dark when we* ***arrived at*** *the station.*

Common mistake: arrive somewhere

Be careful to choose the correct preposition after **arrive**. You **arrive at** a place such as a building.

We arrived at the hotel just after ten o'clock.

You **arrive in** a town, city, or country.

They arrived in Tokyo on Wednesday.
When did David arrive in Australia?

You **arrive** home, here, or there. You do not use a preposition when **arrive** is used before these words.

We arrived home yesterday.
I had a lot of problems when I first arrived here.

arrogance /'ærəgəns/ **noun** [no plural]
behaviour that shows you believe you are better than other people

arrogant /'ærəgənt/ **adj**
believing that you are better than other people

arrow /'ærəʊ/ **noun**
1 a symbol used on signs to show a direction
2 a long stick with a sharp point at one end that is shot from a bow (= curved piece of wood)

arrows

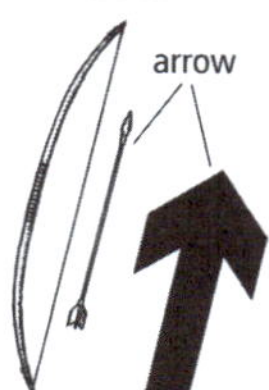

art /ɑːt/ **noun**
1 A2 [no plural] the making of things such as paintings or drawings, or the things that are made: *modern art* ◦ *an art gallery*
2 a skill: *the art of conversation*

article /'ɑːtɪkl/ **noun**
1 B1 a piece of writing in a magazine or newspaper: *I read an* ***article on*** *astrology.*
2 B1 in grammar, used to mean the words 'the', 'a', or 'an'
3 an object: *articles of clothing*

artificial /ˌɑːtɪ'fɪʃəl/ **adj**
not natural, but made by people: *artificial flowers*
• **artificially** **adv** *artificially coloured fruit drinks*

artist /'ɑːtɪst/ **noun**
A2 someone who makes art, especially paintings and drawings

artistic /ɑː'tɪstɪk/ **adj**
1 good at making things, such as paintings and drawings
2 relating to art: *the artistic director of the theatre*

arts /ɑːts/ **plural noun**
1 subjects of study that are not sciences, for example history and languages: *an arts degree*
2 **the arts** activities such as painting, music, film, dance, and writing

as strong /æz/ weak /əz/ **preposition**, **conjunction**
1 A1 used to describe something's purpose or someone's job: *She* ***works as*** *a waitress.*
2 A2 because: *You can go first as you're the oldest.*
3 **as... as** A2 used to compare two things, people, amounts, etc.: *He's not as tall as his brother.* ◦ *She earns three times as much as I do.*
4 B1 while: *I saw James as I was leaving.*
5 B1 in the same way: *This year, as in previous years, tickets sold very quickly.*
6 **as if/as though** used to describe how a situation seems to be: *It looks as if it might rain.*
7 **as for** used to talk about how another person or thing is affected by something: *I was pleased. As for Kyle, I don't care what he thinks.*

ash /æʃ/ **noun** [no plural]
the soft, grey powder that remains when something has burnt: *cigarette ash*

ashamed /ə'ʃeɪmd/ **adj**
B1 feeling angry and disappointed about someone or something, or because you have done something wrong: *I felt* ***ashamed of*** *my behaviour.*

ashtray /ˈæʃˌtreɪ/ **noun**
a small, open container used to put cigarette ash in

aside /əˈsaɪd/ **adv**
1 in a direction to one side: *I gave her some food but she pushed it aside.*
2 If you put or set something aside, you do not use it now, but keep it to use later: *We've put some money aside for the holiday.*

ask /ɑːsk/ **verb**
1 A1 to say something to someone as a question: *I **asked** him **about** his hobbies.* ◦ *I **asked why** the plane was so late.*
2 A2 to invite someone to do something: *She asked him to lunch.*
3 B1 to say to someone that you would like something from them: *He **asked for** a bike for his birthday.*

> **Common mistake: ask for**
>
> When you use **ask** with the meaning of saying you want someone to give you something, remember to use the preposition **for** before the thing that is wanted.
>
> *I'm writing to ask for information about your products.*
>
> ~~*I'm writing to ask information about your products.*~~

4 B1 to say something to someone because you want them to do something: *They **asked** me **to** feed their cat while they're away.*
5 B1 to say something to someone because you want to know if you can do something: *I **asked if** I could go.*
ask *someone* out **phrasal verb**
to invite someone to go out with you: *Jack asked me out to the cinema on Friday.*

asleep /əˈsliːp/ **adj**
B1 sleeping: *The children are asleep.* ◦ *He **fell asleep** in front of the TV.*

aspect /ˈæspekt/ **noun**
one part of a situation, problem, or subject: *His illness affects every aspect of his life.*

aspirin /ˈæspᵊrɪn/ **noun** (plural **aspirin**, **aspirins**)
B1 a common drug used to stop pain and fever

assault /əˈsɔːlt/ **noun**
an attack: *There was an **assault on** a police officer.*
• **assault verb** to attack someone

assembly /əˈsembli/ **noun** (plural **assemblies**)
a meeting of a large group of people

assess /əˈses/ **verb**
to decide how good, important, or serious something is: *The tests are designed to assess reading skills.*
• **assessment noun**

assignment /əˈsaɪnmənt/ **noun**
a piece of work or a job that someone gives you to do: *a written assignment*

assist /əˈsɪst/ **verb**
to help: *The army arrived to **assist in** the search for survivors.*

assistance /əˈsɪstᵊns/ **noun** [no plural] formal
help: *financial assistance*

assistant /əˈsɪstᵊnt/ **noun**
1 B1 someone whose job is to help a person who has a more important job: *I'm the assistant manager.*
2 a sales/shop assistant A2 UK someone who works in a shop

associate /əˈsəʊʃieɪt/ **verb** (**associating**, **associated**)
to relate two things or people in your mind: *Most people **associate** this brand **with** good quality.*
be associated with *something* **phrasal verb**
to be caused by something: *There are many health problems associated with smoking.*

association /əˌsəʊʃiˈeɪʃᵊn/ **noun**
an organization of people with the same interests or purpose: *the Football Association*

assume /əˈsjuːm/ **verb** (**assuming**, **assumed**)
to think that something is true, although you have no proof: *You weren't here so I assumed you were at home.*

assure /əˈʃɔːʳ/ **verb** (**assuring**, **assured**)
to stop someone from worrying by

telling them that something is certain: *She **assured** me **that** she would be safe.*

asterisk /ˈæstərɪsk/ **noun**
the symbol *

asthma /ˈæsmə/ **noun** [no plural]
an illness that makes it difficult to breathe: *an asthma attack*

astonished /əˈstɒnɪʃt/ **adj**
very surprised: *I was **astonished at** the news.*

astonishing /əˈstɒnɪʃɪŋ/ **adj**
very surprising: *What an astonishing thing to say!*

astonishment /əˈstɒnɪʃmənt/ **noun** [no plural]
a feeling of great surprise: *I tried to hide my astonishment.*

astrology /əˈstrɒlədʒi/ **noun** [no plural]
the study of the positions and movements of stars, and the belief that they change people's lives

astronaut /ˈæstrənɔːt/ **noun**
someone who travels into space

astronaut

astronomer /əˈstrɒnəmər/ **noun**
a scientist who studies astronomy

astronomy /əˈstrɒnəmi/ **noun** [no plural]
the scientific study of stars and planets

at strong /æt/ weak /ət/ **preposition**
1 A1 in a particular place or position: *We met at the station.* ◦ *She was sitting at the table.*
2 A1 used to show the time something happens: *The meeting starts at three.*
3 A1 towards: *I threw the ball at him.*
4 A2 used to show the cause of something, especially a feeling: *We were surprised at the news.*
5 B1 used after an adjective to show a person's ability to do something: *He's good at making friends.*
6 used to show the price, speed, or level of something: *He was driving at 80 miles per hour.*
7 A1 the @ symbol, used in email addresses

ate /eɪt/, /et/
past tense of eat

athlete /ˈæθliːt/ **noun**
B1 someone who is good at sports such as running, jumping, or throwing things

athletic /æθˈletɪk/ **adj**
1 strong, healthy, and good at sports
2 relating to athletes or to the sport of athletics

athletics /æθˈletɪks/ **noun** [no plural]
1 B1 UK (US **track and field**) the sports that include running, jumping, and throwing
→ See **Sports 1** on page C15
2 US any sports, for example football and baseball

atlas /ˈætləs/ **noun**
a book of maps: *a road atlas*

ATM /ˌeɪtiːˈem/ **noun** mainly US (UK usually **cash machine**)
a machine that you get money from using a plastic card

atmosphere /ˈætməsfɪər/ **noun**
1 B1 [no plural] the feeling that exists in a place or situation: *The atmosphere in the office is very relaxed.*
2 **the atmosphere** the gases around the Earth

atom /ˈætəm/ **noun**
the smallest unit that an element can be divided into

atomic /əˈtɒmɪk/ **adj**
1 relating to atoms
2 using the energy created when an atom is divided: *atomic power/weapons*

attach /əˈtætʃ/ **verb**
1 B1 to join one thing to another: *She **attached** a picture **to** her letter.*
2 to join a file, such as a document, picture, or computer program, to an email: *The information is in the attached document.*

attached /əˈtætʃt/ **adj**
be attached to *someone/something* to like someone or something a lot: *I'm rather attached to my old car.*

a b c d e f g h i j k l m n o p q r s t u v w x y z

attachment /əˈtætʃmənt/ **noun**
1 a computer file that is sent together with an email message: *Have you **opened** the **attachment**?*
2 a feeling of love or liking for someone or something

attack¹ /əˈtæk/ **noun**
1 B1 a violent act intended to hurt or damage someone or something: *There was a terrorist **attack on** the capital.*
2 a sudden, short illness: *He had a nasty **attack of** flu.*

attack² /əˈtæk/ **verb**
1 B1 to use violence to hurt or damage someone or something: *He was attacked by a gang of youths.*
2 to say that someone or something is bad: *She has attacked the government's new education policy.*

attempt¹ /əˈtempt/ **verb**
B1 to try to do something: *He **attempted to** escape through a window.*

attempt² /əˈtempt/ **noun**
an act of trying to do something: *This is his second **attempt at** passing the exam.*

attend /əˈtend/ **verb** formal
1 B1 to go to an event: *He attended a meeting.*
2 B1 to go regularly to a place such as a school or church: *Which school does your daughter attend?*

attendant /əˈtendᵊnt/ **noun**
someone whose job is to help the public in a public place: *a parking attendant*

attention /əˈtenʃᵊn/ **noun** [no plural]
1 B1 the act of watching or listening to something carefully: *I wasn't **paying attention** (= listening) to what she was saying.* ◦ *Ladies and gentlemen, could I have your attention, please? (= please listen to me)*
2 catch/get *someone's* attention to make someone notice you: *I waved at him to get his attention.*
3 draw (*someone's*) attention to *something/someone* to make someone notice something or someone: *She shouted to draw attention to herself.*

attic /ˈætɪk/ **noun**
a room at the top of a house under the roof

attitude /ˈætɪtjuːd/ **noun**
B1 how you think or feel about something: *He has a very bad **attitude towards** work.*

attorney /əˈtɜːni/ **noun** especially US
a lawyer, especially one who represents someone in court: *You should consult an attorney before making any major decisions.*

attract /əˈtrækt/ **verb**
1 B1 to make people come to a place or do a particular thing: *The museum attracts more than 300,000 visitors a year.*
2 attract attention, interest, etc. B1 to cause people to pay attention, be interested, etc.: *Her ideas have attracted a lot of attention.*
3 to cause someone to be interested, especially sexually: *So what **attracted** you **to** Joe in the first place?* ◦ *I was **attracted to** him straight away.*

attraction /əˈtrækʃᵊn/ **noun**
1 B1 something that makes people come to a place: *a tourist attraction*
2 [no plural] a feeling of liking someone because of the way they look or behave: *physical attraction*

attractive /əˈtræktɪv/ **adj**
1 A2 beautiful or pleasant to look at: *an attractive woman*
2 interesting or useful: *a very attractive offer*

aubergine /ˈəʊbəʒiːn/ **noun** UK (US **eggplant**)
an oval, purple vegetable that is white inside
→ See **Fruit and Vegetables** on page C8

auction¹ /ˈɔːkʃᵊn/ **noun**
a sale in which things are sold to the person who offers the most money

auction² /ˈɔːkʃᵊn/ **verb**
to sell something at an auction

audience /ˈɔːdiəns/ **noun**
B1 the people who sit and watch a performance at a theatre or cinema

audio /ˈɔːdiəʊ/ **adj**
relating to the recording or playing of sound: *audio equipment*

audio-visual /ˌɔːdiəʊˈvɪʒuəl/ **adj**
used to describe something that uses sounds and pictures: *audio-visual equipment*

audition /ɔːˈdɪʃən/ **noun**
a short performance that someone gives to try to get a job as an actor, musician, dancer, etc.: *I have an audition for the play tomorrow.*

August /ˈɔːgəst/ **noun**
A1 the eighth month of the year

aunt /ɑːnt/ **noun**
A2 the sister of someone's mother or father, or the wife of someone's uncle: *I'm going to visit my aunt next week.*

au pair /ˌoʊ ˈpeər/ /ˌəʊ ˈpeər/ **noun**
a young person who stays with a family in another country and looks after their children

authentic /ɔːˈθentɪk/ **adj**
real and not false: *authentic Italian food*

author /ˈɔːθər/ **noun**
B1 someone who writes a book, article, etc.: *a popular author of children's fiction*

authority /ɔːˈθɒrəti/ **noun**
1 [no plural] the official power to make decisions or control people
2 (plural **authorities**) an official group with the power to control a particular public service: *a health authority*

autobiography /ˌɔːtəʊbaɪˈɒgrəfi/ **noun** (plural **autobiographies**)
a book that someone has written about their own life

autograph /ˈɔːtəgrɑːf/ **noun**
a famous person's name, written by that person

automatic /ˌɔːtəˈmætɪk/ **adj**
1 An automatic machine works by itself or with little human control: *automatic doors*
2 done without thinking: *After lots of practice, driving becomes automatic.*

automatically /ˌɔːtəˈmætɪkli/ **adv**
1 If a machine does something automatically, it does it without being controlled by anyone: *The camera automatically puts the time and date on the photo.*
2 without thinking about what you are doing: *I automatically put my hand out to catch it.*

automobile /ˈɔːtəməʊbiːl/ **noun** US (UK **car**)
a vehicle with an engine, four wheels, and seats for a few people

autumn /ˈɔːtəm/ **noun** (also US **fall**)
A2 the season of the year between summer and winter, when leaves fall from the trees: *I'm starting a new job* ***in the autumn***.

auxiliary verb /ɔːgˌzɪliəri ˈvɜːb/ **noun**
a verb that is used with another verb to form tenses, negatives, and questions, for example 'do' and 'must'

available /əˈveɪləbl/ **adj**
A2 If something is available, you can use it or get it: *This information is available free on the Internet.*

avenue /ˈævənjuː/ **noun**
a wide road in a town or city

average[1] /ˈævərɪdʒ/ **adj**
1 B1 An average amount is calculated by adding some amounts together and then dividing by the number of amounts: *The average age of the students is 18.*
2 usual and like the most common type: *an average day*
3 not excellent, although not bad: *The food was pretty average.*

average[2] /ˈævərɪdʒ/ **noun**
1 B1 an amount calculated by adding some amounts together and then dividing by the number of amounts: *They work an average of 30.5 hours per week.*
2 B1 the usual or typical amount: *An eight-hour day at work is about* ***the average***.
3 **on average** usually, or based on an average: *On average, people who don't smoke are healthier than people who do.*

avoid /əˈvɔɪd/ **verb**
1 B1 to stay away from a person or place: *Try to avoid the city centre.*

a b c d e f g h i j k l m n o p q r s t u v w x y z

2 to prevent something from happening: *I braked to avoid hitting the gate.*
3 to not do something because you do not want to: *She managed to avoid answering my question.*

> **Common mistake: avoid doing something**
>
> When **avoid** is followed by a verb, the verb is always in the **-ing** form.
> *I avoided seeing him for several days.*
> ~~*I avoided to see him for several days.*~~

awake /əˈweɪk/ **adj**
B1 not sleeping: *I was awake half the night.*

award¹ /əˈwɔːd/ **noun**
a prize given to someone for something good they have done: *the award for best actress*

award² /əˈwɔːd/ **verb**
to officially give someone something such as a prize or an amount of money: *He was awarded the Nobel Prize for Physics.*

aware /əˈweəʳ/ **adj**
knowing about something: *Were you* ***aware of*** *the problem?*
→ Opposite **unaware** adj

away /əˈweɪ/ **adv**
1 A2 to a different place: *Go away and leave me alone.* ◦ *We moved* ***away from*** *the city.*
2 A2 at a particular distance from a place: *The nearest town is ten miles away.*
3 A2 not at the place where someone usually lives or works: *Sophie is feeding the cat while we're away.*
4 B1 at a particular time in the future: *My exam is only a week away.*
5 B1 in or into the usual or a suitable place, especially one that can be closed: *Please put your toys away.*
6 gradually disappearing until mostly or completely gone: *All the snow has melted away.*

awesome /ˈɔːsəm/ **adj**
1 very big or special and making you feel respect, admiration, or fear: *an awesome responsibility*
2 mainly US informal very good: *You look awesome in those jeans.*

awful /ˈɔːfəl/ **adj**
1 B1 very bad: *an awful place* ◦ *The play was absolutely awful.*
2 an awful lot (of *something*) a very large amount: *It costs an awful lot of money.*

awfully /ˈɔːfəli/ **adv**
very: *We had to get up awfully early.*

awkward /ˈɔːkwəd/ **adj**
1 difficult or causing problems: *an awkward question*
2 embarrassing and not relaxed: *an awkward silence*
3 moving in a way that is not attractive: *His movements were slow and awkward.*

axe /æks/ **noun** (US also **ax**)
a tool with a sharp piece of metal at one end, used for cutting trees or wood

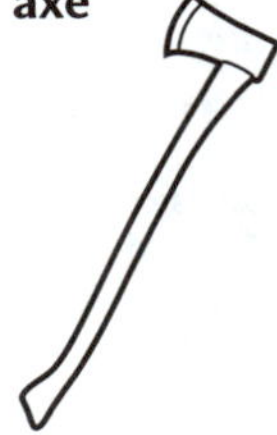

Bb

B, b /biː/
the second letter of the alphabet

baby /ˈbeɪbi/ **noun**
(plural **babies**)
A1 a very young child or animal: *a baby girl*

baby

babysit /ˈbeɪbisɪt/ **verb** (**babysitting**, **babysat**)
B1 to look after children while their parents are not at home
• **babysitting noun** [no plural] B1 *He does babysitting to earn extra money.*

babysitter /ˈbeɪbisɪtəʳ/ **noun**
B1 someone who looks after children while their parents are not at home

bachelor /ˈbætʃᵊləʳ/ **noun**
a man who has never been married

back¹ /bæk/ **adv**
1 A1 to the place where someone or something was before: *When do you go back to college?* ◦ *I put it back in the cupboard.*
2 A2 as a reply or reaction to something: *Can I call you back later?*
3 B1 in a direction behind you: *She stepped back.*
4 B1 to the state something or someone was in before: *Go back to sleep.*
5 to an earlier time: *Looking back, I think we did the right thing.*

back² /bæk/ **noun**
1 A1 the part of something that is away from the front: *Our seats were in the back of the theatre.*
2 A2 the part of your body from your shoulders to your bottom: *He was lying on his back.*
→ See **The Body** on page C2
3 back to front with the back part of something where the front should be: *You've got your trousers on back to front.*
4 in back of behind: *They sat in back of us on the plane.*

back³ /bæk/ **verb**
1 to give support to a person or plan: *He backed Clark in the recent election.*
2 to move or drive backwards: *It's best to* ***back into*** *a parking space.*
back *something* up phrasal verb
1 to prove that something is true: *His theory is backed up by recent evidence.*
2 to make an extra copy of computer information
back *someone* up phrasal verb
1 to support or help someone: *My family backed me up in my fight for compensation.*
2 to say that someone is telling the truth: *That's exactly what happened – Cleo will back me up.*

back⁴ /bæk/ **adj**
A2 at the back of something: *the back garden*

backache /ˈbækeɪk/ **noun** [no plural]
a pain in your back: *Gardening gives me backache.*

background /ˈbækgraʊnd/ **noun**
1 B1 a person's education and family: *He was* ***from*** *a poor* ***background****.*
2 the things at the back of a picture or view: *He had a photo of Paul with his children* ***in the background****.*
3 [no plural] sounds you can hear that are not the main sounds that you are listening to: *background music/noise* ◦ *If you listen carefully, you can hear a flute* ***in the background****.*
4 [no plural] the things that have happened in the past that affect a situation: *Can you give me some* ***background on*** *the issue?*

backpack /ˈbækpæk/ **noun**
B1 a bag that you carry on your back, with two straps that go over your shoulders

backpack

backpacker /ˈbækˌpækəʳ/ **noun**
B1 someone who travels, carrying the

a b c d e f g h i j k l m n o p q r s t u v w x y z

things they need in a backpack: *Lots of backpackers stay at this hostel.*

backpacking /ˈbækˌpækɪŋ/ **noun** [no plural]
B1 the activity of travelling around an area without spending much money, carrying the things you need in a backpack: *He wants to* ***go backpacking*** *in the summer.*

backup /ˈbækʌp/ **noun**
1 an extra copy of computer information: *Have you* ***made*** *a* ***backup*** *of that document?*
2 extra help, support, or equipment that is available if you need it: *Medical staff are available to provide backup in an emergency.*

backward /ˈbækwəd/ **adj**
in the direction behind you: *a backward glance*

backwards /ˈbækwədz/ **adv** mainly UK (also **backward**)
1 B1 towards the direction behind you: *She took a couple of steps backwards.*
2 in the opposite order to what is usual: *'Erehwon' is 'nowhere' spelled backwards.*
3 with the part that is usually at the front at the back: *You've got your skirt on backwards.*
4 **backwards and forwards** in one direction then the opposite way, many times: *I drive backwards and forwards between Oxford and London every day.*

backyard /ˌbækˈjɑːd/ **noun** mainly US
the area behind a house

bacon /ˈbeɪkᵊn/ **noun** [no plural]
B1 meat from a pig that has been treated with salt or smoke, often cut into long, thin slices

bacteria /bækˈtɪəriə/ **plural noun**
very small living things that can cause disease

bad /bæd/ **adj** (**worse**, **worst**)
1 A1 not good or pleasant: *bad weather* ◦ *bad news*
2 A2 of low quality and not acceptable: *The movie was so bad we couldn't watch it.* ◦ *I'm very* ***bad at*** *cooking.*
3 B1 serious: *a bad injury* ◦ *bad flooding*
4 B1 evil or morally unacceptable: *She's not a bad person.* ◦ *Stealing is a bad thing to do.*
5 B1 not lucky, or not happening in a way that you would like: *It was just* ***bad luck*** *that she heard us.* ◦ *I'll call you later if this is a* ***bad time*** *for you.*
6 Food that is bad is not fresh and cannot be eaten.
7 **not bad** A2 fairly good: *'How was your sandwich?' 'Not bad.'*
8 **be bad for *someone*** A2 to be harmful for someone: *Too much fat is bad for you.*
9 **feel bad** B1 to feel guilty: *I felt* ***bad about*** *leaving her by herself.*
10 **too bad** B1 used to say that you are sorry about a situation: *'He didn't get the job.' 'Oh, that's too bad.'*

badge /bædʒ/ **noun**
a small piece of metal, plastic, etc., with words or a picture on it, that is attached to your clothes: *a name badge*

badly /ˈbædli/ **adv**
1 A2 not well: *You're behaving very badly.* ◦ *The team played badly in the first half.* ◦ *Nurses are* ***badly paid*** *(= do not earn much money).*
2 A2 seriously: *He was badly injured in the accident.*
3 A2 very much: *He needs the money very badly.*
4 in an unpleasant way: *I think they treated her very badly.*

badminton /ˈbædmɪntən/ **noun** [no plural]
A2 a sport in which two or four people hit a small object that looks like a ball with feathers over a net

bad-tempered /ˌbædˈtempəd/ **adj** UK
used to describe a person who gets angry and annoyed easily: *She's very bad-tempered in the mornings!*

bag /bæg/ **noun**
A1 a container made of paper, plastic, cloth, or other material, used for carrying things: *a paper bag* ◦ *I was carrying three* ***bags of*** *shopping.*

baggage /ˈbægɪdʒ/ **noun** [no plural]
B1 all the cases and bags that you

bags

carrier bag *UK*, grocery bag *US*

handbag

take with you when you travel: *I waited at baggage collection (= the place where you get your baggage at the airport).*

bake /beɪk/ **verb** (**baking**, **baked**)
A2 to cook something such as bread or a cake in an oven: *I baked a cake for the party.*
→ See picture at **cook**

baked beans /ˌbeɪkt ˈbiːnz/ **plural noun**
beans cooked in a tomato sauce and sold in cans

baker /ˈbeɪkəʳ/ **noun**
B1 someone who makes and sells bread, cakes, etc.

bakery /ˈbeɪkᵊri/ **noun** (plural **bakeries**)
a shop where you can buy bread, cakes, etc.

balance¹ /ˈbæləns/ **noun**
1 [no plural] a state in which weight is spread in such a way that something does not fall over: *I **lost my balance** and fell off the bike.*
2 [no plural] a state in which the correct amount of importance is given to each thing so that a situation is successful: *It's hard to find the **right balance between** doing too much exercise and not doing enough.*
3 the amount of money that you still have to pay, or that you have left to use: *I always pay off the balance on my credit card each month.*

balance² /ˈbæləns/ **verb** (**balancing**, **balanced**)
1 to be in a position where you will not fall to either side, or to put something in this position: *She was trying to balance a book on her head.*
2 to give the same amount of attention to each thing: *I try to balance work and family commitments.*

balcony /ˈbælkəni/ **noun** (plural **balconies**)
B1 an area with a wall or bars around it that is on the outside wall of building on an upper level

bald /bɔːld/ **adj**
B1 with little or no hair: *John started to **go bald** at an early age.*

bald

ball /bɔːl/ **noun**
1 A1 a round object that you throw, kick, or hit in a game, or something with this shape: *a tennis ball* ◦ *a ball of string*
2 a formal occasion where a lot of people dance

ballet /ˈbæleɪ/ **noun** [no plural]
B1 a type of dancing that is done in a theatre and tells a story, usually with music: *She wants to be a ballet dancer.*

ballet

balloon /bəˈluːn/ **noun**
A2 a round rubber thing filled with air or gas that floats in the air

ballpoint pen /ˌbɔːlpɔɪnt ˈpen/ **noun**
a pen with a small ball in the end that rolls ink onto paper

ban¹ /bæn/ **verb** (**banning**, **banned**)
to officially stop a person or many people from doing something: *I think plastic bags should be banned.*

ban² /bæn/ **noun**
an official rule that people must not do or use something: *There is a **ban on** smoking in this restaurant.*

a b c d e f g h i j k l m n o p q r s t u v w x y z

a b c d e f g h i j k l m n o p q r s t u v w x y z

banana /bəˈnɑːnə/ **noun**
A1 a long, white fruit with a yellow skin
→ See **Fruit and Vegetables** on page C8

band /bænd/ **noun**

band

1 A1 a group of musicians who play modern music together: *a jazz band*
2 a line of a different colour or design
3 a piece of material put around something: *an elastic band*

bandage¹ /ˈbændɪdʒ/ **noun**
B1 a long piece of cloth that you wrap around a part of the body that is hurt

bandage² /ˈbændɪdʒ/ **verb** (**bandaging**, **bandaged**)
to put a bandage around a part of the body

Band-Aid /ˈbændeɪd/ **noun** US trademark (UK **plaster**)
a thin piece of material that you stick to the skin to cover a small cut

bang¹ /bæŋ/ **noun**
1 a sudden, loud noise: *The door shut with a bang.*
2 an act of suddenly hitting part of your body on something hard: *She had a painful bang on her head.*

bang² /bæŋ/ **verb**
1 to make a loud noise by hitting something against something hard: *We heard the door bang.*
2 to hit part of your body against something hard: *Ted fell and banged his head.*

bangs /bæŋz/ **noun** US (UK **fringe**)
hair that is cut short and straight at the top of someone's face

banish /ˈbænɪʃ/ **verb**
to send someone away from a place as a punishment

bank¹ /bæŋk/ **noun**
1 A1 a place where you can keep or borrow money: *I need to go to the bank on my way home.*
2 B1 the land along the side of a river

bank² /bæŋk/ **verb**
to put or keep money in a bank: *Who do you **bank with**?*

bank account /ˈbæŋk əˌkaʊnt/ **noun**
B1 an arrangement with a bank to keep your money there and take it out when you need it

banker /ˈbæŋkəʳ/ **noun**
someone who has an important job in a bank

bank holiday /ˌbæŋk ˈhɒlədeɪ/ **noun** UK
an official holiday when all banks and most shops and offices are closed: *Spring bank holiday*

banking /ˈbæŋkɪŋ/ **noun** [no plural]
the business of operating a bank

banknote /ˈbæŋknəʊt/ **noun** mainly UK (US **bill**)
a piece of paper money

bankrupt /ˈbæŋkrʌpt/ **adj**
not having enough money to pay what you owe to others: *He **went bankrupt** after only a year in business.*

baptism /ˈbæptɪzᵊm/ **noun**
a Christian ceremony in which water is put on someone to show that they have become a member of the Church

baptize /bæpˈtaɪz/ **verb** (**baptizing**, **baptized**)
to do a baptism ceremony for someone

bar¹ /bɑːʳ/ **noun**
1 A1 a place where alcoholic drinks are sold and drunk: *I met him in a bar in Soho.*
2 B1 a small block of something solid: *a chocolate bar*
→ See **Quantities** on page C14
3 a long, thin piece of metal or wood: *There were bars on the windows.*

bar² /bɑːʳ/ **verb** (**barring**, **barred**)
to officially stop someone from doing something or going somewhere: *The court **barred** him **from** contacting his children.*

barbecue /ˈbɑːbɪkjuː/ **noun**
1 A2 a party at which you cook food over a fire outdoors
2 A2 a piece of equipment with a

metal frame for cooking food over a fire outdoors
• **barbecue** verb B1 *barbecued steaks*

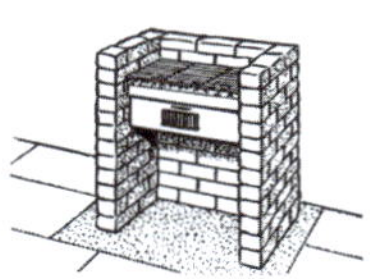
barbecue

barbed wire /ˌbɑːbd ˈwaɪəʳ/ **noun** [no plural]
strong wire with short, sharp points on it to keep people out of a place: *a barbed wire fence*

barbed wire

barber /ˈbɑːbəʳ/ **noun**
someone whose job is to cut men's hair
• **barber's** **noun** a shop where men have their hair cut

bare /beəʳ/ **adj**
1 not covered by clothes: *bare legs*
2 not covered by anything: *The walls were bare.*

barefoot /beəˈfʊt/ **adj**, **adv**
not wearing any shoes or socks: *They ran barefoot along the beach.*

barely /ˈbeəli/ **adv**
only just: *He was barely alive when they found him.*

bargain¹ /ˈbɑːɡɪn/ **noun**
something that is sold for less than its usual price: *At $8.95, it's a bargain.*

bargain² /ˈbɑːɡɪn/ **verb**
to try to agree how much you will pay for something: *We* ***bargained over*** *the price.*

barge /bɑːdʒ/ **noun**
a long, narrow boat with a flat bottom that is used to carry things

bark¹ /bɑːk/ **noun**
1 [no plural] the hard substance that covers the surface of a tree
2 the sound that a dog makes

bark² /bɑːk/ **verb**
if a dog barks, it makes loud, short sounds

barmaid /ˈbɑːmeɪd/ **noun** UK
a woman who serves drinks in a bar

barman /ˈbɑːmən/ **noun** (plural **barmen**) UK
B1 a man who serves drinks in a bar

barn /bɑːn/ **noun**
a large building on a farm where crops or animals are kept

barracks /ˈbærəks/ **noun**
a building or group of buildings where soldiers live: *an army barracks*

barrel /ˈbærəl/ **noun**
1 a large, round container for storing liquids such as oil or wine
2 the tube in a gun that the bullet shoots out of

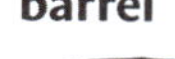

barrel

barrier /ˈbæriəʳ/ **noun**
1 a wall that stops people from going into an area: *Police put up barriers to hold back the crowd.*
2 something that prevents people from doing what they want to do: *Shyness is one of the biggest barriers to making friends.*

bartender /ˈbɑːˌtendəʳ/ **noun** mainly US (UK usually **barman**, **barmaid**)
someone who serves drinks in a bar

base¹ /beɪs/ **noun**
1 the bottom part of something: *We started climbing at the base of the mountain.*
2 the main place where a person lives or works, or from where they do things: *The hotel is an excellent base for exploring the city.*
3 a place where people in the armed forces live and work: *an American Air Force base*

base² /beɪs/ **verb** (**basing**, **based**)
be based at/in If you are based at or in somewhere, that is where you live or work: *The company is based in Geneva.*
base ***something*** **on** ***something*** **phrasal verb**
B1 If you base something on facts or ideas, you use those facts or ideas to develop it: *This book is based on a true story.*

a b c d e f g h i j k l m n o p q r s t u v w x y z

a b c d e f g h i j k l m n o p q r s t u v w x y z

baseball /ˈbeɪsbɔːl/ **noun** [no plural]
A2 a game in which two teams try to win points by hitting a ball and running around four fixed points
→ See **Sports 2** on page C16

basement /ˈbeɪsmənt/ **noun**
part of a building that is under the level of the ground

bases /ˈbeɪsiːz/
plural of basis

basic /ˈbeɪsɪk/ **adj**
1 B1 being the main or most important part of something: *These are basic needs, such as food and water.*
2 B1 very simple, with nothing special added: *The software is very basic.*

basically /ˈbeɪsɪkəli/ **adv**
1 in the most important ways: *The two PCs are basically the same.*
2 used before you explain something simply: *Basically, there aren't enough people.*

basics /ˈbeɪsɪks/ **plural noun**
the most important facts, skills, or needs: *I need to learn* ***the basics of*** *first aid.*

basin /ˈbeɪsən/ **noun**
1 B1 UK the bowl that is fixed to the wall in a bathroom, where you can wash your hands
2 mainly UK a big bowl

basis /ˈbeɪsɪs/ **noun** (plural **bases** /ˈbeɪsiːz/)
1 a way or method of doing something: *Most of the staff here work on a voluntary basis.*
2 **on a daily/monthly/regular basis** how often something is done: *Meetings are held on a weekly basis.*
3 a situation or idea from which something can develop: *Dani's essay can serve as* ***a basis for*** *our discussion.*

basket /ˈbɑːskɪt/ **noun**
B1 a container for carrying things, made of thin pieces of plastic, metal, or wood: *a shopping basket*

baskets

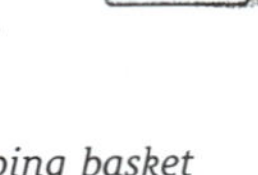

basketball /ˈbɑːskɪtbɔːl/ **noun** [no plural]
A1 a game in which two teams try to win points by throwing a ball through a high net
→ See **Sports 2** on page C16

bass /beɪs/ **adj**
producing low musical notes: *a bass guitar*

bat[1] /bæt/ **noun**
1 A2 a piece of wood used to hit the ball in some sports
2 B1 a small animal like a mouse with wings that flies at night

bat[2] /bæt/ **verb** (**batting**, **batted**)
to try to hit a ball with a bat

bath[1] /bɑːθ/ **noun**
1 A1 UK the container that you fill with water and sit in to wash your body
2 A1 an act of washing your body in a bath: *I'll just* ***have a*** *quick* ***bath.***

bath *UK,* **bathtub** *US*

bath[2] /bɑːθ/ **verb** UK
to wash yourself or someone else in a bath: *I was just bathing the baby.*

bathe /beɪð/ **verb** (**bathing**, **bathed**)
1 to wash yourself in a bath
2 to swim

bathing suit /ˈbeɪðɪŋ ˌsuːt/ **noun** US (UK **swimming costume**)
a piece of clothing that you wear for swimming

bathroom /ˈbɑːθruːm/ **noun**
1 A1 a room with a bath, sink (= bowl for washing), and often a toilet
2 **go to the bathroom** US to use the toilet

bathtub /ˈbɑːθtʌb/ **noun** US
the container that you fill with water and sit in to wash your body

battery /ˈbætəri/ **noun** (plural **batteries**)
A2 an object that provides electricity for things such as radios, toys, or cars

battle[1] /ˈbætl/ **noun**

battery

1 B1 a fight between two armies in a war: *the Battle of Waterloo*
2 a fight against something that is very difficult, or that is hurting you: *a long battle against cancer*

battle[2] /ˈbætl/ **verb** (**battling**, **battled**)
to try very hard to do something difficult: *Both teams **are battling for** a place in the final.*

bay /beɪ/ **noun**
B1 an area of coast where the land curves in: *a sandy bay*

BC /biːˈsiː/
used to show that a particular year came before the birth of Christ: *331 BC*

be[1] strong /biː/ weak /bi/, /bɪ/ **verb** (**being**, **was**, **been**)
1 A1 used to describe someone or something: *I'm Maria (= I am Maria).* ◦ *I'm sixteen.* ◦ *He's German (= He is German).* ◦ *They were ill.* ◦ *Be quiet!*
2 **there is/there are** A1 used to show that someone or something exists: *There are three of us.* ◦ *Is there a bank near here?*
3 A1 used to show where someone or something is: *She's in the kitchen.*
4 **it is, it was, etc.** used to give a fact or your opinion about something: *It's a good idea.* ◦ *It's a big problem.*

be[2] strong /biː/ weak /bi/, /bɪ/ **auxiliary verb** (**being**, **was**, **been**)
1 A2 used with the -ing form of other verbs to describe actions that are or were still happening: *Are you leaving?* ◦ *He was talking to Andrea.*
2 A2 used with other verbs to describe actions that will happen in the future: *I'm going to France next week.* ◦ *I'll be coming back on Tuesday.*
3 A2 used with the past participle of other verbs to show that something happens to someone or something: *He was injured in a car crash.* ◦ *The results will be announced next week.*

beach /biːtʃ/ **noun**
A1 an area of sand or rocks next to the sea

beak /biːk/ **noun**
the hard part of a bird's mouth

beach

beam /biːm/ **noun**
1 a line of light that shines from something: *a laser beam*
2 a long, thick piece of wood that supports weight in a building

bean /biːn/ **noun**
A2 a seed or seed case of some climbing plants, that is used as food: *soya beans* ◦ *coffee beans*

bear[1] /beəʳ/ **verb** (**bearing**, **bore**, **borne**)
1 to accept someone or something bad: *I **can't bear** her (= I dislike her very much).* ◦ *The pain was too much to bear.*
2 to support something: *I don't think that chair will bear his weight.*

bear[2] /beəʳ/ **noun**
A2 a large, strong, wild animal with thick fur

bear

beard /bɪəd/ **noun**
A1 the hair that grows on a man's chin (= the bottom of his face)
→ See **Hair** on page C9

beast /biːst/ **noun** formal
an animal, especially a large or wild one

beat[1] /biːt/ **verb** (**beating**, **beat**, **beaten**)
1 B1 to defeat someone in a competition: *Our team beat Germany 3-1.*
2 B1 When your heart beats, it makes regular movements and sounds: *By the time the doctor arrived, his heart had stopped beating.*
3 to hit a person or animal repeatedly: *They saw him beating his dog with a stick.*
4 to hit against something hard, making a regular sound: *Rain beat against the windows.*
beat *someone* up **phrasal verb**

a b c d e f g h i j k l m n o p q r s t u v w x y z

to hit or kick someone until they are hurt: *He beat up the other prisoners.*

beat[2] /biːt/ **noun**
1 a regular sound that is made by your heart or by something hitting a surface: *the beat of a drum*
2 the main rhythm of a piece of music: *I like music with a strong beat.*

beautiful /ˈbjuːtɪfᵊl/ **adj**

> **Common mistake: beautiful**
> Learners often spell **beautiful** wrong. Remember that it starts with **beau** and has one **l** at the end.

1 A1 very attractive: *a beautiful woman* ◦ *beautiful scenery*
2 A1 very pleasant: *beautiful music* ◦ *It's a beautiful day (= the sun is shining).*
• **beautifully adv** B1 *She sings beautifully.*

beauty /ˈbjuːti/ **noun** [no plural]
B1 the quality of being beautiful: *The area is famous for its natural beauty.*

became /bɪˈkeɪm/
past tense of become

because /bɪˈkɒz/ **conjunction**

> **Common mistake: because**
> Learners often spell **because** wrong. Remember that it has **au** in the middle, like **cause**.

A1 used to give a reason for something: *I'm calling because I need to ask you something.*

because of /bɪˈkɒz əv/ **preposition**
B1 as a result of someone or something: *I'm only here because of you.*

become /bɪˈkʌm/ **verb** (**becoming**, **became**, **become**)
A2 to begin to be something: *They became great friends.*

bed /bed/ **noun**
1 A1 a piece of furniture that you sleep on: *What time did you **go to bed** last night?* ◦ *She's still **in bed**.* ◦ *Have you **made the bed** (= tidied the bed after you have slept in it)?*
2 the ground at the bottom of the sea or a river: *the sea bed*

bed and breakfast /ˌbed ənd ˈbrekfəst/ **noun**
a house where you pay for a room to sleep in for the night and a meal in the morning

bedclothes /ˈbedkləʊðz/ **plural noun**
the sheets and other pieces of cloth that cover you in bed

bedroom /ˈbedruːm/ **noun**
A1 a room used for sleeping in

bedtime /ˈbedtaɪm/ **noun**
the time that you usually go to bed

bee /biː/ **noun**
B1 a yellow and black insect that makes honey (= sweet, sticky food)

bee

beef /biːf/ **noun** [no plural]
B1 the meat of a cow: *roast beef*

been /biːn/, /bɪn/ **verb**
1 past participle of be
2 have been to to have gone to a place and come back: *Have you ever been to Thailand?*

beer /bɪəʳ/ **noun**
A1 an alcoholic drink made from grain: *a pint of beer*

beetle /ˈbiːtl/ **noun**
an insect with a hard, shiny body

beetroot /ˈbiːtruːt/ **noun** UK (US **beet**)
a round, dark red vegetable that is usually cooked and eaten cold

before[1] /bɪˈfɔːʳ/ **preposition**
1 A1 earlier than something or someone: *a week before Christmas* ◦ *She arrived before me.*
2 A1 at a place where you arrive first when going towards another place: *The hospital is just before the bridge.*
3 B1 in front of someone or something in an order or a list: *K comes before L in the English alphabet.*
4 B1 in a position in front of someone or something: *I've never performed this before an audience.*

before[2] /bɪˈfɔːʳ/ **conjunction**
1 A2 earlier than the time when some-

thing happens: *He was a teacher before he became famous.*
2 B1 in order to avoid something bad happening: *Put that stick down before you hurt someone!*
3 B1 until: *It took a few moments before I realized that he was joking.*

before³ /bɪˈfɔːʳ/ **adv**
A2 at an earlier time: *I've never seen her before.*

beg /beg/ **verb** (**begging**, **begged**)
1 to ask someone for food or money, because you do not have any: *Young children were begging on the streets.*
2 to ask for something in a strong and emotional way: *I* ***begged*** *him not* ***to*** *leave.*

began /bɪˈgæn/
past tense of begin

beggar /ˈbegəʳ/ **noun**
a poor person who asks other people for money and food

begin /bɪˈgɪn/ **verb** (**beginning**, **began**, **begun**)
1 A1 to start to happen: *What time does the movie begin?*
2 A2 to start to do something: *She* ***began to*** *cry.*
3 begin with *something* B1 to have something at the start: *Local phone numbers begin with 01224.*
4 to begin with B1 at the start of a situation: *To begin with, I was very nervous.*

beginner /bɪˈgɪnəʳ/ **noun**
A2 someone who is learning or doing something for the first time: *a Spanish class for beginners*

beginning /bɪˈgɪnɪŋ/ **noun**
A2 the start of something: *We met at the* ***beginning of*** *2008.*

begun /bɪˈgʌn/
past participle of begin

behalf /bɪˈhɑːf/ **noun**
on behalf of *someone* for someone or instead of someone: *Will you accept the prize on my behalf?*

behave /bɪˈheɪv/ **verb** (**behaving**, **behaved**)
1 B1 to do or say things in a particular way: *He behaved very badly.* ◦ *You're behaving like a child!*
2 behave *yourself* B1 to be polite and not make a situation difficult: *Did the children behave themselves?*

behaviour /bɪˈheɪvjəʳ/ **noun** [no plural]
B1 the way that you behave: *good/bad behaviour*

behind¹ /bɪˈhaɪnd/ **preposition**
1 A1 at or to the back of someone or something: *Close the door behind you.* ◦ *There's a hotel behind the station.*
2 B1 slower or less successful than someone or something: *Our team is three points behind the winners.*
3 B1 giving your help or support to someone: *The group is 100 percent behind her.*

behind² /bɪˈhaɪnd/ **adv**
1 A2 at or to the back of someone or something: *Somebody pulled me from behind.*
2 A2 in the place where someone or something was before: *When we got to the restaurant, I realized that I had* ***left*** *my purse* ***behind***.

beige /beɪʒ/ **adj**
being a pale brown colour

being¹ /ˈbiːɪŋ/
present participle of be

being² /ˈbiːɪŋ/ **noun**
a living person or imaginary creature: *human beings*

belief /bɪˈliːf/ **noun**
1 an idea that you are certain is true: *political beliefs*
2 a strong feeling that something is true or real: *my belief in God*
3 beyond belief too bad, good, difficult, etc. to be imagined: *The evil of that man is beyond belief.*

believable /bɪˈliːvəbl/ **adj**
If something is believable, you can believe that it could be true or real.

believe /bɪˈliːv/ **verb** (**believing**, **believed**)

Common mistake: believe
Learners often spell **believe** wrong.
Remember that the **i** comes before the **e**.

1 A2 to think that something is true,

or that what someone says is true: *She says she's only thirty, but I don't believe it.* ◦ *Do you believe him?*
2 (A2) to think something, although you are not completely sure: *The murderer is believed to be in his thirties.*
3 believe it or not (B1) used to say that something surprising is true: *He even remembered my birthday, believe it or not.*
4 not believe your eyes/ears (B1) to be very surprised when you see someone or something, or when you hear what someone says: *I couldn't believe my ears when Dan said they were getting married.*

believe in *something* **phrasal verb**
(B1) to be certain that something exists: *Do you believe in life after death?*

believe in *something*/in doing *something* **phrasal verb**
to be confident that something is good and right: *They don't believe in living together before marriage.*

bells

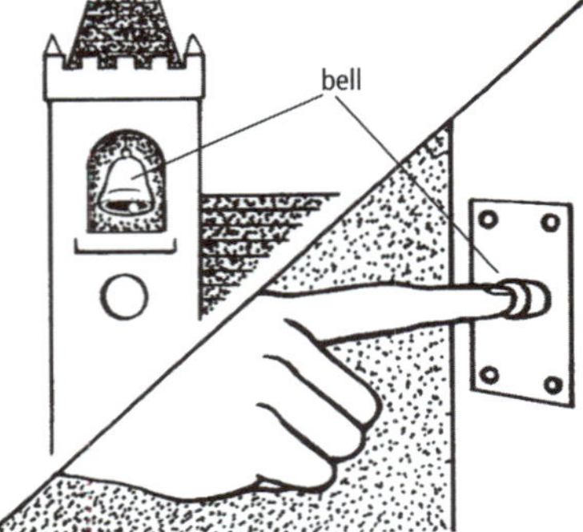

bell /bel/ **noun**
1 (B1) an electrical object that makes a ringing sound when you press a switch: *Please ring the bell for service.*
2 a hollow metal object, shaped like a cup, that makes a ringing sound: *church bells*

belong /bɪˈlɒŋ/ **verb**
1 to be in the right place: *That chair belongs in the dining room.*
2 to feel happy or comfortable in a situation: *I spent two years in Oxford but I never felt that I belonged there.*

belong to *someone* **phrasal verb**
(A2) If something belongs to you, you own it: *This necklace belonged to my grandmother.*

belong to *something* **phrasal verb**
(B1) to be a member of an organization: *We belong to the same health club.*

belongings /bɪˈlɒŋɪŋz/ **plural noun**
the things that you own: *I took a few* ***personal belongings*** *with me.*

below /bɪˈləʊ/ **adv, preposition**
1 (A1) in a lower position than someone or something else: *He could hear people shouting below his window.*
2 (B1) less than an amount or level: *The temperature there rarely drops below 22 degrees.*

belt /belt/ **noun**
(A2) a thin piece of leather or cloth that you wear around the middle of your body

belt

bench /benʃ/ **noun**
a long seat for two or more people, usually made of wood: *a park bench*

bench

bend[1] /bend/ **verb**
(**bent**)
1 to move your body or part of your body so that it is not straight: *Bend your knees when lifting heavy objects.*
2 to become curved, or to make something become curved: *The road bent to the left.*

bend[2] /bend/ **noun**
a curved part of something: *a bend in the road/river*

beneath /bɪˈniːθ/ **adv, preposition**
(B1) under something, or in a lower position than something: *He hid the letter beneath a pile of papers.*

benefit[1] /ˈbenɪfɪt/ **noun**
1 (B1) something good that helps you: *I've had* ***the benefit of*** *a happy childhood.*
2 for *someone's* benefit in order to

help someone: *We bought the piano for the children's benefit.*

benefit² /ˈbenɪfɪt/ **verb**
to help someone: *These changes will benefit the whole company.*

bent¹ /bent/
past tense and past participle of bend

bent² /bent/ **adj**
curved; not straight or flat: *The metal bars were bent and twisted.*

berry /ˈberi/ **noun** (plural **berries**)
a small, round fruit on some plants and trees

beside /bɪˈsaɪd/ **preposition**
A2 next to someone or something: *She lay down beside him.*

besides¹ /bɪˈsaɪdz/ **preposition**
B1 in addition to: *Do you play any other sports besides football?*

besides² /bɪˈsaɪdz/ **adv**
1 B1 used to give another reason for something: *She won't mind if you're late – besides, it's not your fault.*
2 B1 in addition to: *Besides looking after the children, she also runs a successful business.*

best¹ /best/ **adj**
A1 superlative of good: better than any other: *She's one of our best students.* ◦ *Susie is my* ***best friend****.*

best² /best/ **adv**
1 A1 superlative of well: most, or more than any other: *Which of the songs did you like best?*
2 B1 in the most suitable or satisfactory way: *I sleep best with the windows open.*

best³ /best/ **noun**
1 all the best! A2 used to say that you hope someone will be happy, healthy, successful, etc.: *All the best for the game tomorrow!*
2 at its best B1 at the highest level of achievement or quality: *The new building is an example of architecture at its best.*
3 the best B1 someone or something that is better than any other: *He's the best of the new players.*
4 do/try your best B1 to try very hard to do something: *I did my best to persuade him.*
5 make the best of *something* to try to be positive about a situation you do not like but cannot change: *Our hotel room is small, but we'll just have to make the best of it.*

best man /ˌbest ˈmæn/ **noun**
a man who is chosen to help another man on his wedding day

bestseller /ˌbestˈseləʳ/ **noun**
a very popular book that many people have bought: *The 'Harry Potter' novels are all bestsellers.*
• **best-selling adj** *It's the best-selling book of the year.*

bet¹ /bet/ **verb** (**betting**, **bet**)
1 to risk money on the result of a game or competition: *I* ***bet*** *him a dollar* ***that*** *I was right.*
2 I bet informal B1 something you say to show that you are sure something is true or will happen: *I bet he'll be late.*

bet² /bet/ **noun**
an act of risking money on the result of a game or competition: *She won her bet.*

betray /bɪˈtreɪ/ **verb**
to behave in a dishonest way to someone who trusts you

better¹ /ˈbetəʳ/ **adj**
1 A1 comparative of good: of a higher quality or more enjoyable than someone or something else: *He got a better job in the States.* ◦ *Her English is* ***getting better*** *(= improving).*
2 A1 less ill than before: *I feel much better.* ◦ *I hope you* ***get better*** *soon.*
3 be better off richer: *We're better off now that we're both working.*
4 be better off in a better situation: *Steve's an idiot – you'd be better off without him.*

better² /ˈbetəʳ/ **adv**
1 A1 comparative of well: more, or in a more successful way: *I'd like to get to know him better.* ◦ *Helen did much* ***better than*** *me in the exam.*
2 you had better do *something* A2 used to say what someone should do:

a b c d e f g h i j k l m n o p q r s t u v w x y z

a b c d e f g h i j k l m n o p q r s t u v w x y z

You'd better hurry or you'll miss the train.

between[1] /bɪˈtwiːn/ **preposition**
1 A1 in the space that separates two places, people, or things: *The town lies halfway between Florence and Rome.*
2 A1 in the period of time that separates two events or times: *The shop is closed for lunch between 12.30 and 1.30.*
3 A1 involving two or more groups of people: *Tonight's game is between Brazil and Germany.*
4 A2 connecting two or more places or things: *the train service between Glasgow and Edinburgh*
5 A2 used when comparing two people or things: *What's the* ***difference between*** *these two cameras?*
6 A2 If something is between two amounts, it is larger than the first amount but smaller than the second: *The temperature will be between 20 and 25 degrees today.*
7 B1 shared by a particular number of people: *We shared the cake between us.*

between[2] /bɪˈtwiːn/ **adv**
1 B1 in the space that separates two people, places, or things: *The wood is in neat piles with newspaper between.*
2 B1 in the period of time that separates two events or times: *There's a train at 6.15 and one at 10.30 but nothing* ***in between****.*

beware /bɪˈweəʳ/ **verb**
used in order to warn someone to be careful: ***Beware of*** *the dog.*

beyond /biˈɒnd/ **preposition**
1 B1 on the other side of something: *Our house is just beyond the bridge.*
2 B1 continuing after a particular time or date: *Not many people live beyond the age of a hundred.*

the Bible /ˈbaɪbl/ **noun**
1 the holy book of Christianity
2 the holy book of Judaism

bicycle /ˈbaɪsɪkl/ **noun**
A2 a vehicle with two wheels that you sit on and move by turning the two pedals (= parts you press with your feet)
→ See **Sports 2** on page C16

bicycle

bicycle lane /ˈbaɪsɪkl ˌleɪn/ **noun** US (UK **cycle lane**)
a part of a road or a special path that only people riding bicycles can use

bid[1] /bɪd/ **noun**
1 an attempt to do something good: *a successful* ***bid for*** *re-election*
2 an offer to pay a particular amount of money for something: *I made a* ***bid*** *of $150* ***for*** *the painting.*

bid[2] /bɪd/ **verb** (**bidding, bid**)
to offer to pay an amount of money for something: *They* ***bid*** *$500 million* ***for*** *the company.*

big /bɪg/ **adj** (**bigger, biggest**)
1 A1 large in size or amount: *I come from a big family.* ◦ *We're looking for a bigger house.*
→ Opposite **small adj** (1), **little adj** (1)
2 A2 important or serious: *Buying that car was a big mistake.*
3 your big brother/sister informal A2 your older brother or sister

bike /baɪk/ **noun** informal
1 A2 short form of bicycle
2 B1 short form of motorcycle: *He came* ***on*** *his* ***bike****.*

bikini /bɪˈkiːni/ **noun**
a piece of clothing with two parts that women wear for swimming
→ See **Clothes** on page C5

bilingual /baɪˈlɪŋgwəl/ **adj**
using or able to speak two languages: *a bilingual dictionary* ◦ *She's bilingual in English and Spanish.*

bill /bɪl/ **noun**
1 A2 a piece of paper that tells you how much you must pay for something: *Have you* ***paid the*** *electricity* ***bill****?*
2 US (UK **note**) a piece of paper money: *a five-dollar bill*

billion /ˈbɪliən/
B1 the number 1,000,000,000

bin /bɪn/ **noun** UK
a container that is used to put waste in: *I threw it in the bin.*
→ See **The Office** on page C12

bind /baɪnd/ **verb** (**bound**)
to tie something together with string, rope, etc.: *His hands were bound behind his back.*

binoculars /bɪˈnɒkjələz/ **plural noun**
a piece of equipment for looking at things that are far away, made from two tubes with glass at the ends

binoculars

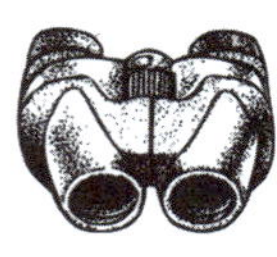

biography /baɪˈɒgrəfi/ **noun** (plural **biographies**)
B1 the story of a person's life written by another person

biological /ˌbaɪəˈlɒdʒɪkᵊl/ **adj**
connected with the natural processes of living things, such as plants and animals: *the biological sciences*

biology /baɪˈɒlədʒi/ **noun** [no plural]
A2 the study of living things
• **biologist noun** a scientist who studies biology

bird /bɜːd/ **noun**
A1 an animal that has wings and feathers and is usually able to fly

bird

Biro /ˈbaɪrəʊ/ **noun** UK trademark
a pen with a small ball in the end that rolls ink onto paper

birth /bɜːθ/ **noun**
1 B1 the time when a baby is born: *a difficult birth* ◦ *What's your* ***date of birth*** *(= the date when you were born)?*
2 give birth to produce a baby from your body: *She* ***gave birth to*** *twins.*

birthday /ˈbɜːθdeɪ/ **noun**
A1 the day of the year on which someone was born: *Her birthday is on March the eighteenth.* ◦ *Happy Birthday!*

biscuit /ˈbɪskɪt/ **noun** UK (US **cookie**)
A1 a thin, flat cake that is dry and usually sweet

bishop /ˈbɪʃəp/ **noun**
an important priest in some Christian churches: *the Bishop of Oxford*

bit[1] /bɪt/
past tense of bite

biscuits

bit[2] /bɪt/ **noun**
1 A2 a small amount or piece of something: *There's a little bit more pasta left.*
2 a bit A2 slightly: *It was a bit too expensive.*
3 a bit informal a short period of time: *I'll see you* ***in a bit.***
4 quite a bit informal B1 a lot: *He does quite a bit of travelling.*
5 bit by bit gradually: *She saved up the money, bit by bit.*
6 a unit of information in a computer

bite[1] /baɪt/ **verb** (**biting**, **bit**, **bitten**)
B1 to cut something using your teeth: *She* ***bit into*** *an apple.* ◦ *He was bitten by a dog.*

bite[2] /baɪt/ **noun**
1 a piece taken from food when you bite it: *She* ***took a bite*** *from her pizza.*
2 an injury caused when an animal or insect bites you: *mosquito bites*

bitten /ˈbɪtən/
past participle of bite

bitter /ˈbɪtəʳ/ **adj**
1 B1 having a strong, unpleasant taste
2 angry and upset: *She is still very* ***bitter about*** *the way she was treated.*
3 very cold
4 making you feel very unhappy or angry: *Failing the test was a bitter disappointment for me.*
• **bitterness noun** [no plural]

bizarre /bɪˈzɑːʳ/ **adj**
very strange and surprising: *bizarre behaviour*
• **bizarrely adv**

black[1] /blæk/ **adj**
1 (A1) being the colour of the sky on a dark night: *a black jacket*
→ See **Colours** on page C6
2 (A2) Someone who is black has the dark skin typical of people from Africa: *black Americans*
3 funny about unpleasant or frightening subjects: *black comedy*
• **blackness noun** [no plural]

black[2] /blæk/ **noun**
(A2) the colour of the sky on a dark night: *She always dresses* ***in black.***
→ See **Colours** on page C6

blackberry /ˈblækbᵊri/ **noun** (plural **blackberries**)
a small, soft, purple fruit with seeds

blackboard /ˈblækbɔːd/ **noun** (also US **chalkboard**)
(A2) a large, black or green board that teachers write on with chalk (= soft, white rock)

blackcurrant /ˌblækˈkʌrᵊnt/ **noun**
a small, round, dark purple fruit

blackmail /ˈblækmeɪl/ **noun** [no plural]
a situation in which someone forces you to do something, or to pay them money, by saying they will tell another person something secret
• **blackmail verb**

blade /bleɪd/ **noun**
1 the flat, sharp, metal part of a knife, tool, or weapon
2 a long, thin leaf of grass: *a blade of grass*

blame[1] /bleɪm/ **verb** (**blaming**, **blamed**)
(B1) to say that someone or something has done something bad: *She still* ***blames*** *him* ***for*** *Tony's death.*

blame[2] /bleɪm/ **noun** [no plural]
take the blame to be the person that everyone thinks has done something bad: *When a team loses it's always the manager who takes the blame.*

bland /blænd/ **adj**
1 boring and without excitement
2 If food is bland, it has no taste.

blank /blæŋk/ **adj**
1 (B1) with no writing, pictures, or sound: *a blank page* ◦ *a blank CD*
2 go blank If your mind goes blank, you suddenly cannot remember or think of something.

blanket /ˈblæŋkɪt/ **noun**
1 (A2) a thick, warm cover that you sleep under
2 a thick layer of something: *a blanket of snow*

blast /blɑːst/ **noun**
1 an explosion: *a bomb blast*
2 a sudden, strong movement of air: *a blast of cold air*

blaze[1] /bleɪz/ **verb** (**blazing**, **blazed**)
to burn or shine very brightly or strongly: *the blazing sun*

blaze[2] /bleɪz/ **noun**
1 a large fire: *The blaze started in the hall.*
2 a blaze of colour a lot of bright colours: *The flowers were a blaze of colour outside her window.*

bled /bled/
past tense and past participle of bleed

bleed /bliːd/ **verb** (**bled**)
(B1) to have blood coming out from a cut in your body

blend[1] /blend/ **verb**
1 to mix two or more things together completely: *Blend the sugar and butter till smooth.*
2 to look, sound, or taste good together: *The flavours blend very well.*

blend[2] /blend/ **noun**
two or more things that are put together: *Their music is a blend of jazz and African rhythms.*

blender /ˈblendəʳ/ **noun**
an electric machine that turns soft foods into a smooth liquid
→ See **The Kitchen** on page C10

bless /bles/ **verb**
1 to ask God to help or protect someone or something: *The priest blessed their marriage.*
2 Bless you! something you say when someone sneezes

blew /bluː/
past tense of blow

blind[1] /blaɪnd/ **adj**
B1 not able to see: *She **went blind** after an accident.*
• **blindness noun** [no plural]

blind[2] /blaɪnd/ **noun**
a cover that you pull down over a window

blink /blɪŋk/ **verb**
to quickly close and open your eyes
• **blink noun**

blister /ˈblɪstəʳ/ **noun**
a raised area of skin that hurts, caused by rubbing or burning

blizzard /ˈblɪzəd/ **noun**
a storm with strong winds and snow

blob /blɒb/ **noun**
a small amount of a thick liquid: *a blob of paint*
→ See **Quantities** on page C14

block[1] /blɒk/ **noun**
1 B1 a large building containing many apartments or offices: *a block of flats*
2 B1 a group of buildings between streets: *They only live two blocks away from the school.*
3 a solid piece of something, in the shape of a square: *a block of wood*

block[2] /blɒk/ **verb**
to stop anyone or anything from passing through a place: *A fallen tree blocked the road.*
block *something* up phrasal verb
to fill a narrow space with something so that nothing can pass through: *In autumn, leaves block the drains up.*
◦ *I've got a **blocked-up nose.***

blog[1] /blɒg/ **noun**
B1 a record of your activities or opinions that you put on the Internet for other people to read and that you change regularly: *There are two or three blogs that I read daily.*

blog[2] /blɒg/ **verb**
B1 to write a blog: *He blogs about travelling around the world.*

blogger /ˈblɒgəʳ/ **noun**
B1 someone who writes a blog: *Bloggers are commenting on the issue.*

blonde (also **blond**) /blɒnd/ **adj**
A2 Blonde hair is yellow.
→ See **Hair** on page C9

blood /blʌd/ **noun** [no plural]
A2 the red liquid that flows around your body

bloom /bluːm/ **verb**
If a plant blooms, its flowers open.

blossom /ˈblɒsᵊm/ **noun**
a small flower, or the small flowers on a tree or plant: *cherry blossom*

blouse /blaʊz/ **noun**
a shirt that women wear

blow[1] /bləʊ/ **verb** (**blowing**, **blew**, **blown**)
1 B1 If the wind blows, it moves and makes currents of air: *The wind blew hard during the storm.*
2 B1 to force air out through your mouth: *I blew on my coffee to cool it.*
3 B1 to make a sound by forcing air out of your mouth and through a musical instrument: *Ann blew a few notes on the trumpet.*
4 If the wind blows something somewhere, it makes it move in that direction: *The storm blew a tree across the road.*
5 blow your nose B1 to clear your nose by forcing air through it into a piece of paper
blow (*something*) away phrasal verb
B1 If something blows away, or if the wind blows something away, that thing moves because the wind blows it: *The letter blew away and I had to run after it.*
blow (*something*) down phrasal verb
B1 If something blows down, or if the wind blows something down, that thing falls to the ground because the wind blows it: *The wind blew our fence down last night.*
blow *something* out phrasal verb
B1 to stop a flame burning by blowing on it: *Emma blew out the candle.*
blow *something* up phrasal verb
1 B1 to destroy something with a bomb: *Terrorists blew up an office building in the city.*
2 to fill something with air

a b c d e f g h i j k l m n o p q r s t u v w x y z

a b c d e f g h i j k l m n o p q r s t u v w x y z

blow² /bləʊ/ **noun**
1 a hard hit with a hand or heavy object: *He received a* ***blow on*** *the head.*
2 a shock or disappointment: *Losing his job was a terrible* ***blow to*** *him.*

blown /ˈbləʊn/
past participle of blow

blue¹ /bluː/ **adj**
A1 being the same colour as the sky when there are no clouds: *a dark blue jacket*
→ See **Colours** on page C6

blue² /bluː/ **noun**
A2 the colour of the sky when there are no clouds
→ See **Colours** on page C6
• **out of the blue** If something happens out of the blue, you did not expect it.

blunt /blʌnt/ **adj**
1 not sharp: *a blunt knife*
2 saying exactly what you think without caring if you upset people
• **bluntness** **noun** [no plural]

blurred /blɜːd/ **adj**
1 not clear: *a blurred photograph*
2 If your sight is blurred, you cannot see clearly: *blurred vision*

blush /blʌʃ/ **verb**
If you blush, your face becomes red because you are embarrassed: *He* ***blushed with*** *shame.*
• **blush** **noun**

board¹ /bɔːd/ **noun**
1 A1 a surface on the wall of a classroom that a teacher writes on: *The teacher wrote an exercise* ***on the board****.*
2 A2 a piece of wood, plastic, etc. on a wall where information can be put: *I put the notice up on the board.*
3 A2 a flat piece of wood, cardboard, etc. for playing games on: *a chess board*
4 B1 a flat object or surface used for a particular purpose: *an ironing board* ◦ *a chopping board*
5 **on board** B1 on a boat, train, or plane
6 [no plural] meals that are provided when you stay in a hotel: *How much is a single room with* ***full board*** *(= all meals)?*
7 a long, thin, flat piece of wood: *He put some boards across the broken window.*
8 a group of people who control a company: *The board approved the plan.*

board² /bɔːd/ **verb**
1 B1 to get on a bus, boat, or plane
2 If a plane or train is boarding, passengers are getting onto it: *The plane is now boarding at gate 26.*

board game /ˈbɔːd ˌgeɪm/ **noun**
A2 a game such as chess that is played on a board: *It rained all day so we played lots of board games.*

boarding pass /ˈbɔːdɪŋ ˌpɑːs/ **noun**
(UK also **boarding card**)
a piece of paper you must show to get on a plane or ship

boast /bəʊst/ **verb**
to talk too proudly about something good that you have done or that you own: *I wish she would stop* ***boasting about*** *her new car.*

boat /bəʊt/ **noun**
A1 a vehicle for travelling on water: *a fishing/sailing boat*

body /ˈbɒdi/ **noun** (plural **bodies**)
1 A1 all of a person or animal: *the human body*
→ See **The Body** on page C2
2 A2 a dead person: *Police found the body in a field.*
3 B1 the main part of a person or animal's body, not the head, arms, or legs: *a dog with a thin body*

boil /bɔɪl/ **verb**
1 A2 If a liquid boils, or if you boil it, it reaches the temperature where bubbles rise up in it and it produces steam: *Could you boil some water for the pasta?* ◦ *boiling water*
2 B1 to cook food in water that is boiling: *Boil the eggs for three minutes.*
→ See picture at **cook**
3 B1 If a container of liquid boils, or if you boil it, it reaches the temperature where bubbles rise up in it and it produces steam: *Could you boil the kettle for me?* ◦ *The pan is boiling.*

boiled /bɔɪld/ **adj**
A2 cooked in water that is boiling: *boiled potatoes*

boiling /ˈbɔɪlɪŋ/ **adj** informal
very hot: *It's boiling in this room!*

bold /bəʊld/ **adj**
1 B1 strong in colour or shape: *a bold design*
2 brave: *It was a bold decision to go and live abroad.*
• **boldly adv**

bolt[1] /bəʊlt/ **noun**
1 a metal bar that you push across a door or window to lock it
2 a piece of metal that is used to attach things together by going through a nut (= piece of metal with a hole in it)

bolt[2] /bəʊlt/ **verb**
to lock a door or window with a bolt: *I bolted the door before going to bed.*

bomb[1] /bɒm/ **noun**
B1 a weapon that explodes and causes damage: *The **bomb went off** (= exploded), destroying the building.*

bomb[2] /bɒm/ **verb**
B1 to attack a place using bombs: *Factories were bombed during the war.*

bomber /ˈbɒməʳ/ **noun**
a person who puts a bomb somewhere to cause an explosion: *The bombers escaped by car.*

bone /bəʊn/ **noun**
B1 one of the hard, white pieces inside the body of a person or animal: *He broke a bone in his hand.*

bone

bonfire /ˈbɒnfaɪəʳ/ **noun**
a large fire that is made outside for pleasure or for burning waste

bonnet /ˈbɒnɪt/ **noun** UK (US **hood**)
the metal cover of a car's engine
→ See **Car** on page C3

bonus /ˈbəʊnəs/ **noun**
1 a pleasant thing in addition to something you were expecting: *The sunny weather was an **added bonus**.*
2 money you receive in addition to the usual amount, often because you have worked hard: *a Christmas bonus*

book[1] /bʊk/ **noun**
1 A1 a set of pages with writing on them fastened together in a cover: *I've just read a really good book.*
2 a set of pages fastened together in a cover and used for writing on: *an address book*

book[2] /bʊk/ **verb**
A2 to arrange to use or do something at a time in the future: *I've booked a hotel room.* ∘ *We've booked a trip to Spain for next month.*
book *someone* in/book *someone* into *something* **phrasal verb**
B1 to arrange for someone to stay at a hotel: *She booked me into a hotel in the town centre.*

bookcase /ˈbʊkkeɪs/ **noun**
A2 a piece of furniture with shelves for putting books on
→ See **The Living Room** on page C11

booking /ˈbʊkɪŋ/ **noun**
B1 an arrangement you make to have a hotel room, tickets, etc. at a particular time in the future: *We **made** the **booking** three months ago.*

bookshelf /ˈbʊkʃelf/ **noun** (plural **bookshelves** /ˈbʊkʃelvz/)
A2 a shelf that you put books on: *There's a bookshelf above our bed.*

bookshop /ˈbʊkʃɒp/ **noun** UK (US **bookstore** /ˈbʊkstɔːʳ/)
A2 a shop that sells books

boom /buːm/ **noun**
1 a loud, deep sound: *We heard a boom in the distance.*
2 a period when there is a big increase in sales or profits: *an economic boom*

boost[1] /buːst/ **verb**
to increase or improve something: *We hope that lower prices will boost sales.*

boost[2] /buːst/ **noun** [usually no plural]
something that makes you feel more confident and happy, or that helps something improve: *Passing my test was a **boost to** my **confidence**.*

boot /buːt/ **noun**
1 A2 a shoe that covers your foot and part of your leg: *a pair of boots*
→ See **Clothes** on page C5

2 B1 UK (US **trunk**) a closed space at the back of a car for storing things in
→ See **Car** on page C3

border /ˈbɔːdəʳ/ **noun**
1 B1 the line that separates two countries or states: *the border between France and Spain*
2 a line around the edge of something: *white plates with a blue border*

bore¹ /bɔːʳ/
past tense of bear

bore² /bɔːʳ/ **verb** (**boring**, **bored**)
to make someone feel bored

bore³ /bɔːʳ/ **noun**
a person or a situation that is boring: *It's a real bore not having a car.*

bored /bɔːd/ **adj**
A1 tired and unhappy because something is not interesting or because you are doing nothing: *I'm* ***bored with*** *doing homework.*

boredom /ˈbɔːdəm/ **noun**
a state of feeling bored: *the boredom of a long car journey*

boring /ˈbɔːrɪŋ/ **adj**
A1 not interesting or exciting: *a boring job* ◦ *The movie was so boring that I fell asleep.*

> **Common mistake: bored or boring?**
>
> **Bored** is used to describe how someone feels.
>
> *He didn't enjoy the lesson because he was bored.*
>
> ~~*He didn't enjoy the lesson because he was boring.*~~
>
> If something or someone is **boring**, they make you feel bored.
>
> *The book was long and boring.*

born /bɔːn/ **verb**
be born A2 When a person or animal is born, they come out of their mother's body and start to exist: *She was born in London in 1973.*

borne /bɔːn/
past participle of bear

borrow /ˈbɒrəʊ/ **verb**
1 A2 to use something that belongs to someone else and then return it to them: *Can I borrow a pen please?*
2 to take money from a person or bank and pay it back over a period of time

boss¹ /bɒs/ **noun**
A2 someone who is responsible for employees and tells them what to do

boss² /bɒs/ **verb** (also **boss around**)
to tell someone what they should do all the time: *She's always bossing her little brother around.*

bossy /ˈbɒsi/ **adj** (**bossier**, **bossiest**)
always telling other people what to do

both /bəʊθ/ **pronoun**, **determiner**
A1 used to talk about two people or things: *Both her parents are dead.* ◦ ***Both of*** *my sisters are teachers.*

bother¹ /ˈbɒðəʳ/ **verb**
1 A2 to annoy someone by talking to them when they are busy: *Don't bother your father when he's working.*
2 to worry or upset someone: *I'm used to living alone – it doesn't bother me.*
3 to make the effort to do something: *He didn't even* ***bother to*** *call.*
4 **can't be bothered** informal If you can't be bothered to do something, you are too lazy or tired to do it: *I can't be bothered to iron my clothes.*

bother² /ˈbɒðəʳ/ **noun** [no plural]
trouble or problems: *I'll drive you there – it's no bother!*

bottle /ˈbɒtl/ **noun**
A2 a container for liquids, usually made of glass or plastic, with a narrow top: *a bottle of wine*

bottled /ˈbɒtld/ **adj**
contained, stored, or sold in bottles: *bottled water*

bottom /ˈbɒtəm/ **noun**
1 A1 the lowest part of something: *Click on the icon* ***at the bottom of*** *the page.*
2 A2 the flat surface on the lowest side of something: *There was a price tag on* ***the bottom of*** *the box.*
3 A2 [no plural] the lowest position in a group or organization: *His team are* ***at the bottom of*** *the first division.*
4 B1 [no plural] the part of an area that is furthest from where you are: *the bottom of the garden*

5 B1 the part of your body that you sit on
6 B1 [no plural] the ground under a river, lake, or sea: *The ship sank to **the bottom of** the sea.*

bought /bɔːt/
past tense and past participle of buy

bounce /baʊns/ **verb** (**bouncing**, **bounced**)
1 to hit a surface and then move quickly away, or to make something do this: *The ball bounced into the air.*
2 to jump up and down many times on a soft surface: *The children love to bounce on the bed.*

bound[1] /baʊnd/
past tense and past participle of bind

bound[2] /baʊnd/ **adj**
bound to do *something* certain to do something, or certain to happen: *You're bound to feel nervous before a test.*

bow[1] /baʊ/ **verb**
to bend your head or body forward in order to show respect or to thank an audience: *The actors all bowed after the performance.*

bow[2] /baʊ/ **noun**
an act of bending your head or body forward: *The actors came back on stage and **took a bow**.*

bow[3] /bəʊ/ **noun**
1 a knot with two circles that is used to tie shoes or as a decoration
2 a piece of curved wood with string attached to both ends, used for shooting arrows
3 a long, thin piece of wood with hair stretched between the ends, used to play some musical instruments

bowl /bəʊl/ **noun**
A2 a round, deep dish used for holding soup and other food

box /bɒks/ **noun**
1 A1 a square or rectangular container: *a cardboard box* ◦ *a **box of** chocolates*
→ See picture at **container**
2 A2 a small square on a page that gives you information or where you write information: *If you would like more information, tick this box.*

boxer /ˈbɒksəʳ/ **noun**
someone who does the sport of boxing

boxer shorts /ˈbɒksə ˌʃɔːts/ **plural noun**
loose underwear for men
→ See **Clothes** on page C5

boxing /ˈbɒksɪŋ/ **noun** [no plural]
B1 a sport in which two people hit each other while wearing big, leather gloves (= pieces of clothing for your hands)

boxing

Boxing Day /ˈbɒksɪŋ ˌdeɪ/ **noun**
26 December, a public holiday in the UK and Canada

boy /bɔɪ/ **noun**
A1 a male child or young man: *We've got three children – a boy and two girls.*

boyfriend /ˈbɔɪfrend/ **noun**
A2 a man or boy who someone is having a romantic relationship with

bra /brɑː/ **noun**
a piece of woman's underwear that supports the breasts
→ See **Clothes** on page C5

bracelet /ˈbreɪslət/ **noun**
B1 a piece of jewellery that you wear around your wrist
→ See picture at **jewellery**

brackets /ˈbrækɪts/ **noun** UK
two curved lines ( ) used around information that is separate from the main part

braid /breɪd/ **noun** US (UK **plait**)
a single piece of hair made by twisting three thinner pieces over and under each other
→ See **Hair** on page C9

brain /breɪn/ **noun**
A2 the part inside your head that controls your

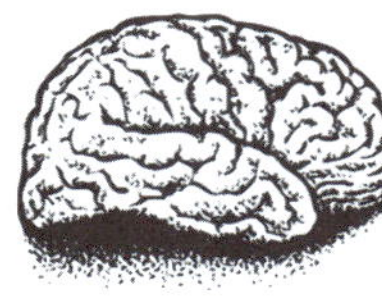
brain

thoughts, feelings, and movements: *brain damage*

brake[1] /breɪk/ **noun**
B1 the part of a vehicle that makes it stop or go more slowly

brake[2] /breɪk/ **verb** (**braking**, **braked**)
B1 to make a car stop by using its brake

branch /brɑːnʃ/ **noun**
1 B1 one of the many parts of a tree that grows out from the main part
→ See picture at **tree**
2 B1 one of many shops or offices that are part of a company: *a bank with branches all over the country*
3 a part of a subject: *Geometry is a **branch of** mathematics.*

brand /brænd/ **noun**
a product that is made by a particular company: *Which brand of toothpaste do you use?*

brand new /ˌbrænd ˈnjuː/ **adj**
B1 completely new: *a brand new sports car*

brandy /ˈbrændi/ **noun** (plural **brandies**)
a strong alcoholic drink made from wine

brass /brɑːs/ **noun** [no plural]
a shiny yellow metal: *a door with a brass handle*

brave /breɪv/ **adj**
B1 Not afraid of dangerous or difficult situations: *He died after a brave fight against cancer.*
• **bravely** **adv**

bravery /ˈbreɪvᵊri/ **noun** [no plural]
actions or behavior that show someone is brave

bread /bred/ **noun** [no plural]
A1 a basic food made by mixing and baking flour and water: *a slice of bread* ◦ *a loaf of white bread*

break[1] /breɪk/ **verb** (**broke**, **broken**)
1 A2 to separate into two or more pieces, or to make something separate into two or more pieces: *They had to break a window to get in.*
2 A2 to damage a bone in your body: *She broke her leg in the accident.*
3 A2 to stop working or to make something stop working: *Who broke the TV?*

break

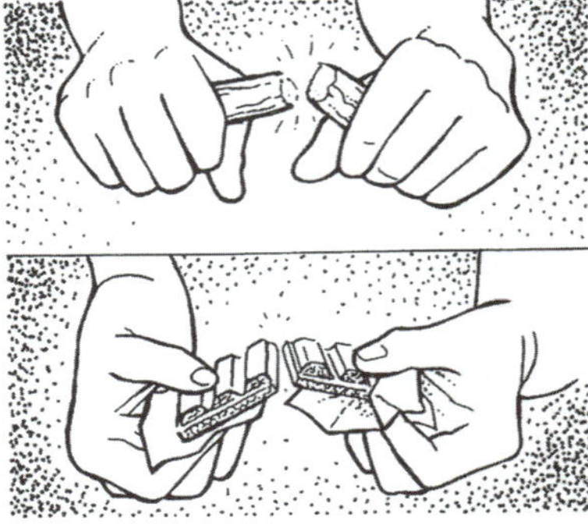

4 to not do something that you should do: *I don't like to **break promises**.*
5 **break the law** to do something that the law says you must not do
6 B1 to stop an activity and have a short rest: *Let's **break for** five minutes.*
7 to come to an end or make something come to an end: *Eventually someone spoke, breaking the silence.*

break down **phrasal verb**
B1 If a car or machine breaks down, it stops working: *My car broke down on the way to work.*

break into *something* **phrasal verb**
B1 to get into a building or car using force, usually to steal something: *Someone broke into the office and stole some computers.*

break off **phrasal verb**
to become separated from something by force: *A large piece of ice had broken off from the iceberg.*

break *something* off **phrasal verb**
1 to separate something from something else by breaking it: *He broke off a piece of chocolate.*
2 to end something suddenly: *She broke off the engagement two weeks before the wedding.*

break out **phrasal verb**
If something dangerous or unpleasant breaks out, it suddenly starts: *The fire broke out in the early morning.* ◦ *War broke out in 1914.*

break up **phrasal verb**

1 B1 to stop having a relationship: *He's just **broken up with** his girlfriend.*
2 B1 UK When schools or colleges break up, the classes end and the holidays begin.

break² /breɪk/ **noun**
1 A2 the act of stopping an activity for a short time, usually to rest: *a coffee break*
2 B1 a holiday or period of time away from work or school: *a weekend break in Paris*
3 B1 a place where a bone has been broken in an accident

breakdown /ˈbreɪkdaʊn/ **noun**
1 (also **nervous breakdown**) a short period of mental illness
2 an occasion when a car or machine stops working

breakfast /ˈbrekfəst/ **noun**
A1 the food you eat in the morning after you wake up

breast /brest/ **noun**
B1 one of the two soft, round parts on a woman's chest

breath /breθ/ **noun**
1 B1 [no plural] the air that comes out of your lungs: *His breath smells of garlic.*
2 an amount of air that goes into or out of your lungs: *She **took a deep breath** before she started.*
3 **be out of breath** to be breathing quickly because you have been doing exercise
4 **hold your breath** to keep air in your lungs and not let it out: *How long can you hold your breath under water?*

> **Common mistake: breath or breathe?**
>
> Be careful not to confuse the noun **breath** with the verb **breathe**.
>
> *I was so excited, I could hardly breathe.*

breathe /briːð/ **verb** (**breathing**, **breathed**)
B1 to take air into and out of your lungs: *breathe in/out* ◦ *breathe deeply*

bred /bred/
past tense and past participle of breed

breed¹ /briːd/ **noun**
a type of dog, sheep, pig, etc.: *a rare breed of cattle*

breed² /briːd/ **verb** (**bred**)
1 If animals breed, they produce babies.
2 to keep animals in order to produce baby animals

breeze /briːz/ **noun**
B1 a gentle wind: *a cool breeze*

bribe /braɪb/ **noun**
money or a present that you give to someone so that they will do something for you: *The politician was accused of **accepting bribes**.*
• **bribe** **verb** (**bribing**, **bribed**)

brick /brɪk/ **noun**
a hard, rectangular block used for building walls: *a brick wall*

brick

bride /braɪd/ **noun**
B1 a woman who is getting married or has just been married

bridegroom /ˈbraɪdgruːm/ **noun**
a man who is getting married

bridesmaid /ˈbraɪdzmeɪd/ **noun**
a woman or girl who helps the bride on her wedding day

bridge

bridge /brɪdʒ/ **noun**
A2 a structure that is built over a river or road so that people can go across it: *Brooklyn Bridge*

brief /briːf/ **adj**
1 B1 lasting only for a short time: *a brief visit*
2 B1 using only a few words: *a brief description*

a b c d e f g h i j k l m n o p q r s t u v w x y z

3 in brief using only a few words: *world news in brief*
• **briefly adv** B1 *They discussed the matter briefly.*

briefcase /ˈbriːfkeɪs/ **noun** a flat, rectangular case with a handle for carrying documents or books

briefcase

bright /braɪt/ **adj**
1 A2 having a strong, light colour: *bright yellow/blue*
2 B1 full of light or shining strongly: *bright sunshine*
3 intelligent: *He's a bright boy.*
4 happy or full of hope: *She has a **bright future**.*
• **brightly adv**
• **brightness noun** [no plural]

brilliant /ˈbrɪliənt/ **adj**
1 A2 UK very good: *We saw a brilliant movie.*
2 B1 very clever: *a brilliant scholar*
3 B1 full of light or colour: *The sky was a brilliant blue.*
• **brilliantly adv** *He played the piano brilliantly.*

bring /brɪŋ/ **verb** (**brought**)
1 A2 to take someone or something with you when you go somewhere: *Did you bring an umbrella with you?* ◦ *He brought me some flowers.*
2 bring (*someone*) happiness, luck, peace, etc. B1 to cause happiness, luck, peace, etc.: *She's brought us so much happiness over the years.*

Common mistake: bring or take?

Use **bring** to talk about moving something or someone towards the speaker or towards the place where you are now.
Did you bring any money?
I've brought you a present.
Use **take** to talk about moving something or someone away from the speaker or away from the place where you are now.
I can take you to the station.
Don't forget to take your umbrella.

bring *something* back phrasal verb A2 to return from somewhere with something: *Look at what I brought back from my trip.*

bring *someone* up phrasal verb B1 to take care of a child until he or she becomes an adult: *Her grandparents brought her up.*

bring *something* up phrasal verb to start to talk about a particular subject: *She's always bringing up her health problems.*

broad /brɔːd/ **adj**
1 B1 wide: *broad shoulders*
2 B1 including many different things: *a broad range of subjects*

broadband /ˈbrɔːdbænd/ **noun** [no plural]
a type of Internet connection that allows large amounts of information to be sent or received very quickly: *We've got broadband at home.*

broadcast¹ /ˈbrɔːdkɑːst/ **noun** a television or radio programme: *a news broadcast*

broadcast² /ˈbrɔːdkɑːst/ **verb** (**broadcast**)
to send out a programme on television or radio: *The concert will be broadcast live next week.*

broccoli /ˈbrɒkəli/ **noun** [no plural]
B1 a green vegetable with a thick stem

brochure /ˈbrəʊʃəʳ/ **noun**
B1 a thin book with pictures and information, usually advertising something: *a holiday brochure*

broke /brəʊk/
past tense of break

broken¹ /ˈbrəʊkən/
past participle of break

broken² /ˈbrəʊkən/ **adj**
1 A2 damaged and separated into pieces: *broken glass*
2 A2 with a damaged bone: *a broken leg*
3 A2 not working: *The TV is broken.*
4 a broken heart a feeling of sadness because of the end of a relationship: *They said she died of a broken heart.*

bronze /brɒnz/ **noun** [no plural]
a shiny orange-brown metal

broom /bruːm/ **noun**
a brush with a long handle used for cleaning the floor

brother /ˈbrʌðəʳ/ **noun**
A1 a boy or man who has the same parents as you: *an* ***older/younger*** *brother* ◦ *my* ***little brother*** *(= younger brother)* ◦ *my* ***big brother*** *(= older brother)*

brother-in-law /ˈbrʌðərɪnlɔː/ **noun** (plural **brothers-in-law**)
the man married to someone's sister, or the brother of someone's husband or wife: *My sister and brother-in-law have two kids.*

brought /brɔːt/
past tense and past participle of bring

brown /braʊn/ **adj**
A1 being the same colour as chocolate: *dark brown hair*
• **brown noun** A2 the colour brown
→ See **Colours** on page C6

browser /ˈbraʊzəʳ/ **noun**
a computer program that allows you to look at pages on the Internet

bruise /bruːz/ **noun**
a dark area on your skin where you have been hurt: *He suffered cuts and bruises after falling off his bike.*
• **bruise verb** (**bruising**, **bruised**) to make someone have a bruise: *He was badly bruised in the accident.*

brushes

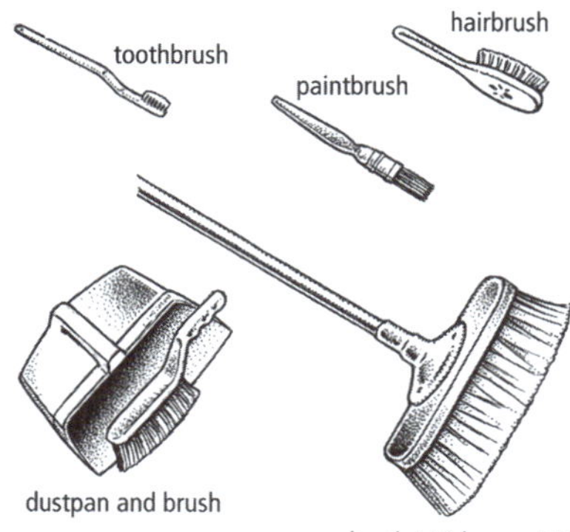

brush¹ /brʌʃ/ **noun**
A2 an object made of short, thin pieces of plastic, wire, etc. attached to a handle and used to arrange hair, to clean, or to paint: *a stiff wire brush*

brush² /brʌʃ/ **verb**
1 A2 to use a brush to clean or tidy something: *to* ***brush your hair/teeth***
2 to lightly touch someone or something as you move past: *Charlotte* ***brushed against*** *him as she left the room.*
3 brush *something* away, off, etc. to move something somewhere using a brush or your hand: *Jackie brushed the hair out of her eyes.* ◦ *He brushed away a tear.*

brutal /ˈbruːtəl/ **adj**
very violent or cruel: *a brutal murder*
• **brutally adv** *brutally murdered*

bubble /ˈbʌbl/ **noun**
a ball of air or gas with liquid around it: *an air bubble*

bubbles

bucket /ˈbʌkɪt/ **noun** (also **pail**)
B1 a round, open container with a handle used for carrying liquids: *a bucket of water*

bucket

buckle /ˈbʌkl/ **noun**
a metal object used to fasten the ends of a belt or strap: *a silver buckle*
→ See **Clothes** on page C5

bud /bʌd/ **noun**
a part of a plant that develops into a leaf or a flower: *In spring the trees are covered in buds.*

Buddhism /ˈbʊdɪzəm/ **noun** [no plural]
a religion based on the ideas that Buddha taught

Buddhist /ˈbʊdɪst/ **noun**
someone whose religion is Buddhism
• **Buddhist adj**

budget /ˈbʌdʒɪt/ **noun**
a plan that shows how much money you have and how you will spend it

budgie /ˈbʌdʒi/ **noun** UK
a small, brightly coloured bird often kept as a pet

buffalo /ˈbʌfəˈləʊ/ **noun** (plural **buffaloes**, **buffalo**)
a large wild animal similar to a cow: *a herd of buffalo*

bug /bʌg/ **noun**
1 B1 a small insect
2 an illness that is caused by bacteria or viruses: *a stomach bug*
3 a mistake in a computer program

buggy /ˈbʌgi/ **noun** (plural **buggies**)
UK (US **stroller**) a chair on wheels that is used to move small children

build /bɪld/ **verb** (**built**)
A2 to make something by putting materials and parts together: *He built his own house.*

builder /ˈbɪldər/ **noun**
B1 someone who makes or repairs buildings as a job

building /ˈbɪldɪŋ/ **noun**
1 A2 a structure with walls and a roof, such as a house or school: *an office building*
2 [no plural] the activity of putting together materials and parts to make structures

building society /ˈbɪldɪŋ səˌsaɪəti/ **noun** (plural **building societies**)
UK an organization similar to a bank that lends you money if you want to buy a house

built /bɪlt/
past tense and past participle of build

bulb /bʌlb/ **noun**
B1 a glass object containing a wire that produces light from electricity: *an electric light bulb*

bulky /ˈbʌlki/ **adj** (**bulkier**, **bulkiest**)
too big and taking up too much space

bull /bʊl/ **noun**
B1 a male cow

bullet /ˈbʊlɪt/ **noun**
a small metal object that is fired from a gun

bulletin board /ˈbʊlətɪn ˌbɔːd/ **noun** US (UK **noticeboard**)
a board on a wall where you put pieces of paper telling people about things: *I saw the ad **on** the **bulletin board**.*

bully¹ /ˈbʊli/ **verb** (**bullying**, **bullied**)
to try to frighten someone who is smaller or weaker than you: *He was bullied at school by some older boys.*
• **bullying** **noun** [no plural] *Bullying is a problem in many schools.*

bully² /ˈbʊli/ **noun** (plural **bullies**)
someone who intentionally frightens a person who is smaller or weaker than them

bump¹ /bʌmp/ **verb**
to hurt part of your body by hitting it against something hard: *I bumped my head on the door.*
bump into *something* **phrasal verb**
to hit something with force: *She kept bumping into things.*
bump into *someone* **phrasal verb**
to meet someone you know without planning it: *I bumped into an old school friend in town today.*

bump² /bʌmp/ **noun**
1 a round, raised area on a surface: *My bike hit a bump in the road.*
2 a raised area on your body where it has been hurt: *a painful bump on the head*

bumper /ˈbʌmpər/ **noun**
a bar attached to the front and back of a car to protect it in an accident

bun /bʌn/ **noun**
1 UK a small, round cake: *a cream bun*
2 a small, round piece of bread: *a hamburger bun*

bunch /bʌnʃ/ **noun**
1 B1 a number of things of the same type that are joined together: *a **bunch of** flowers*
→ See **Quantities** on page C14
2 B1 informal a group of people: *His friends are a nice bunch.*

bundle /ˈbʌndl/ **noun**
a number of things that are tied together: *a bundle of letters/clothes*

bungalow /ˈbʌŋɡəl əʊ/ **noun**
a house that has all its rooms on the ground floor

buoy /bɔɪ/ **noun**
a floating object used in water to mark dangerous areas for boats

burger /ˈbɜːɡər/ **noun**
A2 meat in a round, flat shape, that you eat between bread

burglar /ˈbɜːɡlər/ **noun**
someone who gets into buildings illegally and steals things

burglarize /ˈbɜːɡləraɪz/ **verb** (**burglarizing**, **burglarized**) US
US word for burgle

burglary /ˈbɜːɡləri/ **noun** (plural **burglaries**)
the crime of going into a building illegally and stealing things

burgle /ˈbɜːɡl/ **verb** (**burgling**, **burgled**) UK (US **burglarize**)
to get into a building illegally and steal things: *They've been burgled twice recently.*

burn¹ /bɜːn/ **verb** (**burnt**, **burned**)
1 B1 to destroy something with fire, or to be destroyed by fire: *I burnt all his letters.* ◦ *The factory burned to the ground.*
2 B1 to produce flames: *The fire's burning well.*
3 B1 to be hurt by fire or heat: *He burned his hand on the iron.*
4 to copy music, information or images onto a CD: *He's burnt all his favourite records onto a CD.*
5 to use fuel to produce heat or energy: *to burn fuel*
burn down **phrasal verb**
to be destroyed by fire: *Their house burnt down while they were away on holiday.*

burn² /bɜːn/ **noun**
a place where fire or heat has damaged or hurt something: *She has a nasty burn on her arm.*

burning /ˈbɜːnɪŋ/ **adj**
1 B1 on fire: *Firefighters rushed into the burning house.*
2 very hot: *the burning heat of the desert sun*

burnt¹ /bɜːnt/ mainly UK
past tense and past participle of burn

burnt² /bɜːnt/ **adj**
destroyed or made black by fire or heat: *burnt toast*

burst /bɜːst/ **verb** (**burst**)
1 If a container bursts, or if you burst it, it breaks suddenly, so that what is inside it comes out: *A water pipe burst and flooded the cellar.* ◦ *He burst all the balloons.*
2 **burst into flames** to suddenly start burning
3 **burst into tears** to suddenly start crying: *She burst into tears and ran away.*
4 **burst out laughing** to suddenly start laughing

bury /ˈberi/ **verb** (**burying**, **buried**)
1 B1 to put a dead body into the ground: *He was buried next to his wife.*
2 B1 to hide something in the ground or under something: *buried treasure*

bus /bʌs/ **noun**
A1 a large vehicle that carries passengers by road: *a school bus*
→ See picture at **vehicle**

bush

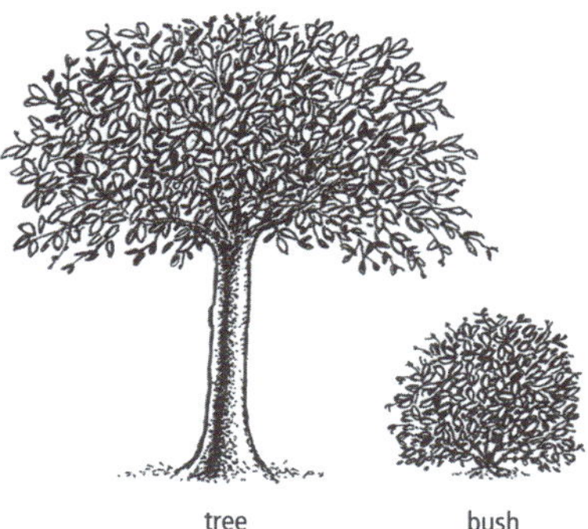

bush /bʊʃ/ **noun**
a short, thick plant with a lot of branches: *a rose bush*

business /ˈbɪznɪs/ **noun**
1 A1 [no plural] the buying and selling of goods or services: *We* ***do*** *a lot of* ***business with*** *China.*
2 A2 an organization that sells goods or services: *He* ***runs a*** *small cleaning* ***business****.*
3 B1 [no plural] work that is part of your job: *a business trip/lunch*

a b c d e f g h i j k l m n o p q r s t u v w x y z

a b c d e f g h i j k l m n o p q r s t u v w x y z

4 be none of *someone's* business to be something private that another person should not be interested in
5 mind your own business used to rudely tell someone that a subject is private and they should not ask you about it

businessman, businesswoman /ˈbɪznɪsmən/, /ˈbɪznɪsˌwʊmən/ **noun** (plural **businessmen, businesswomen**)
A2 someone who works in business, usually having an important job

bus station /ˈbʌs ˌsteɪʃən/ **noun**
A2 the place where a bus starts or ends its journey: *The bus station is in the centre of town.*

bus stop /ˈbʌs ˌstɒp/ **noun**
a place where a bus stops to allow passengers to get on and off: *Wait for me at the bus stop.*

busy /ˈbɪzi/ **adj** (**busier, busiest**)
1 A2 working hard, or giving your attention to a particular activity: *Mum was busy in the kitchen.* ◦ *I've got plenty of jobs to **keep** you **busy**.*
2 A2 full of activity or people: *a busy restaurant*
3 A2 In a busy period, you have a lot of things to do: *I've had a busy day.*

but¹ strong /bʌt/ weak /bət/ **conjunction**
A1 used to introduce something new, especially something that is different from what you have just said: *I'd drive you there, but I don't have my car.* ◦ *The food was good but expensive.*

but² strong /bʌt/ weak /bət/ **preposition**
B1 except: *Everyone but Andrew knows.*

butcher /ˈbʊtʃəʳ/ **noun**
B1 someone who prepares and sells meat

butter /ˈbʌtəʳ/ **noun** [no plural]
A1 a soft, yellow food made from cream that you put on bread
→ See **Food** on page C7

butterfly /ˈbʌtəflaɪ/ **noun** (plural **butterflies**)
B1 an insect with large, coloured wings
→ See picture at **insect**

buttock /ˈbʌtək/ **noun**
one of the two sides of your bottom

button /ˈbʌtᵊn/ **noun**
1 B1 a small, round object that you push through a hole to fasten clothes: *You haven't done your buttons up.*
2 B1 a switch that you press to control a piece of equipment: *Press the play button to listen to your recording.*

buy /baɪ/ **verb** (**buying, bought**)
A1 to get something by giving money for it: *I went to the shop to buy some milk.*

buyer /ˈbaɪəʳ/ **noun**
B1 someone who buys something expensive, such as a house: *He's still looking for a buyer for his house.*

buzz /bʌz/ **verb**
to make a continuous sound like a bee: *I can hear something buzzing.*

by¹ /baɪ/ **preposition**
1 A2 used to show the person or thing that does something: *a painting by Van Gogh* ◦ *The building had been destroyed by fire.*
2 A2 through doing or using something: *I sent it by email.* ◦ *We'll get there by car.*
3 A2 before a particular time or date: *Applications have to be in by the 31st.*
4 B1 near or next to: *I'll meet you by the post office.*
5 holding a particular part of someone or something: *She grabbed me by the arm.*
6 past: *He sped by me on a motorcycle.*
7 used to show measurements or amounts: *twelve by ten feet of floor space* ◦ *I'm paid by the hour.*

by² /baɪ/ **adv**
past: *I sat there, watching people walk by.*

bye /baɪ/ **exclamation** (also **bye-bye**)
A1 goodbye: *Bye, see you tomorrow.*

byte /baɪt/ **noun**
a unit for measuring the amount of information a computer can store

Cc

C, c /siː/
the third letter of the alphabet

C
written abbreviation for Celsius or centigrade: *30°C*

cab /kæb/ **noun** informal
B1 a taxi (= car that you pay to travel in): *We **took a cab** to the theatre.*

cabbage /ˈkæbɪdʒ/ **noun**
B1 a large, round vegetable with a lot of green or white leaves

cabin /ˈkæbɪn/ **noun**
1 B1 the area where most people sit on a plane
2 a small house made of wood: *a log cabin*
3 a small room to sleep in on a ship: *We had a cabin on the top deck.*

cabinet /ˈkæbɪnət/ **noun**
1 a group of people in a government who advise the leader: *A Cabinet minister*
2 a cupboard with shelves or drawers: *kitchen cabinets*

cable /ˈkeɪbl/ **noun**
1 B1 [no plural] the system of sending television programmes or telephone signals along wires in the ground: *cable TV*
2 a wire that carries electricity or telephone signals
3 a metal rope

cactus /ˈkæktəs/ **noun** (plural **cacti** /ˈkæktaɪ/, **cactuses**)
a plant with thick leaves and sharp points that grows in deserts

cactus

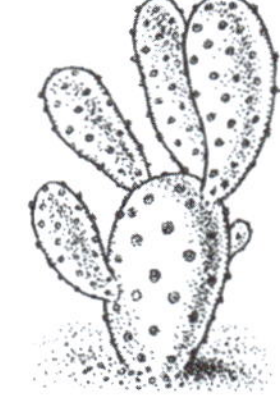

café (also **cafe**) /ˈkæfeɪ/ **noun**
A1 a small restaurant where you buy drinks and small meals

cafeteria /ˌkæfəˈtɪəriə/ **noun**
a restaurant where you pick up and pay for your food and drink before you eat it: *a school cafeteria*

cage /keɪdʒ/ **noun**
B1 a container made of wire or metal bars used for keeping birds or animals in: *a bird cage*

cage

cake /keɪk/ **noun**
A1 a sweet food made from flour, butter, sugar, and eggs mixed together and baked: *a chocolate cake*

cake

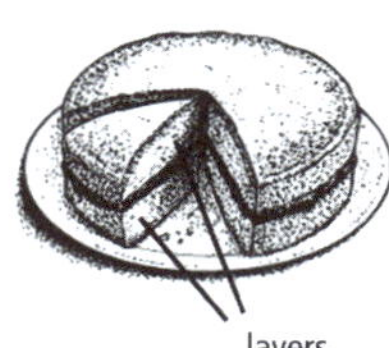

calculate /ˈkælkjəleɪt/ **verb** (**calculating**, **calculated**)
to discover an amount or number using mathematics: *I'm trying to calculate the cost of the trip.*

calculation /ˌkælkjəˈleɪʃən/ **noun**
the use of mathematics to find a number or amount

calculator /ˈkælkjəleɪtər/ **noun**
B1 a small machine that you use to do mathematics

calendar /ˈkæləndər/ **noun**
A2 something that shows all the days, weeks, and months of the year

calf /kɑːf/ **noun** (plural **calves** /kɑːvz/)
1 B1 a young cow
2 the back of your leg below your knee
→ See **The Body** on page C2

call¹ /kɔːl/ **verb**
1 B1 to give someone a name: *They called their first son Joshua.*
2 **be called *something*** A1 to have a particular name: *a boy called Adam* ◦ *Their latest album is called 'In Rainbows'.*
3 A2 to telephone someone: *Call the police.*
4 B1 to shout: *I heard someone call my name.*
5 to describe someone or something in a particular way: *Are you calling me a liar?*

6 to ask someone to come somewhere: *She called me into her office.*
call (*someone*) back phrasal verb
A2 to telephone someone a second time, or to telephone someone who telephoned you earlier
call for *someone* phrasal verb
B1 to go to a place in order to get someone: *I'll call for you at eight.*
call in phrasal verb
B1 to visit a place or person for a short time, usually while you are going somewhere else: *I'll call in on my way home.*
call *something* off phrasal verb
to decide that something that is planned will not happen: *The game was called off because of bad weather.*

call² /kɔːl/ **noun**
1 A2 the act of using the telephone: ***Give me a call*** *at the weekend.* ◦ *I* ***got a call*** *from Sue this morning.*
2 B1 the act of shouting something
3 a sound made by a bird or other animal

caller /ˈkɔːləʳ/ **noun**
someone who makes a telephone call: *an anonymous caller*

call-in /ˈkɔːlɪn/ **noun** US (UK **phone-in**)
a television or radio programme in which the public can ask questions or give opinions over the telephone

calm¹ /kɑːm/ **adj**
1 B1 relaxed and not worried or frightened: *a calm voice*
2 B1 If the weather or the sea is calm, it is quiet and peaceful.
• **calmly** **adv** in a relaxed way: *He spoke slowly and calmly.*

calm² /kɑːm/ **verb**
calm down phrasal verb
to stop feeling angry, upset, or excited: *Calm down and tell me what's wrong.*

calorie /ˈkæləri/ **noun**
a unit for measuring the amount of energy food provides: *I try to eat about 2000 calories a day.*

calves /kɑːvz/
plural of calf

camcorder /ˈkæmˌkɔːdəʳ/ **noun**
a camera that you hold in your hand and that records moving pictures

came /keɪm/
past tense of come

camel /ˈkæməl/ **noun**
B1 a large animal that lives in hot, dry places and has one or two humps (= raised parts on its back)

camera /ˈkæmərə/ **noun**
A1 a piece of equipment used to take photographs

camp¹ /kæmp/ **noun**
1 B1 an area where people stay in tents for a short time, usually on holiday
2 an area containing temporary buildings or tents used for soldiers, prisoners, etc.

camp² /kæmp/ **verb**
A2 to stay in a tent or temporary home: *We camped on the beach for two nights.*

campaign¹ /kæmˈpeɪn/ **noun**
1 a group of activities that are planned to get a result: *an election campaign*
2 a lot of military attacks: *a bombing campaign*

campaign² /kæmˈpeɪn/ **verb**
to organize a group of activities to try to make something happen

camper /ˈkæmpəʳ/ **noun**
1 someone who stays in a tent on holiday
2 a vehicle that you can live in, containing a bed, kitchen equipment, etc.

camping /ˈkæmpɪŋ/ **noun** [no plural]
A2 living in a tent for a holiday

campsite /ˈkæmpsaɪt/ **noun** UK (US **campground** /ˈkæmpgraʊnd/)
B1 an area where people stay in tents for a holiday

a b c d e f g h i j k l m n o p q r s t u v w x y z

campus /ˈkæmpəs/ **noun**
the land and buildings belonging to a college or university

can[1] /kæn/ **noun** (UK also **tin**)
A2 a metal container for food or liquids: *a can of soup*
→ See picture at **container**

can[2] strong /kæn/ weak /kən/, /kn/ **modal verb**

> **Common mistake: cannot**
> Remember that the negative form of **can** is written as one word.
> *They cannot decide what to do.*
> ~~*They can not decide what to do.*~~

1 **A1** to be able to do something: *Can you drive?* ◦ *I can't swim.*
2 **A1** used to request something: *Can I have a glass of water?*
3 **A1** used in polite offers of help: *Can I help you with those bags?*
4 **A1** to be allowed to do something: *You can't park here.* ◦ *Can I go now?*
5 **A2** used to talk about what is possible: *You can get stamps from the local newsagents.*
6 **B1** used to show surprise or lack of belief: *You can't possibly be hungry already!* ◦ *Can you believe it?*

canal /kəˈnæl/ **noun**
B1 a river made by people

cancel /ˈkænsᵊl/ **verb** (**cancelling**, **cancelled**)
B1 to say that an organized event will not happen: *The meeting has been cancelled.*

cancellation /ˌkænsᵊlˈeɪʃᵊn/ **noun**
a decision that an event will not happen

cancer /ˈkænsəʳ/ **noun**
B1 a serious disease that is caused when some cells in the body grow too much and damage other cells: *lung cancer*

candidate /ˈkændɪdət/ **noun**
1 a person who takes part in an election or tries to get a job: *a presidential candidate*
2 **B1** UK someone who is taking an exam

candle

candle /ˈkændl/ **noun**
B1 a stick of wax with string inside it that you burn to make light

candy /ˈkændi/ **noun** (plural **candies**) US
a small piece of sweet food: *a candy bar*

canned /kænd/ **adj** (UK also **tinned**)
Canned food is sold in metal containers: *canned tomatoes*

cannon /ˈkænən/ **noun**
a very large gun

cannot /ˈkænɒt/ **modal verb**
A1 the negative form of 'can': *I cannot say what will happen.*

canoe

canoe /kəˈnuː/ **noun**
a small, thin boat with pointed ends for one or two people

can opener /ˈkæn ˌəʊpᵊnəʳ/ **noun** (UK also **tin opener**)
a piece of kitchen equipment for opening metal food containers

can't /kɑːnt/ **modal verb**
short form of cannot: *I can't drive.*

canteen /kænˈtiːn/ **noun**
B1 a restaurant in an office, factory, or school

canvas /ˈkænvəs/ **noun** [no plural]
a strong cloth

canyon /ˈkænjən/ **noun**
a deep valley with very steep sides

cap /kæp/ **noun**
1 **A2** a hat with a flat part at the front: *a baseball cap*
2 the top part of a bottle or tube that you take off

capable /ˈkeɪpəbl/ **adj**
1 able to do things well: *She's a very capable young woman.*
2 **capable of** able to do something: *I know she is capable of good work.*
→ Opposite **incapable** **adj**

a b c d e f g h i j k l m n o p q r s t u v w x y z

capacity /kəˈpæsəti/ **noun** (plural **capacities**)
1 the largest amount that a container or building can hold: *The restaurant has* ***a capacity of*** *about 200.*
2 the ability to do or feel something: *She has a great* ***capacity for*** *love.*

capital /ˈkæpɪtəl/ **noun**
1 A2 the most important city in a country or state: *Paris is the capital of France.*
2 A2 (also ˌ**capital** ˈ**letter**) a large letter of the alphabet used at the beginning of sentences
3 [no plural] money used in business

captain /ˈkæptɪn/ **noun**
1 B1 the leader of a team
2 the person who controls a ship or plane
3 an officer in the army, navy, or air force

captive /ˈkæptɪv/ **noun**
a prisoner

captivity /kæpˈtɪvəti/ **noun** [no plural]
the state of being kept somewhere and not allowed to leave: *lion cubs born* ***in captivity***

capture /ˈkæptʃər/ **verb** (**capturing**, **captured**)
1 to catch someone and make them your prisoner: *Two soldiers were captured by the enemy.*
2 to show or describe something successfully using words or pictures: *The painting captures the beauty of the landscape.*

car /kɑːr/ **noun**
1 A1 a vehicle with an engine, four wheels, and seats for a few people
→ See **Car** on page C3
2 US (UK **carriage**) one of the separate parts of a train where the people sit

caravan /ˈkærəvæn/ **noun** UK (US **camper**)
a vehicle that people stay in on holiday and which is pulled by a car

carbon /ˈkɑːbən/ **noun** [no plural]
a chemical element that exists in all animals and plants and in coal and oil: *Diamonds are formed from carbon.*

card /kɑːd/ **noun**
1 A2 a piece of folded paper with a picture on the front and some writing inside: *a birthday card*
2 A2 (also **playing card**) a piece of hard paper with numbers and pictures used for playing games: *We spent the evening* ***playing cards*** *(= playing games using cards).*
3 B1 a piece of hard paper or plastic with information on it: *a library card*
4 B1 a part inside a computer which controls how the computer operates: *a sound card*
5 [no plural] UK thick paper

cardboard /ˈkɑːdbɔːd/ **noun** [no plural]
thick, hard paper that is used for making boxes

cardigan /ˈkɑːdɪgən/ **noun**
a piece of clothing like a jacket, often made of wool, that fastens at the front

cardigan

care[1] /keər/ **verb** (**caring**, **cared**)
1 B1 to feel interested in something or worried about it: *I don't* ***care what*** *she thinks.*
2 B1 to love someone: *I only worry about him because I* ***care about*** *him.*
3 who cares? informal used to emphasize that you do not think something is important: *'We're going to be late.' 'Who cares?'*

care for *someone* **phrasal verb**
B1 to look after someone who is young, old, or ill: *The children are being cared for by a relative.*

care[2] /keər/ **noun**
1 [no plural] the process of protecting or looking after someone or something: *A small baby requires constant care.*
2 take care B1 to give a lot of attention to what you are doing, especially something dangerous: *The roads are very icy so take care when you drive home.*

3 take care! informal A2 used when saying goodbye to someone: *See you soon, Bob – take care!*
4 take care of B1 to look after someone or something: *My parents take care of the house while we're away.*

career /kəˈrɪəʳ/ **noun**
B1 a job that you do for a lot of your life, especially one for which you are trained: *a successful career in marketing*

careful /ˈkeəfᵊl/ **adj**
A2 giving a lot of attention to what you are doing so that you do not have an accident or make a mistake: ***Be careful**, Michael – that knife is sharp.*
• **carefully adv** A2 *He carefully lifted the baby.*

careless /ˈkeələs/ **adj**
B1 not giving enough attention to what you are doing: *He was fined £250 for careless driving.*
• **carelessly adv**

cargo /ˈkɑːgəʊ/ **noun** (plural **cargoes**)
things that are carried in a vehicle: *a cargo of oil*

caring /ˈkeərɪŋ/ **adj**
describes someone who is kind and who helps other people: *She's a very caring person.*

carnival /ˈkɑːnɪvᵊl/ **noun**
a public occasion where people wear special clothes and dance in the streets

carol /ˈkærᵊl/ **noun**
a song that people sing at Christmas

car park /ˈkɑː ˌpɑːk/ **noun** UK
A2 a place where you can leave your car for a short time: *I parked in the car park.*

carpet /ˈkɑːpɪt/ **noun**
A2 thick material for covering floors, often made of wool

carriage /ˈkærɪdʒ/ **noun** UK (US **car**)
one of the separate parts of a train where the people sit

carrier bag /ˈkæriə ˌbæg/ **noun** UK
a large paper or plastic bag that you are given in a shop to carry the things you have bought
→ See picture at **bag**

carrot /ˈkærət/ **noun**
A2 a long, thin, orange vegetable that grows in the ground

carrot

carry /ˈkæri/ **verb** (**carrying**, **carried**)
1 A1 to hold something or someone with your hands or on your back and take them somewhere: *He was carrying my bags.*
2 B1 to have something with you all the time: *She still carries his photo in her wallet.*
3 to move someone or something from one place to another: *The plane was carrying 30 passengers.*
4 to have a disease that you might give to someone else: *Mosquitoes carry malaria and other infectious diseases.*
5 to support the weight of something: *Is the ice thick enough to carry my weight?*

carry on phrasal verb
B1 to continue doing something: *We will **carry on with** the game unless it rains.*

be/get carried away phrasal verb
to be so excited about something that you cannot control what you say or do: *There's far too much food – I'm afraid I got carried away!*

carry *something* out phrasal verb
B1 to do or complete something, especially something that you have said you would do or that you have been told to do: *The hospital is carrying out tests to find out what's wrong.*

cart /kɑːt/ **noun** US (UK **trolley**)
a metal structure on wheels that is used for carrying things

carton /ˈkɑːtᵊn/ **noun**
a container for food and drink that is made from strong paper or plastic: *a carton of milk*
→ See picture at **container**

cartoon /kɑːˈtuːn/ **noun**
1 A2 a movie made using characters that are drawn and not real: *Mickey Mouse and other cartoon characters*
2 A2 a funny drawing, especially in a newspaper or magazine

carve /kɑːv/ **verb** (**carving**, **carved**)
1 to make an object or shape by cutting wood or stone: *The statue was* ***carved out of*** *stone.*
2 to cut a piece of cooked meat into thin pieces

case /keɪs/ **noun**
1 A2 a large bag with a handle that you use for carrying clothes in when you are travelling
2 A2 a container for storing or protecting something: *a pencil case*
3 B1 a particular situation or example of something: *We usually ask for references, but in your case it will not be necessary.*
4 something that is decided in a court of law: *a divorce case*
5 a crime that the police are trying to solve: *a murder case* ◦ *Local police have investigated 50 cases of burglary in the past month.*
6 in case B1 because something might happen: *I don't think it will rain, but I'll bring an umbrella* ***just in case****.*
7 in case of *something* B1 in preparation for something happening: *We keep a bucket of water here in case of fire.*
8 be the case B1 to be true: *A poor diet can make you tired, but I don't think that's the case here.*
9 in any case used to give another reason for something you are saying, or that you have done: *I don't want to go, and in any case, I wasn't invited.*
10 in that case because that is the situation: *'Peter will be there.' 'Oh, in that case, I'll come too.'*

cash¹ /kæʃ/ **noun** [no plural]
1 A2 money in the form of coins or notes (= paper money): *I'm taking £50* ***in cash****.*
2 B1 informal money in any form: *I'm* ***short of cash*** *(= I don't have much money).*

cash² /kæʃ/ **verb**
cash a cheque to get money in return for a cheque: *I need to cash a traveller's cheque.*

cash desk /ˈkæʃ ˌdesk/ **noun** UK
the place in a shop where you pay for things

cashier /kæʃˈɪəʳ/ **noun**
someone whose job is to take and pay out money in a shop or bank

cash machine /ˈkæʃ məˌʃiːn/ **noun** (UK also **cashpoint** /ˈkæʃpɔɪnt/)
a machine in a wall that you get money from using a plastic card

cast¹ /kɑːst/ **verb** (**cast**)
1 cast a spell on *someone* to use magic to make something happen to someone: *The witch cast a spell on him.*
2 to choose an actor for a particular part in a movie or play: *Why is he always* ***cast as*** *a criminal?*

cast² /kɑːst/ **noun**
all the actors in a movie, play, or show: *The play has a cast of twenty actors.*

castle /ˈkɑːsl/ **noun**
A2 a large, strong building that was built in the past to protect the people inside from being attacked

castle

casual /ˈkæʒjuəl/ **adj**
1 B1 Casual clothes are comfortable and not formal.
2 not planned: *a casual remark*
3 relaxed and not seeming very interested in someone or something: *a casual manner*
• **casually adv** *She was dressed casually in shorts and a T-shirt.*

cat /kæt/ **noun**
A1 an animal with fur that is kept as a pet

catalogue (also US **catalog**) /ˈkætəlɒg/ **noun**
a book with a list of things that you can buy: *a clothing catalogue*

catastrophe /kəˈtæstrəfi/ **noun**
an extremely bad event that causes a lot of suffering or destruction: *The country is facing a catastrophe.*

catch /kætʃ/ **verb** (**caught**)
1 A1 to stop someone or something that is moving through the air by getting them or it in your hands: *Try to catch the ball.*

2 A1 to get on a bus, train, etc.: *I caught the last train home.*
3 A2 to get an illness or disease: *I think I caught a cold from her.*
4 B1 to find and stop a person or animal who is trying to escape: *He ran after the dog, but couldn't catch him.*
5 to stick somewhere, or to make something stick somewhere: *My dress got caught on a nail and tore.*
6 **catch fire** B1 to start burning
7 **catch *someone*'s attention, interest, etc.** to make someone notice something and feel interested: *All the noise in the street caught his attention.*
8 to discover someone who is doing something wrong or something secret: *She was caught cheating in the exam.*
catch up phrasal verb
to learn and discuss the newest facts about something: *Let's go out for lunch – I want to* ***catch up on*** *all the gossip.*
catch (*someone/something*) up phrasal verb
1 to reach someone or something that is in front of you by moving faster: *We soon* ***caught up with*** *the car in front.*
2 B1 to reach the same level or quality as someone or something else: *She's doing extra work to* ***catch up with*** *the rest of the class.*

category /ˈkætəgəri/ noun (plural **categories**)
a group of people or things of a similar type: *Our customers fall into two main categories.*

catering /ˈkeɪtərɪŋ/ noun [no plural]
providing food and drinks for people: *Who* ***did the catering*** *for the party?*

caterpillar /ˈkætəpɪləʳ/ noun
a small, long animal with many legs that eats leaves

caterpillar

cathedral /kəˈθiːdrəl/ noun
A2 the largest and most important church in an area

Catholic /ˈkæθəlɪk/ noun (also **Roman Catholic**)
a member of the part of the Christian religion whose leader is the Pope
• **Catholic** adj

cattle /ˈkætl/ plural noun
B1 cows kept on a farm for their milk and meat

caught /kɔːt/
past tense and past participle of catch

cauliflower /ˈkɒlɪˌflaʊəʳ/ noun
a round, white vegetable with green leaves around the outside
→ See **Fruit and Vegetables** on page C8

cause¹ /kɔːz/ verb (**causing**, **caused**)
to make something happen, especially something bad: *What caused the fire?*

cause² /kɔːz/ noun
1 someone or something that makes something happen: *They still don't know the* ***cause of*** *the accident.*
2 [no plural] a reason to feel something: *There is no* ***cause for*** *alarm.*
3 a reason for doing something, especially one that involves helping other people: *The money will go to charity – it's a good cause.*

caution /ˈkɔːʃən/ noun [no plural]
great care to avoid danger or bad situations: *Caution! Wet floor.*

cautious /ˈkɔːʃəs/ adj
taking care to avoid danger or bad situations: *a cautious driver*
• **cautiously** adv

cave /keɪv/ noun
B1 a large hole in the ground or in the side of a mountain

CD /ˌsiːˈdiː/ noun
A1 a small disc on which music or information is recorded
→ See **The Office** on page C12

CD player /ˌsiːˈdiː ˌpleɪəʳ/ noun
A1 a machine that is used for playing music CDs

CD-ROM /ˌsiːdiːˈrɒm/ noun
B1 a CD that holds large amounts of information that can be read by a computer: *Cambridge dictionaries are available* ***on CD-ROM****.*

cease /siːs/ verb (**ceasing**, **ceased**)
formal
to stop: *He ordered his men to cease firing.*

a b c d e f g h i j k l m n o p q r s t u v w x y z

ceiling /ˈsiːlɪŋ/ **noun**
A2 the top surface of a room

celebrate /ˈseləbreɪt/ **verb**
(**celebrating**, **celebrated**)
B1 to have a party or a meal because it is a special day or something good has happened: *We went out to celebrate Richard's birthday.*

celebration /ˌseləˈbreɪʃən/ **noun**
B1 an occasion or party that celebrates a special event: *You passed your test? Let's have a celebration.*

celebrity /səˈlebrəti/ **noun** (plural **celebrities**)
B1 a famous person

celery /ˈseləri/ **noun** [no plural]
a vegetable with long, light green stems that can be eaten raw or cooked
→ See **Fruit and Vegetables** on page C8

cell /sel/ **noun**
1 the smallest living part of an animal or a plant: *brain cells*
2 a small room where a prisoner is kept

cellar /ˈseləʳ/ **noun**
a room under the floor of a building

cello /ˈtʃeləʊ/ **noun**
a large, wooden musical instrument that you hold between your knees to play

cell phone /ˈsel fəʊn/ **noun** mainly US (UK usually **mobile**, **mobile phone**)
a telephone that you can carry everywhere with you
→ See picture at **mobile phone**

Celsius /ˈselsiəs/ **noun** [no plural] (written abbreviation **C**)
a measurement of temperature in which water freezes at 0° and boils at 100°

cement /sɪˈment/ **noun** [no plural]
a powder used in building that is mixed with water to make a hard substance

cemetery /ˈsemətri/ **noun** (plural **cemeteries**)
a place where dead people are buried: *She went to the cemetery where her grandfather was buried.*

cent /sent/ **noun**
A2 a coin with a low value that is used in some countries

centigrade /ˈsentɪgreɪd/ **noun** [no plural] (written abbreviation **C**)
a measurement of temperature in which water freezes at 0° and boils at 100°

centimetre (written abbreviation **cm**) /ˈsentɪˌmiːtəʳ/ **noun** UK (US **centimeter**)
A2 a unit for measuring length, equal to 0.01 metres

central /ˈsentrəl/ **adj**
B1 in or near the centre of a place or thing: *central America*
• **centrally** **adv**

central heating /ˌsentrəl ˈhiːtɪŋ/ **noun** [no plural]
B1 a system of heating a building by warming air or water in one place and carrying it to different rooms in pipes: *The house had no central heating.*

centre UK (US **center**) /ˈsentəʳ/ **noun**
1 A2 the middle point or part of something: *Cars are not allowed in the town centre.*
2 A2 a building used for a particular activity: *a health centre*
3 **be the centre of attention** to get more attention than anyone else

century /ˈsentʃəri/ **noun** (plural **centuries**)
A2 a period of 100 years: *the twentieth century*

cereal /ˈsɪəriəl/ **noun**
1 a plant that is grown to produce grain for food
2 A2 a food that is made from grain and eaten with milk, especially in the morning: *breakfast cereals*
→ See **Food** on page C7

ceremony /ˈserɪməni/ **noun**
1 B1 (plural **ceremonies**) a formal event that is performed on important social or religious occasions: *a wedding ceremony*
2 [no plural] formal words and actions that are part of a ceremony

certain /ˈsɜːtᵊn/ **adj**
1 B1 without doubt: *I am certain that you're doing the right thing.* ◦ *It now looks certain that she will resign.*
→ Opposite **uncertain** **adj**
2 B1 some: *The museum is only open at certain times of the day.*

certainly /ˈsɜːtənli/ **adv**
1 A2 definitely: *They certainly deserved to win.* ◦ *'Do you regret what you said?' '**Certainly not**!'*
2 A2 used to politely agree to do something: *'Could you pass the salt, please?' 'Certainly.'*

certificate /səˈtɪfɪkət/ **noun**
B1 an official document that gives details to show that something is true: *a birth certificate*

chain

chain¹ /tʃeɪn/ **noun**
1 A2 a line of metal rings connected together: *She wore a gold chain around her neck.*
2 B1 a number of similar shops, restaurants, etc. owned by the same company: *a chain of hotels*
3 a series of things that happen one after the other: *His arrival set off a surprising chain of events.*

chain² /tʃeɪn/ **verb**
to tie someone or something using a chain: *I **chained** my bike **to** a lamppost.*

chair¹ /tʃeəʳ/ **noun**
A1 a seat for one person, with a back and usually four legs
→ See **The Office** on page C12

chair² /tʃeəʳ/ **verb**
to control a meeting or organization: *Would you like to chair the meeting tomorrow?*

chairman, chairwoman /ˈtʃeəmən/, /ˈtʃeəˌwʊmən/ **noun** (plural **chairmen, chairwomen**) (also **chair**)
a man or woman who controls a meeting or company

chalk /tʃɔːk/ **noun**
1 a small stick of chalk used for writing
2 [no plural] a soft, white rock

challenge¹ /ˈtʃælɪndʒ/ **noun**
1 B1 something difficult that tests your ability: *Managing a large team is quite a challenge.*
2 an invitation to compete in a game or a fight

challenge² /ˈtʃælɪndʒ/ **verb** (**challenging, challenged**)
1 to tell someone you do not accept their rules or you think they are wrong: *The election results are being challenged.*
2 to ask someone to compete in a game or fight: *He **challenged** me **to** a game of tennis.*

challenging /ˈtʃæləndʒɪŋ/ **adj**
B1 difficult, in a way that tests your ability or determination: *This has been a challenging time for us all.*

champagne

champagne /ʃæmˈpeɪn/ **noun** [no plural]
A2 French white wine with a lot of bubbles in it

champion /ˈtʃæmpiən/ **noun**
B1 a person or animal that wins a competition

championship /ˈtʃæmpiənʃɪp/ **noun**
B1 a competition to find the best team or player in a game or sport

chance /tʃɑːns/ **noun**
1 B1 the possibility that something will happen: *There's a **chance that** she'll still be there.* ◦ *She has a small **chance of** passing the exam.*
2 B1 the opportunity to do something: *I didn't **get a chance** to talk to you at the party.*
3 B1 [no plural] the way something happens because of luck, or without being planned: *I saw her **by chance**.*
4 **stand a chance** to have a chance of success or of doing something good: *He stands a good chance of winning.*

a b c d e f g h i j k l m n o p q r s t u v w x y z

change[1] /tʃeɪndʒ/ **verb** (**changing**, **changed**)
1 A1 to stop having one thing, and start having another: *I've changed my doctor.*
2 A2 to become different, or to make someone or something become different: *She's changed a lot in the last few years.* ◦ *The course changed my life.*
3 A2 to take off your clothes and put on different ones: *Is there somewhere I can **get changed**?*
4 A2 to get off one bus, plane, etc. and get on a different one: *I have to change trains at Bristol.*
5 A2 to get one type of money in exchange for a different type: *Where can I change my dollars?*
6 B1 to take something you have bought back to a shop and exchange it for something else: *I had to **change** those shorts I bought **for** a bigger pair.*
7 change the subject to start talking about a different subject: *I'd tried to explain my feelings, but he just changed the subject.*
change *something* around/round **phrasal verb**
to move things such as furniture into different positions: *The room looks very different since you've changed the furniture around.*

change[2] /tʃeɪndʒ/ **noun**
1 A2 the process or result of something becoming different: *We need to **make** a few **changes to** the design.*
2 A2 the process of stopping one thing and starting to have or do another thing: *a **change of** plan*
3 A2 [no plural] the money that you get back when you pay more for something than it costs: *There's your receipt and £3 change.*
4 A2 [no plural] coins, not paper money: *Have you got any change for the parking meter?*
5 B1 something that is pleasant or interesting because it is unusual or new: *It's nice to see her smile **for a change**.*
6 a change of clothes A2 a set of clean clothes you can put on if you need to take off the ones you are wearing: *Make sure you bring a change of clothes.*

changeable /ˈtʃeɪndʒəbl/ **adj**
often changing, or likely to change: *The weather is very changeable.*

changing room /ˈtʃeɪndʒɪŋ ˌruːm/ **noun**
a room in a shop where you can try clothes, or a room where you change into clothes to do sport: *Is the changing room free?*

channel /ˈtʃænəl/ **noun**
1 A2 a number on a television that you choose in order to watch a programme
2 a long passage for water or other liquids to move along

chaos /ˈkeɪɒs/ **noun** [no plural]
a state in which there is confusion and no organization: *The city was in chaos after the earthquake.*

chapel /ˈtʃæpəl/ **noun**
a small church, or a room used as a church in a building

chapter /ˈtʃæptəʳ/ **noun**
B1 one of the parts that a book is divided into

character /ˈkærəktəʳ/ **noun**
1 B1 the qualities that make one person or thing different from another: *The whole character of the town changed after the road was built.*
2 B1 a person in a book, movie, etc.: *a cartoon character*

characteristic /ˌkærɪktəˈrɪstɪk/ **noun**
a typical or noticeable quality of someone or something: *A long neck is a common characteristic of the giraffe.*

charge[1] /tʃɑːdʒ/ **noun**
1 B1 the price of something, especially a service: *delivery charges*
2 be in charge B1 to be responsible for something: *She's in charge of the team.*
3 something written by the police saying that someone has done a crime

charge[2] /tʃɑːdʒ/ **verb** (**charging**, **charged**)
1 B1 to ask for money for something: *How much do you **charge for** delivery?*
2 to officially say that someone has

done a crime: *He has been* ***charged with*** *murder.*
3 to run: *The children charged out of the school.*
4 to attack someone or something by moving forward quickly: *The bull* ***charged at*** *the boy.*
5 to put electricity into something: *My mobile phone needs charging.*

charger /ˈtʃɑːdʒəʳ/ **noun**
a piece of equipment used for putting electricity in a battery: *a phone charger*

charity /ˈtʃærɪti/ **noun**
1 B1 (plural **charities**) an official organization that gives money, food, or help to people who need it: *We're raising money* ***for charity****.*
2 [no plural] money, food, or other help that is given to people

charm /tʃɑːm/ **noun**
1 a quality that makes you like someone or something: *I know why women like him – he has a certain charm.*
2 something that brings you good luck: *a lucky charm*

charming /ˈtʃɑːmɪŋ/ **adj**
B1 nice and attractive: *a charming smile*

chart /tʃɑːt/ **noun**
1 a drawing that shows information in a simple way: *a sales chart*
2 **the charts** an official list of the most popular songs each week: *It's number one* ***in the charts****.*

chase

chase /tʃeɪs/ **verb** (**chasing**, **chased**)
to run after someone or something in order to catch them: *The dog was chasing a rabbit.*

chat[1] /tʃæt/ **verb** (**chatting**, **chatted**)
1 A2 to talk with someone in a friendly way
2 A2 to communicate with someone on the Internet by sending messages that you can read and reply to immediately: *We were chatting till midnight.*

chat[2] /tʃæt/ **noun**
A2 a friendly conversation: *We* ***had*** *a long* ***chat*** *on the phone yesterday.*

chat room /ˈtʃæt ˌruːm/ **noun**
a place on the Internet where people can have a conversation by writing to each other

chat show /ˈtʃæt ˌʃəʊ/ **noun** UK (US **talk show**)
B1 a television or radio programme where people are asked questions about themselves: *I saw her on a chat show last week.*

cheap /tʃiːp/ **adj**
A1 not expensive, or costing less than usual: *a cheap flight*
• **cheaply** **adv** *You can buy a used car very cheaply.*

cheat /tʃiːt/ **verb**
to do something that is not honest, in order to get something: *He* ***cheats at*** *cards.*

check[1] /tʃek/ **verb**
1 A2 to look at something to make sure that it is right or safe: *Check that you've locked the door.*
2 B1 to find out information about something: *I'll check whether Peter knows about the party.*
3 US to put a mark (✓) by an answer to show that it is correct
check in **phrasal verb**
B1 to show your ticket at an airport so they can tell you your seat number
check in/check into ***something*** **phrasal verb**
B1 to say who you are when you arrive at a hotel so that you can be given a key for your room: *Please* ***check in at*** *the reception desk.*
check out **phrasal verb**
B1 to leave a hotel after paying

check[2] /tʃek/ **noun**
1 B1 the act of looking at something

a b c d e f g h i j k l m n o p q r s t u v w x y z

a b c d e f g h i j k l m n o p q r s t u v w x y z

to make sure it is right or safe: *We do safety **checks on** all our equipment.*
2 US (UK **cheque**) a piece of paper printed by a bank that you use to pay for things
3 US (UK **tick**) a mark (✓) that shows that an answer is correct
4 a pattern of squares of different colours

checkbook /ˈtʃekbʊk/ **noun** US (UK **chequebook**)
a book of papers printed by a bank that you use to pay for things

checked /tʃekt/ **adj**
with a pattern of squares of different colours: *a checked shirt*

check-in /ˈtʃekɪn/ **noun** [no plural]
1 B1 the place at an airport where you go to say that you have arrived for your flight: *We went straight to check-in.*
2 the act of showing your ticket at an airport to say that you have arrived for your flight: *There was a queue at the **check-in desk**.*

checkout /ˈtʃekaʊt/ **noun**
1 B1 a place in a large shop where you pay for things: *a supermarket checkout*
2 B1 the place on a website where you order and pay for goods: *After you've chosen what you want, click here to proceed to checkout.*

check-up /ˈtʃekʌp/ **noun**
a general medical examination to see if you are healthy: *I'm going to the doctor for a check-up.*

cheek /tʃiːk/ **noun**
1 B1 one of the two soft parts of your face below your eyes: *Tears ran down his cheeks.*
→ See **The Body** on page C2
2 [no plural] mainly UK rude behaviour that shows you do not respect someone: *She **had the cheek to** ask me to pay for her!*

cheeky /ˈtʃiːki/ **adj** (**cheekier**, **cheekiest**) UK
rude, often in a funny way: *a cheeky little boy*
• **cheekily** **adv**

cheer¹ /tʃɪəʳ/ **verb**
to shout loudly at someone that you like or want to encourage: *The crowd cheered as he ran into the stadium.*
cheer up **phrasal verb**
to stop feeling sad: *Cheer up. It's not the end of the world!*

cheer² /tʃɪəʳ/ **noun**
a shout that shows you like someone or want to encourage them

cheerful /ˈtʃɪəfᵊl/ **adj**
1 B1 happy: *She seemed fairly cheerful.*
2 describes a place or thing that is bright and pleasant and makes you feel happy: *The doctor's waiting room was bright and cheerful.*
• **cheerfully** **adv** *She walked down the road, whistling cheerfully.*

cheers! /tʃɪəz/ **exclamation**
1 B1 something friendly that you say before you start to drink alcohol with someone
2 UK informal used to mean 'thank you': *'I've bought you a drink.' 'Cheers, mate.'*
3 B1 UK informal used to mean 'goodbye': *'Bye.' 'Cheers, see you next week.'*

cheese /tʃiːz/ **noun**
A1 a yellow or white solid food made from milk: *a slice of cheese* ◦ *a cheese sandwich* ◦ *French cheeses*
→ See **Food** on page C7

cheeseburger /ˈtʃiːzˌbɜːgəʳ/ **noun**
a hamburger (= meat cooked in a round, flat shape) eaten between round pieces of bread with a slice of cheese

chef /ʃef/ **noun**
A2 someone who cooks food in a restaurant

chemical¹ /ˈkemɪkᵊl/ **adj**
relating to chemistry or chemicals

chemical² /ˈkemɪkᵊl/ **noun**
a substance that is used in chemistry or produced by chemistry

chemist /ˈkemɪst/ **noun**
1 UK (US **pharmacist**) someone who prepares and sells drugs in a shop
2 B1 a scientist who does work that involves chemistry

chemistry /ˈkemɪstri/ **noun** [no plural]
A2 the scientific study of substances

and how they change when they combine

chemist's /ˈkemɪsts/ **noun** UK (US **drugstore**)
A2 a shop where you can buy medicine, soap, etc.

cheque /tʃek/ **noun** UK (US **check**)
A2 a piece of paper printed by a bank that you use to pay for things: *Are you **paying by cheque**?*

chequebook /ˈtʃekbʊk/ **noun** UK (US **checkbook**)
a book of cheques

cherry /ˈtʃeri/ **noun** (plural **cherries**)
a small, round red or black fruit with a large seed inside

chess /tʃes/ **noun** [no plural]
A2 a game that two people play by moving different pieces around a board of black and white squares

chest /tʃest/ **noun**
1 the front of your body between your neck and your stomach
→ See **The Body** on page C2
2 a big wooden box for keeping things in

chest of drawers /ˌtʃest əv ˈdrɔːz/ **noun** UK (US **bureau**)
B1 a piece of furniture with drawers for keeping clothes in

chew /tʃuː/ **verb**
to break food between your teeth as a part of eating

chewing gum /ˈtʃuːɪŋ ˌɡʌm/ **noun** [no plural]
B1 a sweet that you chew but do not eat

chick /tʃɪk/ **noun**
a baby bird, especially a baby chicken

chicken /ˈtʃɪkɪn/ **noun**
1 A2 a bird kept on a farm for its meat and eggs
2 A2 [no plural] the meat of a chicken

chief¹ /tʃiːf/ **adj**
most important: *The weather was our chief reason for coming here.*

chief² /tʃiːf/ **noun**
the leader of a group

child /tʃaɪld/ **noun** (plural **children** /ˈtʃɪldrən/)
1 A1 a young person who is not yet an adult: *When I was a child I had fair hair.*
2 a son or daughter of any age: *Her children are all grown up now.*

childhood /ˈtʃaɪldhʊd/ **noun**
B1 the part of your life when you are a child: *She **had** a happy **childhood**.*

childish /ˈtʃaɪldɪʃ/ **adj**
silly, like the behaviour of a child: *Don't be so childish!*
• **childishly adv**

childminder /ˈtʃaɪldˌmaɪndəʳ/ **noun** UK
someone whose job is to look after children while their parents are working

children **noun**
the plural of 'child'

chilli (plural **chillies**) UK (US **chili**) /ˈtʃɪli/ **noun**
1 A2 a small, thin, red or green vegetable that tastes very hot: *chilli powder*
2 [no plural] a spicy dish of beans, meat, and chillies

chilly /ˈtʃɪli/ **adj** (**chillier**, **chilliest**)
too cold: *It's chilly outside.*

chimney /ˈtʃɪmni/ **noun**
a pipe that takes smoke from a fire out through a roof

chimney

chimpanzee /ˌtʃɪmpᵊnˈziː/ **noun**
an African animal like a large monkey with no tail

chin /tʃɪn/ **noun**
B1 the bottom part of your face, below your mouth
→ See **The Body** on page C2

china /ˈtʃaɪnə/ **noun** [no plural]
1 the hard substance that plates, cups, bowls, etc. are made from: *a china teapot*
2 cups, plates, bowls, etc. that are made from china: *I use the best china when we have visitors.*

chip[1] /tʃɪp/ **noun**
1 A1 (US **French fry**) a long, thin piece of potato that is cooked in oil: *fish and chips*
→ See **Food** on page C7
2 US (UK **crisp**) a thin, dry slice of fried potato
→ See **Food** on page C7
3 a very small part of a computer that stores information

chip[2] /tʃɪp/ **verb** (**chipping**, **chipped**)
to break a small piece off something that is hard: *a chipped plate*

chocolate /ˈtʃɒkələt/ **noun**
1 A1 [no plural] a sweet, brown food that is usually sold in a block: *a bar of chocolate* ◦ *milk chocolate*
2 a small piece of sweet food covered in chocolate: *a box of chocolates*
3 A2 a sweet drink made with chocolate and hot milk

choice /tʃɔɪs/ **noun**
1 B1 the possibility of choosing between two or more things: *If I had a choice, I'd stop working.*
2 the decision to choose one thing or person and not someone or something else: *In the past women had to **make a choice between** a career or marriage.*
3 B1 the things or people you can choose from: *The dress is available in a **choice of** colours.*
4 B1 the person or thing that someone has chosen: *Harvard was not his **first choice** of college.*

choir /kwaɪəʳ/ **noun**
a group of people who sing together: *a church choir*

choke /tʃəʊk/ **verb** (**choking**, **choked**)
to stop breathing because something is in your throat: *Small children can **choke on** peanuts.*

choose /tʃuːz/ **verb** (**choosing**, **chose**, **chosen**)
1 A1 to decide which thing you want: *Have you chosen a name for the baby?* ◦ *There were lots of books to **choose from**.*
2 **choose to do *something*** to decide to do something: *Manuela chose to take a job in Paris.*

chop

chop[1] /tʃɒp/ **verb** (**chopping**, **chopped**)
to cut something into small pieces: *Chop the onion and pepper.*

chop[2] /tʃɒp/ **noun**
a flat piece of meat with a bone in it: *a lamb chop*

chord /kɔːd/ **noun**
two or more musical notes that are played at the same time

chore /tʃɔːʳ/ **noun**
a boring job that you must do: *the household chores*

chorus /ˈkɔːrəs/ **noun**
the part of a song that is repeated many times

chose /tʃəʊz/
past tense of choose

chosen /ˈtʃəʊzən/
past participle of choose

christen /ˈkrɪsən/ **verb**
to give a baby a name at a Christian ceremony and make them a member of the Christian Church

christening /ˈkrɪsənɪŋ/ **noun**
a ceremony where someone is made a member of the Christian Church

Christian /ˈkrɪstʃən/ **noun**
someone whose religion is Christianity
• **Christian** adj

a b c d e f g h i j k l m n o p q r s t u v w x y z

Christianity /ˌkrɪstiˈænəti/ **noun** [no plural]
a religion based on belief in one God and the ideas that Jesus Christ taught

Christmas /ˈkrɪsməs/ **noun**
the Christian period of celebration around 25 December, when Christians celebrate the birth of Jesus Christ and people give each other presents: *Merry Christmas!*

chunk /tʃʌŋk/ **noun**
a large piece of something: *a chunk of cheese*
→ See **Quantities** on page C14

church /tʃɜːtʃ/ **noun**
A2 a building where Christians go to pray: *We used to go to church every Sunday morning.*

cigar /sɪˈgɑːʳ/ **noun**
a thick tube made from rolled tobacco leaves, that people smoke

cigarette /ˌsɪgəˈret/ **noun**
A2 a thin tube of paper filled with tobacco, that people smoke

cinema /ˈsɪnəmə/ **noun** UK
A1 a building where you go to watch movies

circle /ˈsɜːkl/ **noun**
A2 a round, flat shape like the letter O: *We all sat on the floor* ***in a circle***.
→ See picture at **shape**

circular /ˈsɜːkjələʳ/ **adj**
shaped like a circle

circulate /ˈsɜːkjəleɪt/ **verb** (**circulating**, **circulated**)
to move around: *Hot water circulates through the pipes.*

circulation /ˌsɜːkjəˈleɪʃən/ **noun** [no plural]
the movement of blood around the body

circumstances /ˈsɜːkəmstænsɪz/ **plural noun**
1 the facts or events of a situation: *I think they coped very well* ***under the circumstances*** *(= in that difficult situation).*
2 under no circumstances used to say that something must never happen: *Under no circumstances should you approach the bear.*

circus /ˈsɜːkəs/ **noun**
B1 a show in which people and animals perform in a large tent

citizen /ˈsɪtɪzən/ **noun**
1 someone who lives in a particular town or city: *the citizens of Berlin*
2 someone who has a legal right to live in a particular country: *He applied to become an American citizen.*

city /ˈsɪti/ **noun** (plural **cities**)
A1 a large town

civilization /ˌsɪvəlaɪˈzeɪʃən/ **noun**
the way that people live together, with laws to control their behaviour, education, and a government: *Nuclear war could mean the end of civilization.*

civilized /ˈsɪvəlaɪzd/ **adj**
a civilized society is advanced and has laws, education, and a government

the Civil Service /ˌsɪvəl ˈsɜːvɪs/ **noun** [no plural]
the government departments of a country and the people who work in them: *She works in the Civil Service.*

civil war /ˌsɪvəl ˈwɔːʳ/ **noun**
a war between groups of people who live in the same country

claim¹ /kleɪm/ **verb**
1 to say that something is true: *She* ***claimed that*** *the dog attacked her.*
2 to ask for something because it belongs to you or you have the right to have it: *She claimed $2,500 in travel expenses.*

claim² /kleɪm/ **noun**
1 a statement that something is true: *There were* ***claims that*** *he had lied.*
2 an official demand for something you think you have a right to: *a claim for compensation*

clap /klæp/ **verb** (**clapping**, **clapped**)
B1 to hit your hands together to show that you have enjoyed a performance, talk, etc.: *The crowd clapped and cheered for more.*

clash¹ /klæʃ/ **verb**
1 to fight or argue: *Government troops* ***clashed with*** *rebel soldiers.*
2 If colours clash, they do not look good together.
3 UK If two events clash, they happen

a b c d e f g h i j k l m n o p q r s t u v w x y z

a b c d e f g h i j k l m n o p q r s t u v w x y z

clap

at the same time so that you cannot go to them both: *Emma's party* ***clashes with*** *my brother's wedding.*

clash[2] /klæʃ/ **noun**
1 a fight or argument
2 a loud sound that is made when metal objects hit each other: *the clash of pans in the sink*

clasp /klɑːsp/ **verb**
to hold something or someone tightly: *He clasped his daughter in his arms.*

class /klɑːs/ **noun**
1 A1 a group of students who have lessons together: *We were in the same class at school.*
2 A1 a period of time in which students are taught something: *My first class starts at 8.30.*
3 A2 a group into which products, services, or people are put according to their standard: *second-class post* ◦ *a first-class ticket*
4 one of the groups in a society with the same social and economic position
5 a group of similar or related things, especially plants and animals

classic[1] /ˈklæsɪk/ **adj**
1 A classic book, movie, etc. is one that has been popular for a long time and is very good: *the classic movie 'Gone With the Wind'*
2 typical: *He's a classic example of a child who's clever but lazy.*

classic[2] /ˈklæsɪk/ **noun**
a classic book, movie, etc.

classical /ˈklæsɪkəl/ **adj**
classical music A2 serious music by people like Mozart and Stravinsky

classmate /ˈklɑːsmeɪt/ **noun**
A2 someone who is in your class at school or college

classroom /ˈklɑːsruːm/ **noun**
A1 a room in a school where students have lessons
→ See **The Classroom** on page C4

clause /klɔːz/ **noun**
a group of words containing a subject and a verb, that is usually only part of a sentence

claws

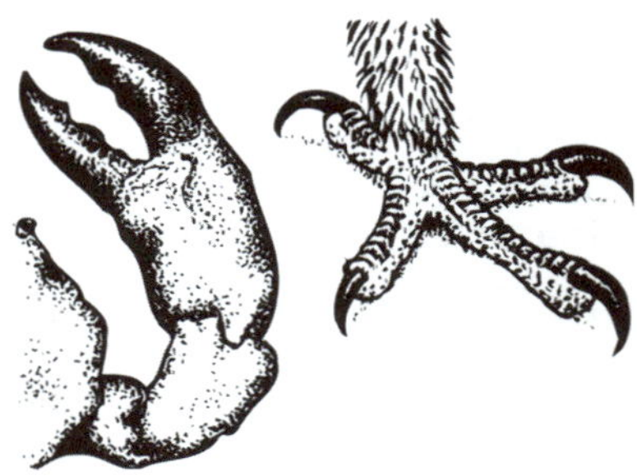

claw /klɔː/ **noun**
one of the sharp, curved nails on the feet of some animals and birds

clay /kleɪ/ **noun** [no plural]
a heavy soil that is hard when it is dry, used for making bricks and containers

clean[1] /kliːn/ **adj**
A1 not dirty: *clean hands*

clean[2] /kliːn/ **verb**
A1 to remove the dirt from something: *I spent the morning cleaning the house.*

cleaner /ˈkliːnəʳ/ **noun**
A2 someone whose job is to clean houses, offices, and other places

clear[1] /klɪəʳ/ **adj**
1 A2 easy to understand: *clear instructions*
2 A2 easy to hear, read, or see: *These photos are very clear.*
3 A2 easy to see through: *clear glass*
4 B1 obvious and not possible to

doubt: *It was* ***clear that*** *he didn't like me.*
5 B1 not covered or blocked by anything: *a clear road* ◦ *a clear sky*

clear² /klɪəʳ/ **verb**
1 B1 to take away all the things or people from a place: *I've completely cleared the room.*
2 If the sky or weather clears, the clouds and rain disappear.
clear ***something*** **out** **phrasal verb**
to tidy a place by throwing away things that you do not want: *We cleared out the attic.*
clear up **phrasal verb**
1 mainly UK to make a place tidy: *Dad was clearing up in the kitchen.*
2 to improve: *If the weather clears up we'll go out.*
3 to give an explanation for something, or to deal with a problem or argument: *They never cleared up the mystery of the missing money.*

clearly /ˈklɪəli/ **adv**
1 A2 in a way that is easy to see, hear, or understand: *He spoke very clearly.*
2 A2 in a way that is not confused: *I'd had two hours' sleep and wasn't thinking clearly.*
3 B1 in a way that you cannot doubt: *He's clearly not interested.*

clerk /klɑːk/ **noun**
someone who works in an office but does not have an important job: *a bank clerk*

clever /ˈklevəʳ/ **adj**
1 A1 good at learning and understanding things: *a clever student*
2 B1 showing intelligence: *a clever idea*
• **cleverly** **adv**

click¹ /klɪk/ **verb**
1 to make a short, sharp sound: *The door clicked shut behind him.*
2 A2 to push part of a computer mouse (= small computer control) to make the computer do something: *To start the program,* ***click on*** *its icon.*

click² /klɪk/ **noun**
1 A2 a short, sharp sound: *the click of a switch*
2 the action of pressing on part of a computer mouse: *You can get the information with a single click.*

client /klaɪənt/ **noun**
someone who pays for services or advice

cliff /klɪf/ **noun**
B1 a high area of rock with a very steep side, often next to a coast

cliff

climate /ˈklaɪmət/ **noun**
B1 the weather conditions of an area: *a hot, dry climate* ◦ *Climate change (= the way the Earth's weather is changing) is the greatest challenge facing the world.*

climax /ˈklaɪmæks/ **noun**
the most exciting or important time: *The* ***climax of*** *her career was winning a gold medal.*

climb

climb /klaɪm/ **verb**
1 A2 to go up something: *Slowly we climbed the hill.*
2 to move into or out of a small space, often with difficulty or effort: *The baby had managed to climb out of his cot.*
• **climb** **noun** *a long climb*

climber /ˈklaɪməʳ/ **noun**
someone who climbs mountains, hills, or rocks as a sport

climbing /ˈklaɪmɪŋ/ **noun** [no plural]
A2 the sport of climbing mountains, hills, or rocks: *mountain climbing* ◦ *climbing boots*

cling /klɪŋ/ **verb** (**clung**)
to hold someone or something tightly: *I* ***clung on to*** *his hand in the dark.*

clinic /ˈklɪnɪk/ **noun**
B1 a place where people go for medical treatment or advice: *an eye clinic*

clip¹ /klɪp/ **noun**
1 a small metal object used for holding things together: *a paper clip*
2 a short part of a film: *They showed clips from his new movie.*
3 a short video recording that you can see on a website: *The site has thousands of TV and movie clips.*

clip² /klɪp/ **verb** (**clipping**, **clipped**)
1 to fix things together with a clip: ***Clip*** *the microphone* ***to*** *your jacket.*
2 to cut small pieces from something

cloak /kləʊk/ **noun**
a loose coat with no parts for the arms

cloakroom /ˈkləʊkruːm/ **noun**
a room where you leave your coat at a theatre, school, etc.

clock /klɒk/ **noun**
A1 a piece of equipment that shows you what time it is: *There was a clock on the wall.*
→ See **The Living Room** on page C11

clockwise

clockwise

anti-clockwise *UK*, counter-clockwise *US*

clockwise /ˈklɒkwaɪz/ **adj**, **adv**
in the same direction as the hands (= parts that point to the numbers) on a clock move
→ Opposite **anti-clockwise** UK, **counter-clockwise** US

close¹ /kləʊz/ **verb** (**closing**, **closed**)
1 A1 If something closes, it moves so that it is not open. If you close something, you move it so that it is not open: *Jane closed the window.* ◦ *Suddenly the door closed.*
2 A2 If a shop, restaurant, etc. closes, people cannot go in it: *The supermarket closes at 8 p.m.*
3 If a business closes, it stops operating.
close down **phrasal verb**
If a business closes down, it stops operating: *So many shops are closing down.*

close² /kləʊs/ **adj**
1 A1 near in distance: *His house is* ***close to*** *the sea.*
2 A1 near in time: *It was* ***close to*** *lunchtime when we arrived.*
3 A2 If people are close, they know each other well and like each other: *close friends*
4 B1 A close relative is someone who is directly related to you, for example your mother, father, or brother: *There weren't many people at the funeral – just close family.*
5 A close competition is one in which people's scores are very similar.
6 looking at or listening to someone or something very carefully: ***Keep a close watch on*** *the children (= watch them carefully).*
• **closely** **adv**

close³ /kləʊs/ **adv**
B1 near in distance: *They sat* ***close together.***

closed /kləʊzd/ **adj**
1 A1 not open for business: *We went to the library but it was closed.*
2 A1 not open: *Her eyes were closed.*

cloth /klɒθ/ **noun**
1 [no plural] material made from cotton, wool, etc., and used, for example, to make clothes or curtains
2 a piece of material used for cleaning or drying things

a b c d e f g h i j k l m n o p q r s t u v w x y z

clothes /kləʊðz/ **plural noun**
A1 things such as shirts and trousers that you wear on your body: *She was **wearing** her sister's **clothes**.*
→ See **Clothes** on page C5

> **Common mistake: clothes**
> Remember that **clothes** is plural. If you want to talk about one particular thing that you wear use **a piece of clothing** or **an item of clothing**.
> *I need some new clothes.*
> *He bought two or three pieces of clothing.*

clothing /ˈkləʊðɪŋ/ **noun** [no plural]
clothes, especially of a particular type: *outdoor clothing*

cloud /klaʊd/ **noun**
cloud
1 A2 one of the white or grey things in the sky that are made of small water drops: *rain clouds*
2 a mass of something such as dust or smoke that looks like a cloud: *A huge cloud of smoke spread across the sky.*

cloudy /ˈklaʊdi/ **adj** (**cloudier**, **cloudiest**)
A2 with many clouds in the sky: *a cloudy day*

clown /klaʊn/ **noun**
A2 someone with funny clothes and a painted face, who makes people laugh by being silly

clown

club /klʌb/ **noun**
1 A2 a group of people who do a sport or other activity together: *a health club*
2 B1 a team of sports players: *Manchester United Football Club*
3 a long, thin stick used to hit the ball in golf
→ See **Sports 2** on page C16
4 a place where people dance late at night

clubbing /ˈklʌbɪŋ/ **noun** [no plural]
the activity of going to clubs where there is music and dancing: *I love **going clubbing**.*

clubs /klʌbz/ **plural noun**
one of the four suits (= groups) of playing cards: *the four of clubs*

clue /kluː/ **noun**
1 something that helps you to solve a problem or answer a question: *Police are searching for **clues to** the murder.*
2 not have a clue informal to know nothing about something: *I haven't a clue what you're talking about.*

clumsy /ˈklʌmzi/ **adj** (**clumsier**, **clumsiest**)
Clumsy people move in a way that is not controlled or careful, and often knock or damage things.

clung /klʌŋ/
past tense and past participle of cling

clutch[1] /klʌtʃ/ **verb**
to hold something tightly: *She clutched a coin in her hand.*

clutch[2] /klʌtʃ/ **noun** [no plural]
the part of a car that you press with your foot when you change gear (= the part that controls how fast the wheels turn)
→ See **Car** on page C3

cm
written abbreviation for centimetre: a unit for measuring length

coach[1] /kəʊtʃ/ **noun**
1 A2 UK a comfortable bus used to take groups of people on long journeys: *a coach trip*
2 B1 someone who gives lessons, especially in a sport: *a tennis coach*

coach[2] /kəʊtʃ/ **verb**
to give someone lessons, especially in a sport or school subject
• **coaching** **noun** [no plural]

coal /kəʊl/ **noun** [no plural]
a hard, black substance that is found in the ground and burnt as fuel: *a lump of coal*

coast /kəʊst/ **noun**
B1 the land next to the sea: *They live **on the** east **coast** of Scotland.*

coat /kəʊt/ **noun**
1 A1 a piece of clothing that you wear

a b c d e f g h i j k l m n o p q r s t u v w x y z

over your other clothes when you are outside: *a winter coat*
→ See **Clothes** on page C5
2 the fur that covers an animal's body
3 a layer of a liquid over a surface: *a coat of paint*

coat hanger /ˈkəʊt ˌhæŋəʳ/ **noun**
a wire, wooden, or plastic thing for hanging clothes on

Coca-Cola /ˌkəʊkəˈkəʊlə/ **noun** trademark
a sweet, brown drink with bubbles

cock /kɒk/ **noun**
an adult male chicken

cocoa /ˈkəʊkəʊ/ **noun** [no plural]
1 the dark brown powder used to make chocolate
2 a drink made by mixing cocoa powder with hot milk

coconut /ˈkəʊkənʌt/ **noun**
B1 a large nut with a hard shell, a white part that you eat, and liquid inside

cod /kɒd/ **noun** (plural **cod**)
B1 a large sea fish that is eaten as food

code /kəʊd/ **noun**
1 a set of letters, numbers, or signs that are used instead of ordinary words to keep a message secret: *It was written* ***in code****.*
2 UK a set of numbers used at the beginning of a telephone number for a particular area

coffee /ˈkɒfi/ **noun**
1 A1 a hot drink made from dark beans that are made into a powder, or a cup of this drink: *Do you want a cup of coffee?*
2 A1 [no plural] the beans from which coffee is made, or the powder made from these beans: *instant coffee*

coffee table /ˈkɒfi ˌteɪbl/ **noun**
a low table in a living room on which people put magazines, drinks, etc.
→ See **The Living Room** on page C11

coffin /ˈkɒfɪn/ **noun**
a box in which a dead body is buried

coin /kɔɪn/ **noun**
B1 a flat, round piece of metal used as money: *a pound coin*

coincidence /kəʊˈɪnsɪdəns/ **noun**
an occasion when two very similar things happen at the same time by chance: *It was just coincidence that we were travelling on the same train.*

Coke /kəʊk/ **noun** trademark
short form of Coca-Cola

cola /ˈkəʊlə/ **noun**
A2 a sweet, dark brown drink with lots of bubbles, or a glass or can of this drink: *a can of cola*

cold[1] /kəʊld/ **adj**
1 A1 having a low temperature: *cold water/weather*
2 B1 unfriendly or showing no emotion: *a cold stare*

cold[2] /kəʊld/ **noun**
1 A2 a common illness that makes your nose produce liquid: *I've got a cold.*
2 the cold B1 cold weather: *Don't go out in the cold!*

collapse /kəˈlæps/ **verb** (**collapsing**, **collapsed**)
to fall down, sometimes breaking into pieces: *The roof collapsed under the weight of the snow.* ◦ *He collapsed and died of a heart attack.*
• **collapse noun** [no plural] *the collapse of a building during the earthquake*

collar /ˈkɒləʳ/ **noun**
1 B1 the part of a shirt or coat that goes around your neck
→ See picture at **jacket**
2 a thin piece of leather that goes around the neck of a dog or a cat

colleague /ˈkɒliːg/ **noun**
A2 someone that you work with

collect[1] /kəˈlekt/ **verb**
1 A2 to get and keep things of one type such as stamps or coins as a hobby: *She collects dolls.*
2 A2 UK to go to a place and bring someone or something away from it: *She* ***collects*** *Anna* ***from*** *school at 3.30.*
3 B1 to get things from different places and bring them together: *Police collected a lot of information during the investigation.*
4 to ask people for money for something, for example a charity (= organi-

zation that helps people): *I'm collecting on behalf of Oxfam.*

collect[2] /kəˈlekt/ **adj, adv** US
If you telephone collect or make a collect telephone call, the person you telephone pays for the call: *She called her parents collect.*

collection /kəˈlekʃən/ **noun**
1 B1 a group of objects of the same type that have been brought together: *a private art collection*
2 the act of something being removed from a place: *rubbish collection*

collector /kəˈlektə^{r}/ **noun**
someone who collects objects because they are interesting or beautiful: *a collector of modern art*

college /ˈkɒlɪdʒ/ **noun**
A2 a place where students are educated after they have stopped going to school: *a teacher-training college*

collision /kəˈlɪʒən/ **noun**
an accident in which vehicles hit each other

colon /ˈkəʊlɒn/ **noun**
a mark (:) used before a list, an example, an explanation, etc.

colony /ˈkɒləni/ **noun** (plural **colonies**)
a country or area controlled by a more powerful country

colour[1] UK (US **color**) /ˈkʌlə^{r}/ **noun**
1 A1 red, blue, green, yellow, etc.: *What colour shall I paint the kitchen?*
→ See **Colours** on page C6
2 [no plural] the colour of a person's skin, which shows their race

colour[2] UK (US **color**) /ˈkʌlə^{r}/ **verb**
A1 to make something a particular colour: *He drew a heart and coloured it red.*

colourful UK (US **colorful**) /ˈkʌləfəl/ **adj**
1 B1 having bright colours
2 interesting and unusual: *The town has a very colourful history.*

column /ˈkɒləm/ **noun**
1 a tall stone post that supports a roof
2 a long, vertical line of something
3 one of the blocks of print into which a page of a newspaper, magazine, or dictionary is divided: *I didn't have time to read the whole article – just the first column.*

comb[1] /kəʊm/ **noun**
A2 a flat piece of metal or plastic with a line of long, narrow parts along one side, that you use to tidy your hair

comb[2] /kəʊm/ **verb**
B1 to tidy your hair using a comb

combination /ˌkɒmbɪˈneɪʃən/ **noun**
a mixture of different people or things: *Strawberries and cream – a perfect combination!*

combine /kəmˈbaɪn/ **verb**
(**combining**, **combined**)
to become mixed or joined, or to mix or join things together: *Combine the sugar and the butter.*

come /kʌm/ **verb** (**coming**, **came**, **come**)
1 A1 to move or travel towards a person who is speaking: *Come here.* ◦ *Can you **come to** my party?* ◦ ***Here comes** Adam (= Adam is coming).*
2 A1 to arrive somewhere: *I've come to see Mr Curtis.* ◦ *Has the paper come yet?*
3 A1 to go somewhere with the person who is speaking: ***Come with** us later.*
4 A2 to be available to buy in a particular colour, size, etc.: *Do these socks **come in** any other colour?*
5 B1 to have a particular position in a competition or list: *Our team came third.*
6 to happen: *Spring has come early.*
7 **come apart/off** to become separated or removed from something: *The book **came apart** in my hands.* ◦ *The handle **came off**.*
8 **how come** used to ask why something has happened: *How come you didn't go to the party?*

come along **phrasal verb**
B1 to go somewhere with someone: *We're going to the zoo. Do you want to come along?*

come back **phrasal verb**

A2 to return to a place: *I've just come back from the dentist's.*

come down phrasal verb
If a price or a level comes down, it becomes lower: *House prices have come down recently.*

come from *something* phrasal verb
A1 to be born, got from, or made somewhere: *She comes from Poland.* ◦ *Milk comes from cows.*

come in phrasal verb
A2 to enter a room or building: *Come in and have a cup of coffee.*

come on phrasal verb
B1 said to encourage someone to do something, especially to hurry or try harder: *Come on, the taxi's waiting.*

come out phrasal verb
1 B1 If a book, movie, etc. comes out, it becomes available for people to buy or see: *When does their new album come out?*
2 B1 If the sun, the moon, or a star comes out, it appears in the sky: *It's really warm when the sun comes out.*

come round phrasal verb UK
A2 to visit someone at their house: *You must come round for dinner some time.*

come up phrasal verb
1 to move towards someone: *A young girl* ***came up to*** *me and asked for money.*
2 to be mentioned or talked about in conversation: *What issues came up at the meeting?*

come up with *something* phrasal verb
to suggest or think of an idea or plan: *She's come up with a great idea to make money.*

comedian /kə'mi:di:ən/ **noun**
someone who entertains people by telling jokes

comedy /'kɒmədi/ **noun** (plural **comedies**)
B1 a funny movie or play: *The movie is described as a romantic comedy.*

comfort[1] /'kʌmfət/ **noun** [no plural]
B1 a nice feeling of being relaxed and without pain: *Now you can watch the latest movies* ***in the comfort of*** *your sitting room.*

comfort[2] /'kʌmfət/ **verb**
to make someone feel better when they are sad: *We comforted Sasha after her dog died.*

comfortable /'kʌmftəbl/ **adj**

> **Common mistake: comfortable**
> Learners often spell **comfortable** wrong. Remember that it begins with **com**.

1 A2 making you feel relaxed and free from pain: *comfortable shoes* ◦ *a comfortable bed*
2 B1 relaxed and without pain: ***Make yourself comfortable*** *while I get you a drink.*
3 If you are comfortable in a situation, you do not have any worries about it: *I don't feel comfortable about leaving the children here alone.*
→ Opposite **uncomfortable adj**
• **comfortably adv**

comic[1] /'kɒmɪk/ **adj**
B1 funny: *a comic novel*

comic[2] /'kɒmɪk/ **noun**
A2 a magazine with stories told in pictures

comma /'kɒmə/ **noun**
B1 a mark (,) used to separate parts of a sentence, or to separate the items in a list

command[1] /kə'mɑ:nd/ **noun**
1 [no plural] control over someone or something and responsibility for them: *Jones was* ***in command*** *(= the leader).*
2 an order to do something

command[2] /kə'mɑ:nd/ **verb** formal
to order someone to do something: *The officer commanded his men to shoot.*

comment[1] /'kɒment/ **noun**
something that you say or write that shows your opinion: *He read my essay and* ***made*** *a few* ***comments****.*

comment[2] /'kɒment/ **verb**
to make a comment: *My mum always* ***comments on*** *what I'm wearing.*

commentary /'kɒmənt^{ə}ri/ **noun** (plural **commentaries**)
a spoken description of an event while

the event is happening: *the football commentary*

commerce /ˈkɒmɜːs/ **noun** [no plural]
the activities involved in buying and selling things

commercial¹ /kəˈmɜːʃəl/ **adj**
1 relating to buying and selling things
2 done in order to make a profit: *The computer was a commercial success (= made a profit).*

commercial² /kəˈmɜːʃəl/ **noun**
an advertisement on the radio or television

commit /kəˈmɪt/ **verb** (**committing**, **committed**)
1 to do something bad or illegal: *He went to prison for a crime he didn't commit.*
2 to make a definite decision to do something: *I said I might be interested in the job but I haven't* ***committed myself*** *yet.*

commitment /kəˈmɪtmənt/ **noun**
1 a promise to do something: *Players must* ***make a commitment to*** *daily training.*
2 [no plural] the willingness to give a lot of time and energy to something

committed /kəˈmɪtɪd/ **adj**
loyal and giving a lot of your time and energy to something: *She's* ***committed to*** *the job.*

committee /kəˈmɪti/ **noun**
a group of people who represent a larger organization and make decisions for it

common¹ /ˈkɒmən/ **adj**
1 B1 happening often or existing in large numbers: *Injuries are common in sports such as hockey.*
2 B1 belonging to two or more people or things: *We don't have any common interests.*

common² /ˈkɒmən/ **noun**
have *something* in common B1 to have the same interests, experiences, or qualities as someone or something else: *Sue and I don't have much in common.*

common sense /ˌkɒmən ˈsens/ **noun** [no plural]
the ability to use good judgment in making decisions: *The kids will be fine as long as they use their common sense.*

communicate /kəˈmjuːnɪkeɪt/ **verb** (**communicating**, **communicated**)
B1 to talk or write to someone in order to share information with them: *I usually* ***communicate with*** *him by email.*

communication /kəˌmjuːnɪˈkeɪʃən/ **noun** [no plural]
B1 the act of communicating with other people: *The school is improving* ***communication between*** *teachers and parents.*

communications /kəˌmjuːnɪˈkeɪʃənz/ **noun**
the different ways of sending information between people and places, such as post, telephones, computers, and radio: *the communications industry*

community /kəˈmjuːnəti/ **noun** (plural **communities**)
1 the people living in a particular area: *the local community*
2 a group of people with the same interests, religion, or nationality: *the Chinese community in London*

commuter /kəˈmjuːtər/ **noun**
someone who regularly travels between work and home: *The train was full of commuters.*

companion /kəmˈpænjən/ **noun**
someone who you spend a lot of time with or go somewhere with: *a travelling companion*

company /ˈkʌmpəni/ **noun**
1 A2 (plural **companies**) an organization that sells things or services: *a software company*
2 [no plural] a state of having a person or people with you: *I enjoy his company.*
3 **keep *someone* company** to stay with someone so that they are not alone: *Come and keep me company, Lauren.*

comparative /kəmˈpærətɪv/ **noun**
A2 the form of an adjective or adverb that is used to show that someone or

something has more of a particular quality than someone or something else. For example 'better' is the comparative of 'good' and 'smaller' is the comparative of 'small'.

compare /kəmˈpeəʳ/ **verb** (**comparing**, **compared**)
1 B1 to examine the ways in which two people or things are different or similar: *The teachers are always* ***comparing me with*** *my sister.*
2 **compared to/with *someone/something*** used when saying how one person or thing is different from another: *Her room is very clean compared to mine.*

comparison /kəmˈpærɪsᵊn/ **noun** the act of comparing two or more people or things: *She's so tall that he looks tiny* ***by/in comparison****.*

compartment /kəmˈpɑːtmənt/ **noun**
1 one of the separate areas inside a train
2 a separate part of a container, bag, etc.: *a fridge with a small freezer compartment*

compass /ˈkʌmpəs/ **noun** a piece of equipment that shows you which direction you are going in

compass

compatible /kəmˈpætɪbl/ **adj** happy or successful when together or combined: *This keyboard is* ***compatible with*** *all of our computers.*

compensation /ˌkɒmpənˈseɪʃᵊn/ **noun** [no plural] money that you give someone because you have hurt them or damaged something that they own

compete /kəmˈpiːt/ **verb** (**competing**, **competed**)
1 B1 to try to win a competition: *She's* ***competing for*** *a place in next year's Olympics.*
2 to try to be more successful than someone or something else: *It's difficult for a small supermarket to* ***compete against/with*** *the big supermarkets.*

competition /ˌkɒmpəˈtɪʃᵊn/ **noun**
1 A2 an event in which people try to win something by being the best, fastest, etc.
2 [no plural] a situation in which people or companies try to be more successful than others: *There's a lot of* ***competition between*** *computer companies.*

competitive /kəmˈpetɪtɪv/ **adj**
1 wanting to win or be better than other people: *She's very competitive.*
2 involving competition: *competitive sports*
3 as good as or better than other prices, services, etc.: *They offer high-quality products at competitive prices.*

competitor /kəmˈpetɪtəʳ/ **noun** B1 someone who is trying to win a competition

complain /kəmˈpleɪn/ **verb** B1 to say that something is wrong or that you are angry about something: *Lots of people have* ***complained about*** *the noise.* ◦ *She* ***complained*** *that no one listened to her.*
complain of *something* **phrasal verb** B1 to tell other people that something is making you feel ill: *She's been complaining of a headache all day.*

complaint /kəmˈpleɪnt/ **noun** B1 a statement that someone makes to say something is wrong or not good enough: *I wish to* ***make a complaint****.*

complete¹ /kəmˈpliːt/ **adj**
1 B1 with all parts: *the complete works of Oscar Wilde*
2 B1 used to make what you are saying stronger: *The meeting was a complete waste of time.*

complete² /kəmˈpliːt/ **verb** (**completing**, **completed**)
1 A2 to finish doing or making something: *The palace took 15 years to complete.*
2 A2 to provide the last part needed to make something whole: *Complete the sentence with one of the adjectives provided.*
3 A2 to write all the necessary details

on a form or other document: *Have you completed your application yet?*

completely /kəmˈpliːtli/ **adv**
B1 in every way or as much as possible: *I completely forgot that you were coming.* ◦ *The sisters are completely different.*

complex /ˈkɒmpleks/ **adj**
made of a lot of different but connected parts; difficult to understand: *a complex network of roads* ◦ *The story was so complex that I couldn't understand it.*

complicated /ˈkɒmplɪkeɪtɪd/ **adj**
B1 with many different parts and difficult to understand: *The instructions were too complicated.*

complication /ˌkɒmplɪˈkeɪʃən/ **noun**
something that makes a situation more difficult

compliment /ˈkɒmplɪmənt/ **noun**
something good that you say about someone, showing that you admire them

compose /kəmˈpəʊz/ **verb**
(**composing**, **composed**)
1 If something is composed of other things, it has those things in it: *The committee is composed of three men and six women.*
2 to write a piece of music

composition /ˌkɒmpəˈzɪʃən/ **noun**
1 B1 a short piece of writing about a particular subject, done by a student: *a 500-word composition*
2 a piece of music that someone has written: *The children played their own compositions in the concert.*

comprehensive school /ˌkɒmprɪˈhensɪv ˌskuːl/ **noun**
a school in the UK for students aged 11 to 18 of all levels of ability

compulsory /kəmˈpʌlsəri/ **adj**
If something is compulsory, you must do it because a rule or law says you must.

computer /kəmˈpjuːtər/ **noun**
A1 an electronic machine that can store and arrange large amounts of information: *We've put all our records **on computer**.*
→ See **The Office** on page C12

computer game /kəmˈpjuːtə ˌɡeɪm/ **noun**
a game that is played on a computer, in which the pictures on the screen are controlled by pressing keys

conceal /kənˈsiːl/ **verb**
to hide something: *I couldn't conceal my anger.*

concentrate /ˈkɒnsəntreɪt/ **verb**
(**concentrating**, **concentrated**)
B1 to think very hard about the thing you are doing and nothing else: *Be quiet – I'm trying to concentrate.* ◦ *I can't **concentrate on** my work. It's too noisy.*

concentration /ˌkɒnsənˈtreɪʃən/ **noun** [no plural]
the ability to think only about something you are doing

concept /ˈkɒnsept/ **noun**
an idea or principle: *It is very difficult to define **the concept of** beauty.*

concern[1] /kənˈsɜːn/ **verb**
1 to be important to someone: *Environmental issues concern us all.*
2 to worry or upset someone: *What concerns me is her lack of experience.*
3 If a story, movie, etc. concerns a particular subject, it is about that subject.

concern[2] /kənˈsɜːn/ **noun**
1 a feeling of worry about something: *I have **concerns about** his health.*
2 something that involves or affects you or is important to you: *Our primary concern is safety.*

concerned /kənˈsɜːnd/ **adj**
1 worried: *I'm a bit **concerned about** her health.*
2 as far as *someone* is concerned used to show what someone thinks about something: *He can do what he wants as far as I'm concerned.*
3 as far as *something* is concerned used to say what you are talking about: *As far as money is concerned, we're doing very well.*

concerning /kənˈsɜːnɪŋ/ **preposition**
about something: *I got a letter concerning my tax payments.*

concert /ˈkɒnsət/ **noun**
A2 a performance of music and singing: *a rock concert*

conclusion /kənˈkluːʒən/ **noun**
1 B1 your opinion after considering all the information about something: *I've* ***come to the conclusion that*** *we'll have to sell the car.*
2 in conclusion used to begin the last part of a speech or a piece of writing: *In conclusion, I would like to thank our speaker for her interesting talk.*

concrete /ˈkɒŋkriːt/ **noun** [no plural]
a wet mixture that is used in building and that becomes hard when it dries: *concrete blocks*

condemn /kənˈdem/ **verb**
to say very strongly that you think something is very bad: *The Prime Minister was quick to condemn the terrorists.*

condition /kənˈdɪʃən/ **noun**
1 B1 the state that something or someone is in: *My bike's a few years old but it's* ***in*** *really* ***good condition****.*
2 conditions B1 the situation in which people live, work, or do things: *What are their* ***living conditions*** *like?* ◦ *The prisoners were kept* ***in*** *terrible* ***conditions****.*
3 an illness: *a heart condition*
4 something that must happen or be agreed before something else can happen: *One of the conditions of the contract is that we can't keep pets.*

conduct¹ /ˈkɒndʌkt/ **noun** [no plural]
the way someone behaves

conduct² /kənˈdʌkt/ **verb**
1 to organize or do something: *We are conducting a survey.*
2 to stand in front of a group of musicians and control how they play

conductor /kənˈdʌktəʳ/ **noun**
someone who stands in front of a group of musicians and controls how they play

cone /kəʊn/ **noun**
1 a solid shape with a round bottom and a pointed top
2 a sweet, hard food shaped like a cone or cup that holds ice cream

conference /ˈkɒnfərəns/ **noun**
B1 a large meeting, often lasting a few days, where people talk about a subject: *the annual sales conference*

confess /kənˈfes/ **verb**
to say that you have done something wrong: *He finally* ***confessed to*** *the murder.*

confession /kənˈfeʃən/ **noun**
a statement someone makes to say that they have done something wrong: *The thief has* ***made*** *a full* ***confession*** *to the police.*

confidence /ˈkɒnfɪdəns/ **noun** [no plural]
the belief that you are able to do things well or be successful: *He's a good student, but he* ***lacks confidence****.*

confident /ˈkɒnfɪdənt/ **adj**
1 B1 certain about your ability to do things well
2 certain that something will happen: *I am* ***confident that*** *we can win this.*
• **confidently adv** *Try to act confidently, even if you feel nervous.*

confirm /kənˈfɜːm/ **verb**
1 B1 to make sure an arrangement or meeting will happen, often by telephone or in writing: *I accepted the job over the phone, but I haven't* ***confirmed in writing*** *yet.*
2 to say or show that something is true: *His wife* ***confirmed that*** *he left the house at 8.00.*

confirmation /ˌkɒnfəˈmeɪʃən/ **noun** [no plural]
a statement or document that shows something is true or certain

conflict¹ /ˈkɒnflɪkt/ **noun**
disagreement or fighting: *The* ***conflict between*** *the two sides lasted for years.*

conflict² /kənˈflɪkt/ **verb**
to be different: *Her views on raising children* ***conflict with*** *mine.*

confuse /kənˈfjuːz/ **verb** (**confusing**, **confused**)
1 to stop someone from understanding something: *My explanation just confused her.*
2 to think that one person or thing is

another person or thing: *People often **confuse** me **with** my brother.*

confused /kən'fju:zd/ **adj**
1 B1 not able to think clearly or to understand something: *Sorry, I'm completely confused.* ◦ *Even the politicians are **confused about** what to do.*
2 not clear: *The witnesses gave confused accounts of what happened.*

confusing /kən'fju:zɪŋ/ **adj**
B1 difficult to understand: *These instructions are really confusing.*

confusion /kən'fju:ʒən/ **noun** [no plural]
1 a state in which people do not understand what is happening or what they should do: *The new system has caused a lot of confusion.*
2 a situation, often with a lot of activity and noise, in which people do not know what to do: *I lost my bag **in the confusion** after the explosion.*

congratulate /kən'grætʃʊleɪt/ **verb** (**congratulating**, **congratulated**)
to tell someone that you are happy about something good that they have done: *I **congratulated** Lulu **on** passing her exam.*

congratulations! /kənˌgrætʃʊ'leɪʃənz/ **exclamation**
A2 something that you say to show someone you are pleased about an event or achievement: *I hear you're getting married. Congratulations!*

congregation /ˌkɒŋgrɪ'geɪʃən/ **noun**
a group of people who worship together regularly

conjunction /kən'dʒʌŋkʃən/ **noun**
a word that is used to connect phrases or parts of a sentence. For example the words 'and' and 'because' are conjunctions.

connect /kə'nekt/ **verb**
B1 to join two things or places together: *A small bridge connects the two parts of the building.*

connection /kə'nekʃən/ **noun**
1 B1 something that joins things together: *Many companies now offer free connection to the Internet.*
2 a relationship between people or things: *The **connection between** smoking and heart disease is clear.*
3 in connection with *something* used to say what something is about: *A man has been arrested in connection with the murder.*
4 a train, bus, or plane that leaves a short time after another arrives, so that people can continue their journey: *The train was ten minutes late and I **missed my connection**.*

conquer /'kɒŋkər/ **verb**
to take control of a country or to defeat people in a war: *Peru was conquered by the Spanish in 1532.*

conquest /'kɒŋkwest/ **noun**
the act of taking control of a country, area, or situation: *the Roman conquest of Britain*

conscience /'kɒnʃəns/ **noun**
the part of your mind that makes you feel bad when you have done something wrong: *a guilty conscience*

conscious /'kɒnʃəs/ **adj**
awake and able to think and notice things: *He's still conscious, but he's very badly injured.*
→ Opposite **unconscious adj**

consciousness /'kɒnʃəsnəs/ **noun** [no plural]
the state of being awake and being able to think and notice things: *He **lost consciousness** (= stopped being conscious) for several minutes.*

consent /kən'sent/ **noun** [no plural]
permission to do something: *You can't come without your parents' consent.*

consequence /'kɒnsɪkwəns/ **noun**
the result of an action, especially a bad result: *If you make him angry, you'll have to **suffer the consequences**.*

consequently /'kɒnsɪkwəntli/ **adv**
as a result: *I had car trouble and was consequently late.*

conservation /ˌkɒnsə'veɪʃən/ **noun** [no plural]
the protection of nature: *wildlife conservation*

conservative /kən'sɜ:vətɪv/ **adj**
not liking sudden changes or new

ideas: *Older people tend to be more conservative.*

consider /kən'sɪdəʳ/ **verb**
1 B1 to think carefully about something: *We're considering buying a new car.*
2 consider *someone/something* (to be) *something* to have a particular opinion about someone or something: *We don't consider her suitable for the job.*

considerable /kən'sɪdərəbl/ **adj**
large or important enough to be noticed: *a considerable amount of money*
• **considerably adv** *He's considerably fatter than he was the last time I saw him.*

consideration /kənˌsɪdəʳ'eɪʃən/ **noun**
1 something that you have to think about when you make decisions: *Safety is our main consideration.*
2 [no plural] the quality of thinking about other people's feelings and trying not to upset them: *They always treated me with consideration.*
3 [no plural] careful thought and attention: *After **careful consideration**, we decided to offer her the job.* ◦ *It may be cheap to buy a used car, but you've got to **take into consideration** the money you'll spend on repairs.*

considering /kən'sɪdərɪŋ/ **preposition, conjunction**
used for saying that you have a particular opinion about something, because of a particular fact about it: *Considering the weather, we got here really quickly.*

consist /kən'sɪst/ **verb**
consist of *something* phrasal verb
B1 to be made from something: *The dessert consisted of fruit and cream.*

console[1] /kən'səʊl/ **verb**
to make someone who is sad feel better: *I tried to console her, but she just kept crying.*

console[2] /'kɒnsəʊl/ **noun**
an object that contains the controls for a piece of equipment: *a video game console*

consonant /'kɒnsənənt/ **noun**
B1 a letter of the alphabet that is not a vowel. (The vowels are a, e, i, o, and u.)

constable /'kʌnstəbl/ **noun** (also **police constable**)
In the UK, a police officer of the lowest rank

constant /'kɒnstənt/ **adj**
happening a lot or all the time: *She's in constant pain.*
• **constantly adv** *She has the television on constantly.*

construct /kən'strʌkt/ **verb**
to build something from many parts: *The building was constructed in 1930.*

construction /kən'strʌkʃən/ **noun**
1 [no plural] the work of building houses, offices, bridges, etc.: *railway construction*
2 something that is built, such as a building: *a large steel construction*

consul /'kɒnsəl/ **noun**
someone whose job is to work in a foreign country and help people from their own country who go there

consult /kən'sʌlt/ **verb**
1 to go to a person or book to get information or advice: *For more information, consult your travel agent.*
2 to talk with someone before you decide something: *Why didn't you consult me about this?*

consume /kən'sjuːm/ **verb**
(**consuming**, **consumed**)
1 to use something: *These lights consume a lot of electricity.*
2 formal to eat or drink something: *People consume too much sugar.*

consumer /kən'sjuːməʳ/ **noun**
someone who buys or uses goods or services: *These price cuts are good news for consumers.*

consumption /kən'sʌmpʃən/ **noun**
[no plural]
the amount of something that someone uses, eats, or drinks: *China's total energy consumption*

contact[1] /'kɒntækt/ **noun**
1 A2 someone you know who can

help you because of their job: *business contacts*
2 B1 [no plural] communication with someone: *We **keep in** close **contact** with our grandparents.*
3 [no plural] the state of two people or things touching each other: *Wash your hands if they **come into contact with** chemicals.*

contact² /ˈkɒntækt/ **verb**
A2 to telephone someone or write to them: *I've been trying to contact you for days.*

contact lens /ˈkɒntækt ˌlenz/ **noun**
a small piece of plastic that you put on your eye to make you see more clearly

contain /kənˈteɪn/ **verb**
B1 If one thing contains another thing, it has that thing inside it: *a box containing a diamond ring*

containers

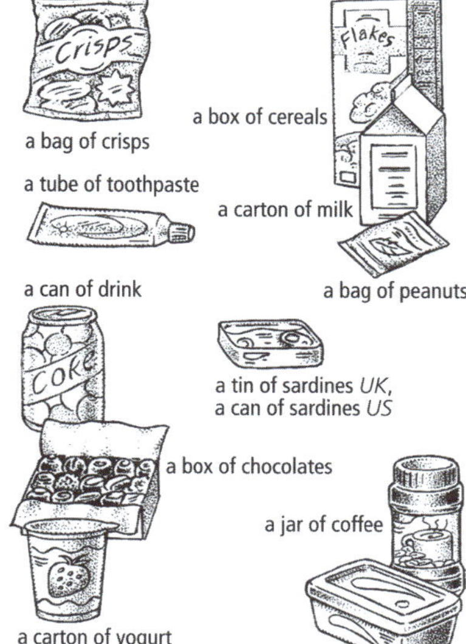

a bag of crisps
a box of cereals
a tube of toothpaste
a carton of milk
a can of drink
a bag of peanuts
a tin of sardines *UK*, a can of sardines *US*
a box of chocolates
a jar of coffee
a carton of yogurt
a tub of margarine

container /kənˈteɪnəʳ/ **noun**
an object such as a box or a bottle that is used for holding something

content¹ /kənˈtent/ **adj**
happy: *I was **content to** stay at home and read.*

content² /ˈkɒntent/ **noun** [no plural]
B1 the ideas that are talked about in a piece of writing, a speech, or a movie: *the **content of** the article*

contented /kənˈtentɪd/ **adj**
happy: *a contented smile*

contents /ˈkɒntents/ **plural noun**
1 B1 all of the things that are contained inside something: *Please empty out the contents of your pockets.*
2 a list in a book that tells you what different parts the book contains: *a table of contents*

contest /ˈkɒntest/ **noun**
B1 a competition

contestant /kənˈtestᵊnt/ **noun**
someone who tries to win a competition: *The quiz contestants come from all over the country.*

context /ˈkɒntekst/ **noun**
all the facts, opinions, etc. relating to a particular thing or event: *This small battle is very important **in the context of** Scottish history.*

continent /ˈkɒntɪnənt/ **noun**
B1 one of the seven main areas of land on the Earth, such as Asia, Africa, or Europe

continual /kənˈtɪnjuəl/ **adj**
happening again and again over a long period of time: *I can't work with these continual interruptions.*
• **continually adv** *Dad continually complains about money.*

continue /kənˈtɪnjuː/ **verb**
(**continuing**, **continued**)
1 B1 to keep happening or doing something: *It **continued to** snow heavily for three days.* ◦ *Ava continued working until June.*
2 B1 to start doing or saying something again, after stopping: *We'll have to continue this discussion tomorrow.*
3 to go further in a particular direction: *Continue down the road until you reach Elm Street.*

continuous /kənˈtɪnjuəs/ **adj**
1 not stopping: *continuous pain*
2 The continuous form of a verb is used to show that an action is con-

a b c d e f g h i j k l m n o p q r s t u v w x y z

tinuing to happen: *the present continuous*
• **continuously** **adv** not stopping: *Their baby cried continuously.*

contract /ˈkɒntrækt/ **noun**
B1 a legal agreement between two people or organizations

contrary /ˈkɒntrəri/ **adj**
contrary to *something* opposite to what someone said or thought: *Contrary to popular belief, he is not a stupid man.*

contrast¹ /ˈkɒntrɑːst/ **noun**
an obvious difference between two people or things: *The* ***contrast between*** *their lifestyles couldn't be greater.*

contrast² /kənˈtrɑːst/ **verb**
to compare two people or things: *If you* ***contrast*** *his early novels* ***with*** *his later work, you can see how his writing has developed.*

contribute /kənˈtrɪbjuːt/ **verb** (**contributing**, **contributed**)
to give something, especially money: *I* ***contributed*** *$20* ***towards*** *Andrea's present.*

contribution /ˌkɒntrɪˈbjuːʃən/ **noun**
an amount of money that is given to help pay for something: *a generous* ***contribution to*** *charity*

control¹ /kənˈtrəʊl/ **noun**
1 [no plural] the power to make a person or thing do what you want: *The new teacher has no* ***control over*** *the class.* ◦ *He* ***lost control of*** *the car.*
2 under control If a situation is under control, things are happening in the way that you want them to: *Don't worry – everything's under control.*
3 out of control behaving very badly and not stopped by anyone: *The children were out of control.*
4 beyond your control/out of control If something is beyond your control or out of control, you cannot influence or direct it: *There's nothing we can do – the situation is beyond our control.* ◦ *The car skidded and* ***went out of control.***
5 a switch or other device used to operate a machine: *Where's the volume control on your phone?*
6 take control to start to rule or govern an area: *The dictator took control of the country in 1933.*

control² /kənˈtrəʊl/ **verb** (**controlling**, **controlled**)
1 **B1** to make a person or thing do what you want: *Can't you control your dogs?*
2 **B1** to stop yourself expressing strong emotions or behaving in a silly way: *You're going to have to learn to control your temper.*
3 to limit the number, amount, or increase of something: *They couldn't control the spread of the disease.*
4 to rule or govern an area: *The police controlled the country during the civil war.*

controversial /ˌkɒntrəˈvɜːʃəl/ **adj**
causing disagreement or discussion: *The book was very controversial.*

convenience /kənˈviːniəns/ **noun**
1 [no plural] the quality of being easy to use and suitable for what you want to do: *the convenience of credit cards*
→ Opposite **inconvenience** **noun**
2 something that makes life easier: *Fortunately, the house has every modern convenience.*

convenient /kənˈviːniənt/ **adj**
1 **B1** easy and helpful: *When would be a convenient time to meet?*
2 **B1** near or easy to get to: *The new supermarket is very convenient for me.*
• **conveniently** **adv**

convent /ˈkɒnvənt/ **noun**
a building where nuns (= religious women) live together

conventional /kənˈventʃənəl/ **adj**
traditional and ordinary: *conventional clothes*

conversation /ˌkɒnvəˈseɪʃən/ **noun**
A1 a talk between two or more people: *a telephone conversation* ◦ *We* ***had a conversation*** *about football.*

convert /kənˈvɜːt/ **verb**
to change something into something else: *The old factory was* ***converted into*** *offices.*

convict /kənˈvɪkt/ **verb**
to decide officially in a court of law that someone has done a crime: *He was **convicted of** murder.*

convince /kənˈvɪns/ **verb** (**convincing**, **convinced**)
B1 to make someone believe that something is true: *He tried to **convince** me **that** I needed a new car.*

convinced /kənˈvɪnst/ **adj**
completely certain about something: *I'm **convinced that** he's wrong.*

cook

cook¹ /kʊk/ **verb**
A1 to make food ready to eat: *Who's cooking this evening?* ◦ *She cooked the meat in a hot pan.*

cook² /kʊk/ **noun**
A2 someone who prepares food for people to eat

cooker /ˈkʊkəʳ/ **noun** UK (US **stove**)
A2 a piece of equipment used to cook food: *an electric cooker*

cookery /ˈkʊkəri/ **noun** [no plural] UK
preparing food for people to eat

cookie /ˈkʊki/ **noun**
a thin, flat cake that is sweet and dry
→ See **Food** on page C7

cooking /ˈkʊkɪŋ/ **noun** [no plural]
A2 preparing food for people to eat: *I do all the **cooking**.*

cool¹ /ku:l/ **adj**
1 B1 slightly cold: *a cool drink*
2 A2 informal good or fashionable: *Cool hat, Maria!*
3 calm and not worried: *She seemed very cool before her exam.*
• **coolness** **noun** [no plural]

cool² /ku:l/ **verb**
to become less hot, or make something become less hot: *Allow the bread to cool before you eat it.*
cool down **phrasal verb**
to become less hot: *We went for a swim to cool down.*

cool³ /ku:l/ **exclamation** informal
A2 used when you like something or agree to something: *'I'll meet you there at 6.00.' 'Cool!'*

cooperate /kəʊˈɒpəreɪt/ **verb** (**cooperating**, **cooperated**)
1 to work together with someone: *Witnesses are **cooperating with** detectives.*
2 to do what someone asks you to do: *We will get there as long as we cooperate.*

cooperation /kəʊˌɒpəˈreɪʃən/ **noun** [no plural]
the activity of working together with someone or doing what they ask you to do: *international cooperation*

cooperative /kəʊˈɒpərətɪv/ **adj**
willing to help or do what people ask: *If I need any help she is usually very cooperative.*

cop /kɒp/ **noun** mainly US informal
a police officer

cope /kəʊp/ **verb** (**coping**, **coped**)
to do something well in a difficult situation: *She has a lot of work but somehow she **copes with** it.*

copper /ˈkɒpəʳ/ **noun** [no plural]
a soft, red-brown metal

copy¹ /ˈkɒpi/ **noun** (plural **copies**)
1 B1 something that is made to look exactly like something else: *Always **make copies of** important documents.*
2 a single book, newspaper, etc. of which many have been made: *a copy of the New York Times*

copy² /ˈkɒpi/ **verb** (**copying**, **copied**)
1 A2 to make something that is the same as something else: *Copy the file onto disk.*

a b c d e f g h i j k l m n o p q r s t u v w x y z

2 to behave like someone else: *He likes to copy his older brother.*
3 to cheat by using someone else's work: *She copied his answers.*

cord /kɔːd/ **noun**
1 thick string, or a piece of this
2 a piece of wire covered in plastic, used to connect electrical equipment to a power supply: *a telephone cord*

core /kɔːʳ/ **noun**
1 the most important part of something: *Lack of money is* ***at the core of*** *the problem.*
2 the hard central part of fruits such as apples, which contains the seeds

cork /kɔːk/ **noun**
1 [no plural] a light material that comes from the outside of a particular tree
2 a small piece of this material put in the top of a wine bottle to close it

corkscrew /ˈkɔːkskruː/ **noun**
a piece of equipment used for pulling corks out of wine bottles

corn /kɔːn/ **noun** [no plural]
1 B1 mainly UK a crop of grain, or the seed from this crop used to make flour: *fields of corn*
2 US (UK **maize**) a tall plant with yellow seeds that are eaten as food

corner /ˈkɔːnəʳ/ **noun**
A2 the point or area where two lines, walls, or roads meet: *the corner of the table* ◦ *There was a television* ***in the corner*** *of the room.* ◦ *The bar is* ***at the corner*** *of Ross Street and Mill Road.*

corporation /ˌkɔːpᵊrˈeɪʃᵊn/ **noun**
a large company or group of companies

corpus /ˈkɔːpəs/ **noun** (plural **corpora**)
an electronic collection of many millions of words that can be studied to show how language works

correct¹ /kəˈrekt/ **adj**
1 A2 accurate, or having no mistakes: *Check that you have the correct information.* ◦ *Was that the correct answer?*
2 B1 suitable for a particular situation: *We have the correct number of players for the game.*
• **correctly** **adv**

correct² /kəˈrekt/ **verb**
to show or tell someone that something is wrong and to make it right: *The students asked the teacher to correct their pronunciation.*

correction /kəˈrekʃᵊn/ **noun**
B1 a change to make something right or better: *She* ***made*** *some* ***corrections*** *before handing the essay in.*

correspond /ˌkɒrɪˈspɒnd/ **verb**
1 to be the same or very similar: *The newspaper story does not* ***correspond with/to*** *what really happened.*
2 to communicate with someone by writing letters: *They had corresponded ever since the war.*

correspondence /ˌkɒrɪˈspɒndəns/ **noun** [no plural]
letters from one person to another: *business correspondence*

corridor /ˈkɒrɪdɔːʳ/ **noun**
a passage in a building or train with rooms on one or both sides

corruption /kəˈrʌpʃᵊn/ **noun** [no plural]
dishonest or immoral behaviour, usually by people who have important positions: *There is widespread corruption in the government.*

cosmetics /kɒzˈmetɪks/ **plural noun**
substances that you put on your face or body to make you look better

cost¹ /kɒst/ **noun**
1 A2 the amount of money that you need to buy or do something: *The* ***cost of*** *rail travel is terrible.*
2 **at all costs** If something must be done at all costs, it is very important that it is done: *We have to succeed at all costs.*

cost² /kɒst/ **verb** (**cost**)
1 A2 If something costs a particular amount of money, you have to pay that in order to buy or do it: *How much do these shoes cost?* ◦ ***It costs*** *$5 to send the package by airmail.*
2 to cause someone to lose something valuable: *Drinking and driving costs lives (= can cause death).* ◦ *His affairs cost him his marriage.*

costume /ˈkɒstjuːm/ **noun**
1 a set of clothes worn in order to look like someone else, especially for a party, or in a movie or play: *The children were dressed in Halloween costumes.*
2 the set of clothes typical of a particular country or period of history: *Japanese* ***national costume***

cosy /ˈkəʊzi/ **adj** (**cosier**, **cosiest**) UK (US **cozy**)
B1 comfortable and warm: *It's nice and cosy in this room.*

cot /kɒt/ **noun** UK (US **crib**)
a bed with high sides for a baby

cot

cottage /ˈkɒtɪdʒ/ **noun**
B1 a small house, usually in the countryside

cotton /ˈkɒtᵊn/ **noun** [no plural]
1 B1 cloth or thread that is made from the cotton plant: *a cotton shirt*
2 a plant used for making thread and cloth

cotton wool /ˌkɒtᵊn ˈwʊl/ **noun** [no plural] UK
a soft mass of cotton, usually used for cleaning your skin
→ See **The Bathroom** on page C1

couch /kaʊtʃ/ **noun**
a long, comfortable piece of furniture that two or more people can sit on

cough¹ /kɒf/ **verb**
B1 to make air come out of your throat with a short sound: *Paul has been coughing and sneezing all day.*

cough² /kɒf/ **noun**
B1 the action or sound of coughing, or an illness that makes you cough: *I* ***have*** *a* ***bad cough***.

could strong /kʊd/ weak /kəd/ **modal verb**
1 A2 used as the past form of 'can' to talk about what someone or something was able or allowed to do: *I couldn't see him.* ◦ *You said I could go!*
2 A2 used as a more polite form of 'can' when asking for permission: *Excuse me, could I say something here?* ◦ *Could I speak to Mr Davis, please?*
3 B1 used to talk about what is possible or might happen: *She could arrive any time now.*
4 B1 used as a more polite form of 'can' when asking someone to give you something or do something: *Could you lend me £5?* ◦ *Could you turn the music down a little, please?*
5 B1 used for making a suggestion: *We could go for a drink after work tomorrow, if you like.*

couldn't /ˈkʊdᵊnt/
short form of could not: *I couldn't understand what he was saying.*

council /ˈkaʊnsᵊl/ **noun**
a group of people who are chosen to control a town, city, or area: *the town council*

councillor /ˈkaʊnsᵊləʳ/ **noun** UK
a member of a town, city, or area council

count¹ /kaʊnt/ **verb**
1 to see how many people or things there are: *I counted the money on the table.*
2 to say numbers in their correct order: *Can you count to twenty in French?*
3 to be important: *Doesn't my opinion* ***count for*** *anything?*
count on *someone* **phrasal verb**
to be certain that you can depend on someone: *I can always count on my parents to help me.*
count *someone/something* up **phrasal verb**
to add together all the people or things in a group

count² /kaʊnt/ **noun**
1 the action of counting something, or the total number you get after counting: ***At the last count*** *the club had 410 members.*
2 **lose count** to forget how many of something there is: *I've lost count of the number of times she's arrived late.*

countable noun /ˈkaʊntəbl ˌnaʊn/ **noun**
B1 a noun that can be used in the sin-

a b c d e f g h i j k l m n o p q r s t u v w x y z

gular and the plural: *'House' is a countable noun.*

counter /ˈkaʊntəʳ/ **noun**
the place in a shop, bank, etc. where people are served: *The woman **behind the counter** took his money.*

counterclockwise /ˌkaʊntəˈklɒkwaɪz/ **adj, adv** US (UK **anti-clockwise**)
in the opposite direction to the way the hands (= parts that point to the numbers) of a clock move
→ Opposite **clockwise**

country /ˈkʌntri/ **noun**
1 A1 (plural **countries**) an area of land that has its own government, army, etc.: *European countries*
2 the country A2 the areas that are away from towns and cities

countryside /ˈkʌntrisaɪd/ **noun** [no plural]
A2 land that is not in towns or cities and has farms, fields, etc.

> **Common mistake: countryside**
> Remember that **countryside** is written as one word.
> *I live in the countryside.*
> ~~*I live in the country side.*~~

county /ˈkaʊnti/ **noun** (plural **counties**)
an area of the UK, Ireland, or the US

couple /ˈkʌpl/ **noun**
1 B1 two or a few: *I went to New York with **a couple of** friends.*
2 B1 two people who are married or having a romantic relationship: *a married couple*

courage /ˈkʌrɪdʒ/ **noun** [no plural]
the quality that makes you able to do dangerous or difficult things: *The soldiers fought **with** great **courage**.* ◦ *She didn't **have the courage** to tell him the truth.*

courageous /kəˈreɪdʒəs/ **adj**
brave: *He was a courageous soldier.*

courgette /kɔːˈʒet/ **noun** UK (US **zucchini**)
a long, green vegetable that is white inside

course /kɔːs/ **noun**
1 of course A1 used to say 'yes' strongly, often to be polite: *'Can you help me?' 'Of course!'*
2 of course B1 used to show that what you are saying is obvious: *Of course, the Olympics are not just about money.*
3 of course not A2 used to say 'no' strongly: *'Do you mind if I borrow your pen?' 'Of course not.'*
4 A1 a set of lessons about a particular subject: *She did a ten-week computer course.*
5 A2 a part of a meal: *a three-course dinner*
6 B1 an area used for horse races or playing golf: *a golf course*
7 the direction in which a ship, plane, etc. is moving: *The boat was blown **off course** (= in the wrong direction).*
8 the way something develops, usually over a long time: *Nuclear weapons have changed **the course of** history.*

coursebook /ˈkɔːsbʊk/ **noun**
a book used by students when they do a particular course of study

court /kɔːt/ **noun**
1 the place where a judge decides if someone has done a crime: *The suspect appeared **in court** charged with robbery.*
2 B1 an area for playing a sport: *a tennis court*

courteous /ˈkɜːtiəs/ **adj**
polite and showing respect

courtesy /ˈkɜːtəsi/ **noun** [no plural]
behaviour that is polite and shows respect

cousin /ˈkʌzᵊn/ **noun**
A2 the child of someone's aunt or uncle: *He comes from a big family and has a lot of cousins.*

cover[1] /ˈkʌvəʳ/ **verb**
1 A2 to put something over something else: *They **covered** him **with** a blanket.* ◦ *He **covered** his face **with** his hands.*
2 B1 to form a layer on the surface of something: *Snow covered the trees.*
3 B1 to include or deal with a subject or piece of information: *The book covers European history from 1789-1914.*

4 to travel a particular distance: *We covered 300 miles in four days.*
5 to be a particular size or area: *The town **covers an area** of 15 square miles.*
6 to report the news about a particular important event: *She's covering the election for BBC television.*
cover *something* up phrasal verb
to put something over something else, in order to hide it: *We used a picture to cover up a hole in the wall.*

cover² /ˈkʌvəʳ/ **noun**
1 B1 the outer part of a book, magazine, etc. that protects the pages: *Her picture was on the cover of Vogue.*
2 B1 something you put over something else, usually to protect it: *an ironing board cover*

covering /ˈkʌvərɪŋ/ **noun** [no plural]
a layer that covers something: *a thick covering of snow*

cow /kaʊ/ **noun**
A1 a large female farm animal kept for milk or meat

coward /kaʊəd/ **noun**
someone who is not brave and does not do dangerous things

cowboy /ˈkaʊbɔɪ/ **noun**
a man whose job is to look after cows in the US, and who rides a horse

cozy /ˈkəʊzi/ **adj** (**cozier**, **coziest**) US (UK **cosy**)
comfortable and warm

crab /kræb/ **noun**
a sea animal with ten legs and a shell

crack¹ /kræk/ **verb**
1 to break something so that thin lines appear on its surface, or to become broken in this way: *Linda cracked her tooth when she fell.* ◦ *The glass cracked in my hand.*
2 to make a sudden, short noise

crack² /kræk/ **noun**
a line on the surface of something that is damaged: *Several cups had cracks in them.*

cracker /ˈkrækəʳ/ **noun**
1 a dry biscuit that is sometimes eaten with cheese: *a plate of cheese and crackers*
2 a coloured paper tube with a small toy inside, that people pull open at Christmas in the UK: *to **pull a cracker***

cradle /ˈkreɪdl/ **noun**
a baby's bed, especially one that moves from side to side

craft /krɑːft/ **noun**
1 an activity in which you make something using a lot of skill, especially with your hands: *traditional crafts such as weaving*
2 (plural **craft**) a boat

cram /kræm/ **verb** (**cramming**, **crammed**)
cram *something* in, into, etc. to force too many things into a small space: *Thousands of people were crammed into the stadium.*

crane /kreɪn/ **noun**
a large machine used for lifting and moving heavy things

crash¹ /kræʃ/ **noun**
1 B1 an accident in which a vehicle hits something: *a car/plane crash*
2 a sudden, loud noise made when something falls or breaks: *I heard a crash and hurried into the kitchen.*

crash² /kræʃ/ **verb**
1 B1 If a vehicle crashes, it hits something by accident: *The van skidded and **crashed into** a tree.*
2 If a computer or computer system crashes, it suddenly stops working.
3 to hit something and make a loud noise: *The waves crashed against the rocks.*

crash helmet /ˈkræʃ ˌhelmət/ **noun**
a hard hat that protects your head when you ride a motorcycle

crate /kreɪt/ **noun**
a large box used for carrying or storing things

crawl /krɔːl/ **verb**
to move on your hands and knees: *I crawled under the desk to plug in the lamp.*

crawl

crayon /ˈkreɪɒn/ **noun**
a stick of coloured wax used for drawing

crazy /ˈkreɪzi/ **adj** (**crazier**, **craziest**)
1 A2 stupid or strange: *a crazy idea*
2 annoyed or angry: *Dad* ***went crazy*** *when I told him what had happened.*
3 be crazy about ***someone/something*** A2 to love someone very much, or to be very interested in something: *Mia's crazy about baseball.*

creak /kriːk/ **verb**
If something such as a door or a piece of wood creaks, it makes a long noise when it moves: *The floorboards creaked under my feet.*

cream[1] /kriːm/ **noun**
1 A2 [no plural] a thick, white liquid that is taken from milk
2 A2 [no plural] a yellow-white colour
3 B1 a soft substance that you put on your skin: *face/hand cream*

cream[2] /kriːm/ **adj**
A2 being a yellow-white colour: *We chose cream paint for the walls.*

create /kriˈeɪt/ **verb** (**creating**, **created**)
B1 to make something happen or exist: *The project will create more than 500 jobs.* ◦ *The snow created further problems.*

creation /kriˈeɪʃᵊn/ **noun**
1 [no plural] the act of making something happen or exist: *the creation of a new political party*
2 something that someone has made: *The museum contains some of his best creations.*

creative /kriˈeɪtɪv/ **adj**
B1 good at thinking of new ideas and making interesting things: *Her book is full of creative ways to decorate your home.*
• **creatively** **adv** *We have to think creatively about this problem.*

creature /ˈkriːtʃəʳ/ **noun**
B1 anything that lives but is not a plant: *Dolphins are intelligent creatures.*

credit /ˈkredɪt/ **noun**
1 B1 [no plural] a way of buying something in which you arrange to pay for it at a later time: *He bought most of the furniture* ***on credit.***
2 B1 [no plural] an amount of money in your bank account or on your mobile phone: *I didn't have enough credit on my phone to call you.*
3 [no plural] praise that is given to someone for something they have done: *I did most of the work but Dan* ***got*** *all* ***the credit!***
4 in credit having money in your bank account

credit card /ˈkredɪt ˌkɑːd/ **noun**
A1 a small plastic card that allows you to buy something and pay for it later: *He paid* ***by credit card.***

creep /kriːp/ **verb** (**crept**)
to move very quietly and carefully: *I crept out of the room.*

crept /krept/
past tense and past participle of creep

crescent /ˈkresᵊnt/ **noun**
a curved shape that is narrow at each end and wider in the middle: *the pale crescent of the moon*

crew /kruː/ **noun**
1 B1 the people who work together on a ship, plane, or train: *a crew member*
2 a team of people with special skills who work together: *an ambulance crew*

crib /krɪb/ **noun** US (UK **cot**)
a bed with high sides for a baby

cricket /ˈkrɪkɪt/ **noun**
1 A2 [no plural] a game in which two teams of eleven people score points by hitting a ball and running between two sets of sticks
→ See **Sports 2** on page C16
2 an insect that jumps and makes a noise by rubbing its wings together

crime /kraɪm/ **noun**
1 B1 [no plural] illegal activities: *violent crime*
2 B1 something someone does that is illegal: *He* ***committed*** *a serious* ***crime.***

criminal /ˈkrɪmɪnᵊl/ **noun**
B1 someone who has done a crime

crisis /ˈkraɪsɪs/ **noun** (plural **crises** /ˈkraɪsiːz/)
a situation or time that is very danger-

ous or difficult: *The country's leadership is **in crisis**.*

crisp[1] /krɪsp/ **adj**
Crisp food is hard and pleasant: *a crisp apple*

crisp[2] /krɪsp/ **noun** UK (US **chip**)
A2 a very thin slice of potato that has been cooked in oil and is eaten cold: *a packet of crisps*
→ See **Food** on page C7

critic /ˈkrɪtɪk/ **noun**
1 someone who says that they do not approve of someone or something: *a critic of the government*
2 someone whose job is to give their opinion of a book, play, movie, etc.: *a theatre critic*

critical /ˈkrɪtɪkᵊl/ **adj**
1 saying that someone or something is bad or wrong: *He is very **critical of** the way I work.*
2 very important for the way things will happen in the future: *a critical decision*
3 very serious or dangerous: *The doctors said her condition was critical.*
• **critically** **adv** *They were both critically injured in the crash.*

criticism /ˈkrɪtɪsɪzᵊm/ **noun**
remarks about the faults of someone or something

criticize /ˈkrɪtɪsaɪz/ **verb** (**criticizing**, **criticized**)
to say that something or someone is bad: *The movie was criticized for being too violent.*

crocodile /ˈkrɒkədaɪl/ **noun**
a big reptile with a long mouth and sharp teeth, that lives in water

croissant /ˈkwæsɒŋ/ **noun**
a soft, curved piece of bread, eaten for breakfast

crooked /ˈkrʊkɪd/ **adj**
not straight: *crooked teeth*

crop /krɒp/ **noun**
B1 a plant such as a grain, fruit, or vegetable that is grown in large amounts by farmers

cross[1] /krɒs/ **verb**
1 A2 to go from one side of something to the other side: *It's not a good place to cross the road.*
2 If two lines, roads, etc. cross, they go over or across each other.
3 cross your arms/fingers/legs to put one of your arms, fingers, or legs over the top of the other
cross *something* out **phrasal verb**
to draw a line through something that you have written, usually because it is wrong: *Cross out that last sentence.*

cross[2] /krɒs/ **noun**
1 A1 a written mark (x), used for showing that something is wrong
2 B1 an object in the shape of a cross, used as a symbol of the Christian religion

cross[3] /krɒs/ **adj**
angry: *Don't be **cross with** me!*

crossing /ˈkrɒsɪŋ/ **noun**
B1 a place where people can go across a road, river, etc.

crossword /ˈkrɒswɜːd/ **noun** (also **crossword puzzle**)
a game in which you write words that are the answers to questions in a pattern of black and white squares

crouch /kraʊtʃ/ **verb**
to move your body close to the ground by bending your knees: *I crouched behind the chair to hide from them.*

crow /krəʊ/ **noun**
a large black bird that makes a loud noise

crowd[1] /kraʊd/ **noun**
A2 a large group of people who are together in one place: *A large crowd had gathered to wait for the mayor.*

crowd[2] /kraʊd/ **verb**
crowd around (*someone/something*) **phrasal verb**
to stand in a group around someone or something: *Everyone crowded around my desk.*

crowded /ˈkraʊdɪd/ **adj**
A2 very full of people: *a crowded train*

crown /kraʊn/ **noun**
a round object made of gold and jewels (= valuable stones) that a king or queen wears on their head

a b c d e f g h i j k l m n o p q r s t u v w x y z

crucial /ˈkru:ʃəl/ **adj** extremely important or necessary: *a crucial decision*

crown

crude /kru:d/ **adj**
1 simple and made without skill: *It's a fairly crude device.*
2 rude: *a crude remark*

cruel /ˈkru:əl/ **adj**
B1 very unkind, or causing people or animals to suffer: *a cruel joke* ◦ *Many people think hunting is* ***cruel to*** *animals.*
• **cruelly** **adv** *They treated her cruelly.*

cruelty /ˈkru:əlti/ **noun** [no plural] cruel behaviour or a cruel action: *laws against cruelty to animals*

cruise /kru:z/ **noun**
B1 a holiday on a ship, sailing from place to place

crumb /krʌm/ **noun** a very small piece of bread, cake, etc.
→ See **Quantities** on page C14

crumble /ˈkrʌmbl/ **verb** (**crumbling**, **crumbled**) to break into small pieces, or to make something break into small pieces: *Buildings crumbled as the earthquake struck.*

crunch /krʌnʃ/ **verb**
1 to make a noise by chewing hard food: *She was* ***crunching on*** *an apple.*
2 to make a sound as if something is being crushed: *The gravel crunched under our feet.*

crush /krʌʃ/ **verb** to press something so hard that it is made flat or broken into pieces: *Her car was crushed by a falling tree.*

crust /krʌst/ **noun** the hard part on the outside of bread or other baked foods

crutch /krʌtʃ/ **noun** a stick that you put under your arm to help you walk if your leg is hurt: *Charles was* ***on crutches*** *(= walking with crutches) for six weeks.*

cry[1] /kraɪ/ **verb** (**crying**, **cried**)
1 A2 to produce tears from your eyes because you are sad: *My baby brother cries all the time.*
2 B1 to speak or say something loudly: *'Look at this!' cried Raj.*

cry

cry[2] /kraɪ/ **noun** (plural **cries**)
B1 a shout: *I could hear the cries of children playing in the street.*

crystal /ˈkrɪstəl/ **noun**
1 a piece of a substance that has become solid, with a regular shape: *ice crystals*
2 [no plural] a type of glass of high quality: *a crystal vase*

cub /kʌb/ **noun** a young animal, such as a bear, fox, or lion

cube /kju:b/ **noun** a solid object with six square sides of the same size
→ See picture at **shape**

cucumber /ˈkju:kʌmbəʳ/ **noun**
B1 a long, green vegetable that you eat in salads
→ See **Fruit and Vegetables** on page C8

cuddle /ˈkʌdl/ **verb** (**cuddling**, **cuddled**) to put your arms around someone to show them that you love them: *Her mother cuddled her until she stopped crying.*
• **cuddle** **noun**

cuff /kʌf/ **noun** the bottom part of a sleeve that goes around your wrist
→ See picture at **jacket**

cultivate /ˈkʌltɪveɪt/ **verb** (**cultivating**, **cultivated**) to prepare land and grow crops on it
• **cultivation** /ˌkʌltɪˈveɪʃən/ **noun** [no plural]

cultural /ˈkʌltʃərəl/ **adj**
1 B1 relating to the habits, traditions, and beliefs of a society: *cultural differences* ◦ *Australia has its own cultural identity.*
2 B1 relating to music, art, theatre, literature, etc.: *cultural events*

• **culturally** adv *The two countries are culturally very different.*

culture /ˈkʌltʃəʳ/ **noun**
1 B1 the habits, traditions, and beliefs of a country or group of people: *American/Japanese culture*
2 B1 [no plural] music, art, theatre, literature, etc.: *popular culture*

cunning /ˈkʌnɪŋ/ **adj**
skilful at getting what you want, especially by tricking people

cups

cup /kʌp/ **noun**
1 A1 a small, round container with a handle on the side, used to drink from: *a cup of tea*
2 B1 a prize given to the winner of a competition

cupboard /ˈkʌbəd/ **noun**
A2 a piece of furniture with a door on the front and shelves inside, used for keeping things in
→ See **Kitchen** on page C10

curb /kɜːb/ **noun** US (UK **kerb**)
the edge of the raised path at the side of the road

cure¹ /kjʊəʳ/ **noun**
B1 something that makes someone with an illness healthy again: *They are trying to find **a cure for** cancer.*

cure² /kjʊəʳ/ **verb** (**curing**, **cured**)
B1 to make someone with an illness healthy again

curiosity /ˌkjʊəriˈɒsəti/ **noun** [no plural]
the feeling of wanting to know or learn about something: *Just **out of curiosity**, how did you get my address?*

curious /ˈkjʊəriəs/ **adj**
B1 wanting to know or learn about something: *I was **curious about** his life in India.*

curiously /ˈkjʊəriəsli/ **adv**
1 B1 in a way that shows you want to know more about something: *'What are you doing?' she asked curiously.*
2 strangely: *a curiously shaped insect*

curl¹ /kɜːl/ **noun**
something with a small, curved shape, especially a piece of hair: *a child with blonde curls*

curl² /kɜːl/ **verb**
to make something into the shape of a curl, or to be this shape: *The cat curled its tail around its body.*
curl up **phrasal verb**
to sit or lie in a position with your arms and legs close to your body: *She curled up and went to sleep.*

curly /ˈkɜːli/ **adj** (**curlier**, **curliest**)
B1 with many curls: *curly hair*
→ See **Hair** on page C9

currant /ˈkʌrᵊnt/ **noun**
a small, black dried fruit used in cooking

currency /ˈkʌrᵊnsi/ **noun** (plural **currencies**)
B1 the units of money used in a particular country: *foreign currency*

current¹ /ˈkʌrᵊnt/ **adj**
happening or existing now: *What is your current address?*
• **currently** **adv** *The factory currently (= now) employs 750 people.*

current² /ˈkʌrᵊnt/ **noun**
1 the natural flow of air or water in one direction: *a current of air*
2 the flow of electricity through a wire: *an electrical current*

current affairs /ˌkʌrᵊnt əˈfeəz/ **plural noun** UK (US **current events**)
important political or social events that are happening in the world at the present time

curriculum /kəˈrɪkjələm/ **noun** (plural **curricula** /kəˈrɪkjələ/)
B1 all the subjects taught in a school,

a b c d e f g h i j k l m n o p q r s t u v w x y z

college, etc., or on an educational course: *the school curriculum*

curriculum vitae /kəˌrɪkjʊləm ˈviːtaɪ/ **noun** (also **CV**)
formal a document that describes your qualifications and the jobs you have done, which you send to an employer that you want to work for

curry /ˈkʌri/ **noun** (plural **curries**)
A2 a type of food from India, made of vegetables or meat cooked with hot spices

cursor /ˈkɜːsəʳ/ **noun**
a symbol on a computer screen that shows the place where you are working

curtain /ˈkɜːtᵊn/ **noun**
A2 a piece of material that hangs down to cover a window, stage, etc.
→ See **The Living Room** on page C11

curve[1] /kɜːv/ **noun**
a line that bends around like part of a circle: *a road with gentle curves*

curve[2] /kɜːv/ **verb** (**curving**, **curved**)
to move in a curve or form a curve: *The road curves to the left.*

curved /kɜːvd/ **adj**
bent in a shape like part of a circle: *a curved handle*
→ See picture at **flat**

cushion /ˈkʊʃᵊn/ **noun**
B1 a cloth bag filled with something soft that you put on a chair
→ See **The Living Room** on page C11

custom /ˈkʌstəm/ **noun**
B1 a habit or tradition

customer /ˈkʌstəməʳ/ **noun**
A2 a person or organization that buys things or services from a shop or business

customs /ˈkʌstəmz/ **noun** [no plural]
B1 the place where your bags are examined when you are going into a country

cut[1] /kʌt/ **verb** (**cutting**, **cut**)
1 A2 to use a knife or other sharp tool to divide something or make a hole in something: *Cut the meat into small pieces.* ◦ *He cut the piece of wood in half.* ◦ *I had my hair cut.*

cut

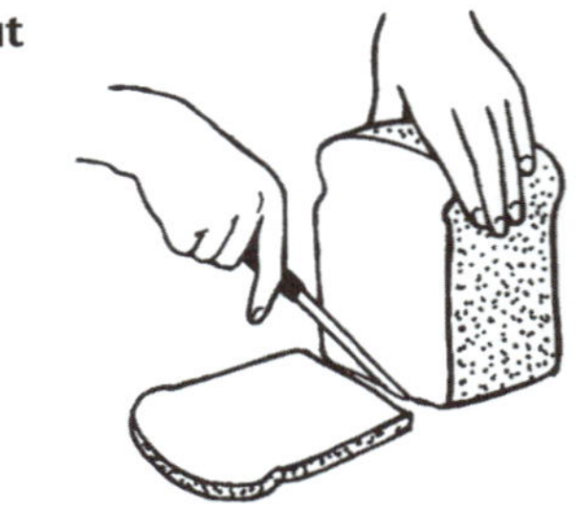

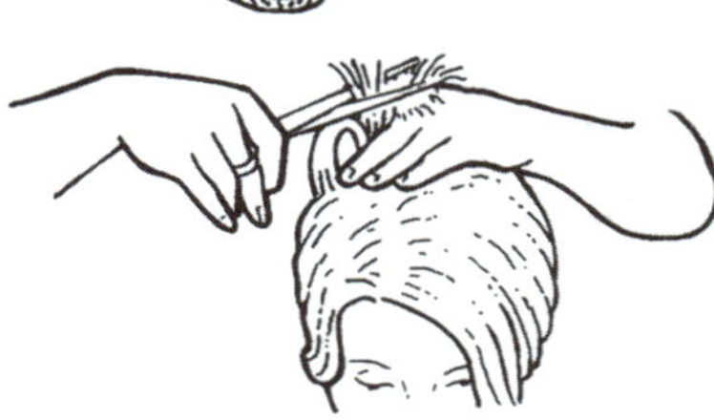

2 B1 to hurt yourself on a sharp object that makes you bleed: *She cut her finger on some broken glass.*
3 to reduce the size or amount of something: *Prices have been cut by 25%.*
4 to remove part of a movie or piece of writing: *The movie was too long, so they cut some scenes.*

cut back (*something*) **phrasal verb**
to reduce the amount of money being spent on something: *We have had to* ***cut back on*** *training this year.*

cut *something* down **phrasal verb**
to make a tree or other plant fall to the ground by cutting it near the bottom

cut down (*something*) **phrasal verb**
to eat or drink less of a particular thing, usually in order to improve your health: *I'm trying to* ***cut down on*** *the amount of sugar I eat.*

cut *someone/something* off **phrasal verb**
to stop providing something such as electricity or water: *If we don't pay the gas bill, we'll be cut off.*

cut *something* out **phrasal verb**
to remove something made of paper or cloth: *She cut his picture out of the magazine.*

cut *something* up **phrasal verb**
B1 to cut something into pieces

cut[2] /kʌt/ **noun**
1 B1 an injury made when the skin is cut with something sharp: *He got some cuts and bruises in the accident.*
2 a reduction in the number or amount of something: *job cuts*
3 an opening made with a sharp tool: *She made a cut in the material.*
4 a situation in which the supply of something is stopped: *a power cut*

cutlery /ˈkʌtlᵊri/ **noun** [no plural]
knives, forks, and spoons

CV /ˌsiːˈviː/ **noun** UK (US **résumé**)
B1 a document that describes your qualifications and the jobs you have done, which you send to an employer that you want to work for: *Send me your CV.*

cycle /ˈsaɪkl/ **verb** (**cycling**, **cycled**)
B1 to ride a bicycle
• **cycling noun** [no plural] A2 the activity of riding a bicycle
→ See **Sports 2** on page C16

cycle lane /ˈsaɪkl ˌleɪn/ **noun** UK (US **bicycle lane**, **bike lane**)
a part of a road or a special path that only people riding bicycles can use

cyclist /ˈsaɪklɪst/ **noun**
B1 someone who rides a bicycle

cylinder /ˈsɪlɪndəʳ/ **noun**
a shape with circular ends and long, straight sides
→ See picture at **shape**

a b c d e f g h i j k l m n o p q r s t u v w x y z

Dd

D, d /diː/
the fourth letter of the alphabet

dad /dæd/ **noun** informal
A1 father: *My dad has curly brown hair.*

daddy /ˈdædi/ **noun** (plural **daddies**)
a word for 'father', used mainly by children

daft /dɑːft/ **adj** UK informal
silly: *That's a daft idea.*

daily /ˈdeɪli/ **adj**, **adv**
A2 happening or made every day or once a day: *a daily newspaper* ◦ *He exercises daily.*

dairy /ˈdeəri/ **adj**
relating to milk or to products made using milk: *dairy products*

dam /dæm/ **noun**
a strong wall built across a river to stop the water and make a lake

damage1 /ˈdæmɪdʒ/ **noun** [no plural]
B1 harm or injury: *The strong wind caused serious* ***damage to*** *the roof.*

damage2 /ˈdæmɪdʒ/ **verb** (**damaging**, **damaged**)
B1 to harm or break something: *Many buildings were damaged in the storm.*

damn1 /dæm/ **adj** informal
used to express anger: *He didn't listen to a damn thing I said.*

damn2 /dæm/ **exclamation** informal
B1 used to express anger or disappointment: *Damn! I've forgotten the tickets.*

damp /dæmp/ **adj**
slightly wet, usually in a bad way: *It was cold and damp outside.* ◦ *damp socks*

dance1 /dɑːns/ **verb** (**dancing**, **danced**)
A1 to move your feet and body to the rhythm of music: *She's dancing with Steven.*

dance2 /dɑːns/ **noun**
1 A1 an occasion when you dance: *I had a dance with my dad.*
2 A2 [no plural] the activity or skill of dancing: *a dance class*
3 B1 a set of movements that you do to music
4 a social event where people dance to music

dancer /ˈdɑːnsəʳ/ **noun**
1 A2 someone who dances either as a job or for pleasure: *He's a dancer in the San Francisco Ballet.*
2 someone who is dancing or who dances in a particular way: *The dancers looked strong and graceful.* ◦ *I'm not a good dancer.*

dancing /ˈdɑːnsɪŋ/ **noun** [no plural]
A1 the activity of moving your feet and body to the rhythm of music: *Let's* ***go dancing*** *on Friday night.*

dandruff /ˈdændrʌf/ **noun** [no plural]
small pieces of dead skin in someone's hair or on their clothes

danger /ˈdeɪndʒəʳ/ **noun**
1 A2 the possibility that someone will be harmed or killed: *the dangers of rock climbing* ◦ *The soldiers were* ***in*** *serious* ***danger****.*
2 B1 something or someone that may harm you: *Icy roads are a* ***danger to*** *drivers.*

dangerous /ˈdeɪndʒərəs/ **adj**
A2 If someone or something is dangerous, they could harm you: *It's dangerous to ride a motorcycle without a helmet.*
• **dangerously adv** B1 *dangerously close to the edge*

dare /deəʳ/ **verb** (**daring**, **dared**)
1 dare (to) do *something* to be brave enough to do something: *I didn't dare tell Dad that I'd scratched his car.*
2 dare *someone* to do *something* to try to make someone do something dangerous: *She dared her friend to climb onto the roof.*
3 Don't you dare! used to tell someone angrily not to do something: *Don't you dare try to stop me!*
4 How dare she, you, etc. said when you are very angry about something someone has done: *How dare you talk to me like that!*

a b c d e f g h i j k l m n o p q r s t u v w x y z

dark¹ /dɑːk/ **adj**
1 A1 nearer to black than white in colour: *dark blue/green*
2 A2 with no light or not much light: *It doesn't **get dark** until nine o'clock in the evening.*
3 having black or brown hair or brown skin
→ See **Hair** on page C9

dark² /dɑːk/ **noun**
1 the dark B1 a lack of light in a place: *He's scared of the dark.*
2 before/after dark B1 before or after it becomes night: *She doesn't let her children out after dark.*

darkness /ˈdɑːknəs/ **noun** [no plural] a state in which there is little or no light: *He stumbled around in the darkness looking for the light switch.*

darling /ˈdɑːlɪŋ/ **noun** used when you speak to someone you love: *Are you feeling all right, darling?*

dart /dɑːt/ **verb** to move somewhere quickly and suddenly: *A cat darted across the street.*

darts /dɑːts/ **noun** [no plural] a game played by throwing small arrows at a round board

dash¹ /dæʃ/ **verb** to run somewhere suddenly: *She dashed back into the house to grab her sunglasses.*

dash² /dæʃ/ **noun**
1 a mark (–) used to separate parts of sentences
2 the action of running somewhere suddenly: *As the rain started, we **made a dash for** shelter.*

dashboard /ˈdæʃbɔːd/ **noun** the part at the front of a car with equipment to show things such as how fast you are going
→ See **Car** on page C3

data /ˈdeɪtə/ **noun** [no plural]
1 information or facts about something: *financial data*
2 information in the form of text, numbers, or symbols that can be used by or stored in a computer: *He transferred the data to a disk.*

date¹ /deɪt/ **noun**
1 A1 a particular day of the month or year: *'What's the date today?' 'It's the fifth.'* ◦ *Please give your name, address, and **date of birth**.*
2 B1 a romantic meeting when two people go out somewhere: *He's asked her out **on a date**.*
3 B1 a time when something has been arranged to happen: *Let's **make a date** to have lunch.*
4 out of date B1 old and no longer useful, correct, or fashionable: *I have a map, but I think it's out of date.*
5 up to date B1 modern, recent, or containing the latest information: *Is the information in your files up to date?*
6 a sweet, sticky brown fruit with a long seed inside

date² /deɪt/ **verb**
B1 to write or print the day's date on something: *Thank you for your letter dated August 30th.*
date back **phrasal verb** to have existed for a particular length of time or since a particular time: *This house **dates back to** 1780.*
date from *something* **phrasal verb** to have existed since a particular time: *The castle dates from the 11th century.*

daughter /ˈdɔːtəʳ/ **noun** A1 someone's female child: *Their daughter is seven years old.*

daughter-in-law /ˈdɔːtərɪnlɔː/ **noun** (plural **daughters-in-law**) the wife of someone's son: *Our son and daughter-in-law are coming to visit.*

dawn /dɔːn/ **noun** [no plural] the early morning when light first appears in the sky: *We woke **at dawn**.*

day /deɪ/ **noun**
1 A1 a period of 24 hours: *the days of the week* ◦ *I saw her **the day before yesterday**.*
2 A2 the period during the day when there is light from the sun: *a bright, sunny day*
3 A2 the time that you usually spend at work or school: *It's been a very busy day at the office.* ◦ *I have a **day off** (= when I am not at work) tomorrow.*
4 one day A2 used to talk about

something that happened in the past: *One day, I came home to find my windows smashed.*
5 these days A2 used to talk about the present period of time: *I don't go out much these days.*
6 for days B1 for a long time: *I haven't seen Jack for days.*
7 one day/one of these days B1 used to talk about something you think will happen in the future: *One of these days I'll tell her what really happened.*
8 the other day B1 a few days ago: *I saw Terry in the bank the other day.*
9 day after day every day for a long period of time: *Day after day they marched through the mountains.*

daydream /ˈdeɪdriːm/ **verb**
to spend time thinking good thoughts about something you wish would happen

daylight /ˈdeɪlaɪt/ **noun** [no plural]
the natural light from the sun during the day

day return /ˌdeɪ rɪˈtɜːn/ **noun** UK
a ticket for a bus or train that you use to go somewhere and come back on the same day: *a day return to London*

daytime /ˈdeɪtaɪm/ **noun** [no plural]
the period of the day when there is light from the sun, or the period when most people are at work: *a daytime telephone number*

dead /ded/ **adj**
1 A2 not now alive: *She's been dead for twenty years now.* ◦ *There were two firefighters among **the dead**.*
2 If a piece of equipment is dead, it is not working: *a dead battery* ◦ *The phone suddenly **went dead**.*
3 informal If a place is dead, it is too quiet and nothing interesting is happening there.

deadline /ˈdedlaɪn/ **noun**
a time by which something must be done: *The deadline for entering the competition is tomorrow.*

deadly /ˈdedli/ **adj**
causing death: *a deadly virus*

deaf /def/ **adj**
B1 not able to hear: *Many deaf people use sign language.* ◦ *He goes to a school for **the deaf**.*
• **deafness noun** [no plural]

deal[1] /diːl/ **noun**
1 an arrangement or an agreement, for example in business or politics: *a business deal* ◦ *I'll **make a deal with** you – you wash the car, and I'll let you use it tonight.*
2 a good/great deal a lot: *A great deal of time and effort went into organizing this party.*

deal[2] /diːl/ **verb** (**dealt**)
to give cards to players in a game: *Whose turn is it to deal?*
deal with *someone* phrasal verb
to find a way to talk to someone or work with someone, especially as part of your job: *She's good at dealing with difficult customers.*
deal with *something* phrasal verb
B1 to do something to make a situation work or to solve a problem: *How will we deal with these problems?*

dealer /ˈdiːləʳ/ **noun**
a person or company that buys and sells things for profit: *a car dealer*

dealt /delt/
past tense and past participle of deal

dear[1] /dɪəʳ/ **adj**
1 A1 used at the beginning of a letter, before the name of the person you are writing to: *Dear Amy* ◦ *Dear Sir/Madam*
2 liked very much: *She is a very dear friend.*
3 UK expensive: *The hotel was very dear.*

dear[2] /dɪəʳ/ **exclamation**
Oh dear! A2 used to express surprise and disappointment: *Oh dear! I forgot my keys!*

death /deθ/ **noun**
1 B1 the end of life: *After the death of her husband she lost interest in life.* ◦ *We need to reduce the number of deaths from heart attacks.*
2 bored, frightened, etc. to death extremely bored, frightened, etc.: *She's scared to death of dogs.*

debate[1] /dɪˈbeɪt/ **noun**
talk or arguments about a subject:

There has been a lot of public ***debate about*** *the safety of food.*

debate² /dɪˈbeɪt/ **verb** (**debating**, **debated**)
1 to talk about a subject in a formal way: *These issues need to be debated.*
2 to try to make a decision about something: *I'm still debating whether to go out tonight or not.*

debit card /ˈdebɪt ˌkɑːd/ **noun**
a plastic card used to pay for things directly from your bank account

debt /det/ **noun**
1 an amount of money that you owe someone: *She's working in a bar to try to* ***pay off*** *her* ***debts****.*
2 [no plural] the situation of owing money to someone: *We don't want to* ***get into debt****.* ◦ *He's* ***in debt****.*

decade /ˈdekeɪd/ **noun**
a period of ten years

decaffeinated /diːˈkæfɪneɪtɪd/ **adj**
Decaffeinated coffee or tea does not contain caffeine (= a chemical that makes you feel more awake).

decay /dɪˈkeɪ/ **verb**
to gradually become bad or be destroyed: *Sugar makes your teeth decay.*
• **decay** **noun** [no plural] *tooth decay*

deceive /dɪˈsiːv/ **verb** (**deceiving**, **deceived**)
to make someone believe something that is not true: *The company deceived customers by selling old computers as new ones.*

December /dɪˈsembəʳ/ **noun**
A1 the twelfth month of the year

decent /ˈdiːsənt/ **adj**
1 of a quality or level that is good enough: *a decent meal*
2 honest and good: *He seemed like a very decent man.*

decide /dɪˈsaɪd/ **verb** (**deciding**, **decided**)
A2 to choose something after thinking about the possibilities: *She* ***decided to*** *take the job.* ◦ *Have you decided what to wear?*

decision /dɪˈsɪʒən/ **noun**
B1 a choice that you make about something after thinking about many possibilities: *What was your decision – are you coming or not?* ◦ *We need to* ***make a decision****.*

deck /dek/ **noun**
1 one of the floors of a ship, bus, or plane: *The children like to sit on the top deck of the bus.*
2 (also **pack**) a set of cards used for playing games

deckchair /ˈdektʃeəʳ/ **noun**
a folding chair that you use outside

deckchair

declaration /ˌdekləˈreɪʃən/ **noun**
something that someone says officially, giving information about something: *a declaration of independence*

declare /dɪˈkleəʳ/ **verb** (**declaring**, **declared**)
1 B1 to officially tell someone the value of something, for example at an airport, because you may have to pay tax: *Do you have anything to declare?*
2 to announce something publicly or officially: *Scientists have* ***declared that*** *the process is safe.* ◦ *The country has* ***declared war on*** *its neighbour.*

decline¹ /dɪˈklaɪn/ **noun** [no plural] (**declining**, **declined**)
a reduction in the amount, importance, quality, or strength of something: *a steady* ***decline in*** *sales*

decline² /dɪˈklaɪn/ **verb**
to become less in amount, importance, quality, or strength: *Sales of CDs have declined steadily.*

decorate /ˈdekəreɪt/ **verb** (**decorating**, **decorated**)
1 B1 to make something look more attractive by putting things on it: *They* ***decorated*** *the room* ***with*** *balloons for her party.*
2 B1 to put paint or paper on the walls of a room or building: *The whole house needs decorating.*

a b c d e f g h i j k l m n o p q r s t u v w x y z

decoration /ˌdekəˈreɪʃən/ **noun**
the act or process of making something look more attractive by putting things on it, or something that you use to do this: *Christmas decorations* ◦ *She hung some pictures around the room* ***for decoration****.*

decrease /dɪˈkriːs/ **verb** (**decreasing**, **decreased**)
B1 to become less, or to make something become less: *Prices have decreased.*
• **decrease** /ˈdiːkriːs/ **noun** B1 *There has been a* ***decrease in*** *the number of violent crimes.*
→ Opposite **increase** verb

deed /diːd/ **noun** formal
something that you do: *good deeds*

deep

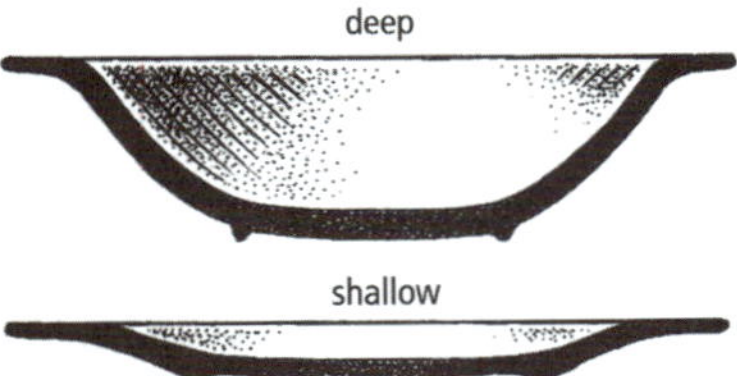

deep¹ /diːp/ **adj**
1 A2 having a long distance from the top to the bottom or from the front to the back: *The water is a lot deeper than it seems.*
2 one metre, six feet, etc. deep A2 one metre, six feet, etc. from the top to the bottom, or from the front to the back: *This end of the pool is two metres deep.*
3 B1 A deep colour is strong and dark: *deep brown eyes*
4 A deep sound is low: *a deep voice*
5 A deep feeling is very strong: *deep affection*
6 a deep sleep the action of someone sleeping in a way that makes it difficult to wake them up

deep² /diːp/ **adv**
B1 a long way into something from the top or outside: *They travelled deep into the forest.*

deeply /ˈdiːpli/ **adv**
very much: *I have fallen deeply in love with her.*

deer /dɪəʳ/ **noun** (plural **deer**)
a large, wild animal that has antlers (= long horns) if it is male

deer

defeat¹ /dɪˈfiːt/ **verb**
B1 to win against someone in a fight or competition: *She was defeated in the first round of the tournament.*

defeat² /dɪˈfiːt/ **noun**
B1 the action of someone losing a fight or competition

defence /dɪˈfens/ **noun** UK (US **defense**)
1 protection, or something that provides protection against attack or criticism: *the body's* ***defences against*** *infection*
2 B1 the part of a sports team that tries to prevent the other team from scoring points: *I play* ***in defence****.*

defend /dɪˈfend/ **verb**
1 B1 to protect someone or something from being attacked, especially by fighting: *She tried to defend herself with a knife.*
2 to support someone or something that is being criticized: *They are fighting to defend their rights.*

defender /dɪˈfendəʳ/ **noun**
someone in a sports team who tries to prevent the other team from scoring points, goals, etc.: *He ran past the defenders and scored a goal.*

define /dɪˈfaɪn/ **verb** (**defining**, **defined**)
to say exactly what something means: *Your duties are clearly defined in the contract.*

definite /ˈdefɪnət/ **adj**
certain, clear, and not likely to change: *We need a definite answer by tomorrow.*

definite article /ˌdefɪnət ˈɑːtɪkl/ **noun**
B1 in grammar, used to mean the word 'the'

definitely /ˈdefɪnətli/ **adv**
B1 without any doubt: *This book is definitely worth reading.*

definition /ˌdefɪˈnɪʃᵊn/ **noun**
an explanation of the meaning of a word or phrase: *a dictionary definition*

defrost /ˌdiːˈfrɒst/ **verb**
If frozen food defrosts, or if you defrost it, it becomes warmer and no longer frozen: *You need to defrost the fish before you cook it.*

defy /dɪˈfaɪ/ **verb** (**defying**, **defied**)
to refuse to obey someone or something

degree /dɪˈgriː/ **noun**
1 A2 a unit for measuring temperatures or angles, shown by the symbol ° written after a number
2 B1 a qualification given for completing a course of study at a college or university: *He has a **degree in** physics.*
3 [no plural] an amount or level of something: *There was some **degree of** truth in what she said.*

delay¹ /dɪˈleɪ/ **verb**
1 A2 to make something happen at a later time than you planned: *Can you delay your departure until next week?*
2 B1 to make someone or something late: *I was delayed by traffic.*

delay² /dɪˈleɪ/ **noun**
1 A2 the action of having to wait longer than expected: *An accident caused long delays on the motorway.*
2 without delay B1 immediately: *We need to deal with this problem without delay.*

delete /dɪˈliːt/ **verb** (**deleting**, **deleted**)
B1 to remove something, especially on a computer: *I deleted the file by mistake.*

deliberate /dɪˈlɪbᵊrət/ **adj**
If an action is deliberate, you wanted or planned to do it: *This was a deliberate attempt by them to deceive us.*

deliberately /dɪˈlɪbᵊrətli/ **adv**
If you do something deliberately, you wanted or planned to do it: *He deliberately lied to the police.*

delicate /ˈdelɪkət/ **adj**
1 easy to damage or break: *a delicate shell*
2 soft, light, or gentle: *a delicate shade of pink*

delicatessen /ˌdelɪkəˈtesᵊn/ **noun**
a shop that sells foods such as cheeses and cold cooked meat

delicious /dɪˈlɪʃəs/ **adj**
B1 very good to eat or drink: *This soup is really delicious.*

delight¹ /dɪˈlaɪt/ **noun** [no plural]
happiness and excited pleasure: *The children screamed with delight.*

delight² /dɪˈlaɪt/ **verb**
to make someone feel very pleased: *The new discovery has delighted scientists everywhere.*

delighted /dɪˈlaɪtɪd/ **adj**
B1 very pleased: *They are **delighted with** their new car.*

delightful /dɪˈlaɪtfᵊl/ **adj**
very pleasant or attractive: *We had a delightful evening.*

deliver /dɪˈlɪvəʳ/ **verb**
1 B1 to take letters or things to a person or place: *They can deliver the sofa on Wednesday.*
2 deliver a baby to help take a baby out of its mother when it is being born

delivery /dɪˈlɪvᵊri/ **noun** (plural **deliveries**)
B1 the act of taking letters or things to a person or place: *Is there a charge for delivery?*

demand¹ /dɪˈmɑːnd/ **noun**
1 B1 a strong request or need for something: *There was not much **demand for** ice cream in winter.*
2 in demand wanted or needed in large numbers: *Good teachers are always in demand.*

demand² /dɪˈmɑːnd/ **verb**
1 B1 to ask for something in an angry way: *I demanded an explanation.*
2 to need something such as time and effort: *This work demands a lot of concentration.*

demanding /dɪˈmɑːndɪŋ/ **adj**
needing a lot of time, attention, or effort: *This is a very demanding job.*

democracy /dɪˈmɒkrəsi/ **noun** (plural **democracies**)
a system of government in which all the people choose their leaders, or a country with this system

democrat /ˈdeməkræt/ **noun**
1 someone who supports democracy
2 Democrat someone who supports the Democratic Party in the US

democratic /ˌdeməˈkrætɪk/ **adj**
following or supporting the political system of democracy: *a democratic society*

demolish /dɪˈmɒlɪʃ/ **verb**
to destroy something such as a building: *The factory is dangerous, and will have to be demolished.*

demonstrate /ˈdemənstreɪt/ **verb** (**demonstrating**, **demonstrated**)
1 to show someone how to do something: *She demonstrated how to use the new software.*
2 to show that something exists or is true: *The experiment clearly **demonstrates that** there are positive benefits.*
3 to walk or stand with a group of people to show that you have a strong opinion about something: *Thousands of people gathered to **demonstrate against** the new proposals.*

demonstration /ˌdemənˈstreɪʃᵊn/ **noun**
1 an event at which a group of people walk or stand together to show that they have a strong opinion about something: *They're taking part in a **demonstration against** the war.*
2 an act of showing how to do something: *We asked the sales assistant to give us a demonstration.*

demonstrator /ˈdemənstreɪtəʳ/ **noun**
someone who takes part in a demonstration to show their opinion about something: *Police arrested several of the demonstrators.*

denim /ˈdenɪm/ **noun** [no plural]
thick, strong cotton cloth, used to make clothes: *denim jeans*

dense /dens/ **adj**
1 with a lot of people or things close together: *dense forest*
2 thick and difficult to see through: *dense fog*
• **densely adv**

dent¹ /dent/ **noun**
an area in a hard surface that has been hit and pushed inward: *The car door had a dent in it.*

dent² /dent/ **verb**
to push an area of a hard surface inward by hitting it with something: *The side of the car was dented in the accident.*

dental /ˈdentᵊl/ **adj**
relating to the teeth: *a dental appointment*

dentist /ˈdentɪst/ **noun**
A2 someone who looks at and repairs teeth: *I've got an appointment at **the dentist's** (= where the dentist works) tomorrow.*

dentist

dentures /ˈdentʃəz/ **plural noun**
artificial teeth that fit inside the mouth of someone who does not have their own teeth: *I have dentures.*

deny /dɪˈnaɪ/ **verb** (**denying**, **denied**)
to say that something is not true, or that you have not done something: *She denies any involvement in the attack.*

deodorant /diˈəʊdᵊrᵊnt/ **noun**
something that you put on your body to stop bad smells

depart /dɪˈpɑːt/ **verb** formal
B1 to leave a place: *The train to Lincoln will **depart from** platform 9.*

department /dɪˈpɑːtmənt/ **noun**
A2 a part of an organization that does a particular type of work: *the sales department*

department store /dɪˈpɑːtmənt ˌstɔːʳ/ **noun**
A2 a large shop that sells different types of things

departure /dɪˈpɑːtʃəʳ/ **noun**
B1 the action of someone or something leaving a place: *the departure of flight BA117*

depend /dɪˈpend/ **verb**
it/that depends B1 used to say that you are not certain about something because other things affect your answer: *'Are you coming out tonight?' 'It depends where you're going.'*
depend on *someone/something* **phrasal verb**
1 B1 to need the help of someone or something: *Our economy depends on the car industry.*
2 to be affected by someone or something: *What you buy depends on how much you can spend.*
3 to trust someone or something and know that they will help you or do what you want or expect them to do: *You can always depend on her in a crisis.*

> **Common mistake: depend on something**
>
> Be careful to choose the correct preposition after **depend**.
>
> *I might go – it depends on the weather.*
>
> ~~*I might go – it depends of the weather.*~~
>
> ~~*I might go – it depends from the weather.*~~

dependant /dɪˈpendənt/ **noun** UK (US **dependent**)
someone, usually a child, who needs your money to live: *The pension provides for him and all his dependants.*

dependent /dɪˈpendənt/ **adj**
needing the help of someone or something: *She's completely **dependent on** her parents for money.*

deposit[1] /dɪˈpɒzɪt/ **noun**
1 B1 a payment that you make immediately when you decide to buy something: *They've put down a **deposit on** a house.*
2 money that you pay into a bank: *to **make** a **deposit***
3 money that you pay when you rent something, and that is returned to you if you do not damage anything

deposit[2] /dɪˈpɒzɪt/ **verb**
1 to put something down somewhere: *He **deposited** his books **on** the table.*
2 to put money into a bank: *She **deposited** $150,000 **in** a Swiss bank account.*

depot /ˈdepəʊ/ **noun**
a place where vehicles or goods are kept

depress /dɪˈpres/ **verb**
to make someone feel very sad: *This place really depresses me.*

depressed /dɪˈprest/ **adj**
B1 very sad, often for a long time: *She's been very depressed since her marriage broke up.*

depressing /dɪˈpresɪŋ/ **adj**
making you feel sad and without any hope for the future: *The news is very depressing.*

depression /dɪˈpreʃᵊn/ **noun**
a feeling of sadness, or a mental illness that makes you feel very sad: *Nearly three million people suffer from depression every year.*

deprive /dɪˈpraɪv/ **verb** (**depriving**, **deprived**)
to take something, especially something necessary or pleasant, away from someone: *They were **deprived of** food for long periods of time.*

depth /depθ/ **noun**
1 B1 the distance from the top of something to the bottom: *Dig a hole 10 cm **in depth**.*
2 the quality of having a lot of knowledge or of being able to think seriously about something: *Her writing shows astonishing depth.*
3 **in depth** in a very detailed way: *I have studied this subject in depth.*

deputy /ˈdepjəti/ **noun** (plural **deputies**)
someone who has the second most important job in an organization: *the deputy Prime Minister*

descend /dɪˈsend/ **verb** formal
to move down or go down

a b c d e f g h i j k l m n o p q r s t u v w x y z

descendant /dɪˈsendənt/ **noun**
someone who is related to someone who lived a long time ago

describe /dɪˈskraɪb/ **verb** (**describing**, **described**)
A2 to say what someone or something is like: *I described what I had seen.*

description /dɪˈskrɪpʃᵊn/ **noun**
B1 words that tell you what someone or something is like: *I **gave** the police a **description of** the stolen jewellery.*

desert¹ /ˈdezət/ **noun**
A2 a large, hot, dry area of land with very few plants: *the Sahara Desert*

desert² /dɪˈzɜːt/ **verb**
1 to leave a place, so that it is empty: *People desert the city on summer weekends and go to the beaches.*
2 to leave the army without permission: *He deserted his post.*
3 to leave someone and never come back: *He deserted his wife and children.*

deserted /dɪˈzɜːtɪd/ **adj**
A deserted place has no people in it: *a deserted street*

deserve /dɪˈzɜːv/ **verb** (**deserving**, **deserved**)
B1 If you deserve something good or bad, it should happen to you because of the way you have behaved: *He deserves to be locked up for life.*

design¹ /dɪˈzaɪn/ **noun**
1 B1 the way in which something is planned and made: *Engineers are working on the new designs.*
2 B1 a pattern or decoration: *a design of fish and sea shells*
3 B1 [no plural] the art of making plans or drawings for something: *He's studying fashion design at college.*

design² /dɪˈzaɪn/ **verb**
1 B1 to draw or plan something before making it: *She designs furniture.*
2 be designed for/to do *something* to have been planned or done for a particular purpose: *This dictionary is designed for learners of English.*

designer¹ /dɪˈzaɪnəʳ/ **noun**
B1 someone who draws and plans how something will be made: *a fashion designer*

designer² /dɪˈzaɪnəʳ/ **adj**
designer jeans, sunglasses, etc. expensive clothes or things

desire /dɪˈzaɪəʳ/ **noun**
wanting something very much: *the desire to have children*

desk /desk/ **noun**
A1 a table that you sit at to write or work

desk

despair /dɪˈspeəʳ/ **noun** [no plural]
a feeling of having no hope: *She shook her head **in despair**.*
• **despair** **verb**

desperate /ˈdespᵊrət/ **adj**
1 feeling that you have no hope and will do anything to change the situation you are in: *He was **desperate to** get her back.*
2 needing or wanting something very much: *By two o'clock I was **desperate for** something to eat.*
• **desperately** **adv**
• **desperation** /ˌdespəˈreɪʃᵊn/ **noun** [no plural]

despise /dɪˈspaɪz/ **verb** (**despising**, **despised**)
to hate someone or something and have no respect for them: *The two groups despise each other.*

despite /dɪˈspaɪt/ **preposition**
B1 although something happened or is true: *I'm still pleased with the house despite all the problems we've had.* ◦ *The company has been forced to reduce its price, **despite the fact that** the offer has been very popular.*

dessert /dɪˈzɜːt/ **noun**
A2 sweet food that is eaten after the main part of a meal

destination /ˌdestɪˈneɪʃᵊn/ **noun**
B1 the place where someone or something is going: *Spain is a very popular holiday destination.*

destroy /dɪˈstrɔɪ/ **verb**
B1 to damage something so badly that it cannot be used or does not

desserts

exist: *Many books were destroyed in the fire.*

destruction /dɪˈstrʌkʃən/ **noun** [no plural]
the act or process of destroying something: *We are all responsible for the* ***destruction of*** *the forest.*

detach /dɪˈtætʃ/ **verb**
to take a part of something off so that it is separate: *Please complete and detach the form below.*

detail /ˈdiːteɪl/ **noun**
1 B1 a piece of information about something: *Please send me* ***details of*** *your training courses.*
2 in detail B1 including every part of something: *He explained it all in great detail.*
3 go into detail to tell or include all the facts about something: *I won't go into detail over the phone, but I've had a few problems recently.*

detailed /ˈdiːteɪld/ **adj**
giving a lot of information: *a detailed description*

detect /dɪˈtekt/ **verb**
to discover or notice something: *This special camera can detect movement.*

detective /dɪˈtektɪv/ **noun**
B1 someone whose job is to discover information about a crime

detergent /dɪˈtɜːdʒənt/ **noun**
a liquid or powder that is used to clean things

determination /dɪˌtɜːmɪˈneɪʃən/ **noun** [no plural]
the action of continuing to try to do something, although it is very difficult: *He'll need great determination and skill to win this match.*

determined /dɪˈtɜːmɪnd/ **adj**
wanting so much to do something that you keep trying very hard: *He's* ***determined to*** *win this match.*

determiner /dɪˈtɜːmɪnəʳ/ **noun**
in grammar, a word that is used before a noun to show which person or thing you mean: *In the phrases 'my first boyfriend' and 'that strange woman', the words 'my' and 'that' are determiners.*

detest /dɪˈtest/ **verb**
to hate someone or something: *They used to be friends, but now they absolutely detest each other.*

detour /ˈdiːtʊəʳ/ **noun**
a different, longer route to a place that is used to avoid something or to visit a place

develop /dɪˈveləp/ **verb**
1 B1 to change and become better, or to make someone or something become better: *He's* ***developing into*** *a very good tennis player.*
2 B1 to make something new, such as a product: *Scientists are developing new drugs all the time.*
3 to start to have a problem or feeling: *Shortly after take-off the plane developed engine trouble.*
4 to use special chemicals on a piece of film to make photographs appear

developed /dɪˈveləpt/ **adj**
describes a country or region of the world with an advanced level of technology, industry, etc.: *a developed country*

developing /dɪˈveləpɪŋ/ **adj**
describes a country or region of the world that is poor and has few industries: *the developing countries*

development /dɪˈveləpmənt/ **noun**
1 B1 the action of someone or something changing and becoming better: *There have been some major developments in technology recently.*
2 B1 [no plural] the process of developing something new: *the development of new drugs*
3 something new that happens and

changes a situation: *Have there been any more developments since I left?*

device /dɪˈvaɪs/ **noun**
a piece of equipment: *an electronic device for sending messages*

devil /ˈdev^{ə}l/ **noun**
1 the Devil the most powerful evil spirit, according to the Christian and Jewish religions
2 an evil spirit

devote /dɪˈvəʊt/ **verb** (**devoting**, **devoted**)
1 to use time or energy for a particular person: *She devotes most of her free time to charity work.*
2 to use a space or area for a particular purpose: *Most of the magazine was devoted to photos of the wedding.*

dew /djuː/ **noun** [no plural]
drops of water that form on surfaces outside during the night

diabetes /ˌdaɪəˈbiːtiːz/ **noun** [no plural]
a serious medical condition in which your body cannot control the amount of sugar in your blood

diabetic /ˌdaɪəˈbetɪk/ **noun**
a person who has diabetes
• **diabetic adj** *a diabetic patient*

diagonal /daɪˈæg^{ə}n^{ə}l/ **adj**
going from the top corner to the bottom corner on the other side
• **diagonally adv**

diagram /ˈdaɪəgræm/ **noun**
B1 a simple picture showing what something looks like or explaining how something works

dial[1] /daɪəl/ **noun**
a round part on a clock or piece of equipment that shows you the time or other measurement

dial[2] /daɪəl/ **verb** (**dialling**, **dialled**)
B1 to make a telephone call to a particular number: *Dial 0 for the operator.*

dialect /ˈdaɪəlekt/ **noun**
a form of a language that people speak in a particular part of a country

dialogue /ˈdaɪəlɒg/ **noun**
the talking in a book, play, or movie

diameter /daɪˈæmɪtə^{r}/ **noun**
a straight line that goes from one side of a circle to the other side and through the centre: *The cake was about 30 centimetres* ***in diameter***.

diamond /ˈdaɪəmənd/ **noun**
1 a very hard, transparent stone that is very valuable and is often used in jewellery: *a diamond ring*
2 a shape with four straight sides of equal length that join to form two large angles and two small angles

diamonds

diamonds /ˈdaɪəməndz/ **plural noun**
one of the four suits (= groups) of playing cards: *the three of diamonds*

diaper /ˈdaɪəpə^{r}/ **noun** US (UK **nappy**)
a thick piece of paper or cloth worn by a baby on its bottom

diarrhoea /ˌdaɪəˈriːə/ **noun** [no plural]
an illness that makes a person go to the toilet more often

diary /ˈdaɪəri/ **noun** (plural **diaries**)
1 A2 a book in which you write things that you must remember to do: *According to my diary, I've got two meetings on Monday.*
2 a book in which you write about what you have done and your thoughts and feelings: *She* ***kept a diary*** *of her trip to Egypt.*

dice /daɪs/ **noun** (plural **dice**)
a small object with six equal square sides, each with between one and six spots on it, used in games

dice

dictate /dɪkˈteɪt/ **verb** (**dictating**, **dictated**)
to say or read something for someone to write down: *Tony was busy* ***dictating*** *letters* ***to*** *his secretary.*

dictation /dɪkˈteɪʃ^{ə}n/ **noun**
1 [no plural] the act of saying something for someone else to write down
2 a test where a teacher reads something for students to write down

a b c d e f g h i j k l m n o p q r s t u v w x y z

dictator /dɪkˈteɪtəʳ/ **noun**
a leader who has complete power in a country

dictionary /ˈdɪkʃənəri/ **noun** (plural **dictionaries**)
A1 a book that contains a list of words in alphabetical order with their meanings explained and sometimes written in another language: *Use your dictionaries to look up any words you don't understand.*

did /dɪd/
past tense of do

didn't /ˈdɪdənt/
short form of did not

die /daɪ/ **verb** (**dying**, **died**)
1 A1 to stop living: *Many of the refugees* ***died of*** *hunger.*
2 be dying for *something*; be dying to do *something* informal B1 to want to have or do something very much: *I'm dying for a drink.*

Common mistake: died or dead?

Be careful not to confuse the verb and adjective forms of these words. **Died** is the past of the verb 'to die', which means 'to stop living'.

My cat died last week.

Dead is an adjective and is used to talk about people or things that are not alive.

My cat is dead.

die out **phrasal verb**
to become more and more rare and then disappear completely: *Dinosaurs died out about 65 million years ago.*

diesel /ˈdiːzəl/ **noun** [no plural]
fuel used in the engines of some vehicles

diet /daɪət/ **noun**
1 B1 the type of food that someone usually eats: *His diet isn't very healthy.*
2 B1 the practice of someone eating a particular type or amount of food for a special reason, such as being ill or wanting to become thinner: *No cake for me, thanks – I'm* ***on a diet****.*

difference /ˈdɪfərəns/ **noun**
1 A2 the way in which two people or things are not the same: *What's the* ***difference between*** *an ape and a monkey?*
2 B1 the amount by which one thing is different from another: *There's a big difference in age between them.*
3 make any difference to have an effect on a situation: *Do what you like, it doesn't make any difference.*
4 tell the difference to notice the way in which two things are different: *This coffee is half the price of that one, but I can't tell the difference.*

different /ˈdɪfərənt/ **adj**
1 A1 not the same as someone or something else: *Jo's very* ***different from*** *her sister, isn't she?*
2 B1 used to talk about separate things or people of the same type: *eight different flavours of ice cream*
• **differently** **adv**

Common mistake: different

Different is usually followed by the preposition **from**. In British English people also use **to**.

The UK is very different from/to my country.

difficult /ˈdɪfɪkəlt/ **adj**
1 A1 not easy to do or understand: *Japanese is a difficult language to learn.*
2 B1 not friendly or easy to deal with: *a difficult teenager*

difficulty /ˈdɪfɪkəlti/ **noun** (plural **difficulties**)
B1 a problem: *I had difficulty finding somewhere to park.*

dig /dɪg/ **verb** (**digging**, **dug**)

dig

1 to make a hole in the ground by moving some of the ground or soil away: *They've dug a huge hole in the road.*
2 B1 to break up and move soil using a tool, a machine, or your hands: *Digging in the garden is good exercise.*

digest /daɪˈdʒest/ **verb**
to change food in your stomach into substances that your body can use: *Your stomach contains acid to help you digest your food.*
• **digestion** **noun**

a b c d e f g h i j k l m n o p q r s t u v w x y z

digit /ˈdɪdʒɪt/ **noun**
any of the numbers from 0 to 9, especially when they form part of a longer number: *a seven-digit phone number*

digital /ˈdɪdʒɪtəl/ **adj**
1 A2 using an electronic system that changes sounds or images into numbers before it stores or sends them: *digital television*
2 B1 A digital clock or watch shows the time in the form of numbers.

digital camera /ˌdɪdʒɪtəl ˈkæmrə/ **noun**
A2 a type of camera that records images that you can use and store on a computer: *These pictures were taken using a digital camera.*

dilute /daɪˈluːt/ **verb** (**diluting**, **diluted**)
to make a liquid thinner by adding another liquid to it: *You need to dilute this juice before you drink it.*

dim /dɪm/ **adj** (**dimmer**, **dimmest**)
not bright or clear: *He could hardly see her in the dim light.*
• **dimly** **adv** *a* ***dimly lit*** *room*

dinghy /ˈdɪŋi/ **noun** (plural **dinghies**)
a small boat

dining room /ˈdaɪnɪŋ ˌruːm/ **noun**
A1 a room where you eat your meals

dinner /ˈdɪnəʳ/ **noun**
A1 the main meal of the day that people eat in the evening

dinosaur /ˈdaɪnəsɔːʳ/ **noun**
A2 a very large animal that used to live millions of years ago

dip /dɪp/ **verb** (**dipping**, **dipped**)
to put something into a liquid for a short time: *She* ***dipped*** *the brush* ***into*** *the paint.*

diploma /dɪˈpləʊmə/ **noun**
A2 an official document showing that someone has completed a course of study: *a diploma in art and design*

direct[1] /dɪˈrekt/ **adj**, **adv**
1 B1 going straight from one place to another without turning or stopping: *We went by the most direct route.*
2 with no other person or thing involved or between: *direct sunlight*
→ Opposite **indirect** **adj**

direct[2] /dɪˈrekt/ **verb**
1 B1 to tell the actors in a movie or play what to do: *a movie directed by Alfred Hitchcock*
2 B1 to show or tell someone how to get to a place: *Can you* ***direct*** *me* ***to*** *the manager's office please?*

direction /dɪˈrekʃən/ **noun**
1 B1 the way that someone or something is going or facing: *The car sped away* ***in the direction of*** *the airport.*
2 **in *someone's* direction** towards someone: *She keeps looking in my direction.*

directions /dɪˈrekʃənz/ **plural noun**
A2 instructions that tell you how to get to a place, or how to do something: *We stopped to ask for directions.*

directly /dɪˈrektli/ **adv**
B1 with no other person or thing involved or between: *Why don't you speak to him directly?*

director /dɪˈrektəʳ/ **noun**
1 B1 an important manager in an organization or company: *Meet the new sales director.*
2 B1 someone who tells the actors in a movie or play what to do

directory /dɪˈrektəri/ **noun** (plural **directories**)
a book or list of names and numbers: *a telephone directory*

dirt /dɜːt/ **noun** [no plural]
B1 a substance that makes something not clean: *You've got some dirt on your trousers.*

dirty /ˈdɜːti/ **adj** (**dirtier**, **dirtiest**)
A2 not clean: *dirty clothes/dishes*

disabled /dɪˈseɪbld/ **adj**
B1 having an illness or condition that makes it difficult to do the things that other people do: *They are demanding equal rights for* ***the disabled.***

disadvantage /ˌdɪsədˈvɑːntɪdʒ/ **noun**
B1 something that makes a situation more difficult: *One* ***disadvantage of*** *living in the country is the lack of public transport.*

disagree /ˌdɪsəˈgriː/ **verb** (**disagreeing**, **disagreed**)
B1 to have a different opinion from someone else: *I* ***disagree with*** *most of what he said.* ◦ *Experts* ***disagree about/on*** *the causes of the disease.*

disagreement /ˌdɪsəˈgriːmᵊnt/ **noun**
a situation in which people have a different opinion about something or have an argument: *They* ***had*** *a* ***disagreement*** *about money.*

disappear /ˌdɪsəˈpɪəʳ/ **verb**
1 B1 to suddenly go somewhere and be impossible to see or find: *She watched him* ***disappear into*** *the crowd.* ◦ *Her husband disappeared in 1991.*
2 to no longer exist: *These flowers are* ***disappearing from*** *our countryside.*

disappearance /ˌdɪsəˈpɪərəns/ **noun**
the fact of someone or something suddenly going somewhere and becoming impossible to see or find: *Police are investigating the girl's disappearance.*

disappoint /ˌdɪsəˈpɔɪnt/ **verb**
B1 to make someone feel sad because someone or something was not as good as they had expected: *We don't want to disappoint the fans.*

disappointed /ˌdɪsəˈpɔɪntɪd/ **adj**
B1 sad because something was not as good as you expected: *I was very disappointed that he didn't come.*

disappointing /ˌdɪsəˈpɔɪntɪŋ/ **adj**
B1 making you feel disappointed: *a disappointing performance*

disappointment /ˌdɪsəˈpɔɪntmənt/ **noun**
1 B1 [no plural] the feeling of being disappointed
2 B1 someone or something that disappoints you: *I'm sorry I'm such* ***a disappointment to*** *you.*

disapproval /ˌdɪsəˈpruːvᵊl/ **noun** [no plural]
a feeling of thinking that someone or something is bad or wrong

disapprove /ˌdɪsəˈpruːv/ **verb** (**disapproving**, **disapproved**)
to think that someone or something is bad or wrong: *Her family* ***disapproved of*** *the marriage.*

disaster /dɪˈzɑːstəʳ/ **noun**
1 a very bad situation, especially something that causes a lot of harm or damage: *floods and other natural disasters*
2 something that is a failure or negative result: *His idea was a total disaster.*

disastrous /dɪˈzɑːstrəs/ **adj**
bad and causing big problems: *a disastrous week*

disc /dɪsk/ **noun**
1 B1 a record or CD
2 a flat, round shape or object

discipline /ˈdɪsəplɪn/ **noun** [no plural]
the action of controlling people's behaviour using rules and punishments: *There should be better discipline in schools.*

disc jockey /ˈdɪsk ˌdʒɒki/ **noun** (also **DJ**)
B1 someone who plays music on the radio or at nightclubs.

disco /ˈdɪskəʊ/ **noun**
A2 a place or event where people dance to pop music

disconnect /ˌdɪskəˈnekt/ **verb**
to separate a machine from the electricity supply or from another machine: *Switch off the PC before* ***disconnecting*** *it* ***from*** *the power supply.*

discount /ˈdɪskaʊnt/ **noun**
A2 a reduction in the price of something: *They offer a 10 percent* ***discount on*** *travel for students.*

discourage /dɪˈskʌrɪdʒ/ **verb** (**discouraging**, **discouraged**)
1 to try to persuade someone to stop doing something: *a campaign to discourage people from smoking*
2 to make someone less confident or enthusiastic about something: *The thought of how much work she had to do discouraged her.*

discover /dɪˈskʌvəʳ/ **verb**
B1 to find something or get information about something for the first time: *The body was discovered in a river.* ◦ *She* ***discovered that*** *he had been married three times before.*

discovery /dɪˈskʌvəri/ **noun** (plural **discoveries**)
finding something or someone for the first time: *Scientists have* ***made*** *some important* ***discoveries*** *about genetics.*

discrimination /dɪˌskrɪmɪˈneɪʃən/ **noun** [no plural]
unfair treatment because of a person's sex, race, age, etc.

discuss /dɪˈskʌs/ **verb**
A2 to talk about something with someone and tell each other your ideas or opinions: *Have you discussed this matter with anyone else?*

> **Common mistake: discuss**
>
> **Discuss** is not followed by a preposition.
> *We discussed the plans for the wedding.*
> ~~*We discussed about the plans for the wedding.*~~
> You can **discuss something with someone.**
> *Can I discuss this report with you?*

discussion /dɪˈskʌʃən/ **noun**
B1 a talk in which people tell each other their ideas or opinions: *They were* ***having*** *a* ***discussion*** *about football.*

disease /dɪˈziːz/ **noun**
B1 an illness: *heart disease*

disgrace /dɪsˈgreɪs/ **noun** [no plural]
1 the action of someone doing something very bad that makes people stop respecting them: *They were sent home* ***in disgrace****.*
2 be a disgrace to be very bad: *It's a* ***disgrace that*** *money is being wasted like this.*

disgraceful /dɪsˈgreɪsfəl/ **adj**
very bad: *disgraceful behaviour*

disguise[1] /dɪsˈgaɪz/ **noun**
things that you wear to change the way you look so that people cannot recognize you: *She usually goes out* ***in disguise*** *to avoid being recognized.*

disguise[2] /dɪsˈgaɪz/ **verb** (**disguising**, **disguised**)
to change the way you look so that people cannot recognize you: *He managed to escape by* ***disguising*** *himself* ***as*** *a woman.*

disgust /dɪsˈgʌst/ **noun** [no plural]
a very strong feeling of dislike: *She walked out* ***in disgust****.*
• **disgust verb**

disgusted /dɪsˈgʌstɪd/ **adj**
feeling extreme dislike of something: *I'm totally* ***disgusted with*** *your behaviour.*

disgusting /dɪsˈgʌstɪŋ/ **adj**
B1 extremely unpleasant: *What's that disgusting smell?*

dish /dɪʃ/ **noun**
1 A2 a container for food that you eat from and cook food in
2 A2 part of a meal: *She cooked a very nice chicken dish.*
3 the dishes A2 dirty plates and other objects that have been used for cooking or eating food: *Who's going to* ***wash the dishes****?*

dishcloth /ˈdɪʃklɒθ/ **noun**
a cloth used for washing dirty dishes

dishonest /dɪˈsɒnɪst/ **adj**
not honest and likely to lie

dishwasher /ˈdɪʃˌwɒʃər/ **noun**
B1 a machine that washes plates, glasses, and other kitchen equipment
→ See **The Kitchen** on page C10

disinfectant /ˌdɪsɪnˈfektənt/ **noun**
a chemical substance that destroys bacteria

disk /dɪsk/ **noun**
B1 a round flat object that records and keeps computer information: *How much free space is there* ***on the disk****?*

dislike /dɪˈslaɪk/ **verb** (**disliking**, **disliked**)
B1 to not like someone or something: *Why do you dislike her so much?*
• **dislike noun** *He has a strong* ***dislike of*** *perfume.*

dismal /ˈdɪzməl/ **adj**
very bad or unpleasant and making you feel sad: *What dismal weather!*

dismay /dɪˈsmeɪ/ **noun** [no plural]
a feeling of sadness and disappointment: ***To our dismay****, it started raining.*
• **dismayed adj**

dismiss /dɪˈsmɪs/ **verb**
1 to officially make someone leave their job: *Anyone who breaks company rules will be dismissed.*
2 to give someone official permission to leave: *The bell rang and the teacher dismissed the class.*

disobedient /ˌdɪsəʊˈbiːdiənt/ **adj** refusing to do what someone in authority tells you to do: *a disobedient child*

disobey /ˌdɪsəʊˈbeɪ/ **verb** to not do what you are told to do by someone in authority: *How dare you disobey me!*

disorganized /dɪˈsɔːgənaɪzd/ **adj** not good at planning or organizing things: *She's extremely disorganized.*

display¹ /dɪˈspleɪ/ **noun**
1 B1 a performance or a collection of things for people to look at: *a firework display* ◦ *a display of paintings*
2 **on display** B1 If something is on display, it is there for people to look at: *Many old planes are on display at the museum.*
3 B1 the part of a piece of electronic equipment that shows information, such as a computer screen: *The display shows the time and date.*

display² /dɪˈspleɪ/ **verb**
1 B1 to arrange something somewhere so that people can see it: *There were some family photographs displayed on his desk.*
2 to show something on a computer screen: *The text can be displayed on screen.*

disposal /dɪˈspəʊzəl/ **noun** [no plural]
1 the act of getting rid of something: *waste disposal*
2 **at *someone's* disposal** available for someone to use at any time: *You will have a car at your disposal for the whole trip.*

dispose /dɪˈspəʊz/ **verb** (**disposing, disposed**)
dispose of *something* **phrasal verb** to get rid of something: *How did they dispose of the body?*

dispute /ˈdɪspjuːt/ **noun** a disagreement, especially one that lasts a long time: *A man stabbed his neighbour in a **dispute over** noise.*

disrupt /dɪsˈrʌpt/ **verb** to interrupt something and stop it continuing as it should: *Heavy snow disrupted the city's transport system.*

dissatisfied /dɪsˈsætɪsfaɪd/ **adj** not happy with something: *Are you **dissatisfied with** our service?*

dissolve /dɪˈzɒlv/ **verb** (**dissolving, dissolved**) If a solid dissolves, it becomes part of a liquid, and if you dissolve it, you make it become part of a liquid: *These tablets dissolve in water.*

distance /ˈdɪstəns/ **noun**
1 B1 the length of the space between two places: *We're only a short **distance from** my house.*
2 [no plural] somewhere that is far away: *I could see Mary **in the distance**.*

distant /ˈdɪstənt/ **adj** far away in space or time: *distant galaxies* ◦ *We hope to see you in the not too distant future (= soon).*

distinct /dɪˈstɪŋkt/ **adj**
1 different and separate: *This word has three distinct meanings.*
2 clear and easy to see or hear: *The voices gradually became louder and more distinct.*
• **distinctly** **adv**

distinguish /dɪˈstɪŋgwɪʃ/ **verb**
1 to see or understand the differences between two people, ideas, or things: *Children must learn to **distinguish between** right and wrong.*
2 to make one person or thing seem different from another: *His great skill **distinguishes** him **from** the rest of the team.*
3 to be able to see, hear or understand something: *I couldn't distinguish anything in the darkness.*

distinguished /dɪˈstɪŋgwɪʃt/ **adj** famous or admired: *a distinguished writer*

distract /dɪˈstrækt/ **verb** to make someone stop giving their attention to something: *Stop distracting me – I'm trying to finish my essay.*

a b c d e f g h i j k l m n o p q r s t u v w x y z

distress /dɪˈstres/ **noun** [no plural]
1 the feeling of being very upset or worried: *The newspaper reports caused her a great deal of distress.*
2 the fact of someone or something being in danger and needing help: *an aircraft* ***in distress***
• **distress verb** to make someone feel upset or worried
• **distressing adj** *a distressing experience*

distribute /dɪˈstrɪbjuːt/ **verb** (**distributing, distributed**)
to give something out to a lot of people or places: *The books will be* ***distributed to*** *local schools.*
• **distribution** /ˌdɪstrɪˈbjuːʃᵊn/ **noun**

district /ˈdɪstrɪkt/ **noun**
B1 a part of a city or country: *the New York fashion district*

disturb /dɪˈstɜːb/ **verb**
1 to stop what someone is doing or make problems for them, often by making a noise: *Georgia is working, so try not to disturb her.*
2 to upset someone or make them feel worried: *He was disturbed by the violence in the movie.*

disused /dɪˈsjuːzd/ **adj**
not used now: *a disused warehouse*

ditch /dɪtʃ/ **noun**
a long, narrow hole in the ground next to a road or field which water can flow through

dive /daɪv/ **verb** (**diving, dived**)
1 B1 to jump into water with your head and arms going in first: *He dived off the side of the boat into the sea.*
2 B1 to swim under water, usually with breathing equipment

diver /ˈdaɪvəʳ/ **noun**
B1 someone who swims under water, usually with breathing equipment

divide /dɪˈvaɪd/ **verb** (**dividing, divided**)
1 B1 to separate into parts or groups, or to make something separate into parts or groups: *We* ***divided up into*** *teams.*
2 to separate a place into two areas: *There's a narrow alley which* ***divides*** *our house* ***from*** *the one next door.*

dive

3 divide *something* (up) among/between *someone* to separate something into parts and give a part to each person in a group: *The prize money will be divided equally among the winners.*
4 to calculate how many times a number can go into another number: *12* ***divided by*** *6 equals 2.*

divine /dɪˈvaɪn/ **adj**
relating to or coming from God or a god

diving /ˈdaɪvɪŋ/ **noun** [no plural]
1 B1 the activity or sport of swimming under water, usually using special breathing equipment: *We* ***went diving*** *in the Red Sea.*
2 the activity or sport of jumping into water with your arms and head going in first

division /dɪˈvɪʒᵊn/ **noun**
1 [no plural] the act of separating something into parts or groups: *the equal division of wealth*
2 one of the groups in an organization: *the sales division*
3 one of the groups of teams in a league: *a Second Division club*
4 [no plural] the process of dividing one number by another number

divorce /dɪˈvɔːs/ **noun**
B1 the legal ending of a marriage: *My parents are* ***getting a divorce.***

• **divorce** verb (**divorcing**, **divorced**)
B1 *She's divorcing her husband.*

divorced /dɪˈvɔːst/ **adj**
1 B1 married before but not married now
2 **get divorced** to officially stop being married: *My parents got divorced when I was seven.*

DIY /ˌdiːaɪˈwaɪ/ **noun** [no plural]
the activity of building, decorating, or doing repairs in your own home

dizzy /ˈdɪzi/ **adj** (**dizzier**, **dizziest**)
feeling like everything is turning around and as if you might fall

DJ /ˈdiːˌdʒeɪ/ **noun**
B1 someone who plays music on the radio or at nightclubs

do[1] strong /duː/ weak /də/ **auxiliary verb** (**doing**, **did**, **done**)
1 A1 used with another verb to form questions and negative phrases: *Do you need any help?* ◦ *I don't know.*
2 A2 used at the end of a sentence to make it into a question: *Sarah lives near here, doesn't she?*
3 B1 used to avoid repeating a verb that has just been used: *'I hate that song.' 'So do I.'*
4 used to make the main verb stronger: *He does like you, he's just shy.*

do[2] /duː/ **verb** (**doing**, **did**, **done**)
1 A1 to perform an action: *Go upstairs and do your homework.*
2 A1 to perform a type of exercise or activity: *She does yoga in her spare time.*
3 A1 to study a subject: *Diana did history at university.*
4 A2 to make or prepare something: *Max's Café does great sandwiches.*
5 A2 used for talking about how healthy, happy, or successful someone is: *'How is Sarah doing?' 'She's doing really well, thanks.'*
6 **do the cleaning, cooking, etc.** A1 to perform a job in the house: *I do the cooking but Joe does the cleaning.*
7 **what does *someone* do?** A1 used to ask what someone's job is: *'What do you do?' 'I'm a doctor.'*
8 **do badly/well** B1 to not succeed or to succeed: *Sam did very well in her exams.*
9 **be/have to do with *something*** to be related to something: *She lacks confidence and I think that has to do with her childhood.*
10 **do your hair, make-up, etc.** B1 to make your hair, make-up, etc. look nice: *It takes him half an hour to do his hair in the morning.*
11 **do *someone* good** to have a good effect on someone: *A holiday would do you good.*
12 **will do** will be satisfactory: *You don't have to pay now. Next week will do.*
13 **could do with *someone* or *something*** to need or want someone or something: *I could do with a few days off work.*

Common mistake: do or make?

Do generally means to perform an activity or job.
I should do more exercise.
~~*I should make more exercise.*~~
Make generally means to create or produce something.
Did you make the dress yourself?
~~*Did you do the dress yourself?*~~

do *something* up **phrasal verb**
1 mainly UK to fasten something: *Do your coat up. It's cold outside.*
2 to repair or decorate a building so that it looks attractive

do without (*someone/something*) **phrasal verb**
to do something well without having someone or something: *Jack's the kind of player we can't do without.*

do with *something* **phrasal verb**
used to ask where someone put something: *What did you do with my keys?*

dock /dɒk/ **noun**
the place where ships stop and goods are taken off or put on
• **dock** **verb** to arrive at a dock

doctor /ˈdɒktəʳ/ **noun**
A1 a person whose job is to treat people who are ill or hurt

document /ˈdɒkjəmənt/ **noun**
1 A2 a piece of paper with official information on it

2 B1 a piece of text produced on a computer: *How do I create a new document?*

documentary /ˌdɒkjəˈmentᵊri/ **noun** (plural **documentaries**)
B1 a film or television programme that gives facts about a real situation

dodge /dɒdʒ/ **verb** (**dodging**, **dodged**)
1 to move quickly to avoid someone or something: *He managed to* ***dodge past*** *the security guard.*
2 to avoid doing something you should do: *The minister dodged questions about his relationship with the actress.*

does strong /dʌz/ weak /dəz/
present simple of do, used with 'he', 'she', and 'it'

doesn't /ˈdʌzᵊnt/
short form of does not: *Keith doesn't like mushrooms or garlic.*

dog /dɒg/ **noun**
A1 an animal with fur, four legs, and a tail, that is kept as a pet

doll /dɒl/ **noun**
A1 a child's toy that looks like a small person

dollar /ˈdɒləʳ/ **noun**
A1 the unit of money used in the US, Canada, and some other countries; $

dolphin /ˈdɒlfɪn/ **noun**
B1 an intelligent sea animal that breathes air and looks like a large fish

dolphin

dome /dəʊm/ **noun**
a curved, round roof of a building

domestic /dəˈmestɪk/ **adj**
1 relating to the home and family relationships: *domestic violence*
2 inside one country: *a domestic flight*
3 A domestic animal is kept as a pet.

dominate /ˈdɒmɪneɪt/ **verb** (**dominating**, **dominated**)
to control or have power over someone or something: *You often find that one person dominates at a meeting.*

donate /dəʊˈneɪt/ **verb** (**donating**, **donated**)
to give something, mainly money, to a person or organization that needs help: *Four hundred new computers were donated to the college.*

done¹ /dʌn/
past tense and past participle of do

done² /dʌn/ **adj**
finished or completed: *Did you get your essay done in time?*

donkey /ˈdɒŋki/ **noun**
B1 an animal that looks like a small horse with long ears

donkey

donor /ˈdəʊnəʳ/ **noun**
someone who gives something to a person or organization that needs help

don't /dəʊnt/
short form of do not: *Please don't talk during the exam.*

> **Common mistake: don't**
>
> Remember that **don't** is always written with an apostrophe.
>
> ~~*Please dont talk during the exam.*~~

donut **noun**
US spelling of doughnut (= a small fried cake)

doodle /ˈduːdl/ **verb** (**doodling**, **doodled**)
to draw little pictures or patterns on something without thinking about it
• **doodle** **noun**

doodles

door /dɔːʳ/ **noun**
A1 the part of a building or room that you open or close to get inside it or out of it: *Please shut the door behind you.*

doorbell /ˈdɔːbel/ **noun**
a button that you press next to a door that makes a noise to let someone know that you are there

doorknob /ˈdɔːnɒb/ **noun**
a round object on a door that you use to open or close it

doorway /ˈdɔːweɪ/ **noun**
an entrance to a building or room through a door

dorm /dɔːm/ **noun** US (UK **hall of residence**)
short form of dormitory: a large building containing many bedrooms, usually for students

dormitory /ˈdɔːmɪtᵊri/ **noun** (plural **dormitories**)
1 a large bedroom with a lot of beds, especially in a school
2 US the full form of dorm

dosage /ˈdəʊsɪdʒ/ **noun**
how much medicine you should take and how often you should take it: *the recommended daily dosage*

dose /dəʊs/ **noun**
a measured amount of medicine that is taken: *What is the recommended dose?*

dot /dɒt/ **noun**
1 a small, round mark or spot: *a pattern of blue and green dots*
2 B1 [no plural] the spoken form of '.' in an Internet address: *dot co dot uk (= .co.uk)*
3 on the dot at that exact time: *We have to leave at 7.30 on the dot.*

double[1] /ˈdʌbl/ **adj**
1 having two parts of the same type or size: *My number is four, two, six, double two, five (= 426225).*
2 A2 twice the amount, number, or size of something: *a double hamburger*
3 made to be used by two people: *a double bed* ◦ *a double room in a hotel*

double[2] /ˈdʌbl/ **determiner**
B1 twice as much or as many: *Our new house is double the size of the old one.*

double[3] /ˈdʌbl/ **verb** (**doubling**, **doubled**)
to increase and become twice the original size or amount, or to make something do this: *Our house has almost **doubled in** value.*

double-click /ˌdʌblˈklɪk/ **verb**
to quickly press a button twice on a mouse to make something happen on a computer screen: *Double-click on the icon to start the program.*

double-decker /ˌdʌblˈdekəʳ/ **noun**
a tall bus with two levels: *a **double-decker bus***

doubt[1] /daʊt/ **noun**
1 B1 a state of being uncertain about something, or not trusting someone or something: *I **have** some **doubts about** his ability to do the job.*
2 have no doubt B1 to be certain: *I **have no doubt that** I made the right decision.*
3 there is no doubt B1 it is certain: ***There is no doubt that** he's a good player.*
4 be in doubt to not be certain: *The future of the project is in doubt.*
5 without (a) doubt certainly: *She is without doubt a great writer.*
6 no doubt used to say that something is very likely: *No doubt she'll spend the money on her son.*

doubt[2] /daʊt/ **verb**
to not feel certain about something or think that something will not happen: *I **doubt that** I'll get the job.*

doubtful /ˈdaʊtfᵊl/ **adj**
1 If something is doubtful, it probably will not happen: *It's **doubtful whether** he'll be able to come.*
2 not feeling certain about something: *The teacher is **doubtful about** having parents working as classroom assistants.*

doubtless /ˈdaʊtləs/ **adv**
probably: *He will doubtless be criticized by journalists.*

doughnut (also US **donut**) /ˈdəʊnʌt/ **noun**
a small, round, fried cake, sometimes with a hole in the middle

doughnut

dove /dʌv/ **noun**
a white bird, sometimes used as a symbol of peace

a b c **d** e f g h i j k l m n o p q r s t u v w x y z

down¹ /daʊn/ **adv, preposition**
1 A1 moving from above and onto a surface: *Put that box down on the floor.*
2 A2 towards or in a lower place: *I bent down to have a look.*
3 A2 towards or at a lower level or amount: *Can you turn the music down?*
4 **down the road, river, etc.** A2 along or further along the road, river, etc.: *There's another pub further down the street.*
5 **note/write** ***something*** **down** B1 to write something on a piece of paper: *Can I write down your phone number?*

down² /daʊn/ **adj**
unhappy or unable to feel excited or energetic about anything: *She's been really down since her husband died.*

downhill /ˌdaʊnˈhɪl/ **adv**
towards the bottom of a hill or slope: *It's so much easier cycling downhill.*

download¹ /ˈdaʊnləʊd/ **verb**
A2 to copy computer programs, music, or information electronically, usually from the Internet or from a larger computer: *You can download this software free from their website.*

download² /ˈdaʊnləʊd/ **noun**
B1 a computer program, music, or other information that is downloaded: *a free download*

downstairs¹ /ˌdaʊnˈsteəz/ **adv**
A2 on or to a lower level of a building: *She went downstairs to see who was at the door.*

downstairs² /ˈdaʊnsteəz/ **adj**
B1 on or at a lower level of a building, especially the ground floor: *The burglars had got in through a downstairs window.*

downtown /ˌdaʊnˈtaʊn/ **adj, adv** US
in or to the central part or main business area of a city: *downtown Chicago* ◦ *I work downtown.*

downwards (also **downward**) /ˈdaʊnwədz/ **adv** mainly UK
towards a lower place or level: *The road slopes downwards to the river.*

doze /dəʊz/ **verb** (**dozing, dozed**)
to sleep lightly
doze off **phrasal verb**
to gradually start sleeping, usually during the day: *He dozed off during the movie.*

dozen /ˈdʌzᵊn/ **noun, determiner**
1 B1 twelve, or a group of twelve: *There were about* ***a dozen*** *people at the party.*
2 **dozens** informal a lot: *She's got* ***dozens of*** *friends.*

Dr
A2 written abbreviation for doctor: *Dr Anna Prescott*

draft /drɑːft/ **noun**
1 a piece of writing or a plan that is not yet in its finished form: *He made several changes to the* ***first draft****.*
2 the US spelling of draught

drag /dræg/ **verb** (**dragging, dragged**)
1 to pull something or someone along the ground somewhere, usually with difficulty: *The table was too heavy to lift, so we had to drag it out.*
2 B1 to move something somewhere on a computer screen using a mouse
3 **drag and drop** B1 to move something on a computer screen using a mouse and place it where you want it to be: *You can drag and drop photos from one folder to another.*
4 (also **drag on**) to continue for too much time in a boring way: *The talks dragged on for months.*

dragon /ˈdrægᵊn/ **noun**
a big imaginary creature that breathes out fire

dragon

drain¹ /dreɪn/ **verb**
1 to remove the liquid from something, usually by pouring it away: *Drain the pasta and add the tomatoes.*
2 If something drains, liquid flows away or out of it.

drain² /dreɪn/ **noun**
a pipe or hole that takes away waste liquids or water: *She poured the dirty water down the drain.*

drama /ˈdrɑːmə/ **noun**
1 B1 a play in a theatre or on television or radio: *a historical drama*
2 B1 [no plural] plays and acting generally: *modern drama*
3 B1 the fact of something exciting happening: There was a bit of drama at work today.

dramatic /drəˈmætɪk/ **adj**
1 very sudden or exciting: *a dramatic change/improvement*
2 relating to plays and acting
• **dramatically** **adv** *Your life changes dramatically when you have a baby.*

drank /dræŋk/
past tense and past participle of drink

draught /drɑːft/ **noun** UK (US **draft**)
cold air coming into a room: *There's a draught coming from under the door.*

draw /drɔː/ **verb** (**drew**, **drawn**)
1 A1 to make a picture with a pen or pencil: *She drew a picture of a tree.*
2 to attract someone to a place or person: *He's an excellent speaker who always draws a crowd.*
3 to pull something or someone in a particular direction: *He took her hand and drew her towards him.*
4 **draw near/close** to become nearer in space or time: *Her birthday's drawing nearer every day.*
5 to move somewhere, usually in a vehicle: *The train drew into the station.*
6 UK to finish a game or competition with each team or player having the same score: *England drew 2-2 against Italy.*
7 **draw the curtains** to pull curtains open or closed
draw back **phrasal verb**
to move away from someone or something: *She drew back in disgust when she saw the snake.*
draw *something* up **phrasal verb**
to prepare something by writing it: *He drew up some plans for the new office.*

drawer /drɔːʳ/ **noun**
A2 a container like a box that is part of a piece of furniture and moves in and out

drawing /ˈdrɔːɪŋ/ **noun**
1 a picture made with a pencil or pen: *There were some drawings on the wall.*
2 A2 [no plural] the skill or activity of making pictures using a pencil or pen: *Do you want to do some drawing?*

drawing pin /ˈdrɔːɪŋ ˌpɪn/ **noun** UK (US **thumbtack**)
a pin with a wide, flat top, used for fastening pieces of paper to a wall

drawn /drɔːn/
past tense and past participle of draw

dreadful /ˈdredfəl/ **adj**
very bad

dreadfully /ˈdredfəli/ **adv**
1 very badly: *The children behaved dreadfully.*
2 mainly UK formal very: *I'm dreadfully sorry.*

dream[1] /driːm/ **noun**
1 A2 events and images in your mind while you are sleeping: *I **had** a very strange **dream** last night.*
2 B1 something that you want to happen although it is not very likely: *It was his dream to become an actor.*
3 **be in a dream** to not notice things that are around you because you are thinking about something else: *I didn't hear what you were saying – I was in a dream.*

dream[2] /driːm/ **verb** (**dreamed**, **dreamt**)
1 A2 to experience events and images in your mind while you are sleeping: *Last night I dreamed that I was flying.*
2 B1 to imagine something that you would like to happen: *I dream of living on a desert island.*

dress[1] /dres/ **verb**
1 A2 to put clothes on yourself or someone else: *I usually **get dressed** before having breakfast.*
→ Opposite **undress** verb
2 B1 to wear a particular type, style, or colour of clothes: *She was **dressed in** black.*
dress up **phrasal verb**
1 to wear formal clothes for a special occasion: *Weddings are a great opportunity to dress up.*
2 to wear special clothes for a game

or party: *He **dressed up as** Superman for the party.*

dress² /dres/ **noun**
1 A1 a piece of clothing for women that covers the top of the body and hangs down over the legs
→ See **Clothes** on page C5
2 [no plural] a particular style of clothes: *casual dress*

dressed /drest/ **adj**
1 A2 wearing clothes and not naked: *I usually **get dressed** before I eat breakfast.* ◦ *He was **dressed in** a grey suit.*
2 B1 wearing clothing of a particular type: *a well-dressed man*

dressing /ˈdresɪŋ/ **noun**
1 a sauce, especially a mixture of oil and vinegar for salad
2 a covering that protects an injury

dressing gown /ˈdresɪŋ ˌgaʊn/ **noun** UK
a piece of clothing, like a long coat, that you wear at home when you are not dressed

dressing room /ˈdresɪŋ ˌruːm/ **noun**
1 a room where actors or sports teams get dressed before a performance or game
2 a room in a shop where you can try on clothes

drew /druː/
past tense and past participle of draw

dried /draɪd/
past tense and past participle of dry

drift /drɪft/ **verb**
to be moved slowly somewhere by wind or water: *The boat drifted towards the beach.*

drill /drɪl/ **noun**
a machine for making holes in a hard substance: *an electric drill*
• **drill verb**

drink¹ /drɪŋk/ **verb** (**drank, drunk**)
1 A1 to put liquid into your mouth and swallow it: *He drank a glass of milk.*
2 A2 to drink alcohol, usually regularly: *She doesn't smoke or drink.*

drink² /drɪŋk/ **noun**
1 A1 a liquid or an amount of liquid that you drink: *a cold drink*
2 A2 alcoholic liquid: *Do you want to **have a drink** to celebrate?*

drip /drɪp/ **verb** (**dripping, dripped**)
1 to fall in drops: *There was water **dripping from** the ceiling.*
2 to produce drops of liquid: *The candle's dripping.*

drive¹ /draɪv/ **verb** (**driving, drove, driven**)
1 A1 to make a car, bus, or train move, and control what it does: *She's learning to drive.*
2 A1 to travel somewhere in a car, or to take someone somewhere in a car: *Annie drove me home last night.*
3 drive *someone* mad, crazy, etc. to make someone extremely annoyed: *He leaves dirty clothes all over the floor and it's driving me mad.*

drive² /draɪv/ **noun**
1 B1 a journey in a car: *The drive from Boston to New York took four hours.*
2 B1 a part of a computer that can keep information: *Save your work on the C drive.*
3 the area of ground that you drive on to get from your house to the road: *You can park on the drive.*

driven /ˈdrɪvᵊn/
past participle of drive

driver /ˈdraɪvəʳ/ **noun**
A1 someone who drives a vehicle: *a bus/train driver*

driving licence /ˈdraɪvɪŋ ˌlaɪsᵊns/ **noun** UK (US **driver's license** /ˈdraɪvəz ˌlaɪsᵊns/)
A2 an official document that allows you to drive a car

drop

drop¹ /drɒp/ **verb** (**dropping, dropped**)
1 B1 to fall or let something fall: *She tripped and dropped the vase.*

2 If you drop a plan, activity, class, or idea, you stop doing or planning it: *Plans for a new supermarket have been dropped.* ◦ *Is it too late to drop your art class?*
3 If a level or amount drops, it becomes less: *Unemployment has dropped from 8% to 6% in the last year.*
4 (also **drop off**) to take someone or something to a place, usually by car as you travel somewhere else: *I can drop you at the station on my way to work.*
drop by/in **phrasal verb**
to visit someone for a short time, usually without arranging it: *I* ***dropped in on*** *Pam on my way home.*
drop *someone/something* off **phrasal verb**
to take someone or something to a place, usually by car
drop out **phrasal verb**
to stop doing something before you have completely finished: *He* ***dropped out of*** *school at 14.*

drop² /drɒp/ **noun**
1 B1 a small, round-shaped amount of liquid: *I felt a few drops of rain.*
→ See **Quantities** on page C14
2 a fall in the level or amount of something: *There has been a* ***drop in*** *crime recently.*

drought /draʊt/ **noun**
a long period when there is no rain and people do not have enough water: *A severe drought ruined the crops.*

drove /drəʊv/
past tense of drive

drown /draʊn/ **verb**
to die because you are under water and cannot breathe, or to kill someone in this way

drug /drʌg/ **noun**
1 an illegal substance that people take to make them feel happy: *a drug dealer*
2 a chemical substance used as a medicine: *Scientists are developing a new drug to treat cancer.*

drug addict /ˈdrʌg ˌædɪkt/ **noun**
someone who cannot stop taking drugs

drugstore /ˈdrʌgstɔːʳ/ **noun** US (UK **chemist's**)
a shop that sells medicines and also things such as soap and beauty products

drum /drʌm/ **noun**
1 A2 a round, hollow musical instrument that you hit with your hands or with sticks

drum

2 a large, round container for holding things such as oil or chemicals

drunk¹ /drʌŋk/
past participle of drink

drunk² /drʌŋk/ **adj**
not able to behave or speak normally because you have drunk too much alcohol: *He often* ***gets drunk*** *at parties.*

dry¹ /draɪ/ **adj** (**drier**, **driest**)
1 A2 without water or liquid on the surface: *dry paint* ◦ *Is your hair dry yet?*
2 without rain: *a dry summer*
3 Dry wine is not sweet.

dry² /draɪ/ **verb** (**drying**, **dried**)
A2 to become dry, or to make something become dry: *He dried his hands on a towel.*

dry-clean /ˌdraɪˈkliːn/ **verb**
to clean clothes using a special chemical, not water: *This dress has to be dry-cleaned.*

duchess /ˈdʌtʃɪs/ **noun**
a woman of very high social rank in some European countries: *the Duchess of Windsor*

duck¹ /dʌk/ **noun**
A2 a bird with short legs that lives in or near water, or the meat from this bird

ducks

duck² /dʌk/ **verb**
to move your body down quickly to avoid being hit or seen: *Billy ducked behind a car when he saw his teacher.*

duckling /ˈdʌklɪŋ/ **noun**
a young duck

a b c d e f g h i j k l m n o p q r s t u v w x y z

a b c d e f g h i j k l m n o p q r s t u v w x y z

due /djuː/ **adj**
1 B1 expected or planned: *When is the baby due (= expected to be born)?* ◦ *He was **due to** fly back this morning.*
2 due to *something* B1 because of something: *The train was late due to snow.*
3 owed to someone: *The rent is due today.* ◦ *He didn't get the praise and recognition that was **due to** him.*
4 be due for *something* If you are due for something, it should happen very soon: *She's due for a pay rise.*

duet /djuˈet/ **noun**
a piece of music for two people to perform together

dug /dʌg/
past tense and past participle of dig

duke /djuːk/ **noun**
a man of very high social rank in some European countries: *the Duke of Beaufort*

dull /dʌl/ **adj**
1 B1 not interesting: *a dull place*
2 not bright: *dull colours*
3 A dull sound is not loud or clear: *a dull thud*

dumb /dʌm/ **adj**
not able to talk

dummy /ˈdʌmi/ **noun** (plural **dummies**) UK (US **pacifier**)
a small rubber object that you put in a baby's mouth to stop it crying

dump[1] /dʌmp/ **verb**
1 to put something somewhere to get rid of it: *The company was fined for illegally dumping toxic chemicals.*
2 to quickly put something somewhere: *He dumped his bag on the table.*

dump[2] /dʌmp/ **noun**
a place where people take things that they do not want

dune /djuːn/ **noun**
a hill of sand in the desert or on the coast

dungarees /ˌdʌŋgəˈriːz/ **plural noun** UK (US **overalls**)
trousers with a part that covers your chest and straps that go over your shoulders

during /ˈdjʊərɪŋ/ **preposition**
1 A2 for the whole of a period of time: *Emma's usually at home during the day.*
2 A2 at a particular moment in a period of time: *We'll arrange a meeting some time during the week.*

> **Common mistake: during or for?**
>
> Use **during** to talk about a period of time when something happens.
>
> *I'm at work during the day, so it's better to phone in the evening.*
>
> *Please don't take photos during the performance.*
>
> Use **for** to say how long something happens or continues, for example 'for two hours', 'for three days'.
>
> *I've been in Cambridge for six months now.*
>
> *We waited for an hour and then left.*
>
> ~~*We waited during an hour and then left.*~~

dusk /dʌsk/ **noun** [no plural]
the time in the evening when it starts to become dark

dust[1] /dʌst/ **noun** [no plural]
B1 a powder that you see on a surface or in the air: *The shelves were covered in a thick layer of dust.*

dust[2] /dʌst/ **verb**
to remove dust from something: *I tidied and dusted the shelves.*

dustbin /ˈdʌstbɪn/ **noun** UK
B1 a large container for rubbish kept outside your house

duster /ˈdʌstəʳ/ **noun**
a cloth used for removing dust from furniture and other objects

dustpan /ˈdʌstpæn/ **noun**
a flat container with a handle, used with a brush for removing dirt from a floor

dusty /ˈdʌsti/ **adj** (**dustier**, **dustiest**)
B1 covered with dust

duty /ˈdjuːti/ **noun** (plural **duties**)
1 B1 something you must do because the law says you must or because it is right: *The police **have a duty** to protect the public.*
2 something you do as part of your job or because of your position: *professional duties*

3 on/off duty If a doctor, police officer, etc. is on duty, he or she is working, and if he or she is off duty, he or she is not working: *I'm on duty tomorrow night.*

duty-free /ˌdjuːtiˈfriː/ **adj**
B1 Duty-free goods are things that you can buy and bring into a country without paying tax.

duvet /ˈdjuːveɪ/ **noun** mainly UK
B1 a cover filled with feathers or warm material that you sleep under

DVD /ˌdiːviːˈdiː/ **noun**
A1 a small disc for storing movies, games, or other information: *Is this movie available **on DVD**?* ◦ *I just bought a new **DVD player**.*

dwarf /dwɔːf/ **noun**
an imaginary creature like a little man, in children's stories

dye[1] /daɪ/ **noun**
a substance that is used to change the colour of something

dye[2] /daɪ/ **verb** (**dyeing**, **dyed**)
to change the colour of something by using a dye: *I dyed my hair blonde.*

dying /ˈdaɪɪŋ/
present participle of die

dynamite /ˈdaɪnəmaɪt/ **noun** [no plural]
a type of explosive: *a stick of dynamite*

Ee

E, e /iː/
the fifth letter of the alphabet

each /iːtʃ/ **pronoun, determiner**
A1 every one in a group: ***Each of** the teams has four players.* ◦ *Each student received a new pen.* ◦ *The bill comes to £79 so that's about £10 each.*

each other /ˌiːtʃ ˈʌðəʳ/ **pronoun**
used to show that each person in a group of two or more people does something to the others: *The children are always arguing with each other.*

eager /ˈiːgəʳ/ **adj**
wanting to do or have something very much: *Sam was **eager to** go home.*
• **eagerly adv** *The results were eagerly awaited.*
• **eagerness noun** [no plural]

eagle /ˈiːgl/ **noun**
a large wild bird with a big, curved beak, that hunts smaller animals

eagle

ear /ɪəʳ/ **noun**
A1 one of the two things on your head that you hear with: *She whispered something in his ear.*
→ See **The Body** on page C2

earache /ˈɪəreɪk/ **noun** [no plural]
B1 pain in your ear: *I've got earache.*

early /ˈɜːli/ **adj, adv** (**earlier, earliest**)
1 A1 near the beginning of a period of time, process, etc.: *the early 1980s*
2 A2 before the usual time or the time that was planned: *The plane arrived ten minutes early.*
3 early on in the first stage or part of something: *I lost interest quite early on in the book.*

earn /ɜːn/ **verb**
1 A2 to get money for doing work: *She earns about £40,000 a year.*
2 earn a/your living to work to get money for the things you need
3 to get something good that you deserve: *As a teacher you have to earn the respect of your students.*

earphones /ˈɪəfəʊnz/ **plural noun**
a piece of electronic equipment that you put in your ears so that you can listen to music, etc.
→ See picture at **headphones**

earring /ˈɪərɪŋ/ **noun**
A2 a piece of jewellery that you wear on your ear: *silver earrings*

earring

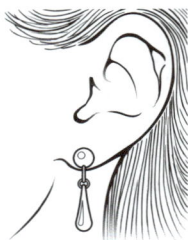

earth /ɜːθ/ **noun**
1 B1 (also **the Earth**) the planet that we live on
2 [no plural] soil or ground: *a pile of earth*
3 how, what, why, etc. on earth informal used when you are extremely surprised, confused, or angry about something: *How on earth did this happen?* ◦ *Why on earth didn't you tell me before?*

earthquake /ˈɜːθkweɪk/ **noun**
a sudden movement of the Earth's surface, often causing damage

ease¹ /iːz/ **noun**
1 [no plural] If you do something with ease, it is very easy for you to do it: *Luca passed his exams **with ease**.*
2 at ease feeling relaxed: *I felt completely at ease with him.*

ease² /iːz/ **verb** (**easing, eased**)
to become less bad, or to make something become less bad: *The pain eased after a few minutes.*

easily /ˈiːzɪli/ **adv**
A2 with no difficulty: *She makes friends very easily.*

east, East /iːst/ **noun** [no plural]
1 A2 the direction that you face to see the sun rise: *Which way is east?*
2 the east A2 the part of an area that is farther towards the east than the rest: *She's from the east of England.*
• **east adj** A2 *the east side of the city*
• **east adv** A2 *They sailed east.*

Easter /ˈiːstəʳ/ **noun**
a holiday in March or April when Christians celebrate the return to life of Jesus Christ: *the Easter holidays*

Easter egg /ˈiːstər ˌeg/ **noun**
a decorated egg, or an egg made of chocolate, that people eat at Easter

eastern, Eastern /ˈiːstᵊn/ **adj**
B1 in or from the east part of an area: *eastern Europe*

easy¹ /ˈiːzi/ **adj** (**easier**, **easiest**)
A1 not difficult: *The exam was easy.* ◦ *It's easy to see why he's so popular.*
→ Opposite **difficult** adj

easy² /ˈiːzi/ **adv**
take it easy B1 to relax and not work hard: *I'm going to take it easy this weekend.*

easy-going /ˌiːziˈgəʊɪŋ/ **adj**
B1 usually relaxed and calm, not worried or upset: *Flavio has an easy-going personality.*

eat /iːt/ **verb** (**ate**, **eaten**)
1 A1 to put food into your mouth and then swallow it: *Who ate all the cake?* ◦ *Let's have* ***something to eat*** *(= some food).*
2 A1 to have a meal: *We usually eat at about 7 o'clock.*
eat out phrasal verb
B1 to eat at a restaurant: *Let's eat out tonight.*
eat *something* up phrasal verb
to eat all the food you have been given: *Be good and eat up your dinner.*

echo¹ /ˈekəʊ/ **verb**
If a sound echoes, you hear it again and again, usually because you are in a large, empty space: *Their voices echoed around the room.*

echo² /ˈekəʊ/ **noun** (plural **echoes**)
a sound that you hear more than once because you are in a big, empty space

eclipse /ɪˈklɪps/ **noun**
an occasion when the sun is covered by the moon, or the moon is covered by the Earth's shadow

ecological /ˌiːkəˈlɒdʒɪkᵊl/ **adj**
relating to the environment: *an ecological disaster*
• **ecologically** **adv**

economic /ˌiːkəˈnɒmɪk/ **adj**
relating to trade, industry, and money: *economic policies*
• **economically** **adv** *The country would benefit economically.*

economical /ˌiːkəˈnɒmɪkᵊl/ **adj**
using little money, fuel, etc.: *It's a very economical car.*
• **economically** **adv**

economics /ˌiːkəˈnɒmɪks/ **noun** [no plural]
B1 the study of the way in which trade, industry, and money are organized: *She studies economics at York University.*

economy /ɪˈkɒnəmi/ **noun** (plural **economies**)
the system by which a country makes and uses goods and money: *the US economy* ◦ *a global economy*

economy class /ɪˈkɒnəmi ˌklɑːs/ **noun** [no plural]
the cheapest and least comfortable type of seats on a plane: *We are travelling* ***in economy class.***

edge /edʒ/ **noun**
B1 the part around something that is furthest from the centre: *Rick was sitting on the edge of the bed.* ◦ *She ran down to the water's edge.*

edible /ˈedɪbl/ **adj**
safe to eat: *edible berries*

edition /ɪˈdɪʃᵊn/ **noun**
many books or newspapers that are the same and were made at the same time: *a new edition*

editor /ˈedɪtəʳ/ **noun**
1 someone who is in charge of a newspaper or magazine
2 someone who prepares books, etc. so that they can be published

educate /ˈedʒʊkeɪt/ **verb** (**educating**, **educated**)
1 to teach someone at a school or college: *She was educated at the Perse School.*
2 to give people information about something: *Children must be* ***educated about*** *the dangers of smoking.*

education /ˌedʒʊˈkeɪʃᵊn/ **noun**
B1 teaching and learning in a school

or college: *More money should be spent on education.*
• **educational** adj providing education: *the educational system*

eel /iːl/ **noun**
a long fish that looks like a snake

effect /ɪˈfekt/ **noun**
1 B1 a change or result that is caused by something: *The accident **had** a huge **effect** on her life.* ◦ *We don't know the long-term **effects of** this drug.*
2 take effect to start to produce results or changes: *They had to wait for the anaesthetic to take effect.*

effective /ɪˈfektɪv/ **adj**
getting the result that you want: *What is the most effective way of teaching?*

effectively /ɪˈfektɪvli/ **adv**
in a way that gets what you want: *Teachers need to be able to communicate ideas effectively.*

efficient /ɪˈfɪʃᵊnt/ **adj**
B1 working well and not wasting time or energy: *Email is a quick and efficient way of contacting people.*
• **efficiently** adv

effort /ˈefət/ **noun**
1 B1 an attempt to do something: *He was **making an effort** to be sociable.*
2 B1 [no plural] the energy that you need to do something: *I **put** a lot of **effort into** organizing the party.*

EFL /ˌiːefˈel/ **noun** [no plural]
abbreviation for English as a Foreign Language: the teaching of English to students whose first language is not English: *Which shop has the largest selection of EFL books?*

e.g. (also **eg**) /ˌiːˈdʒiː/
used to give an example of what you mean: *green vegetables e.g. spinach and cabbage*

egg /eg/ **noun**
1 A1 an oval object made by a female chicken, that you eat as food: *a boiled/fried egg*

egg

2 an oval object with a hard shell that contains a baby bird, insect, or other creature: *The bird **lays** its **eggs** in a nest.*

eggplant /ˈegplɑːnt/ **noun** US (UK **aubergine**)
an oval, purple vegetable that is white inside

eight /eɪt/
A1 the number 8

eighteen /ˌeɪˈtiːn/
A1 the number 18

eighteenth /ˌeɪˈtiːnθ/
18th written as a word

eighth¹ /eɪtθ/
A2 8th written as a word

eighth² /eɪtθ/ **noun**
one of eight equal parts of something; 1/8

eighties /ˈeɪtiz/ **plural noun**
1 the eighties the years from 1980 to 1989: *CDs became popular **in the eighties**.*
2 be in your eighties to be aged between 80 and 89: *My grandmother is **in her eighties**.*

eighty /ˈeɪti/
A2 the number 80
• **eightieth** 80th written as a word

either¹ /ˈaɪðəʳ/, /ˈiːðəʳ/ **conjunction**
either... or B1 used when you are giving a choice of two or more things: *Either you or I can go.*

either² /ˈaɪðəʳ/, /ˈiːðəʳ/ **pronoun, determiner**
1 B1 one of two people or things, when it is not important which: *'A hot or a cold drink?' – 'Oh, either.'*
2 both: *There are trees on either side of the house.*

either³ /ˈaɪðəʳ/, /ˈiːðəʳ/ **adv**
B1 used in negative sentences to mean that something else is also true: *The food was bad and it wasn't cheap either.*

elaborate /ɪˈlæbᵊrət/ **adj**
complicated or with a lot of details: *an elaborate design*
• **elaborately** adv

elastic /ɪˈlæstɪk/ **adj**
Something that is elastic can stretch

and return to its original size: *Your skin is more elastic when you are young.*

elastic band /ɪˌlæstɪk ˈbænd/ **noun** UK
a thin circle of rubber used to hold things together

elbow /ˈelbəʊ/ **noun**
B1 the part in the middle of your arm where it bends
→ See **The Body** on page C2

elder[1] /ˈeldə^r/ **adj**
elder brother, daughter, sister, etc.
B1 the older of two brothers, daughters, sisters, etc.: *Their elder daughter lives in South America.*

elder[2] /ˈeldə^r/ **noun**
1 the elder the oldest of two people: *He's the elder of two sons.*
2 your elders people older than you: *I was taught to respect my elders.*

elderly /ˈeldəli/ **adj**
B1 Elderly people are old: *an elderly man*

eldest /ˈeldɪst/ **adj**
eldest child, daughter, brother, etc.
B1 the oldest child, daughter, brother, etc.: *My eldest brother is a doctor.*

elect /ɪˈlekt/ **verb**
to choose someone for a particular job or position by voting: *He was elected president in 2008.*

election /ɪˈlekʃən/ **noun**
B1 a time when people vote in order to choose someone for a political or official job

electric /ɪˈlektrɪk/ **adj**
A2 using or giving electricity: *an electric heater* ◦ *an electric socket*

electrical /ɪˈlektrɪkəl/ **adj**
B1 using or relating to electricity: *electrical goods* ◦ *an electrical engineer*

electrician /ɪˌlekˈtrɪʃən/ **noun**
someone whose job is to put in or repair electrical equipment

electricity /ɪˌlekˈtrɪsəti/ **noun** [no plural]
A2 a type of energy that can produce light and heat, or make machines work: *The electricity was turned off.*

electronic /ɪˌlekˈtrɒnɪk/ **adj**
1 B1 Electronic equipment consists of things such as computers, televisions, and radios.
2 B1 done by computers: *electronic communication*
• **electronically adv** *electronically controlled gates*

electronics /ˌɪlekˈtrɒnɪks/ **noun** [no plural]
the science of making electronic equipment: *the electronics industry*

elegant /ˈelɪgənt/ **adj**
stylish and attractive: *an elegant dining room* ◦ *She's a very elegant woman.*
• **elegantly adv** *She was elegantly dressed.*

element /ˈelɪmənt/ **noun**
1 a part of something: *This book has all the elements of a good story.*
2 an element of *something* a small amount of something: *There's an element of truth in what she says.*
3 a simple substance that you cannot reduce to smaller chemical parts: *Iron is a common element.*

elementary /ˌelɪˈmentəri/ **adj**
B1 relating to the early stages of studying a subject: *students at elementary level*

elephant /ˈelɪfənt/ **noun**
A2 a very large, grey animal with big ears and a very long nose

elephant

elevator /ˈelɪveɪtə^r/ **noun** US (UK **lift**)
a machine that carries people up and down in tall buildings

eleven /ɪˈlevən/
A1 the number 11

eleventh[1] /ɪˈlevənθ/
11th written as a word

eleventh[2] /ɪˈlevənθ/ **noun**
one of eleven equal parts of something; 1/11

else /els/ **adv**
1 A2 in addition to someone or some-

thing: *Would you like* ***anything else*** *to eat?* ◦ ***What else*** *did he say?*
2 A2 different from someone or something: *I don't like it here. Let's go* ***somewhere else****.*
3 A2 other things or people: *I forgot my toothbrush, but I remembered* ***everything else****.*
4 or else used to say what will happen if another thing does not happen: *We must be there by six, or else we'll miss the beginning.*

elsewhere /ˌelsˈweəʳ/ **adv**
in or to another place: *If we can't find it here, we'll have to* ***go elsewhere****.*

email[1] (also **e-mail**) /ˈiːmeɪl/ **noun**
1 A1 [no plural] a way of sending messages electronically, from one computer to another: *What's your* ***email address****?*
2 A1 a message sent to a computer: *I got an email from Danielle yesterday.*

email[2] (also **e-mail**) /ˈiːmeɪl/ **verb**
A2 to send a message using email: *I'll email you tomorrow.* ◦ *Has he emailed you that list of addresses yet?*

embarrass /ɪmˈbærəs/ **verb**
to make someone feel ashamed or shy: *My dad's always embarrassing me in front of my friends.*

embarrassed /ɪmˈbærəst/ **adj**
B1 feeling ashamed or shy: *I was too embarrassed to admit that I was scared.*

embarrassing /ɪmˈbærəsɪŋ/ **adj**
B1 making you feel embarrassed: *I forgot his name – it was very embarrassing.*

embarrassment /ɪmˈbærəsmənt/ **noun** [no plural]
shy, ashamed, or uncomfortable feelings: *He blushed with embarrassment.*

embassy /ˈembəsi/ **noun** (plural **embassies**)
B1 the official group of people who live in a foreign country and represent their government there, or the building where they work

embrace /ɪmˈbreɪs/ **verb** (**embracing**, **embraced**)
to put your arms around someone: *They embraced and kissed each other.*

embryo /ˈembriəʊ/ **noun**
a human or an animal that is starting to grow inside its mother

emerald /ˈemᵊrᵊld/ **noun**
a valuable bright green stone that is used in jewellery

emerge /ɪˈmɜːdʒ/ **verb** (**emerging**, **emerged**)
to appear from somewhere or come out of somewhere: *A figure* ***emerged from*** *the shadows.*

emergency /ɪˈmɜːdʒᵊnsi/ **noun** (plural **emergencies**)
B1 a serious or dangerous situation that needs immediate action: *In an emergency, call this number.* ◦ *an emergency exit*

emergency brake /ɪˈmɜːdʒᵊnsi ˌbreɪk/ **noun** US (UK **handbrake**)
a stick inside a car that you pull up to stop the car from moving

emergency room /ɪˈmɜːdʒᵊnsi ˌruːm/ **noun** US (UK **A&E**)
the part of a hospital where people go when they need treatment quickly: *She was taken to the emergency room.*

emigrate /ˈemɪgreɪt/ **verb** (**emigrating**, **emigrated**)
to leave your own country to live in a different one: *He* ***emigrated to*** *New Zealand.*
• **emigration** /ˌemɪˈgreɪʃᵊn/ **noun** [no plural]

emotion /ɪˈməʊʃᵊn/ **noun**
a strong feeling such as love or anger: *He finds it hard to express his emotions.*

emotional /ɪˈməʊʃᵊnᵊl/ **adj**
1 relating to emotions: *a child's emotional development*
2 showing strong feelings: *an emotional speech*
• **emotionally adv** *She spoke emotionally about her experiences as a nurse.*

emphasis /ˈemfəsɪs/ **noun** (plural **emphases** /ˈemfəsiːz/)
the particular importance or attention that you give to something: *Schools are starting to* ***place*** *greater* ***emphasis on*** *passing exams.*

emphasize /ˈemfəsaɪz/ **verb** (**emphasizing**, **emphasized**)
to show that something is important or needs special attention: *He emphasized the importance of learning foreign languages.*

empire /ˈempaɪəʳ/ **noun**
a group of countries that is ruled by one person or government

employ /ɪmˈplɔɪ/ **verb**
B1 to pay someone to work for you: *The company employs 2500 workers.*

employee /ɪmˈplɔɪiː/ **noun**
B1 someone who is paid to work for a person or company: *How many employees does the firm have?*

employer /ɪmˈplɔɪəʳ/ **noun**
B1 a person or company that pays people to work for them

employment /ɪmˈplɔɪmənt/ **noun** [no plural]
B1 work that a person or company pays you to do: *It is not easy to* ***find employment*** *in the countryside.*

empty[1] /ˈempti/ **adj** (**emptier**, **emptiest**)
A2 with nothing or no one inside: *an empty house* ◦ *empty bottles*
→ See picture at **full adj**
• **emptiness noun** [no plural]

empty[2] /ˈempti/ **verb** (**emptying**, **emptied**) (also **empty out**)
to remove everything that is inside something: *Where can I empty this ashtray?*

enable /ɪˈneɪbl/ **verb** (**enabling**, **enabled**)
to make someone able to do something: *This money enabled me to buy a new computer.*

enclose /ɪnˈkləʊz/ **verb** (**enclosing**, **enclosed**)
to send something in the same envelope or parcel as something else: *I enclose a map of the area.*

encourage /ɪnˈkʌrɪdʒ/ **verb** (**encouraging**, **encouraged**)
1 B1 to say good things to someone that will make them confident about doing something: *My parents* ***encouraged*** *me* ***to*** *try new things.*
2 B1 to make something more likely to happen: *We hope the new hotel will encourage tourism.*

encouragement /ɪnˈkʌrɪdʒmənt/ **noun** [no plural]
good things that you say to someone in order to make them more confident: *Children need lots of encouragement from their parents.*

end[1] /end/ **noun**
1 A1 the final part of something: *I'll pay you at the end of next month.*
2 A2 the furthest part: *They live at the other end of the street.*
3 in the end B1 finally: *We thought we might go away for Christmas, but in the end we stayed at home.*
4 a situation in which something stops happening or existing: *They are calling for* ***an end to*** *the violence.*
5 put an end to *something* to make something stop: *We must put an end to this violence.*

end[2] /end/ **verb**
A2 to stop, or to make something stop: *What time does the concert end?* ◦ *These talks do not look likely to end the war.*
end up phrasal verb
B1 to finally be in a particular place or situation: *He ended up in prison.*

ending /ˈendɪŋ/ **noun**
1 B1 the last part of a story: *I hope this movie has a happy ending.*
2 B1 a part added to the end of a word: *To make the plural of 'dog', you add the ending '-s'.*

endless /ˈendləs/ **adj**
never seeming to stop: *We used to have endless arguments about politics.*
• **endlessly adv**

endure /ɪnˈdjʊəʳ/ **verb** (**enduring**, **endured**) formal
to experience something difficult or unpleasant: *She's already had to endure three painful operations on her leg.*

enemy /ˈenəmi/ **noun** (plural **enemies**)
B1 a person or country that you are arguing or fighting with: *I try not to* ***make enemies.***

energetic /ˌenəˈdʒetɪk/ **adj**
having or needing a lot of energy: *an energetic young woman*

energy /ˈenədʒi/ **noun** [no plural]
1 B1 the ability to be very active without becoming tired: *Looking after children takes up a lot of time and energy.* ◦ *I didn't even have the energy to get out of bed.*
2 B1 the power that comes from electricity, gas, etc.: *nuclear energy*

engaged /ɪnˈgeɪdʒd/ **adj**
1 B1 If two people are engaged, they have agreed to marry each other: *When did they* ***get engaged****?*
2 B1 UK If a telephone line or a toilet is engaged, it is already being used.

engagement /ɪnˈgeɪdʒmənt/ **noun**
1 an agreement to get married to someone: *an engagement ring*
2 an arrangement to meet someone

engine /ˈendʒɪn/ **noun**
A2 the part of a vehicle that uses oil, electricity, or steam to make it move

engineer /ˌendʒɪˈnɪəʳ/ **noun**
A2 someone whose job is to design, build, or repair machines, roads, bridges, etc.: *a mechanical engineer*

engineering /ˌendʒɪˈnɪərɪŋ/ **noun** [no plural]
B1 the work of an engineer, or the study of this work

English /ˈɪŋglɪʃ/ **noun**

> **Common mistake: English**
>
> Remember that **English** is always written with a capital letter.

1 [no plural] the language that is spoken in the UK, the US, and in many other countries
2 **the English** the people of England

enjoy /ɪnˈdʒɔɪ/ **verb**
1 A1 If you enjoy something, it makes you feel happy: *I hope you enjoy your meal.* ◦ *I really enjoyed being with him.*
2 **enjoy** ***yourself*** A2 to like something that you are doing: *It was a great party – I really enjoyed myself.*

> **Common mistake: enjoy doing something**
>
> When **enjoy** is followed by a verb, the verb must be in the **-ing** form.
>
> *My parents enjoy walking in the mountains.*
>
> ~~*My parents enjoy to walk in the mountains.*~~

enjoyable /ɪnˈdʒɔɪəbl/ **adj**
B1 If something is enjoyable, it makes you feel happy: *We had a very enjoyable evening.*

enjoyment /ɪnˈdʒɔɪmənt/ **noun** [no plural]
the feeling of enjoying something: *She gets a lot of enjoyment from music.*

enlarge /ɪnˈlɑːdʒ/ **verb** (**enlarging**, **enlarged**)
to make something become bigger: *I want to get this photo enlarged.*

enormous /ɪˈnɔːməs/ **adj**
B1 very large: *They have an enormous house.*
• **enormously** **adv** very or very much: *The show was enormously popular.*

enough¹ /ɪˈnʌf/ **pronoun, quantifier**
1 A2 as much as you need: *Have you had enough to eat?* ◦ *She brought enough clothes for the trip.*
2 A2 as much as or more than is wanted: *Stop. You've made* ***enough of*** *a mess already.* ◦ *You've eaten* ***more than enough*** *already.*

enough² /ɪˈnʌf/ **adv**
1 A2 as much as you need: *Are you old enough to vote?* ◦ *You're not going fast enough.*
2 **funnily, strangely, etc. enough** although it may seem funny, strange, etc.: *Strangely enough, I was just speaking to him the other day.*

enquire (**enquiring**, **enquired**) UK (UK/US **inquire**) /ɪnˈkwaɪəʳ/ **verb**
to ask someone for information about something: *I* ***enquired about*** *dentists in the area.*

enquiry /ɪnˈkwaɪəri/ **noun** (plural **enquiries**)
another spelling of inquiry

en suite /ˌɒn ˈswiːt/ **adj** UK
An en suite bathroom is directly connected to a bedroom.

ensure /ɪnˈʃɔːʳ/ **verb** (**ensuring**, **ensured**)
to make certain that something happens: *Please* ***ensure that*** *you have completed the forms correctly.*

enter /ˈentəʳ/ **verb**
1 A2 to go into a place: *The police entered by the back door.*
2 B1 to put information into a computer, book, or document: *You have to enter a password to access this file.*
3 B1 to do a competition: *Are you going to enter the photography competition?*

entertain /ˌentəˈteɪn/ **verb**
1 B1 to keep someone interested and help them to have an enjoyable time: *We hired a clown to entertain the children.*
2 to invite someone to be your guest and give them food and drink: *We don't entertain as much as we used to.*

entertainer /ˌentəˈteɪnəʳ/ **noun**
someone whose job is to make people laugh and enjoy themselves by singing, telling jokes, etc.

entertaining /ˌentəˈteɪnɪŋ/ **adj**
interesting and helping someone to have an enjoyable time: *an entertaining and informative book*

entertainment /ˌentəˈteɪnmənt/ **noun** [no plural]
B1 shows, movies, television, or other performances or activities that entertain people: *There is live entertainment in the bar every night.*

enthusiasm /ɪnˈθjuːziæzᵊm/ **noun** [no plural]
a feeling of interest and excitement about something: *She has always had a lot of* ***enthusiasm for*** *her work.*

enthusiastic /ɪnˌθjuːziˈæstɪk/ **adj**
showing enthusiasm: *The teacher was very* ***enthusiastic about*** *my project.*
• **enthusiastically** **adv** *Everyone cheered enthusiastically.*

entire /ɪnˈtaɪəʳ/ **adj**
whole or complete: *She spent her entire life caring for other people.*

entirely /ɪnˈtaɪəli/ **adv**
completely: *It was entirely my fault.*

entrance /ˈentrəns/ **noun**
1 A2 a door or other opening that you use to go in somewhere: *I'll meet you* ***at the*** *main* ***entrance****.*
2 B1 [no plural] the right to enter a place or join an organization: *Entrance is free, but you have to pay for your drinks.*
3 the act of going into a place: *Everyone went quiet when he* ***made his entrance*** *(= came in).*

entry /ˈentri/ **noun**
1 B1 (plural **entries**) a piece of work that you do to try to win a competition: *The first ten correct entries will receive a prize.*
2 B1 (plural **entries**) a separate piece of information that is recorded in a dictionary, diary, or list: *Dictionary entries are arranged in alphabetical order.*
3 B1 [no plural] the right or ability to come into or go into a place: *There's free entry to the exhibition for students after 6 p.m.*
4 B1 [no plural] the act of joining an organization or taking part in a competition: *Have you filled in your* ***entry form*** *yet?*

envelope /ˈenvələʊp/ **noun**
A2 a flat paper container for a letter
→ See **The Office** on page C12

envious /ˈenviəs/ **adj**
wanting something that someone else has: *She was* ***envious of*** *his success.*

environment /ɪnˈvaɪərᵊnmənt/ **noun**
1 **the environment** B1 the air, land, and water where people, animals, and plants live: *The new road may cause damage to the environment.*
2 the situation that you live or work in, and how it changes how you feel: *We are working in a very competitive environment.*

a b c d e f g h i j k l m n o p q r s t u v w x y z

environmental /ɪnˌvaɪərᵊnˈmentᵊl/ **adj**
B1 relating to the environment: *environmental issues*
• **environmentally** **adv** ***environmentally friendly*** *products (= that do not harm the environment)*

envy¹ /ˈenvi/ **noun** [no plural]
the feeling of wanting something that someone else has: *I watched with envy as he climbed into his brand new car.*

envy² /ˈenvi/ **verb** (**envying**, **envied**)
to want something that someone else has: *I envy her good looks.*

epic /ˈepɪk/ **noun**
a story or movie that is very long and has a lot of action

epidemic /ˌepɪˈdemɪk/ **noun**
a situation in which a large number of people get the same disease at the same time: *the AIDS epidemic*

episode /ˈepɪsəʊd/ **noun**
one of the parts into which a story is divided, mainly on television or radio: *Did you see last week's episode of The Vampire Diaries?*

equal¹ /ˈiːkwəl/ **adj**
1 B1 the same in amount, number, or size: *The sides are of equal length.* ◦ *One metre is* ***equal to*** *39.37 inches.*
2 the same in importance and deserving the same treatment: *All people are equal.*

equal² /ˈiːkwəl/ **verb** (**equalling**, **equalled**)
to have the same value, size, etc. as something else, often shown using a symbol (=): *Two plus two equals four.*

equal³ /ˈiːkwəl/ **noun**
someone who has the same ability or rights as someone else: *The teacher treats us all as equals.*

equality /ɪˈkwɒləti/ **noun** [no plural]
a situation in which everyone is equal and has the same rights: *racial/sexual equality*

equator /ɪˈkweɪtəʳ/ **noun** [no plural]
the imaginary line around the Earth that divides it into equal north and south parts

equip /ɪˈkwɪp/ **verb** (**equipping**, **equipped**)
be equipped with ***something*** to include the things that are needed for a particular purpose: *The new trains are equipped with all the latest technology.*

equipment /ɪˈkwɪpmənt/ **noun**
1 B1 [no plural] the things that are used for an activity or purpose: *kitchen/office equipment*
2 **a piece of equipment** a tool or object used for an activity or purpose

er /ɜːʳ/ **exclamation** UK spoken
something that you say while you are thinking what to say next: *Well, er, I'm not too sure about that.*

era /ˈɪərə/ **noun**
a period of time in history that is special for a particular reason: *the Victorian era* ◦ *a new era of peace*

eraser /ɪˈreɪzəʳ/ **noun**
a small object that is used to remove pencil marks from paper
→ See **The Classroom** on page C4

erotic /ɪˈrɒtɪk/ **adj**
making you feel strong sexual feelings: *an erotic movie*

errand /ˈerənd/ **noun**
a short journey to a place such as a shop to buy or do something for yourself or someone else: *I need to* ***run*** *a few* ***errands*** *this morning.*

error /ˈerəʳ/ **noun**
a mistake: *a computer error/human error* ◦ *to* ***make*** *an* ***error***

erupt /ɪˈrʌpt/ **verb**
If a volcano erupts, it suddenly throws out fire and melted rocks.
• **eruption** /ɪˈrʌpʃᵊn/ **noun** *a volcanic eruption*

escalator

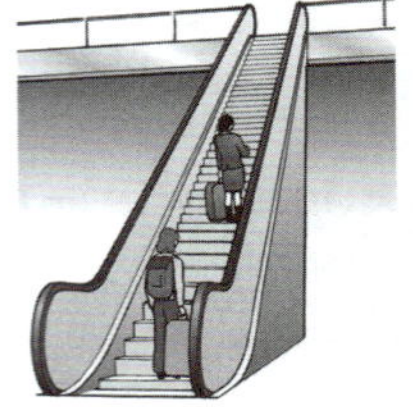

escalator /ˈeskəleɪtəʳ/ **noun**
moving stairs that take people from one level of a building to another: *We took the escal-*

a b c d e f g h i j k l m n o p q r s t u v w x y z

ator down to the basement.

escape[1] /ɪˈskeɪp/ **verb** (**escaping, escaped**)
1 B1 to succeed in getting away from a place where you do not want to be: *The two killers* ***escaped from*** *prison last night.*
2 to avoid a dangerous or unpleasant situation: *She was lucky to escape serious injury.*

escape[2] /ɪˈskeɪp/ **noun**
a successful attempt to get out of a place or a dangerous or bad situation: *He made his escape while no one was watching.*

especially /ɪˈspeʃəli/ **adv**
1 A2 more than other things or people: *I liked all the food but I especially liked the dessert.*
2 for one particular person, purpose, or reason: *I cooked this meal* ***especially for*** *you.*

essay /ˈeseɪ/ **noun**
B1 a short piece of writing about a subject, especially one written by a student: *He wrote an* ***essay on*** *modern Japanese literature.*

essential /ɪˈsenʃəl/ **adj**
B1 very important and necessary: *Computers are an essential part of our lives.* ◦ *It is absolutely* ***essential that*** *she gets this message.*

establish /ɪˈstæblɪʃ/ **verb**
to start a company or organization that will continue for a long time: *The company was established in 1822.*

estate /ɪˈsteɪt/ **noun**
1 a large area of land in the country that is owned by a family or an organization and is often used for growing crops or keeping animals: *a country estate*
2 an area with a lot of buildings of the same type: *an industrial estate (= a group of factories)*

estate agent /ɪˈsteɪt ˌeɪdʒənt/ **noun**
UK (US **real estate agent**)
someone who sells buildings and land as their job

estimate[1] /ˈestɪmət/ **noun**
a guess of what the size, value, amount, cost, etc. of something might be: *This is only a* ***rough estimate****.*

estimate[2] /ˈestɪmeɪt/ **verb** (**estimating, estimated**)
to guess the cost, size, or value of something: *They* ***estimate that*** *90 people were killed in the accident.*

etc. /etˈsetərə/
used after a list of words to show that other similar words could be added: *This shelf here is for pens, paper, etc.*

eternal /ɪˈtɜːnəl/ **adj**
continuing forever: *eternal youth*

euro /ˈjʊərəʊ/ **noun**
A2 a unit of money that is used in many European countries; €

eve /iːv/ **noun**
Christmas Eve/New Year's Eve the day or night before Christmas Day or New Year's Day

even[1] /ˈiːvən/ **adj**
flat, level, or smooth: *Find an even surface to work on.*
→ Opposite **uneven** adj

even[2] /ˈiːvən/ **adv**
1 A2 used to emphasize something that is surprising: *Everyone danced, even Mick.* ◦ *I said hello, but he didn't even look at me.*
2 **even better, faster, smaller, etc.** B1 used when comparing things, to emphasize the difference: *Alex will be even taller than his father.*
3 **even if** used to say that nothing will change if something happens: *Even if you take a taxi, you'll still miss your train.*
4 **even though** although: *He went to work even though he wasn't well.*

evening /ˈiːvnɪŋ/ **noun**
A1 the part of the day between the afternoon and the night: *Are you doing anything this evening?*

evening class /ˈiːvnɪŋ ˌklɑːs/ **noun**
a class for adult students that happens in the evening: *I've been going to evening classes to improve my Spanish.*

evenly /ˈiːvənli/ **adv**
into equal amounts: *They divided the prize money evenly between them.*

even number /ˌiːvᵊn ˈnʌmbəʳ/ **noun**
a number that can be exactly divided by two, for example four, six, or eight
→ Opposite **odd number** noun

event /ɪˈvent/ **noun**
1 B1 something that happens, especially something important or strange: *Local people have been shocked by recent events in the town.*
2 B1 a race, party, competition, etc. that has been organized for a particular time: *They organize a lot of **social events**.*

eventually /ɪˈventʃuəli/ **adv**
in the end, especially after a long time: *We all hope that an agreement can be reached eventually.*

ever /ˈevəʳ/ **adv**
1 A2 at any time: *Have you ever been skiing?* ◦ *No one ever calls me.*
2 ever since B1 always since that time: *We met at school and have been friends ever since.*
3 hardly ever B1 almost never: *We hardly ever go out these days.*
4 for ever UK B1 for all time in the future: *I'm not going to live here for ever.*
→ See also **forever**
5 ever so/ever such a very/a very: *It was ever so kind of you to meet us at the airport.* ◦ *She's ever such a good dancer.*

every /ˈevri/ **determiner**
1 A1 each one of a group of people or things: *He knows the name of every child in the school.*
2 A1 used to show that something is repeated regularly: *They go camping every summer.*

everybody /ˈevriˌbɒdi/ **pronoun**
A2 another word for everyone

everyone /ˈevriwʌn/ **pronoun** (also **everybody**)
A2 every person: *I've received a reply from everyone now.* ◦ *Everyone agreed with the decision.*

everything /ˈevriθɪŋ/ **pronoun**
1 A2 all things or each thing: *They lost everything in the fire.* ◦ *What's the matter, Nick, is everything all right?*
2 everything else all the other things: *The meat tasted strange, but everything else was okay.*

everywhere /ˈevriweəʳ/ **adv**
A2 in or to every place: *I've looked everywhere, but I still can't find that letter.*

evidence /ˈevɪdᵊns/ **noun** [no plural]
1 something that makes you believe that something is true or exists: ***evidence of** global warming* ◦ *There is no scientific evidence that the drug is harmful.*
2 information that is given or things that are shown in a court of law to help to prove that someone has done a crime: *He was arrested despite the lack of **evidence against** him.*
3 give evidence to give information and answer questions in a court of law: *She was called to give evidence at his trial.*

evident /ˈevɪdᵊnt/ **adj** formal
obvious to everyone and easy to see or understand: *It was evident from his voice that he was upset.*

evil[1] /ˈiːvᵊl/ **adj**
very bad and cruel: *an evil monster*

evil[2] /ˈiːvᵊl/ **noun** [no plural]
a force that is very bad or makes bad things happen: *The theme of the play is the battle between good and evil.*

evolution /ˌiːvəˈluːʃᵊn/ **noun** [no plural]
1 the way in which living things gradually change and develop over millions of years: *Darwin's theory of evolution*
2 a gradual process of change and development: *the **evolution of** language* ◦ *the painter's artistic evolution*

ex- /eks-/ **prefix**
used to show that someone is no longer what they were: *my ex-girlfriend*

exact /ɪgˈzækt/ **adj**
B1 completely correct: *I don't know the exact price.*

exactly /ɪgˈzæktli/ **adv**
1 A2 used when you are giving or asking for information that is completely correct: *What exactly is the*

a b c d e f g h i j k l m n o p q r s t u v w x y z

problem? ◦ The train got in at exactly ten o'clock.
2 B1 used to make stronger what you are saying: *I found a dress that's exactly the same colour as my shoes.*
3 something you say when you agree completely with someone: *'Surely they should have told us about this problem sooner?' 'Exactly.'*
4 not exactly used to say that something is not completely true: *'Did you give her your book?' 'Not exactly, I lent it to her.'*

exaggerate /ɪgˈzædʒəreɪt/ **verb** (**exaggerating, exaggerated**)
to make something seem larger, better, or worse than it really is: *Don't exaggerate – it didn't cost that much!*

exam /ɪgˈzæm/ **noun**
A2 an official test of how much you know about something, or how well you can do something: *a maths exam ◦ to fail/pass an exam*

examination /ɪgˌzæmɪˈneɪʃən/ **noun**
1 A2 formal an exam: *a written examination*
2 the process of looking at something very carefully: *a medical examination*

examine /ɪgˈzæmɪn/ **verb** (**examining, examined**)
1 to look at someone or something very carefully, especially to try to discover something: *She picked up the knife and examined it carefully.*
2 formal to test someone to see how much they know or how well they can do something: *You'll be examined in three main areas: speaking, listening, and reading.*

examiner /ɪgˈzæmɪnər/ **noun**
B1 someone who tests how much you know about something, or how well you can do something

example /ɪgˈzɑːmpl/ **noun**
1 A1 something that is typical of the group of things that you are talking about: *This is a good* ***example of*** *the architecture of the period.*
2 for example A1 used to give an example of what you are talking about: *Some people, students for example, can get cheaper tickets.*

exceed /ɪkˈsiːd/ **verb**
to be more than a particular number or amount: *Sales have exceeded $1 million so far this year.*

excellent /ˈeksələnt/ **adj**
A2 very good, or of a very high quality: *That was an excellent meal.*

except /ɪkˈsept/ **preposition**
A2 not including a particular fact, thing, or person: *He works every day except Sunday. ◦ Everyone passed the exam* ***except for*** *Camilla.*

exception /ɪkˈsepʃən/ **noun**
1 someone or something that is not included in a rule, group, or list: *There are* ***exceptions to*** *every rule. ◦ I like all kinds of movies,* ***with the exception of*** *horror movies.*
2 make an exception to treat someone differently from all other people: *I don't usually accept credit cards but for you I'll make an exception.*

exceptional /ɪkˈsepʃənəl/ **adj**
very good and better than most other people or things: *an exceptional student*
• **exceptionally adv** *an exceptionally clever child*

excess /ɪkˈses/ **noun**
more of something than is usual or needed: *There's a charge for* ***excess baggage*** *on a plane.*

exchange[1] /ɪksˈtʃeɪndʒ/ **noun**
1 B1 an occasion when you give something to someone and they give you something else: *an* ***exchange of*** *ideas ◦ They were given food and shelter* ***in exchange for*** *work.*
2 B1 a period when students and teachers from one country go to stay with students and teachers in another: *I have happy memories of going on an exchange to France.*

exchange[2] /ɪksˈtʃeɪndʒ/ **verb** (**exchanging, exchanged**)
1 B1 to give something to someone and get something similar from them: *The two teams usually exchange shirts after the game.*
2 to take something back to the shop where you bought it and get some-

a b c d e f g h i j k l m n o p q r s t u v w x y z

thing else: *Could I **exchange** this shirt **for** a larger size?*
3 exchange looks, opinions, views, etc. If two people exchange looks, opinions, views, etc., they look at each other, talk to each other, etc.: *The group meets every month to exchange views on a book they have all read.*

exchange rate /ɪks'tʃeɪndʒ ˌreɪt/ **noun**
B1 how much of a country's money you can buy with a particular amount of another country's money

excited /ɪk'saɪtɪd/ **adj**
A1 feeling very happy and interested, or showing this: *happy, excited faces* ◦ *The children are getting really **excited about** the party.*
• **excitedly adv** B1 *She ran excitedly to meet her cousins.*

> **Common mistake: excited or exciting?**
>
> **Excited** is used to describe how someone feels.
> *She was very excited about the visit.*
> ~~*She was very exciting about the visit.*~~
> **Exciting** is used to describe the thing that makes you excited.
> *I've had some exciting news!*

excitement /ɪk'saɪtmənt/ **noun** [no plural]
B1 a feeling of happiness and interest: *The competition is causing a lot of excitement.*

exciting /ɪk'saɪtɪŋ/ **adj**
A1 making you feel very happy and interested: *an exciting football match* ◦ *You're going to Africa? How exciting!*

exclamation /ˌekskləˈmeɪʃᵊn/ **noun**
something that you say loudly and suddenly because you are surprised or angry: *an exclamation of delight*

exclamation mark /ˌekskləˈmeɪʃᵊn ˌmɑːk/ **noun**
a mark (!) used at the end of a sentence to show surprise or excitement

exclude /ɪks'kluːd/ **verb** (**excluding, excluded**)
1 to not allow someone or something to do an activity or enter a place: *Women are still **excluded from** the club.*
2 to not include something: *The insurance cover excludes particular medical conditions.*

excluding /ɪks'kluːdɪŋ/ **preposition**
not including: *That's $600 per person for seven days, excluding travel costs.*

exclusive /ɪks'kluːsɪv/ **adj**
expensive and only for people who are rich or important: *an exclusive club*

excuse[1] /ɪk'skjuːz/ **verb** (**excusing, excused**)
1 B1 to forgive someone for something that is not very serious: *Please excuse my appearance, I've been painting.*
2 to say that someone does not have to do something: *Could I be excused from football training today?*
3 excuse me A1 used to politely get someone's attention: *Excuse me, does this bus go to Oxford Street?*
4 excuse me A2 used to say sorry for something that you have done: *Oh, excuse me, did I take your seat?*

excuse[2] /ɪk'skjuːs/ **noun**
1 B1 a reason that you give to explain why you did something wrong: *I hope he's got a good **excuse for** being so late.*
2 B1 a false reason that you give to explain why you do something: *Nick was just looking for an excuse to call her.*

execute /'eksɪkjuːt/ **verb** (**executing, executed**)
to kill someone as a legal punishment: *He was executed for murder.*

execution /ˌeksɪ'kjuːʃᵊn/ **noun**
the killing of someone as a legal punishment

executive /ɪg'zekjətɪv/ **noun**
someone who has an important job in a business

exercise[1] /'eksəsaɪz/ **noun**
1 A2 activity that you do with your body to make your body strong: *Swimming is my favourite form of exercise.*
2 A2 a piece of written work that helps you learn something: *For your homework, do exercise 3 on page 24.*

exercise[2] /ˈeksəsaɪz/ **verb** (**exercising**, **exercised**)
A2 to do activities with your body to make your body strong and healthy: *I try to exercise every day.*

exercise book /ˈeksəsaɪz ˌbʊk/ **noun**
a book that students use at school for writing in
→ See **The Classroom** on page C4

exhausted /ɪɡˈzɔːstɪd/ **adj**
B1 very tired: *He looks exhausted.*

exhausting /ɪɡˈzɔːstɪŋ/ **adj**
making you feel very tired: *What an exhausting day!*

exhaustion /ɪɡˈzɔːstʃən/ **noun** [no plural]
a feeling of being very tired: *The star was suffering from exhaustion.*

exhibition /ˌeksɪˈbɪʃən/ **noun**
B1 an event at which things such as paintings are shown to the public: *There's a new* ***exhibition of*** *sculpture on at the city gallery.*

exile /ˈeksaɪl/ **noun** [no plural]
a situation in which someone has to leave their home and live in another country, often for political reasons: *He spent the war years* ***in exile*** *in Paris.*

exist /ɪɡˈzɪst/ **verb**
B1 to be real or present: *Poverty still exists in this country.*

existence /ɪɡˈzɪstəns/ **noun** [no plural]
the fact of something or someone existing: *The theatre company that we started is still* ***in existence*** *today.*

exit[1] /ˈeksɪt/ **noun**
1 A2 a door, window, or other opening that allows you to leave a structure or a vehicle: *a fire exit* ◦ *a plane's emergency exits*
2 A2 a road that you use to leave another, larger road such as a motorway: ***Take*** *the third* ***exit*** *and follow the signs to the park.*

exit[2] /ˈeksɪt/ **verb**
1 B1 to stop using a program on a computer: *Press 'escape' to exit the game.*
2 to leave a place: *Please exit by the side doors.*

exotic /ɪɡˈzɒtɪk/ **adj**
unusual, interesting, and often foreign: *exotic fruit*

expand /ɪkˈspænd/ **verb**
to get larger, or to make something get larger: *The company has expanded.*

expansion /ɪkˈspænʃən/ **noun** [no plural]
the action of getting larger: *the rapid expansion of the software industry*

expect /ɪkˈspekt/ **verb**
1 B1 to think that something will happen: *He didn't* ***expect to*** *see me.* ◦ *I* ***expect that*** *she'll be very angry about this.*
2 be expecting ***someone/something*** B1 to be waiting for someone or something to arrive: *We've been expecting you.*
3 to think that someone should do a particular thing: *You will be* ***expected to*** *work some weekends.*
4 I expect mainly UK used to show that you think that something is true: *'Will you be coming to the party?'* ***'I expect so.'***
5 be expecting to be going to have a baby: *I'm expecting my first baby in May.*

expedition /ˌekspɪˈdɪʃən/ **noun**
B1 an organized journey, especially a long one for a particular purpose: *Peary led the first expedition to the North Pole.*

expel /ɪkˈspel/ **verb** (**expelling**, **expelled**)
to make someone leave a school, organization, or country: *He was* ***expelled from*** *school* ***for*** *fighting.*

expense /ɪkˈspens/ **noun**
the money that you spend on something: *You have to pay your own medical expenses.*

expensive /ɪkˈspensɪv/ **adj**
A1 costing a lot of money: *expensive jewellery*
→ Opposite **cheap** adj
• **expensively** **adv** *expensively dressed*

experience[1] /ɪkˈspɪəriəns/ **noun**
1 B1 [no plural] knowledge that you get from doing a job, or from doing, seeing, or feeling something: *Do you*

have any ***experience of*** working with children? ◦ He knows ***from experience*** how difficult she can be.

2 B1 something that happens to you that affects how you feel: *My trip was an experience I'll never forget.*

experience[2] /ɪkˈspɪəriəns/ **verb** (**experiencing**, **experienced**)
B1 If you experience something, it happens to you, or you feel it: *It was the worst pain I had ever experienced.*

experienced /ɪkˈspɪəriənst/ **adj**
B1 having skill and knowledge because you have done something many times: *Karsten's a very experienced ski instructor.*
→ Opposite **inexperienced adj**

experiment[1] /ɪkˈsperɪmənt/ **noun**
B1 a test, especially a scientific one, that you do in order to discover if something is true: *We **do** lots of **experiments** in class.*

experiment[2] /ɪkˈsperɪment/ **verb**
1 to try something in order to discover what it is like: *Did he ever **experiment with** drugs?*
2 to do an experiment: *He's against **experimenting on** animals.*

expert[1] /ˈekspɜːt/ **noun**
B1 someone who has a lot of skill in something or a lot of knowledge about something: *He's **an expert on** Japanese literature.*

expert[2] /ˈekspɜːt/ **adj**
having or showing a lot of knowledge or skill: *He's an expert fisherman.*

explain /ɪkˈspleɪn/ **verb**
A2 to make something clear or easy to understand by giving reasons for it: *Can you **explain why** you did this?* ◦ *Can you **explain to** me how this phone works?* ◦ *He **explained that** he was going to stay with his sister.*

> **Common mistake: explain something**
>
> **Explain** is followed by the thing you are explaining.
> *I'll explain the situation.*
> Remember to use the preposition **to** before a person.
> *I'll explain the situation to my parents.*
> ~~*I'll explain my parents the situation.*~~

explanation /ˌekspləˈneɪʃᵊn/ **noun**
B1 the details or reasons that someone gives to make something clear or easy to understand: *What's your **explanation for** the team's poor performance?* ◦ *Could you give me a quick **explanation of** how it works?*

explode /ɪkˈspləʊd/ **verb** (**exploding**, **exploded**)
B1 If a bomb explodes, it bursts with noise and force: *One of the bombs did not explode.*

explore /ɪkˈsplɔːʳ/ **verb** (**exploring**, **explored**)
1 B1 to go around a place where you have never been in order to find out what is there: *The children love exploring.* ◦ *The best way to explore the countryside is on foot.*
2 to find out more about something, especially something that you might do in the future: *We're exploring the possibility of buying a house abroad.*
• **exploration** /ˌekspləˈreɪʃᵊn/ **noun** *She's always loved travel and exploration.*

explorer /ɪkˈsplɔːrəʳ/ **noun**
someone who travels to places where no one has ever been in order to find out what is there

explosion /ɪkˈspləʊʒᵊn/ **noun**
the action of something such as a bomb exploding: *Forty people were killed in the explosion.*

explosive /ɪkˈspləʊsɪv/ **adj**
able to cause an explosion: *The explosive device was hidden in a suitcase.*

export[1] /ˈekspɔːt/ **noun**
a product that you sell in another country: *Scottish beef exports to Japan*
→ Opposite **import**

export[2] /ɪkˈspɔːt/ **verb**
to send goods to another country in order to sell them there: *Singapore exports large quantities of rubber.*
→ Opposite **import**
• **exporter noun** *Brazil is the world's largest exporter of coffee.*

expose /ɪkˈspəʊz/ **verb** (**exposing**, **exposed**)
1 to show something by removing its

a b c d e f g h i j k l m n o p q r s t u v w x y z

cover: *He removed the bandage to expose the wound.*
2 be exposed to *something* to experience something or be affected by something: *It was the first time I'd been exposed to violence.*

express /ɪkˈspres/ **verb**
to show what you think or how you feel using words or actions: *I'm simply expressing my opinion.*

expression /ɪkˈspreʃən/ **noun**
1 the look on someone's face showing what they feel or think: *He had a sad expression on his face.*
2 a group of words that has a special meaning: *'A can of worms' is an expression meaning 'a difficult situation'.*

extend /ɪkˈstend/ **verb**
1 to make something bigger or longer: *We're going to extend our kitchen.*
2 to make an activity, agreement, etc. last for a longer time: *They have extended the deadline by one week.*

extension /ɪkˈstenʃən/ **noun**
1 a telephone that is connected to the main telephone in an office or other large building: *Call me **on extension** 3104.*
2 extra time that you are given to do or use something: *I've applied for an **extension to** my visa.*
3 UK a new room or rooms that are added to a building: *You could build an extension on to the back of the house.*

extensive /ɪkˈstensɪv/ **adj**
large in amount or size: *Fire caused extensive damage to the building.*

extent /ɪkˈstent/ **noun** [no plural]
1 the size or importance of something: *They are just beginning to realize the full extent of the damage.*
2 to a great, large, etc. extent mainly: *Her book is based to a large extent on real events.*
3 to some extent/to a certain extent used to say that something is true, but is not the whole truth: *To some extent she was responsible for the accident.* ◦ *I agree with you to a certain extent.*

exterior /ɪkˈstɪəriəʳ/ **noun**
the outside part of something or someone: *The exterior of the house was painted white.*
• **exterior adj** *an exterior wall*
→ Opposite **interior noun**

external /ɪkˈstɜːnəl/ **adj**
1 relating to the outside part of something: *the external walls of the house*
→ Opposite **internal adj**
2 coming from or relating to another country, group, organization, etc.: *We don't want any external interference in our affairs.*
• **externally adv** *The cream should only be **applied externally** (= on the skin).*

extinct /ɪkˈstɪŋkt/ **adj**
If a type of animal is extinct, it does not now exist.

extinguish /ɪkˈstɪŋgwɪʃ/ **verb**
to make something stop burning: *The fire took two hours to extinguish.*

extra[1] /ˈekstrə/ **adj**
A2 more, or more than usual: *Can I invite a few extra people?*

extra[2] /ˈekstrə/ **adv**
B1 more: *They pay her extra for working late.*

extra[3] /ˈekstrə/ **noun**
B1 something that you can get with something else if you pay a little more money: *The car comes with **optional extras** such as a CD player.*

extract[1] /ɪkˈstrækt/ **verb** formal
to remove or take something out, especially using force: *He's going to the dentist's to have a tooth extracted.*

extract[2] /ˈekstrækt/ **noun**
a short part taken from a book, poem, etc.: *The teacher read out an extract from 'Brave New World'.*

extraordinary /ɪkˈstrɔːdənəri/ **adj**
B1 very special or strange: *She was an extraordinary young woman.*
• **extraordinarily adv** *She is extraordinarily (= very) beautiful.*

extravagant /ɪkˈstrævəgənt/ **adj**
spending too much money: *the extravagant lifestyle of a movie star*

extreme /ɪkˈstriːm/ **adj**
1 the worst or most serious: *extreme weather conditions*

a b c d e f g h i j k l m n o p q r s t u v w x y z

2 very large in amount or degree: *extreme pain*
3 at the furthest point of something: *in the extreme south of the island*

extremely /ɪkˈstriːmli/ **adv**
B1 very: *extremely beautiful* ◦ *He works extremely hard.*

extreme sports /ɪkˌstriːm ˈspɔːts/ **noun**
B1 activities that are exciting and dangerous: *I love most extreme sports, such as snowboarding.*

eye /aɪ/ **noun**
1 A1 one of the two organs in your face that you use to see with: *Sara has black hair and brown eyes.* ◦ *She closed her eyes and fell asleep.*

eye

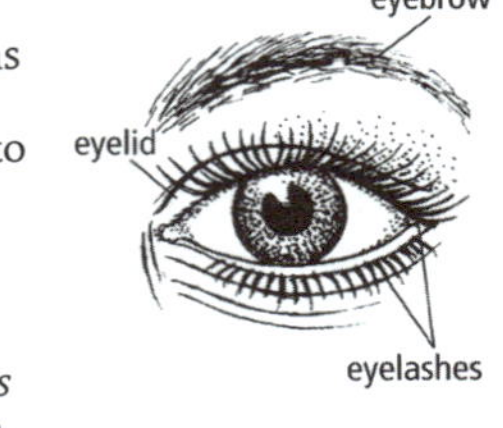

2 the small hole at the end of a needle that you put the thread through
3 keep an eye on *someone/something* to watch or look after someone or something: *Could you keep an eye on the kids for a moment?*
4 in *someone's* eyes in someone's opinion: *In my parents' eyes, I'll always be a child.*

eyebrow /ˈaɪbraʊ/ **noun**
the thin line of hair that is above each eye

eyelash /ˈaɪlæʃ/ **noun** (also **lash**)
one of the short hairs that grow from the edge of your eyelids: *false eyelashes*

eyelid /ˈaɪlɪd/ **noun**
the piece of skin that covers your eyes when you close them

eyesight /ˈaɪsaɪt/ **noun** [no plural]
the ability to see: *My eyesight is getting worse.*

Ff

F, f /ef/
the sixth letter of the alphabet

F
written abbreviation for Fahrenheit: a measurement of temperature: *a body temperature of 98.6°F*

fable /ˈfeɪbl/ **noun**
a short story that shows people how to behave

fabric /ˈfæbrɪk/ **noun**
cloth: *a light cotton fabric*

fabulous /ˈfæbjələs/ **adj**
very good: *They've got a fabulous house.*

face[1] /feɪs/ **noun**
1 A1 the front part of the head where the eyes, nose, and mouth are: *She's got a long, thin face.*
2 the front or surface of something: *the north face of the mountain* ◦ *a clock face*
3 face to face B1 being with someone in the same place: *We need to talk face to face.*
4 make a face B1 to show with your face that you do not like someone or something: *Joe made a face when he saw what was for lunch.*
5 to *someone's* face If you say something to someone's face, you say it to them directly, when you are with them: *If you have something to say, say it to my face.*

face

face[2] /feɪs/ **verb** (**facing**, **faced**)
1 B1 to be or turn in a particular direction: *The room faces south.* ◦ *She turned to face him.*
2 to have a problem: *Passengers could face long delays.*
3 to accept that something unpleasant is true and start to deal with the situation: *I think he has to* ***face the fact that*** *she no longer loves him.*
4 let's face it used before you say something that is bad but true: *Let's face it, we are not going to win this game.*
5 can't face (doing) *something* to not want to do something or deal with something because it is difficult or unpleasant: *I can't face walking up all those steps again.*
face up to *something* **phrasal verb**
to accept that a difficult situation exists and is something you must deal with: *Eventually he faced up to his money problems.*

face-to-face /ˌfeɪstəˈfeɪs/ **adj**
B1 between people who are in the same place: *a face-to-face meeting*

facilities /fəˈsɪlətiz/ **plural noun**
B1 buildings, equipment, or services that are provided for a particular purpose: *sports/washing facilities*

fact /fækt/ **noun**
1 A2 something that you know is true, exists, or has happened: *No decision will be made until we know all the facts.* ◦ *The real problem is* ***the fact that*** *we cannot agree.*
2 in fact/in actual fact B1 used to say what is really true: *I was told there were some tickets left, but in actual fact they were sold out.*
3 real events and experiences, not things that are imagined: *The movie is based on historical facts.*
4 the fact is used to tell someone that something is the truth: *The fact is that we don't have enough money.*

factor /ˈfæktər/ **noun**
one of the things that has an effect on a particular situation, decision, event, etc.: *Safety is an important* ***factor in*** *car design.*

factory /ˈfæktəri/ **noun** (plural **factories**)
A1 a building or group of buildings where things are made or put together: *a toy factory*

fade /feɪd/ **verb** (**fading**, **faded**)
If a colour or sound fades, it gradually becomes less bright or strong: *The music fades at the end of the song.*
fade away **phrasal verb**
to gradually become less strong or clear and then disappear: *As the years*

a b c d e f g h i j k l m n o p q r s t u v w x y z

a b c d e f g h i j k l m n o p q r s t u v w x y z

passed, her memories of her childhood faded away.

Fahrenheit /ˈfærᵊnhaɪt/ **noun** [no plural] (written abbreviation **F**)
a measurement of temperature in which water freezes at 32° and boils at 212°

fail /feɪl/ **verb**
1 A2 to not pass a test or an exam: *I've just failed my driving test.*
2 to not be successful: *Dad's business failed after just three years.*
→ Opposite **succeed** verb
3 fail to do *something* to not do what is expected: *He failed to turn up for football practice yesterday.*
4 to stop working normally, or to become weaker: *The brakes failed and the car crashed into a tree.*

failure /ˈfeɪljəʳ/ **noun**
1 [no plural] a situation in which someone or something does not succeed: *Their attempt to climb the mountain ended in failure.*
2 someone or something that does not succeed: *I felt like a failure after losing the race.*
→ Opposite **success** noun
3 [no plural] a situation in which you do not do something that you are expected to do: ***Failure to** pay within 14 days will result in a fine.*

faint¹ /feɪnt/ **adj**
1 slight and not easy to notice: *a faint smell of smoke*
2 feel faint to feel very weak and as if you might fall down: *Seeing all the blood made me feel faint.*

faint² /feɪnt/ **verb**
to suddenly become unconscious for a short time

fair¹ /feəʳ/ **adj**
1 A2 Fair hair or skin, or a person who has it, is pale or light in colour: *a boy with fair hair*
→ See **Hair** on page C9
2 B1 treating everyone in the same way: *a fair trial*
→ Opposite **unfair**
3 B1 acceptable, reasonable, or right: *He offered me a fair price for the car.*
4 a fair amount, number, etc. a fairly large amount, number, etc.: *There's still a fair amount of work to be done on the house.*
5 good, but not very good: *He has a fair chance of winning.*
6 sunny and not raining
7 fair enough used for saying that you can understand and accept someone's opinion or decision: *'He says he'll only work on Sunday if he gets paid extra.' 'Fair enough.'*

fair² /feəʳ/ **noun**
B1 a place outside where you can ride on big machines for pleasure and play games to win prizes

fair

fairly /ˈfeəli/ **adv**
1 B1 more than average, but less than very: *a fairly large family*
2 done in a fair or honest way: *The company says that all of its workers are treated fairly.*

fairness /ˈfeənəs/ **noun** [no plural]
the fact of treating everyone in the same way

fairy /ˈfeəri/ **noun** (plural **fairies**)
a small, imaginary person with wings who has magic powers

fairy

fairy tale /ˈfeəri ˌteɪl/ **noun**
a story told to children that has magic in it and a happy ending

faith /feɪθ/ **noun**
1 [no plural] the belief that someone or something is good and can be trusted: *I have great **faith in** her ability to do well in the exam.*
2 a religion: *the Jewish faith*
3 [no plural] strong belief in a god or gods: *Throughout her illness, she never lost her **faith in** God.*

faithful /ˈfeɪθfᵊl/ **adj**
always liking and supporting someone or something: *She's a faithful friend.*

faithfully /ˈfeɪθfəli/ **adv**
Yours faithfully used to end a formal letter to someone whose name you do not know

fake[1] /feɪk/ **adj**
not real, but made to look or seem real: *She was carrying a fake passport.*

fake[2] /feɪk/ **noun**
a copy of something that is intended to make people think it is real: *Experts say that the painting is a fake.*

fall[1] /fɔːl/ **verb** (**fell**, **fallen**)
1 A2 to move down towards the ground: *Huge snowflakes were **falling from** the sky.*
2 to suddenly go down and hit the ground: *She **fell off** her bike.*
3 B1 to become less in number or amount: *House prices have fallen by 15% this year.*
4 fall asleep B1 to start to sleep
fall apart phrasal verb
to break into pieces: *These old boots are falling apart.*
fall down phrasal verb
B1 to fall onto the ground: *The wall is in danger of falling down.*
fall out phrasal verb
to argue with someone: *She has **fallen out with** Sam again.*
fall over phrasal verb
B1 to fall to the ground: *She fell over and hurt her knee.*
→ See **Phrasal Verbs** on page C13

fall[2] /fɔːl/ **noun**
1 B1 a situation when the number or amount of something becomes smaller: *There's been a sharp **fall in** prices.*
2 a drop from a higher level to a lower level: *a heavy fall of snow*
3 US (UK **autumn**) the season of the year between summer and winter, when leaves fall from the trees

fallen /ˈfɔːlən/
past participle of fall

false /fɔːls/ **adj**
1 B1 not true or correct: *He gave false information to the police.*
2 not real: *false teeth*

fame /feɪm/ **noun** [no plural]
a state of being known by many people

familiar /fəˈmɪliər/ **adj**
1 B1 If something is familiar, you know it well or have seen it before: *This street looks **familiar to** me.*
2 be familiar with *something* to know about something or have done or seen it many times before: *Are you familiar with his poetry?*

family /ˈfæməli/ **noun** (plural **families**)
1 A1 a group of people who are related to each other, especially parents and children: *My family originally came from Poland.*
2 B1 the children of two parents: *They have a large family.*

famine /ˈfæmɪn/ **noun**
a lack of food for a long time in a particular place

famous /ˈfeɪməs/ **adj**
A1 known by many people: *a famous actress*

fans

fan /fæn/ **noun**
1 A2 someone who likes a person or thing very much: *He's a big **fan of** country music.*
2 B1 something that is used to move the air around so it feels cooler: *an electric fan*

fancy /ˈfænsi/ **verb** (**fancying**, **fancied**)
1 B1 UK to want to have or do something: *Do you fancy a drink?*
2 UK informal to feel sexually attracted to someone: *I fancied him the first time I saw him.*

fancy dress /ˌfænsi ˈdres/ **noun** [no plural] UK
special clothes that people wear for a

a b c d e **f** g h i j k l m n o p q r s t u v w x y z

party, which make them look like a different person: *a fancy dress party*

fantastic /fæn'tæstɪk/ **adj** informal
A2 very good: *He looks fantastic in that suit.*
• **fantastically adv** *They're doing fantastically (= very) well.*

fantasy /'fæntəsi/ **noun** (plural **fantasies**)
a pleasant situation or event that you imagine, which is not real or true: *Steve's fantasy was to have a big house and an expensive car.*

FAQ /ˌefeɪ'kjuː/ **noun**
a set of questions that many people ask when they use the Internet or a computer program, or a document containing these questions and their answers

far[1] /fɑːʳ/ **adv**
1 A2 used to talk about how distant something is: ***How far** is it to the supermarket?*
2 very much: *Young people are far more independent these days.*
3 as far as I know used to say what you think is true, although you do not know all the facts: *As far as I know, they are coming to the party.*
4 by far used to say that something is very much the biggest, the best, etc.: *This is his best book by far.*
5 so far B1 until now: *So far, we haven't made much progress on the project.*

far[2] /fɑːʳ/ **adj** (**farther** or **further**, **farthest** or **furthest**)
describing the part of something that is most distant from you: *His office is at the far end of the corridor.*

fare /feəʳ/ **noun**
B1 the price that you pay to travel on a plane, train, bus, etc.: *plane/bus fares*

farm /fɑːm/ **noun**
A1 land and buildings used for growing crops and keeping animals: *a dairy farm (= where cows are raised for milk)*

farmer /'fɑːməʳ/ **noun**
A2 someone who owns or looks after a farm

farming /fɑːmɪŋ/ **noun** [no plural]
B1 the job of working on a farm

farmyard /'fɑːmjɑːd/ **noun**
an area of land with farm buildings around it

farther /'fɑːðəʳ/ **adj, adv**
comparative of far: more distant: *I couldn't walk any farther.*

farthest /'fɑːðɪst/ **adj, adv**
superlative of far: most distant: *Which planet is farthest from the sun?*

fascinated /'fæsɪneɪtɪd/ **adj**
very interested: *They were absolutely fascinated by the video game.*

fascinating /'fæsɪneɪtɪŋ/ **adj**
very interesting: *a fascinating story*

fashion /'fæʃᵊn/ **noun**
1 A2 the most popular style of clothes or behaviour at a particular time: *Long hair is **in fashion** now.* ◦ *Fur coats have gone **out of fashion**.*
2 B1 [no plural] the business of making and selling clothes: *fashion magazines*

fashionable /'fæʃᵊnəbl/ **adj**
B1 popular at a particular time: *fashionable clothes*
→ Opposite **unfashionable adj**

fast[1] /fɑːst/ **adj**
1 A1 quick: *fast cars* ◦ *a fast swimmer*
→ Opposite **slow adj**
2 If a clock or watch is fast, it shows a time that is later than the correct time: *My watch is five minutes fast.*

fast[2] /fɑːst/ **adv**
1 A2 quickly: *We ran as fast as we could.*
2 fast asleep completely asleep
3 in a firm or tight way: *He tried to get away, but she held him fast.*

fasten /'fɑːsᵊn/ **verb**
1 B1 to close or attach something: *Fasten your seat belts.*
2 to attach one thing to another: *He fastened the shelf to the wall.*

fast food /ˌfɑːst 'fuːd/ **noun** [no plural]
A2 hot food that is served very quickly in a restaurant because it is already made

fat[1] /fæt/ **adj** (**fatter**, **fattest**)
A1 Someone who is fat weighs too

much: *She eats all the time but never **gets fat**.*
→ Opposite **thin** adj

fat[2] /fæt/ **noun**
a solid or liquid substance like oil that is taken from plants or animals and used in cooking: *animal/vegetable fat*

fatal /ˈfeɪtᵊl/ **adj**
1 A fatal accident or illness makes someone die: *a fatal car crash*
2 Fatal actions have very bad effects: *He made the **fatal error** of deleting the file.*

fate /feɪt/ **noun** [no plural]
1 a power that some people believe controls what will happen: *I believe it was fate that caused us to meet again.*
2 something that happens to someone, especially something bad: *The election will **decide** his **fate**.*

father /ˈfɑːðəʳ/ **noun**
A1 someone's male parent: *My father and mother met at university.*

Father Christmas /ˌfɑːðə ˈkrɪsməs/ **noun** UK
a kind, fat, old man in red clothes who children believe brings presents at Christmas

father-in-law /ˈfɑːðərɪnlɔː/ **noun** (plural **fathers-in-law**)
the father of someone's husband or wife: *My father-in-law has always been very kind to me.*

fault /fɔːlt/ **noun**
1 ***someone's* fault** **B1** If something bad that happened is someone's fault, they made it happen: *The accident was not my fault.*
2 something that is wrong with something: *The car has a serious design fault.*
3 something that is wrong with someone's character: *He has many faults, but laziness isn't one of them.*

faulty /ˈfɔːlti/ **adj** (**faultier**, **faultiest**)
not working correctly: *faulty brakes*

favour /ˈfeɪvəʳ/ **noun**
1 **B1** something that you do to help someone: *Could you **do me a favour** please?*
2 **be in favour of *something*** to agree with a plan or idea: *Most people are in favour of reducing traffic in cities.*

favourite[1] UK (US **favorite**) /ˈfeɪvᵊrət/ **adj**
A1 Your favourite person or thing is the one that you like best: *What's your favourite colour?*

favourite[2] /ˈfeɪvᵊrət/ **noun**
B1 a thing that someone likes best or enjoys most: *These chocolates are my favourites.*

fax /fæks/ **noun**
1 a document that is sent using a special machine and a telephone line
2 a machine that is used to send and receive faxes
→ See **The Office** on page C12
• **fax** **verb** **B1** *I faxed the changes to my publisher.*

fear[1] /fɪəʳ/ **noun**
B1 a strong, bad feeling that you get when you think that something bad might happen: *She was trembling **with fear**. ◦ There are **fears that** the disease will spread.*

fear[2] /fɪəʳ/ **verb**
1 to be worried or frightened that something bad might happen or might have happened: *Police **fear that** she drowned in the river.*
2 to be frightened of something or someone unpleasant: *Many older people fear death.*

feast /fiːst/ **noun**
a large meal, especially to celebrate something special

feather /ˈfeðəʳ/ **noun**
one of the soft, light things that cover a bird's skin

feature[1] /ˈfiːtʃəʳ/ **noun**
1 an important part of something: *This phone has some new features.*
2 a part of a person's face: *His eyes are his best feature.*

feature[2] /ˈfiːtʃəʳ/ **verb**
to include someone or something as an important part: *a new movie featuring Sandra Bullock*

February /ˈfebruᵊri/ **noun**
A1 the second month of the year

a b c d e f g h i j k l m n o p q r s t u v w x y z

fed /fed/
past tense and past participle of feed

federal /ˈfedᵊrᵊl/ **adj**
1 A federal system of government consists of a group of regions that can make their own laws, but are also controlled by a national government.
2 relating to the national government of a country such as the United States, and not to the government of one of its states: *the* ***federal government*** ◦ *a federal employee*

fed up /ˌfed ˈʌp/ **adj** informal
bored or annoyed by something that you have done for too long: *I'm* ***fed up with*** *my job.*

fee /fiː/ **noun**
B1 an amount of money that you pay to do or use something: *university fees*

feeble /ˈfiːbl/ **adj**
very weak: *She was too feeble to get out of bed.*

feed /fiːd/ **verb** (**fed**)
B1 to give food to a person, group, or animal: *Have you fed the cat yet?*

feel /fiːl/ **verb** (**felt**)
1 A1 to experience happiness, sadness, fear, etc.: *I feel guilty about shouting at her.* ◦ *He's feeling lonely.* ◦ *I felt sorry for her.*
2 A1 to experience a touch, a pain, or something else that is physical: *I felt a sharp pain in my foot.* ◦ *Do you feel sick?*
3 B1 to have an opinion about something: *I* ***feel that*** *she's the best person for the job.*
4 **feel like *someone/something*** B1 to seem to be similar to a type of person, thing, or situation: *Your hands feel like ice.*
5 **feel as if/feel like** B1 to have a feeling or idea about something that you have experienced, even though it might not be true: *It feels like I've been here forever, but it's only been a week.*
6 **feel like *something*** B1 to want something: *I feel like a sandwich.*
7 **feel like doing *something*** B1 to want to do something: *Jane felt like crying.*
8 to touch something in order to examine it: *He felt her ankle to see if it was broken.*
9 **feel different, strange, etc.** If a place, situation, etc. feels different, strange, etc., that is how it seems to you: *It felt strange to see him again after so long.* ◦ *The house feels empty without the kids.*

feeling /ˈfiːlɪŋ/ **noun**
1 B1 something that you feel in your mind when you are happy, sad, afraid, etc.: *Sitting by the lake gives me a nice, peaceful feeling.* ◦ *He tries to hide his feelings.*
2 B1 something that you feel in your body: *I had a strange feeling in my fingers.*
3 B1 an idea that something is true or exists: *I* ***had the feeling*** *that we had met before.* ◦ *I* ***got the feeling*** *that she was unhappy.*
4 an opinion or belief: *My feeling is that we should not hire him.*

feelings /ˈfiːlɪŋz/ **plural noun**
hurt *someone's* feelings B1 to upset someone by insulting them: *Say you like the cake, or you'll hurt her feelings.*

feet /fiːt/
plural of foot

fell /fel/
past tense of fall

fellow /ˈfeləʊ/ **adj**
used to describe people with the same interests or situation: *her fellow students*

felt /felt/
past tense and past participle of feel

female /ˈfiːmeɪl/ **adj**
B1 belonging to the sex that can have babies: *a female butterfly*
• **female noun**

feminine /ˈfemɪnɪn/ **adj**
showing qualities that people think are typical of women: *feminine beauty*

fence

fence /fens/ **noun**
a wood or metal structure that goes

around an area: *We put up a fence around the garden.*

ferry /ˈferi/ **noun** (plural **ferries**)
B1 a boat that regularly carries people and vehicles across an area of water: *a **car/passenger ferry***

fertile /ˈfɜːtaɪl/ **adj**
1 Fertile land or soil produces a lot of healthy plants.
2 If people or animals are fertile, they are able to have babies.

fertilizer /ˈfɜːtɪlaɪzəʳ/ **noun**
something that you put on land in order to make plants grow well

festival /ˈfestɪvəl/ **noun**
1 B1 a series of special events or performances: *a dance/music festival*
2 B1 a special day or period when people celebrate something, especially a religious event: *the Jewish festival of Hanukkah*

fetch /fetʃ/ **verb**
B1 to go to another place to get something or someone: *Can you fetch my glasses from the bedroom?*

fever /ˈfiːvəʳ/ **noun**
B1 a high body temperature that happens because someone is ill

feverish /ˈfiːvərɪʃ/ **adj**
having a fever

few /fjuː/ **quantifier**
1 a few A2 some, or a small number of: *I'm only here for a few days.* ◦ *I've met **a few of** her friends.*
2 quite a few A2 quite a large number of: *Quite a few people have had the same problem.*
3 B1 not many, or only a small number of: ***Very few** people can afford to pay those prices.*

fiancé /fiˈɑːnseɪ/ **noun**
A woman's fiancé is the man that she will marry.

fiancée /fiˈɑːnseɪ/ **noun**
A man's fiancée is the woman that he will marry.

fibre UK (US **fiber**) /ˈfaɪbəʳ/ **noun**
one of the thin threads that cloth is made of: *The fibres are woven into fabric.*

fiction /ˈfɪkʃən/ **noun** [no plural]
B1 books and stories about imaginary people and events: *She is a writer of children's fiction.*

field /ˈfiːld/ **noun**
1 A2 an area of land used for growing crops or keeping animals
2 B1 an area of grass where you can play a sport: *a football field*
3 an area of study or activity: *He's an expert in the field of chemistry.*

field hockey /ˈfiːld ˌhɒki/ **noun** [no plural] US (UK **hockey**)
a game that two teams play on grass, in which players hit a ball with long curved sticks

fierce /fɪəs/ **adj**
1 violent or angry: *a fierce dog* ◦ *a fierce attack*
2 very strong or powerful: *fierce wind*
3 showing strong feeling or energetic activity: *There is fierce competition among computer companies.*

fifteen /ˌfɪfˈtiːn/
A1 the number 15

fifteenth /ˌfɪfˈtiːnθ/
15th written as a word

fifth[1] /fɪfθ/
A2 5th written as a word

fifth[2] /fɪfθ/ **noun**
B1 one of five equal parts of something; 1/5

fifties /ˈfɪftiz/ **plural noun**
1 the fifties the years from 1950 to 1959: *He was born **in the fifties**.*
2 be in your fifties to be aged between 50 and 59: *My dad is **in his fifties**.*

fifty /ˈfɪfti/
A2 the number 50
• **fiftieth** 50th written as a word

fig /fɪg/ **noun**
a dark, sweet fruit with lots of seeds

fight[1] /faɪt/ **verb** (**fought**)
1 B1 to try to hurt someone using your body or weapons: *Two men were fighting outside the bar.*
2 to argue: *Don't fight in front of the children!*
3 to take part in a war: *Thousands of young men fought in the war.*

a b c d e f g h i j k l m n o p q r s t u v w x y z

4 to try hard to stop something bad happening: *She* ***fought against*** *racism.*
5 to try hard to get or achieve something: *They are* ***fighting for*** *their freedom.*

fight² /faɪt/ **noun**
1 B1 a situation in which people try to hurt each other using their body or weapons: *He gets into a lot of fights.*
2 an argument: *My parents had a big fight about money.*
3 a situation in which people try very hard to achieve something or to stop something: *She was brave in her* ***fight against*** *cancer.* ◦ *a* ***fight for*** *freedom*

fighting /faɪtɪŋ/ **noun** [no plural]
a situation in which people fight, especially in a war: *Thousands of people were killed in the fighting.*

figure¹ /ˈfɪgəʳ/ **noun**
1 B1 a symbol for a number: *Write down the amount in words and figures.*
2 B1 the shape of someone's body, usually an attractive shape: *That big coat hides her figure.*
3 a person that you cannot see clearly: *I could see two figures in the distance.*
4 a particular type of person, often someone important or famous: *Kennedy was a major figure in American politics.*

figure² /ˈfɪgəʳ/ **verb** (**figuring**, **figured**)
figure *something/someone* out phrasal verb
to think about and then understand something or someone: *I can't figure this map out.*

file¹ /faɪl/ **noun**
1 A2 a collection of information stored electronically: *Do you want to download these files?*
2 A2 a box or folded piece of thick paper used to store documents: *files full of personal papers*
→ See **The Office** on page C12
3 a small tool with a rough edge that is used to make a surface smooth: *a nail file*

file² /faɪl/ **verb** (**filing**, **filed**)
1 to put documents into an ordered system so that you can easily find them: *She filed her tax returns under T.*
2 to rub something with a rough tool in order to make it smooth

filing cabinet /ˈfaɪlɪŋ ˌkæbɪnət/ **noun**
a piece of office furniture with deep drawers for storing documents
→ See **The Office** on page C12

fill /fɪl/ **verb**
1 A2 to make a container or space full, or to become full: *He filled the bucket with water.* ◦ *The bath should fill in five minutes.*
2 B1 If people or things fill a space, there are a lot of them in it: *The streets were* ***filled with*** *tourists.*
3 B1 If light, sound, or a smell fills a place, you can easily notice it: *The smell of smoke filled the room.*
fill *something* in/out phrasal verb
A2 to write all the information that is needed on a document: *Please fill out this form.*
fill (*something*) up phrasal verb
B1 to become full, or to make something become full: *The restaurant soon filled up with people.*

filling /ˈfɪlɪŋ/ **noun**
a hard substance that is put in a hole in a tooth

film¹ /fɪlm/ **noun**
1 A1 (also **movie**) a story that is shown in moving pictures on a screen, usually at a cinema or on television: *a cowboy film*
2 special thin plastic used for making photographs

film² /fɪlm/ **verb**
B1 to record moving pictures with a camera, usually to make a movie: *They filmed for a week in Spain.*

film star /ˈfɪlm ˌstɑːʳ/ **noun**
a famous cinema actor or actress

filter /ˈfɪltəʳ/ **noun**
a device that you pass liquid through in order to remove particular substances: *a coffee filter*
• **filter verb**

filthy /ˈfɪlθi/ **adj** (**filthier**, **filthiest**)
very dirty: *filthy clothes*

fin /fɪn/ **noun**
a thin, flat part on a fish that helps it to swim

final¹ /ˈfaɪnəl/ **adj**
A2 last or coming at the end: *the final paragraph* ◦ *They scored a goal in the final minute.*

final² /ˈfaɪnəl/ **noun**
1 B1 the last part of a competition to decide who will win: *the European Cup Final*
2 finals UK exams that you take at the end of a university course

finally /ˈfaɪnəli/ **adv**
1 A2 after a long time: *We finally got home at midnight.*
2 B1 used before you say the last point or idea: *Finally, I'd like to thank everyone for coming.*

finance¹ /ˈfaɪnæns/ **noun** [no plural]
the control of the way large amounts of money are spent: *She wants to get a job in finance.*

finance² /ˈfaɪnæns/ **verb** (**financing**, **financed**)
to give the money that is needed to do something: *Who is financing the project?*

finances /ˈfaɪnænsɪz/ **plural noun**
the money that a person, company, or country earns and spends: *They need to keep better track of their finances.*

financial /faɪˈnænʃəl/ **adj**
B1 relating to money or how money is used: *financial advice*
• **financially adv** *He's still financially dependent on his parents.*

find /faɪnd/ **verb** (**found**)
1 A1 to discover something or someone that you have been looking for: *I can't find my car keys.*
2 A2 to discover something by chance: *I found some money in my coat pocket.*
3 B1 to become aware of something: *I came home to find the kitchen window had been broken.*
4 B1 to think or feel a particular way about someone or something: *I find exams very stressful.*
5 find *someone* guilty to judge that someone is guilty in a law court: *She was found guilty of murder.*
6 find *yourself* somewhere/doing *something* to become aware that you have gone somewhere or done something without intending to: *I woke up and found myself in a hospital bed.*
7 be found to exist or be present somewhere: *Many animals are found only in Australia.*
find (*something*) out phrasal verb
A2 to get information about something: *I must find out the train times.*

fine¹ /faɪn/ **adj**
1 A1 well, healthy, or happy: *'How are you?' 'I'm fine, thanks. And you?'*
2 (that's) fine A1 used to agree with a suggestion: *'Shall we meet at eight o'clock?' 'Yes, that's fine by me.'*
3 A2 good enough: *'Is the soup okay?' 'Yes, it's fine.'*
4 B1 sunny and not raining: *It will be a fine day tomorrow.*
5 excellent, or of very good quality: *fine wines*
6 thin: *fine brown hair*

fine² /faɪn/ **noun**
B1 an amount of money that you must pay for doing something wrong: *a parking fine*
• **fine verb** (**fining**, **fined**) to punish someone by making them pay some money

finely /ˈfaɪnli/ **adv**
into small pieces: *finely chopped onions*

finger /ˈfɪŋgər/ **noun**
A2 one of the five long parts at the end of your hand

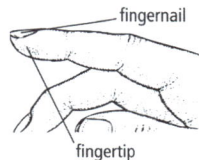

finger

fingernail /ˈfɪŋgəneɪl/ **noun**
the hard, thin part on the top of the end of your finger

fingerprint /ˈfɪŋgəprɪnt/ **noun**
the mark made on something by the pattern of curved lines on the end of someone's finger: *The police found fingerprints on the murder weapon.*

a b c d e f g h i j k l m n o p q r s t u v w x y z

a b c d e f g h i j k l m n o p q r s t u v w x y z

fingertip /ˈfɪŋɡətɪp/ **noun**
the end of your finger

finish[1] /ˈfɪnɪʃ/ **verb**
1 A1 to stop doing something because nothing more needs to be done: *I've finished my homework.* ◦ *We finished planting the garden.*
2 A1 to end: *The meeting will finish at five o'clock.*
3 B1 (also **finish off/up**) to eat, drink, or use something completely: *They finished their coffee and left the restaurant.*
finish *something* off **phrasal verb**
to do the last part of something: *I have to finish off this report by Friday.*

finish[2] /ˈfɪnɪʃ/ **noun**
B1 the end of a race, or the last part of something: *I enjoyed the movie **from start to finish**.*

fir /fɜːʳ/ **noun**
a tree with very thin, straight leaves that do not fall off in winter

fire[1] /faɪəʳ/ **noun**
1 A2 heat, light, and flames that are made when something burns: *Three people were killed in the fire.*

fire

2 catch fire
B1 to start burning: *Dry grass can catch fire easily.*
3 be on fire B1 to be burning: *That house is on fire.*
4 set fire to *something* to make something start burning: *Enemy troops set fire to the village.*
5 B1 a pile of wood or coal that is burning to produce heat: *He sat close to the fire to keep warm.*
6 open fire (on *someone*) to start shooting with guns, usually at a group of people: *Suddenly, the soldiers opened fire on the enemy.*

fire[2] /faɪəʳ/ **verb** (**firing**, **fired**)
1 to shoot a bullet from a gun: *She **fired** three shots **at** the target.*
2 to tell someone that they must leave their job: *She was **fired for** stealing from the company.*

fire brigade /ˈfaɪə brɪˌɡeɪd/ **noun**
mainly UK
an organization of people whose job is to stop fires

fire engine /ˈfaɪər ˌendʒɪn/ **noun**
a vehicle for carrying firefighters and equipment for stopping large fires

fire escape /ˈfaɪər ɪsˌkeɪp/ **noun**
a set of metal stairs on the outside of a building that people can use to leave if there is a fire

fire extinguisher /ˈfaɪər ɪk ˌstɪŋwɪʃəʳ/ **noun**
a piece of equipment that is used to stop small fires

firefighter /ˈfaɪəfaɪtəʳ/ **noun**
B1 someone whose job is to stop fires burning

fireman /ˈfaɪəmən/ **noun** (plural **firemen**)
a man whose job is to stop fires burning

fireplace /ˈfaɪəpleɪs/ **noun**
the open part of a wall in a room where you can make a fire
→ See **The Living Room** on page C11

fire station /ˈfaɪə ˌsteɪʃən/ **noun**
a building where fire engines are kept, and firefighters wait when they are not fighting fires

fireworks

firework /ˈfaɪəwɜːk/ **noun**
B1 a small object that explodes and

makes a loud noise and bright colours in the sky: *a fireworks display*

firm[1] /fɜːm/ **adj**
1 not soft, but not completely hard: *A firm bed is better for your back.*
2 strongly fixed in place: *Make sure the ladder is firm before you go up.*
3 If you are firm, you show people that you are strong and in control: *My parents were always **firm with** me.*
4 certain and not likely to change: *We don't have any firm plans for the weekend.*
• **firmly adv** *The door was firmly shut.* ◦ *'Let me do it,' she said firmly.* ◦ *I am firmly convinced that we should keep going.*

firm[2] /fɜːm/ **noun**
B1 a company that sells goods or services: *a law firm*

first[1] /ˈfɜːst/ **adj**
1 A1 coming before all others: *Ken was the first person to arrive.*
2 A2 most important: *Sheila won **first prize** in the photo competition.*
3 A2 1st written as a word

first[2] /ˈfɜːst/ **adv**
1 A1 before everything or everyone else: *Jason **came first** in the race (= he won).*
2 B1 for the first time: *I first met him last year.*
3 at first B1 at the beginning of a situation or period of time: *I didn't like her at first, but now we are friends.*
4 first; first of all B1 before doing anything else: *First of all, make sure you have all the ingredients.*

first[3] /ˈfɜːst/ **noun, pronoun**
the first B1 the first person or thing: *I liked the second movie more than the first.* ◦ *I was the first to arrive.*

first aid /ˌfɜːst ˈeɪd/ **noun** [no plural]
basic help that a person who is not a doctor can give to a person who is hurt or ill: *The police officer **gave** him **first aid** before the ambulance arrived.*

first-class /ˌfɜːstˈklɑːs/ **adj**
relating to the best and most expensive quality or service: *a first-class ticket* ◦ *a first-class stamp*
• **first class adv** *I want to send this letter first class.*

first floor /ˌfɜːst ˈflɔːʳ/ **noun UK**
B1 the level of a building directly above the ground level
• **first-floor adj** B1 *He jumped from a first-floor window.*

first language /ˌfɜːst ˈlæŋgwɪdʒ/ **noun**
the language that someone learns to speak first: *Madeleine's first language is French.*

first name /ˈfɜːst ˌneɪm/ **noun**
A2 the name that comes before your family name: *What is Mrs Jackson's first name?*

fish[1] /fɪʃ/ **noun** (plural **fish, fishes**)
A1 an animal that lives only in water, swims, and can be eaten as food
→ See **Food** on page C7

fish[2] /fɪʃ/ **verb**
B1 to try to catch fish

fisherman /ˈfɪʃəmən/ **noun** (plural **fishermen**)
someone who catches fish as a job or as a hobby

fishing /ˈfɪʃɪŋ/ **noun** [no plural]
A2 the sport or job of catching fish: *Dad loves to **go fishing**.* ◦ *a fishing boat*

fist /fɪst/ **noun**
a hand closed into a ball with the fingers and thumb curled tightly together: *He banged his fist angrily on the table.*

fist

fit[1] /fɪt/ **verb** (**fitting, fitted**)
1 B1 to be the right shape or size for someone or something: *This shirt doesn't fit me any more.*
2 B1 If people or things fit somewhere, that place is big enough for them: *How many people can fit in your car?*
3 UK to put or fix something some-

where: *You ought to fit a smoke alarm in the kitchen.*

> **Common mistake: fit or suit?**
>
> Remember that the verb **fit** means to be the right shape or size.
>
> *This jacket doesn't fit me. It's too tight.*
>
> Use the verb **suit** when you want to say that something is right for someone or makes them look more attractive.
>
> *That dress looks lovely. Red really suits you.*
>
> *Life in the big city didn't suit him.*
>
> ~~*Life in the big city didn't fit him.*~~

fit[2] /fɪt/ **adj** (**fitter**, **fittest**)
1 A2 healthy, especially because you exercise a lot: *He's very fit for his age.*
→ Opposite **unfit** adj
2 good enough for a particular purpose: *Is this water **fit to** drink?*

fitness /ˈfɪtnəs/ **noun** [no plural]
B1 the condition of being physically strong and healthy: *I'm trying to improve my fitness by cycling.*

fitted /ˈfɪtɪd/ **adj**
UK made or cut to fill a particular space exactly: ***fitted carpets/kitchens***

five /faɪv/
A1 the number 5

fix /fɪks/ **verb**
1 B1 to repair something: *Can you fix my watch?*
2 to decide a date or price: *Let's fix a day to have lunch together.*
3 to fasten something in a particular place: *They fixed the bookcase to the wall.*
4 mainly US to prepare a drink or meal: *I'll fix you a sandwich.*

fixed /fɪkst/ **adj**
arranged or decided already and not able to be changed: *a fixed price*

fizzy /ˈfɪzi/ **adj** (**fizzier**, **fizziest**)
A fizzy drink has lots of bubbles of gas in it.

fizzy

flag /flæg/ **noun**
B1 a piece of cloth with a special design and colours, that is the symbol of a country or group

flag

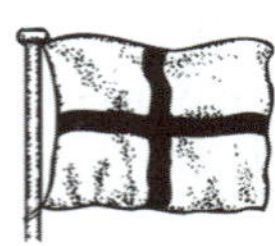

flake /fleɪk/ **noun**
a small, flat, thin piece of something: *flakes of skin*

flame /fleɪm/ **noun**
hot, bright, burning gas made by something on fire: *The car crashed and **burst into flames** (= suddenly started burning).*

flap[1] /flæp/ **noun**
something that hangs over an opening and is attached on one side

flap[2] /flæp/ **verb** (**flapping**, **flapped**)
If a bird flaps its wings, it moves them up and down.

flash[1] /flæʃ/ **verb**
1 to shine brightly and suddenly, or to make something shine in this way: *The doctor flashed a light into my eye.*
2 (also **flash up**) to appear for a short time, or to make something appear for a short time: *An icon flashed up on the screen.*

flash[2] /flæʃ/ **noun**
1 a sudden bright light: *The bomb exploded in a **flash of** yellow light.*
2 a piece of camera equipment that produces a bright light when you take a photograph in a dark place

flask /flɑːsk/ **noun** UK
a special container that keeps drinks hot or cold: *a flask of coffee*

flask

flat[1] /flæt/ **noun** UK
(US **apartment**)

A1 a set of rooms to live in, with all the rooms on one floor: *a large block of flats*

flat[2] /flæt/ **adj** (**flatter**, **flattest**)
1 B1 smooth and level with nothing sticking up: *a flat surface* ◦ *The countryside around here is very flat.*
2 If a tyre is flat, it does not contain enough air.

flat[3] /flæt/ **adv**
in a horizontal or level position: *She spread the cloth flat across the table.*

flat

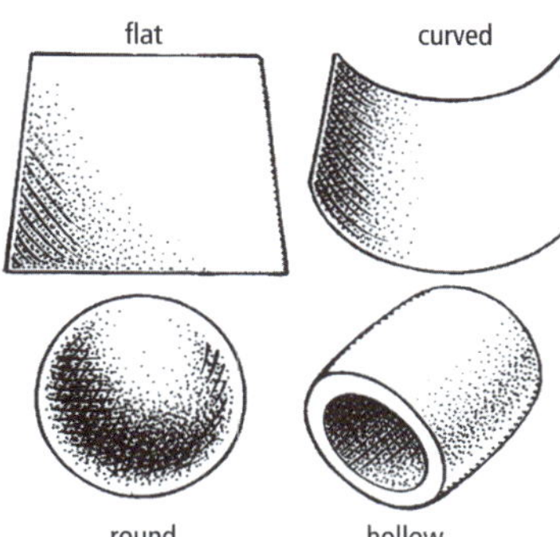

flatmate /ˈflætmeɪt/ **noun** UK (US **roommate**)
someone who you share a flat with

flatter /ˈflætəʳ/ **verb**
to say nice things to someone to please them, or because you want something from that person: *He flattered me with his compliments.*

flattering /ˈflætərɪŋ/ **adj**
making you look more attractive than usual: *a flattering dress*

flavour UK (US **flavor**) /ˈfleɪvəʳ/ **noun**
B1 the taste of a type of food or drink: *We sell 50 different flavours of ice cream.*

flea /fliː/ **noun**
a small, jumping insect that lives on animals or people and drinks their blood

flee /fliː/ **verb** (**fleeing**, **fled**)
to leave a place quickly because you are in danger: *He fled the country during the war.*

fleece /fliːs/ **noun**
1 a warm, soft jacket, or the material used to make it
2 the thick covering of wool on a sheep

fleet /fliːt/ **noun**
a group of ships

flesh /fleʃ/ **noun** [no plural]
the soft part under the skin of a person's or animal's body

flew /fluː/
past tense of fly

flexible /ˈfleksɪbl/ **adj**
1 able to change or be changed easily according to the situation: *I'd like a job with more flexible hours.*
2 able to bend easily without breaking

flight /flaɪt/ **noun**
A2 a journey in a plane

flight attendant /ˈflaɪt əˌtendənt/ **noun**
someone whose job is to look after passengers on a plane

fling /flɪŋ/ **verb** (**flinging**, **flung**)
to suddenly throw something: *She flung her jacket on the sofa.*

flirt /flɜːt/ **verb**
to behave as if you are sexually attracted to someone: *She was* ***flirting with*** *a guy at the bar.*

float

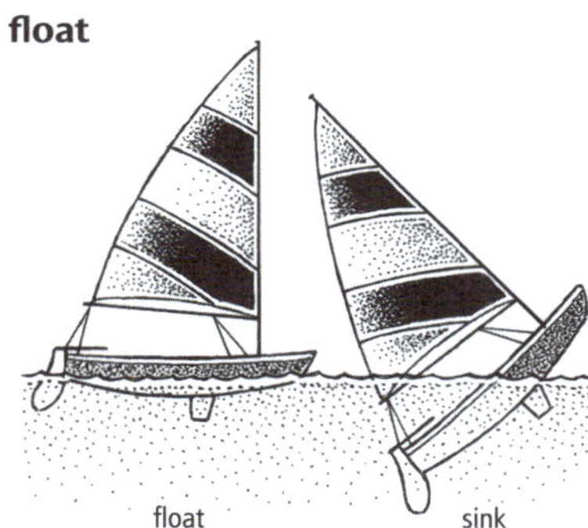

float /fləʊt/ **verb**
1 B1 to stay on the surface of a liquid and not go under: *I like floating on my back in the pool.*
2 B1 to move gently through the air: *A balloon floated across the sky.*

flock /flɒk/ **noun**
a group of birds or sheep: *a flock of geese*

flood[1] /flʌd/ **verb**
1 B1 to become covered with water: *Our basement flooded during the storm.*
2 to fill or enter a place in large numbers or amounts: *She opened the curtains and sunlight flooded the room.*

flood[2] /flʌd/ **noun**
B1 a large amount of water that covers an area that is usually dry: *The flood destroyed thousands of homes.*

flood

floodlights /ˈflʌdlaɪts/ **noun**
powerful lights used at night to light up sports fields or the outside of buildings

floor /flɔːʳ/ **noun**
1 (A1) a surface that you walk on inside a building: *a wooden floor*
2 (A2) a particular level of a building: *the **second/third floor***
3 (B1) an area where a particular activity happens: *a dance floor*

florist /ˈflɒrɪst/ **noun**
1 someone who sells and arranges flowers in a shop
2 a shop that sells flowers

flour /flaʊəʳ/ **noun** [no plural]
(B1) a powder made from grain that is used to make bread and cakes

flourish /ˈflʌrɪʃ/ **verb**
to grow or develop well: *The tourist industry is flourishing.*

flow /fləʊ/ **verb**
(B1) If a liquid flows, it moves somewhere in a smooth, continuous way: *The river flows to the sea.*
• **flow noun** the continuous, smooth movement of something: *the flow of traffic through the town*

flower /flaʊəʳ/ **noun**
(A1) the attractive coloured part of a plant where the seeds grow: *a bunch of flowers*

flown /fləʊn/
past participle of fly

flu /fluː/ **noun** [no plural]
an illness like a very bad cold that causes pains and fever

fluent /ˈfluːənt/ **adj**
1 able to use a language naturally and well: *She is **fluent in** six languages.*
2 produced or done in a smooth, natural style: *He speaks fluent Korean.*
• **fluency noun** *The job requires fluency in French.*
• **fluently adv** *I'd like to speak English fluently.*

fluff /flʌf/ **noun** [no plural]
small, loose bits of wool or other soft material

fluffy /ˈflʌfi/ **adj** (**fluffier**, **fluffiest**)
very light and soft to touch: *a fluffy kitten*

fluid /ˈfluːɪd/ **noun**
a liquid: *Drink plenty of fluids.*

flush /flʌʃ/ **verb**
to clean something, especially a toilet, by sending water through it: *Remember to **flush** the **toilet** when you are done.*

flute /fluːt/ **noun**
(B1) a musical instrument that you hold out to the side and play by blowing into it

flutter /ˈflʌtəʳ/ **verb**
to move quickly and gently in the air: *The flag was fluttering in the breeze.*

fly¹ /flaɪ/ **verb** (**flying**, **flew**, **flown**)
1 (A2) to move through the air: *The bird flew up into a tree.*
2 (A1) to travel through the air in a plane: *I'm flying to Delhi tomorrow.*
3 to control a plane or other aircraft in the sky: *He learned to fly in the military.*
4 to move somewhere very quickly: *He grabbed some clothes and flew down the stairs.*

fly² /flaɪ/ **noun** (plural **flies**)
1 (B1) a small insect with two wings
→ See picture at **insect**
2 (also UK **flies**) the part where trousers open and close at the front: *a button fly*

foam /fəʊm/ **noun** [no plural]
a lot of small, white bubbles on the surface of a liquid

focus[1] /ˈfəʊkəs/ **noun**
1 in focus If a picture is in focus, it is clear: *Try to get your subject in focus.*
2 out of focus If a picture is out of focus, it is not clear: *The photos were all out of focus.*
3 the person or thing that is getting most attention in a situation or activity: *He is the focus of a police investigation.*

focus[2] /ˈfəʊkəs/ **verb**
to adjust something, such as a camera, so that the picture is clear: *This camera is easy to focus.*
focus on *someone/something* **phrasal verb**
to give most of your attention to someone or something: *Try to focus on the most important facts.*

fog /fɒg/ **noun** [no plural]
A2 a thick cloud close to the ground that makes it difficult to see: *The fog should lift (= clear) by this afternoon.*
• **foggy adj** (**foggier**, **foggiest**) A2 *a foggy day*

foil /fɔɪl/ **noun** [no plural]
metal made into very thin sheets like paper, used mainly for covering food: *aluminium foil*

fold[1] /fəʊld/ **verb**
1 B1 to bend something so that one part of it lies flat on top of another part: *Can you help me fold the sheets?*
2 fold your arms to bend your arms across your chest, with one crossing over the other: *He sat with his arms folded.*

fold[2] /fəʊld/ **noun**
a line made where paper or cloth is folded: ***Make** a **fold** across the centre of the card.*

folder /ˈfəʊldəʳ/ **noun**
1 a folded piece of plastic or thick paper used to store loose papers
→ See **The Office** on page C12
2 B1 a place on a computer where particular files (= documents, pictures) are kept

folk[1] /fəʊk/ **noun** UK informal (US **folks**)
people: *old folk*

folk[2] /fəʊk/ **adj**
B1 typical of the people of a particular group or country: *folk music*

follow /ˈfɒləʊ/ **verb**
1 A2 to move behind someone or something and go where they go: *She followed me into the kitchen.*
2 B1 to happen or come after something: *There was a bang, **followed by** a cloud of smoke.*
3 follow a path/road B1 to travel along a path or road: *Follow the main road down to the traffic lights.*
4 follow instructions/orders B1 to do what instructions or orders say you should do: *Did you follow the instructions on the packet?*
5 B1 to understand something: *Could you say that again? I didn't quite follow.*
6 as follows used to introduce a list or description: *The main reasons are as follows.*

following[1] /ˈfɒləʊɪŋ/ **adj**
the following day, morning, etc. B1 the next day, morning, etc.

following[2] /ˈfɒləʊɪŋ/ **preposition**
after or as a result of: *Following a long illness, he died in October.*

fond /fɒnd/ **adj**
1 be fond of *someone/something* B1 to like someone or something: *We're very fond of each other.*
2 causing happy feelings: *I have fond memories of my childhood.*

food /fuːd/ **noun**
A1 something that people and animals eat to keep them alive: *baby/dog food* ◦ *You should eat healthy food.*

fool[1] /fuːl/ **noun**
1 B1 a stupid person
2 make a fool of *yourself* to behave in a silly or embarrassing way: *He got drunk and made a fool of himself.*

fool[2] /fuːl/ **verb**
to trick someone: *He fooled the old man into giving him the money.*
fool around/about **phrasal verb**
to behave in a silly way: *Stop fooling around – this is serious!*

a b c d e f g h i j k l m n o p q r s t u v w x y z

foolish /ˈfuːlɪʃ/ **adj**
silly: *a foolish mistake* ◦ *It would be foolish to ignore his advice.*
• **foolishly adv** *I foolishly didn't write her phone number down.*

foot /fʊt/ **noun**
1 A1 (plural **feet**) one of the two flat parts on the ends of your legs that you stand on: *bare feet*
→ See **The Body** on page C2
2 on foot A2 walking: *I usually go to school on foot.*
3 B1 (plural **foot**, **feet**) (written abbreviation **ft**) a unit for measuring length, equal to 0.3048 metres or 12 inches: *Alex is about six feet tall.*
4 the foot of *something* the bottom of something: *He was standing at the foot of the stairs.*

football /ˈfʊtbɔːl/ **noun**
1 A1 [no plural] UK (US **soccer**) a game in which two teams of players kick a round ball and try to score goals: *a football match/team*
→ See **Sports 2** on page C16
2 A1 a large ball for kicking
3 [no plural] US (UK **American football**) a game for two teams in which players move a ball along the field by running with it or throwing it
• **footballer noun** UK someone who plays football, especially as their job

footpath /ˈfʊtpɑːθ/ **noun** UK
a path or track for people to walk along, especially in the countryside: *a public footpath*

footprint /ˈfʊtprɪnt/ **noun**
a mark made by a foot or shoe

footstep /ˈfʊtstep/ **noun**
the sound of a foot hitting the ground when someone walks: *I heard footsteps behind me and quickly turned round.*

for strong /fɔːʳ/ weak /fəʳ/ **preposition**
1 A1 to be given to or used by someone or something: *I bought a dress for their new baby.* ◦ *We need some curtains for the bedroom.*
2 A1 used to show an amount of time or distance: *We walked for miles.* ◦ *I lived with my parents for a year.*
3 A2 having a particular purpose: *What are those large scissors for?*
4 A2 because of something: *Scotland is famous for its beautiful countryside.*
5 A2 in exchange for something, especially an amount of money: *How much did you pay for your computer?*
6 A2 on the occasion of: *What did you buy him for his birthday?*
7 A2 at a particular time: *I've booked a table at the restaurant for nine o'clock.*
8 A2 towards or in the direction of: *Just follow the signs for the airport.*
9 A2 meaning or representing something: *What's the German word for 'cut'?*
10 B1 in order to help someone: *I'll carry those bags for you.*
11 B1 representing a country or organization: *He plays football for Arsenal.*
12 used when comparing something to a particular fact: *She's quite tall for her age.*

forbid /fəˈbɪd/ **verb** (**forbidding**, **forbade**, **forbidden**)
to tell someone that they must not do something: *The school **forbids** students **from** smoking.* ◦ *National Park regulations forbid hunting.*
• **forbidden adj** B1 *Smoking is forbidden (= not allowed) in this area.*

force[1] /fɔːs/ **noun**
1 [no plural] physical power or strength: *The army has gained power **by force**.*
2 a group of people who work together for a particular purpose, for example in military service: *the police force* ◦ *the Royal Air Force*

force[2] /fɔːs/ **verb** (**forcing**, **forced**)
1 to make someone do something that they do not want to do: *You can't **force** her **to** eat.*
2 to make an object move by pushing or pulling it hard: *She forced the window shut.*

forecast[1] /ˈfɔːkɑːst/ **noun**
B1 something that says what will happen in the future: *the weather forecast*

forecast[2] /ˈfɔːkɑːst/ **verb** (**forecast**)
to say what will happen in the future: *They forecast more snow for this area.*
• **forecaster noun** *a weather forecaster*

forehead /ˈfɔːhed/ **noun**
B1 the part of your face between your eyes and your hair
→ See **The Body** on page C2

foreign /ˈfɒrən/ **adj**
A2 from a country that is not yours: *a foreign language/student*

foreigner /ˈfɒrənəʳ/ **noun**
B1 a person from another country

foresee /fɔːˈsiː/ **verb** (**foreseeing**, **foresaw**, **foreseen**)
to think that something will happen in the future: *I don't foresee any problems with the project.*

forest /ˈfɒrɪst/ **noun**
A2 a large area of trees growing close together: *a pine forest*

forever /fəˈrevəʳ/ **adv**
B1 for all time in the future: *I want to live here forever.*

forgave /fəˈgeɪv/
past tense of forgive

forge /fɔːdʒ/ **verb** (**forging**, **forged**)
to make an illegal copy of something in order to deceive people: *She forged his signature.*

forgery /ˈfɔːdʒəri/ **noun**
1 (plural **forgeries**) an illegal copy of something
2 [no plural] the crime of making an illegal copy of something: *He was found guilty of forgery.*

forget /fəˈget/ **verb** (**forgetting**, **forgot**, **forgotten**)
1 A2 to not bring something with you because you did not remember it: *I've forgotten my umbrella.*
2 B1 to not remember something: *I've forgotten his name.* ◦ *Don't forget to feed the cat.*
3 B1 (also **forget about**) to stop thinking about someone or something: *Let's try to forget about work.*

> **Common mistake: forget or leave?**
> With **forget**, you do not mention the place where you left the thing.
> ~~*I forgot my phone at home.*~~
> You use **leave** to say that you forgot an object when you left a place or when you got off the bus, train, etc.
> *I left my umbrella on the bus.*
> ~~*I forgot my umbrella on the bus.*~~

forgetful /fəˈgetfəl/ **adj**
often forgetting things: *She's 84 now and a bit forgetful.*

forgive /fəˈgɪv/ **verb** (**forgiving**, **forgave**, **forgiven**)
B1 to decide not to be angry with someone, or not to punish them for something bad they have done: *Jane never* ***forgave*** *her mother* ***for*** *lying to her.*

forgot /fəˈgɒt/
past tense of forget

forgotten /fəˈgɒtən/
past participle of forget

fork /fɔːk/ **noun**
A2 a small tool with three or four points and a handle, used to eat with: *a knife and fork*

form¹ /fɔːm/ **noun**
1 A2 a printed document with spaces for you to write information: *Please* ***fill in the form*** *using black ink.*
2 B1 a way of writing or saying a word that shows if it is singular or plural, past or present, etc.: *'Isn't' is the short form of 'is not'.*
3 B1 UK a school class for students of the same age or ability: *the third form*
4 a type of something or way of doing something: *Swimming is the best* ***form of*** *exercise.*

form² /fɔːm/ **verb**
1 B1 to make something by putting different parts together: *In English you form the present participle by adding '-ing' to the verb.*
2 to begin to exist, or to make something begin to exist: *This plant forms new leaves in the spring.*
3 to start an organization or business: *Brown formed her own company eleven years ago.*
4 to make a shape: *Hold hands and form a circle.*

formal /ˈfɔːməl/ **adj**
1 used about clothes, language, and behaviour that are serious or very polite: *a formal dinner party*
2 public or official: *a formal announcement*

formation /fɔːˈmeɪʃən/ **noun**
[no plural] the development of some-

a b c d e f g h i j k l m n o p q r s t u v w x y z

thing into a particular thing or shape: *the formation of a star*

former /ˈfɔːməʳ/ **adj**
B1 happening or existing in the past but not now: *the former Soviet Union*

formerly /ˈfɔːməli/ **adv**
in the past: *The European Union was formerly called the European Community.*

formula /ˈfɔːmjələ/ **noun** (plural **formulas, formulae**)
a list of the substances that something is made of: *What is the formula for water?*

forties /ˈfɔːtiz/ **plural noun**
1 the forties the years from 1940 to 1949: *My family left India* ***in the forties.***
2 be in your forties to be aged between 40 and 49: *She's probably* ***in her early forties.***

fortieth /ˈfɔːtiθ/
40th written as a word

fortnight /ˈfɔːtnaɪt/ **noun** UK
B1 two weeks: *a fortnight's holiday*

fortunate /ˈfɔːtʃᵊnət/ **adj**
lucky: *It was* ***fortunate that*** *our plane was not late.*
→ Opposite **unfortunate adj**

fortunately /ˈfɔːtʃᵊnətli/ **adv**
B1 happening because of good luck: *Fortunately, no one was hurt in the crash.*
→ Opposite **unfortunately adv**

fortune /ˈfɔːtʃuːn/ **noun**
1 a lot of money: *Nick's new car must have cost a fortune!*
2 the good or bad things that happen to you: *The family's fortunes changed suddenly.*

forty /ˈfɔːti/
A2 the number 40

forward /ˈfɔːwəd/ **adv** (also **forwards**)
B1 towards the direction that is in front of you: *She leaned forward to make sure I could hear her.* ◦ *Please step forward when I call your name.*

fought /fɔːt/
past tense and past participle of fight

foul /faʊl/ **adj**
very dirty or bad: *a foul smell*

found¹ /faʊnd/
past tense and past participle of find

found² /faʊnd/ **verb**
to start an organization, especially by giving money: *He founded the charity in 1861.*

foundations /faʊnˈdeɪʃᵊns/ **noun** UK
the part of a building that is under the ground and supports it: *concrete foundations*

fountain /ˈfaʊntɪn/ **noun**
B1 a structure that forces water up into the air as a decoration

fountain

four /fɔːʳ/
A1 the number 4

fourteen /ˌfɔːˈtiːn/
A1 the number 14

fourteenth /ˌfɔːˈtiːnθ/
14th written as a word

fourth¹ /fɔːθ/
A2 4th written as a word

fourth² /fɔːθ/ **noun** mainly US
a quarter

fox /fɒks/ **noun**
a wild animal like a dog with brown fur and a long thick tail

fraction /ˈfrækʃᵊn/ **noun**
a number less than 1, such as 1/2 or 3/4

fracture /ˈfræktʃəʳ/ **verb** (**fracturing, fractured**)
to break a bone: *She's fractured her ankle.*
• **fracture noun**

fragile /ˈfrædʒaɪl/ **adj**
easy to break: *a fragile china cup*

fragment /ˈfrægmənt/ **noun**
a small piece of something larger: *fragments of pottery*

fragrance /ˈfreɪgrəns/ **noun**
a good smell: *the delicate fragrance of roses*

fragrant /ˈfreɪgrənt/ **adj**
with a good smell: *fragrant flowers*

frail /freɪl/ **adj**
not strong or healthy: *a frail old lady*

frame

frame¹ /freɪm/ **noun**
1 A2 a structure that goes around the edge of something, such as a picture or window: *a window frame*
2 the main structure of a building or vehicle that other parts are added onto: *a bicycle frame*

frame² /freɪm/ **verb** (**framing**, **framed**)
to put something such as a picture into a frame: *I'm going to frame this picture.*

frank /fræŋk/ **adj**
honest and saying what you really think: *It was a frank discussion.*

frankly /ˈfræŋkli/ **adv**
in an honest way: ***Quite frankly**, I think you're making a big mistake.*

fraud /frɔːd/ **noun** [no plural]
something illegal a person does in order to get money: *credit card fraud*

fray /freɪ/ **verb**
If material frays, the threads at the edge break and become loose.

freak /friːk/ **noun**
1 informal someone who is very interested in something: *My brother is a computer freak.*
2 someone who looks strange or behaves in a strange way: *They made me feel like a freak.*

freckle /ˈfrekl/ **noun**
a light brown spot on a person's skin

freckles

free¹ /friː/ **adj**
1 A2 costing no money: *Entry is free for children.*
2 A2 not busy doing anything: *Are you free on Friday?* ◦ *free time*
3 able to do things without being controlled: *People should be **free to** say what they think.*
4 not in prison or in a cage: *He opened the cage and **set** the birds **free**.*
5 not being used by anyone: *Is this seat free?*
• **freely** **adv** *For the first time in months she could move freely.*

free² /friː/ **adv**
1 A2 without paying money: *Children under five travel free.*
2 in a way that is not tied up, limited, or controlled: *I let the dogs run free in the park.*

free³ /friː/ **verb** (**freeing**, **freed**)
to allow someone to leave a prison or place where they have been kept: *The hostages were finally freed yesterday.*

freedom /ˈfriːdəm/ **noun** [no plural]
the right to live in the way you want without being controlled by anyone else

freeway /ˈfriːweɪ/ **noun** US (UK **motorway**)
a long, wide road between cities, usually used by cars travelling fast

freeze /friːz/ **verb** (**freezing**, **froze**, **frozen**)
1 B1 If something freezes, it becomes hard and solid because it is very cold: *The pond froze overnight.*
2 B1 to make food last a long time by making it very cold and hard: *Freeze any bread that you have left over.*
3 to feel very cold: *You'll freeze if you don't wear a coat.*

a b c d e f g h i j k l m n o p q r s t u v w x y z

4 to suddenly stop moving, especially because you are frightened: *She saw someone outside the window and froze.*

freezer /ˈfriːzəʳ/ **noun**
B1 a large electric container in which food can be frozen and stored
→ See **The Kitchen** on page C10

freezing /ˈfriːzɪŋ/ **adj** informal
B1 very cold: *It's absolutely freezing in here.*

French fries /ˌfrentʃ ˈfraɪz/ **plural noun** US (UK **chips**)
long, thin pieces of potato that have been cooked in hot oil

frequency /ˈfriːkwənsi/ **noun** [no plural]
the number of times something is repeated: *Hurricanes have increased in frequency over the last few years.*

frequent /ˈfriːkwənt/ **adj**
B1 happening often: *He is a frequent visitor to the US.*

frequently /ˈfriːkwəntli/ **adv** formal
B1 often: *I see him very frequently.*

fresh /freʃ/ **adj**
1 **A2** Fresh food has been made or collected recently and has not been frozen or dried: *fresh fruit/vegetables* ◦ *fresh bread*
2 **B1** new or different from what was there before: *fresh ideas*
3 **B1** smelling clean or feeling cool: *a fresh breeze* ◦ *fresh air*
4 recently made, done, arrived, etc., and especially not yet changed by time: *a fresh coat of paint* ◦ *We should take a fresh look at the budget.*

Friday /ˈfraɪdeɪ/ **noun**
A1 the day of the week after Thursday and before Saturday

fridge /frɪdʒ/ **noun**
A2 a large electric cupboard that keeps food cold
→ See **The Kitchen** on page C10

fried /fraɪd/ **adj**
A2 cooked in hot oil or fat: *a fried egg*

friend /frend/ **noun**
1 **A1** someone that you know well and like: *Sarah is my* ***best friend*** *(= the friend I like most).*
2 **A2** a person you write to on an Internet site: *I've just added Adam as a friend on Facebook.*
3 **make friends (with *someone*)** **B1** to begin to know and like someone: *He's shy and finds it difficult to make friends.*
4 **be friends (with *someone*)** **B1** to know and like someone: *I've been friends with Lynne for years.*
5 **old friend** someone that you have known and liked for a long time: *Ricardo and I are old friends.*

friendly /ˈfrendli/ **adj** (**friendlier**, **friendliest**)
behaving in a pleasant, kind way towards someone: *a friendly face/smile*
→ Opposite **unfriendly** **adj**
• **friendliness** **noun** [no plural] **A2** *The city is famous for the friendliness of its people.*

friendship /ˈfrendʃɪp/ **noun**
B1 a relationship between friends: *a close friendship*

fries /fraɪz/ **plural noun** mainly US (also UK **chips**)
long, thin pieces of potato that have been cooked in hot oil

fright /fraɪt/ **noun** [no plural]
a sudden feeling of shock and fear: *She was shaking with fright.*

frighten /ˈfraɪtᵊn/ **verb**
to make someone afraid or nervous: *It frightens me when he drives so fast.*

frightened /ˈfraɪtᵊnd/ **adj**
B1 afraid or nervous: *I've always been* ***frightened of*** *going to the dentist.*

frightening /ˈfraɪtᵊnɪŋ/ **adj**
B1 making you feel afraid or nervous: *a frightening movie*

fringe /frɪndʒ/ **noun**
1 UK (US **bangs**) hair that is cut short and straight at the top of someone's face
→ See **Hair** on page C9
2 loose threads that hang along the edge of cloth as a decoration

frog /frɒg/ **noun**
B1 a small, green animal with long back legs for jumping, that lives in or near water

from strong /frɒm/ weak /frəm/ **preposition**
1 A1 used to show the place where someone or something started: *Did you walk all the way from the beach?* ◦ *We'll go* ***from*** *Prague* ***to*** *Berlin by train.*
2 A1 used to show the time when something starts or the time when it was made or first existed: *The museum is open* ***from*** *9.30* ***to*** *6.00.*
3 A1 used to say where someone was born, or where someone lives or works: *Steve's father is from Poland.*
4 A1 used to say how far away something is: *The house is about five miles from the city.*
5 A1 used to say who gave or sent something to someone: *Who are your flowers from?*
6 A2 used to say what something is made of: *juice made from oranges*
7 If you take something from a person, place, or amount, you take it away: *He took a knife from the drawer.*
8 used to show a change in the state of someone or something: *Things went* ***from*** *bad* ***to*** *worse.*

front[1] /frʌnt/ **noun**
1 the front A2 the side of something that faces forward: *Write the address* ***on the front of*** *the envelope.*
2 the front A2 the part of something that is furthest forward: *He was standing right* ***at the front****.*
3 in front of *something* A2 close to the front part of something: *He parked the car in front of the house.*
4 in front B1 further forward than someone or something else: *He was sitting* ***in front of*** *me.*

front[2] /frʌnt/ **adj**
B1 in or at the front of something: *the front door/garden*

frontier /frʌnˈtɪəʳ/ **noun**
a line or border between two countries or areas

frost /frɒst/ **noun** [no plural]
a thin, white layer of ice that forms on very cold surfaces

frosty /ˈfrɒsti/ **adj** (**frostier**, **frostiest**)
very cold, with a thin layer of white ice covering everything: *a frosty morning*

frown /fraʊn/ **verb**
to look angry or worried by moving your eyebrows close together: *She frowned when I mentioned his name.*

froze /frəʊz/
past tense of freeze

frozen[1] /ˈfrəʊzᵊn/
past participle of freeze

frozen[2] /ˈfrəʊzᵊn/ **adj**
1 B1 Frozen food has been made very cold so that it will last a long time: *frozen peas*
2 B1 turned into ice: *The pond was frozen this morning.*
3 B1 informal If a person or a part of their body is frozen, they are very cold: *Is there any heating in here? I'm frozen!*

fruit /fruːt/ **noun** [no plural]
A1 things such as apples or oranges that grow on a tree or a bush, contain seeds, and can be eaten as food: *dried/fresh fruit*

fruit salad /ˌfruːt ˈsæləd/ **noun**
a mixture of pieces of different types of fruit, eaten at the end of a meal

frustrated /frʌsˈtreɪtɪd/ **adj**
annoyed because you cannot achieve or do what you want: *Are you feeling* ***frustrated with*** *your job?*

frustrating /frʌsˈtreɪtɪŋ/ **adj**
making you feel annoyed because you cannot achieve or do what you want: *a frustrating situation* ◦ *It's frustrating to see money being wasted like that.*

frustration /frʌsˈtreɪʃᵊn/ **noun**
the feeling of being annoyed because you cannot achieve or do what you want: *I could sense his* ***frustration at*** *not being able to help.*

fry /fraɪ/ **verb** (**frying**, **fried**)
B1 to cook something in hot oil or fat: *Fry the onions for two minutes.*
→ See picture at **cook**

frying pan /ˈfraɪɪŋ ˌpæn/ **noun**
B1 a flat, metal pan with a long handle that is used for frying food
→ See **The Kitchen** on page C10

ft
written abbreviation for foot: a unit for measuring length

fuel /ˈfjuːəl/ **noun**
B1 a substance that is burned to give heat or power

fulfil /fʊlˈfɪl/ **verb** (**fulfilling**, **fulfilled**)
to do something that you have promised or planned to do: *I finally fulfilled my ambition.*

full /fʊl/ **adj**
1 **A2** If a container or a space is full, it contains as many things or people as possible: *a full bottle of red wine*
2 **A2** containing a lot of things or people: *The room was **full of** people.*
3 **A2** complete and including every part: *Please give your full name and address.*
4 **B1** the greatest possible: *We were driving at full speed all the way.*
5 **in full** **B1** completely and with nothing missing: *The bill must be paid in full by the end of the month.*
6 informal (also UK **full up**) having eaten enough food: *No more for me, thanks, I'm full.*

full

full empty

full stop /ˌfʊl ˈstɒp/ **noun** UK (US **period**)
B1 a mark (.) used at the end of a sentence, or to show that the letters before it are an abbreviation

full-time /ˌfʊlˈtaɪm/ **adj**
B1 happening or working for the whole of the working week and not only part of it: *a full-time job/student*

fully /ˈfʊli/ **adv**
B1 completely: *The restaurant is fully booked this evening.*

fun¹ /fʌn/ **noun** [no plural]
1 **A1** enjoyment or pleasure, or something that gives you enjoyment or pleasure: *Did you **have fun** at the party?* ◦ *That was fun!*
2 **for fun** **B1** for pleasure and not for any other reason: *I took part in the race, but it was just for fun.*
3 **make fun of *someone/something*** to make a joke about someone or something in an unkind way: *The other children used to make fun of his red hair.*

fun² /fʌn/ **adj** informal
A2 enjoyable or entertaining: *There are lots of fun things to do here.*

function /ˈfʌŋkʃᵊn/ **noun**
the purpose of something or someone: *Each button has a different function.*

fund /fʌnd/ **noun**
an amount of money that is collected or given for a purpose: *a pension fund*

funeral /ˈfjuːnᵊrəl/ **noun**
a ceremony for honouring a person who has died, before the body is buried or burned: *The funeral will be held next Friday.*

funfair /ˈfʌnfeəʳ/ **noun** (also **fair**)
a place outside where you can ride on big machines for pleasure and play games to win prizes

fungus /ˈfʌŋgəs/ **noun** (plural **fungi**)
a type of plant without leaves that gets its food from other living or decaying things: *The mushroom is a fungus.*

funnel /ˈfʌnᵊl/ **noun**
a tube with a wide part at the top that you use to pour liquid into a small opening

funnel

funny /ˈfʌni/ **adj** (**funnier**, **funniest**)
1 **A1** making you smile or laugh: *a funny story*

Common mistake: fun or funny?

Use **fun** to talk about something that you enjoy doing.
Going to the cinema is fun.
Use **funny** to describe something that makes you laugh.
The film was really funny.

2 B1 strange or unusual and not what you expect: *This chicken tastes a bit funny.*

fur /fɜːʳ/ **noun** [no plural]
B1 the thick hair that covers the bodies of some animals like cats and rabbits

furious /ˈfjʊəriəs/ **adj**
very angry: *My boss was* ***furious with*** *me.*
• **furiously** **adv** *'Get out of here!' she shouted furiously.*

furnace /ˈfɜːnɪs/ **noun**
a large piece of equipment that is used to melt metals

furnished /ˈfɜːnɪʃt/ **adj**
If a room, flat, etc. is furnished, there is furniture in it: *a fully furnished apartment*

furniture /ˈfɜːnɪtʃəʳ/ **noun** [no plural]
A2 things such as chairs, tables, and beds that you put into a room or building

Common mistake: furniture

Remember you cannot make **furniture** plural. Do not say 'furnitures'.

I want to buy some new furniture for my bedroom.

furry /ˈfɜːri/ **adj** (**furrier**, **furriest**)
covered with fur

further¹ /ˈfɜːðəʳ/ **adv**
1 more: *He refused to discuss the matter further.*
2 B1 comparative of far: at or to a place or time that is a longer distance away: *Let's walk a bit further down the road.*

further² /ˈfɜːðəʳ/ **adj**
A2 more or extra: *For further details about the offer, call this number.*

furthest /ˈfɜːðɪst/ **adj**, **adv**
B1 superlative of far: most distant: *What is the furthest distance you can run?*

fury /ˈfjʊəri/ **noun** [no plural]
very strong anger: *He could hardly control his fury.*

fuse /fjuːz/ **noun**
a small object that stops electrical equipment from working if there is too much electricity going through it: *a fuse box*

fuss /fʌs/ **noun** [no plural]
1 excitement or worry about something that is not important: *What's all the fuss about?*
2 **make a fuss** to complain about something: *He made such a fuss because I was five minutes late.*
3 **make a fuss of** ***someone*** to give someone a lot of attention and treat them well: *My uncle always makes a big fuss of the children.*

fussy /ˈfʌsi/ **adj** (**fussier**, **fussiest**)
very difficult to please and only liking particular things: *She is a fussy eater (= does not like many foods).*

future¹ /ˈfjuːtʃəʳ/ **noun**
1 **the future** A2 in grammar, the form of a verb that is used to talk about something that will happen
2 **the future** B1 the time that is to come: *At some point* ***in the future*** *we'll probably move.*
3 **in future** UK (US **in the future**) B1 beginning from now: *In future, I'll be more careful.*
4 B1 things that will happen to someone or something in the time that is to come: *We need to discuss the future of the company.*

future² /ˈfjuːtʃəʳ/ **adj**
B1 happening or existing in the time that is to come: *in future years*

a b c d e f g h i j k l m n o p q r s t u v w x y z

Gg

G, g /dʒiː/
the seventh letter of the alphabet

g
written abbreviation for gram: a unit for measuring weight

gadget /ˈgædʒɪt/ **noun**
a small piece of equipment that does a particular job: *a kitchen gadget*

gain /geɪn/ **verb**
1 B1 to get something good: *You'll gain a lot of experience working there.*
2 to increase: *He's gained a lot of weight in the last few months.*

gale /geɪl/ **noun**
a very strong wind

gallery /ˈgæləri/ **noun** (plural **galleries**)
B1 a room or building that is used for showing paintings and other art to people: *an art gallery*

gallon /ˈgælən/ **noun**
a unit for measuring liquid, equal to 4.546 litres in the UK and 3.785 litres in the US

gallop /ˈgæləp/ **verb**
If a horse gallops, it runs very fast.

gamble[1] /ˈgæmbl/ **verb** (**gambling**, **gambled**)
to try to win money by saying who will win a game, race, or competition: *He gambled all of our savings.*
• **gambler** **noun** someone who gambles
• **gambling** **noun** [no plural] *People can become addicted to gambling.*

gamble[2] /ˈgæmbl/ **noun**
the act of doing something that you hope will have a good result, although you know that this might make something bad happen: *Buying this place was a big gamble.*

game /geɪm/ **noun**
1 A1 an activity or sport that people play, usually with rules and needing skill: *a computer game* ◦ *Football is such an exciting game.* ◦ *Do you want to **play** a different **game**?*
2 A2 a particular occasion when people play a game: *We **had a game of** cards.* ◦ *Who won yesterday's game?*

game show /ˈgeɪm ˌʃəʊ/ **noun**
a programme on television in which people play games to try to win prizes

gang /gæŋ/ **noun**
1 a group of young people who spend time together, often fighting with other groups: *a member of a gang*
2 a group of criminals who work together: *a gang of armed robbers*
3 informal a group of young friends

gangster /ˈgæŋstəʳ/ **noun**
one of a group of violent criminals

gap /gæp/ **noun**
1 B1 an empty space or hole in the middle of something, or between two things: *There's a big **gap between** the door and the floor.* ◦ *The sun was shining through a **gap in** the curtains.*
2 something that is absent and stops something from being complete: *There are still huge gaps in my knowledge.*
3 a period of time spent doing something different: *After a gap of five years, Jen decided to go back to work.*
4 a difference between two groups of people or two situations: *an age gap* ◦ *The **gap between** rich and poor is increasing.*

garage /ˈgærɑːʒ/ **noun**
1 A2 a small building where you put your car
2 B1 a place where cars are repaired or sold and sometimes fuel is sold

garbage /ˈgɑːbɪdʒ/ **noun** [no plural] US (UK **rubbish**)
1 things that you throw away because you do not want them: *Could you take out the garbage?* ◦ *a **garbage can** (= a container for rubbish)*
2 something that is wrong or very bad: *There's so much garbage on TV.*

garden[1] /ˈgɑːdᵊn/ **noun** UK (US **yard**)
A1 an area of ground next to a house, often with grass, flowers, or trees: *the front/back garden* ◦ *Dad's outside **in the garden**.*

garden[2] /ˈgɑːdᵊn/ **verb**
to work in a garden, growing plants and making it look attractive

a b c d e f g h i j k l m n o p q r s t u v w x y z

garden centre /ˈɡɑːdᵊn ˌsentəʳ/ **noun** UK
a place where you can buy things such as plants and equipment for your garden

gardening /ˈɡɑːdᵊnɪŋ/ **noun** [no plural]
the work that you do in a garden in order to grow plants and keep it attractive

garlic /ˈɡɑːlɪk/ **noun** [no plural]
A2 a vegetable like a small onion with a very strong taste and smell
→ See **Fruit and Vegetables** on page C8

gas /ɡæs/ **noun**
1 A2 [no plural] a substance in a form that is like air and is used for cooking and burning: *a gas cooker*
2 a substance in a form that is like air and not solid or liquid: *poisonous gases*
3 [no plural] US (UK **petrol**) a liquid fuel used in cars: *a tank of gas*

gasp /ɡɑːsp/ **verb**
to make a noise by suddenly breathing in because you are shocked or surprised: *She gasped in amazement.*
• **gasp noun** *a gasp of surprise*

gas station /ˈɡæs ˌsteɪʃᵊn/ **noun** US (UK **petrol station**)
a place where you can buy fuel for cars

gate /ɡeɪt/ **noun**
1 A2 a door in a fence or outside wall: *Please shut the gate.*
2 B1 the part of an airport where you get on or off a plane: *The flight to Dublin is now boarding at gate 8.*

gather /ˈɡæðəʳ/ **verb**
1 to join other people somewhere to make a group: *Crowds of fans gathered at the stadium for the big match.*
2 to collect a lot of things together, often from different places or people: *She **gathered** her things **together** and left.*
3 to think something is true, although you are not completely sure: *I gather they're arriving on Friday.*

gathering /ˈɡæðərɪŋ/ **noun**
a party or a meeting where many people get together as a group: *a family gathering*

gave /ɡeɪv/
past tense of give

gay /ɡeɪ/ **adj**
B1 attracted to people of the same sex: *Our neighbours are gay.* ◦ *a gay club (= for gay people)*

gaze /ɡeɪz/ **verb** (**gazing**, **gazed**)
gaze at, into, etc. to look at someone or something for a long time: *They gazed into each other's eyes.*
• **gaze noun**

GCSE /ˌdʒiːsiːesˈiː/ **noun**
in the UK, an exam in one subject that students take at the age of 16, or the qualification itself: *Katie got nine GCSEs.*

gear /ɡɪəʳ/ **noun**
1 the parts in a car or bicycle that control how fast the wheels turn: *I have a mountain bike with 21 gears.* ◦ *I **changed gear**.*
2 first, second, third, etc. gear a particular position of the gears in a car, bicycle, etc. that controls how fast the wheels turn: *I left the car **in** first **gear**.*
3 [no plural] the clothes and things that you use for a particular purpose: *sports gear*

gearstick /ˈɡɪəstɪk/ **noun** UK (US **gearshift** /ˈɡɪəʃɪft/)
a stick with a handle that you use to change from one gear to another in a vehicle
→ See **Car** on page C3

geese /ɡiːs/
plural of goose

gel /dʒel/ **noun** [no plural]
a thick, clear liquid that you use to wash your body or to make you hair stay in the right position: *shower gel* ◦ *hair gel*

gender /ˈdʒendəʳ/ **noun**
1 the state of being male or female
2 the division of words into groups corresponding to masculine, feminine, etc.: *In English, nouns don't have gender, but in Spanish, they do.*

gene /dʒiːn/ **noun**
a part of a cell that is passed on from a parent to a child and that controls

a b c d e f g h i j k l m n o p q r s t u v w x y z

particular characteristics: *Red hair is **in** my **genes**.*

general[1] /ˈdʒenᵊrᵊl/ **adj**
1 B1 with the most basic or necessary information but no details: *These leaflets contain some general information about the school.*
2 relating to or involving all or most people, things, or places: *There seems to be general agreement on this matter.*
3 in general considering the whole of someone or something: *I still have a sore throat, but I feel much better in general.*
4 in general B1 usually, or in most situations: *In general, the weather here is good.*

general[2] /ˈdʒenᵊrᵊl/ **noun**
a very important officer in the army or air force

general election /ˌdʒenᵊrᵊl ɪˈlekʃᵊn/ **noun**
a big election in which the people living in a country vote to decide who will represent them in the government

general knowledge /ˌdʒenᵊrᵊl ˈnɒlɪdʒ/ **noun** [no plural]
knowledge of many different subjects

generally /ˈdʒenᵊrᵊli/ **adv**
1 B1 usually or mostly: *I generally wake up early.* ◦ *The children were generally very well behaved.*
2 considering the whole of someone or something, and not just a particular part of them: *My health is generally very good.*
3 by most people, or to most people: *He is generally believed to be their best player.*

generate /ˈdʒenᵊreɪt/ **verb** (**generating, generated**)
1 to make something exist: *This movie has generated a lot of interest.*
2 to make energy: *We need to generate more electricity.*

generation /ˌdʒenəˈreɪʃᵊn/ **noun**
1 B1 all the people who are about the same age: *the older/younger generation* ◦ *This is the story of three generations of women.*
2 a period of about 25 to 30 years; the time it takes for children to become adults and take the place of their parents in society: *Our family has lived in this village **for generations**.*

generator /ˈdʒenᵊreɪtəʳ/ **noun**
a machine that produces electricity

generosity /ˌdʒenᵊˈrɒsəti/ **noun** [no plural]
the quality of being generous

generous /ˈdʒenᵊrəs/ **adj**
B1 often giving people money or presents: *It was very generous of you to buy her flowers.*
• **generously adv** *He generously offered to pay for dinner.*

genetic /dʒəˈnetɪk/ **adj**
relating to genes: *genetic research*

genetics /dʒəˈnetɪks/ **noun** [no plural]
the scientific study of genes

genius /ˈdʒiːniəs/ **noun**
someone who is extremely intelligent or extremely good at doing something: *Einstein was a genius.*

gentle /ˈdʒentl/ **adj**
1 B1 kind and careful not to hurt or upset anyone: *My mother was such a gentle, loving person.*
2 B1 not strong or unpleasant: *a gentle breeze*
• **gently adv** *He gently stroked her cheek.*

gentleman /ˈdʒentlmən/ **noun** (plural **gentlemen**)
1 a very polite man: *He was a perfect gentleman.*
2 a polite word for 'man': *There's a gentleman here to see you.*

genuine /ˈdʒenjuɪn/ **adj**
real or true: *a genuine antique* ◦ *Was her disappointment genuine?*
• **genuinely adv** used to say that something really is true: *I think she was genuinely concerned.*

geography /dʒiˈɒgrəfi/ **noun** [no plural]
A2 the study of all the countries of the world, and of the surface of the Earth

geology /dʒiˈɒlədʒi/ **noun** [no plural]
the study of rocks and soil and how they were made

geometry /dʒiˈɒmɪtri/ **noun** [no plural]
a type of mathematics that deals with points, lines, angles, and shapes

germ /dʒɜːm/ **noun**
a very small living thing that causes disease: *Wash your hands before you cook so you don't spread germs.*

gesture[1] /ˈdʒestʃəʳ/ **noun**
1 a movement you make with your hand, arm, or head to show what you are thinking or feeling: *He made a rude gesture at the crowd.*
2 something you do to show people how you feel about a person or situation: *It would be a nice gesture to invite her to dinner.*

gesture[2] /ˈdʒestʃəʳ/ **verb** (**gesturing**, **gestured**)
to point at something or show something using your hand, arm, or head: *He gestured towards the window.*

get /get/ **verb** (**getting**, **got**)
1 A1 to obtain or buy something: *Where did you get your shoes?* ◦ *I got you a ticket.*
2 A1 to receive something: *Did you get anything nice for your birthday?* ◦ *Ben still hasn't got my email.*
3 get a bus, train, taxi, etc. A1 to travel somewhere in a bus, train, taxi, or other vehicle: *Shall we get a taxi to the station?*
4 A1 to arrive somewhere: *What time do you get home from work?*
5 A2 to go somewhere and bring back someone or something: *Wait here while I get the car.*
6 get ill, rich, wet, etc. B1 to become ill, rich, wet, etc.: *It's getting late – we should go.*
7 B1 to become ill: *You can get malaria from mosquitoes.*
8 get caught, bitten, etc. B1 If you get caught, bitten, etc., someone or something catches you, bites you, etc.: *He got killed in the war.*
9 B1 to arrange for someone to do something for you: *I need to get my hair cut.*
10 B1 to move to a different place or into a different position: *I saw her **getting into** his car.*
11 B1 to deal with or answer a ringing telephone, a knock on the door, etc.: *Could you get the phone?*
12 get *someone/something* to do *something* to make something happen, or make someone or something do something: *I can't get my computer to work.* ◦ *I got my dad to pick me up from the station.*
13 get to do *something* to have the chance to do something: *I never got to meet her.*
14 to understand something: *He never gets any of my jokes.*

get along **phrasal verb**
1 If two or more people get along, they like each other and are friends: *Chris and Jack don't get along.*
2 to manage or deal with a situation: *How are you getting along in your new flat?*

get around **phrasal verb**
to move from place to place: *I used my brother's car to get around.*

get at *something* **phrasal verb**
B1 to be able to reach or get something: *Put the cake on a high shelf where the kids can't get at it.*

get away **phrasal verb**
1 to leave or escape from a place or person, often when it is difficult to do this: *We walked to the next beach to **get away from** the crowds.*
2 to go somewhere to have a holiday, often because you need to rest: *I just need to get away for a few days.*

get away with *something* **phrasal verb**
to do something bad without being punished for it: *If he's rude to you, don't let him get away with it.*

get back **phrasal verb**
A2 to return to a place after you have been somewhere else: *We got back home late last night.*

get *something* back **phrasal verb**
B1 to be given something again that you had before: *Don't lend him money – you'll never get it back.*

get in **phrasal verb**
1 B1 to succeed in entering a place, especially a building: *The thieves got in through the bathroom window.*
2 B1 to arrive at a place at a particular time: *My train gets in at 9.45 p.m.*

3 B1 to succeed in being chosen or elected: *He wanted to go to Cambridge University but he didn't get in.*

get into *something* phrasal verb
to succeed in being chosen to study at a school or to join an organization: *He got into Oxford University.*

get off (*something*) phrasal verb
A2 to leave a bus, train, plane, or boat: *We should get off at the next stop.*

get on phrasal verb UK
1 B1 If two or more people get on, they like each other and are friends: *Karen and Dianne don't get on.*
2 B1 to manage or deal with a situation: *How are you getting on in your new flat?*

get on (*something*) phrasal verb
A2 to go onto a bus, train, plane, or boat: *I think we got on the wrong bus.*

get out phrasal verb
B1 to move out of a car: *I'll get out when you stop at the traffic lights.*

get over *something* phrasal verb
to feel better after being ill or sad: *She's just getting over a cold.*

get through *something* phrasal verb
to succeed in an exam or competition: *She got through her exams without too much trouble.*

get together phrasal verb
B1 to meet in order to do something or spend time together: *Let's get together next week for a game of tennis.*

get (*someone*) up phrasal verb
A1 to wake up and get out of bed, or to make someone do this: *I had to get up at five o'clock this morning.*

get up phrasal verb
to stand up: *The whole audience got up and started clapping.*

ghetto /ˈgetəʊ/ **noun** (plural **ghettos**)
a poor part of a city where many people of the same race or background live

ghost

ghost /gəʊst/ **noun**
B1 a dead person's spirit, which some people believe they can see: *Do you believe in ghosts?* ◦ *a ghost story*

giant[1] /ˈdʒaɪənt/ **adj**
B1 very big: *a giant spider*

giant[2] /ˈdʒaɪənt/ **noun**
a very big person in children's stories

gift /gɪft/ **noun**
1 A2 something that you give to someone, usually on a special day: *a birthday/wedding gift*
2 a natural ability: *She **has a gift for** art.*

gift shop /ˈgɪft ˌʃɒp/ **noun**
a shop that sells things that are suitable for giving as presents

gig /gɪg/ **noun** informal
a concert where music is performed: *Our band has a gig on Friday night.*

gigantic /dʒaɪˈgæntɪk/ **adj**
very big: *a gigantic teddy bear*

giggle /ˈgɪgl/ **verb** (**giggling**, **giggled**)
to laugh in a nervous or silly way: *She started giggling and couldn't stop.*
• **giggle** noun

ginger[1] /ˈdʒɪndʒəʳ/ **noun** [no plural]
a root with a strong taste that is used in cooking

ginger[2] /ˈdʒɪndʒəʳ/ **adj** UK
Ginger hair is an orange-brown colour.

giraffe

giraffe /dʒɪˈrɑːf/ **noun**
B1 a large African animal with a very long neck and long, thin legs

girl /gɜːl/ **noun**
A1 a female child or young woman: *We have three children – a boy and two girls.*

girlfriend /ˈgɜːlfrend/ **noun**
1 A2 a woman or girl who someone is having a romantic relationship with: *Have you met Steve's new girlfriend?*
2 a female friend, especially of a woman

give /gɪv/ **verb** (**giving**, **gave**, **given**)
1 A1 to provide someone with something: *I gave her a bike for her birthday.* ◦ *Do you **give** money **to** charity?*
2 A2 to put something in someone's

hand so that they can use it or look at it: *Can you give me that pen?*
3 A2 to tell someone something: *Can you give Jo a message?*
4 B1 to do an action: *He gave her a kiss.*
5 B1 to produce or cause something: *What you said has given me an idea.*
6 B1 to allow someone to have something, such as a right or an opportunity: *We didn't really give him a chance to explain.*
7 B1 to allow someone or something a particular amount of time: *I'm nearly ready – just give me a few minutes.*
8 B1 to pay someone a particular amount of money for something: *I gave him £20 for his old camera.*
9 to perform or speak in public: *Tony gave a great speech.*
10 give *someone* a call/ring A2 to telephone someone

give *something* away phrasal verb
1 B1 to give something to someone without asking for payment: *They're giving away a CD with this magazine.*
2 to tell people something secret, often without intending to: *I promise not to give away your secret.*

give *something* back phrasal verb
A2 to give something to the person who gave it to you: *Has she given you those books back yet?*

give in phrasal verb
1 B1 to finally agree to do something that someone wants: *We will never* ***give in to*** *terrorists' demands.*
2 B1 to accept that you have been defeated and agree to stop competing or fighting: *You'll never guess the answer – do you give in?*

give *something* in phrasal verb
B1 to give a piece of written work, etc. to someone to read: *Have you given that essay in yet?*

give *something* out phrasal verb
B1 to give something to a lot of people: *He gave out copies of the report.*

give up *something* phrasal verb
1 B1 If you give up something bad, such as smoking, you stop doing it or having it: *I gave up smoking two years ago.*
2 B1 to stop doing an activity or piece of work before you have completed it, usually because it is too difficult: *I've given up trying to help her.*
3 B1 to stop doing a regular activity or job: *Are you going to give up work when you have your baby?*

glacier /ˈglæsiəʳ/ **noun**
a very large piece of ice that moves very slowly

glad /glæd/ **adj**
1 A2 happy about something: *I'm very* ***glad that*** *you like your present.*
2 very willing to do something: *I'd be* ***glad to*** *help.*

gladly /ˈglædli/ **adv**
If you would gladly do something, you would like to do it: *I would gladly pay extra for better service.*

glamorous /ˈglæmᵊrəs/ **adj**
attractive in an exciting and special way: *She's very glamorous.*

glamour (also US **glamor**) /ˈglæməʳ/ **noun** [no plural]
the quality of being attractive, exciting, and special: *the glamour of Hollywood*

glance¹ /glɑːns/ **verb** (**glancing**, **glanced**)
1 B1 to look somewhere for a short time: *He* ***glanced at*** *his watch.*
2 to read something quickly: *She* ***glanced through*** *the newspaper.*

glance² /glɑːns/ **noun**
a quick look: *She* ***had*** *a quick* ***glance*** *around the restaurant.*

glare¹ /gleəʳ/ **noun**
a long, angry look

glare² /gleəʳ/ **verb** (**glaring**, **glared**)
to look at someone in an angry way: *She* ***glared at*** *him.*

glass /glɑːs/ **noun**
1 A1 [no plural] a hard, clear substance that objects such as windows and bottles are made of: *broken glass* ◦ *glass jars*
2 A1 a container made of glass that is used for drinking: *Would you like* ***a glass of*** *water?*

a b c d e f g h i j k l m n o p q r s t u v w x y z

a b c d e f g h i j k l m n o p q r s t u v w x y z

glass

glass

The window is made of glass.

glasses

glasses /ˈɡlɑːsɪz/ **plural noun**
A1 a piece of equipment with two transparent parts that you wear in front of your eyes to help you see better: *a* ***pair of glasses*** ◦ *She was* ***wearing glasses****.*

gleam /ɡliːm/ **verb**
to shine in a pleasant, soft way: *Her new car gleamed in the sun.*

glide /ɡlaɪd/ **verb** (**gliding**, **glided**)
to move somewhere smoothly and quietly: *The train slowly glided out of the station.*

glimmer /ˈɡlɪməʳ/ **noun**
1 a glimmer of happiness, hope, etc. a small sign of something good
2 a light that shines in a weak way

glimpse /ɡlɪms/ **noun**
a look at something or someone for a very short time: *He* ***caught a glimpse of*** *her as she got into the car.*
• **glimpse verb** (**glimpsing**, **glimpsed**) to see something or someone for a very short time: *She glimpsed him out of the corner of her eye.*

glisten /ˈɡlɪsᵊn/ **verb**
If something glistens, it shines, often because it is wet: *Their faces were* ***glistening with*** *sweat.*

glitter /ˈɡlɪtəʳ/ **verb**
to shine with small flashes of light: *Snow glittered on the mountains.*

glittering /ˈɡlɪtᵊrɪŋ/ **adj**
1 shining with small flashes of light: *glittering jewels*
2 successful and exciting: *a glittering career*

global /ˈɡləʊbᵊl/ **adj**
relating to the whole world: *global problems*

global warming /ˌɡləʊbᵊl ˈwɔːmɪŋ/ **noun** [no plural]
an increase in the temperature of the air around the world that is caused by pollution

globe /ɡləʊb/ **noun**
1 the globe the world: *This event was watched by 200 million people around the globe.*
2 a model of the world shaped like a ball with a map of all the countries on it

globe

gloomy /ˈɡluːmi/ **adj** (**gloomier**, **gloomiest**)
1 sad or without hope: *a gloomy face* ◦ *gloomy predictions*
2 dark in a bad way: *a gloomy room*
• **gloomily adv**

glorious /ˈɡlɔːriəs/ **adj**
1 beautiful or very good: *We had four days of glorious sunshine.* ◦ *glorious colours*
2 getting praise and respect: *a glorious career*

glory /ˈɡlɔːri/ **noun** [no plural]
praise and respect you get from other people for doing something very brave and good

glove /ɡlʌv/ **noun**
A2 a piece of clothing that covers your fingers and hand: *a pair of gloves*
→ See picture at **pair**

glow¹ /ɡləʊ/ **noun**
1 a soft, warm light: *the warm glow of the moon*
2 a pink colour on your face that makes it appear happy and healthy: *Sam's face had lost its usual glow.*

glow² /ɡləʊ/ **verb**
1 to produce a soft, warm light: *toys that glow in the dark*
2 to have a warm and healthy appearance: *She glows with health.*

3 glow with happiness, pride, etc. to feel very happy, proud, etc.: *Glowing with pride, she showed me her painting.*

glue[1] /gluː/ **noun** [no plural]
a substance used to stick things together: *Put a bit of glue on both edges and hold them together.*
→ See **The Classroom** on page C4

glue[2] /gluː/ **verb** (**glueing**, **glued**)
to stick something to something else with glue: *Do you think you can* ***glue*** *this vase back* ***together****?*

glum /glʌm/ **adj**
sad: *Why are you looking so glum today?*
• **glumly adv**

GMT /ˌdʒiːemˈtiː/ **noun** [no plural]
abbreviation for Greenwich Mean Time: the time at Greenwich in London, which is used as an international measurement for time

go[1] /gəʊ/ **verb** (**going**, **went**, **gone**)
1 A1 to move or travel somewhere: *I'd love to go to America.* ◦ *We went into the house.* ◦ *Are you* ***going by*** *train?*
2 A1 to move or travel somewhere in order to do something: *Let's* ***go for*** *a walk.*
3 go running, swimming, etc. A2 to go somewhere to do a particular activity: *We went skating yesterday.*
4 be going to do/be *something* A2 to intend to do or be something: *I'm going to phone her tonight.* ◦ *I'm going to be a dancer when I grow up.*
5 be going to do *something* A2 used to say that something is expected to happen in the future: *It's going to snow tonight.*
6 go badly, well, etc. B1 to happen in a particular way: *My exams went really well.*
7 B1 to disappear or no longer exist: *When I turned round the man had gone.*
8 B1 If a road, path, etc. goes in a particular direction, it leads there: *This road* ***goes to*** *Birmingham.*
9 go bald, blind, etc. B1 to become bald, blind, etc.: *He went bald when he was thirty.*
10 B1 If two things go, they match each other: *Does the jacket* ***go with*** *the trousers?*
11 to work correctly: *I managed to get the car going.*
12 to have a particular tune or words: *I can't remember how his latest song goes.*
13 If time goes, it passes: *The day went very quickly.*

go ahead phrasal verb
1 to start to do something: *We have permission to go ahead with the project.*
2 something that you say to someone to allow them to do something: *'Can I borrow your book?' 'Yes, go ahead.'*

go away phrasal verb
1 B1 to leave a place: *Just go away and leave me alone.*
2 B1 to leave your home in order to spend time in a different place: *We're going away for a few weeks in the summer.*

go back phrasal verb
B1 to return to a place where you were or where you have been before: *When are you* ***going back to*** *Paris?*

go by phrasal verb
If time goes by, it passes: *The days went by really slowly.*

go down phrasal verb
1 B1 to become lower in level: *Food prices have gone down recently.*
2 B1 When the sun goes down, it moves down in the sky until it cannot be seen any more: *I sat and watched the sun go down.*

go for *something* phrasal verb
B1 to choose something: *I don't know whether to go for the fish or the steak.*

go in phrasal verb
A2 to enter a place: *I looked through the window but I didn't go in.*

go into *something* phrasal verb
to describe, discuss, or examine something in a detailed way: *She didn't* ***go into detail*** *about the job.*

go off phrasal verb
1 B1 to leave a place and go somewhere else: *She went off with Laurie.*
2 B1 If a light or machine goes off, it stops working: *The heating goes off at ten o'clock.*
3 If a bomb or gun goes off, it explodes or fires.

4 If something that makes a noise goes off, it suddenly starts making a noise: *His car alarm goes off every time it rains.*
5 If food goes off, it stops being good to eat because it is too old: *That milk has gone off.*
go on phrasal verb
1 B1 to last for a particular period of time: *The speech seemed to go on forever.*
2 to continue doing something: *We can't go on living like this.*
3 B1 to happen: *What's going on?*
go out phrasal verb
1 A1 to leave a place in order to go somewhere else: *Are you going out tonight?*
2 B1 If two people go out together, they have a romantic relationship with each other: *Tina is **going out with** Peter.*
3 B1 If a light or something that is burning goes out, it stops producing light or heat: *I'm sorry – I let the fire go out.*
go over *something* phrasal verb
to examine something, such as a piece of writing or some numbers, in order to make sure that they are correct: *I'm just going over my essay one more time.*
go through *something* phrasal verb
to have a difficult or bad situation: *She's going through a difficult time with her job.*
go up phrasal verb
B1 to become higher in level: *House prices keep going up.*

go² /gəʊ/ **noun** (plural **goes**)
1 UK the act of trying to do something: *I **had a go at** catching a fish.*
2 B1 mainly UK a time when you do something in a game: *Throw the dice, Jane, it's your go.*

goal /gəʊl/ **noun**
1 A2 a point scored in sports such as football, by sending a ball into a particular area, such as between two posts: *He scored two goals in the second half.*
2 A2 in some sports, the area between two posts where players try to send the ball
→ See **Sports 2** on page C16
3 B1 something that you want to do in the future: *Andy's goal is to run in the New York Marathon.*

goalkeeper /ˈgəʊlˌkiːpəʳ/ **noun**
B1 the player in a sport such as football who tries to stop the ball from going into the goal

goalkeeper

goat /gəʊt/ **noun**
B1 an animal with horns that is kept for the milk it makes

god /gɒd/ **noun**
1 **God** A2 in certain religions, the being that made the universe and controls it
2 **Oh my God!** informal B1 used to emphasize how surprised, angry, shocked, etc. you are: *Oh my God! The car's been stolen.*
3 **thank God** informal B1 something you say when you are happy because something bad did not happen: *Thank God nobody was hurt in the accident.*
4 a spirit, especially a male one, that people pray to: *the ancient Greek gods and goddesses*

goddess /ˈgɒdes/ **noun**
a female spirit that people pray to: *the ancient goddess of love*

goggles /ˈgɒglz/ **noun**
special glasses for protecting your eyes: *a pair of goggles*

gold¹ /gəʊld/ **noun** [no plural]
A2 a valuable, shiny, yellow metal used to make jewellery

gold² /gəʊld/ **adj**
1 A2 made of gold: *gold jewellery*
2 A2 being the shiny yellow colour of gold: *gold paint*

golden /ˈgəʊldᵊn/ **adj**
A2 being a bright yellow colour: *golden hair*

goldfish /ˈgəʊldfɪʃ/ **noun** (plural **goldfish**)
a small orange fish that is often kept as a pet

a b c d e f g h i j k l m n o p q r s t u v w x y z

golf /ɡɒlf/
noun [no plural]
A2 a game you play by hitting a small ball with a long, thin stick into holes on a large area of grass
• **golfer** noun

golf

golf course /ˈɡɒlf ˌkɔːs/ **noun**
an area of land used for playing golf

gone /ɡɒn/
past participle of go

good[1] /ɡʊd/ **adj** (**better**, **best**)
1 A1 enjoyable or nice: *a good book* ◦ *Did you have a good time at the party?*
2 A1 of a high quality: *The food at this restaurant is very good.*
3 A1 able to do something well: *Anna is a good cook.*
4 A1 kind or helpful: *She's a good friend.*
5 A1 something you say when you are pleased about something: *Oh good, he's arrived at last.*
6 A1 having a positive or useful effect: *Fruit is **good for** you.*
7 A1 informal something that you say when a person asks how you are or how someone you know is: *'How are you, Emily?' 'I'm good, thanks!'*
8 A2 A good child or animal behaves well.
9 A2 suitable or satisfactory: *When would be a good time to call?*
10 B1 morally right: *a good person*

> **Common mistake: good or well?**
> **Good** is an adjective and is used to describe nouns.
> *She's a **good** cook.*
> *Her children had a **good** education.*
> **Well** is an adverb and is used to describe verbs.
> *She cooks **well**.*
> *Her children were **well** educated.*

good[2] /ɡʊd/ **noun**
1 [no plural] what people think is morally right: *Children don't always understand the difference between good and bad.*
2 something that is an advantage or help to a person or situation: *It's hard work, but it's **for your own good**.*
3 **do *someone* good** to be useful or helpful to someone: *A holiday will do you good.*
4 **for good** forever: *When he was 20, he left home for good.*

goodbye /ɡʊdˈbaɪ/ **exclamation**
A1 something you say when you leave someone or when they leave you: *Goodbye Vicki! See you next week.*

good evening /ˌɡʊd ˈiːvnɪŋ/ **exclamation**
A1 something you say to someone in the evening

good-looking /ˌɡʊdˈlʊkɪŋ/ **adj**
A2 attractive: *a good-looking woman*

good morning /ˌɡʊd ˈmɔːnɪŋ/ **exclamation**
A1 something you say to someone when you meet them in the morning

goodness /ˈɡʊdnəs/ **noun**
1 [no plural] the quality in people that makes them behave well and treat other people kindly: *She believes in the goodness of human nature.*
2 informal something you say when you are surprised: ***My goodness**, he's a big baby, isn't he?*

good night /ˌɡʊd ˈnaɪt/ **exclamation**
A1 something you say when you leave someone in the evening or when someone is going to bed

goods /ɡʊdz/ **plural noun**
B1 items that are made to be sold: *We sell pies, cakes, and other baked goods.*

goose /ɡuːs/ **noun** (plural **geese**)
a large water bird similar to a duck

gorgeous /ˈɡɔːdʒəs/ **adj**
B1 very beautiful or pleasant: *You look gorgeous in that dress!*

gorilla /ɡəˈrɪlə/ **noun**
a big, black, hairy animal, like a large monkey

gossip[1] /ˈɡɒsɪp/ **noun** [no plural]
conversation about other people's private lives that might not be true: *an interesting piece of gossip*

gossip[2] /ˈgɒsɪp/ **verb** (**gosipping**, **gosipped**)
to talk about other people's private lives

got /gɒt/
past tense and past participle of get

govern /ˈgʌv(ə)n/ **verb**
to officially control a country: *The country is now governed by the army.*

government /ˈgʌv(ə)nmənt/ **noun**
1 B1 the group of people who officially control a country: *The government has cut taxes.*
2 [no plural] the method or process of governing a country: *The country has returned to democratic government.*

governor /ˈgʌv(ə)nə(r)/ **noun**
someone who controls a region or organization: *the governor of Texas*

GP /ˌdʒiːˈpiː/ **noun** mainly UK
abbreviation for general practitioner: a doctor who treats people in the local area, not in a hospital

GPS /ˌdʒiːpiːˈes/ **noun** [no plural]
abbreviation for global positioning system: a system that uses satellites (= devices that move around the Earth) to show the position of a person or thing anywhere in the world

grab /græb/ **verb** (**grabbing**, **grabbed**)
1 B1 to take hold of something or someone suddenly with your hand: *He grabbed my arm and pulled me away.*
2 informal to quickly take the opportunity to get, use, or enjoy something: *We'd better get there early, or someone else will grab the best seats.*

grace /greɪs/ **noun** [no plural]
the quality of moving in a smooth and attractive way: *She moved **with** such **grace**.*

graceful /ˈgreɪsf(ə)l/ **adj**
moving in a smooth and attractive way: *graceful movements*
• **gracefully** **adv**

grade[1] /greɪd/ **noun**
1 B1 a number or letter that shows how good your work is: *Carla got a grade A in German.*
2 a level of quality, size, importance, etc.: *I applied for a position a grade higher than my current job.*
3 US (UK **form**) a school class for students of the same age or ability: *My son is in fifth grade.*

grade[2] /greɪd/ **verb** (**grading**, **graded**)
to separate people or things into different levels of quality, size, importance, etc.: *The fruit is washed and then **graded by** size.*

graded /ˈgreɪdɪd/ **adj**
arranged in order according to difficulty: *a series of graded readers (= books for people learning a language)*

gradual /ˈgrædʒuəl/ **adj**
happening slowly: *a gradual change*

gradually /ˈgrædʒuəli/ **adv**
slowly over a period of time: *Gradually he got better.*

graduate[1] /ˈgrædʒuət/ **noun**
1 UK someone who has studied for and got a degree (= qualification) from a university: *a science graduate*
2 US someone who has completed their education at a school or university successfully: *a high school graduate*

graduate[2] /ˈgrædjueɪt/ **verb** (**graduating**, **graduated**)
to complete your education successfully at a university, college, or, in the US, at school: *He **graduated from** Cambridge University in 2006.*

graduation /ˌgrædʒuˈeɪʃ(ə)n/ **noun**
1 a formal event at which students receive a certificate for successfully completing a course of study: *We all went to the **graduation ceremony**.*
2 [no plural] the act of successfully completing your education or course of study: *What do you plan to do after graduation?*

graffiti /grəˈfiːti/ **noun** [no plural]
writing or pictures painted on walls and public places, usually illegally: *The walls are covered in graffiti.*

grain /greɪn/ **noun**
1 a seed or seeds from types of grass that are eaten as food: *grains of wheat/rice*
2 a very small piece of something: *a grain of sand/sugar*

gram /græm/ **noun** (written abbreviation **g**)
A2 a unit for measuring weight, equal to 0.001 kilograms

grammar /ˈgræməʳ/ **noun** [no plural]
A2 the way you combine words and change their form and position in a sentence, or the rules of this

grammatical /grəˈmætɪkəl/ **adj**
obeying the rules of grammar: *a grammatical sentence*

grand /grænd/ **adj**
very large and special: *a grand hotel*

grandad /ˈgrændæd/ **noun** mainly UK informal
A2 another word for grandfather

grandchild /ˈgrændtʃaɪld/ **noun** (plural **grandchildren**)
A2 the child of someone's son or daughter: *We have three children and seven grandchildren.*

granddaughter /ˈgrændˌdɔːtəʳ/ **noun**
A2 the daughter of someone's son or daughter: *We're excited to see our new baby granddaughter.*

grandfather /ˈgrændˌfɑːðəʳ/ **noun**
A2 the father of someone's mother or father: *My grandfather lived to the age of 92.*

grandma /ˈgrændmɑː/ **noun** informal
A2 another word for grandmother

grandmother /ˈgrændˌmʌðəʳ/ **noun**
A2 the mother of someone's mother or father: *His grandmother sent him some money for his birthday.*

grandpa /ˈgrændpɑː/ **noun** informal
A2 another word for grandfather

grandparent /ˈgrændˌpeərənt/ **noun**
A2 the parent of someone's mother or father: *Her grandparents lived far away from her family.*

grandson /ˈgrændsʌn/ **noun**
A2 the son of someone's son or daughter: *Our grandson is doing well in school.*

granny /ˈgræni/ **noun** (plural **grannies**)
A2 informal another word for grandmother

grant¹ /grɑːnt/ **verb** formal
to give or allow someone something, usually in an official way: *He was granted a visa.*
• **take *something/someone* for granted** to expect something and not understand that you are lucky to have it: *Most of us take our freedom for granted.*

grant² /grɑːnt/ **noun**
B1 an amount of money that an organization gives you for a special purpose: *They received a grant for the project.*

grape /greɪp/ **noun**
A2 a small, round fruit that grows in large groups and is used to make wine: *a bunch of grapes*
→ See **Fruit and Vegetables** on page C8

grapefruit /ˈgreɪpfruːt/ **noun** (plural **grapefruit, grapefruits**)
a large, round, yellow fruit with a sour taste

graph /grɑːf/ **noun**
a picture that shows different amounts by using a line or many lines

graph

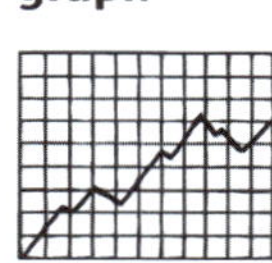

graphics /ˈgræfɪks/ **plural noun**
B1 images shown on a computer screen: *computer graphics*

grapple /ˈgræpl/ **verb** (**grappling, grappled**)
grapple with *something* **phrasal verb**
to try to understand something difficult

grasp /grɑːsp/ **verb**
1 to take hold of something firmly with your hand: *He grasped my hand.*
2 to understand something: *I didn't grasp what she was saying.*

grass /grɑːs/ **noun** [no plural]
A1 a common plant with thin green leaves that grows close to the ground: *We like to lie on the grass in the sun.*

a b c d e f g h i j k l m n o p q r s t u v w x y z

grate /greɪt/ **verb** (**grating**, **grated**)
to break food such as cheese into small, thin pieces by rubbing it against a grater (= kitchen tool with holes): *grated cheese*

grateful /ˈgreɪtfəl/ **adj**
B1 wanting to say 'thank you' to someone who has done something good for you: *I'm really* ***grateful to*** *you* ***for*** *all your help.*
→ Opposite **ungrateful adj**
• **gratefully adv**

grater /ˈgreɪtəʳ/ **noun**
a kitchen tool with a surface full of holes, used to grate (= break into small pieces) food such as cheese
→ See **The Kitchen** on page C10

gratitude /ˈgrætɪtjuːd/ **noun** [no plural]
a feeling of being grateful to someone who has done something good for you

grave[1] /greɪv/ **noun**
a place in the ground where a dead body is buried

grave[2] /greɪv/ **adj**
very serious: *grave doubts* ◦ *a grave mistake*

gravel /ˈgrævəl/ **noun** [no plural]
small pieces of stone used to make paths and roads

gravestone /ˈgreɪvstəʊn/ **noun**
a stone that shows the name of a dead person who is buried under it

graveyard /ˈgreɪvjɑːd/ **noun**
an area of land where dead bodies are buried, usually next to a church

gravity /ˈgrævəti/ **noun** [no plural]
1 the force that makes objects fall to the ground: *the laws of gravity*
2 formal the seriousness of a problem

gravy /ˈgreɪvi/ **noun** [no plural]
a warm, brown sauce that you put on meat

graze[1] /greɪz/ **verb** (**grazing**, **grazed**)
1 to eat grass
2 UK to hurt your skin by rubbing it against something rough: *I fell and grazed my knee.*

graze[2] /greɪz/ **noun** mainly UK
an injury on your skin caused by rubbing against something: *She has a nasty* ***graze on*** *her elbow.*

grease /griːs/ **noun** [no plural]
a substance such as oil or fat

greasy /ˈgriːsi/ **adj** (**greasier**, **greasiest**)
containing or covered with fat or oil: *greasy food*

great /greɪt/ **adj**
1 A1 very good: *We had a great time.*
2 A2 large: *a great crowd of people*
3 B1 extreme: *He has great difficulty walking.*
4 important or famous: *a great actor*
5 great big, long, etc. very big, long, etc.: *They've got a great big house.*

great- /greɪt/ **prefix**
1 great-grandfather/-grandmother the father or mother of your grandfather or grandmother
2 great-aunt/-uncle the aunt or uncle of your mother or father
3 great-grandchild, -granddaughter, etc. the child, daughter, etc. of your grandson or granddaughter
4 great-niece/-nephew the daughter or son of your niece or nephew

greatly /ˈgreɪtli/ **adv**
very much: *We will miss her greatly.*

greed /griːd/ **noun** [no plural]
a desire for a lot more food, money, or things than you need

greedy /ˈgriːdi/ **adj** (**greedier**, **greediest**)
wanting a lot more food, money, etc. than you need: *greedy, selfish people*

green[1] /griːn/ **adj**
1 A1 being the same colour as grass
→ See **Colours** on page C6
2 B1 covered with grass or other plants: *green spaces*
3 relating to nature and protecting the environment: *green issues*

green[2] /griːn/ **noun**
A2 the colour of grass
→ See **Colours** on page C6

greengrocer /ˈgriːnˌgrəʊsəʳ/ **noun** UK
1 someone who sells fruit and vegetables

2 greengrocer's a shop where you buy fruit and vegetables

greenhouse /ˈgriːnhaʊs/ **noun** a building made of glass for growing plants in

greenhouse

greet /griːt/ **verb** B1 to say hello to someone who has arrived in a place: *He greeted me at the door.*

greeting /ˈgriːtɪŋ/ **noun** B1 something friendly or polite that you say or do when you see someone

grew /gruː/ past tense of grow

grey[1] UK (US **gray**) /greɪ/ **adj** A1 being a colour that is a mixture of black and white: *grey clouds* ◦ *an old man with grey hair*
→ See **Colours** on page C6

grey[2] UK (US **gray**) /greɪ/ **noun** A2 a colour that is a mixture of black and white
→ See **Colours** on page C6

grief /griːf/ **noun** [no plural] the great sadness that you feel when someone dies

grieve /griːv/ **verb** (**grieving**, **grieved**) to feel very sad because someone has died: *He is still* ***grieving for*** *his wife.*

grill[1] /grɪl/ **noun** B1 a piece of equipment that cooks food using heat from above

grill[2] /grɪl/ **verb** B1 to cook food using direct heat: *Grill the fish for two minutes on each side.*
→ See picture at **cook**
• **grilled adj** A2 *grilled fish*

grim /grɪm/ **adj** (**grimmer**, **grimmest**)
1 worrying and bad: *grim news*
2 sad and serious: *a grim expression*
3 A grim place is ugly and unpleasant.

grin /grɪn/ **verb** (**grinning**, **grinned**) to smile a big smile: *He* ***grinned at*** *me.*
• **grin noun** *She had a big grin on her face.*

grind /graɪnd/ **verb** (**ground**) to make something change into powder by rubbing it between two hard things: *to grind coffee*

grip[1] /grɪp/ **noun** an act of holding something tightly: *She tightened her* ***grip on*** *my arm.*

grip[2] /grɪp/ **verb** (**gripping**, **gripped**)
1 to hold something tightly: *She gripped his arm.*
2 to keep someone's attention completely: *This trial has gripped the nation.*

gripping /ˈgrɪpɪŋ/ **adj** very interesting and exciting: *a gripping movie*

groan /grəʊn/ **verb** to make a long, low sound because you are sad or in pain: *He collapsed, groaning with pain.*
• **groan noun**

groceries /ˈgrəʊsəriz/ **plural noun** the food and other things for your home that you buy in a food store: *a bag of groceries*

groom /gruːm/ **noun** (also **bridegroom**) B1 a man who is getting married

grope /grəʊp/ **verb** (**groping**, **groped**) to try to get hold of something with your hand, usually when you cannot see it: *I* ***groped*** *in my bag* ***for*** *my keys.*

ground[1] /graʊnd/ past tense and past participle of grind

ground[2] /graʊnd/ **noun**
1 the ground B1 the surface of the Earth: *I sat down* ***on the ground****.*
2 B1 an area of land used for a particular activity: *a football ground*
3 [no plural] the soil in an area: *soft ground*

ground floor /ˌgraʊnd ˈflɔːʳ/ **noun** UK (US **first floor**) B1 the level of a building that is on the ground

grounds /graʊndz/ **plural noun**
a reason for doing or believing something: *I refused* ***on the grounds that*** *(= because) it was too risky.* ◦ *We have grounds to believe that you have been lying to us.*

group /gruːp/ **noun**
1 A1 a number of people or things that are together in one place: *She was with a* ***group of*** *friends.*
2 A1 a few musicians or singers who perform together, usually playing popular music: *a rock group*

grow /grəʊ/ **verb** (**grew**, **grown**)
1 A2 to become bigger or taller as time passes: *Children grow very quickly.*
2 A2 If a plant grows, or you grow it, it develops from a seed to a full plant: *These plants grow well in sandy soil.*
3 B1 to increase: *The problem grows every year.*
4 to become: *We've grown older.*
5 B1 If your hair or nails grow, or if you grow them, they get longer.
grow up **phrasal verb**
A2 to become older or an adult: *She grew up in Madrid.*

growing /ˈgrəʊɪŋ/ **adj**
increasing in size or quantity: *A growing number of people are shopping on the Internet.*

growl /graʊl/ **verb**
If a dog growls, it makes a deep, angry noise.
• **growl** **noun**

grown /grəʊn/
past participle of grow

grown-up[1] /ˈgrəʊnʌp/ **noun**
an adult, used especially when talking to children: *Ask a grown-up to cut the shape out for you.*

grown-up[2] /ˌgrəʊnˈʌp/ **adj**
adult: *Anne has a grown-up son of 24.*

growth /grəʊθ/ **noun**
1 the process of getting bigger or developing: *population growth*
2 something that grows on your skin or inside your body, that should not be there

grumble /ˈgrʌmbl/ **verb** (**grumbling**, **grumbled**)
to keep complaining about something: *She's always* ***grumbling about*** *something.*
• **grumble** **noun**

grumpy /ˈgrʌmpi/ **adj** (**grumpier**, **grumpiest**)
easily annoyed and often complaining: *a grumpy old man*

grunt /grʌnt/ **verb**
If a pig grunts, it makes short, low sounds.

guarantee[1] /ˌgærənˈtiː/ **verb** (**guaranteeing**, **guaranteed**)
1 to promise that something is true or will happen: *We can't guarantee that it will arrive in time.*
2 If a company guarantees a product, it promises to repair it or give you a new one if it has a fault: *The TV is guaranteed for twelve months.*

guarantee[2] /ˌgærənˈtiː/ **noun**
1 a written promise made by a company to repair one of its products or give you a new one if it has a fault: *a three-year guarantee*
2 a promise that something will be done or will happen: *There's no guarantee that it actually works.*

guard[1] /gɑːd/ **noun**
B1 someone whose job is to protect a person or make sure that a person does not escape: *prison guards*
• **be on your guard** to be ready to do something if a problem happens: *Companies were warned to be on their guard for suspicious packages.*

guard[2] /gɑːd/ **verb**
1 to protect someone or something so that no one attacks the person or thing, or steals the thing: *Soldiers guarded the main doors of the embassy.*
2 to watch someone and make certain that they do not escape: *Five prison officers guarded the prisoners.*

guardian /ˈgɑːdiən/ **noun**
someone who is legally responsible for someone else's child

guerrilla /gəˈrɪlə/ **noun**
a soldier who fights to achieve their political beliefs: *guerrilla warfare*

guess[1] /ges/ **verb**
1 A2 to give an answer or opinion about something without knowing all the facts: *Guess how old he is.*
2 A2 to say something that is right without knowing all the facts: *How did you guess I was pregnant?*
3 guess what? informal A2 used before telling someone something interesting or surprising: *Guess what? We're going to Hawaii!*
4 I guess B1 used when you think something is probably true: *I guess you're angry with me.*
5 I guess so/not used when you agree or disagree but are not completely certain about something: *'It would be better to buy a new car than to try to fix this one.' 'Yeah, I guess so.'*

guess[2] /ges/ **noun**
1 B1 an attempt to give the right answer when you are not certain: *How old do you think John is? Go on,* ***have a guess****.*
2 an opinion that you have formed by guessing: *My guess is she probably won't come.*

guest /gest/ **noun**
1 A2 someone who comes to visit you: *We've got some guests coming this weekend.*
2 A2 someone who is staying in a hotel: *The hotel has room for 200 guests.*
3 a famous person who has been invited to appear on television, etc.: *Our special guest on the show tonight is Robert De Niro.*

guesthouse /ˈgesthaʊs/ **noun**
a small, cheap hotel

guidance /ˈgaɪdᵊns/ **noun** [no plural]
help or advice: *I need some careers guidance.*

guide[1] /gaɪd/ **noun**
1 A2 someone whose job is to show interesting places to visitors: *a tour guide*
2 B1 a book that gives information about something or tells you how to do something: *a hotel/restaurant guide* ◦ *a user's guide*

guide[2] /gaɪd/ **verb** (**guiding**, **guided**)
B1 to help someone or something go somewhere: *He gently guided her back to her chair.*

guidebook /ˈgaɪdbʊk/ **noun**
A2 a book that gives visitors information about a particular place

guided tour /ˌgaɪdɪd ˈtʊəʳ/ **noun**
a visit to a place such as a museum with a guide who explains facts about the place

guilt /gɪlt/ **noun** [no plural]
1 the bad feeling you get when you know you have done something bad, such as upsetting someone: *He had feelings of guilt about leaving his children.*
2 the fact that someone has done something illegal: *He was never convinced of her guilt.*
→ Opposite **innocence** **noun**

guilty /ˈgɪlti/ **adj** (**guiltier**, **guiltiest**)
1 B1 feeling bad because you have done something wrong: *I feel so guilty about missing her party.*
2 having broken a law: *The jury* ***found her guilty*** *(= decided that she was guilty of a crime).* ◦ *They found him* ***guilty of*** *murder.*
→ Opposite **innocent** **adj**

guitar /gɪˈtɑːʳ/ **noun**
A1 a musical instrument with strings that you play by pulling the strings: *an electric guitar*

guitarist /gɪˈtɑːrɪst/ **noun**
B1 someone who plays the guitar

gulf /gʌlf/ **noun**
a large area of sea that has land almost all the way around it: *the Gulf of Mexico*

gulp /gʌlp/ **verb** (also **gulp down**)
to drink or eat something quickly: *I just had time to gulp down a coffee.*
• **gulp** **noun** an amount of something that you swallow: *He* ***took a gulp of*** *water.*

gum /gʌm/ **noun**
the hard pink part inside your mouth that your teeth grow out of

gun /gʌn/ **noun**
B1 a weapon that you fire bullets out of

gush /gʌʃ/ **verb**
If liquid gushes from an opening, a lot of it comes out quickly: *Blood was gushing from the wound.*

gust /gʌst/ **verb**
If winds gust, they blow strongly.
• **gust noun** a sudden, strong movement of wind: *a gust of air*

guts /gʌts/ **plural noun** informal
the courage that you need to do something difficult or frightening: *It takes guts to admit that you were wrong.*

gutter /ˈgʌtəʳ/ **noun**
the edge of a road where water flows away

guy /gaɪ/ **noun** informal
A2 a man: *What a nice guy!*

gym /dʒɪm/ **noun**
1 B1 a building with equipment for doing exercises: *Nick goes to the gym three times a week.*
2 B1 [no plural] exercises done inside, especially as a school subject: *my gym teacher*

gymnast /ˈdʒɪmnæst/ **noun**
someone who does gymnastics: *an Olympic gymnast*

gymnastics

gymnastics /dʒɪmˈnæstɪks/ **noun** [no plural]
B1 a sport in which you do physical exercises on the floor and on different pieces of equipment

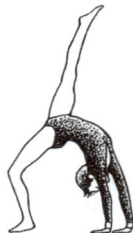

H, h /eɪtʃ/
the eighth letter of the alphabet

habit /ˈhæbɪt/ **noun**
B1 something that you often do, almost without thinking about it: *I got into the **habit of** drinking coffee every morning.*

hack /hæk/ **verb**
to use a computer to illegally get into someone else's computer system

had strong /hæd/ weak /həd/ **verb**
past tense and past participle of have

hadn't /ˈhædᵊnt/
short form of had not: *I hadn't seen Megan since college.*

hail¹ /heɪl/ **noun** [no plural]
small, hard balls of ice that fall from the sky like rain

hail² /heɪl/ **verb**
it hails If it hails, small, hard balls of ice fall from the sky like rain.

hailstone /ˈheɪlstəʊn/ **noun**
a small, hard ball of ice that falls from the sky like rain

hair /heəʳ/ **noun**
1 A1 [no plural] the thin threads that grow on the head and body of people and animals: *a girl with long, dark hair*
2 one of the thin threads that grow on a person's or animal's skin: *My skirt was covered with cat hairs.*

hairbrush /ˈheəbrʌʃ/ **noun**
a brush that you use to make your hair look tidy
→ See picture at **brush noun**

haircut /ˈheəkʌt/ **noun**
1 B1 an act of having your hair cut: *I really need a haircut.*
2 the style in which your hair has been cut: *I like your new haircut.*

hairdresser /ˈheəˌdresəʳ/ **noun**
1 B1 someone whose job is to cut people's hair
2 **hairdresser's** the place where you go to have your hair cut, coloured, etc.

hairdryer /ˈheəˌdraɪəʳ/ **noun**
B1 a piece of electrical equipment for drying your hair with hot air

hairstyle /ˈheəstaɪl/ **noun**
the style in which someone's hair is cut and arranged: *Do you like my new hairstyle?*

hairy /ˈheəri/ **adj** (**hairier**, **hairiest**)
covered in hair: *a hairy chest*

half¹ /hɑːf/ **noun**, **determiner** (plural **halves** /hɑːvz/)
1 A2 one of two equal parts of something; 1/2: *Divide the lemons into halves.* ◦ *It'll take **half an hour** to get there.* ◦ *Jenny lived in Beijing for a year and a half.*
2 **half past one, two, etc.** mainly UK A1 30 minutes past one o'clock, two o'clock, etc.: *We got back to our hotel at half past seven.*
3 **break, cut, etc. *something* in half** B1 to divide something into two equal parts: *Fold the piece of paper in half.*
4 informal a lot: *I don't even know where she is **half of the time**.*

half² /hɑːf/ **adv**
B1 partly, but not completely: *The room was half empty.* ◦ *Sophia is half Greek and half Spanish (= she has one Greek parent and one Spanish parent).*

half-price /ˌhɑːfˈpraɪs/ **adj**, **adv**
A2 costing half the usual price: *I got some half-price pizzas at the supermarket.* ◦ *Children under the age of 16 can travel half-price on most trains.*

half-term /hɑːfˈtɜːm/ **noun** UK
a short holiday in the middle of a school term (= one of the periods the school year is divided into)

half-time /ˌhɑːfˈtaɪm/ **noun** [no plural]
a short period of rest between the two halves of a game

halfway /ˌhɑːfˈweɪ/ **adj**, **adv**
in the middle between two places, or in the middle of a period of time: ***halfway between** London and Oxford* ◦ *We were already halfway through the week.*

hall /hɔːl/ **noun**
1 A2 a room that leads to other

rooms: *Her office is at the end of the hall.*
2 A2 a large room or building where meetings, concerts, etc. happen: *The concert was held in Carnegie Hall.* ◦ *the school hall*
3 (also **hall of residence**) a building where university or college students live

hall of residence /ˌhɔːl əv ˈrezɪdᵊns/ **noun** UK (US **dorm**)
a building where university or college students live

Halloween /ˌhæləʊˈiːn/ **noun** [no plural]
the night of October 31 when children dress in special clothes and visit houses to ask for sweets, and people try to frighten each other

halt[1] /hɒlt/ **noun**
the action of stopping something moving or happening: *The car* ***came to a halt****.*

halt[2] /hɒlt/ **verb** formal
to stop or make something stop: *Work on the project was halted immediately.*

halve /hɑːv/ **verb** (**halving**, **halved**)
to divide something into two equal parts: *Peel and halve the potatoes.*

ham /hæm/ **noun**
A2 meat from a pig's leg: *a ham sandwich*

hamburger /ˈhæmˌbɜːgəʳ/ **noun**
meat that is cooked in a round, flat shape and eaten between round pieces of bread: *a hamburger and fries*

hammer /ˈhæməʳ/ **noun**
a tool with a heavy metal part at the top that you use to hit nails into something

hammer

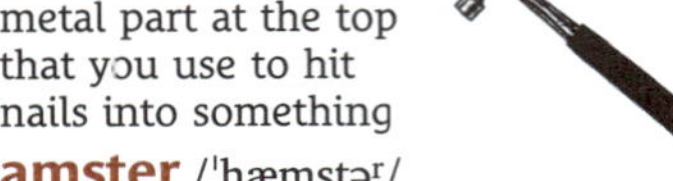

hamster /ˈhæmstəʳ/ **noun**
a small animal with soft fur and no tail that is often kept as a pet

hand[1] /hænd/ **noun**
1 A1 the part of your body on the end of your arm that has fingers: *I had my hands in my pockets.*
→ See **The Body** on page C2
2 hold hands If two people hold hands, they hold each other's hand.
3 by hand B1 done or made by a person and not a machine: *This sweater has to be washed by hand.*
4 one of the long, thin pieces that point to the numbers on a clock or watch
5 give *someone* a hand B1 to help someone: *Could you give me a hand with these suitcases?*
6 on the one hand... on the other hand used when you are comparing two different ideas or opinions: *On the one hand, I'd like more money, but on the other hand, I don't want to work.*

hand[2] /hænd/ **verb**
B1 to give something to someone: *Could you hand me that book, please?*
hand *something* in **phrasal verb**
B1 to give your finished work to a teacher: *Have you handed your history essay in yet?*
hand *something* out **phrasal verb**
B1 to give something to all the people in a group: *The teacher handed out worksheets to the class.*
hand *someone/something* over **phrasal verb**
to give someone or something to someone else: *We were ordered to hand over our passports.*

handbag /ˈhændbæg/ **noun**
A2 a bag carried by a woman with her money, keys, etc. inside
→ See picture at **bag**

handbrake /ˈhændbreɪk/ **noun** (US **emergency brake**)
a stick inside a car that you pull up to stop the car from moving: *You should* ***put*** *the* ***handbrake on*** *whenever you stop on a hill.*
→ See **Car** on page C3

handcuffs /ˈhænd kʌfs/ **plural noun**
two metal rings joined by a chain that are used for holding a prisoner's hands together

handcuffs

handful /ˈhændfʊl/ **noun**
1 the amount of something that you

can hold in one hand: *a handful of nuts*
2 a handful of *something* a small number of people or things: *Only a handful of people came to the meeting.*

handheld[1] /ˈhændheld/ **adj**
B1 describes something that is designed to be held and used easily with one or two hands: *a handheld computer*

handheld[2] /ˈhændheld/ **noun**
a small computer or electronic device that is designed to be held and used easily with one or two hands

handicap /ˈhændɪkæp/ **noun**
1 something that is wrong with your mind or body permanently: *a mental/physical handicap*
2 something that makes it more difficult for you to do something: *Not having a car was a real handicap in the countryside.*

handicapped /ˈhændɪkæpt/ **adj**
not able to use part of your body or your mind because it has been damaged: *mentally/physically handicapped*

handkerchief /ˈhæŋkətʃiːf/ **noun**
B1 a small piece of cloth or soft paper that you use to dry your eyes or nose

handle[1] /ˈhændl/ **verb** (**handling**, **handled**)
1 B1 to take action to improve a difficult situation: *He handled the situation very well.*
2 to touch, hold, or pick up something: *You must wash your hands before handling food.*

handle[2] /ˈhændl/ **noun**
the part of something that you use to hold it or open it: *a door handle* ◦ *the handle on a suitcase*

handlebars /ˈhændlbɑːz/ **plural noun**
the metal bars at the front of a bicycle or motorcycle that you hold on to

handlebars

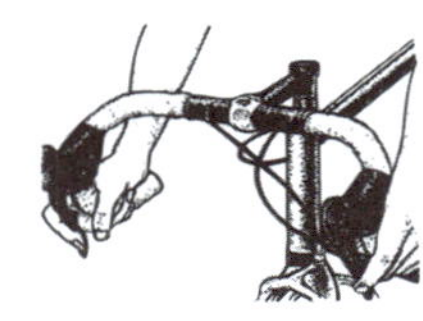

handles

hand luggage /ˈhænd ˌlʌgɪdʒ/ **noun** [no plural]
small bags that you can carry onto a plane with you: *How many items of hand luggage can I take onto the plane?*

handout /ˈhændaʊt/ **noun**
a copy of a document that is given to all the people in a class or meeting: *You will find the exercises on page two of your handout.*

handsome /ˈhændsəm/ **adj**
B1 A handsome man is attractive: *He was tall, dark, and handsome.*

handwriting /ˈhændˌraɪtɪŋ/ **noun** [no plural]
B1 the way that someone forms letters when they write with a pen or pencil

handy /ˈhændi/ **adj** (**handier**, **handiest**)
1 useful or easy to use: *a handy container/tool*
2 UK informal near to a place: *It's a nice house and it's **handy for** the station.*

hang /hæŋ/ **verb** (**hung**)
1 B1 to fasten something so that the top part is fixed but the lower part is free to move: *He **hung** his coat **on** the hook behind the door.*
2 to kill someone by putting a rope around their neck and making them drop
hang about/around **phrasal verb** informal
B1 to spend time somewhere, usually doing little: *Teenagers hang around on street corners.*

a b c d e f g h i j k l m n o p q r s t u v w x y z

hang on **phrasal verb** informal
B1 to wait for a short time: *Hang on – I'm coming.*

hang out **phrasal verb** informal
B1 to spend a lot of time in a place or with someone: *I've been* ***hanging out with*** *my cousins.*

hang up **phrasal verb**
B1 to finish talking on the telephone

hang ***something*** **up** **phrasal verb**
B1 to put something such as a coat somewhere where it can hang: *You can hang up your jacket over there.*

hanger /ˈhæŋəʳ/ **noun** (also **coat hanger**)
a wire, wooden, or plastic object for hanging clothes on

happen /ˈhæpᵊn/ **verb**
1 A2 If an event or situation happens, it exists or starts to be done: *Accidents can happen to anyone.* ◦ *We can't let a mistake like this happen again.* ◦ *Did you hear what* ***happened to*** *Jamie?*
2 A2 to be the result of an action, situation, or event that someone or something experiences: ***What happens*** *if we miss the flight?*

happily /ˈhæpɪli/ **adv**
1 B1 in a happy way: *They are very happily married.*
2 in a way that is very willing: *I'd happily drive you to the airport.*

happiness /ˈhæpinəs/ **noun** [no plural]
B1 the feeling of being happy

happy /ˈhæpi/ **adj** (**happier**, **happiest**)
1 A1 pleased and in a good mood, especially because something good has happened: *She looked really happy.*
→ Opposite **unhappy** **adj**
2 **happy birthday, New Year, etc.** A1 something friendly that you say to someone on a special day or holiday
3 A2 satisfied and not worried: *Are you* ***happy with*** *your exam results?*
4 **happy to do** ***something*** A2 to be willing to do something: *I'd be very happy to help if you need a hand.*

harbour UK (US **harbor**) /ˈhɑːbəʳ/ **noun**
B1 an area of water near the coast where ships are kept

harbour

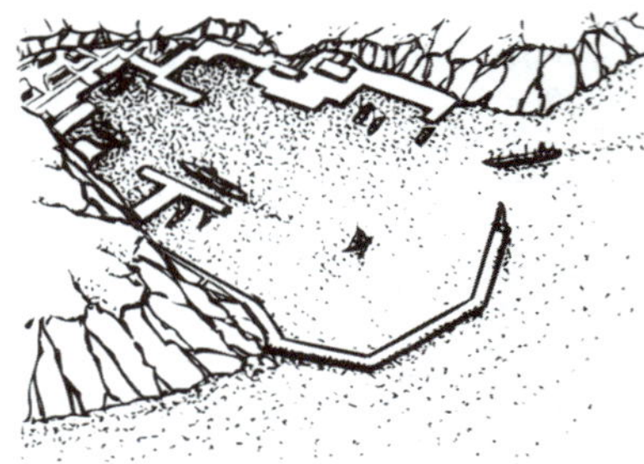

hard¹ /hɑːd/ **adj**
1 A2 firm and not easy to press or bend: *a hard surface* ◦ *The seats were really hard.*
→ Opposite **soft** **adj**
2 A1 difficult to do or understand: *It must be hard to study with all this noise.*
→ Opposite **easy** **adj**
3 B1 needing or using a lot of physical or mental effort: *It was* ***hard work*** *on the farm, but satisfying.*
4 **be hard on** ***someone*** to criticize someone too much, or to treat them unfairly: *Don't be too hard on him – he's only trying to help.*

hard² /hɑːd/ **adv**
1 A1 with a lot of effort: *She tried so hard.* ◦ *You must work harder.*
2 B1 with a lot of force: *She kicked the ball hard.*

hard drive /ˈhɑːd ˌdraɪv/ **noun** (also **hard disk** /ˌhɑːd ˈdɪsk/)
the part inside a computer that is not removed and keeps very large amounts of information

harden /ˈhɑːdᵊn/ **verb**
to become hard and stiff, or to make something become hard and stiff

hardly /ˈhɑːdli/ **adv**
1 B1 almost not, or only a very small amount: *I was so tired that I could hardly walk.* ◦ *There's* ***hardly any*** *food left in the fridge.*
2 certainly not: *It's hardly my fault that it's raining!*

hardware /ˈhɑːdweəʳ/ **noun** [no plural]
B1 the machines or equipment that

your computer system is made from, not the programs

hard-working /ˌhɑːdˈwɜːkɪŋ/ **adj**
doing a job seriously and with a lot of effort: *She was always a very hard-working student.*

harm¹ /hɑːm/ **noun**
1 [no plural] hurt or damage: *Smoking can **cause** serious **harm to** the lungs.*
2 not come to any harm to not be hurt or damaged

harm² /hɑːm/ **verb**
to hurt someone or damage something: *Luckily, no one was harmed in the accident.*

harmful /ˈhɑːmfᵊl/ **adj**
causing damage or injury: *Smoking is **harmful to** your health.*

harmless /ˈhɑːmləs/ **adj**
not causing hurt or damage: *Taken in small doses, this drug is completely harmless.*

harmony /ˈhɑːməni/ **noun** [no plural]
a situation in which people are peaceful and agree with each other, or in which different things seem right or suitable together: *the desire to live together **in** peace and **harmony***

harsh /hɑːʃ/ **adj**
1 cruel or unkind: *harsh criticism*
2 too strong, bright, loud, etc.: *harsh chemicals* ◦ *harsh lighting*
• **harshly adv** *She felt that she had been treated harshly.*

harvest¹ /ˈhɑːvɪst/ **noun**
1 the job of cutting and collecting crops from fields
2 the amount of crops that are collected

harvest² /ˈhɑːvɪst/ **verb**
to cut and collect crops when they are ready

has strong /hæz/ weak /həz/
present simple of have, used with 'he', 'she' and 'it'

hasn't /ˈhæzᵊnt/
short form of has not: *It hasn't rained for three weeks.*

hassle¹ /ˈhæsl/ **noun**
a problem: *It's such a hassle finding a place to park.*

hassle² /ˈhæsl/ **verb** (**hassling**, **hassled**)
to annoy someone, mainly by asking for something again and again: *He's always **hassling** me **for** money.*

haste /heɪst/ **noun** [no plural]
speed in doing something, especially because you do not have much time: *In their haste to escape, they left behind all their belongings.*

hasty /ˈheɪsti/ **adj** (**hastier**, **hastiest**)
done very quickly: *I don't want to make a hasty decision.*

hat /hæt/ **noun**
A1 something that you wear to cover your head: *a cowboy hat*
→ See **Clothes** on page C5

hatch /hætʃ/ **verb**
to come out of an egg: *When will the chicks hatch?*

hate /heɪt/ **verb** (**hating**, **hated**)
A2 to dislike someone or something very much: *I hate going to the dentist's.*

hatred /ˈheɪtrɪd/ **noun** [no plural]
a great dislike of someone or something: *He developed an intense **hatred of** all women.*

haul /hɔːl/ **verb**
to pull something somewhere slowly and with difficulty: *They hauled the piano into the living room.*

haunt /hɔːnt/ **verb**
1 If a ghost haunts a place, it appears there often: *a haunted house*
2 If an unpleasant memory or feeling haunts you, you think about or feel it often: *It was an experience that haunted him for the rest of his life.*

have¹ strong /hæv/ weak /həv/ **auxiliary verb** (**having**, **had**)
A2 used with the past participle of another verb to make the present perfect and past perfect tenses: *Have you seen Roz?* ◦ *I've (= I have) passed my test.* ◦ *He hasn't (= has not) visited London before.*

a b c d e f g **h** i j k l m n o p q r s t u v w x y z

have[2] strong /hæv/ weak /həv/ **verb**
(**having**, **had**)
1 A1 (also **have got**) to own something: *I have two horses.* ◦ *Laura has got beautiful blue eyes.*
2 A1 (also **have got**) If you have a particular illness, you are suffering from it: *I have a bad cold.*
3 A1 to eat or drink something: *Can I have a drink of water?*
4 B1 used to say that someone is holding something: *He had a pen in his hand.* ◦ *She had a baby with her.*
5 B1 to cause something to be in a particular state: *He had dinner ready by the time we got home.*
6 have to do *something*; have got to do *something* A2 to need to do something: *I have to go to Manchester tomorrow.* ◦ *Do we have to finish this today?*
7 have a bath, sleep, walk, etc. A2 used with nouns to say that someone does something: *Can I have a quick shower?*
8 have difficulty, fun, problems, etc. A2 used with nouns to say that someone experiences something: *We had a great time in Barcelona.*
9 have a baby A2 to give birth to a baby
10 have *something* cleaned, cut, repaired, etc. B1 to arrange for someone to do something for you: *I'm having my hair cut this afternoon.*
11 have *something* stolen, taken, etc. B1 If you have something stolen, taken, etc., someone takes something that belongs to you: *She had her car stolen last week.*
have (got) *something* on **phrasal verb**
B1 If you have clothes or shoes on, you are wearing them: *He's got a red shirt on.*

hay /heɪ/ **noun** [no plural]
dried grass for animals to eat

hay fever /ˈheɪ ˌfiːvəʳ/ **noun** [no plural]
an illness like a cold, caused by pollen (= a powder made by flowers): *She gets really bad hay fever.*

hazard /ˈhæzəd/ **noun**
something that is dangerous: *a fire hazard* ◦ *a health hazard*

hazardous /ˈhæzədəs/ **adj**
dangerous: *hazardous chemicals*

haze /heɪz/ **noun** [no plural]
smoke or water in the air, making it difficult to see: *There was a haze over the horizon.*

he strong /hiː/ weak /hi/ **pronoun**
A1 used when talking about a man or male animal who has already been talked about: *'When is Paul coming?' 'He should be here soon.'*

head[1] /hed/ **noun**
1 A1 the part of your body that contains your brain, eyes, ears, mouth, nose, etc.: *He fell and hit his head on the table.*
→ See **The Body** on page C2
2 A2 (also **headteacher**) UK the person in charge of a school
3 B1 your mind: *All these thoughts were going round in my head.*
4 B1 the person who is in charge of an organization: *Her father is the head of an oil company.*
5 the front or top part of something: *Who is that at the head of the table?*
• **come to a head** If a problem comes to a head, it becomes very bad.
• **go over *someone*'s head** to be too difficult for someone to understand: *All this talk about philosophy went right over my head.*

head[2] /hed/ **verb**
1 to move in a particular direction: *I was **heading towards** the park.* ◦ *I think we ought to **head home** now, before it gets too dark.*
2 to be in charge of a group, organization, etc.: *She heads the country's leading travel company.*

headache /ˈhedeɪk/ **noun**
A2 pain inside your head: *I've got a bad headache.*

heading /ˈhedɪŋ/ **noun**
words at the top of a piece of writing that tell you its subject

headlight /ˈhedlaɪt/ **noun**
one of the two large lights on the front of a car
→ See picture at **light** noun

headline /ˈhedlaɪn/ **noun**
1 B1 the title of a newspaper story

that is printed in large letters above it: *a front-page headline*
2 the headlines the main stories in newspapers, on television, etc.: *That story was **in the headlines** all over the world.*

headmaster /ˌhedˈmɑːstəʳ/ **noun** UK
a man who is in charge of a school

headmistress /ˌhedˈmɪstrəs/ **noun** UK
a woman who is in charge of a school

headphones

headphones /ˈhedfəʊnz/ **plural noun**
a piece of equipment that you wear over your ears so that you can listen to music: *a pair of headphones*

headquarters /ˈhedˌkwɔːtəz/ **noun** (plural **headquarters**)
the place from where an organization is controlled: *police headquarters*

headteacher /ˌhedˈtiːtʃəʳ/ **noun** UK (US **principal**)
A2 the person in charge of a school

heal /hiːl/ **verb** (also **heal up**)
If an injury heals, it becomes healthy again, and if something heals it, it makes it healthy again: *The wound on his head had begun to heal.*

health /helθ/ **noun** [no plural]
A2 the condition of your body: *She is in poor health.*

health care (also **healthcare**) /ˈhelθ ˌkeəʳ/ **noun** [no plural]
the set of services provided by a country or an organization for treating people who are ill

health club /ˈhelθ ˌklʌb/ **noun**
a private club where people can go to do exercise to keep fit

healthy /ˈhelθi/ **adj** (**healthier**, **healthiest**)
1 A2 not sick: *Maria is a normal, healthy child.*
2 A2 good for your health: *a healthy diet*

heap /hiːp/ **noun**
an untidy pile of things: *a heap of rubbish*

hear /hɪəʳ/ **verb** (**heard**)
1 A1 to be aware of a sound through your ears: *I could hear his voice in the distance.*
2 A2 to listen to someone or something: *I heard a programme about tigers on the radio this morning.*
3 B1 to be told some information: *When did you first **hear about** this?* ◦ *Have you heard the news?*
have heard of *something* **phrasal verb**
to know that someone or something exists: *It's a tiny country that most people have never heard of.*
hear from *someone* **phrasal verb**
B1 to get a letter, telephone call, or other message from someone: *Have you heard from Helena recently?*

hearing /ˈhɪərɪŋ/ **noun** [no plural]
the ability to hear sounds: *He lost his hearing when he was a child.*

heart /hɑːt/ **noun**
1 A2 the organ inside your chest that sends blood around your body: *My heart was beating fast.*
2 B1 the centre of something: *Her office is **in the heart of** Tokyo.*
3 B1 someone's deepest feelings and true character: *She has a kind heart.*
4 a shape that is used to mean love
→ See picture at **shape**
5 with all your heart used to say that

you feel something very strongly: *I thank you with all my heart.*
• **break *someone's* heart** to make someone very unhappy

heart attack /ˈhɑːt əˌtæk/ **noun**
B1 a serious medical condition in which the heart stops working correctly: *John **had a heart attack** three years ago.*

heartbeat /ˈhɑːtbiːt/ **noun**
the regular movement of the heart as it moves blood around the body

heartless /ˈhɑːtləs/ **adj**
cruel and not caring about other people

hearts /hɑːts/ **plural noun**
one of the four suits (= groups) of playing cards: *the five of hearts*

heat¹ /hiːt/ **noun**
1 B1 [no plural] the quality of being hot or warm: *the heat of his body*
2 **the heat** hot weather or hot conditions: *I don't really like the heat.*
3 B1 the temperature of something: *Cook on a low heat.*
4 a competition, especially a race, that decides who will be in the final event

heat² /hiːt/ **verb** (also **heat up**)
to make something become hot or warm: *I'll just heat up some soup.*

heater /ˈhiːtəʳ/ **noun**
B1 a machine that heats air or water

heating /ˈhiːtɪŋ/ **noun** [no plural] UK (US **heat**)
A2 the system that keeps a building warm

heaven /ˈhevᵊn/ **noun** [no plural]
1 the place where some people think good people go when they die
→ Opposite **hell** **noun**
2 informal something very nice that gives you great pleasure: *I just lay in the sun and did nothing – it was heaven.*

heavily /ˈhevɪli/ **adv**
1 B1 a lot or to a great degree: *She's heavily involved in politics.*
2 **drink/smoke heavily** to drink or smoke a lot
3 **rain/snow heavily** to rain or snow a lot

heavy /ˈhevi/ **adj** (**heavier**, **heaviest**)
1 A2 Heavy objects weigh a lot: *heavy bags*
→ Opposite **light** **adj**
2 A2 used to say how much someone or something weighs: *How heavy are you?*
3 B1 large in amount or degree: *heavy traffic*
4 **a heavy drinker/smoker** someone who drinks or smokes a lot
5 **heavy snow/rain** a large amount of snow or rain

hectare /ˈhekteəʳ/ **noun**
a unit for measuring area, equal to 10,000 square metres

hectic /ˈhektɪk/ **adj**
very busy and full of activity: *I've had a very hectic day.*

he'd /hiːd/
1 short form of he had: *We knew he'd taken the money.*
2 short form of he would: *No one thought he'd get the job.*

hedge /hedʒ/ **noun**
a row of bushes growing close together

hedge

heel /hiːl/ **noun**
1 the back part of your foot
→ See **The Body** on page C2
2 B1 the part of a shoe that is under your heel: *high heels*

height /haɪt/ **noun**
1 B1 how tall or high something or someone is: *The tower measures 27.28 metres **in height**.*
→ See picture at **length**
2 B1 how far above the ground something is: *The plane was flying at a height of about 6,000 metres.*

held /held/
past tense and past participle of hold

helicopter /ˈhelɪkɒptəʳ/ **noun**
A2 a plane that flies using long, thin parts on top of it that turn around very fast

helicopter

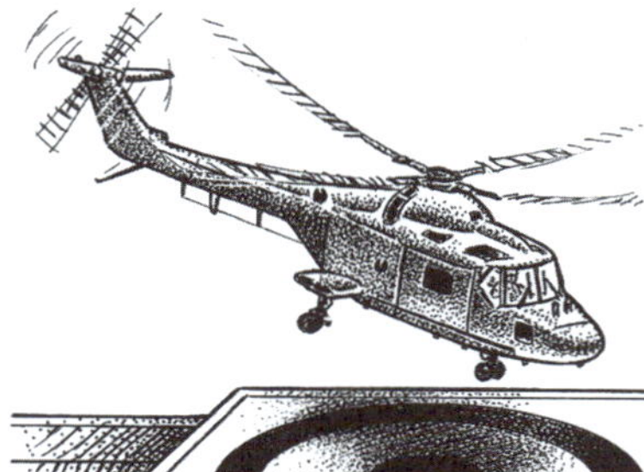

hell /hel/ **noun**
1 [no plural] the place where some people think bad people go when they die
→ Opposite **heaven** **noun**
2 [no plural] informal an experience that is very bad: *It's hell working with him.*
3 the hell informal used to emphasize something in a rude or angry way: ***What the hell** are you doing here?*

he'll /hiːl/
short form of he will: *He'll be home soon.*

hello /helˈəʊ/ **exclamation**
1 A1 said when you meet someone or start talking with someone: *Hello, Christina. How are you?*
2 A1 used when you start speaking on the telephone: *Hello, this is Alex.*

helmet /ˈhel mət/ **noun**
a hard hat that protects your head: *a cycling helmet*

helmet

help¹ /help/ **verb**
1 A1 to do something for someone: *Thank you for helping.* ◦ *Dad always **helps** me **with** my homework.*
2 A2 to provide advice, money, support, etc. to make it possible or easier for someone to do something: *My mum said she would **help with** the costs of buying a house.*
3 to make something better or easier: *When you're nervous or frightened, it helps to breathe slowly.*

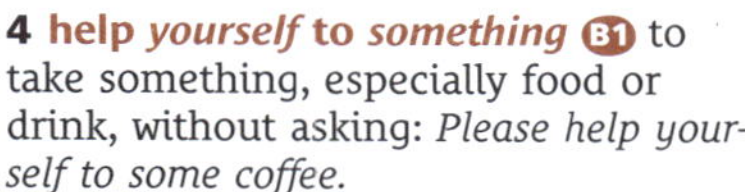

4 help *yourself* to *something* B1 to take something, especially food or drink, without asking: *Please help yourself to some coffee.*
5 can't/couldn't help *something* B1 to not be able to stop doing something: *I couldn't help laughing.*
help (*someone*) out **phrasal verb**
to help someone, especially by giving them money or working for them: *Sophia has been helping out in the shop this week.*

help² /help/ **noun**
1 A2 [no plural] things you do to make it easier for another person to do something: *Do you want any help?*
2 with the help of *something* B1 using something: *We managed to open the box with the help of a knife.*
3 something or someone that makes things easier for you: *Dave has been a great help to me.*

help³ /help/ **exclamation**
A2 something that you shout when you are in danger: *Help! I'm drowning!*

helper /helpəʳ/ **noun**
someone who helps another person to do something: *The school needs more helpers for the concert.*

helpful /ˈhelpfᵊl/ **adj**
1 B1 useful: *helpful advice*
2 B1 willing to help: *The staff here are very helpful.*
→ Opposite **unhelpful** **adj**

helping /ˈhelpɪŋ/ **noun**
an amount of food given to one person at one time: *She gave me a very large helping of pasta.*

helpless /ˈhelpləs/ **adj**
not able to do things for yourself or protect yourself: *a helpless animal*

hem /hem/ **noun**
the edge of a piece of clothing or cloth that has been folded under and sewn

hen /hen/ **noun**
a female bird, especially a chicken

her¹ strong /hɜːʳ/ weak /həʳ/ **pronoun**
A1 used to mean a woman or girl who you have already talked about: *Where's Katie – have you seen her?*

her2 strong /hɜːʳ/ weak /həʳ/ **determiner**
A1 belonging to a woman or girl who you have already talked about: *That's her house on the corner.* ◦ *It's not her fault.*

herb /hɜːb/ **noun**
B1 a plant that is used in cooking to add flavour to food

herd1 /hɜːd/ **noun**
a large group of animals such as cows that live and eat together: *a herd of cattle/deer*

herd2 /hɜːd/ **verb**
to move a group of people or animals somewhere: *The passengers were quickly herded onto a bus.*

here /hɪəʳ/ **adv**
1 A1 in the place where you are: *Does Lucy live near here?* ◦ *Come here!*
2 A1 used when saying who you are on the telephone: *Hello, Tim here.*
3 here you are A2 used when you are giving someone something: *'Please pass me the bread.' 'Here you are.'*
4 here you are, here it is, etc. A2 used when you see someone or something you have been looking for or waiting for: *Here's our bus.* ◦ *I've lost my watch – oh, here it is.*
5 at this point in a discussion or piece of writing: *I don't have time to examine the issue here.*
6 here and there in many different places: *Trees were growing here and there.*

hero /ˈhɪərəʊ/ **noun** (plural **heroes**)
1 B1 a very brave person, often a man, that a lot of people admire: *He became a national hero for his part in the revolution.*
2 B1 the main man in a book or movie: *the hero of her new novel*

heroic /hɪˈrəʊɪk/ **adj**
very brave: *a heroic figure*

heroine /ˈherəʊɪn/ **noun**
1 a very brave woman that a lot of people admire
2 B1 the main woman in a book or movie: *the heroine of the movie 'Alien'*

hers /hɜːz/ **pronoun**
A2 the things that belong to a woman or girl: *That's Sara's coat over there – at least I think it's hers.*

herself /həˈself/ **pronoun**
1 A2 used to show that the woman or girl who does the action is also the person who is affected by it: *She looked at herself in the mirror.*
2 by herself A2 alone or without anyone else's help: *She fixed the bike by herself.*
3 used to show that a particular woman or girl did something: *She baked the cake herself.*

he's /hiːz/
1 short form of he is: *He's my best friend.*
2 short form of he has: *Sam must be tired – he's been dancing all night!*

hesitate /ˈhezɪteɪt/ **verb** (**hesitating**, **hesitated**)
1 to stop before you do something, especially because you are nervous or not sure: *Richard hesitated before answering.*
2 don't hesitate to do *something* used to encourage someone to do something: *If you need any help, don't hesitate to call me.*

hesitation /ˌhezɪˈteɪʃᵊn/ **noun**
a pause before you do something, especially because you are not sure: *After a moment's hesitation, he unlocked the door.*

hey /heɪ/ **exclamation** informal
A2 used to get someone's attention or to show that you are interested, excited, or angry: *Hey, Helen, look at this!* ◦ *Hey, wait a minute!*

hi /haɪ/ **exclamation** informal
A1 hello: *Hi! How are you?*

hiccups /ˈhɪkʌps/ **plural noun**
sudden noises you make in your throat when a muscle in your chest moves: *I **got hiccups** from drinking too quickly.*

hidden /ˈhɪdᵊn/ **adj**
B1 A hidden thing or place is not easy to find: *There were hidden microphones in the room.*

hide /haɪd/ **verb** (**hiding**, **hid**, **hidden**)
1 B1 to put something in a place

where no one can see it: *I hid the money in a drawer.*
2 B1 to go to a place where no one can see you: *She hid behind a tree.*
3 B1 to keep a feeling or information secret: *He couldn't hide his embarrassment.*

hideous /ˈhɪdiəs/ **adj**
very ugly: *a hideous monster*
• **hideously** **adv**

hi-fi /ˈhaɪfaɪ/ **noun**
a set of electronic equipment for playing recorded music

high[1] /haɪ/ **adj**
1 A2 having a long distance from the bottom to the top: *a high building/mountain*
→ Opposite **low** **adj**
2 B1 a long distance above the ground or the level of the sea: *The village was* ***high up*** *in the mountains.*
3 used to say how long the distance is from the top of something to the bottom: *How high is it?* ◦ *It's ten feet high.*
4 B1 great in amount or level: *a high temperature* ◦ *high prices*
→ Opposite **low** **adj**
5 B1 very good: *of high quality* ◦ *She got high marks in her last exam.*
6 A high sound or note is near the top of the set of sounds that people can hear.
→ Opposite **low** **adj**
7 important, powerful, or at an upper level of something: *a high rank in the army*

high[2] /haɪ/ **adv**
1 B1 at or to a long distance above the ground: *He threw the ball high into the air.* ◦ *We flew* ***high above*** *the city.*
2 B1 at or to a large amount or level: *Temperatures rose as high as 40 degrees.*

higher education /ˌhaɪər ˌedʒʊˈkeɪʃən/ **noun** [no plural]
education at a college or university

high heels /ˌhaɪ ˈhiːlz/ **plural noun**
women's shoes that have heels that are raised high off the ground: *I'm going to wear high heels tonight.*

highlight[1] /ˈhaɪlaɪt/ **noun**
the best or most important part of something: *The boat trip was one of the* ***highlights of*** *the holiday.*

highlight[2] /ˈhaɪlaɪt/ **verb**
to emphasize something or make people notice something: *The report* ***highlights*** *the* ***problems*** *with the project.*

highlighter /ˈhaɪˌlaɪtər/ **noun**
a pen containing brightly coloured ink that is used to mark words in a text
→ See **The Office** on page C12

highly /ˈhaɪli/ **adv**
very: *a highly intelligent child*

Highness /ˈhaɪnəs/ **noun**
Her/His/Your Highness used when you are speaking to or about a royal person: *Thank you, Your Highness.*

high school /ˈhaɪ ˌskuːl/ **noun**
a school in the US that children go to between the ages of 14 and 18

high street /ˈhaɪ ˌstriːt/ **noun** UK
the main road in the centre of a town where there are shops

highway /ˈhaɪweɪ/ **noun** mainly US
a main road, especially between two cities

hijack /ˈhaɪdʒæk/ **verb**
to take control of a plane during a flight, especially using violence: *The plane was hijacked by terrorists.*
• **hijacker** **noun**

hill /hɪl/ **noun**
A2 a high area of land that is smaller than a mountain: *They climbed up the hill to get a better view.*

him strong /hɪm/ weak /ɪm/ **pronoun**
A1 used to mean a man or boy who you have already talked about: *I'm looking for Al – have you seen him?*

himself /hɪmˈself/ **pronoun**
1 A2 used to show that the man or boy who does the action is also the person who is affected by it: *John always cuts himself when he's shaving.*
2 **by himself** A2 alone or without anyone else's help: *My three-year-old son can tie his shoelaces by himself.*
3 used to show that a particular man or boy did something: *He baked the cake himself.*

a b c d e f g h i j k l m n o p q r s t u v w x y z

hinder /ˈhɪndəʳ/ **verb**
to make it difficult to do something: *Our progress was hindered by bad weather.*

Hindu /ˈhɪnduː/ **noun**
someone whose religion is Hinduism
• **Hindu adj**

Hinduism /ˈhɪnduːɪzᵊm/ **noun** [no plural]
the main religion of India, based on belief in one or more gods, and the belief that when a person dies his or her spirit returns to life in another body

hinge /ˈhɪndʒ/ **noun**
a metal fastening that joins the edge of a door or window and allows you to open or close it

hint[1] /hɪnt/ **noun**
1 something you say that suggests what you think or want, but not in a direct way: *He* ***dropped*** *(= made) several* ***hints*** *that he wanted a computer for his birthday.*
2 a small piece of advice: *The magazine gives lots of useful hints on how to save money.*

hint[2] /hɪnt/ **verb**
to suggest something, but not in a direct way: *He* ***hinted that*** *he wanted to leave the company.*

hip /hɪp/ **noun**
one of the two parts of your body above your leg and below your waist
→ See **The Body** on page C2

hippopotamus /ˌhɪpəˈpɒtəməs/ **noun**
a very large animal with thick skin that lives near water in parts of Africa

hire[1] /haɪəʳ/ **verb** (**hiring**, **hired**) UK
1 B1 to pay money in order to use something for a short time: *They hired a car for a few weeks.*
2 to employ someone or pay them to do a particular job: *We hired a new secretary last week.*

hire[2] /haɪəʳ/ **noun** [no plural]
an arrangement to use something for a short time by paying for it: *Do you have bikes* ***for hire****?*

his[1] strong /hɪz/ weak /ɪz/ **determiner**
A1 belonging to a man or boy who you have already talked about: *Phillip is sitting over there with his daughter.* ◦ *It's not his fault.*

his[2] /hɪz/ **pronoun**
A2 the things that belong to a man or boy: *That's Brian's coat – at least I think it's his.*

hiss /hɪs/ **verb**
to make a long noise like the letter 's': *The gas hissed through the pipes.*

historic /hɪˈstɒrɪk/ **adj**
B1 important in history: *historic buildings* ◦ *a historic day*

historical /hɪˈstɒrɪkᵊl/ **adj**
B1 relating to the past: *historical documents*

history /ˈhɪstᵊri/ **noun** [no plural]
1 A2 events that happened in the past: *American history*
2 A2 the study of events in the past: *a history book*

hit

hit[1] /hɪt/ **verb** (**hitting**, **hit**)
1 A2 to touch something quickly and with force, usually hurting or damaging something: *The ball hit him on the head.* ◦ *As she fell, she hit her head on the pavement.*

2 to affect something in a bad way: *The city has been* ***hit hard*** *by the crisis.*
• **hit it off** informal If people hit it off, they like each other immediately.

hit² /hɪt/ **noun**
1 B1 a very successful song, movie, book, etc.: *The movie 'Titanic' was a big hit.*
2 B1 an occasion when you touch something or when something touches you quickly and with force
3 an occasion when someone visits a website on the Internet, which is then counted to find the number of people who look at the page

hitchhike /ˈhɪtʃhaɪk/ **verb** (**hitch-hiking, hitch-hiked**)
B1 to get free rides in other people's cars by waiting next to the road
• **hitchhiker noun**

hitchhike

hi-tech /haɪˈtek/ **adj**
another spelling of high-tech

HIV /ˌeɪtʃaɪˈviː/ **noun** [no plural]
a virus that causes AIDS (= a serious disease that destroys the body's ability to fight infection)

hive /haɪv/ **noun** (also **beehive**)
a special container for keeping bees

hoard /hɔːd/ **verb**
to collect a lot of something, often secretly: *He hoarded antique books in the attic.*
• **hoard noun** a lot of something that someone keeps secretly: *Police found a* ***hoard of*** *stolen jewellery in the car.*

hoarse /hɔːs/ **adj**
If you are hoarse, your voice sounds rough, often because you are ill: *I was hoarse from shouting.*

hobby /ˈhɒbi/ **noun** (plural **hobbies**)
A2 an activity that you like and often do when you are not working: *Do you have any hobbies?*

hockey /ˈhɒki/ **noun** [no plural]
1 A2 UK (US **field hockey**) a game that two teams play on grass, in which players hit a ball with long curved sticks
2 US (UK **ice hockey**) a game that two teams play on ice, in which players hit a flat round object with long curved sticks

hold¹ /həʊld/ **verb** (**held**)
1 A2 to have something in your hand or arms: *He was holding a glass of wine.* ◦ *She held the baby in her arms.*
2 B1 to keep something in a particular position: *Can you hold the door open, please?* ◦ *Hold your hand up if you know the answer.*
3 B1 to organize an event: *They are holding an election.*
4 B1 to contain something: *The bucket holds about ten litres.*
5 to keep someone in a place so that the person cannot leave: *I was* ***held prisoner*** *in a tiny room.*
6 Hold it! informal used to tell someone to wait: *Hold it! I've forgotten my coat.*
7 hold your breath to stop breathing for a time

hold on phrasal verb informal
B1 to wait: *Hold on! I'll just check my diary.*

hold *something/someone* up phrasal verb
B1 to make something or someone slow or late: *Sorry I'm late. I got held up in traffic.*

hold² /həʊld/ **noun**
1 the act of holding something in your hand: *Keep a tight hold on your tickets.*
2 catch, grab, etc. hold of *something/someone* to start holding something or someone: *He tried to escape, but I grabbed hold of his jacket.*
3 get hold of *something/someone* to get something: *I got hold of the book at the local library.*
4 an area on a plane or ship for storing things: *a cargo hold*

hold-up /ˈhəʊldʌp/ **noun**
1 something that makes you move slowly or makes you late: *There were several hold-ups on the motorway.*

2 the action of stealing money from a bank, shop, car, etc. using force

hole /həʊl/ **noun**
B1 a hollow space in something, or an opening in something: *There's a* ***hole in*** *the roof.* ◦ *We dug a hole to plant the tree.*

holiday /ˈhɒlədeɪ/ **noun** UK (US **vacation**)
1 A1 a time when you do not have to go to work or school: *the school holidays*
2 A1 a long visit to a place away from where you live, for pleasure: *a skiing holiday* ◦ *Are you* ***going on holiday*** *this year?*

hollow /ˈhɒləʊ/ **adj**
having a hole or empty space inside: *a hollow shell/tube*
→ See picture at **flat adj**
→ Opposite **solid adj**

holy /ˈhəʊli/ **adj** (**holier**, **holiest**)
1 relating to a religion or a god: *the holy city of Jerusalem*
2 very religious or pure: *a holy man*

home¹ /həʊm/ **noun**
1 A1 the place where you live: *He wasn't* ***at home****.*
2 a place where people who need special care live: *an old people's home*
3 **feel at home** B1 to feel happy and confident in a place or situation: *After a month I felt at home in my new job.*

home² /həʊm/ **adv**
A2 to the place where you live: *He didn't* ***come home*** *until midnight.* ◦ *I* ***went home*** *to visit my parents.*

> **Common mistake: home**
>
> When you use verbs of movement with **home**, for example 'go' or 'come', you do not use a preposition.
>
> *What time did you go home?*
>
> *I'll call you as soon as I get home.*
>
> When you use the verbs **be** or **stay** with **home**, use the preposition **at**.
>
> *I was at home all afternoon.*
>
> *I'll stay at home to look after the children.*

home³ /həʊm/ **adj**
1 **home address/phone number** an address or telephone number for the place where someone lives
2 made or used in the place where someone lives: *home cooking*

homeless /ˈhəʊmləs/ **adj**
without a place to live: *10,000 people were made homeless by the floods.*

homemade /ˌhəʊmˈmeɪd/ **adj**
made at home and not bought from a shop: *homemade bread*

home page /ˈhəʊm ˌpeɪdʒ/ **noun**
the first page that you see when you look at a website on the Internet

homesick /ˈhəʊmsɪk/ **adj**
feeling sad because you are away from your home

homework /ˈhəʊmwɜːk/ **noun** [no plural]
A1 work that teachers give students to do at home: *Have you* ***done*** *your* ***homework*** *yet?*

honest /ˈɒnɪst/ **adj**
1 B1 sincere and truthful: *What is your honest opinion?*
2 B1 not likely to lie, cheat, or steal: *I'm just an honest man, trying to live my life.*
3 **to be honest** informal B1 used to say your real opinion: *To be honest, I didn't really enjoy the party.*

honestly /ˈɒnɪstli/ **adv**
1 B1 used to say that you are telling the truth: *I honestly couldn't eat any more.*
2 without lying or stealing: *We will always deal honestly with our customers.*

honesty /ˈɒnɪsti/ **noun** [no plural]
the quality of being honest: *I appreciate your honesty.*

honey /ˈhʌni/ **noun**
1 A2 [no plural] a sweet, sticky food that is made by bees
→ See **Food** on page C7
2 a name that you call someone you love or like very much

honeymoon /ˈhʌnimuːn/ **noun**
B1 a holiday for two people who have just got married: *We went to Paris* ***on our honeymoon****.*

honour UK (US **honor**) /ˈɒnəʳ/ **noun**
1 [no plural] qualities such as goodness, honesty, and bravery that make people respect you: *a man of honour*
2 in honour of *someone/something* in order to show great respect for someone or something: *a dinner in honour of the President*
3 something that makes you feel proud and pleased: *I had the great **honour of** meeting the King.*

hood /hʊd/ **noun**
1 a part of a coat or jacket that covers your head and neck: *a waterproof jacket with a hood*
2 US (UK **bonnet**) the metal part that covers a car engine
→ See **Car** on page C3

hoof /huːf/ **noun** (plural **hooves**, **hoofs**)
the hard part on the foot of a horse and some other large animals

hook /hʊk/ **noun**
a curved piece of metal or plastic used for hanging something on, or a similar object used for catching fish: *His coat was hanging from a hook on the door.*

hooligan /ˈhuːlɪgᵊn/ **noun**
someone who behaves badly or violently and causes damage in a public place

hooray /hʊˈreɪ/ **exclamation**
something that you shout when you are happy because of something that has just happened: *We won – hooray!*

hoot¹ /huːt/ **noun**
a short sound made by an owl (= bird) or by a car horn

hoot² /huːt/ **verb** UK
to make a short sound with your car's horn: *The van driver hooted his horn.*

Hoover /ˈhuːvəʳ/ **noun** UK trademark
(UK/US **vacuum cleaner**)
an electric machine that cleans floors by taking up dirt
• **hoover verb** to use a Hoover to clean a floor

hooves /huːvz/
plural of hoof

hop¹ /hɒp/ **verb** (**hopping**, **hopped**)
1 to jump on one foot
2 If an animal hops, it moves by jumping on two or four feet at the same time: *Rabbits were hopping across the field.*

hop² /hɒp/ **noun**
a short jump, especially on one leg

hope¹ /həʊp/ **verb** (**hoping**, **hoped**)
1 A2 to want something to happen or be true: *I **hope that** the bus won't be late.* ◦ *We had **hoped for** better weather than this.* ◦ *'Is he coming?' 'I hope so.'*
2 hope to do *something* B1 to want to do something: *Dad hopes to retire next year.*

hope² /həʊp/ **noun**
1 B1 a good feeling about the future, or something that you want to happen: *a message full of hope* ◦ *What are your **hopes for** the future?*
2 a person or thing that could help you and make you succeed: *Doctors say his only hope is an operation.*
3 in the hope of/that because you want something good to happen: *She went to Paris in the hope of improving her French.*

hopeful /ˈhəʊpfᵊl/ **adj**
B1 feeling good or confident about something in the future: *Many teenagers do not feel **hopeful about** the future.* ◦ *Police are still **hopeful that** they will find the missing girl.*

hopefully /ˈhəʊpfᵊli/ **adv**
1 B1 used when you are saying what you would like to happen: *Hopefully it won't rain.*
2 in a hopeful way: *'Are there any tickets left?' she asked hopefully.*

hopeless /ˈhəʊpləs/ **adj**
1 B1 very bad and probably not going to improve: *a hopeless situation*
2 very bad at a particular activity: *I'm **hopeless at** sports.*

horizon /həˈraɪzᵊn/ **noun**
the line in the distance where the sky and the land or sea seem to meet

horizontal /ˌhɒrɪˈzɒntᵊl/ **adj**
level and flat, or parallel to the ground: *a horizontal line*

horizontal/vertical

hormone /ˈhɔːməʊn/ **noun**
one of many chemicals made in your body that make the body grow and develop

horn /hɔːn/ **noun**
1 one of the two long, hard things on the heads of cows, goats, and some other animals
2 a piece of equipment used to make a loud sound as a warning: *a car horn*
3 a musical instrument that you blow into to make a sound

horoscope /ˈhɒrəskəʊp/ **noun**
a description of what might happen to someone in the future, based on the position of the stars and planets: *What does your horoscope say?*

horrible /ˈhɒrəbl/ **adj**
A2 very unpleasant or bad: *What's that horrible smell?*

horrific /hɒrˈɪfɪk/ **adj**
very bad and shocking: *a horrific crime* ◦ *horrific injuries*

horrify /ˈhɒrɪfaɪ/ **verb** (**horrifying**, **horrified**)
to make someone feel very shocked: *I was horrified to hear about her accident.*

horror /ˈhɒrəʳ/ **noun**
1 a strong feeling of shock or fear: *She watched* ***in horror*** *as the car skidded across the road.*
2 **a horror film/movie/story** **B1** a movie or story that entertains people by shocking or frightening them: *I love reading horror stories.*

horse /hɔːs/ **noun**
A1 a large animal with four legs that people ride or use to pull heavy things

horseback /ˈhɔːsbæk/ **noun**
on horseback riding a horse: *police on horseback*

horse riding /ˈhɔːs ˌraɪdɪŋ/ **noun** [no plural] UK
the sport or activity of riding a horse
→ See **Sports 1** on page C15

hose /həʊz/ **noun**
a long pipe made of plastic and used for putting water somewhere, usually onto a garden or fire

hospitable /hɒsˈpɪtəbl/ **adj**
A hospitable person or place is friendly and pleasant for people who visit.

hospital /ˈhɒspɪtᵊl/ **noun**
A1 a place where sick or injured people go to be treated by doctors and nurses: *He was* ***in hospital*** *for two weeks.*

host /həʊst/ **noun**
1 someone who is having a party
2 someone who presents a television programme

hostage /ˈhɒstɪdʒ/ **noun**
someone who is kept as a prisoner and may be hurt or killed in order to make other people do something

hostel /ˈhɒstᵊl/ **noun**
B1 a cheap hotel where you can live when you are away from home: *a youth hostel*

hostess /ˈhəʊstes/ **noun**
a woman who is having a party

hostile /ˈhɒstaɪl/ **adj**
not friendly and not liking or agreeing with something: *Some politicians were very* ***hostile to*** *the idea.*

hot /hɒt/ **adj** (**hotter**, **hottest**)
1 **A1** very warm: *a hot summer's day* ◦ *a hot drink* ◦ *I'm too hot in this jacket.*
→ Opposite **cold** **adj**
2 **B1** Hot food contains strong spices that cause a burning feeling in your mouth: *The sauce is very hot – be careful!*
→ Opposite **mild** **adj**

a b c d e f g h i j k l m n o p q r s t u v w x y z

hot dog /ˈhɒt ˌdɒg/ **noun**
a cooked sausage that you usually eat inside bread

hotel /həʊˈtel/ **noun**
A1 a place where you pay to stay when you are away from home

hour /aʊəʳ/ **noun**
1 A1 a period of time equal to 60 minutes: *It's a six-hour flight.*
2 the period of time when a particular activity happens or when a shop, business, etc. is open: *working hours* ◦ *Our opening hours are from 8 to 6.*
3 hours informal B1 a long time: *I spent hours doing my homework.*

> **Common mistake: hour or time?**
> An **hour** is a period of 60 minutes.
> *The journey takes about three hours.*
> *We went for a two-hour walk.*
> **Time** is measured in hours and minutes. We use **time** to refer to a particular point during the day or night, or to say when something happens.
> *What time do you get up in the morning?*
> *There's only one bus at that time of night.*
> Remember to use **time**, not 'hour', when you are talking about what time it is.
> *'What time is it?' 'Two o'clock.'*
> ~~*'What hour is it?' 'Two o'clock.'*~~

hourly /ˈaʊəli/ **adj, adv**
1 happening every hour: *There is an hourly bus service.*
2 for each hour: *an hourly rate/wage*

house /haʊs/ **noun** (plural **houses** /ˈhaʊzɪz/)
A1 a building where people live, usually one family or group: *We went to my aunt's house for dinner.*

household /ˈhaʊshəʊld/ **noun**
a family or group of people who live together in a house

housewife /ˈhaʊswaɪf/ **noun** (plural **housewives** /ˈhaʊswaɪvz/)
A2 a woman who stays at home to cook, clean, and take care of her family

housework /ˈhaʊswɜːk/ **noun** [no plural]
B1 the work that you do to keep your house clean: *I can't stand **doing housework**.*

hover /ˈhɒvəʳ/ **verb**
to stay up in the air but without moving anywhere: *A helicopter hovered over us.*

how /haʊ/ **adv**
1 A1 used to ask about quantity, size, or age: *How big is the house?* ◦ *How old are they?* ◦ *How much (= what price) was that dress?*
2 how are you? A1 used to ask someone if they are well and happy: *'How are you, Ellie?' 'Oh, not so bad, thanks.'*
3 A2 used to ask about the way something happens or is done: *How did he die?* ◦ *How do you keep the house so clean?*
4 how about..? A2 used to make a suggestion: *How about going to the cinema?*
5 how do you do? A2 a polite thing to say to someone you are meeting for the first time
6 B1 used to ask about what an experience or event was like: *How was your flight?*
7 B1 used for emphasis: *How nice to see you!* ◦ *I was amazed at how quickly she finished.*

> **Common mistake: how or what?**
> In these expressions we use **what**. Be careful not to use 'how'.
> **what something is called**
> *I don't know what it's called in English.*
> ~~*I don't know how it's called in English.*~~
> **what something/someone looks like**
> *I'd like to see what it looks like before I buy it.*
> *What does your brother look like?*

however /haʊˈevəʳ/ **adv**
1 A2 but: *This is one solution to the problem. However, there are others.*
2 however cold, difficult, slowly, etc. used to say that it does not make any difference how cold, difficult, slowly, etc.: *We're not going to get there in time, however fast we drive.*

howl /haʊl/ **verb**
to make a long, high sound: *He **howled in** pain.*
• **howl** noun

a b c d e f g h i j k l m n o p q r s t u v w x y z

huddle /ˈhʌdl/ **verb** (**huddling, huddled**)
to move closer to other people because you are cold or frightened: *They huddled around the fire to keep warm.*

hug¹ /hʌg/ **verb** (**hugging, hugged**)
B1 to put your arms around someone and hold them, usually because you love them: *They hugged and kissed each other.*

hug

hug² /hʌg/ **noun**
B1 the action of putting your arms around someone and holding them: *She **gave** me a big **hug** before she left.*

huge /hjuːdʒ/ **adj**
B1 very large: *a huge house*

hum¹ /hʌm/ **verb** (**humming, hummed**)
1 to sing without opening your mouth: *He was humming a tune.*
2 to make a continuous, low sound: *The computers were humming in the background.*

hum² /hʌm/ **noun**
a low, continuous sound: *the hum of traffic*

human¹ /ˈhjuːmən/ **adj**
B1 relating to people: *the human body* ◦ *human behaviour*

human² /ˈhjuːmən/ **noun** (also **human being**)
B1 a man, woman, or child: *The disease affects both humans and animals.*

humble /ˈhʌmbl/ **adj**
not believing that you are important: *He's very humble about his success.*

humid /ˈhjuːmɪd/ **adj**
B1 Humid air or weather is hot and slightly wet: *It's very humid today.*

humorous /ˈhjuːmᵊrəs/ **adj**
funny, or making you laugh: *a humorous book*

humour UK (US **humor**) /ˈhjuːməʳ/ **noun** [no plural]
1 the ability to laugh and know that something is funny: *He's got a great **sense of humour**.*
2 things that are funny: *His speech was full of humour.*

hump /hʌmp/ **noun**
a round, hard part on an animal's or a person's back: *a camel's hump*

hundred /ˈhʌndrəd/
1 A2 the number 100: *There were over **a hundred** people at the party.* ◦ *Water boils at **one hundred** degrees Celsius.*
2 hundreds informal a lot: ***Hundreds of** people wrote in to complain.*

hundredth /ˈhʌndrədθ/
one of a hundred equal parts of something

hung /hʌŋ/
past tense and past participle of hang

hunger /ˈhʌŋgəʳ/ **noun** [no plural]
1 B1 the feeling that you want to eat
2 the state of not having enough food: *Many of the refugees **died of hunger**.*

hungry /ˈhʌŋgri/ **adj** (**hungrier, hungriest**)
A1 wanting or needing food: *I'm hungry. What's for dinner?*
• **hungrily** /ˈhʌŋgrɪli/ **adv**

hunt /hʌnt/ **verb**
1 B1 to chase and kill wild animals: *They are hunting rabbits.*
2 to search for something: *The children **hunted for** shells on the beach.*
• **hunting noun** *deer hunting*

hunter /ˈhʌntəʳ/ **noun**
a person who hunts wild animals

hurricane /ˈhʌrɪkən/ **noun**
a violent storm with very strong winds

hurry¹ /ˈhʌri/ **verb** (**hurrying, hurried**)
A2 to move or to do things quickly: *Please hurry, the train is about to leave.*
hurry up phrasal verb
B1 to start moving or doing something more quickly: *Hurry up! We're going to be late.*

hurry² /ˈhʌri/ **noun**
be in a hurry B1 If you are in a

hurry, you need to do something quickly: *I was in a hurry so I took a taxi.*

hurt /hɜːt/ **verb** (**hurt**)
1 A2 to cause someone pain or to injure someone: *Simon hurt his knee playing football.*
2 A2 If a part of your body hurts, it is painful: *My eyes really hurt.*
3 B1 to upset someone: *I hope I didn't hurt him with my remarks.*

husband /ˈhʌzbənd/ **noun**
A1 the man that someone is married to

hush /hʌʃ/ **noun** [no plural]
a period of silence: *A hush fell over the room.*

hut /hʌt/ **noun**
B1 a small, simple building, often made of wood: *a mountain hut*

hymn /hɪm/ **noun**
a song sung by Christians in church

hype /haɪp/ **noun** [no plural]
discussion that makes something seem more important or exciting than it actually is: *media hype* ◦ *There's been a lot of* ***hype surrounding*** *his latest movie.*

hyphen /ˈhaɪfᵊn/ **noun**
a mark (-) used to join two words together, or to show that a word continues on the next line

hypnotize /ˈhɪpnətaɪz/ **verb**
(**hypnotizing**, **hypnotized**)
to place someone in a mental state in which you can influence what they think and do

hysterical /hɪˈsterɪkᵊl/ **adj**
not able to control your behaviour because you are very frightened, angry, excited, etc.: *hysterical laughter* ◦ *As soon as Wendy saw the blood, she became hysterical.*

I i

I, i /aɪ/
the ninth letter of the alphabet

I /aɪ/ **pronoun**

> **Common mistake: I**
> Remember that **I** is always written with a capital letter.

A1 used when the person speaking or writing is the subject of the verb: *I've bought some chocolate.* ◦ *I'll see you later.*

ice /aɪs/ **noun** [no plural]
1 **A2** water that is so cold it has become solid: *Would you like ice and lemon in your drink?*
2 **break the ice** to make people who have not met before feel more relaxed with each other: *I told everyone a joke, which helped to break the ice.*

iceberg /ˈaɪsbɜːg/ **noun**
a very large piece of ice that floats in the sea

ice cream /ˌaɪs ˈkriːm/ **noun**
A1 a sweet, cold food made from frozen milk: *vanilla ice cream*

ice cream

ice cube /ˈaɪs ˌkjuːb/ **noun**
a small piece of ice that you put into a drink to make it cold

ice hockey /ˈaɪs ˌhɒki/ **noun** [no plural] UK (US **hockey**)
B1 a game that two teams play on ice, in which players hit a flat round object with long curved sticks: *He plays ice hockey.*
→ See **Sports 1** on page C15

ice skate /ˈaɪs ˌskeɪt/ **noun**
a boot with a metal part on the bottom, used for moving across ice
• **ice skating** **noun** [no plural]

icicle /ˈaɪsɪkl/ **noun**
a long, thin piece of ice that hangs down from something

icing /ˈaɪsɪŋ/ **noun** [no plural]
a sweet mixture used to cover or fill cakes

icicles

icon /ˈaɪkɒn/ **noun**
1 a small picture on a computer screen that you choose in order to make the computer do something: *Click on the print icon.*
2 a person or thing that is famous because it represents a particular idea or way of life: *a fashion icon*

icy /ˈaɪsi/ **adj**
1 covered in ice: *icy roads*
2 very cold: *an icy wind*

ID /ˌaɪˈdiː/ **noun**
A2 an official document that shows or proves who you are: *Make sure you carry some ID with you.* ◦ *You will need a passport or an **ID card**.*

I'd /aɪd/
1 short form of I had: *Everyone thought I'd gone.*
2 short form of I would: *I'd like to buy some stamps, please.*

idea /aɪˈdɪə/ **noun**
1 **A2** a suggestion or plan: *What a good idea!* ◦ *It was Kate's idea to hire a car.*
2 **B1** an opinion or belief: *We have very different **ideas about** politics.*
3 **have no idea** **B1** to not know: *'Where's Matt?' 'I have no idea.'*
4 an understanding, thought, or picture in your mind: *I think you've got the wrong idea about this.*

ideal /aɪˈdɪəl/ **adj**
perfect, or the best possible: *She is the ideal person for the job.*

ideally /aɪˈdɪəli/ **adv**
1 in a perfect way: *She's ideally suited to the job.*
2 used to talk about how something would be in a perfect situation: *Ideally, I'd like to work at home.*

identical /aɪˈdentɪkəl/ **adj**
exactly the same: *She found a dress **identical to** the one in the picture.*

identification /aɪˌdentɪfɪˈkeɪʃᵊn/ **noun** [no plural]
1 A2 an official document that shows or proves who you are: *Do you have any identification on you?*
2 the act of recognizing and naming someone or something: *Most of the bodies were badly burned, making identification almost impossible.*

identify /aɪˈdentɪfaɪ/ **verb** (**identifying**, **identified**)
to say what someone's name is or what something's name is: *The victim has not yet been identified.*
identify with *someone/something* **phrasal verb**
to feel that you are similar to someone and can understand them or their situation: *Readers can identify with the hero of the novel.*

identity /aɪˈdentəti/ **noun** (plural **identities**)
1 who someone is: *They kept her identity secret.*
2 the things that make one person or group of people different from others: *a sense of national identity*

identity card /aɪˈdentɪti ˌkɑːd/ **noun**
B1 a card that shows your name, photograph, and information to prove who you are: *Her identity card was stolen.*

idiom /ˈɪdiəm/ **noun**
a group of words used together with a meaning that you cannot guess

idiot /ˈɪdiət/ **noun**
a stupid person: *This idiot ran in front of my car.*
• **idiotic** /ˌɪdiˈɒtɪk/ **adj** stupid: *an idiotic idea*

idol /ˈaɪdᵊl/ **noun**
1 someone that you admire and respect very much: *a pop idol*
2 a picture or object that people pray to as part of their religion

i.e. /ˌaɪˈiː/
used to explain exactly what you mean: *The price must be more realistic, i.e. lower.*

if /ɪf/ **conjunction**
1 A2 used to say that something will happen only after something else happens or is true: *We'll have the party in the garden if the weather's good.*
2 B1 used to talk about something that might happen or be true: *What will we do if this doesn't work?*
3 B1 whether: *I wonder if he'll get the job.*
4 B1 used to mean 'always' or 'every time': *If you mention his mother, he always cries.*
5 if not A2 used to say what the situation will be if something does not happen: *I hope to see you there but, if not, I'll call you.*
6 if you like A2 used when you offer someone something: *If you like, I could drive you there.*
7 if I were you B1 used when you give someone advice: *I think I'd take the money if I were you.*
8 if only B1 used to express a wish for something that is impossible or unlikely to happen: *If only I knew the answer!*
9 if so if this is the case: *It might rain this afternoon. If so, we'll have the party indoors.*

ignorance /ˈɪgnᵊrᵊns/ **noun** [no plural]
a lack of knowledge about something: *I was shocked by her ignorance of the subject.*

ignorant /ˈɪgnᵊrᵊnt/ **adj**
not knowing enough about something: *She's completely* ***ignorant about*** *computers.*

ignore /ɪgˈnɔːʳ/ **verb** (**ignoring**, **ignored**)
to not give attention to something or someone: *I said hello but she ignored me.*

ill /ɪl/ **adj**
A2 not feeling well, or suffering from a disease: *He was in bed, ill.*

I'll /aɪl/
short form of I will: *I'll see you tomorrow.*

illegal /ɪˈliːgᵊl/ **adj**
not allowed by law: *illegal drugs* ◦ *It is* ***illegal to*** *sell cigarettes to anyone under 16.*
→ Opposite **legal** **adj**
• **illegally** **adv** *an illegally parked car*

a b c d e f g h **i** j k l m n o p q r s t u v w x y z

illegible /ɪˈledʒəbl/ **adj**
Illegible writing is impossible to read.
→ Opposite **legible adj**

illiterate /ɪˈlɪtᵊrət/ **adj**
not able to read or write

illness /ˈɪlnəs/ **noun**
1 B1 a disease: *He has a serious illness.*
2 [no plural] being ill: *Unfortunately I couldn't go because of illness.*

illusion /ɪˈluːʒᵊn/ **noun**
something that is not really what it seems to be: *There is a large mirror at one end to create the illusion of space.*

illustrate /ˈɪləstreɪt/ **verb** (**illustrating**, **illustrated**)
to draw pictures for a book

illustration /ˌɪləˈstreɪʃᵊn/ **noun**
a picture in a book

I'm /aɪm/
short form of I am: *I'm Fiona.* ◦ *I'm too hot.*

Common mistake: I'm
Remember that **I'm** is always written with an apostrophe.
I'm pleased you could come.
~~*Im too hot.*~~

image /ˈɪmɪdʒ/ **noun**
1 the way that other people think someone or something is: *They want to improve the* ***public image of*** *the police.*
2 a picture, especially in movies or television or in a mirror: *television images of starving children*
3 a picture in your mind: *I have an* ***image of*** *the way I want the garden to look.*

imaginary /ɪˈmædʒɪnᵊri/ **adj**
not real but imagined in your mind: *The story takes place in an imaginary world.*

imagination /ɪˌmædʒɪˈneɪʃᵊn/ **noun**
1 B1 [no plural] the ability to have ideas or pictures in your mind: *The job needs someone with a bit of imagination.*
2 B1 the part of your mind that creates ideas or pictures of things that are not real or that you have not seen: *My son has a very vivid (= active) imagination.*

imagine /ɪˈmædʒɪn/ **verb** (**imagining**, **imagined**)
1 B1 to make an idea or picture of something in your mind: *Imagine being able to do all your shopping from home.*
2 to believe that something is probably true: *I imagine he is quite difficult to live with.*
3 B1 to have an idea of what something is like or might be like: *Can you* ***imagine how*** *it feels to be blind?*
4 B1 to think that you hear or see something that does not really exist: *'Did you hear a noise?' 'No, you're* ***imagining things.****'*

imitate /ˈɪmɪteɪt/ **verb** (**imitating**, **imitated**)
to copy someone: *He was imitating the president.*

imitation /ˌɪmɪˈteɪʃᵊn/ **noun**
a copy of something that looks like the real thing: *It wasn't a genuine Gucci handbag, just* ***a cheap imitation.***

immature /ˌɪməˈtjʊəʳ/ **adj**
behaving like a younger person: *Some boys are so immature for their age.*

immediate /ɪˈmiːdiət/ **adj**
1 happening now or very soon after something else: *The drugs had an immediate effect.*
2 important now and needing attention: *Our* ***immediate concern*** *is getting food to the refugees.*

immediately /ɪˈmiːdiətli/ **adv**
A2 now, without waiting: *She asked him to come home immediately.*

immense /ɪˈmens/ **adj**
very big: *He won an immense amount of money.*

immensely /ɪˈmensli/ **adv**
very: *He was immensely popular.*

immigrant /ˈɪmɪgrᵊnt/ **noun**
someone who comes to live in a different country

immigration /ˌɪmɪˈgreɪʃᵊn/ **noun** [no plural]
1 B1 the place where people's official documents are checked when they

enter a country, for example, at an airport: *After you've been through immigration, you can get your luggage.*
2 the process of coming to live in a different country: *immigration policy*

immoral /ɪˈmɒrəl/ **adj**
not correct, honest, or good: *immoral behaviour*

immune /ɪˈmjuːn/ **adj**
If you are immune to a disease, you will not get it: *Once you've had the virus, you are* ***immune to*** *it.*

immunize /ˈɪmjənaɪz/ **verb** (**immunizing**, **immunized**)
to stop someone from getting a disease by giving them medicine: *He was* ***immunized against*** *the disease as a child.*

impact /ˈɪmpækt/ **noun** [no plural]
the effect that a person, event, or situation has on someone or something: *She has* ***had a major impact on*** *today's pop music.*

impatient /ɪmˈpeɪʃənt/ **adj**
1 If you are impatient, you get angry with people who make mistakes or you hate waiting for things: *I get very* ***impatient with*** *the children when they won't do their homework.*
→ Opposite **patient** adj
2 wanting something to happen as soon as possible: *People are* ***impatient for*** *change in this country.*
• **impatiently** **adv** *We waited impatiently for the show to begin.*

imperative /ɪmˈperətɪv/ **adj**
An imperative form of a verb is used to say an order. In the sentence 'Stop the machine!', the verb 'stop' is an imperative verb.
• **imperative** **noun** the imperative form of a verb

imply /ɪmˈplaɪ/ **verb** (**implying**, **implied**)
to suggest or show something, without saying it directly: *She* ***implied that*** *she wasn't happy at work.*

impolite /ˌɪmpəlˈaɪt/ **adj** formal
rude

import¹ /ɪmˈpɔːt/ **verb**
to bring something into your country for people to buy: *We import about 20 percent of our food.*

import² /ˈɪmpɔːt/ **noun**
something that one country gets from another country: *Japanese imports*

importance /ɪmˈpɔːtəns/ **noun** [no plural]
B1 how important someone or something is: *Do you understand* ***the importance of*** *what I'm saying?*

important /ɪmˈpɔːtənt/ **adj**
1 **A1** valuable, useful, or necessary: *My family is very* ***important to*** *me.*
2 **B1** having a lot of power: *an important person*

importantly /ɪmˈpɔːtəntli/ **adv**
in a way that is important: *They provided showers and, more importantly, clean clothes.*

impossible /ɪmˈpɒsəbl/ **adj**
B1 not able to happen: *It is impossible to work with all this noise.*
→ Opposite **possible** adj

impress /ɪmˈpres/ **verb**
to make someone admire or respect you: *I was hoping to* ***impress*** *him* ***with*** *my knowledge.*

impression /ɪmˈpreʃən/ **noun**
1 an idea, feeling, or opinion about something or someone: *What was your impression of Carla's husband?* ◦ *I* ***got*** *the* ***impression*** *that he was bored.*
2 [no plural] the way that something seems, looks, or feels to a particular person: *It* ***makes*** *a very bad* ***impression*** *if you're late for an interview.* ◦ *Monica* ***gives the impression*** *of being shy.*
3 **be under the impression** to think or understand something: *I was under the impression that you didn't like him.*

impressive /ɪmˈpresɪv/ **adj**
Someone or something that is impressive makes you admire and respect them: *an impressive performance*

imprison /ɪmˈprɪzən/ **verb**
to put someone in prison: *Taylor was imprisoned in 1969 for burglary.*

a b c d e f g h i j k l m n o p q r s t u v w x y z

improve /ɪmˈpruːv/ **verb** (**improving, improved**)
A2 to get better or to make something better: *Scott's behaviour has improved a lot lately.*

improvement /ɪmˈpruːvmənt/ **noun**
1 B1 the process or result of something getting better: *There's been a big* ***improvement in*** *her work this term.*
2 B1 a change to something that makes it better: *home improvements*

impulse /ˈɪmpʌls/ **noun**
a sudden feeling that you must do something: *Her first impulse was to run away.*

impulsive /ɪmˈpʌlsɪv/ **adj**
doing things suddenly, without planning or thinking carefully: *It was an impulsive response.*

in[1] /ɪn/ **preposition**
1 A1 inside a container or place: *a shop in Manhattan.* ◦ *He put his hand in his pocket.*
2 A1 during a period of time: *We're going to Italy in April.*
3 A2 needing or using no more time than a particular amount of time: *I finished the job in two weeks.*
4 A2 after a particular amount of time in the future: *Dinner will be ready in ten minutes.*
5 A2 forming a part of something: *I've been waiting in this queue for a long time.*
6 B1 connected with a particular subject: *advances in medical science*
7 B1 wearing: *Do you know that man in the grey suit?*
8 B1 experiencing an emotion or condition: *She's in a good mood this morning.* ◦ *They are in danger.*
9 B1 arranged in a particular way: *Is this list in alphabetical order?* ◦ *We all sat down in a circle.*
10 B1 expressed or written in a particular way: *They spoke in Russian the whole time.*
11 involved in a particular type of job: *He wants a career in politics.*

in[2] /ɪn/ **adv**
1 A2 into an area or space from the outside of it: *She took off her shoes and socks and jumped in.*
2 B1 at the place where a person usually lives or works: *I called, but she wasn't in.*
3 B1 If a train, plane, etc. is in, it has arrived at the place it was going to: *My train gets in at 9.54.*

in.
written abbreviation for inch: a unit for measuring length

inability /ˌɪnəˈbɪləti/ **noun** [no plural]
the state of not being able to do something: *her inability to answer the question*

inaccurate /ɪnˈækjərət/ **adj**
not correct or exact: *inaccurate information*
→ Opposite **accurate adj**

inadequate /ɪˈnædɪkwət/ **adj**
not enough or not good enough: *Her skills were* ***inadequate for*** *the job.*
→ Opposite **adequate adj**

inappropriate /ˌɪnəˈprəʊpriət/ **adj**
not suitable: *inappropriate behaviour*
→ Opposite **appropriate adj**

incapable /ɪnˈkeɪpəbl/ **adj**
not able to do something: *I think he is* ***incapable of*** *listening.*
→ Opposite **capable adj**

inch /ɪnʃ/ **noun** (written abbreviation **in.**)
B1 a unit for measuring length, equal to 2.54 centimetres

incident /ˈɪnsɪdᵊnt/ **noun** formal
something that happens, especially something bad: *Police are investigating the incident.*

incidentally /ɪnsɪˈdentᵊli/ **adv**
used when you say something that is not as important as the main thing that you are talking about but is connected to it: *Incidentally, talking of Stephen, have you met his girlfriend?*

inclined /ɪnˈklaɪnd/ **adj**
inclined to do *something* often behaving in a particular way: *Tom is inclined to be forgetful.*

include /ɪnˈkluːd/ **verb** (**including, included**)
1 A2 to have something or someone as part of something larger: *The price*

includes flights and three nights' accommodation.
2 to allow someone to take part in an activity: *Local residents were **included in** the planning discussions.*
→ Opposite **exclude** verb

including /ɪnˈkluːdɪŋ/ **preposition**
A2 used to show that someone or something is part of something larger: *It's £24.99, including postage and packing.*
→ Opposite **excluding** preposition

income /ˈɪŋkʌm/ **noun**
the money that you regularly get, for example from your job: *Many families are on low incomes.*

income tax /ˈɪŋkʌm ˌtæks/ **noun**
money that the government takes from the money that you earn

incomplete /ˌɪnkəmˈpliːt/ **adj**
not finished, or with parts missing: *The building is still incomplete.*
→ Opposite **complete** adj

inconsiderate /ˌɪnkənˈsɪdᵊrət/ **adj**
not caring when you make problems for other people: *He shouldn't keep us waiting like this – it's very inconsiderate.*

inconvenience /ˌɪnkənˈviːniəns/ **noun**
problems: *I apologized for any inconvenience caused.*

inconvenient /ˌɪnkənˈviːniənt/ **adj**
causing problems: *It is very inconvenient living so far away from the shops.*
→ Opposite **convenient** adj

incorrect /ˌɪnkᵊrˈekt/ **adj**
B1 wrong: *His answers were incorrect.*
• **incorrectly** **adv** *My name was spelled incorrectly.*
→ Opposite **correct** adj

increase[1] /ɪnˈkriːs/ **verb** (**increasing**, **increased**)
B1 to get bigger or to make something bigger: *Smoking increases the risk of serious illnesses.* ◦ *Sales of computers have **increased by** 15%.*
→ Opposite **decrease** verb

increase[2] /ˈɪnkriːs/ **noun**
a rise in the amount or size of something: *a price increase* ◦ *We are seeing **an increase in** standards of living.*
→ Opposite **decrease**

increasingly /ɪnˈkriːsɪŋli/ **adv**
more and more: *The sport is becoming increasingly popular.*

incredible /ɪnˈkredɪbl/ **adj**
1 B1 informal very good and exciting: *The city itself is incredible.*
2 very large in amount or high in level: *She earned an incredible amount of money.* ◦ *The planes make an incredible noise.*
3 If a fact is incredible, it is so strange that you cannot believe it: *It seems incredible that she didn't know what was happening.*
• **incredibly** **adv** very: *The team played incredibly well.*

indeed /ɪnˈdiːd/ **adv**
1 B1 used to make the word 'very' stronger: *Many people are very poor indeed.*
2 B1 used when saying that something is correct: *'Is this your dog?' 'It is indeed.'*

indefinite /ɪnˈdefɪnət/ **adj**
with no definite end: *He will be staying here for an indefinite period.*

indefinite article /ɪnˌdefɪnət ˈɑːtɪkl/ **noun**
B1 in grammar, a phrase used to mean the words 'a' or 'an'

independence /ˌɪndɪˈpendəns/ **noun** [no plural]
1 a situation in which individuals look after themselves and do not need help from other people: *Teenagers need a certain amount of independence.*
2 a situation in which a country has its own government and is not ruled by another country: *Mexico gained its independence from Spain in 1821.*

independent /ˌɪndɪˈpendənt/ **adj**
1 B1 not wanting or needing anyone else to help you: *She's a very independent four-year-old.*
→ Opposite **dependent** adj
2 not controlled or ruled by anyone else: *an independent state*
3 not influenced or controlled in any way by other people, events, or things:

an independent organization ◦ *The group is* ***independent of*** *any political party.*
• **independently** **adv** *The two scientists both made the same discovery independently.*

index /ˈɪndeks/ **noun** (plural **indexes**)
a list of subjects or names at the end of a book, showing on what page in the book you can find them

indicate /ˈɪndɪkeɪt/ **verb** (**indicating**, **indicated**)
1 to show that something exists or is true: *Recent evidence* ***indicates that*** *the skeleton is about a million years old.*
2 to point to someone or something: *He indicated a man in a dark coat.*
3 UK to show that you are going to turn left or right when you are driving: *The driver turned right without indicating.*

indication /ˌɪndɪˈkeɪʃən/ **noun**
a sign showing that something exists or is true: *She* ***gave*** *no* ***indication that*** *she was unhappy.*

indicator /ˈɪndɪkeɪtəʳ/ **noun** UK
a light that flashes on a car to show that the driver is turning right or left
→ See **Car** on page C3

indigestion /ˌɪndɪˈdʒestʃən/ **noun** [no plural]
a painful or uncomfortable feeling in your stomach after you have eaten something

indignant /ɪnˈdɪgnənt/ **adj**
angry because of something that is wrong or not fair: *He was very indignant when I suggested that he had made a mistake.*

indirect /ˌɪndɪˈrekt/ **adj**
connected with something, but not directly: *Her health problems are an indirect result of her job.*
→ Opposite **direct** **adj**

individual¹ /ˌɪndɪˈvɪdʒuəl/ **adj**
1 B1 considered separately from other things in a group: *Read out the individual letters of each word.*
2 B1 relating to one particular person or thing: *He gets more individual attention from his teacher.*
• **individually** **adv** separately and not as a group: *Ask the students to work individually.*

individual² /ˌɪndɪˈvɪdʒuəl/ **noun**
a person, especially when considered separately and not as part of a group: *We try to treat our students as individuals.*

indoor /ˌɪnˈdɔːʳ/ **adj**
A2 in a building: *an indoor pool*
→ Opposite **outdoor** **adj**

indoors /ˌɪnˈdɔːz/ **adv**
B1 into or inside a building: *If you're feeling cold, we can go indoors.*
→ Opposite **outdoors** **adv**

industrial /ɪnˈdʌstriəl/ **adj**
connected with industry: *an industrial city*

industry /ˈɪndəstri/ **noun**
1 B1 (plural **industries**) all the companies involved in a particular type of business: *the entertainment industry*
2 [no plural] the making of things in factories

inefficient /ˌɪnɪˈfɪʃənt/ **adj**
inefficient people or things waste time, money, or effort, and do not achieve as much as they should: *an inefficient heating system*
→ Opposite **efficient** **adj**

inevitable /ɪˈnevɪtəbl/ **adj**
If something is inevitable, you cannot avoid or stop it: *It was* ***inevitable that*** *his crime would be discovered.*
• **inevitably** **adv** *Inevitably, there was a certain amount of fighting between the groups.*

inexpensive /ˌɪnɪkˈspensɪv/ **adj**
B1 cheap but of good quality: *inexpensive children's clothes*

inexperienced /ˌɪnɪkˈspɪəriənst/ **adj**
not having done something often: *Kennedy was young and inexperienced.*
→ Opposite **experienced** **adj**

infant /ˈɪnfənt/ **noun** formal
a baby or very young child

infect /ɪnˈfekt/ **verb**
to give someone a disease: *Thousands of people were infected with the virus.*

infection /ɪnˈfekʃən/ **noun**
a disease that is caused by bacteria or a virus: *a throat infection*
• **infectious adj** An infectious disease can be given by one person to another.

inferior /ɪnˈfɪəriəʳ/ **adj**
not as good as someone or something else: *These are inferior products.*
→ Opposite **superior adj**

infinite /ˈɪnfɪnət/ **adj**
very large or without limits: *God's power is infinite.*

infinitely /ˈɪnfɪnətli/ **adv**
very or very much: *The book was infinitely better than the movie.*

infinitive /ɪnˈfɪnətɪv/ **noun**
B1 in grammar, the basic form of a verb that usually follows 'to'. In the sentence 'She decided to leave', 'to leave' is an infinitive.

inflammable /ɪnˈflæməbl/ **adj**
Something that is inflammable burns very easily.

inflate /ɪnˈfleɪt/ **verb** (**inflating**, **inflated**)
to fill something with air or gas: *Inflate the tyres.*

inflation /ɪnˈfleɪʃən/ **noun** [no plural]
the rate at which prices increase, or an increase in prices: *rising inflation*

influence[1] /ˈɪnfluəns/ **noun**
1 the power to change people or things: *The drug companies have a lot of **influence on** doctors.*
2 someone or something that changes another person or thing: *Her father was a big **influence on** her.*

influence[2] /ˈɪnfluəns/ **verb** (**influencing**, **influenced**)
to change the way that someone thinks or the way that something develops: *Were you influenced by anybody when you were younger?*

influential /ˌɪnfluˈenʃəl/ **adj**
having the power to change people or things: *an influential figure in jazz*

inform /ɪnˈfɔːm/ **verb**
B1 to tell someone about something: *He **informed** us **that** we would have to leave.* ◦ *Patients should be **informed about** the risks.*

informal /ɪnˈfɔːməl/ **adj**
1 relaxed and friendly: *an informal meeting*
2 suitable for normal situations: *informal clothes* ◦ *informal language*
→ Opposite **formal adj**
• **informally adv** *We chatted informally (= in a relaxed, friendly way) before the interview.*

information /ˌɪnfəˈmeɪʃən/ **noun** [no plural]
A2 facts about a situation, person, event, etc.: *Do you have any **information about** local schools?* ◦ *This was an important **piece of information**.*

> **Common mistake: information**
> Remember you cannot make **information** plural. Do not say 'informations'.
> *Could you send me some information about your courses?*

informative /ɪnˈfɔːmətɪv/ **adj**
having a lot of useful facts: *a very informative book*

ingredient /ɪnˈgriːdiənt/ **noun**
B1 one of the different foods that a particular type of food is made from: *I don't have the ingredients for a cake.*

inhabit /ɪnˈhæbɪt/ **verb** formal
to live in a place: *The islands are inhabited by birds and small animals.*

inhabitant /ɪnˈhæbɪtənt/ **noun**
someone who lives somewhere: *a city with ten million inhabitants*

inherit /ɪnˈherɪt/ **verb**
to get money or things from someone after they die: *He inherited the house from his uncle.*
• **inheritance noun** money or things that you get from someone after they die

initial[1] /ɪˈnɪʃəl/ **adj**
first, or happening at the start: *My initial reaction was one of anger.*

initial[2] /ɪˈnɪʃəl/ **noun**
B1 the first letter of a name, especially when used to represent a name: *He wrote his initials, P. M. R., at the bottom of the page.*

a b c d e f g h i j k l m n o p q r s t u v w x y z

a b c d e f g h i j k l m n o p q r s t u v w x y z

initially /ɪˈnɪʃəli/ **adv**
at the start: *Initially we thought it would cost six thousand euros.*

inject /ɪnˈdʒekt/ **verb**
to put a drug into someone's body using a needle
• **injection noun** the act of putting a drug into someone's body using a needle: *I* ***had*** *an* ***injection****.*

injure /ˈɪndʒəʳ/ **verb** (**injuring**, **injured**)
B1 to hurt a person or animal: *She injured her ankle when she fell.* ◦ *No one was injured in the accident.*
• **injured adj** B1 *She was told to stay in bed to rest her injured back.*

injury /ˈɪndʒəri/ **noun** (plural **injuries**)
damage to someone's body: *head injuries* ◦ *The passenger in the car escaped with minor injuries.*

injustice /ɪnˈdʒʌstɪs/ **noun**
a situation or action in which people are not treated fairly: *the fight against racial injustice*

ink /ɪŋk/ **noun** [no plural]
B1 a coloured liquid that you use for writing, printing, or drawing

inland /ˈɪnlənd/ **adj**, **adv**
away from the sea: *The landscape changed as we drove further inland.*

inn /ɪn/ **noun**
a small hotel, especially one in the countryside

inner /ˈɪnəʳ/ **adj**
1 on the inside, or near the middle of something: *Leading off the main hall is a series of inner rooms.*
→ Opposite **outer adj**
2 Inner feelings or thoughts are ones that you do not show or tell other people: *Karen always seemed to have a deep sense of inner peace.*

innocence /ˈɪnəsəns/ **noun** [no plural]
the fact of not having done a crime: *She fought to prove her innocence.*
→ Opposite **guilt noun**

innocent /ˈɪnəsənt/ **adj**
1 If someone is innocent, they have not done a crime: *The jury decided he was innocent.*
→ Opposite **guilty adj**
2 not having much experience of life and not knowing about the bad things that can happen: *an innocent young woman*

inquire (**inquiring**, **inquired**) formal (also UK **enquire**) /ɪnˈkwaɪəʳ/ **verb**
to ask someone for information about something: *I am* ***inquiring about*** *French classes in the area.*

inquiry (plural **inquiries**) (also UK **enquiry**) /ɪnˈkwaɪəri/ **noun**
1 B1 formal a question that you ask to get information: *The company has received a lot of* ***inquiries about*** *its new service.*
2 an official process to try to discover the facts about something bad that has happened: *There will be an official* ***inquiry into*** *the train crash.*

inquisitive /ɪnˈkwɪzətɪv/ **adj**
wanting to know as much as you can about things: *an inquisitive child*

insane /ɪnˈseɪn/ **adj**
crazy or very silly: *She must be insane going out in this weather!*

insects

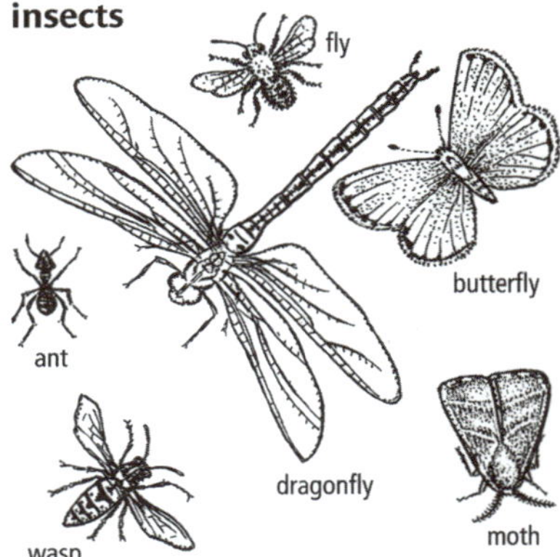

insect /ˈɪnsekt/ **noun**
A2 a small creature with six legs, for example a bee or a fly

insensitive /ɪnˈsensətɪv/ **adj**
not noticing when other people are upset: *an insensitive remark*

insert /ɪnˈsɜːt/ **verb** formal
to put something into something else: *Insert the coin in the slot.*

inside¹ /ˌɪnˈsaɪd/ **adv, preposition**
1 A1 in or into a room, building, or container: *There were some keys inside the box.* ◦ *I'm cold – let's go back inside.*
2 If you have a feeling inside, people do not know about it if you do not tell them: *She looked calm but was feeling nervous inside.*

inside² /ˌɪnˈsaɪd/ **adj**
in or on the part of something under its surface: *This jacket has an inside pocket.*

inside³ /ˌɪnˈsaɪd/ **noun**
1 the inside the part of something that is under its surface: *The inside of her house is nice.*
2 inside out If a piece of clothing is inside out, the part that is usually outside is on the inside: *You've got your sweater on inside out.*

insist /ɪnˈsɪst/ **verb**
1 B1 to say that something is certainly true, especially when other people do not believe you: *Mia* ***insisted that*** *she and Carlo were just friends.*
2 to say that something must be done: *She* ***insisted on*** *seeing her lawyer.*

inspect /ɪnˈspekt/ **verb**
to look carefully at something to see if there is anything wrong: *Clara inspected her make-up in the mirror.*
• **inspection noun**

inspector /ɪnˈspektəʳ/ **noun**
1 someone whose job is to visit places and see if things are being done correctly: *a school inspector*
2 a police officer

inspiration /ˌɪnspəʳˈeɪʃən/ **noun**
someone or something that gives you ideas for doing something: *Africa is a source of* ***inspiration for*** *his painting.*

inspire /ɪnˈspaɪəʳ/ **verb** (**inspiring, inspired**)
1 to make someone feel that they want to do something: *A teacher had inspired Sam to become an actor.*
2 to give someone an idea for a book, play, painting, etc.: *This television drama was inspired by a true story.*
• **inspiring adj** giving you new ideas and making you feel you want to do something: *an inspiring book*

install /ɪnˈstɔːl/ **verb**
1 B1 to put a piece of equipment somewhere and make it ready to use: *The school has installed a burglar alarm.*
2 B1 to put software onto a computer

instalment /ɪnˈstɔːlmənt/ **noun**
1 a regular payment: *You can pay for your computer* ***in*** *six monthly* ***instalments****.*
2 one part of a story that you can see every day or week in a magazine or on television

instance /ˈɪnstəns/ **noun**
for instance B1 for example: *Many teenagers earn money, for instance by babysitting or cleaning cars.*

instant /ˈɪnstənt/ **adj**
1 happening immediately: *The book was an instant success in the US.*
2 Instant food or drink can be made quickly: *instant coffee*
• **instantly adv** immediately: *A car hit them, killing them both instantly.*

instead /ɪnˈsted/ **adv**
A2 in the place of someone or something else: *Why don't you help* ***instead of*** *complaining?*

instinct /ˈɪnstɪŋkt/ **noun**
the force that makes people and animals do things without first thinking: *It's the mother's instinct to protect her children.*

institute /ˈɪnstɪtjuːt/ **noun**
a place where people do scientific or teaching work: *the Massachusetts Institute of Technology*

institution /ˌɪnstɪˈtjuːʃən/ **noun**
a large and important organization, such as a university or bank: *It is one of the country's top medical institutions.*

instruct /ɪnˈstrʌkt/ **verb**
1 to officially tell someone to do something: *Staff are instructed not to use the telephones for personal calls.*
2 formal to teach someone about something

a b c d e f g h i j k l m n o p q r s t u v w x y z

instructions /ɪnˈstrʌkʃənz/ **plural noun**
A2 information that explains how to do or use something: *I just **followed** the **instructions**.*

instructor /ɪnˈstrʌktəʳ/ **noun**
someone who teaches a particular sport or activity: *a driving instructor*

instrument /ˈɪnstrəmənt/ **noun**
1 A2 an object that is used for playing music, for example a piano
2 a tool that is used for doing something: *scientific instruments*

insult /ɪnˈsʌlt/ **verb**
to say or do something rude to someone and upset them: *He annoyed me by insulting one of my friends.*
• **insulting adj** rude: *an insulting remark*
• **insult** /ˈɪnsʌlt/ **noun** something rude that you say or do to someone: *They shouted insults at each other.*

insurance /ɪnˈʃʊərəns/ **noun** [no plural]
an agreement in which you pay a company money and they in the future give you money if you have an accident, are hurt, etc.: *We need car insurance.*

insure /ɪnˈʃʊəʳ/ **verb** (**insuring**, **insured**)
to buy insurance from a company: *I need to get my car insured.*

intellectual /ˌɪntəlˈektjuəl/ **adj**
relating to your ability to think and to understand things, especially complicated ideas: *I like detective stories and romances – nothing too intellectual.*

intelligence /ɪnˈtelɪdʒəns/ **noun** [no plural]
the ability to learn and understand things: *a child of low intelligence*

intelligent /ɪnˈtelɪdʒənt/ **adj**
B1 able to learn and understand things easily: *She is a highly intelligent young woman.*
• **intelligently adv**

intend /ɪnˈtend/ **verb**
1 B1 to want and plan to do something: *How long do you **intend to** stay in Paris?*
2 be intended for *someone*; be intended as *something* to be made for a particular person or reason: *The books are intended for young children.*

intense /ɪnˈtens/ **adj**
extreme or very strong: *intense heat*
• **intensely adv** very much: *I dislike him intensely.*

intensive /ɪnˈtensɪv/ **adj**
involving a lot of work in a little time: *ten weeks of intensive training*

intention /ɪnˈtenʃən/ **noun**
something that you want and plan to do: *I **have no intention** of seeing him again.*

intentional /ɪnˈtenʃənəl/ **adj**
planned: *I'm sorry I didn't let you know – it wasn't intentional.*
• **intentionally adv** *I didn't ignore her intentionally – I just didn't recognize her.*

interactive /ˌɪntərˈæktɪv/ **adj**
Interactive computer programs react to the person using them.

interest¹ /ˈɪntrəst/ **noun**
1 B1 the feeling of wanting to know more about something: *I have always had an **interest in** science.* ◦ *After a while he simply **lost interest in** (= stopped being interested in) his studies.*
2 B1 something you enjoy doing: *We share a lot of the same interests.*
3 B1 [no plural] the quality that makes you think that something is interesting: *Would this book **be of** any **interest to** you (= are you interested in reading it)?*
4 [no plural] the extra money that you must pay to a bank if you borrow money, or that you receive from the bank if you keep your money there: *low interest rates*

interest² /ˈɪntrəst/ **verb**
B1 If someone or something interests you, you want to give them your attention and know more about them: *History doesn't really interest me.*

interested /ˈɪntrəstɪd/ **adj**
A2 wanting to do something or know more about something: *Sarah's only **interested in** boys and clothes.*

Common mistake: interested and interesting

Learners often spell **interesting** and **interested** wrong. Remember that they begin with **inter**.

interesting /ˈɪntrəstɪŋ/ **adj**
A1 keeping your attention: *an interesting person*
→ Opposite **boring** adj

Common mistake: interesting or interested?

Interested is used to describe how someone feels about a person or thing.
I'm interested in theatre.
~~*I'm interesting in theatre.*~~
If a person or thing is **interesting**, they make you feel interested.
It was an interesting film.

interestingly /ˈɪntrəstɪŋli/ **adv**
used to show that the speaker finds something interesting: *Interestingly, he never actually said he was innocent.*

interfere /ˌɪntəˈfɪəʳ/ **verb**
(**interfering**, **interfered**)
to try to become involved in a situation that you should not be involved in: *You shouldn't **interfere in** other people's business.*
interfere with *something* phrasal verb
to spoil something: *I try not to let my dancing interfere with my studies.*
• **interference** noun [no plural]

interior /ɪnˈtɪəriəʳ/ **noun**
the inside part of something: *I have never seen the interior of the hotel.*
→ Opposite **exterior** noun

intermediate /ˌɪntəˈmiːdiət/ **adj**
B1 between the highest and lowest levels of knowledge or skill: *intermediate students*

internal /ɪnˈtɜːnəl/ **adj**
inside a place, or inside your body: *internal injuries*
→ Opposite **external** adj

international /ˌɪntəˈnæʃənəl/ **adj**
A2 relating to or involving two or more countries: *an international team of scientists* ◦ *international politics*
• **internationally** adv

the Internet /ˈɪntənet/ **noun** [no plural] (also **the Net**)
A1 a system that connects computers around the world so you can share information with other people: *Cambridge dictionaries are available **on the Internet**.*

interpret /ɪnˈtɜːprɪt/ **verb**
to change what someone has said into another language: *We had to ask the guide to interpret for us.*

interpretation /ɪnˌtɜːprɪˈteɪʃən/ **noun**
an explanation or opinion of what something means: *These are traditional **interpretations of** the Bible.*

interpreter /ɪnˈtɜːprɪtəʳ/ **noun**
someone whose job is to change what someone else is saying into another language

interrupt /ˌɪntəˈrʌpt/ **verb**
B1 to stop someone while they are talking or doing something, by saying or doing something yourself: *Sorry to interrupt, but what time is it?*

interruption /ˌɪntəˈrʌpʃən/ **noun**
something that causes someone to stop talking or doing something: *Due to constant interruptions, the meeting finished late.*

interval /ˈɪntəvəl/ **noun**
B1 a period of time between two things: *After an interval of three days the peace talks started again.*

interview[1] /ˈɪntəvjuː/ **noun**
1 B1 a meeting in which someone asks you questions to see if you are suitable for a job or course: *I **had an interview** last week for a job in London.*
2 B1 a meeting in which someone asks a famous person questions for a newspaper, television, etc.: *There's an **interview with** the director in this magazine.*

interview[2] /ˈɪntəvjuː/ **verb**
1 B1 to ask someone questions to see if they are suitable for a job or course: *They interviewed several candidates for the job.*
2 B1 to ask someone questions for a

a b c d e f g h **i** j k l m n o p q r s t u v w x y z

newspaper, television, etc.: *She always refuses to be interviewed.*
• **interviewer** **noun** *The interviewer asked me some difficult questions.*

into /ˈɪntə/, /ˈɪntu/ **preposition**
1 A1 towards the inside or middle of something: *Get into bed!* ◦ *I went into the hotel.*
2 A2 used to show a change from one condition to another or from one kind of thing to another: *Chop the apple into small pieces.* ◦ *We **turned** the smallest bedroom **into** an office.*
3 B1 in the direction of something or someone: *She looked into his eyes.*
4 B1 moving towards something or someone and hitting it or them: *I lost control of the car and crashed into a fence.*
5 involving or about something: *There was an investigation into the cause of the fire.*
6 **be into *something*** B1 informal to be very interested in something: *Will's really into jazz.*

intranet /ˈɪntrənet/ **noun**
a system that connects the computers in an organization so that people can share information

introduce /ˌɪntrəˈdjuːs/ **verb** (**introducing**, **introduced**)
1 B1 to tell someone another person's name the first time that they meet: *He took me around the room and **introduced** me **to** everyone.*
2 to make something exist or happen for the first time: *We have introduced a new training scheme for employees.*

introduction /ˌɪntrəˈdʌkʃən/ **noun**
1 [no plural] the first time something has happened or existed: *the introduction of a new policy*
2 the first part of a book, which tells you what the book is about
3 a book or course that gives basic knowledge about a subject: *an introduction to statistics*

invade /ɪnˈveɪd/ **verb** (**invading**, **invaded**)
to enter a country by force in order to take control of it: *Portugal was invaded by the French in 1807.*

invalid /ɪnˈvælɪd/ **adj**
An invalid document or ticket is not legally acceptable.

invasion /ɪnˈveɪʒən/ **noun**
an occasion when an army enters a country by force in order to take control of it

invent /ɪnˈvent/ **verb**
1 B1 to design or make something new: *Who invented the television?*
2 to think of a story or explanation that is not true: *I didn't invent the story – everything I told you is true.*

invention /ɪnˈvenʃən/ **noun**
1 B1 something that has been designed or made for the first time: *A lot of great inventions have come from America.*
2 B1 [no plural] the creation or design of something that has not existed before: *the invention of printing*

inventor /ɪnˈventər/ **noun**
someone who designs and makes new things

inverted commas /ɪnˌvɜːtɪd ˈkɒməz/ **noun** UK
a pair of marks (' ') used before and after a group of words to show that they are spoken or that someone else wrote them

invest /ɪnˈvest/ **verb**
1 to give money to a bank or business, or to buy something, because you hope to get a profit: *He's **invested** a million pounds **in** the project.*
2 to use a lot of time, effort, or emotions because you want to succeed: *She has **invested** a lot of time and energy **in** her job.*

investigate /ɪnˈvestɪgeɪt/ **verb** (**investigating**, **investigated**)
to try to get all the facts about something, especially a crime or accident: *Police are investigating the murder.*
• **investigation** /ɪnˌvestɪˈgeɪʃən/ **noun** effort by police to get all the facts about something, especially a crime or accident: *Police have begun an **investigation into** his death.*

invisible /ɪnˈvɪzəbl/ **adj**
Something that is invisible cannot be seen.

→ Opposite **visible** adj

invitation /ˌɪnvɪˈteɪʃᵊn/ **noun**
A2 If someone gives you an invitation, they are asking whether you would like to do a particular thing or go to a particular event or place: *I've had an **invitation to** Celia's party.*

invite /ɪnˈvaɪt/ **verb** (**inviting**, **invited**)
A1 to ask someone to come to your house, to a party, etc.: *They've **invited** us **to** the wedding.*

invoice /ˈɪnvɔɪs/ **noun**
a list that shows you how much you have to pay for work someone has done or for things someone has given you

involve /ɪnˈvɒlv/ **verb** (**involving**, **involved**)
1 B1 If a situation or activity involves something, that thing is a part of it: *The trips often involve a lot of walking.* ◦ *There are a lot of risks involved.*
2 B1 to affect or include someone or something in an activity: *The event involves hundreds of people.*

involved /ɪnˈvɒlvd/ **adj**
be/get involved in *something* to do things and be part of an activity or event: *How did you get involved in acting?*

involvement /ɪnˈvɒlvmənt/ **noun** [no plural]
the fact of being part of an activity or event

inward[1] /ˈɪnwəd/ **adj**
towards the centre or the inside of something
→ Opposite **outward** adj

inward[2] /ˈɪnwəd/ **adv**
towards the inside or the centre: *The door slowly opened inward.*

IPA /ˌaɪpiːˈeɪ/ **noun** [no plural]
a system of symbols for showing how words are spoken

IQ /ˌaɪˈkjuː/ **noun**
a person's intelligence when measured by a special test: *a high/low IQ*

iron /aɪən/ **noun**
1 B1 [no plural] a dark grey metal
2 B1 a piece of electrical equipment that you use for making clothes smooth
• **iron verb** B1 to make clothes smooth using an iron

ironing /ˈaɪənɪŋ/ **noun** [no plural]
B1 the activity of making clothes smooth using an iron: *John was **doing the ironing**.*

ironing board /ˈaɪənɪŋ ˌbɔːd/ **noun**
a thin table that you use for ironing

irregular /ɪˈregjələʳ/ **adj**
1 B1 not following the general rules in grammar: *irregular verbs*
→ Opposite **regular** adj
2 Irregular actions or events happen with a different amount of time between each one: *an irregular heart-beat*
3 not smooth or straight, or having parts that are different sizes: *irregular teeth*

irrelevant /ɪˈreləvᵊnt/ **adj**
not important in a particular situ-ation: *irrelevant information*
→ Opposite **relevant** adj

irresponsible /ˌɪrɪˈspɒnsəbl/ **adj**
not thinking about the possible bad results of what you are doing: *an irre-sponsible attitude*

irritate /ˈɪrɪteɪt/ **verb** (**irritating**, **irritated**)
1 to make someone slightly angry: *His comments really irritated me.*
2 to make a part of your body hurt: *The smoke irritated her eyes.*

irritating /ˈɪrɪˌteɪtɪŋ/ **adj**
making you feel annoyed: *an irritating habit*

is strong /ɪz/ weak /z/
present simple of be, used with 'he', 'she', 'it'

Islam /ˈɪzlɑːm/ **noun** [no plural]
a religion based on belief in one God and shown to people through Muhammad
• **Islamic** /ɪzˈlæmɪk/ **adj**

island /ˈaɪlənd/ **noun**
A2 an area of land that has water around it: *the Hawaiian Islands*

a b c d e f g h i j k l m n o p q r s t u v w x y z

isn't /ˈɪzᵊnt/
short form of is not: *Mike isn't coming with us.*

isolated /ˈaɪsəleɪtɪd/ **adj**
a long way from other places: *He lives in an isolated village in the mountains.*

issue¹ /ˈɪʃuː/ **noun**
1 B1 an important subject or problem that people are talking about: *environmental issues*
2 the newspaper, magazine, etc. from a particular day, month, etc.

issue² /ˈɪʃuː/ **verb** (**issuing**, **issued**)
to officially give something to someone: *All members will be* ***issued with*** *a membership card.*

it /ɪt/ **pronoun**
1 A1 used to mean the thing, situation, or idea that has already been talked about: *'Have you seen my bag?' 'It's in the hall.'* ◦ *It was a bad experience and I don't want to talk about it.*
2 A1 used before some adjectives, nouns, or verbs to introduce an opinion or description of a situation: *It's unlikely that she'll arrive on time.* ◦ *It's a pity you can't come with us.*
3 A2 used with a verb in sentences giving the time, date, weather, or distances: *It rained all day.* ◦ *What time is it?*
4 used to say the name of a person or thing when the person you are speaking to does not know: *It's your Dad on the phone.*

IT /ˌaɪˈtiː/ **noun** [no plural]
A2 the use of computers and other electronic equipment to keep and send information

itch /ɪtʃ/ **verb**
If a part of your body itches, you want to rub it with your nails: *Woollen sweaters make my arms itch.*
• **itch noun** *I've* ***got an itch*** *in the middle of my back.*

itchy /ˈɪtʃi/ **adj**
If a part of your body is itchy, you want to rub it: *an itchy nose*

it'd /ˈɪtəd/
1 short form of it would: *It'd be great if we could meet next week.*
2 short form of it had: *It'd taken us an hour to find Bruce's house.*

item /ˈaɪtəm/ **noun**
1 B1 a single thing in a set or on a list: *This is the last item on the list.* ◦ *Various stolen items were found.*
2 a piece of news on television or radio, or in a newspaper: *a small item on the back page of the newspaper*

it'll /ˈɪtᵊl/
short form of it will: *It'll take about twenty minutes to get there.*

its /ɪts/ **determiner**
A1 belonging to or relating to the thing that has already been talked about: *The house has its own swimming pool.*

> **Common mistake: its or it's?**
>
> **It's** is short for 'it is', and is always written with an apostrophe.
>
> *It's cold today.*
>
> **Its** means 'of it'.
>
> *The snake put out its tongue.*

it's /ɪts/
1 short form of it is: *'What time is it?' 'It's one o'clock.'*
2 short form of it has: *It's been hard work.*

itself /ɪtˈself/ **pronoun**
1 A2 used to show that the thing or animal that does the action is also the thing or animal that is affected by it: *The cat licked itself clean.*
2 B1 the thing that you are talking about: *The garden is enormous but the house itself is very small.*
3 (by) itself B1 alone or without help: *The dog was in the house by itself for several days.*

I've /aɪv/
short form of I have: *I've decided not to go.*

ivory /ˈaɪvᵊri/ **noun** [no plural]
a hard, white substance from the long teeth of an elephant

ivy /ˈaɪvi/ **noun** [no plural]
a dark green plant that grows up walls

J, j /dʒeɪ/
the tenth letter of the alphabet

jab[1] /dʒæb/ **verb** (**jabbing**, **jabbed**)
to push something quickly into another thing or towards another thing: *He **jabbed** a finger **into** her back.*

jab[2] /dʒæb/ **noun** UK informal
an injection (= when a drug is put into your body using a needle): *a flu jab*

jack /dʒæk/ **noun**
a playing card that has a picture of a young man on it: *the jack of diamonds*

jacket

jacket /ˈdʒækɪt/ **noun**
A2 a short coat: *a leather jacket*

jagged /ˈdʒægɪd/ **adj**
very rough and sharp: *jagged rocks*

jail /dʒeɪl/ **noun**
B1 a place where criminals are kept as a punishment: *He is **in jail**.*

jam[1] /dʒæm/ **noun**
1 A2 [no plural] a sweet food made from fruit, that you put on bread: *a jar of strawberry jam*
→ See **Food** on page C7
2 (also **traffic jam**) a line of cars, trucks, etc. that are moving slowly or not moving: *We were stuck **in a jam** for hours.*

jam[2] /dʒæm/ **verb** (**jamming**, **jammed**)
1 to push something somewhere firmly and tightly: *She **jammed** her hands **into** her pockets.*
2 If a machine or something that moves jams, or you jam it, it stops moving or working: *The paper keeps jamming in the machine.*
3 to fill a place completely: *The streets were **jammed with** cars.*

January /ˈdʒænjuəri/ **noun**
A1 the first month of the year

jar /dʒɑːʳ/ **noun**
B1 a glass container used for keeping food: *a jar of jam*
→ See picture at **container**

javelin /ˈdʒævəlɪn/ **noun**
a long, pointed stick that you throw as a sport
→ See **Sports 1** on page C15

jaw /dʒɔː/ **noun**
either of the two bones in your mouth that contain your teeth
→ See **The Body** on page C2

jazz /dʒæz/ **noun** [no plural]
A2 music with a strong beat that people often play without looking at written music: *a jazz band*

jealous /ˈdʒeləs/ **adj**
1 B1 upset and angry because someone you love seems to like another person: *a jealous husband*
2 not happy because you want something that someone else has: *I'm **jealous of** your new car.*
• **jealously** **adv** *She looked jealously at Gwen's ring.*

jealousy /ˈdʒeləsi/ **noun** [no plural]
jealous feelings

jeans /dʒiːnz/ **plural noun**
A1 trousers made from denim (= a strong, usually blue, material): *a pair of jeans*
→ See **Clothes** on page C5

> **Common mistake: jeans**
> **Jeans** is a plural word.
> *These jeans are too big for me.*

a b c d e f g h i **j** k l m n o p q r s t u v w x y z

a b c d e f g h i j k l m n o p q r s t u v w x y z

jelly /ˈdʒeli/ **noun** (plural **jellies**) UK (US trademark **Jell-O** /ˈdʒeləʊ/)
a soft sweet food that shakes when you move it: *jelly and ice cream*

jerk[1] /dʒɜːk/ **verb**
to move very quickly and suddenly, or to make something move like this: *The truck jerked forward.*

jerk[2] /dʒɜːk/ **noun**
a quick, sudden movement: *a sudden jerk of the head*

Jesus Christ /ˌdʒiːzəs ˈkraɪst/ **noun**
the holy man that Christians believe is the Son of God

jet /dʒet/ **noun**
1 B1 a plane that flies very fast
2 water or gas that is forced out of something in a thin, strong line

Jew /dʒuː/ **noun**
someone whose religion is Judaism, or who is related to the ancient people of Israel

jewel /ˈdʒuːəl/ **noun**
a valuable stone that is used to make jewellery

jewellery *UK*, **jewelry** *US*

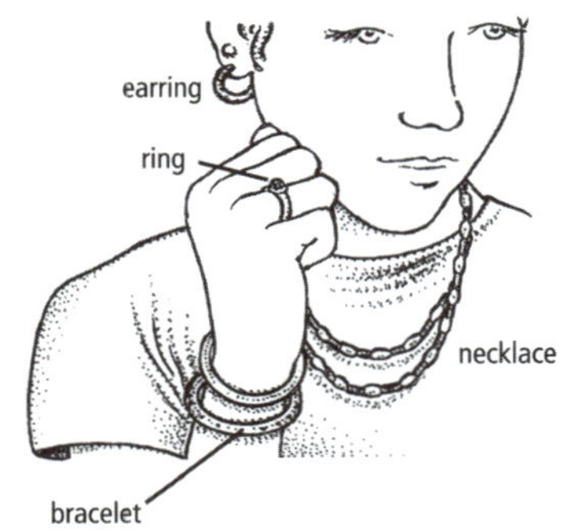

jewellery UK (US **jewelry**) /ˈdʒuːəlri/ **noun** [no plural]
A2 objects made from gold, silver, and valuable stones that you wear for decoration

Jewish /ˈdʒuːɪʃ/ **adj**
relating to the religion of Judaism or to Jews

jigsaw /ˈdʒɪɡsɔː/ **noun** (also **jigsaw puzzle**)
a picture in many small pieces that you put together as a game

jigsaw

jingle /ˈdʒɪŋɡl/ **verb** (**jingling**, **jingled**)
to make the sound of small metal objects hitting against each other: *a pocket full of jingling coins*

job /dʒɒb/ **noun**
1 A1 the work that you do in order to get money: *She **got** a **job** as a cleaner.*
2 A2 a piece of work: *I **did** a few **jobs** around the house.*
3 something that you have to do: *It's my job to water the plants.*
4 do/make a bad, good, etc. job of *something* to do something badly, well, etc.: *She did an excellent job of organizing the event.*

jockey /ˈdʒɒki/ **noun**
someone who rides horses in races

jog /dʒɒɡ/ **verb** (**jogging**, **jogged**)
B1 to run slowly for exercise: *I jog through the park every morning.*
• **jog noun** a slow run that you do for exercise: *We could **go for a jog**.*
• **jogging noun** [no plural] B1 *I **go jogging** every morning.*

join /dʒɔɪn/ **verb**
1 A2 to become a member of an organization: *He joined the army when he was 18.*
2 A2 to do something or go somewhere with someone: *Would you like to join us for dinner?*
3 B1 to fasten or connect things together: ***Join** the ends **together** with glue.*
4 B1 to meet at a particular point: *This is the point where the two rivers join.*
join in (*something*) phrasal verb
B1 to do an activity with other people: *We're playing cards. Would you like to join in?*

joint[1] /dʒɔɪnt/ **adj**
belonging to or done by two or more

people: *The project was a **joint effort** by all the children in the class.*
• **jointly** **adv** *The two states are jointly responsible for the tunnel.*

joint² /dʒɔɪnt/ **noun**
1 a place in your body where two bones meet: *the knee joint*
2 UK a large piece of meat, usually cooked in the oven: *a joint of beef*
3 a place where parts of something are connected

joint

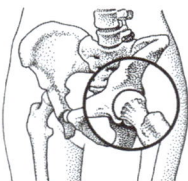

joke¹ /dʒəʊk/ **noun**
B1 a short funny story that someone tells to make people laugh: *Ben was **telling jokes** at the bar.*

joke² /dʒəʊk/ **verb** (**joking**, **joked**)
1 B1 to say funny things, or not be serious: *She always **jokes about** her husband's cooking.*
2 **You must be joking!** informal B1 used to say that something is certainly not true: *'Does Jim do much cooking?' 'You must be joking – he never cooks!'*

jolly /ˈdʒɒli/ **adj** (**jollier**, **jolliest**)
happy or enjoyable: *We had a very jolly evening.*

jolt¹ /dʒəʊlt/ **noun**
a sudden, violent movement: *With a sudden jolt the train started moving.*

jolt² /dʒəʊlt/ **verb**
to make someone or something suddenly move forward: *We were jolted forward when the bus stopped suddenly.*

jot /dʒɒt/ **verb** (**jotting**, **jotted**)
jot *something* down **phrasal verb**
to write something quickly: *I jotted down some notes during his speech.*

journalism /ˈdʒɜːnəlɪzəm/ **noun** [no plural]
the work of writing for newspapers, magazines, television, or radio

journalist /ˈdʒɜːnəlɪst/ **noun**
B1 someone whose job is writing for newspapers, magazines, television, or radio

journey /ˈdʒɜːni/ **noun**
A2 a trip from one place to another: *a train journey*

joy /dʒɔɪ/ **noun**
1 [no plural] a feeling of strong happiness: *The children have brought her so much joy.*
2 something or someone that makes you feel very happy: *She's a joy to work with.*

joyful /ˈdʒɔɪfəl/ **adj**
very happy, or making people feel very happy: *joyful news*

Jr **adj** mainly US
abbreviation for junior: the younger of two men in a family with the same name: *John F. Kennedy Jr*

Judaism /ˈdʒuːdeɪɪzəm/ **noun** [no plural]
a religion based on belief in one God and on the Talmud and Torah

judge¹ /dʒʌdʒ/ **noun**
1 B1 someone who controls a court and decides how criminals should be punished: *The judge ruled that he was not guilty of murder.*
2 B1 someone who decides which person or thing wins a competition: *the Olympic judges*

judge² /dʒʌdʒ/ **verb** (**judging**, **judged**)
1 B1 to have or develop an opinion about something or someone, usually after thinking carefully: *The meeting was judged to be a great success.* ◦ *You shouldn't **judge** people **on** their appearance.* ◦ *He was judged guilty/insane.*
2 B1 to decide the winner or results of a competition: *I was asked to judge the art contest.*
3 **judging by/from** used for saying the reasons why you have a particular opinion: *She must be popular, judging by the number of letters that she gets.*

judgment (also **judgement**) /ˈdʒʌdʒmənt/ **noun**
1 an opinion about someone or something after thinking carefully: *He has to **make a judgment** about who will win the contest.*

2 [no plural] the ability to make good decisions or to be right in your opinions: *I trust her judgment.*
3 an official decision made by a judge

judo /ˈdʒuːdəʊ/ **noun** [no plural]
a sport from Japan in which two people try to throw each other to the ground

jug /dʒʌg/ **noun** UK (US **pitcher**)
B1 a container with a handle used for pouring out liquids: *a jug of water*

jug

juggle /ˈdʒʌgl/ **verb** (**juggling**, **juggled**)
1 to try to do many things at the same time: *Many women have to juggle work and family.*
2 to throw two or more things, such as balls, into the air and catch them continuously

juice /dʒuːs/ **noun** [no plural]
A1 the liquid that comes from fruit or vegetables

juicy /ˈdʒuːsi/ **adj** (**juicier**, **juiciest**)
B1 full of juice: *juicy apples*

July /dʒʊˈlaɪ/ **noun**
A1 the seventh month of the year

jumble¹ /ˈdʒʌmbl/ **noun** [no plural]
a lot of things together in an untidy group: *He looked at the jumble of papers on his desk.*

jumble² /ˈdʒʌmbl/ **verb** (**jumbling**, **jumbled**) (also **jumble up**)
to mix things together in an untidy way: *Her clothes were all jumbled up in the suitcase.*

jump¹ /dʒʌmp/ **verb**
1 A2 to push your body up and away from the ground using your feet and legs: *The children were jumping up and down with excitement.* ◦ *They jumped into the water.*
2 A2 to go over something by moving up into the air: *Can you **jump across** this puddle?*
3 B1 to move somewhere suddenly and quickly: *She jumped into a taxi and rushed to the station.*
4 to make a sudden movement because you are frightened or surprised: *Her scream **made me jump**.*

jump² /dʒʌmp/ **noun**
B1 the act of pushing your body up into the air using your feet and legs: *He won with a jump of 8.5 metres.*

jumper /ˈdʒʌmpəʳ/ **noun** UK (US **sweater**)
A2 a warm piece of clothing that covers the top of your body and is pulled on over your head
→ See **Clothes** on page C5

junction /ˈdʒʌŋkʃᵊn/ **noun** UK
the place where two roads or railway lines meet

June /dʒuːn/ **noun**
A1 the sixth month of the year

jungle /ˈdʒʌŋgl/ **noun**
B1 an area of land in a hot country where trees and plants grow close together

junior /ˈdʒuːniəʳ/ **adj**
1 less important than other people doing the same job: *a junior minister*
→ Opposite **senior** **adj**
2 for or relating to young people: *a junior tennis tournament*

junk /dʒʌŋk/ **noun** [no plural]
old or useless things that no one wants

junk food /ˈdʒʌŋk ˌfuːd/ **noun** [no plural]
food that is bad for your body but quick to prepare and eat

jury /ˈdʒʊəri/ **noun** (plural **juries**)
a group of people in a court of law who decide if someone has done a crime

just¹ strong /dʒʌst/ weak /dʒəst/ **adv**
1 A2 a very short time ago: *I've just seen him.* ◦ *We've only just begun.*
2 A2 now or very soon: *The movie is just beginning.* ◦ *I'm just coming!*
3 B1 only: *I'll just have a small piece.* ◦ *He just wants to win.* ◦ *The movie is not just about love.*

4 B1 used to make something you are saying strong: *I just hate it!*
5 B1 almost not: *This dress* ***only just*** *fits.*
6 B1 exactly: *Tim looks just like his father.*
7 just about B1 almost: *I think I've remembered just about everything.*
8 be just about to do *something* B1 to be going to do something very soon: *I was just about to phone you.*
9 just as bad, good, clever, etc. (as *someone/something*) B1 equally bad, good, clever, etc.: *He's just as clever as his brother.*
10 just before, over, under, etc. B1 a little before, over, under, etc. something else: *It costs just under £10.*
11 it's just as well used to say that it is lucky that something happened: *It's just as well we brought an umbrella.*

just[2] /dʒʌst/ **adj**
fair or morally right: *a just society*

justice /ˈdʒʌstɪs/ **noun** [no plural]
1 treatment of people that is fair: *She tried to bring about fairness and justice for all.*
→ Opposite **injustice** **noun**
2 the system of laws that judges or punishes people: *the criminal justice system*

a b c d e f g h i **j** k l m n o p q r s t u v w x y z

K k

K, k /keɪ/
the eleventh letter of the alphabet

kangaroo /ˌkæŋgᵊrˈuː/ **noun**
a large Australian animal that moves by jumping on its back legs

kangaroo

karaoke /ˌkæriˈəʊki/ **noun** [no plural]
a type of entertainment in which people sing songs with recorded music that is played by a machine: *We're having a karaoke night tonight.*

karate /kəˈrɑːti/ **noun** [no plural]
a sport from Japan in which people fight with the hands or feet

kebab /kɪˈbæb/ **noun**
a dish of meat cooked on a metal stick: *We went for a kebab after the movie.*

keen /kiːn/ **adj**
1 B1 liking something very much: *a keen photographer* ◦ *He's very **keen on** travelling.*
2 B1 wanting to do something very much: *The shop is keen to attract new customers.*

keep /kiːp/ **verb** (**kept**)
1 A2 to have something always, as your own: *You can keep that dress if you like it.* ◦ *I've kept every letter he ever sent to me.*
2 keep *something* in, on, etc. A2 to always put something in a particular place: *I keep the keys in the drawer.*
3 keep (*someone/something*) awake, clean, safe, etc. A2 to make someone or something stay in a particular state: *This coat should keep you warm.* ◦ *He keeps his car very clean.*
4 keep doing *something* B1 to continue to do something, or to often do something: *I keep telling her not to do it.* ◦ *He keeps hitting me.*
5 B1 to delay someone or prevent them from doing something: *He's very late. What's keeping him?* ◦ *I'm so sorry to keep you waiting.*
6 keep a secret B1 to not tell anyone a secret
7 to write something down in order to remember it: *Remember to keep a record of how much money you spend.* ◦ *Keep a note of what's missing.*
8 If food or drink keeps, it remains fresh.
9 to have and look after animals: *Our neighbours keep chickens.*

keep at *something* **phrasal verb**
to continue working hard at something difficult: *Learning a language is hard but you've just got to keep at it.*

keep *something* down **phrasal verb**
to stop the number, level, or size of something from increasing: *I have to exercise to keep my weight down.*

keep *someone* in **phrasal verb**
B1 to make a child stay inside, often as a punishment, or to make someone stay in hospital: *She kept the children in as it was so cold.*

keep (*someone/something*) off *something* **phrasal verb**
B1 to not go onto an area, or to stop someone or something from going onto an area: *Keep off the grass.*

keep on doing *something* **phrasal verb**
B1 to continue to do something, or to do something again and again: *She kept on asking me questions.*

keep (*someone/something*) out **phrasal verb**
B1 to not go into a place, or to stop someone or something from going into a place: *The sign said 'Danger – Keep out'.*

keep up **phrasal verb**
1 to stay with someone who is moving forward by moving as quickly as them: *She was walking so fast I couldn't **keep up with** her.*
2 to increase as quickly as something or someone else: *Prices have risen very fast and wages haven't kept up.*
3 to be able to understand or deal with something that is happening or changing very fast: *It's important to **keep up with** international news.*

keep *something* up **phrasal verb**

B1 to not allow something that is good, strong, etc. to become less good, strong, etc.: *Keep up the good work!*

keeper /ˈkiːpər/ **noun**
1 B1 a person who takes care of a place and the things, people, or animals there: *a zoo keeper*
2 B1 informal short form of goalkeeper (= the player in a sport such as football who tries to stop the ball from going into the goal)

kennel /ˈkenəl/ **noun**
a small building for a dog to sleep in

kennel

kept /kept/
past tense and past participle of keep

kerb /kɜːb/ **noun** UK (US **curb**)
the edge of the raised path at the side of the road

ketchup /ˈketʃʌp/ **noun** [no plural]
a cold, red sauce made from tomatoes

kettle /ˈketl/ **noun**
B1 a metal or plastic container with a lid, used for boiling water: *Charlotte* ***put the kettle on*** *to make some tea.*
→ See **The Kitchen** on page C10

key¹ /kiː/ **noun**
1 A1 a piece of metal that you use for locking a door or starting an engine: *I've lost my car keys.*

keys

2 A2 a list of answers to an exercise or game: *The answer key is on page 134.*
3 B1 one of the parts you press on a keyboard or musical instrument to produce letters and numbers, or to make a sound
4 a set of musical notes based on one particular note: *the key of D major*
5 the key to *something* B1 the thing that you must do in order to achieve something: *Hard work is the key to success.*

key² /kiː/ **adj**
very important in influencing or achieving something: *a key factor in solving the problem*

key³ /kiː/ **verb**
key *something* in **phrasal verb**
B1 to put information into a computer using a keyboard: *Key in your name and password.*

keyboard /ˈkiːbɔːd/ **noun**
1 A2 a set of keys on a computer that you press to make it work, or the row of keys on a piano
2 an electronic musical instrument similar to a piano: *Laurie plays keyboards in the band.*

keyhole /ˈkiːhəʊl/ **noun**
a hole in a lock where you put a key

kg
written abbreviation for kilogram: a unit for measuring weight

kick¹ /kɪk/ **verb**
1 A1 to hit or move something or someone with your foot: *The boys were kicking a ball around.*
2 to move your feet and legs forwards or backwards quickly: *The baby lay kicking on the mat.*
kick *someone* out **phrasal verb** informal
to make someone leave a place or an organization: *His wife kicked him out of the house.*

kick² /kɪk/ **noun**
1 A2 the act of hitting something with your foot: *He* ***gave*** *her a* ***kick*** *in the ribs.*
2 informal a feeling of excitement and energy: *She* ***gets a kick out of*** *performing live.*

kid /kɪd/ **noun**
1 B1 informal a child: *school kids*
2 a young goat

kidnap /ˈkɪdnæp/ **verb** (**kidnapping**, **kidnapped**)
to take someone away using force, saying that you will only bring them back if someone gives you money
• **kidnapper** **noun**

kidney /ˈkɪdni/ **noun**
one of the two parts in your body that remove bad things from the blood

kill /kɪl/ **verb**
1 A2 to make someone or something die: *Their son was killed in a road accident.*
2 informal to hurt a lot: *My feet are killing me.*

killer /ˈkɪlər/ **noun**
B1 someone who kills, or a disease or animal that kills: *Cancer is the UK's biggest killer.*

killing /ˈkɪlɪŋ/ **noun**
B1 an act of killing someone: *a series of brutal killings*

kilo /ˈkiːləʊ/ **noun**
A2 short form of kilogram

kilobyte /ˈkɪləʊbaɪt/ **noun**
a unit for measuring the amount of information you can put on a computer

kilogram /ˈkɪləʊɡræm/ **noun** (also **kilogramme**) (written abbreviation **kg**)
A2 a unit for measuring weight, equal to 1000 grams

kilometre UK (US **kilometer**) /kɪˈlɒmɪtər/ **noun** (written abbreviation **km**)
A2 a unit for measuring distance, equal to 1000 metres

kin /kɪn/ **noun** formal
the people in your family

kind[1] /kaɪnd/ **noun**
1 A1 a type of thing or person: *What **kind of** music do you like?*
2 all kinds of A2 many different types of something: *All kinds of people come to our church.*
3 some kind of used to talk about something when you are not sure of its exact type: *She has some kind of medical problem.*
4 that kind of thing B1 used to show that what you have just said is only an example from a larger group of things: *I like pasta, pizza – that kind of thing.*
5 kind of informal used when you are trying to explain or describe something, but you cannot be exact: *It's kind of unusual.*

kind[2] /kaɪnd/ **adj**
A2 Kind people do things to help others and show that they care about them: *Your mother was very **kind to** us.* ◦ *It was very **kind of** you to come and see me.*
→ Opposite **unkind** **adj**

kindergarten /ˈkɪndəˌɡɑːtən/ **noun**
1 in the UK, a school for children aged under five: *Chloe goes to kindergarten.*
2 in the US, a class in school for children aged five or six

kindly /ˈkaɪndli/ **adv**
B1 in a kind way: *She kindly offered to cook me lunch.*

kindness /ˈkaɪndnəs/ **noun** [no plural]
behaviour that is kind: *I wanted to thank her for her kindness.*

king /kɪŋ/ **noun**
1 A2 a man who rules a country and is part of the royal family: *the kings and queens of England*
2 a playing card that has a picture of a king on it: *the king of hearts*

kingdom /ˈkɪŋdəm/ **noun**
1 a country with a king or queen: *the Kingdom of Belgium*
2 the animal kingdom all animals considered together

kiosk /ˈkiːɒsk/ **noun**
a small building where things like tickets or newspapers are sold through an open window

kiss[1] /kɪs/ **verb**
A2 to put your lips against another person's lips or skin because you love or like that person: *He kissed her cheek.* ◦ *I **kissed** her **goodbye**.*

kiss

kiss[2] /kɪs/ **noun**
A2 the action of kissing someone: *She ran up and **gave** me **a** big **kiss**.*

kit /kɪt/ **noun**
1 A2 UK the clothes that you wear for a particular sport: *a football kit*

2 B1 things that you keep in a container ready for a particular use: *a tool kit*
3 a set of parts that you put together to make something: *He's making a model car from a kit.*

kitchen /ˈkɪtʃɪn/ **noun**
A1 a room used to prepare and cook food in

kite /kaɪt/ **noun**
A2 a toy made of paper or cloth that flies in the air on the end of a long string

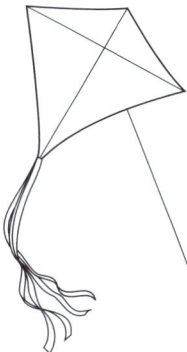

kite

kitten /ˈkɪtᵊn/ **noun**
B1 a young cat

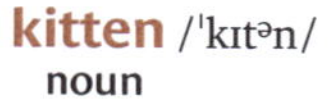

kiwi /ˈkiːwiː/ **noun** (also **kiwi fruit**)
a small fruit that is green inside and has black seeds and brown, hairy skin

km
written abbreviation for kilometre: a unit for measuring distance

knee /niː/ **noun**
B1 the middle part of your leg where it bends: *a knee injury*

knee

kneel /niːl/ **verb** (**knelt**)
to bend your legs and put one knee or both knees on the floor: *She knelt down beside the child.*

knew /njuː/
past tense of know

knickers /ˈnɪkəz/ **noun** UK
B1 women's underwear that covers the bottom

knife /naɪf/ **noun** (plural **knives** /naɪvz/)
A1 a sharp metal tool used for cutting: *a knife and fork*

knit /nɪt/ **verb** (**knitting**, **knitted**, **knitted**)
B1 to make clothes using thick thread and two long needles to join the thread together: *She was knitting him a jumper.*
• **knitting** **noun** [no plural] B1 *She sat **doing** her **knitting**.*

knit

knob /nɒb/ **noun**
a round handle, or a round button on a machine: *a door knob* ◦ ***Turn** the black **knob** to switch on the radio.*

knock[1] /nɒk/ **verb**
1 B1 to hit a door with your closed hand so that people know you are there: *There's someone **knocking at/on** the door.*
2 B1 to hit something or someone and make them move or fall down: *He accidentally knocked the plate off the table.*
knock *someone* down **phrasal verb** UK
B1 to hit someone with a car and hurt or kill them: *She was knocked down by a bus.*
knock *something* down **phrasal verb**
to destroy a building or part of a building: *They knocked down the old factory and built a cinema.*
knock *someone* out **phrasal verb**
1 to make someone become unconscious, usually by hitting them on the head: *He was knocked out halfway through the fight.*
2 to defeat a person or team in a competition so that they cannot take part

any more: *The French team were knocked out in the semifinal.*

knock *something/someone* over **phrasal verb**
to hit or push something or someone, especially accidentally, so that they fall to the ground or onto their side: *I knocked a bottle of wine over.*

knock[2] /nɒk/ **noun**
a sudden short noise made when something or someone hits a surface: *There was a* ***knock at*** *the door.*

knot /nɒt/ **noun**
a place where pieces of string, rope, etc. have been tied

knot

know /nəʊ/ **verb**
(**knew**, **known**)
1 A1 to have information about something in your mind: *'How old is she?' 'I don't know.'* ◦ *He* ***knew that*** *she was lying.*
2 A1 used to ask someone to tell you a piece of information: *Do you know where the post office is?*
3 A2 to be certain: *I know she'll be really pleased to hear the news.*
4 A2 to be able to do something: *Do you* ***know how to*** *ski?*
5 B1 to have spent time with someone or in a place so that the person or place is not new to you: *I've known Al since we were children.* ◦ *I grew up in Brussels so I know it well.*
6 let *someone* know A2 to tell someone something: *Let me know if you're going to the party.*
7 I know used when you agree with something someone has just said: *'It's a lovely day, isn't it?' 'I know – let's hope it lasts.'*
8 you know B1 used to make sure someone understands which person or thing you are talking about: *I was talking about Rachel – you know, the tall woman with the blond hair.*
9 B1 (also **know about**) If you know a subject, you are familiar with it and understand it: *Ask Andy to fix it – he knows about computers.*
10 be known as *something* B1 to be called: *California is also known as the Sunshine State.*
11 get to know *someone/something* B1 to gradually learn more about someone or something: *I got to know Frank at work.*
12 as far as I know used to say that you think something is true, but cannot be sure: *As far as I know, he isn't married.*

Common mistake: know or find out?

To **know** something means to already have information about something.
Kelly knows what time the train leaves.
His parents already know about the problem.
To **find out** something means to learn new information for the first time.
Can you find out what time the train leaves?
His parents were angry when they found out about the problem.

Common mistake: meet, get to know, and know

When you **meet someone**, you see or speak to them for the first time. When you **get to know someone**, you learn more about them. After this you can say that you **know** them.
I met Nick on holiday.
~~*I knew Nick on holiday.*~~
We got to know each other and became good friends.
~~*We knew each other and became friends.*~~
How long have you known Nick?
~~*How long have you got to know Nick?*~~

knowledge /ˈnɒlɪdʒ/ **noun** [no plural]
B1 information and understanding that you have in your mind: *His* ***knowledge of*** *history is amazing.*

knowledgeable /ˈnɒlɪdʒəbl/ **adj**
knowing a lot: *He's very* ***knowledgeable about*** *art.*

known /nəʊn/
past participle of know

knuckle /ˈnʌkl/ **noun**
one of the parts of a finger that bends

koala /kəʊˈɑːlə/ **noun**
an Australian animal like a small bear with grey fur that lives in trees

the Koran /kɒrˈɑːn/ **noun**
the holy book of Islam

Ll

L, l /el/
the twelfth letter of the alphabet

l
written abbreviation for litre: a unit for measuring liquid

lab /læb/ **noun**
B1 short form of laboratory: a room used for scientific work

label¹ /ˈleɪbəl/ **noun**
1 B1 a piece of paper or material that is attached to something and gives you information about it: *There are washing instructions on the label.*
2 B1 a company that makes things for sale, mainly clothes: *Her favourite* ***designer label*** *(= company that makes expensive clothes) is Armani.*

label² /ˈleɪbəl/ **verb** (**labelling, labelled**)
A2 to attach a small piece of paper or material to something that gives information about it: *Was the package clearly labelled?*

laboratory /ləˈbɒrətəri/ **noun** (plural **laboratories**)
B1 a room used for scientific work: *research laboratories*

labour UK (US **labor**) /ˈleɪbər/ **noun**
1 [no plural] work that you do with your hands and body: *Does that price include the cost of labour?*
2 [no plural] people who work: *cheap labour*
3 the process of giving birth to a baby

labourer UK (US **laborer**) /ˈleɪbərər/ **noun**
a worker who does hard work with his or her hands and body: *a farm labourer*

lace /leɪs/ **noun**
1 [no plural] a thin, white cloth with a pattern of holes in it: *a lace curtain*
2 a string used to tie shoes: *I'll just* ***tie*** *my* ***laces****.*

lack¹ /læk/ **noun** [no plural]
lack of ***something*** B1 not having something, or not having enough of something: *My only problem is lack of money.*

lack² /læk/ **verb**
to not have something, or to not have enough of something: *She really lacks confidence.*

lad /læd/ **noun** informal
a boy or young man: *He's a nice young lad.*

ladder /ˈlædər/ **noun**
B1 a thing that you climb up when you want to reach a high place, which has two long pieces joined together by shorter pieces

ladder

lady /ˈleɪdi/ **noun** (plural **ladies**)
1 B1 a polite way of saying 'woman': ***Ladies and gentlemen****, can I have your attention please?*
2 Lady a title used before the name of a woman of high social rank in the UK: *Lady Alison Weir*

lager /ˈlɑːgər/ **noun**
a type of light, yellow beer: *A pint of lager, please.*

laid /leɪd/
past tense and past participle of lay

lain /leɪn/
past participle of lie

lake /leɪk/ **noun**
A2 a large area of water that has land all around it: *Lake Windermere*

lamb /læm/ **noun**
1 B1 a young sheep
2 B1 [no plural] meat from a young sheep

lame /leɪm/ **adj**
A lame animal or person cannot walk because their foot or leg is hurt: *a lame horse*

lamp /læmp/ **noun**
A2 an object that makes light: *I have a lamp next to my bed.*
→ See **The Living Room** on page C11

lamppost /ˈlæmppəʊst/ **noun**
a tall post with a light at the top that

you see on roads where there are houses

lampshade /ˈlæmpʃeɪd/ **noun**
a cover for an electric light
→ See **The Living Room** on page C11

land[1] /lænd/ **noun**
1 B1 [no plural] an area of ground: *agricultural land*
2 [no plural] the surface of the Earth that is not sea: *We travelled over land and sea.*
3 literary a country: *a land of ice and snow*

land[2] /lænd/ **verb**
1 B1 The action of a plane arriving on the ground after flying: *We should **land in** Madrid at 7 a.m.*
2 **land in, on, etc.** If an object or person lands somewhere, they fall to the ground there: *She landed flat on her back.*

landing /ˈlændɪŋ/ **noun**
1 the act of bringing a plane to the ground: *The plane had to make an emergency landing in Chicago.*
2 the area of floor at the top of a set of stairs

landlady /ˈlændˌleɪdi/ **noun** (plural **landladies**)
a woman who owns the house that you live in and who you pay rent to

landlord /ˈlændlɔːd/ **noun**
a man who owns the house that you live in and who you pay rent to

landmark /ˈlændmɑːk/ **noun**
1 a building or place that is easy to recognize, especially one that helps you recognize where you are: *a familiar landmark*
2 a structure that is famous or that is a particularly important example of its type

landscape /ˈlændskeɪp/ **noun** [no plural]
B1 the appearance of an area of land, especially in the countryside: *The landscape is very beautiful.*

lane /leɪn/ **noun**
one of the parts of a big road that is shown by a painted line: *He was driving in the fast lane.*

language /ˈlæŋgwɪdʒ/ **noun**
1 A1 the words used by the people of a country: *How many **languages** do you **speak**?*
2 B1 [no plural] words that people use to speak or write: *The way that children's language develops is fascinating.*

lap /læp/ **noun**
1 the top part of your legs when you are sitting down: *His little daughter was sitting on his lap.*
2 one journey around a race track: *He's two laps behind the leaders.*

laptop /ˈlæp tɒp/ **noun**
A2 a small computer that you can carry around with you

laptop

large /lɑːdʒ/ **adj**
A2 big: *a large number of people* ◦ *He won a large amount of money.* ◦ *She comes from quite a large family.*
→ Opposite **small** **adj**, **little** **adj** (1)

laser /ˈleɪzəʳ/ **noun**
a very strong line of light that is used in machines and for repairing parts of the body: *a laser beam* ◦ *a laser printer*

lashes /ˈlæʃɪz/ **noun**
the small hairs on the edges of your eyes: *She's got lovely, long lashes.*

last[1] /lɑːst/ **adj, determiner**
1 **last week, year, Monday, etc.** A1 the week, year, Monday, etc. before the present one: *I went to Barcelona last month.*
2 A2 the most recent: *What was the last movie you saw?* ◦ *It's rained for the last three days.*
3 A2 Your last book, house, job, etc. is the one before the one that you have now: *My last house was half this size.*
4 A2 happening or coming at the end: *It's the last room on the left.* ◦ *That's the last programme of the series.* ◦ *I was the last person to arrive.*
→ Opposite **first** **adj**
5 B1 only remaining: *Who wants the last piece of cake?*

6 the last person, thing, etc. a person or thing that you do not want or expect: *Three extra people to feed – that's the last thing I need!*

last² /lɑːst/ **adv**

1 B1 used to talk about the most recent time you did something: *When did you last see her?* ◦ *I think it was July when I last spoke to him.*

2 after everything or everyone else: *I came last in the race.* ◦ *We've still got to check the figures but we'll do that last.*

→ Opposite **first** adv

• **last but not least** something you say before you say the last person or thing on a list: *This is Jeremy, this is Olivia and, last but not least, this is Eva.*

last³ /lɑːst/ **noun, pronoun**

1 at last B1 finally: *At last, I've found a jacket I like.*

2 the last a person or thing that comes after all the others: *We were the last to get there.*

3 the last of *something* the only part of something that remains: *We've just finished the last of the wine.*

last⁴ /lɑːst/ **verb**

1 B1 to continue to happen or exist: *How long will the meeting last?* ◦ *The batteries last about ten hours.* ◦ *Enjoy the sun while it lasts!*

2 to be enough for a period of time: *We've got enough food to last a week.*

lasting /ˈlɑːstɪŋ/ **adj**
continuing to exist for a long time: *lasting peace*

lastly /ˈlɑːstli/ **adv**
finally: *And lastly, I'd like to thank everyone who took part in the event.*

last-minute /ˈlɑːstˌmɪnɪt/ **adj**
done at the latest possible time: *I was just doing some last-minute preparation.*

last name /ˈlɑːst ˌneɪm/ **noun**
the name that you and your family all have

late /leɪt/ **adj, adv**

1 A1 after the usual time or the time that was arranged: *I was **late for** work this morning.* ◦ *We got there too late and all the food was gone.* ◦ *We had a late lunch.*

2 A1 near the end of a period of time: *It was built in the late 19th century.* ◦ *It was late at night.*

3 it's late A1 something that you say when it is near the end of a day: *It's late – I really should be going.*

lately /ˈleɪtli/ **adv**
B1 recently: *Lately, I've been walking to work.*

later¹ /ˈleɪtəʳ/ **adj**

1 after some time: *I arranged it for a later date.*

2 more recent: *I'm not so familiar with his later work.*

later² **adv**

1 after some time: *He arrived later that night.* ◦ *I'll be joining them later.*

2 later on at a time in the future: *What are you doing later on today?*

3 see you later A1 used for saying goodbye to someone you are going to meet again soon: *I'm off now – see you later!*

latest¹ /ˈleɪtɪst/ **adj**
A2 most recent: *She wears all the latest fashions.*

latest² /ˈleɪtɪst/ **noun**
at the latest If you tell someone to do something by a particular time at the latest, you mean they must do it before that time: *You need to be there by eight o'clock at the latest.*

Latin /ˈlætɪn/ **noun** [no plural]
the language used by ancient Romans

latitude /ˈlætɪtjuːd/ **noun**
the distance of a place north or south of the Equator (= imaginary line around the Earth's middle): *The latitude of Helsinki is 60 degrees north.*

the latter /ˈlætəʳ/ **noun** [no plural]
the second of two people or things that you have just talked about: *She offered me more money or a car, and I chose the latter.*

laugh¹ /lɑːf/ **verb**
A2 to smile and make sounds with your voice because something is funny: *You never **laugh at** my jokes.* ◦ *She really **makes** me **laugh**.*

laugh at *someone/something* **phrasal verb**

a b c d e f g h i j k l m n o p q r s t u v w x y z

B1 to show that you think someone or something is stupid: *The other children laughed at him because of his strange clothes.*

laugh² /lɑːf/ **noun**
1 B1 the action of smiling and making sounds with your voice because something is funny: *He gave a nervous laugh.* ◦ *At the time I was embarrassed, but I* ***had a good laugh*** *(= laughed a lot) about it later.*
2 for a laugh informal If you do something for a laugh, you do it because it will be funny: *Just for a laugh, I pretended that I'd forgotten his birthday.*

laughter /ˈlɑːftəʳ/ **noun** [no plural]
the sound or act of laughing: *I heard the sound of laughter in the room next door.*

launch /lɔːnʃ/ **verb**
1 to send a spacecraft into the sky, or to send a ship into the water
2 to begin an important activity: *They have launched an inquiry into his death.*
3 to start selling a product: *The book was launched last February.*

launderette /ˌlɔːndᵊrˈet/ **noun** UK
a place where you pay to wash and dry your clothes

laundry /ˈlɔːndri/ **noun** [no plural]
clothes, sheets, etc. that need to be washed: *a laundry basket*

lavatory /ˈlævətᵊri/ **noun** (plural **lavatories**) UK formal
a toilet: *public lavatories*

law /lɔː/ **noun**
1 B1 the subject or job of understanding and dealing with the laws of a country: *I studied law at college.*
2 an official rule in a country: *There are* ***laws against*** *drinking in the street.*
3 by law If you have to do something by law, it is illegal not to do it: *Children have to go to school by law.*
4 the law the system of official rules in a country: *You're* ***breaking the law.*** ◦ *It's* ***against the law*** *(= illegal) not to wear seat belts.*

lawn /lɔːn/ **noun**
an area of grass that is often cut

lawn mower /ˈlɔːn ˌməʊəʳ/ **noun**
a machine that you use to cut grass

lawyer /ˈlɔɪəʳ/ **noun**
B1 someone whose job is to explain the law to people and give advice

lay¹ /leɪ/
past tense of lie¹

lay² /leɪ/ **verb** (**laying**, **laid**)
1 to put something down somewhere: *She laid the baby on the bed.* ◦ *He laid the plate on the table.*
2 lay the table UK B1 to put plates, knives, forks, etc. on the table before a meal
3 lay eggs If an animal lays eggs, eggs come out of its body.

> **Common mistake: lay and lie**
>
> Be careful not to confuse these verbs. **Lay** means 'put down carefully' or 'put down flat'. This verb is always followed by an object. **Laying** is the present participle. **Laid** is the past simple and the past participle.
>
> *She laid the papers on the desk.*
>
> **Lie** means 'be in a horizontal position' or 'be in a particular place'. This verb is irregular and is never followed by an object. **Lying** is the present participle. **Lay** is the past simple and **lain** is the past participle.
>
> *The papers were lying on the desk.*
>
> ~~*The papers were laying on the desk.*~~
>
> *I lay down and went to sleep.*
>
> ~~*I laid down and went to sleep.*~~
>
> The regular verb **lie** means 'not say the truth'.
>
> *He lied to me about his age.*

layer /leɪəʳ/ **noun**
something that covers a surface, or something that is between two things: *The shelf was covered in a thick layer of dust.*
→ See picture at **cake**

lazy /ˈleɪzi/ **adj** (**lazier**, **laziest**)
A2 Someone who is lazy does not like working: *He's too lazy to make his bed in the morning.*
• **laziness noun** [no plural]

lb
written abbreviation for pound: a unit for measuring weight

lead[1] /liːd/ **verb** (**led**)
1 B1 to show someone where to go, usually by taking them to a place: *You lead and we'll follow.* ◦ *She* ***led*** *them* ***down*** *the hall.*
2 If a path or road leads somewhere, it goes there: *That path* ***leads to*** *the beach.*
3 to be winning a game: *They were* ***leading by*** *11 points at half-time.*
4 to be in control of a group, country, or situation: *Amy was leading the discussion.*
5 to live in a particular way: *He led a normal life despite his illness*
lead to *something* **phrasal verb**
to make something happen: *A bad diet can lead to health problems.*

lead[2] /liːd/ **noun**
1 the state of winning a competition: *She's* ***in the lead*** *(= winning).* ◦ *France have a three-goal lead.*
2 the main person in a movie or play: *She* ***plays the lead*** *in both movies.*
3 UK (US **leash**) a rope, piece of leather, etc. that you fix to a dog's neck and hold in order to control the dog: *Dogs must be kept* ***on a lead****.*

lead[3] /led/ **noun**
1 [no plural] a soft, heavy, grey metal
2 the black part inside a pencil

leader /ˈliːdəʳ/ **noun**
B1 a person in control of a group, country, or situation: *a religious leader* ◦ *He is the new* ***leader of*** *the Party.*

leadership /ˈliːdəʃɪp/ **noun** [no plural]
the job of being in control of a group, country, or situation: *She took over the* ***leadership of*** *the Republican Party.* ◦ *leadership skills*

leading /ˈliːdɪŋ/ **adj**
very important: *He's a leading Hollywood producer.*

leaf /liːf/ **noun** (plural **leaves** /liːvz/)
B1 a flat, green part of a plant that grows from a stem or branch: *an oak leaf* ◦ *the falling leaves*

leaf

leaflet /ˈliːflət/ **noun**
a piece of folded paper that has information printed on it

league /liːg/ **noun**
B1 a group of teams that compete against each other in a sport: *Which team are top of the league?*

leak[1] /liːk/ **verb**
1 If a container leaks, it allows liquid or gas to come out when it should not: *The bottle had leaked and the bag was all wet.*
2 to tell people information that is secret: *Details of the report had been* ***leaked to*** *the press.*

leak[2] /liːk/ **noun**
1 a hole in something that a liquid or gas comes out of: *There is a leak in the roof.*
2 an act of telling people secret information

lean[1] /liːn/ **verb** (**leaned**, **leant**)
to move the top part of your body in a particular direction: *She leaned forward to speak to the child.* ◦ *He was leaning out of the window.*
lean (*something*) against/on *something* **phrasal verb**
to sit or stand with part of your body against something, or to put something against a wall or other surface: *He was leaning against the wall.* ◦ *Lean the ladder against the wall.*

lean[2] /liːn/ **adj**
1 thin and healthy: *lean and fit*
2 Lean meat has very little fat on it.

leant /lent/
past tense of lean

leap /liːp/ **verb** (**leapt**)
1 to suddenly move somewhere: *I leapt up to answer the phone.*
2 to jump somewhere: *She leapt over the wall.*

leapt /lept/
past tense and past participle of leap

leap year /ˈliːp ˌjɪəʳ/ **noun**
a year that happens every four years, in which February has 29 days and not 28

learn /lɜːn/ **verb** (**learned**, **learnt**)
1 A1 to get knowledge or a new skill:

I ***learned*** *a lot* ***about*** *computers.* ◦ *I'm* ***learning to*** *drive.*
2 B1 to make yourself remember some writing: *How do actors learn all those lines?*
3 B1 to be told facts or information that you did not know: *We were all shocked to* ***learn of*** *his death.* ◦ *I only* ***learned about*** *the accident later.*
4 to start to understand that you must change the way you behave: *She'll soon* ***learn that*** *she can't treat people so badly.* ◦ *You learn from your mistakes.*

learner /ˈlɜːnəʳ/ **noun**
someone who is getting knowledge or a new skill: *learners of English*

least[1] /liːst/ **adv**
1 B1 less than anyone or anything else: *Which car costs least?* ◦ *I chose the least expensive restaurant.*
2 at least A2 as much as, or more than, a number or amount: *You'll have to wait at least an hour.*
3 at least B1 something that you say when you are telling someone about a good thing in a bad situation: *It's a small house but at least there's a garden.*
4 at least B1 even if nothing else happens or is true: *If you can't manage to clean the whole house, at least make sure the kitchen is clean.*
5 at least used to reduce the effect of a statement: *I've met the President – at least, he shook my hand once.*
6 not in the least not at all: *I don't mind staying at home, not in the least.*

least[2] /liːst/ **quantifier**
the smallest amount: *She earns the least money of all of us.*

leather /ˈleðəʳ/ **noun** [no plural]
A2 the skin of animals that is used to make shoes and bags: *a leather jacket*

leave[1] /liːv/ **verb** (**leaving**, **left**)
1 A1 to go away from a place: *I leave work at five o'clock.* ◦ *They* ***left for*** *Paris last night.* ◦ *She left school at 16.*
2 A2 to not take something with you when you go away from a place: *I left my jacket in the car.* ◦ *She left a letter for me in the kitchen.*
3 A2 to not use all of something: *They drank all the wine but they left some food.*
4 A2 to put something in a place where it will stay: *You can leave your bags at the station.*
5 A2 to put something somewhere for another person to have later: *I left some sandwiches for them.*
6 B1 to end a relationship with a husband, wife, or partner and stop living with them: *I'll never leave you.* ◦ *She* ***left*** *him* ***for*** *a younger man.*
7 to give something to someone after you die: *His aunt left him a lot of money.* ◦ *He* ***left*** *the house* ***to*** *Julia.*
8 leave *someone* alone to stop speaking to someone: *Leave me alone! I'm trying to work.*
9 leave *something* open, on, off, etc. to make something stay open, on, off, etc.: *Who left the window open?*
be left out phrasal verb
to be sad because other people are doing something without you: *The older children had gone upstairs to play and she felt left out.*
leave *someone/something* behind phrasal verb
A2 to leave a place without taking someone or something with you: *We were in a hurry and I left my keys behind.*
leave *someone/something* out phrasal verb
to not include someone or something: *Have I left anyone out?*

leave[2] /liːv/ **noun** [no plural]
time when you do not go to work: *She's* ***on*** *sick* ***leave****.*

leaves /liːvz/
plural of leaf

lecture /ˈlektʃəʳ/ **noun**
B1 a talk to a group of people about a subject: *We went to a* ***lecture on*** *Italian art.*

led /led/
past tense and past participle of lead

ledge /ledʒ/ **noun**
a long, flat surface that comes out under a window

leek /liːk/ **noun**
a long, white and green vegetable that is similar to an onion

left¹ /left/
past tense and past participle of leave

left² /left/ **adj, adv**
A2 on or towards the side of your body where your heart is: *She had a beautiful ring on her left hand.* ◦ ***Turn left*** *at the end of the corridor.*
→ Opposite **right** **adj**

left³ /left/ **noun** [no plural]
A2 the left side of your body, or the direction towards this side: *Ted was sitting* ***on*** *my* ***left****.*
→ Opposite **right** **noun**

left-hand /ˌleftˈhænd/ **adj**
A2 on the left: *The swimming pool is on* ***the left-hand side*** *of the road.*

left-handed /ˌleftˈhændɪd/ **adj**
using your left hand to do most things
→ Opposite **right-handed** **adj**

leg /leg/ **noun**
1 A1 one of the parts of the body that is used for walking: *My legs are tired after so much walking.* ◦ *He broke his leg in the accident.*
→ See **The Body** on page C2
2 one of the parts that support a chair, table, etc.: *a table leg*

legal /ˈliːgᵊl/ **adj**
1 relating to the law: *legal advice*
2 allowed by law: *Is it legal to carry a gun?*
→ Opposite **illegal** **adj**
• **legally** **adv** *Children under sixteen are not legally allowed to buy cigarettes.*

legend /ˈledʒənd/ **noun**
1 a story from a time in the past that was very long ago: *the legend of King Arthur*
2 a famous person: *Jazz legend Ella Fitzgerald once sang in this bar.*

leggings /ˈlegɪŋz/ **plural noun**
tight trousers that are made of soft material that stretches and are worn mainly by women: *a pair of leggings*
→ See **Clothes** on page C5

legible /ˈledʒəbl/ **adj**
If writing is legible, you can read it.
→ Opposite **illegible** **adj**

leisure /ˈleʒəʳ/ **noun** [no plural]
B1 the time when you are not working: *Do you have a lot of leisure time?*

leisure centre /ˈleʒə ˌsentəʳ/ **noun** UK
a building with a swimming pool and other areas where you can exercise and play sports

lemon /ˈlemən/ **noun**
A2 an oval, yellow fruit that has sour juice: *lemon juice*
→ See **Fruit and Vegetables** on page C8

lemon

lemonade /ˌleməˈneɪd/ **noun**
A2 a cold drink that tastes of lemon

lend /lend/ **verb** (**lent**)
1 A2 to give something to someone for a period of time: *I* ***lent*** *my bike* ***to*** *Sara.* ◦ *She lent me her car for the weekend.*
2 If a bank lends money, it gives money to someone who then pays the money back in small amounts over a period.

> **Common mistake: lend and borrow**
>
> Be careful not to confuse these two verbs.
> **Lend** means to give something to someone for a period of time.
>
> *It was raining so she lent me her umbrella.*
>
> **Borrow** means to use something that belongs to someone else and give it back later.
>
> *Can I borrow your umbrella? It's raining.*
> ~~*Can I lend your umbrella? It's raining.*~~

length /leŋθ/ **noun**
1 B1 how long something is from one end to the other: *The room is over eight metres* ***in length****.* ◦ *What length are the curtains?*
2 B1 the amount of time that

length

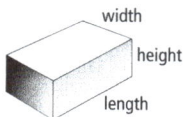

width
height
length

something lasts: *the length of a movie*

lengthen /ˈleŋθən/ **verb**
to become longer or to make something longer: *The days started to lengthen.*

lens /lenz/ **noun**
a curved piece of glass in cameras, glasses, and scientific equipment used for looking at things

lent /lent/
past tense and past participle of lend

leopard

leopard /ˈlepəd/ **noun**
a large wild animal of the cat family, with yellow fur and dark spots

less[1] /les/ **adv**
A2 not as much: *You should eat less.*

less[2] /les/ **quantifier**
A2 a smaller amount: *She gets about £50 a week or less.* ◦ *I prefer my coffee with a little less sugar.*

lessen /ˈlesᵊn/ **verb**
to become less or to make something less: *Exercise lessens the chance of heart disease.*

lesson /ˈlesᵊn/ **noun**
A1 a period of time when a teacher teaches people: *I am* ***taking*** *guitar* ***lessons****.* ◦ *Lessons start at 9 a.m.*
• **teach *someone* a lesson** to punish someone so that they will not behave badly again

let /let/ **verb** (**letting**, **let**)
1 B1 to allow someone to do or have something: *She let me use her camera.* ◦ *I let her have some money.*
2 let's A2 something that you say to ask someone if they want to do something with you: *Let's go shopping.*
3 let *someone* know A2 to tell someone something: *I'll let you know where we are meeting nearer the time.*
4 let (*something*) go to stop holding something: *I* ***let go of*** *the rope.*
5 let *someone/something* in, past, through, etc. to allow someone or something to move to a particular place: *They won't let us past the gate.*
6 If you let a building, you allow someone to live there and they give you money: *I* ***let*** *the top floor of my house* ***to*** *a student.*

let *someone* down **phrasal verb**
to not do something that you promised to do: *I promised Sophie I would meet her and I can't let her down.*

let *someone* in **phrasal verb**
to allow someone to enter a room or building, often by opening the door: *Could you go down and let Rosa in?*

let *someone* off **phrasal verb**
to not punish someone who has done something wrong: *I'll let you off this time, but don't ever lie to me again.*

let *someone/something* out **phrasal verb**
to allow a person or animal to leave somewhere, especially by opening a door

lethal /ˈliːθᵊl/ **adj**
able to kill someone: *a lethal weapon*

letter /ˈletəʳ/ **noun**
1 A1 some writing that you send to someone, usually by post: *I got a letter from Paul this morning.*
2 A2 one of the symbols (for example, a, j, p) that we use to write words: *the letter K*

lettuce /ˈletɪs/ **noun**
B1 a plant with green leaves, that you eat in salads
→ See **Fruit and Vegetables** on page C8

level[1] /ˈlevᵊl/ **noun**
1 A2 how good someone is at doing something compared to other people: *Students at this level need a lot of help.*
2 how high something is: *the water level*
3 the amount or number of something: *The level of iron in her blood was too low.*
4 a floor in a building: *The store had three levels.*

level[2] /ˈlevᵊl/ **adj**
1 flat or horizontal: *Make sure the*

camera is level before you take the picture.
2 at the same height: *I got down till my face was **level with** his.*

lever /ˈliːvəʳ/ **noun**
1 a handle that you push or pull to make a machine work
2 a long bar that you use to lift or move something by pressing one end

liable /ˈlaɪəbl/ **adj**
be liable to do *something* to be likely to do something: *He is liable to get cross if you wake him.*

liar /ˈlaɪəʳ/ **noun**
someone who tells lies

liberal /ˈlɪbᵊrᵊl/ **adj**
accepting beliefs and behaviour that are new or different from your own: *Her parents were very liberal.*

liberty /ˈlɪbəti/ **noun** [no plural]
the freedom to live, work, and travel as you want to: *Many people fight to preserve their liberty.*

library /ˈlaɪbrᵊri/ **noun** (plural **libraries**)
A2 a place with a lot of books that you can read or borrow

lice /laɪs/
plural of louse

licence UK (US **license**) /ˈlaɪsᵊns/ **noun**
A2 a piece of paper that allows you to do or have something: *Can I see your driving licence?*

license /ˈlaɪsᵊns/ **verb** (**licensing**, **licensed**)
to allow someone officially to do or have something: *Are they licensed to carry guns?*

lick /lɪk/ **verb**
to move your tongue across something: *She licked her lips* ◦ *We licked the chocolate off our fingers.*

lick

lid /lɪd/ **noun**
the top part of a container that you can take off: *Can you get the lid off this jar?*

lie¹ /laɪ/ **verb**
1 A2 (**lying**, **lay**, **lain**) to put your body flat on something, or to be in this position: *He lay on the bed.* ◦ *She was lying on her side.*
2 B1 (**lying**, **lay**, **lain**) to be in a place: *The river lies 30 miles to the south of the city.*
3 B1 (**lying**, **lay**, **lain**) to be on a particular surface: *A pen lay on the desk.*
4 B1 (**lying**, **lied**) to say or write something that you know is not true: *Are you **lying to** me?* ◦ *He **lied about** his qualifications for the job.*
lie down **phrasal verb**
A2 to move into a position in which your body is flat, usually in order to sleep or rest: *I'm not feeling well – I'm going to lie down.*

lie² /laɪ/ **noun**
B1 something that you say or write which you know is not true: *I **told a lie** when I said I liked her hair.*

lie-in /ˈlaɪˌɪn/ **noun** UK
a time when you stay in bed in the morning longer than usual: *I **had a** long **lie-in** this morning.*

life /laɪf/ **noun** (plural **lives** /laɪvz/)
1 A1 the time between a person's birth and his or her death: *He **had** a happy **life**.* ◦ *Do you want to **spend** the rest of your **life** with him?*
2 B1 [no plural] living things, such as animals and plants: *human life* ◦ *Is there life in outer space?*
3 B1 a way of living: *You **lead** an exciting **life**.*
4 the state of being alive: *She was badly injured, but the doctor **saved** her **life**.*
5 [no plural] energy and activity: *Like all small children, she was always so **full of life**.*
6 that's life something you say that means bad things happen and you cannot stop them: *You don't get everything you want but that's life, isn't it?*

lifeboat /ˈlaɪfbəʊt/ **noun**
a small boat that is used to help people who are in danger at sea

a b c d e f g h i j k l m n o p q r s t u v w x y z

lifestyle /ˈlaɪfstaɪl/ **noun**
the way that you live: *She has a very unhealthy lifestyle.*

lifetime /ˈlaɪftaɪm/ **noun**
the period of time that someone is alive: *She saw such huge changes in her lifetime.*

lift¹ /lɪft/ **verb**
B1 to put something or someone in a higher position: *She **lifted** the baby **up** and put him in his chair.* ◦ *He lifted his glass to his lips.*

lift² /lɪft/ **noun**
1 A2 UK (US **elevator**) a machine that carries people up and down in tall buildings: *Shall we use the stairs or take the lift?*
2 a free ride somewhere, usually in a car: *Can you **give** me **a lift** to the airport?*

lights

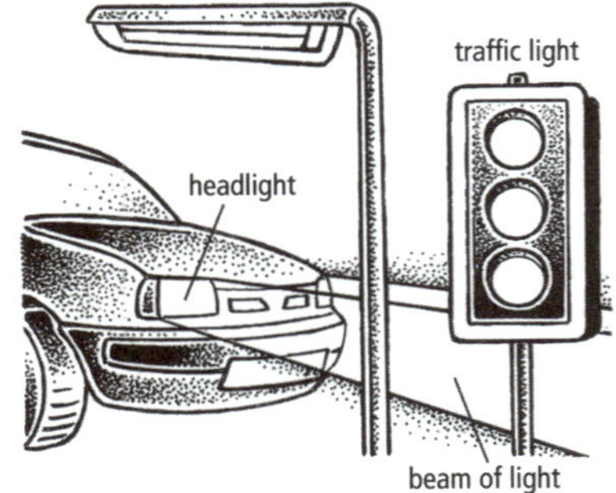

light¹ /laɪt/ **noun**
1 A2 an object that produces light: *car lights* ◦ *Could you turn the kitchen light off?*
2 B1 [no plural] the brightness that shines from the sun, from fire, or from an object, allowing you to see things: *bright light* ◦ *This room gets a lot of light in the morning.*

light² /laɪt/ **adj**
1 A1 Light colours are pale: *a light blue shirt*
→ Opposite **dark** adj
2 A2 not heavy: *My bag is very light.*
3 B1 small in amount: *light rain* ◦ *I only had a light lunch.*
4 it is light B1 bright from the sun: *Let's go now while it's still light.*
5 not strong: *a light breeze*
• **lightness** **noun** [no plural]

light³ /laɪt/ **verb** (**lit**)
1 B1 to start to burn, or to make something start to burn: *She lit a cigarette.* ◦ *The wood won't light.*
2 to make light somewhere so that you can see things: *The room was lit by a single light bulb.*

light bulb /ˈlaɪt ˌbʌlb/ **noun**
a glass object containing a wire that produces light from electricity

light bulb

lighten /ˈlaɪtᵊn/ **verb**
to become less dark, or to make something less dark: *The sun had lightened her hair.*

lighter /ˈlaɪtəʳ/ **noun**
B1 a small object that makes fire and is used to make cigarettes start burning

lighthouse /ˈlaɪthaʊs/ **noun**
a tall building with a large light that shows ships where there are rocks

lighthouse

lighting /ˈlaɪtɪŋ/ **noun** [no plural]
the light that is used in a room or building

lightly /ˈlaɪtli/ **adv**
1 B1 gently, without force: *He kissed her lightly on the cheek.*
2 not much: *I like lightly cooked vegetables.*

lightning /ˈlaɪtnɪŋ/ **noun** [no plural]
B1 sudden, bright light in the sky during a storm: *thunder and lightning*

like¹ /laɪk/ **preposition**
1 A2 similar to someone or something: *He looks like his father.* ◦ *They were acting like children.* ◦ *It sounded like Michelle.*
2 what is *someone/something* like?

A2 something you say when you want someone to describe someone or something: *I haven't met him – what's he like?* ◦ *What's your new dress like?*
3 B1 for example: *She looks best in bright colours like red and pink.*
4 typical or characteristic of: *It's not like you to be so quiet – are you okay?*

like² /laɪk/ **verb** (**liking**, **liked**)
1 A1 to enjoy something or think that someone or something is nice: *I like to paint in my spare time.* ◦ *He really likes her.* ◦ *What do you **like about** him?*
→ Opposite **dislike** verb
2 would like *something* A1 to want something: *I'd **like to** meet him.* ◦ *I'd like some bread, please.*
3 would you like...? A1 used to offer someone something: *Would you like a drink?* ◦ *Would you like to eat now?*
4 if you like A2 used when you offer someone something: *If you like, I can drive you there.*

like³ /laɪk/ **conjunction** informal
B1 in the same way as: *Do it exactly like I told you to.*

likeable /ˈlaɪkəbl/ **adj**
If you are likeable, you are nice and people like you.

likely /ˈlaɪkli/ **adj**
1 B1 expected: *I'm **likely to** forget if you don't remind me.* ◦ *It's **likely that** he'll say no.*
2 probably true: *This is the most likely explanation.*
→ Opposite **unlikely** adj

likes /laɪks/ **plural noun**
likes and dislikes B1 things that you like and things that you do not like

likewise /ˈlaɪkwaɪz/ **adv**
in the same way: *Water these plants twice a week and likewise the ones in the bedroom.*

limb /lɪm/ **noun**
a leg or an arm of a person

lime /laɪm/ **noun**
a small, green fruit that is sour like a lemon

limit¹ /ˈlɪmɪt/ **noun**
B1 the largest amount of something that is possible or allowed: *a time limit* ◦ *There's a **limit to** how much time we can spend on this.*

limit² /ˈlɪmɪt/ **verb**
to control something so that it is less than a particular amount or number: *We'll have to limit the number of guests.*

limited /ˈlɪmɪtɪd/ **adj**
B1 small in amount or number: *There is a **limited choice** of drinks.*

limp¹ /lɪmp/ **adj**
soft and weak: *Her arms were limp, hanging by her side.*

limp² /lɪmp/ **verb**
to walk with difficulty because one of your legs or feet is hurt
• **limp** noun *She walks **with a limp**.*

line¹ /laɪn/ **noun**
1 A2 a long, thin mark: *Sign your name on the line.* ◦ *Draw a line around your hand.*
2 B1 a row of words on a page, for example in a song or poem: *The same line is repeated throughout the poem.*
3 B1 a track that a train travels along: *Which train line do you take to work?*
4 a row of people or things: *a **line of** trees* ◦ *There was a long line of people outside the shop.*
5 a piece of rope or wire with a special purpose: *a fishing line*
6 lines the marks that older people have on their faces, when the skin is loose

line² /laɪn/ **verb** (**lining**, **lined**)
1 to form a row along the side of something: *Trees and cafés lined the street.*
2 be lined with *something* to cover the inside of a piece of clothing with a material: *a jacket lined with fur*

linen /ˈlɪnɪn/ **noun** [no plural]
1 a light cloth that is like rough cotton: *a linen jacket*
2 pieces of cloth that you use to cover tables and beds: *bed linen*

linger /ˈlɪŋɡəʳ/ **verb**
to stay somewhere for a long time: *The smell of onions lingers.*

a b c d e f g h i j k l m n o p q r s t u v w x y z

lining /ˈlaɪnɪŋ/ **noun**
a material that covers the inside of something: *a jacket lining*

link[1] /lɪŋk/ **noun**
1 a connection between two people, things, or ideas: *There's a direct* ***link between*** *smoking and cancer.* ◦ *Their* ***links with*** *Britain are still strong.*
2 one ring of a chain
3 B1 a connection between documents or areas on the Internet: *Click on this link to visit our online bookstore.*

link[2] /lɪŋk/ **verb**
to make a connection between two or more people, things, or ideas: *The drug has been* ***linked to*** *the deaths of several athletes.* ◦ *The two offices will be linked by computer.*

lion

lion /laɪən/ **noun**
A2 a large wild animal of the cat family, with light brown fur

lip /lɪp/ **noun**
B1 one of the two soft, red edges of the mouth: *He licked his lips.*
→ See **The Body** on page C2

lipstick /ˈlɪpstɪk/ **noun**
make-up that people put on their lips

liquid /ˈlɪkwɪd/ **noun**
B1 a substance, for example water, that is not solid and that you can pour easily
• **liquid adj** *liquid fuel*

list[1] /lɪst/ **noun**
A2 a lot of words that are written one under the other: *a shopping list* ◦ *Is your name* ***on the list****?* ◦ ***Make a list*** *of everything you need.*

list[2] /lɪst/ **verb**
to make a list: *All names are listed alphabetically.*

listen /ˈlɪsᵊn/ **verb**
1 A1 to give attention to someone or something in order to hear them: *I* ***listen to*** *the radio while I have breakfast.* ◦ *She does all the talking – I just sit and listen.* ◦ *Listen, if you need money, I can give you some.*
2 B1 to pay attention to what someone tells you and accept what they say: *Why didn't you* ***listen to*** *me when I told you to be careful?*

> **Common mistake: listen, listen to, or hear?**
>
> Use **hear** when you want to say that sounds, music, etc. come to your ears. You can **hear** something without wanting to.
> *I could hear his music through the wall.*
> Use **listen** to say that you pay attention to sounds or try to hear something.
> *The audience listened carefully.*
> *Ssh! I'm listening!*
> Use **listen to** when you want to say what it is that you are trying to hear.
> *The audience listened to the speaker.*
> *Ssh! I'm listening to the radio!*

listener /ˈlɪsᵊnəʳ/ **noun**
someone who listens, especially to the radio: *The new radio station already has twelve million listeners.*

lit /lɪt/
past tense and past participle of light

literally /ˈlɪtᵊrᵊli/ **adv**
1 having the original meaning of a word or phrase: *There are literally hundreds of people here.*
2 used to emphasize what you are saying: *My computer is literally an antique (= it is very old).*

literature /ˈlɪtrətʃəʳ/ **noun** [no plural]
B1 books, poems, etc. that are considered to be art: *classical literature*

litre UK (US **liter**) /ˈliːtəʳ/ **noun** (written abbreviation **l**)
A2 a unit for measuring liquid

litter /ˈlɪtəʳ/ **noun** [no plural]
pieces of paper and other waste that are left in public places: *Please use the* ***litter bin*** *(= a container that is used for rubbish) provided.*

little[1] /ˈlɪtl/ **adj**
1 A1 small in size or amount: *I have a*

little bag. ◦ *She's so little.* ◦ *I had* ***a little bit of*** *cake.*
→ Opposite **big** adj (1), **large** adj
2 A1 young: *When I was little, my hair was curly.*
3 B1 not important: *It's only a little problem.*
4 short in time or distance: *Sit down* ***for a little while.*** ◦ *Let's have a little break.*
5 used to show affection or dislike for someone or something: *What a sweet little house!* ◦ *He's a nasty little man.*

little² /ˈlɪtl/ **quantifier**
B1 not much or not enough: *There's so little time.*

Common mistake: little
When **little** is used as a quantifier, it can only be used with uncountable nouns.

little³ /ˈlɪtl/ **pronoun**
1 B1 not much, or not enough: *We did* ***very little*** *on Sunday.*
2 **a little** B1 a small amount: *'More wine?' 'Just a little, please.'*

little⁴ /ˈlɪtl/ **adv**
1 **a little** A2 slightly: *There's only a little further to go.*
2 not much or not enough: *She ate very little at dinner.*

live¹ /lɪv/ **verb** (**living**, **lived**)
1 A1 to have your home somewhere: *They live in York.* ◦ *Where do you live?*
2 B1 to be alive: *I hope I live to see my grandchildren.*
3 B1 to spend your life in a particular way: *My grandmother lives alone.*

Common mistake: live or life?
Live cannot be used as a noun. The correct noun to use is **life**.
It was the best day of my life.

live together **phrasal verb**
If two people live together, they share a house and have a sexual relationship but are not married: *Now many young people live together before they get married.*

live with *someone* **phrasal verb**
to share a home with someone and have a sexual relationship with them although you are not married: *She's living with her boyfriend.*

live² /laɪv/ **adj**
1 B1 A live performance is done with people watching or listening: *a live concert* ◦ *live music*
2 having life: *live animals*

lively /ˈlaɪvli/ **adj** (**livelier**, **liveliest**)
B1 full of energy and interest: *It was a lively debate.* ◦ *a lively child*

liver /ˈlɪvəʳ/ **noun**
1 a part in your body that cleans your blood
2 [no plural] the liver of an animal that is eaten by people

lives /laɪvz/
plural of life

living /ˈlɪvɪŋ/ **noun** [no plural]
the money that you get from your job: *Like everyone else, I have to* ***make a living.*** ◦ *What does he* ***do for a living*** *(= how does he get money)?*

living room /ˈlɪvɪŋ ˌruːm/ **noun** (also UK **sitting room**)
A1 the room in a house where people sit to relax
→ See **The Living Room** on page C11

lizard /ˈlɪzəd/ **noun**
a small animal with thick skin, a long tail, and four short legs

load¹ /ləʊd/ **noun**
1 things that are carried, often by a vehicle: *We were behind a truck carrying a load of coal.*
2 **a load/loads** informal B1 a lot of something: *There were loads of people there.* ◦ *Have some more food – there's loads.*

load² /ləʊd/ **verb**
1 to put a lot of things into a vehicle or machine: *I was just loading the washing machine.*
2 to put film in a camera or bullets in a gun

loaf /ləʊf/ **noun** (plural **loaves** /ləʊvz/)
bread that has been made in one large piece: *a* ***loaf of bread***

loan¹ /ləʊn/ **noun**
B1 money that someone borrows: *a bank loan* ◦ *a student loan*

loan² /ləʊn/ **verb**
to give something to someone for a

period of time: *My dad loaned me the money.*

loathe /ləʊð/ **verb** (**loathing**, **loathed**)
to hate someone or something: *I loathe housework.*

loaves /ləʊvz/
plural of loaf

lobby /ˈlɒbi/ **noun** (plural **lobbies**)
a room at the main entrance of a building: *a hotel lobby*

lobster /ˈlɒbstəʳ/ **noun**
a sea animal that has two claws (= sharp, curved parts) and eight legs, or the meat of this animal

local /ˈləʊkᵊl/ **adj**
B1 relating to an area near you: *She goes to the local school.*
• **locally** **adv** *locally grown vegetables*

locate /ləʊˈkeɪt/ **verb** (**locating**, **located**) formal
1 **be located** B1 to be in a particular place: *Both schools are located in the town.*
2 to find the exact position of someone or something: *Police are still trying to locate the criminal.*

location /ləʊˈkeɪʃᵊn/ **noun**
B1 a place or position: *Have they decided on **the location of** the factory?*

lock[1] /lɒk/ **verb**
1 B1 to fasten something with a key: *Did you lock the door?*
→ Opposite **unlock** **verb**
2 to put something or someone in a place or container that is fastened with a key: *She locked herself in her bedroom.*

lock[2] /lɒk/ **noun**
B1 the thing that you use to close a door, window, etc. that needs a key to open it: *I heard someone turn a key in the lock.* ◦ *safety locks*

locker /ˈlɒkəʳ/ **noun**
a small cupboard in a public area where you can keep things: *a luggage locker* ◦ *a gym locker*

lodge /lɒdʒ/ **verb** (**lodging**, **lodged**)
1 to become stuck somewhere: *The bullet had lodged near his heart.*
2 to live in someone's home and give them money for it: *He **lodges with** a French family.*

loft /lɒft/ **noun**
the space under the roof of a house or other building

log[1] /lɒg/ **noun**
a thick piece of wood that has been cut from a tree: *We need more logs for the fire.*

log[2] /lɒg/ **verb** (**logging**, **logged**)
log in/on **phrasal verb**
to connect a computer to a system of computers by typing your name and a password
log off/out **phrasal verb**
to stop a computer being connected to a computer system, usually to stop working

logical /ˈlɒdʒɪkᵊl/ **adj**
using reason and good judgment: *a logical choice*

logo /ˈləʊgəʊ/ **noun**
B1 a special design that a company uses to sell its products: *the company's logo*

lollipop /ˈlɒlipɒp/ **noun**
a large, hard sweet on a stick

lonely /ˈləʊnli/ **adj** (**lonelier**, **loneliest**)
B1 sad because you are not with other people: *She gets lonely now that the kids have all left home.*

long[1] /lɒŋ/ **adj**
1 A1 having a large distance from one end to the other: *long hair* ◦ *long legs* ◦ *a long dress*
→ Opposite **short** **adj**
2 A1 continuing for a large amount of time: *a long movie* ◦ *I waited a long time.*
→ Opposite **short** **adj**
3 A2 describes a piece of writing that has a lot of pages or words: *a long book*
4 used when asking for or giving information about the distance or time of something: *It's about three metres long.* ◦ *The concert was three hours long.* ◦ *How long was the skirt?* ◦ *How long is the movie?*

shower
shower curtain
bathroom cabinet *UK*, medicine cabinet *US*
towel
soap
sink
toilet paper
bath *UK*, bathtub *US*
toilet
scales *UK*, scale *US*
bath mat
toothbrush
nail brush
toothpaste
razor
cotton wool
shaver

THE BODY

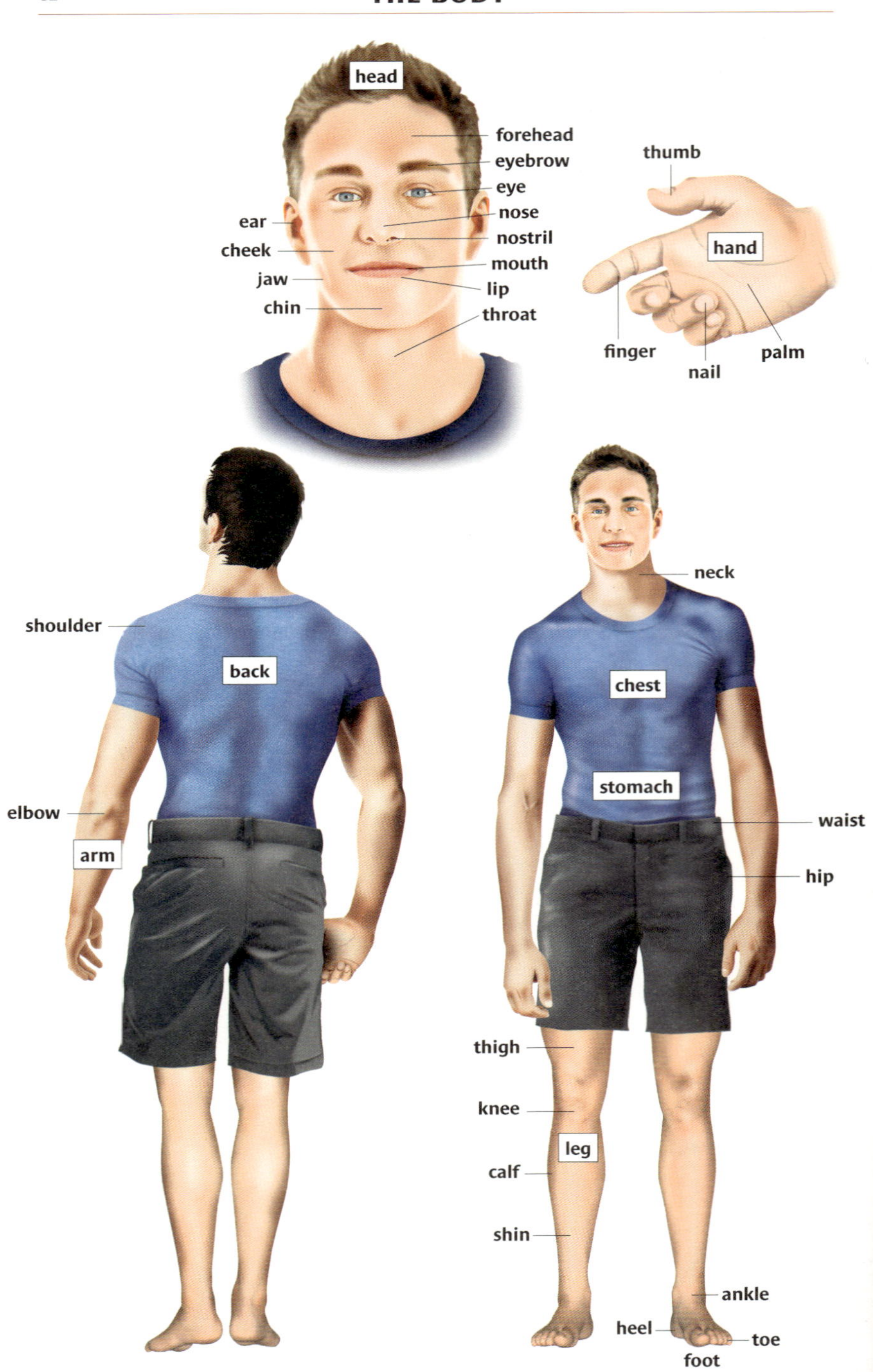
head
forehead
eyebrow
eye
ear
nose
nostril
cheek
mouth
jaw
lip
chin
throat
thumb
hand
finger
palm
nail
neck
shoulder
back
chest
stomach
elbow
waist
arm
hip
thigh
knee
leg
calf
shin
ankle
heel
toe
foot

aerial *UK*, antenna *US*
rear window
number plate *UK*, license plate *US*
boot *UK*, trunk *US*
bonnet *UK*, hood *US*
indicator
tyre *UK*, tire *US*

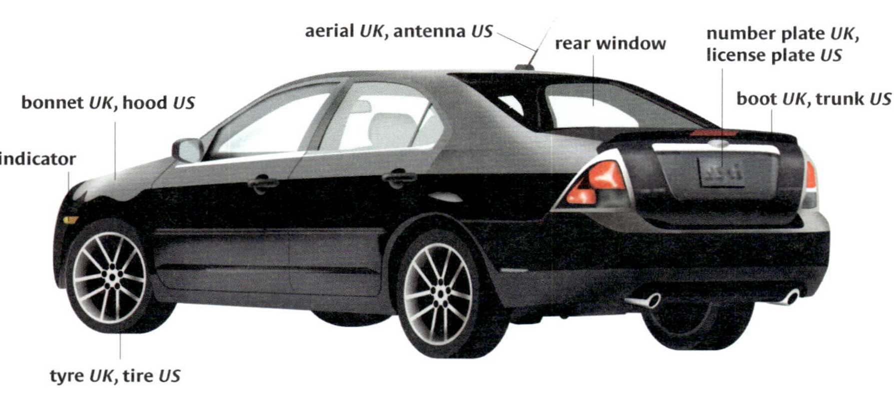

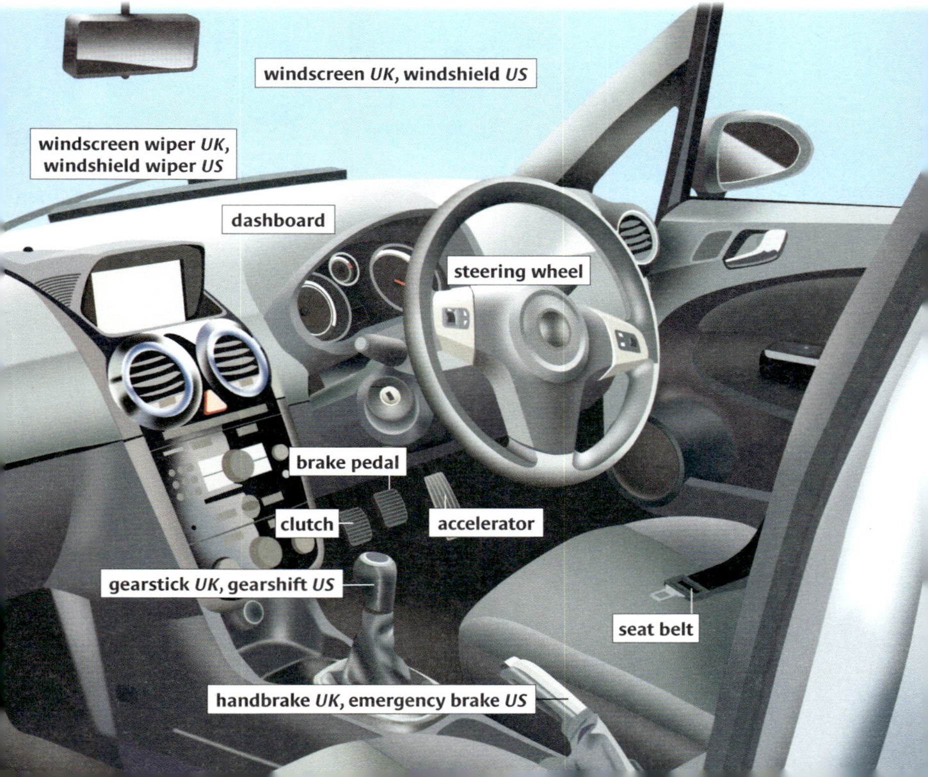

windscreen *UK*, windshield *US*
windscreen wiper *UK*, windshield wiper *US*
dashboard
steering wheel
brake pedal
clutch
accelerator
gearstick *UK*, gearshift *US*
seat belt
handbrake *UK*, emergency brake *US*

THE CLASSROOM

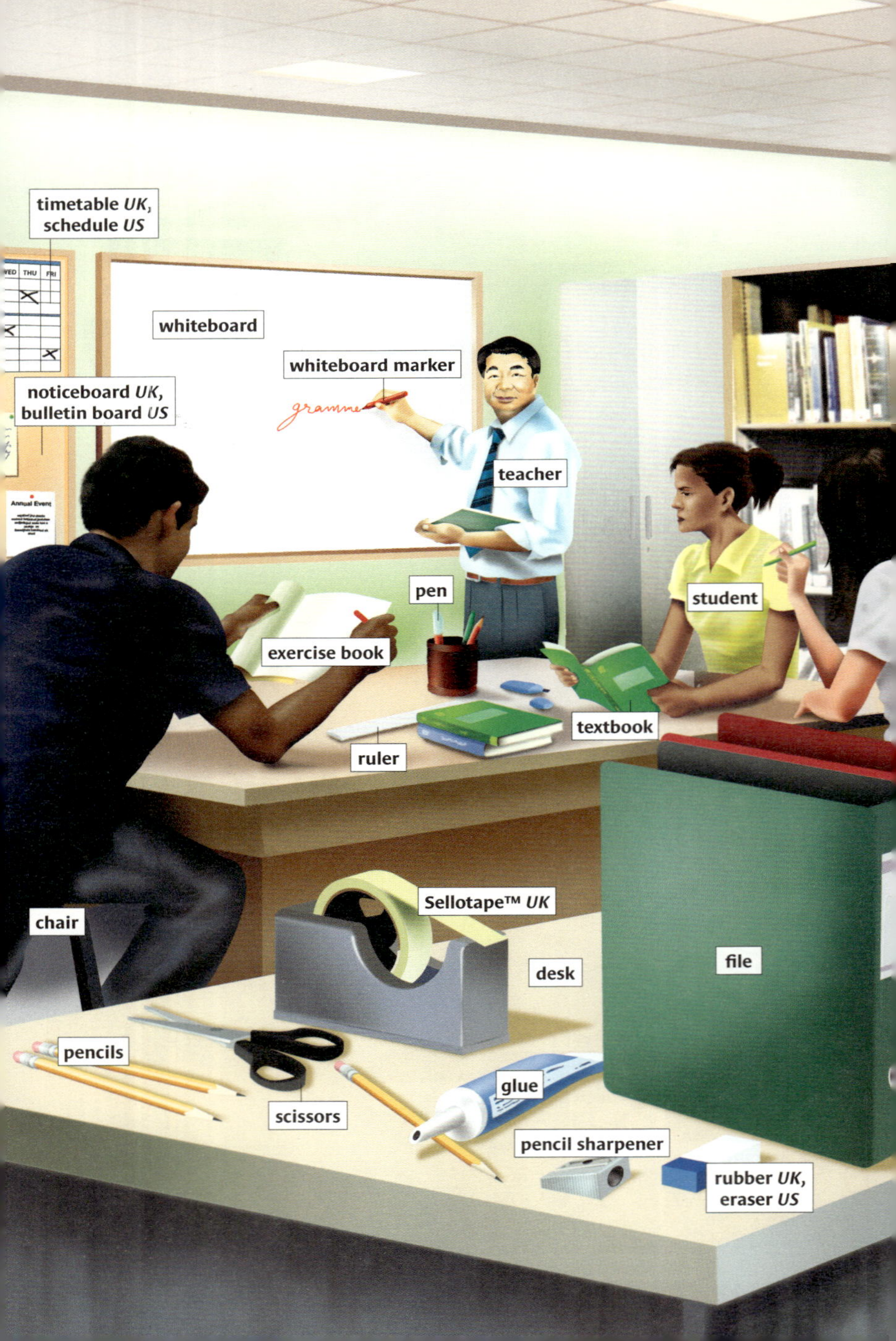
timetable *UK*, schedule *US*
whiteboard
whiteboard marker
gramme
noticeboard *UK*, bulletin board *US*
WED
THU
FRI
Annual Event
teacher
student
pen
exercise book
textbook
ruler
Sellotape™ *UK*
chair
desk
file
pencils
scissors
glue
pencil sharpener
rubber *UK*, eraser *US*

shirt
T-shirt
coat
dress
miniskirt
sweatshirt
jumper UK, sweater US
cardigan
skirt
waterproof jacket
belt
waistcoat
tie
scarf
scarf
sandals
jacket
buckle
shorts
shoes
boots
trainers UK
trousers
jeans
cycling shorts
leggings
stockings
tights UK, pantyhose US
socks
bra
pants UK, panties US
boxer shorts
underpants
hat
bikini
sunglasses
trunks
vest
cap

red
blue
green
yellow
brown
black
grey *UK*,
gray *US*
white
purple
pink
orange
navy blue

roll *UK*

sandwich

soup

biscuits *UK*, cookies *US*

cake

salad

vegetables

pizza

cereal

rice

chips *UK*, French fries *US*

pasta

peanuts

crisps *UK*, chips *US*

jam

honey

fish

butter

eggs

yoghurt

cheese

meat

apples
bananas
grapes
pears
oranges
pineapples
lemons
melons
sweetcorn
carrots
tomatoes
potatoes
celery
lettuce
cucumbers
garlic
onions
cauliflower
mushrooms
aubergines *UK*,
eggplants *US*
peppers

blonde/fair
brown
black
red
grey *UK*, gray *US*
straight
curly
wavy
spiky
fringe *UK*,
bangs *US*
moustache
beard
ponytail
plait *UK*,
braid *US*
long
short
bald

THE KITCHEN

utensils

toaster

scales *UK*,
scale *US*

tin opener *UK*,
can opener *US*

teapot

grater

kettle

blender

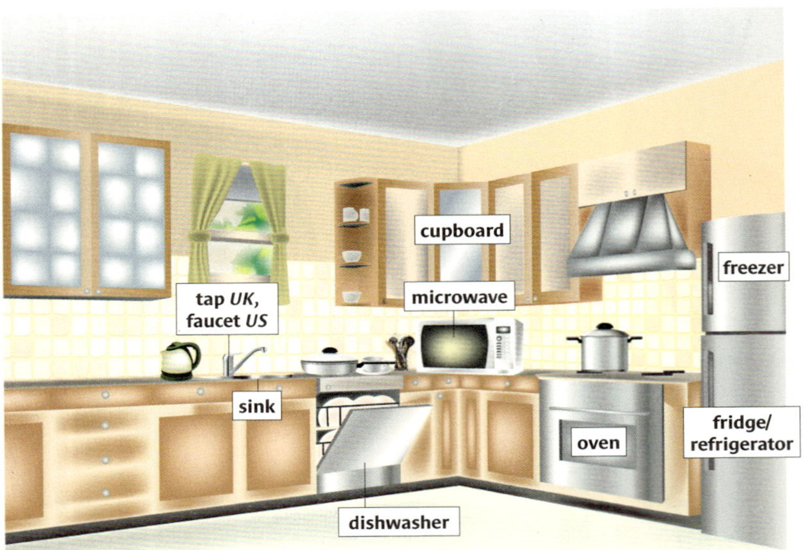

baking tray

saucepan

frying pan

THE LIVING ROOM

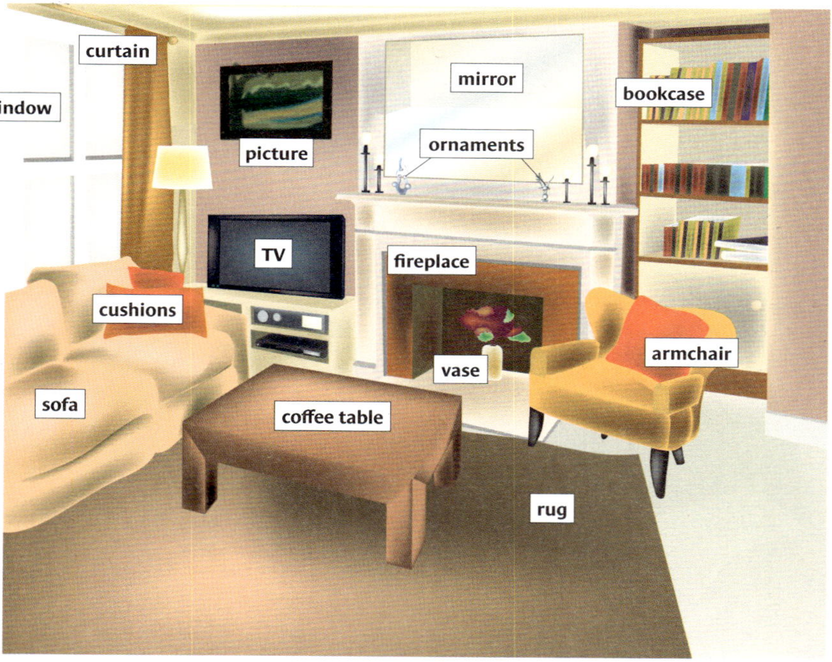

curtain
window
picture
mirror
bookcase
ornaments
TV
fireplace
cushions
armchair
vase
sofa
coffee table
rug

remote control

DVD player

candles

lampshade

lamp

speaker

stereo

11 12 1
10 2
9 3
8 4
7 6 5

clock

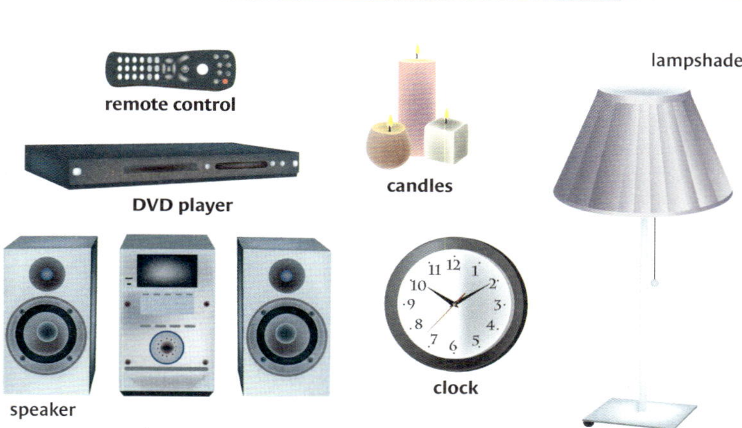

fax
photocopier
monitor
screen
in-tray
paper clips
envelope
file
CD
mouse
keyboard
desk
telephone
folder
highlighter
filing cabinet
computer
chair
files
bin *UK*,
wastepaper basket *US*

wake up
get up
put on
take off
lie down
sit down
stand up
put down
pick up
throw away
put away
wash up
tell off
eat out
turn on
turn off
get on
get off
fall over
work out

QUANTITIES

a slice of... **a bar of...**

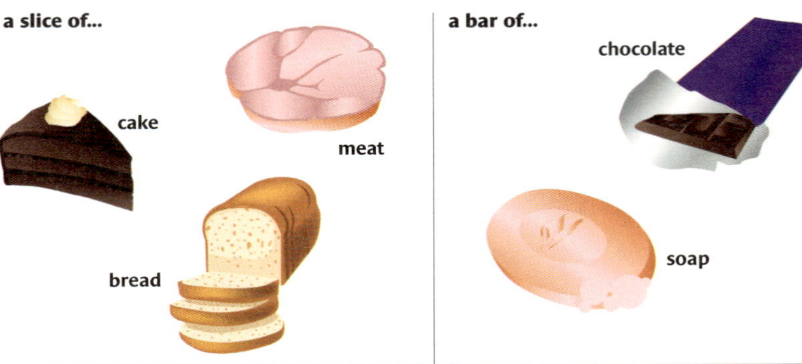

a bunch of...

a piece of...

a chunk of **a blob of...**

crumb **a pinch of...** **a drop of...**

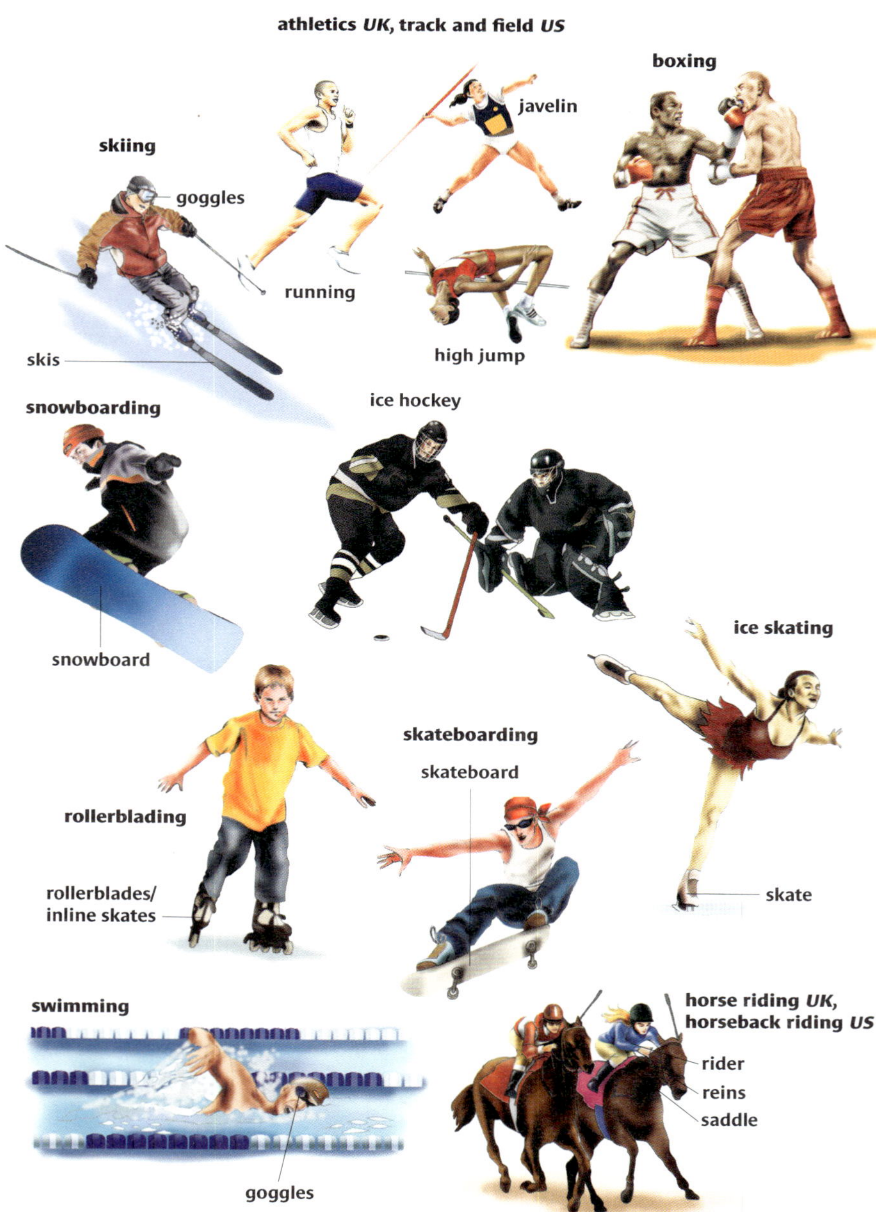
athletics *UK*, track and field *US*
boxing
javelin
skiing
goggles
running
high jump
skis
snowboarding
ice hockey
snowboard
ice skating
skateboarding
skateboard
rollerblading
rollerblades/
inline skates
skate
swimming
horse riding *UK*,
horseback riding *US*
rider
reins
saddle
goggles

SPORTS (2)

football *UK*, soccer *US*
goal
goalkeeper
referee
American football *UK*, football *US*
helmet
rugby
club
golf
cricket
basketball
basket
baseball
cap
tennis
racket
net
helmet
cycling
net
bicycle
volleyball

long[2] /lɒŋ/ **adv**
1 A2 for a long time: *Did you have to wait long for the train?*
2 as long as B1 used when you are talking about something that must happen before something else can happen: *You can play football as long as you do your homework first.*
3 no longer B1 in the past but not now: *The school is no longer used.*
4 before (very/too) long soon: *They'll be home before very long.*

long[3] /lɒŋ/ **noun** [no plural]
a large amount of time: *She won't be away for long.*

long[4] /lɒŋ/ **verb** formal
to want something very much: *She* ***longed to*** *see him again.* ◦ *I'm* ***longing for*** *some sun.*

longing /ˈlɒŋɪŋ/ **noun**
a feeling of wanting something or someone very much: *He gazed at her, his eyes full of longing.*

longitude /ˈlɒndʒɪtjuːd/ **noun** [no plural]
the distance of a place east or west of an imaginary line from the top to the bottom of the Earth

long-term /ˌlɒŋˈtɜːm/ **adj**
continuing a long time into the future: *Seriously ill people need long-term care.*

look[1] /lʊk/ **verb**
1 A1 to turn your eyes in the direction of something or someone so that you can see it or them: ***Look at*** *the picture on page two.* ◦ *He was looking out of the window.*
2 A1 to try to find someone or something: *I'm* ***looking for*** *my keys.* ◦ *I've looked everywhere but I can't find my bag.*
3 look nice, strange, etc. A2 used to describe the appearance of a person or thing: *That food looks nice.* ◦ *You look tired.*
4 look like B1 used to describe the appearance of a person or thing: *He looks like a friendly person.*
5 it looks like; it looks as if B1 used to say that something will probably happen: *It looks as if he isn't coming.*
6 look! something you say when you are annoyed and you want people to listen to you: *Look! I've had enough of your complaints.*
7 look as if/as though used to describe the appearance of a person or thing: *She looked as if she was going to cry.*

Common mistake: look, see, or watch?

See means to notice people and things with your eyes.

She saw a big spider and screamed.

Did you see anyone you knew at the party?

Look (at) is used when you are trying to see something or someone. **Look** cannot be followed by an object.

I've looked everywhere, but I can't find my keys.

He looked at the map to find the road.

~~He looked the photographs.~~

Watch means to look at something for a period of time, usually something that moves or changes.

He watched television all evening.

I watched them playing football.

look after *someone/something* **phrasal verb**
A2 to take care of someone or something: *Could you look after the children while I'm out?*

look around/round (*something*) **phrasal verb**
B1 to visit a place and look at the things in it: *She spent the afternoon looking round the town.*

look at *something* **phrasal verb**
1 to think about a subject carefully so that you can make a decision about it: *Our manager is looking at ways of reducing costs.*
2 to read something in order to check it or see how good it is: *Can you look at my essay?*
3 to examine something: *Did the doctor look at your knee?*

look forward to *something* **phrasal verb**
1 B1 to feel happy and excited about something that is going to happen: *I'm really looking forward to seeing him.*
2 formal used at the end of a formal

letter to say you hope to hear from or see someone soon, or that you expect something from them: *I **look forward to hearing from you**.*

Common mistake: look forward to

Remember always to use the preposition **to** when you use this verb.

We are looking forward to your visit.

~~*We are looking forward your visit.*~~

look into *something* **phrasal verb**
to examine the facts about a situation: *They are looking into the causes of the accident.*

look out! **phrasal verb**
B1 something you say when someone is in danger: *Look out – there's a car coming!*

look *something* up **phrasal verb**
B1 to look at a book or computer in order to find information: *I looked it up on the Internet.*

look² /lʊk/ **noun**

1 B1 the act of looking at someone or something: ***Take a look** at these pictures.* ◦ *Can I **have a look**?*
2 B1 the act of looking for someone or something: *I **had** another **look for** the watch, but couldn't find it.*
3 an expression on someone's face: *She had a worried look on her face.*
4 ***someone's* looks** a person's appearance, especially how attractive he or she is: *I liked his looks.*
5 the look of *someone/something* the appearance of someone or something: *They liked the look of the hotel, but it was too expensive.*

loop /lu:p/ **noun**
a circle of something long and thin, such as a piece of string or wire

loose /lu:s/ **adj**

Common mistake: loose or lose?

Be careful! These two words look and sound similar but have completely different meanings. **Loose** is an adjective, meaning 'not fixed or not tight'.

These trousers are a bit loose.

Be careful not to use **loose** when you really mean the verb **lose**.

I hope he doesn't lose his job.

~~*I hope he doesn't loose his job.*~~

1 B1 Loose clothes are large and not tight: *a loose dress*
2 not firmly attached: *One of my buttons is loose.*
3 An animal that is loose is free to move around: *Two lions escaped and are still loose.*

loosen /ˈlu:s^{ə}n/ **verb**
to become loose or make something loose: *He loosened his tie.*

lord /lɔ:d/ **noun**
1 (also **Lord**) in the UK, a title for a man of high social rank: *Lord Lichfield*
2 the Lord God or Christ

lorry /ˈlɒri/ **noun** (plural **lorries**) UK (UK/US **truck**)
B1 a large road vehicle for carrying things from place to place
→ See picture at **vehicle**

lose /lu:z/ **verb** (**losing**, **lost**)
1 A2 to not be able to find someone or something: *I've lost my passport.* ◦ *She's always losing her keys.*
2 B1 to stop having something that you had before: *She lost a leg in a car accident.* ◦ *He lost his job.*
3 B1 to have less of something than you had before: *She's lost a lot of weight.* ◦ *He's losing his hair.*
4 B1 If you lose a game, the team or person that you are playing against wins: *Chelsea lost by a goal.* ◦ *They're losing 3-1.*
5 lose interest, patience, etc. to stop feeling something: *I've lost interest in the subject.* ◦ *He kept on crying, and I lost my patience.*
6 to waste something such as time or an opportunity: *Because of illness, she lost the chance of a place in the team.*

loser /ˈlu:zə^{r}/ **noun**
1 someone who does not win a game or competition
2 informal someone who is not successful in anything they do

loss /lɒs/ **noun**
1 a state of not having something that you had before: *loss of memory* ◦ *job losses*
2 a situation in which a company spends more money than it earns:

*Both companies **suffered losses** this year.*
3 the death of a person: *They never got over the loss of their son.*

lost[1] /lɒst/
past tense and past participle of lose

lost[2] /lɒst/ **adj**
1 A2 not knowing where you are: *I **got lost** on the way.*
2 B1 If something is lost, no one knows where it is: *The letter **got lost** in the post.*

lost property /ˌlɒst ˈprɒpəti/ **noun** [no plural] UK
things that people have left in public places

lot /lɒt/ **noun**
1 a lot; lots A1 a large number or amount of people or things: *There were **a lot of** people outside the building.* ◦ *He earns **lots of** money.* ◦ *I've got a lot to do this morning.*

Common mistake: a lot of something
Remember to use the preposition **of** before the thing that there is a large number of.
A lot of people enjoy travelling to other countries.
~~*A lot people enjoy travelling to other countries.*~~

2 a lot A1 a large amount or very often: *We used to go there a lot.*
3 a lot better, older, quicker, etc. much better, older, quicker, etc.: *He looks a lot older than his wife.* ◦ *It's a lot quicker by train.*

lotion /ˈləʊʃᵊn/ **noun**
a liquid that you put on your skin to make it soft or healthy: *suntan lotion*

lottery /ˈlɒtᵊri/ **noun** (plural **lotteries**)
B1 a competition in which people buy tickets with numbers on them and win money if their ticket has a particular number: *the national lottery*

loud[1] /laʊd/ **adj**
A2 making a lot of noise: *a loud noise* ◦ *a loud voice*
• **loudly adv** B1 *They were all talking loudly.*

loud[2] /laʊd/ **adv**
1 B1 in a way that makes a lot of noise: *Could you speak louder, please?*
2 out loud B1 If you say or read something out loud, you say or read it so that other people can hear you: *I had to read the poem out loud in front of the whole class.*

loudspeaker /ˌlaʊdˈspiːkəʳ/ **noun**
something that is used for making voices or sounds louder

lounge /laʊndʒ/ **noun** UK
a room with chairs where you can sit and relax

louse /laʊs/ **noun** (plural **lice** /laɪs/)
a small insect that lives on the bodies or in the hair of people or animals

lousy /ˈlaʊzi/ **adj** (**lousier**, **lousiest**) informal
very bad: *The food in the hotel was lousy.*

lovable (also **loveable**) /ˈlʌvəbl/ **adj**
very nice and easy to love: *a lovable child*

love[1] /lʌv/ **verb** (**loving**, **loved**)
1 A1 to like someone very much and have sexual feelings for them: *Last night he told me he loved me.*
2 A1 to like a friend or a person in your family very much: *I'm sure he loves his kids.*
3 A1 to like something very much: *He loves his music.* ◦ *She loves animals.*
4 would love *something*/to do *something* A2 used to say that you want something very much: *I'd love some chocolate!* ◦ *I'd love to be an actor.*
5 I'd love to used to say that you would very much like to do something that someone is offering: *'I wondered if you'd like to meet up sometime?' 'I'd love to.'*

love[2] /lʌv/ **noun**
1 B1 [no plural] the feeling of liking someone very much and having sexual feelings for them: *a love song*
2 in love B1 having a strong feeling that you love someone: *I'm **in love with** him.* ◦ *I was 20 when I first **fell in love** (= started to love someone).*
3 make love to have sex
4 B1 [no plural] the feeling of liking a

a b c d e f g h i j k l m n o p q r s t u v w x y z

friend or person in your family very much: *Nothing is as strong as the **love** you have **for** your kids.*
5 something that interests you a lot: *his love of books*
6 love from; all my love A2 something you write at the end of a letter to a friend or someone in your family: *Love from Mum.*
7 B1 a person that you love and feel attracted to: *She was my first love.*

lovely /ˈlʌvli/ **adj** (**lovelier, loveliest**)
1 A2 very nice or enjoyable: *We had a lovely day together.* ◦ *What lovely weather!*
2 A2 very attractive: *a lovely dress* ◦ *You look lovely!*

lover /ˈlʌvəʳ/ **noun**
1 B1 If two people are lovers, they have a sexual relationship but they are not married.
2 B1 someone who likes something very much: *She's a cat lover.*

loving /ˈlʌvɪŋ/ **adj**
showing that you love someone: *a loving father*

low /ləʊ/ **adj**
1 A2 under the usual level: *Their prices are very low.* ◦ *a low number*
2 B1 near the ground, not high: *low aircraft* ◦ *low ceilings*
3 A low sound is deep or quiet: *a low voice* ◦ *a low note*

lower¹ /ˈləʊəʳ/ **adj**
being the bottom part of something: *I've got a pain in my lower back.*

lower² /ˈləʊəʳ/ **verb**
1 to make something less in amount: *They have lowered the price.*
2 to move something into a low position: *The flag is lowered every night.*

loyal /lɔɪəl/ **adj**
always liking and supporting someone or something: *a loyal supporter* ◦ *She's very **loyal to** her friends.*

loyalty /ˈlɔɪəlti/ **noun** [no plural]
the quality of always liking and supporting someone or something: *Your **loyalty to** the company is impressive.*

Ltd
written abbreviation for limited company: used after the name of some companies: *Pinewood Supplies Ltd*

luck /lʌk/ **noun** [no plural]
1 A2 good and bad things caused by chance and not by your own actions: *It was just luck that we got on the same train.* ◦ *He has had a lot of **bad luck** in his life.*
2 success: *He's been trying to find work but with no luck so far.*
3 good luck! something you say to someone when you hope they will do well: *Good luck with your exam!*

luckily /ˈlʌkəli/ **adv**
B1 happening because of good luck: *Luckily I had some money with me.*

lucky /ˈlʌki/ **adj** (**luckier, luckiest**)
A2 having good things happen to you: *'I'm going on holiday.' 'Lucky you!'* ◦ *You're **lucky to** live in such a beautiful city.*
→ Opposite **unlucky** adj

luggage

backpack

holdall *UK*, carryall *US*

suitcase

luggage /ˈlʌɡɪdʒ/ **noun** [no plural]
A2 bags that you carry with you when you travel

lukewarm /ˌluːkˈwɔːm/ **adj**
A liquid that is lukewarm is only slightly warm.

lump /lʌmp/ **noun**
a bit of something solid with no particular shape: *a lump of coal* ◦ *She found a lump in her breast.*

lunatic /ˈluːnətɪk/ **noun**
someone who behaves in a crazy way: *He drives like a lunatic.*

lunch /lʌntʃ/ **noun**
A1 the food that you eat in the middle of the day: *Shall we* ***have lunch****?*

lunchtime /ˈlʌnʃtaɪm/ **noun**
A2 the time when you eat lunch

lung /lʌŋ/ **noun**
one of the two parts inside your chest that are used for breathing: *lung cancer*

luxurious /lʌgˈʒʊəriəs/ **adj**
very comfortable and expensive: *a luxurious hotel*

luxury /ˈlʌkʃəri/ **noun**
1 B1 [no plural] very expensive and beautiful things: *They live* ***in luxury*** *in a fabulous apartment in Paris.*
2 (plural **luxuries**) something that you like having but do not need: *Having a car each is a luxury really.*
3 [no plural] something that gives you a lot of pleasure, but which you cannot often do: *A day off work is luxury.*

lying /ˈlaɪɪŋ/
present participle of lie[1,2]

lyrics /ˈlɪrɪks/ **plural noun**
the words of a song

M m

M, m /em/
the thirteenth letter of the alphabet

m
written abbreviation for metre: a unit for measuring length

mac /mæk/ **noun** UK
a coat that you wear in the rain

machine /məˈʃiːn/ **noun**
1 A2 a piece of equipment with moving parts that uses power to do a particular job: *a fax machine* ◦ *a coffee machine*
2 a computer

machine gun /məˈʃiːn ˌɡʌn/ **noun**
a gun that fires a lot of bullets very quickly

machinery /məˈʃiːnəri/ **noun** [no plural]
machines, often large machines: *farm machinery*

mad /mæd/ **adj** (**madder, maddest**)
1 B1 (US usually **crazy**) mentally ill: *I think I'm* ***going mad****.*
2 B1 informal stupid or crazy: *You are* ***mad to*** *walk home alone at night.*
3 A2 mainly US angry: *Were your parents* ***mad at*** *you when you came home late?*
4 be mad about ***someone/something*** mainly UK informal B1 to love something or someone: *Jo is mad about skiing.*
5 go mad UK informal to become very angry: *Dad will go mad when he finds out you took the car.*
6 like mad informal If you run, work, etc. like mad, you do it very quickly.

madam /ˈmædəm/ **noun** formal
1 B1 used to be polite when you speak or write to a woman who you do not know: *This way, madam.*
2 Dear Madam a way of beginning a formal letter to a woman whose name you do not know

made /meɪd/
past tense and past participle of make

madly /mædli/ **adv**
1 with a lot of energy and enthusiasm: *We cheered madly as the team came out onto the field.*
2 be madly in love to love someone very much: *He's madly in love with Denise.*

madness /ˈmædnəs/ **noun** [no plural]
stupid or dangerous behaviour: *It is madness to drive that fast.*

magazine /ˌmæɡəˈziːn/ **noun**
A2 a big, thin book that you can buy every week or month, that has pictures and writing: *a fashion magazine*

magazine

magic¹ /ˈmædʒɪk/ **noun** [no plural]
1 A2 special powers that can make things happen that seem impossible: *Do you believe in magic?*
2 A2 tricks that a person performs while other people watch, such as making things disappear: *My daughter loves doing magic.*
3 a quality that makes something or someone seem special or exciting: *Everyone enjoys the magic of this wonderful city.*

magic² /ˈmædʒɪk/ **adj**
1 A2 relating to magic: *a magic show*
2 B1 with special powers that make impossible things happen: *a magic spell*

magical /ˈmædʒɪkəl/ **adj**
1 with special powers: *Diamonds were once thought to have* ***magical powers****.*
2 special or exciting: *It was a magical night.*

magician /məˈdʒɪʃən/ **noun**
someone who performs tricks as entertainment, such as making things disappear

magnet /ˈmæɡnət/ **noun**
an iron object that makes other pieces of iron move towards it

magnetic /mæɡˈnetɪk/ **adj**
with the power of a magnet: *a magnetic field*

magnet

magnificent /mæɡˈnɪfɪsᵊnt/ **adj**
B1 very good or very beautiful: *The view from our room was magnificent.*

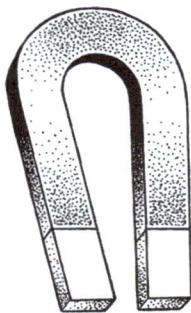

magnify /ˈmæɡnɪfaɪ/ **verb** (**magnifying**, **magnified**)
to make an object look bigger than it is: *The cells are first magnified under a microscope.*

magnifying glass /ˈmæɡ nɪˌfaɪɪŋ ˌɡlɑːs/ **noun**
a piece of curved glass that makes objects look bigger than they are

magnifying glass

maid /meɪd/ **noun**
a woman who cleans or cooks in a hotel or in someone's home

maiden name /ˈmeɪdᵊn ˌneɪm/ **noun**
the family name that a woman has before she gets married

mail[1] /meɪl/ **noun** [no plural]
1 A2 letters and parcels that come by post: *We got loads of mail this morning.*
2 A2 mainly US the system by which letters and parcels are taken and brought: *The book came **in** yesterday's **mail**.*
3 A2 email: *You've got mail.*

mail[2] /meɪl/ **verb** mainly US
to send a letter or parcel or to email something: *Could you **mail** it **to** me?*

mailbox /ˈmeɪlbɒks/ **noun** US
1 a small box outside your home where letters are put
2 (UK **post box**) a large, metal container in a public place where you can post letters

mailman /ˈmeɪlmæn/ **noun** (plural **mailmen**) US (UK **postman**)
a man who takes and brings letters and parcels as a job

main /meɪn/ **adj**
1 B1 most important or largest: *Our main problem is lack of money.* ◦ *The main airport is 15 miles from the capital.*
2 **the main thing** the most important fact in a situation: *You're happy, and that's the main thing.*

main course /ˈmeɪn ˌkɔːs/ **noun**
A2 the largest or most important part of a meal: *I had fish **for** my **main course**.*

mainly /ˈmeɪnli/ **adv**
B1 mostly: *The people are mainly French.*

main road /ˌmeɪn ˈrəʊd/ **noun**
a large road that goes from one town to another: *They live on the main road out of town.*

main street /ˈmeɪn striːt/ **noun** US (UK **high street**)
the main road in the centre of a town where there are shops

maintain /meɪnˈteɪn/ **verb**
1 to make a situation or activity continue in the same way: *The army has been brought in to maintain order in the region.*
2 to keep a building or area in good condition: *A large house is very expensive to maintain.*

maintenance /ˈmeɪntᵊnəns/ **noun** [no plural]
the work that you do to keep something in good condition: *car maintenance*

maize /meɪz/ **noun** [no plural] UK (US **corn**)
a tall plant with yellow seeds that are eaten as food

majesty /ˈmædʒəsti/ **noun**
His/Her/Your Majesty used when you are speaking to or about a king or queen: *His Majesty King Edward VII*

major[1] /ˈmeɪdʒəʳ/ **adj**
important or big: *a major problem* ◦ *a major city*

→ Opposite **minor** **adj**

major² /ˈmeɪdʒəʳ/ **noun**
an officer of middle rank in the army or air force

majority /məˈdʒɒrəti/ **noun** [no plural]
more than half of a group of people or things: ***The majority of*** *people in this country own their houses.*
→ Opposite **minority** **noun**

make /meɪk/ **verb** (**making**, **made**)
1 A1 to create something: *Shall I make some coffee?* ◦ *They've made a movie about her life.* ◦ *Butter is* ***made from*** *milk.*
2 be made of *something* A2 to consist of a particular material: *The ring is made of gold.*
3 A2 to perform an action: *I must make a telephone call.* ◦ *Someone's made a mistake.*
4 B1 to cause something to happen or cause a particular state: *He really makes me laugh.* ◦ *This heat makes me very tired.*
5 make *someone* do *something* B1 to force someone to do something: *You can't make me go.*
6 make *someone/something* happy, sad, difficult, etc. to cause someone or something to become happy, sad, difficult, etc.: *You've made me very happy.*
7 If you make an amount of money, you earn it: *He makes £30,000 a year.*
8 If two or more numbers make a particular amount, that is the amount when they are added together: *That makes $40 altogether.*
9 make the bed to make the sheets and covers on a bed tidy
10 make it informal B1 to arrive at a place at the right time: *Will we make it in time for the movie?*
11 make it informal to be successful: *Very few actors actually make it.*
make *something* into *something* **phrasal verb**
to change something into something else: *They've made the spare room into an office.*
make *something/someone* out **phrasal verb**
to be able to see, hear, or understand something or someone: *We could just make out a building through the trees.*
make *something* up **phrasal verb**
to say or write something that is not true: *I made up an excuse because I didn't want to go.*

maker /ˈmeɪkəʳ/ **noun**
the person or company that makes a product: *They're the biggest maker of computers in the country.*

make-up /ˈmeɪkʌp/ **noun** [no plural]
A2 coloured substances that you put on your face in order to make yourself more attractive: *She doesn't* ***wear*** *much* ***make-up****.*

male¹ /meɪl/ **adj**
B1 belonging to or relating to the sex that cannot have babies: *a male colleague*
→ Opposite **female** **adj**

male² /meɪl/ **noun**
a male person or animal

mall /mɔːl/ **noun** (also **shopping mall**)
B1 a large, covered shopping area

mammal /ˈmæməl/ **noun**
an animal that drinks milk from its mother's body when it is young

man /mæn/ **noun** (plural **men**)
1 A1 an adult male human: *a young man* ◦ *men and women*
2 [no plural] used to refer to both men and women: *Man is still more intelligent than the cleverest robot.*

manage /ˈmænɪdʒ/ **verb** (**managing**, **managed**)
1 B1 to do something that you have been trying to do: *I* ***managed to*** *persuade him to come.*
2 B1 to be in control of an office, shop, team, etc.: *He used to manage the bookshop on King Street.*

management /ˈmænɪdʒmənt/ **noun**
1 [no plural] being in control of an office, shop, team, etc.: *management skills*
2 the people who are in control of an office, shop, team, etc.: *Management have accepted the proposal.*

manager /ˈmænɪdʒəʳ/ **noun**
A2 someone in control of an office,

shop, team, etc.: *She's the manager of the local sports club.*

mane /meɪn/ **noun**
the long hair on the necks of animals such as horses or lions

manipulate /mə'nɪpjəleɪt/ **verb** (**manipulating**, **manipulated**)
to control someone or something in a clever way: *She knows how to manipulate the press.*

mankind /mæn'kaɪnd/ **noun** [no plural]
all people, considered as a group: *the history of mankind*

man-made /ˌmæn'meɪd/ **adj**
not natural, but made by people: *man-made fibres*

manner /'mænəʳ/ **noun** [no plural]
1 the way in which a person talks and behaves with other people: *She has a very friendly manner.*
2 the way something happens or something is done: *They dealt with the problem* ***in a*** *very efficient* ***manner****.*

manners /'mænəz/ **plural noun**
ways of behaving with other people: *It is bad manners to be late.*

mansion /'mænʃᵊn/ **noun**
a very large house

manual[1] /'mænjuəl/ **adj**
using your hands: *manual work*
• **manually adv**

manual[2] /'mænjuəl/ **noun**
a book that tells you how to use something or do something: *an online training manual*

manufacture /ˌmænjə'fæktʃəʳ/ **verb** (**manufacturing**, **manufactured**)
to make something, usually in large numbers in a factory: *He works for a company that manufactures plastic products.*
• **manufacture noun** [no plural] *the manufacture of computers*

manufacturer /ˌmænjə'fæktʃᵊrəʳ/ **noun**
a company that makes something: *a shoe manufacturer*

manufacturing /ˌmænjʊ'fækʃərɪŋ/ **noun** [no plural]
the business of producing goods in large numbers in a factory: *car manufacturing*

many /'meni/ **pronoun, quantifier**
1 A1 a large number of: *I don't have many clothes.* ◦ *Were there many cars on the road?* ◦ *I've got* ***so many*** *things to do this morning.*
2 how many? A1 used in questions to ask about the number of something: *How many hours a week do you work?*

> **Common mistake: many, much, or a lot of?**
>
> **Many** is used with countable nouns in negative sentences and questions. **Much** is used with uncountable nouns in negative sentences and questions.
>
> *Do you have many friends?*
> *I don't earn much money.*
>
> **A lot of** can be used to mean **much** or **many.** In positive sentences it sounds formal to use **much** or **many.** You can use **a lot of** instead.
>
> ~~*There was much enthusiasm for the project.*~~
> *There was a lot of enthusiasm for the project.*

map /mæp/ **noun**
A2 a picture that shows where countries, towns, roads, etc. are: *a road map* ◦ *a map of Europe*

marathon /'mærəθᵊn/ **noun**
a race in which people run for 26.2 miles/42 km

marble /'mɑːbl/ **noun** [no plural]
hard, smooth stone that is often used for decoration

march[1] /mɑːtʃ/ **noun**
an organized event where people walk in a group to show that they disagree with something: *We* ***went on a march*** *to protest against the new law.*

march[2] /mɑːtʃ/ **verb**
1 to walk somewhere as a group to show that you disagree with something: *They marched to London to protest against the war.*
2 When soldiers march, they walk together with regular steps.

map

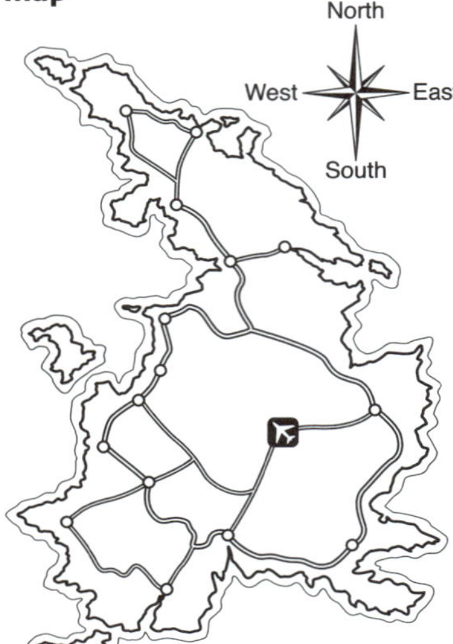

3 to walk somewhere fast: *She marched off angrily.*

March /mɑːtʃ/ **noun**
A1 the third month of the year

margarine /ˌmɑːdʒəˈriːn/ **noun** [no plural]
a soft food that you put on bread and use in cooking

margin /ˈmɑːdʒɪn/ **noun**
an empty space down the side of a page of writing: *You can make notes* ***in the margin****.*

mark[1] /mɑːk/ **noun**
1 A2 a number or letter that is written on a piece of work, saying how good the work is: *She always gets good marks in English.*
2 a dirty area on something: *He's left dirty marks all over the carpet.*

mark[2] /mɑːk/ **verb**
1 to show where something is by drawing or putting something somewhere: *I've marked my street on the map for you.*
2 to read a piece of written work and write on it how good or bad it is: *I marked essays last night.*

marker /ˈmɑːkəʳ/ **noun**
a thick pen used especially for writing on boards
→ See **The Classroom** on page C4

market

market[1] /ˈmɑːkɪt/ **noun**
1 A2 a place where people go to buy or sell things, often outside: *a flower market* ◦ *a market stall*
2 all the people who want to buy a particular thing, or the area where they live: *South America is our largest market.*
3 **on the market** ready to buy: *His house is on the market.*

market[2] /ˈmɑːkɪt/ **verb**
to try to sell things using advertising: *They market their products very cleverly.*
• **marketing noun** [no plural] *a marketing campaign*

marmalade /ˈmɑːməleɪd/ **noun** [no plural]
a sweet soft food made with oranges or lemons that you put on bread: *a jar of marmalade*

marriage /ˈmærɪdʒ/ **noun**
1 B1 the legal relationship of two people who are married: *It was a very happy marriage.*
2 the ceremony at which two people marry

married /ˈmærid/ **adj**
1 If someone is married, they are in a legal relationship with someone else as their husband or wife: *a married couple* ◦ *She's been* ***married to*** *David for nearly ten years.*

a
b
c
d
e
f
g
h
i
j
k
l
m
n
o
p
q
r
s
t
u
v
w
x
y
z

2 get married to begin a legal relationship with someone as your husband or wife: *We got married last year.*

marry /ˈmæri/ **verb** (**marrying**, **married**)
B1 to begin a legal relationship with someone as their husband or wife: *Will you marry me?* ◦ *He never married.*

marsh /mɑːʃ/ **noun**
an area of soft, wet land

martial art /ˌmɑːʃəl ˈɑːt/ **noun**
a sport that is based on traditional forms of fighting from Asia: *Kung fu and karate are martial arts.*

marvellous UK (US **marvelous**) /ˈmɑːvələs/ **adj**
B1 very good: *What a marvellous idea!*

masculine /ˈmæskjəlɪn/ **adj**
having qualities that are like a man: *She had a rather masculine voice.*

mash /mæʃ/ **verb**
to crush food until it is soft: *mashed potatoes*

mask

mask /mɑːsk/ **noun**
a cover for the face: *a surgeon's mask*

mass[1] /mæs/ **noun**
1 a lot of something together, with no clear shape: *Her hair was a mass of blond curls.*
2 masses informal a large amount or number of something: *There was **masses of** food.*

mass[2] /mæs/ **adj**
affecting a lot of people: *mass destruction* ◦ *a mass murderer*

massacre /ˈmæsəkər/ **noun**
the killing of a lot of people
• **massacre verb** (**massacring**, **massacred**) to kill a lot of people

massage /ˈmæsɑːdʒ/ **noun**
the action of pressing and rubbing parts of someone's body in order to make them relax: *She gave me a foot massage.*
• **massage verb** (**massaging**, **massaged**)

massive /ˈmæsɪv/ **adj**
very big: *a massive building*

mast /mɑːst/ **noun**
a tall pole on a boat that supports its sails

master[1] /ˈmɑːstər/ **noun**
1 In the past, a servant's master was the man that they worked for.
2 someone who does something very well: *He was a **master of** disguise.*

master[2] /ˈmɑːstər/ **verb**
to learn how to do something well: *I lived in Italy for a year but didn't master the language.*

mat /mæt/ **noun**
a piece of material that you put on the floor, in order to protect it

match[1] /mætʃ/ **noun**
1 A2 a sports competition in which two people or teams compete against each other: *a football match*
2 a thin, wooden stick that makes fire when you rub one end of it against a rough surface: *a box of matches*

match[2] /mætʃ/ **verb**
1 B1 If two things match, they are the same colour or type: *I can't find anything to match my green shirt.* ◦ *Your socks don't match.*
2 B1 to choose someone or something that is suitable for a particular person, activity, or purpose: *In this exercise you have to match each capital city to its country.*

mate[1] /meɪt/ **noun**
1 B1 UK informal a friend: *She's my best mate.*
2 UK informal You call a man 'mate' when you are speaking to him informally: *Thanks, mate.*
3 an animal's sexual partner

mate[2] /meɪt/ **verb** (**mating**, **mated**)
When animals mate, they have sex in order to produce babies.

material /məˈtɪəriəl/ **noun**
1 B1 cloth for making clothes, curtains, etc.: *Her dress was made of a soft, silky material.*
2 B1 documents, recorded information, etc. that are used for a particular activity: *She writes all her own teaching materials.*
3 a solid substance from which things can be made: *building materials*

maternal /məˈtɜːnəl/ **adj**
1 like a mother
2 A maternal relation is part of your mother's family: *He's my maternal grandfather.*

mathematical /ˌmæθəmˈætɪkəl/ **adj**
relating to mathematics

mathematics /mæθəmˈætɪks/ **noun**
[no plural] formal
maths

maths /mæθs/ **noun** [no plural] (US **math**)
A2 the study or science of numbers and shapes: *Are you good at maths?*

matter¹ /ˈmætəʳ/ **noun**
1 a subject or situation that you need to think about or do something about: *Could I talk to you about a personal matter?* ◦ *This is a matter of some importance.*
2 [no plural] In science, matter is the physical substances that exist in the universe.
3 what's the matter? A2 used to ask about the reason for a problem: *What's the matter with your leg?*
4 no matter how, what, when, etc. used to say that something cannot be changed: *I never manage to lose any weight, no matter how hard I try.*
5 as a matter of fact used to say that something is true, especially when it is surprising: *As a matter of fact, I used to live near him.*

matter² /ˈmætəʳ/ **verb**
A2 to be important: *We were late, but it didn't seem to matter.* ◦ *It doesn't* ***matter to*** *me whether he comes or not.*

mattress /ˈmætrəs/ **noun**
the soft part of a bed that you lie on

mature¹ /məˈtjʊəʳ/ **adj**
1 completely grown or developed: *mature trees*
2 behaving well, like an adult: *She seems very mature for 13.*
→ Opposite **immature adj**

mature² /məˈtjʊəʳ/ **verb** (**maturing, matured**)
1 to become completely grown or developed
2 to start to behave well, like an adult: *Girls mature sooner than boys.*

maximum¹ /ˈmæksɪməm/ **adj**
B1 the largest that is allowed or possible: *the maximum temperature*
→ Opposite **minimum adj**

maximum² /ˈmæksɪməm/ **noun**
B1 the largest amount that is allowed or possible: *The school has* ***a maximum of*** *30 students per class.*

may /meɪ/ **verb**
1 A2 used to talk about what is possibly true or will possibly happen: *There may be other problems that we don't know about.* ◦ *I think I may have a cold.*
2 B1 formal used when you ask if you can do something or say that someone can do something: *May I be excused, please?* ◦ *You may begin.*

> **Common mistake: may be or maybe?**
>
> **May be** is written as two separate words when **be** is used as a verb.
> *I may be late this evening.*
> *~~I maybe late this evening.~~*
> **Maybe** is an adverb, and is written as one word.
> *Maybe we should do it tomorrow.*
> *~~May be we should do it tomorrow.~~*

May /meɪ/ **noun**
A1 the fifth month of the year

maybe /ˈmeɪbi/ **adv**
1 A2 possibly: *Maybe we're too early.* ◦ *It could take a month, or maybe more, to complete.*

2 A2 used to suggest something politely: *Maybe we should start again.*

mayonnaise /ˌmeɪəˈneɪz/ **noun** [no plural]
a thick, white, cold sauce that is made from eggs and oil

mayor /meəʳ/ **noun**
the leader of the group that is in charge of a town or city

me /miː/ **pronoun**
A1 the person who is speaking or writing: *She gave me some money.* ◦ *She never gave it to me.* ◦ *Lydia is three years younger than me.*

meal /miːl/ **noun**
A1 an occasion when you sit down to eat food, or the food that you eat at that time: *a three-course meal* ◦ *We* ***had*** *a nice* ***meal*** *together.*

mean[1] /miːn/ **verb** (**meant**)
1 A2 to have a particular meaning: *What does this word mean?* ◦ *The green light means go.*
2 I mean A2 something that you say in order to correct yourself: *We went there in May – I mean June.*
3 mean to do *something* B1 to want to do something: *I didn't mean to hurt her.*
4 be meaning to do *something* B1 to be planning to do something: *I've been meaning to call you for weeks.*
5 B1 to have a particular result: *These changes will mean better health care for everyone.*
6 B1 to intend to express a fact or opinion: *I didn't* ***mean*** *that* ***as*** *a criticism.* ◦ *What exactly do you* ***mean by*** *'old-fashioned'?*
7 B1 to have an important emotional effect on someone: *It wasn't a valuable picture but it* ***meant a lot to*** *me.*

> **Common mistake: mean**
> When you want to ask the meaning of something, remember to use **does** or **do**.
> *What does this word mean?*
> ~~*What means this word?*~~

mean[2] /miːn/ **adj**
1 not kind: *I thought my sister was being* ***mean to*** *me.*
2 UK A mean person does not like spending money, especially on other people: *He's too mean to buy her a ring.*

meaning /ˈmiːnɪŋ/ **noun**
1 B1 The meaning of words, signs, or actions is what they represent or show: *The word has several meanings.*
2 purpose: *She felt that her life had no meaning.*

means /miːnz/ **noun**
1 (plural **means**) a way of doing something: *We had no* ***means of*** *communication.*
2 money: *We don't have* ***the means to*** *buy the house.*
3 by no means not at all: *I am by no means an expert.*

meant /ment/
past tense and past participle of mean

meantime /ˈmiːnˌtaɪm/ **noun**
in the meantime in the time between two things happening, or while something else is happening: *Your computer will arrive on Friday. In the meantime, you can use Julie's.*

meanwhile /ˈmiːnˌwaɪl/ **adv**
B1 in the time between two things happening, or while something else is happening: *The mother is ill. The child, meanwhile, is with her grandparents.*

measure[1] /ˈmeʒəʳ/ **verb** (**measuring**, **measured**)
1 to find the size, weight, amount, or speed of something: *I've measured all the windows.*
2 to be a certain size: *The whale measured around 60 feet in length.*

measure[2] /ˈmeʒəʳ/ **noun**
something that is done so that a bad situation is stopped: *We must* ***take measures*** *to stop the spread of the disease.* ◦ *security measures*

measurement /ˈmeʒəmənt/ **noun**
the size and shape of something: *I've* ***taken measurements*** *of all the rooms.*

meat /miːt/ **noun** [no plural]
A1 the soft parts of animals, used as food: *I don't eat meat.*
→ See **Food** on page C7

mechanic /məˈkænɪk/ **noun**
A2 someone whose job is to repair machines: *a car mechanic*

mechanical /məˈkænɪkəl/ **adj**
relating to or operated by machines: *a mechanical engineer*
• **mechanically** **adv**

medal /ˈmedəl/ **noun**
a piece of metal given as a prize in a competition or given to someone who has been very brave: *a bronze medal* ◦ *an Olympic medal*

the media /ˈmiːdiə/ **plural noun**
television, newspapers, magazines, and radio considered as a group: *The issue has been much discussed* ***in the media****.*

medical /ˈmedɪkəl/ **adj**
relating to medicine and different ways of curing illness: *medical treatment* ◦ *a medical student*
• **medically** **adv**

medicine /ˈmedɪsən/ **noun**
1 A2 something that you drink or eat when you are ill, to stop you being ill: *cough medicine* ◦ *Have you* ***taken*** *your* ***medicine*** *today?*
2 B1 [no plural] the science of treating and preventing illness

medieval /ˌmediˈiːvəl/ **adj** (also **mediaeval**)
relating to the period in Europe between about AD 500 and AD 1500: *a medieval building*

medium /ˈmiːdiəm/ **adj**
B1 in the middle of a group of different amounts or sizes: *people of medium weight* ◦ *The shirt comes in small, medium, and large.*

meet /miːt/ **verb** (**met**)
1 A1 to come to the same place as someone else: *We met for coffee last Sunday.* ◦ *I met an old friend at a party last Saturday.*
2 A1 to see and speak to someone for the first time: *'This is Helen.' 'Pleased to meet you.'*
3 B1 to wait at a place for someone or something to arrive: *They met me at the airport.*
4 B1 If a group of people meet, they come to a place in order to do something: *The group meets every Thursday.*

> **Common mistake: meet or visit?**
>
> You **meet** a person, but not a place or thing.
>
> *I met John's parents for the first time last week.*
>
> You **visit** a person, place, or thing.
>
> *I visited my aunt today.*
>
> *We visited Paris and the Eiffel Tower.*

meet up **phrasal verb**
to meet another person in order to do something together: *I* ***met up with*** *a few friends yesterday.*

meeting /ˈmiːtɪŋ/ **noun**
A2 an occasion when people come together for a reason, usually to talk about something: *We're having a meeting on Thursday to discuss the problem.* ◦ *He's* ***in a meeting****.*

melody /ˈmelədi/ **noun** (plural **melodies**)
a song or tune

melon /ˈmelən/ **noun**
A2 a large, round, sweet fruit with a thick, green or yellow skin
→ See **Fruit and Vegetables** on page C8

melt /melt/ **verb**
to change from a solid into a liquid because of heat: *The sun soon melted the ice on the pond.* ◦ *The chocolate had melted in my pocket.*

member /ˈmembər/ **noun**
A2 a person who belongs to a group or an organization: *family members* ◦ *He was a* ***member of*** *the university rowing club.*

membership /ˈmembəʃɪp/ **noun** [no plural]
the fact of belonging to a group or an organization: *I've applied for membership of the union.* ◦ *a membership card*

memorable /ˈmemərəbl/ **adj**
If an occasion is memorable, you will remember it for a long time because it is so good: *That was a memorable evening!*

memorize /ˈmeməraɪz/ **verb** (**memorizing**, **memorized**)
to learn something so that you

remember it exactly: *I've memorized all my friends' birthdays.*

memory /ˈmemᵊri/ **noun** (plural **memories**)
1 B1 your ability to remember things: *I have a good* ***memory for*** *names.*
2 B1 something that you remember: *I have nice* ***memories of*** *my childhood.*
3 A2 the part of a computer where information is stored, or the amount of information that can be stored there: *This computer is more expensive because it has a bigger memory.*

Memory Stick /ˈmemᵊri ˌstɪk/ **noun** trademark
a small piece of equipment that stores information and that can be put into a computer, mobile phone, etc.

men
plural of man

mend /mend/ **verb**
B1 to repair something that is broken or not working correctly: *We need to get the chair mended.*

mental /ˈmentᵊl/ **adj**
relating to the mind: *mental illness*
• **mentally adv** *a mentally ill person*

mention /ˈmenʃᵊn/ **verb**
1 B1 to speak or write a few words about something or someone: *She didn't mention her daughter.* ◦ *He* ***mentioned that*** *he liked skiing.*
2 not to mention used to emphasize the importance of something that you are adding to a list: *The resort has great hotels, not to mention some of the best skiing in the region.*

> **Common mistake: mention**
> Do not use a preposition after the verb **mention.**
> *He didn't mention the price.*
> ~~*He didn't mention about the price.*~~

menu /ˈmenju:/ **noun**
1 A2 a list of food and drinks that you can get in a restaurant: *a dinner menu*
2 A2 a list of choices on a computer screen

meow noun
US spelling of miaow (= the sound that a cat makes)

mercy /ˈmɜ:si/ **noun** [no plural]
kindness that makes you forgive someone and not punish them: *The prisoners pleaded for mercy.*

mere /mɪəʳ/ **adj**
used to emphasize that something is not large or important: *It costs* ***a mere*** *twenty dollars.*

merely /ˈmɪəli/ **adv**
only: *I'm not arguing with you – I'm merely explaining the problem.*

merge /mɜ:dʒ/ **verb**
to join together: *The city's smaller libraries will* ***merge into*** *a large one.*

merit /ˈmerɪt/ **verb** formal
to be important enough to get attention or punishment: *Her crimes were serious enough to merit a prison sentence.*

merry /ˈmeri/ **adj** (**merrier, merriest**)
happy: *Merry Christmas!*

mess[1] /mes/ **noun**
1 B1 an untidy or dirty place or thing: *The house is* ***in a mess.*** ◦ *He* ***makes*** *such* ***a mess*** *in the kitchen.*
2 a situation in which there are a lot of problems: *She told me that her life was a mess.*

mess[2] /mes/ **verb**
mess about/around phrasal verb informal
to do silly things that are not important: *Stop messing around and do your homework!*
mess ***something*** **up phrasal verb** informal
to spoil something, or to do something badly: *Susan messed up the arrangements for the trip.*

message /ˈmesɪdʒ/ **noun**
A1 a piece of written or spoken information that one person gives to another: *Did you* ***get*** *my* ***message****?* ◦ *I called her and left a message.*

messenger /ˈmesɪndʒəʳ/ **noun**
someone who takes a message between two people

messy /ˈmesi/ **adj** (**messier, messiest**)
B1 untidy or dirty: *messy hair* ◦ *a messy house/car*

met /met/
past tense and past participle of meet

metal /ˈmetᵊl/ **noun**
B1 a hard, shiny material such as iron, gold, or silver

meter /ˈmiːtəʳ/ **noun**
1 a piece of equipment for measuring the amount of something such as electricity, time, or light: *a gas meter* ◦ *a parking meter*
2 US spelling of metre

method /ˈmeθəd/ **noun**
B1 a way of doing something, often one that involves a system or plan: *What's the best* ***method of*** *solving this problem?* ◦ *traditional teaching methods*

metre UK (US **meter**) /ˈmiːtəʳ/ **noun** (written abbreviation **m**)
A2 a unit for measuring length, equal to 100 centimetres: *Our bedroom is five metres wide.*

metric /ˈmetrɪk/ **adj**
The metric system of measurement uses units based on the gram, metre, and litre.

metro /ˈmetrəʊ/ **noun**
an underground railway system in a large city: *the Paris metro*

miaow UK (US **meow**) /ˌmiːˈaʊ/ **noun**
the sound that a cat makes

mice /maɪs/
plural of mouse

microphone /ˈmaɪkrəfəʊn/ **noun**
a piece of electrical equipment for recording sounds, or for making sounds louder

microphone

microscope /ˈmaɪkrəskəʊp/ **noun**
a piece of scientific equipment that uses lenses (= pieces of curved glass) to make very small objects look bigger

microwave /ˈmaɪkrəʊweɪv/ **noun**
an electric oven that uses waves of energy to quickly cook food or make it warmer
→ See **The Kitchen** on page C10

microscope

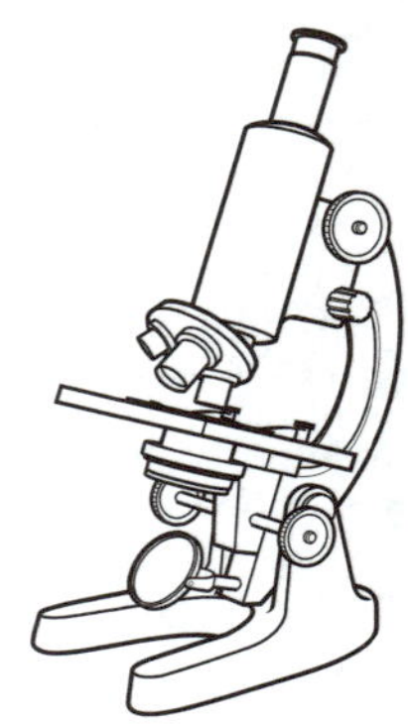

midday /ˌmɪdˈdeɪ/ **noun** [no plural]
A2 twelve o'clock in the middle of the day: *Beware the heat of the midday sun.*

middle¹ /ˈmɪdl/ **noun**
1 A2 the centre of something: *We live right* ***in the middle*** *of the town.*
2 B1 not the beginning or the end but the time in between: *The letter should arrive by* ***the middle of*** *next week.*
3 be in the middle of doing *something* B1 to be busy: *I can't talk now – I'm in the middle of cooking a meal.*

middle² /ˈmɪdl/ **adj**
in a central position: *The middle layer is made of plastic.*

middle-aged /ˌmɪdlˈeɪdʒd/ **adj**
B1 in the middle of your life before you are old: *a middle-aged couple*

midnight /ˈmɪdnaɪt/ **noun** [no plural]
A2 twelve o'clock at night

might /maɪt/ **verb**
1 A2 used to talk about what will possibly happen: *I might come.* ◦ *It might be finished by Thursday.*
2 B1 used to talk about what is possibly true: *I think Isabel might be pregnant.*

mighty /ˈmaɪti/ **adj**
very powerful or successful

migraine /ˈmaɪgreɪn/ **noun**
a very bad pain in the head, often one that makes you feel sick: *I have a migraine.*

migrate /maɪˈgreɪt/ **verb** (**migrating**, **migrated**)
When birds or animals migrate, they travel from one place to another at

the same time each year: *Many birds migrate to Africa for the winter.*

migration /maɪˈɡreɪʃᵊn/ **noun** [no plural]
the travel of birds or animals from one place to another at the same time each year.

mild /maɪld/ **adj**
1 B1 If the weather in winter is mild, it is not cold.
2 Mild food does not have a strong taste: *a mild curry*
→ Opposite **hot** **adj**

mile /maɪl/ **noun**
B1 a unit for measuring distance, equal to 1609 metres or 1760 yards: *The nearest station is two miles from here.*

military /ˈmɪlɪtri/ **adj**
relating to the army, navy, or air force: *military service*

military service /ˌmɪlɪtri ˈsɜːvɪs/ **noun** [no plural]
army training that young people must do in some countries: *He has to* ***do*** *his* ***military service*** *before going to university.*

milk[1] /mɪlk/ **noun** [no plural]
A1 a white liquid that babies and baby animals drink that comes from their mothers' bodies: *a carton of milk* ◦ *breast milk*

milk[2] /mɪlk/ **verb**
to take milk from a cow using your hands or a machine

milkshake /ˈmɪlkʃeɪk/ **noun**
a sweet drink made of milk and chocolate or fruit, and also sometimes ice cream: *a chocolate milkshake*

mill /mɪl/ **noun**
1 a place where grain is pressed and made into flour: *a flour mill*
2 a factory where one material is made: *a cotton mill* ◦ *a paper mill*

millennium /mɪˈleniəm/ **noun** (plural **millennia**)
a period of 1000 years

millilitre UK (US **milliliter**) /ˈmɪlɪˌliːtəʳ/ **noun** (written abbreviation **ml**)
A2 a unit for measuring liquid, equal to 0.001 litres

millimetre UK (US **millimeter**) /ˈmɪlɪˌmiːtəʳ/ **noun**
B1 a unit for measuring length, equal to 0.001 metres

million /ˈmɪljən/
1 A2 the number 1,000,000
2 **millions** informal a lot: *I've seen that movie millions of times.*

millionaire /ˌmɪljəˈneəʳ/ **noun**
a very rich person

mime /maɪm/ **verb** (**miming**, **mimed**)
to act or tell a story without speaking, using movements of your hands, body, and face
• **mime** **noun** *a mime artist*

mimic /ˈmɪmɪk/ **verb** (**mimicking**, **mimicked**)
to copy the way someone talks and behaves, usually to make people laugh: *He's always getting into trouble for mimicking his teachers.*

mince[1] /mɪns/ **noun** [no plural] UK
meat, usually from a cow, that has been cut into very small pieces

mince[2] /mɪns/ **verb** (**mincing**, **minced**)
to cut food into small pieces in a machine: *Mince the garlic and add it to the onions.* ◦ *minced beef/onions*

mind[1] /maɪnd/ **noun**
1 B1 someone's memory or their ability to think and feel emotions: *She has a very logical mind.*
2 **make your mind up** B1 to make a decision: *I haven't made up my mind whether to go yet.*
3 **change your mind** B1 to change a decision or opinion: *We've changed our minds about selling the house.*
4 **cross *someone's* mind** If an idea crosses your mind, you think about it for a short time: *It crossed my mind that she might not want to go.*
5 **have/keep an open mind** to wait until you know all the facts before you form an opinion about something or judge someone: *We're keeping an open mind about the causes of the fire.*
6 **have *something* on your mind** to worry about something: *Jim has a lot on his mind at the moment.*
7 **bear/keep *someone/something* in**

mind to remember someone or something that may be useful in the future: *I'll keep you in mind if another job comes up.*
8 be out of your mind informal to be crazy or very stupid: *You must be out of your mind going out in this weather.*
9 put/set *someone's* mind at rest to say something to someone to stop them worrying: *Talking to the doctor put my mind at rest.*

mind² /maɪnd/ **verb**
1 do you mind?/would you mind? A2 something you say when politely asking someone to do something: *Do you mind not smoking in here, please?*
2 never mind A2 used to tell someone not to worry about something they have done: *'I forgot to bring any money.' 'Never mind, you can pay me next week.'*
3 I don't mind A2 used to say the choice is not important when responding to an offer or suggestion: *'Would you like tea or coffee?' 'I don't mind.'*
4 B1 to be angry or worried about something: *Would he mind if I borrowed his book?* ◦ *I don't mind driving.*
5 B1 something you say when telling someone to be careful with something dangerous: *Mind the iron – it's hot!*
6 mind you something you say before saying the opposite of what you have just said: *We had a really nice holiday. Mind you, the weather was terrible.*

mine¹ /maɪn/ **pronoun**
A2 the thing or things belonging to the person who is speaking or writing: *'Whose book is this?' 'It's mine.'* ◦ *Can I use your pen? Mine's not working.*

mine² /maɪn/ **noun**
1 a hole in the ground where people dig out coal, gold, etc.
2 a bomb hidden in the ground or water that explodes when it is touched: *He was killed when he drove over a mine.*

miner /ˈmaɪnəʳ/ **noun**
someone who works in a hole in the ground, digging out coal, gold, etc.: *a coal miner*

mineral /ˈmɪnᵊrᵊl/ **noun**
1 a valuable or useful substance that is dug out of the ground: *the region's rich mineral deposits*
2 a chemical that your body needs to stay healthy

mineral water /ˈmɪnᵊrᵊl ˌwɔːtəʳ/ **noun**
A2 water that is taken from the ground

mingle /ˈmɪŋgl/ **verb** (**mingling**, **mingled**)
to mix, or be mixed: *The smell of fresh coffee mingled with cigarette smoke.*

miniature /ˈmɪnətʃəʳ/ **adj**
very small: *a miniature camera*

minibus /ˈmɪnibʌs/ **noun**
a small bus with seats for about ten people

minimum¹ /ˈmɪnɪməm/ **adj**
B1 the smallest that is allowed or possible: *There is a minimum charge of $5 for postage.*
→ Opposite **maximum adj**

minimum² /ˈmɪnɪməm/ **noun**
B1 the smallest amount that is allowed or possible: *Please keep noise to an absolute minimum.*
→ Opposite **maximum noun**

mining /ˈmaɪnɪŋ/ **noun** [no plural]
the process of digging coal, gold, etc. out of the ground

miniskirt /ˈmɪniˌskɜːt/ **noun**
a very short skirt
→ See **Clothes** on page C5

minister /ˈmɪnɪstəʳ/ **noun**
1 a politician who has an important position in the government: *a health minister*
2 a religious leader in some Christian churches

ministry /ˈmɪnɪstri/ **noun** (plural **ministries**)
a government department that is responsible for a particular subject: *the Ministry of Defence*

minor /ˈmaɪnəʳ/ **adj**
not important or serious: *There are a few minor problems.* ◦ *He suffered only minor injuries.*
→ Opposite **major adj**

minority /maɪˈnɒrəti/ **noun** (plural **minorities**)
less than half of a group of people or things: *The violence was caused by a* ***small minority*** *of football supporters.* ◦ *I agreed to the suggestion, but I was* ***in the minority****.*
→ Opposite **majority** noun

mint /mɪnt/ **noun**
1 a sweet with a fresh, strong taste
2 [no plural] a plant whose leaves are used to add flavour to food and drinks

minus[1] /ˈmaɪnəs/ **preposition**
1 A2 used when the second of two numbers should be taken away from the first: *Five minus three is two.*
2 without something: *She arrived at the meeting minus her briefcase.*

minus[2] /ˈmaɪnəs/ **adj**
A minus number is less than zero: *The temperature last night was minus ten.*

minute[1] /ˈmɪnɪt/ **noun**
1 A1 a period of time equal to 60 seconds: *It'll take you thirty minutes to get to the airport.* ◦ *She was ten minutes late for her interview.*
2 A2 a very short period of time: *I'll be with you* ***in a minute****.*
3 wait/just a minute B1 used when asking someone to wait for a short time: *Just a minute – I've left my coat in the restaurant.*
4 at the last minute at the latest time possible: *The concert was cancelled at the last minute.*
5 (at) any minute very soon: *Her train will be arriving any minute.*

minute[2] /maɪˈnjuːt/ **adj**
very small: *Her hands are minute.*

miracle /ˈmɪrəkl/ **noun**
1 something that is very surprising or difficult to believe: *It's a* ***miracle that*** *he's still alive.*
2 something very strange that happens which you cannot explain

miraculous /mɪˈrækjələs/ **adj**
very surprising or difficult to believe: *He made a miraculous recovery from his illness.*
• **miraculously** **adv** *One person miraculously survived the crash.*

mirror /ˈmɪrəʳ/ **noun**
A2 a piece of special glass in which you can see yourself: *a bathroom mirror* ◦ *He looked at himself* ***in the mirror****.*
→ See **The Living Room** on page C11

misbehave /ˌmɪsbɪˈheɪv/ **verb** (**misbehaving**, **misbehaved**)
to behave badly

mischief /ˈmɪstʃɪf/ **noun** [no plural]
behaviour, usually of a child, that is slightly bad

mischievous /ˈmɪstʃɪvəs/ **adj**
behaving in a way that is slightly bad but not serious: *a mischievous five-year-old*

miserable /ˈmɪzᵊrəbl/ **adj**
1 B1 sad: *I woke up feeling miserable.*
2 bad and making you sad: *People are living in miserable conditions.*

misery /ˈmɪzᵊri/ **noun** [no plural]
sadness and suffering: *The war brought misery to millions of people.*

misfortune /mɪsˈfɔːtʃuːn/ **noun**
something bad that happens to you: *He* ***had the misfortune*** *to fall in love with a married woman.*

misleading /mɪsˈliːdɪŋ/ **adj**
making someone believe something that is not true: *misleading information*

miss /mɪs/ **verb**
1 A2 to feel sad about someone or something that you have stopped seeing or having: *I'll miss you when you go.* ◦ *He misses having a room of his own.*
2 A2 to not go to something: *I missed my class this morning.*
3 A2 to arrive too late to get on a bus, train, or plane: *If I don't leave now, I'll miss my train.*
4 B1 to not see or hear something: *I missed that. Could you repeat it?*
5 miss a chance/opportunity B1 to not use an opportunity to do something: *She missed the chance to speak to him.*
6 to fail to hit or catch something, or to score a goal: *The bomb missed its target.* ◦ *It should have been such an easy goal but he missed.*

miss *someone/something* out **phrasal verb** UK
to not include someone or something

Miss /mɪs/ **noun**
(A1) a title for a girl or woman who is not married: *Miss Olivia Allenby* ◦ *Tell Miss Russell I'm here.*

missile /ˈmɪsaɪl/ **noun**
an explosive weapon that can travel long distances through the air: *nuclear missiles*

missing /ˈmɪsɪŋ/ **adj**
1 (A2) lost, not in the usual place: *Her daughter* ***went missing*** *a week ago.*
2 (B1) not included in something: *There are a couple of things* ***missing from*** *the list.*

mission /ˈmɪʃᵊn/ **noun**
an important job, usually travelling somewhere: *The soldiers' mission is to destroy the bridge.*

mist /mɪst/ **noun**
small drops of water in the air that make it difficult to see objects that are not near: *Gradually the mist cleared and the sun began to shine.*

mistake¹ /mɪˈsteɪk/ **noun**
1 (A2) something that you do or think that is wrong: *a spelling mistake* ◦ *He* ***made*** *a lot of* ***mistakes*** *in his test.*
2 **by mistake** (B1) If you do something wrong by mistake, you do it without wanting to: *I picked up someone else's book by mistake.*

Common mistake: mistake
Remember to use the correct verb with this word.
I always ***make mistakes*** *in my essays.*
~~*I always do mistakes in my essays.*~~

mistake² /mɪˈsteɪk/ **verb** (**mistaking**, **mistook**, **mistaken**)
to not understand something correctly: *I think you mistook what I said.*
mistake *someone* for *someone* **phrasal verb**
to think that someone is a different person: *People sometimes mistake him for a girl.*

misty /ˈmɪsti/ **adj** (**mistier**, **mistiest**)
If the weather is misty, there is a cloud of small drops of water in the air: *a cold and misty morning*

misunderstand /ˌmɪsʌndəˈstænd/ **verb** (**misunderstood**)
to not understand someone or something correctly: *He misunderstood the question completely.*

misunderstanding /ˌmɪsʌndəˈstændɪŋ/ **noun**
a situation in which someone does not understand something correctly: *I think there's been a misunderstanding. I never ordered these chairs.*

mix¹ /mɪks/ **verb**
1 (A2) to put different things together in order to make something new: ***Mix*** *the powder* ***with*** *water to form a paste.* ◦ *Put the chocolate, butter, and egg in a bowl and* ***mix*** *them all* ***together.***
2 (B1) to have two or more qualities, or to do two or more activities, etc. at the same time: *a feeling of anger mixed with sadness*
3 to meet and talk to people: *She enjoys going to parties and* ***mixing with*** *people.*
mix *something* up **phrasal verb**
to make a group of things untidy: *The books were all mixed up in a box.*

mix² /mɪks/ **noun** [no plural]
(B1) a combination of things or people, often in a group: *There's a good* ***mix of*** *nationalities in the class.*

mixed /mɪkst/ **adj**
1 combining different things: *a mixed salad* ◦ *The study produced mixed results.*
2 UK for both males and females: *Our children go to a* ***mixed school.***

mixture /ˈmɪkstʃəʳ/ **noun**
1 two or more different things or people that have been put together: *Add milk to the mixture and stir until smooth.* ◦ *an odd mixture of people*
2 [no plural] a combination of two or more ideas, qualities, styles, etc.: *Their house is decorated in a mixture of styles.*

ml
written abbreviation for millilitre: a unit for measuring liquid

mm
written abbreviation for millimetre: a unit for measuring length

moan /məʊn/ **verb**
1 to say that something is wrong or that you are angry about something: *She's always* ***moaning about*** *work.*
2 to make a low sound, especially because part of your body hurts: *He lay on the floor moaning.*
• **moan** **noun**

mobile phone UK (also **mobile**) (US usually **cell phone**, **cell**)
A1 a telephone that you can carry everywhere with you: *Call me* ***on*** *my* ***mobile****.*

mobile phone *UK*, **cell phone** *US*

mock /mɒk/ **verb**
to laugh at someone in a way that is not kind: *The other children mocked him whenever he spoke.*

modal verb /ˌməʊdəl ˈvɜːb/ **noun** (also **modal**)
B1 a verb, for example 'can', 'might', or 'must', that is used before another verb to show that something is possible, necessary, etc.

model[1] /ˈmɒdəl/ **noun**
1 A2 a smaller copy of a real object: *He makes models as a hobby.*
2 A2 a particular type of machine or car that a company makes: *I think her car is a slightly older model.*
3 B1 someone whose job is wearing clothes for photographs or fashion shows: *a top fashion model*

model[2] /ˈmɒdəl/ **verb** (**modelling**, **modelled**)
to wear clothes in fashion shows and photographs as a model: *She's been modelling for years.*

modem /ˈməʊdem/ **noun**
a piece of equipment that is used to send information from a computer through a telephone system

moderate /ˈmɒdərət/ **adj**
average in size or amount and not too much: *Eating a moderate amount of fat is healthy.*
• **moderately** **adv**

modern /ˈmɒdən/ **adj**
1 A2 designed and made using the most recent ideas and methods: ***modern art/architecture***
2 B1 relating to the present time and not to the past: *modern society* ◦ *the stresses of modern life*

modest /ˈmɒdɪst/ **adj**
A modest person does not talk about how good they are: *He's very modest about his achievements.*
• **modestly** **adv** *She spoke modestly about her work.*

moist /mɔɪst/ **adj**
slightly wet: *Keep the soil moist but not wet.*

moisture /ˈmɔɪstʃər/ **noun** [no plural]
very small drops of water in the air or on a surface

mold **noun**
US spelling of mould

moldy **noun**
US spelling of mouldy

mole /məʊl/ **noun**
1 a small, dark mark on the skin
2 a small animal with black fur that lives under the ground

molecule /ˈmɒlɪkjuːl/ **noun**
the smallest unit of a substance, with one or more atoms

mom /mɒm/ **noun** US informal (UK **mum**)
mother: *Can we go now, Mom?*

moment /ˈməʊmənt/ **noun**
1 A2 a very short period of time: *I'll be back* ***in a moment****.* ◦ ***For a moment****, I thought it was Anna.* ◦ *Could you* ***wait a moment****?*
2 B1 a point in time: *Just* ***at that moment****, the phone rang.*
3 **at the moment** A2 now: *She's not here at the moment.*
4 **for the moment** If you do something for the moment, you are doing it now, but might do something different in the future: *Let's carry on with what we agreed for the moment.*

a b c d e f g h i j k l m n o p q r s t u v w x y z

monarch /ˈmɒnək/ **noun**
a king or queen

monarchy /ˈmɒnəki/ **noun** (plural **monarchies**)
a system of government in which a country is ruled by a king or queen

monastery /ˈmɒnəstᵊri/ **noun** (plural **monasteries**)
a building where men live as a religious group

Monday /ˈmʌndeɪ/ **noun**
A1 the day of the week after Sunday and before Tuesday

money /ˈmʌni/ **noun** [no plural]
A1 the coins or pieces of paper that are used for buying things: *How much money have you got?* ◦ *He* ***spends*** *all his* ***money*** *on clothes.* ◦ *The company's not* ***making*** *(= earning) any* ***money*** *at the moment.*

monitor /ˈmɒnɪtəʳ/ **noun**
a screen that shows information or pictures, usually connected to a computer: *a colour monitor*
→ See **The Office** on page C12

monk /mʌŋk/ **noun**
a member of a group of religious men living away from other people

monkey /ˈmʌŋki/ **noun**
A2 a hairy animal with a long tail that lives in hot countries and climbs trees

monolingual /ˌmɒnəʊˈlɪŋgwᵊl/ **adj**
speaking or using only one language: *This is a monolingual dictionary.*

monotonous /məˈnɒtᵊnəs/ **adj**
always the same and boring: *The work is very monotonous.*

monsoon /mɒnˈsuːn/ **noun**
the season when there is a lot of rain in Southern Asia

monster /ˈmɒnstəʳ/ **noun**
B1 an imaginary creature that is large, ugly, and frightening

month /mʌnθ/ **noun**
1 A1 one of the twelve periods of time that a year is divided into: *Next month will be very busy.*
2 A1 a period of approximately four weeks: *She'll be working here for six months.*

monthly /ˈmʌnθli/ **adj, adv**
B1 happening or made once a month: *a monthly magazine*

monument /ˈmɒnjəmənt/ **noun**
1 something that is built to make people remember a famous person or something important that happened: *a national monument*
2 B1 an old building or place that is important in history: *an ancient monument*

moo /muː/ **noun**
the sound that a cow makes
• **moo verb**

mood /muːd/ **noun**
1 B1 the way someone feels at a particular time: *You're* ***in a good mood****!* ◦ *Ignore him – he's* ***in a bad mood****.*
2 be in the mood for ***something*** to want to do something: *I'm not really in the mood for shopping.*

moon /muːn/ **noun**
A2 the round object that shines in the sky at night and moves around the Earth

moonlight /ˈmuːnlaɪt/ **noun** [no plural]
light that comes from the moon: *In the moonlight she looked even more beautiful.*

mop[1] /mɒp/ **noun**
a thing for cleaning floors that has a long handle and thick strings at one end

mop[2] /mɒp/ **verb** (**mopping**, **mopped**)
to use a mop: *I mopped the floor.*

moped /ˈməʊped/ **noun**
a small vehicle with two wheels and an engine that is less powerful and smaller than a motorcycle

moral[1] /ˈmɒrᵊl/ **adj**
relating to beliefs about what behaviour is good and what behaviour is bad: *He has very high moral standards.*
• **morally adv** *morally wrong*

moral[2] /ˈmɒrᵊl/ **noun**
something that teaches you how to behave better: *The moral of the story is: never lie.*

morals /ˈmɒrəlz/ **plural noun**
beliefs that you should behave well

and treat other people well: *He doesn't care what he does, he has no morals at all.*

more¹ /mɔːʳ/ **quantifier**
1 A1 something extra to what you have now: *Is there any more soup?* ◦ *Would anyone like some more food?*
2 A1 a greater number or amount of people or things: *There are* ***a lot more*** *people here today than there were yesterday.* ◦ *He knows more about computers than I do.*
3 more and more an increasing number: *More and more people are choosing not to get married.*

> **Common mistake: more**
> The opposite of **more** is **fewer** for plural nouns and **less** for uncountable nouns.
> *He takes more exercise now.*
> *He takes less exercise now.*
> *He smokes fewer cigarettes.*

more² /mɔːʳ/ **adv**
1 more beautiful, difficult, interesting, etc. A1 used to show that someone or something has a greater amount of a quality than someone or something else: *It's* ***more*** *expensive* ***than*** *the others.* ◦ *She's* ***far more*** *intelligent than her sister.*
2 B1 used to show that something happens a greater number of times than before: *We eat out a lot* ***more than*** *we used to.*
3 more and more more as time passes: *It's becoming more and more difficult to pass the exam.*
4 more or less almost: *We've more or less finished work on the house.*

> **Common mistake: more**
> **More** is used to form the comparative of many adjectives and adverbs that have two or more syllables.
> *a more expensive hotel*
> *Could you drive more slowly please?*
> ~~*an expensiver hotel*~~
> The opposite of the adverb **more** is **less**.
> *a less expensive hotel*

moreover /mɔːrˈəʊvəʳ/ **adv** formal also and more importantly: *It is a cheap and, moreover, effective way of dealing with the problem.*

morning /ˈmɔːnɪŋ/ **noun**
1 A1 the first half of the day, from the time when the sun rises until the middle of the day: *Friday morning* ◦ *tomorrow morning* ◦ *I got up late this morning.* ◦ *I listen to the radio* ***in the morning.*** ◦ *I'll pack my bags* ***in the morning*** *(= tomorrow morning).*
2 (good) morning A1 used to say hello to someone in the morning: *Good morning, Sarah!*
3 two, three, etc. o'clock in the morning B1 two, three, etc. o'clock at night: *My car alarm went off at three o'clock in the morning.*

Moslem /ˈmɒzləm/ another spelling of Muslim

mosque /mɒsk/ **noun**
A2 a building where Muslims say their prayers

mosquito /məˈskiːtəʊ/ **noun** (plural **mosquitoes**)
B1 a small flying insect that drinks your blood, and can cause diseases

moss /mɒs/ **noun**
a very small, green plant that grows on the surface of rocks, trees, etc.

most¹ /məʊst/ **adv**
1 the most important, popular, etc. A2 used to show that someone or something has the greatest amount of a quality: *She's the most beautiful girl I've ever seen.* ◦ *There are various reasons but this is the most important.*
2 A2 more than anyone or anything else: *Which subject do you like most?* ◦ *I liked all the cities but I liked Venice* ***most of all.***

> **Common mistake: most**
> The adverb **most** is used to form the superlative of many adjectives and adverbs.
> *the most beautiful actress in the world*

most² /məʊst/ **quantifier**
1 A2 almost all of a group of people or things: *Most people like her.* ◦ *She wears jeans* ***most of*** *the time.*
2 a larger amount than anyone or anything else: *This one costs the most.* ◦ *Which of you earns most?*
3 make the most of ***something*** to

enjoy something as much as you can because it will end soon: *We should make the most of this good weather.*
4 at the most not more than a particular amount or number: *The journey will take an hour at the most.*

most[3] /məʊst/ **determiner**
1 A2 almost all: *I don't eat meat, but I like most types of fish.*
2 B1 the largest amount: *Mike earns the most money of all of us.*

mostly /məʊstli/ **adv**
B1 mainly or most of the time: *The students are mostly Spanish.* ◦ *It's mostly quiet at nights.*

moth /mɒθ/ **noun**
an insect with large wings that often flies at night
→ See picture at **insect**

mother /ˈmʌðəʳ/ **noun**
A1 someone's female parent: *My mother and father are divorced.*

motherhood /ˈmʌðəhʊd/ **noun** [no plural]
being a mother

mother-in-law /ˈmʌðᵊrɪnˌlɔː/ **noun** (plural **mothers-in-law**)
the mother of someone's husband or wife: *My mother-in-law gave me a nice birthday card.*

motion /ˈməʊʃᵊn/ **noun** [no plural]
the action of something moving: *The motion of the boat made him feel sick.*

motivate /ˈməʊtɪveɪt/ **verb** (**motivating**, **motivated**)
to make someone want to do something: *Teaching is all about **motivating** people **to** learn.*

motivated /ˈməʊtɪveɪtɪd/ **adj**
working hard and wanting to succeed: *She is a very motivated student.*

motive /ˈməʊtɪv/ **noun**
a reason for doing something: *The police don't yet know the **motive for** the killing.*

motor /ˈməʊtəʳ/ **noun**
the part of a machine or car, etc. that makes it work: *an electric motor*

motorcycle /ˈməʊtəˌsaɪkl/ **noun** (also **motorbike** /ˈməʊtəbaɪk/)
A2 a vehicle with two wheels and an engine

motorist /ˈməʊtᵊrɪst/ **noun**
someone who drives a car

motorway /ˈməʊtəweɪ/ **noun** UK (US **highway**, **freeway**)
A2 a long, wide road, usually used by traffic travelling fast

mould[1] UK (US **mold**) /məʊld/ **noun**
1 [no plural] a green or black substance that grows in wet places or on old food
2 a container that is used to make something in a particular shape: *a chocolate mould*

mould[2] UK (US **mold**) /məʊld/ **verb**
to make a soft substance a particular shape: *You mould the clay while it is wet.*

mouldy (**mouldier**, **mouldiest**) UK (US **moldy**) /ˈməʊldi/ **adj**
covered with mould: *mouldy cheese*

mound /maʊnd/ **noun**
1 a large pile of something: *There was a mound of clothes on the floor.*
2 a higher area of soil, like a small hill: *an ancient burial mound*

mount /maʊnt/ **verb**
to increase in amount or level: *Concern is mounting over fighting in the region.* ◦ *mounting problems*
mount up phrasal verb
to become a large amount: *My homework is really mounting up this week.*

Mount /maʊnt/ **noun**
used in the names of mountains: *Mount Everest*

mountain

mountain /ˈmaʊntɪn/ **noun**
A2 a very high hill: *to climb a mountain*

mountain bike /ˈmaʊntɪn ˌbaɪk/ **noun**
a bicycle with thick tyres that you can use to ride on hills and rough ground

a b c d e f g h i j k l **m** n o p q r s t u v w x y z

mourn /mɔːn/ **verb**
to feel very sad because someone has died: *He **mourned for** his dead son every day.*

mourning /ˈmɔːnɪŋ/ **noun** [no plural]
a feeling of sadness because someone has died: *The whole nation was **in mourning**.*

mouse /maʊs/ **noun** (plural **mice** /maɪs/)
1 A2 a thing that you move with your hand to control what a computer does
2 A2 a small animal with fur and a long, thin tail

mouse

moustache /məˈstɑːʃ/ **noun** UK (US **mustache**)
B1 a line of hair that some men grow above their mouths

moustache

mouth /maʊθ/ **noun**
1 A1 the part of the face that is used for eating and speaking
→ See **The Body** on page C2
2 the opening or entrance of a cave, tunnel, etc.
3 where a river goes into the sea

mouthful /ˈmaʊθfʊl/ **noun**
the amount of food or drink that you can put into your mouth at one time

move /muːv/ **verb** (**moving**, **moved**)
1 A2 to change place or position, or to make something change place or position: *We **moved** the chairs **to** another room.* ◦ *Someone was **moving around** upstairs.*
2 B1 to go to a different place: *Eventually, she **moved to** Germany.* ◦ *She's **moving into** a new apartment.*
3 move house UK B1 to leave your home in order to live in a new one
4 to make someone feel sad: *I was deeply moved by his speech.*
move in **phrasal verb**
B1 to begin living in a new home: *We're moving in next week.*
move out **phrasal verb**
B1 to stop living in a particular home: *He moved out when he was only 18.*

movement /ˈmuːvmənt/ **noun**
1 a group of people with the same beliefs who work together to do something: *the women's movement*
2 a change of position or place: *His movements were rather clumsy.*

movie /ˈmuːvi/ **noun**
A1 a film: *a Hollywood movie*

movie theater /ˈmuːvi ˌθɪətəʳ/ **noun** US (UK **cinema**)
a building where you go to watch movies

moving /ˈmuːvɪŋ/ **adj**
causing strong feelings of sadness or sympathy: *It's a very moving story.*

mow /məʊ/ **verb** (**mowed**, **mown**)
to cut grass using a machine: *He was mowing the lawn.*

MP /ˌemˈpiː/ **noun**
abbreviation for Member of Parliament: someone who has been elected to represent an area in the UK

MP3 player /empiːˈθriː ˌpleɪəʳ/ **noun**
A2 a piece of electronic equipment that holds and plays music as computer files: *I listened to the song **on** my **MP3 player**.*

mph
written abbreviation for miles per hour: a unit for measuring speed: *a 30 mph speed limit*

Mr /ˈmɪstəʳ/ **noun**
A1 a title for a man, used before his family name or full name: *Good morning, Mr Smith.*

Mrs /ˈmɪsɪz/ **noun**
A1 a title for a married woman, used before her family name or full name: *Hello, Mrs. Jones.*

Ms /mɪz/ **noun**
A2 a title for a woman, used before her family name or full name: *Ms Holly Fox*

Common mistake: Mr, Mrs, Ms, Miss

All these titles are used before someone's name. **Mr** is used for men. **Mrs** is used for women who are married. **Miss** is used for girls or for women who are not married. **Ms** is used for women and does not show if a woman is married. Many women prefer to use this title to **Miss** or **Mrs**. We do not use these titles on their own as a way of speaking to someone. Usually, we use no name.

Can I help you?

~~*Can I help you, Mrs?*~~

much[1] /mʌtʃ/ **quantifier**
1 A1 In questions, 'much' is used to ask about the amount of something: ***How much*** *money will I need?*
2 A2 In negative sentences, 'much' is used to say that there is not a large amount of something: *She doesn't earn much money.* ◦ *Pete didn't say much at dinner.* ◦ *'Is there any coffee left?'* ***'Not much.'***
3 too much/so much A2 a large amount of something, often more than you want: *I'd love to come, but I've got too much work.* ◦ *They have so much money.*

much[2] /mʌtʃ/ **adv**
1 very much A1 a large amount or degree: *I like her very much.*
2 B1 often or a lot: *I don't like curry very much.*
3 much better, bigger, smaller, etc. B1 a lot better, bigger, smaller, etc.: *Their old house was much bigger.*

mud /mʌd/ **noun** [no plural]
wet soil: *He'd been playing football and was covered in mud.*

muddle[1] /ˈmʌdl/ **noun**
a situation in which things are not organized and people do not understand what they should do: *There was a big muddle over who was buying the tickets.* ◦ *I'm* ***in*** *such* ***a muddle*** *with these bills.*

muddle[2] /ˈmʌdl/ **verb** (**muddling**, **muddled**)
get *someone/something* muddled up to think that a person or thing is someone or something else: *I often get Jonathan and his brother muddled up.*

muddy /ˈmʌdi/ **adj** (**muddier**, **muddiest**)
covered with mud: *muddy boots*

mug[1] /mʌg/ **noun**
A2 a large cup with straight sides, used for hot drinks: *a coffee mug*

mug

mug[2] /mʌg/ **verb** (**mugging**, **mugged**)
to attack someone and take something from them in a public place: *He was mugged as he walked across the park.*

mugger /ˈmʌgə^r/ **noun**
a person who attacks people in order to steal their money

multiply /ˈmʌltɪplaɪ/ **verb** (**multiplying**, **multiplied**)
to add one number to itself a particular number of times: *Three* ***multiplied by*** *six equals eighteen.*

mum /mʌm/ **noun** UK informal (US **mom**)
A1 mother: *Can we go now, Mum?*

mumble /ˈmʌmbl/ **verb** (**mumbling**, **mumbled**)
to speak too quietly and not clearly: *He mumbled something about it being a waste of time.*

mummy /ˈmʌmi/ **noun** (plural **mummies**) UK informal
a word for 'mother', used especially by children: *Come here, Mummy!*

murder[1] /ˈmɜːdə^r/ **noun**
B1 the crime of killing someone

murder[2] /ˈmɜːdə^r/ **verb**
B1 to kill someone

murderer /ˈmɜːd^{ə}rə^r/ **noun**
B1 someone who has killed someone

murmur /ˈmɜːmə^r/ **verb**
to speak very quietly: *'Go to sleep now,' she murmured.*

muscle /ˈmʌsl/ **noun**
one of many parts in the body that are connected to your bones and help you to move: *stomach muscles*

museum /mjuːˈziːəm/ **noun**
A1 a building where you can look at important objects connected with art,

history, or science: *a museum of modern art*

mushroom /ˈmʌʃruːm/ **noun**
A2 a type of fungus (= organism like a plant) with a short stem and a round top, some types of which can be eaten

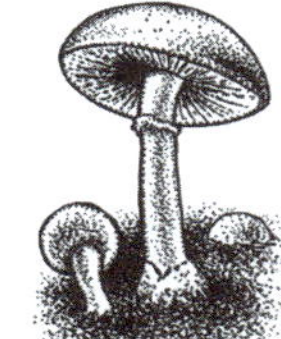
mushrooms

music /ˈmjuːzɪk/ **noun** [no plural]
1 A1 a pattern of sounds that is made by playing instruments or singing, or a recording of this: *pop/dance music* ◦ *classical music* ◦ *He likes* ***listening to music****.* ◦ *a music lesson/teacher*
2 written signs that represent sounds which can be sung or played with instruments: *I never learned to* ***read music*** *(= understand written music).*

musical[1] /ˈmjuːzɪkəl/ **adj**
1 A2 relating to music: *a musical instrument*
2 good at playing music: *She comes from a very musical family.*

musical[2] /ˈmjuːzɪkəl/ **noun**
a play or movie with singing and dancing: *a Broadway musical*

musician /mjuːˈzɪʃən/ **noun**
B1 someone who plays a musical instrument, often as a job: *a jazz musician*

Muslim (also **Moslem**) /ˈmʊzlɪm/ **noun**
someone whose religion is Islam
• **Muslim** **adj**

must strong /mʌst/ weak /məst/ **verb**
1 A2 used to say that it is necessary that something happens or is done: *The meat must be cooked thoroughly.*
2 B1 used to show that you think it is a good idea for someone to do something: *We must meet for lunch.*
3 used to show that you are certain something is true: *You must be exhausted!* ◦ *She must be very wealthy.*

mustache /mʊsˈtæʃ/ **noun**
US spelling of moustache

→ See **Hair** on page C9

mustard /ˈmʌstəd/ **noun** [no plural]
a spicy yellow or brown sauce often eaten in small amounts with meat

mustn't /ˈmʌsənt/
short form of must not: *You mustn't let her know I'm coming.*

mutter /ˈmʌtər/ **verb**
to speak quietly, often when complaining about something: *She walked past me, muttering to herself.*

my /maɪ/ **determiner**
A1 belonging to the person who is speaking or writing: *Tom's my older son.* ◦ *It's not my fault.*

myself /maɪˈself/ **pronoun**
1 A2 used to show that it is the person who is speaking who is affected by an action: *I bought myself a new coat.* ◦ *I looked at myself in the mirror.*
2 **(all) by myself** A2 alone or without anyone else's help: *I live by myself in a small flat.* ◦ *Mummy, I got dressed all by myself!*
3 used to give more attention to the word 'I': *I'll tell her myself.* ◦ *Jack always drinks red wine but I prefer white, myself.*

mysterious /mɪˈstɪəriəs/ **adj**
strange and not explained or understood: *the mysterious death of her son*
• **mysteriously** **adv** *The car was mysteriously in a different place from where we left it.*

mystery /ˈmɪstəri/ **noun** (plural **mysteries**)
B1 something strange that cannot be explained or understood: *They never did solve the mystery of his disappearance.*

myth /mɪθ/ **noun**
1 an ancient story about gods and brave people, often one that explains an event in history or the natural world: *a Greek myth*
2 an idea that is not true but is believed by many people: *It's a myth that men are better drivers than women.*

a b c d e f g h i j k l **m** n o p q r s t u v w x y z

Nn

N, n /en/
the fourteenth letter of the alphabet

nag /næg/ **verb** (**nagging**, **nagged**)
to keep asking someone to do something: *She keeps nagging me to clean my room.*

nail /neɪl/ **noun**
1 a thin piece of metal with a sharp end, used to join pieces of wood together: *a hammer and nails*
2 the hard part at the end of your fingers and toes: *She* ***bites*** *her* ***nails****.*

nails

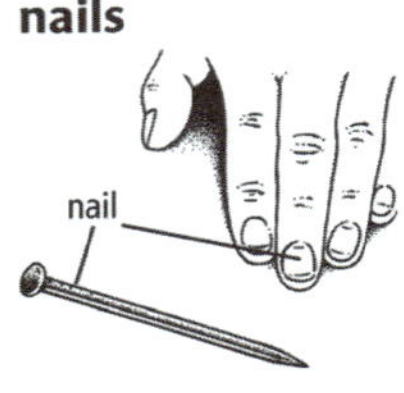

nail polish /ˈneɪl ˌpɒlɪʃ/ **noun** [no plural] (UK also **nail varnish**)
coloured liquid that you put on your nails

naked /ˈneɪkɪd/ **adj**
without clothes: *naked bodies*

name[1] /neɪm/ **noun**
A1 the word or group of words that is used to refer to a person, thing, or place: *What's your name?* ◦ *My name is Alexis.* ◦ *I can't remember the name of the street.*

name[2] /neɪm/ **verb** (**naming**, **named**)
1 B1 to give someone or something a name: *We named our son Edward.*
2 B1 to say what the name of someone or something is: *Can you name three types of monkey?*

nap /næp/ **noun**
a short sleep, especially during the day: *He likes to* ***take a nap*** *after lunch.*

napkin /ˈnæpkɪn/ **noun**
a piece of cloth or paper that you use when you eat to clean your mouth and hands, and keep your clothes clean

nappy /ˈnæpi/ **noun** (plural **nappies**)
UK (US **diaper**)
a thick piece of paper or cloth worn by a baby on its bottom: *She had to* ***change*** *the baby's* ***nappy****.*

narrow

wide

narrow /ˈnærəʊ/ **adj**
B1 not wide, being only a small distance from one side to the other: *a narrow street* ◦ *narrow shoulders*

narrowly /ˈnærəʊli/ **adv**
only by a small amount: *An apple fell from the tree,* ***narrowly missing*** *my head.*

nasty /ˈnɑːsti/ **adj** (**nastier**, **nastiest**)
1 B1 very bad: *He had a nasty cut above his eye.* ◦ *There's a nasty smell in here.*
2 B1 not kind: *She's always being* ***nasty to*** *her little brother.*

nation /ˈneɪʃᵊn/ **noun**
a country or the people living in a country: *African/Asian nations* ◦ *The entire nation mourned her death.*

national /ˈnæʃᵊnᵊl/ **adj**
A2 relating to or shared by all parts of a country: *a national newspaper*

national anthem /ˌnæʃᵊnᵊl ˈænθəm/ **noun**
the official song of a country

nationality /ˌnæʃᵊnˈæləti/ **noun** (plural **nationalities**)
A1 If you have American, British, Swiss, etc. nationality, you are legally a member of that country: *What nationality is she?*

a b c d e f g h i j k l m n o p q r s t u v w x y z

nationwide¹ /ˌneɪʃənˈwaɪd/ **adj**
existing or happening in all parts of a country: *a nationwide search*

nationwide² /ˌneɪʃənˈwaɪd/ **adv**
in all parts of a country: *Schools nationwide don't have enough teachers.*

native¹ /ˈneɪtɪv/ **adj**
1 Your native town or country is the place where you were born: *He returned to his native Algeria.*
2 Your native language is the first language you learn as a child: *native speakers of English*

native² /ˈneɪtɪv/ **noun**
someone who was born in a particular place: *He's* ***a native of*** *Texas.*

native speaker /ˌneɪtɪv ˈspiːkər/ **noun**
someone who has spoken a particular language since he or she was a baby, and not learned it later: *Some of our teachers are native speakers of other languages.*

natural /ˈnætʃərəl/ **adj**
1 B1 made or caused by nature and not by people or machines: *natural gas* ◦ *This product contains only natural ingredients.*
2 normal or expected: *It's natural to feel sad when you leave home.*
→ Opposite **unnatural adj**

naturally /ˈnætʃərəli/ **adv**
1 as you would expect: *Naturally, he was disappointed to fail the exam.*
2 in a normal way: *Relax and try to act naturally.*
3 existing or happening as part of nature and not made or done by people: *Most fruit is naturally sweet.*

nature /ˈneɪtʃər/ **noun**
1 A2 [no plural] all the plants, creatures, and things that exist in the world that are not made by people: *I like to get out and enjoy nature.*
2 someone's character: *It is not* ***in his nature*** *to be rude.*

nature reserve /ˈneɪtʃə rɪˌzɜːv/ **noun**
an area of land where animals and plants live and are protected

naughty /ˈnɔːti/ **adj** (**naughtier, naughtiest**)
If a child is naughty, he or she behaves badly: *a naughty little girl*

naval /ˈneɪvəl/ **adj**
relating to the ships that are used for fighting wars at sea: *a naval officer*

navigate /ˈnævɪgeɪt/ **verb** (**navigating, navigated**)
to find the right direction to travel by using maps or other equipment: *He navigated the ship back to Plymouth.*

navigation /ˌnævɪˈgeɪʃən/ **noun** [no plural]
the act of finding the right direction to travel by using maps or other equipment

navy /ˈneɪvi/ **noun**
1 (plural **navies**) ships and soldiers used for fighting wars at sea: *He joined the navy.*
2 navy blue

navy blue /ˌneɪvi ˈbluː/ **adj** (also **navy**)
B1 very dark blue: *a navy blue sweater*
• **navy blue noun**

near¹ /nɪər/ **adv, preposition**
1 A1 not far away in distance: *Could you come a bit nearer, please?* ◦ *I stood near the window.*
2 not far away in time: *We can decide nearer the time.*

near² /nɪər/ **adj**
1 B1 not far away in distance or time: *The library is very near.* ◦ *The nearest garage is ten miles away.*
2 in the near future at a time that is not far away: *Space travel may become very common in the near future.*

nearby /ˌnɪəˈbaɪ/ **adj, adv**
B1 not far away: *a nearby town*

nearly /ˈnɪəli/ **adv**
A2 almost: *I've nearly finished.* ◦ *Nearly all the food had gone when I arrived.*

neat /niːt/ **adj**
1 B1 tidy and clean: *He always looks very* ***neat and tidy****.*
2 US informal good: *What a neat idea!*

neatly /ˈniːtli/ **adv**
in a tidy way: *He was neatly dressed.*

a b c d e f g h i j k l m **n** o p q r s t u v w x y z

necessary /ˈnesəsᵊri/ **adj**
B1 needed in order to do something: *Is it really **necessary to** spend so much?* ◦ *The police are prepared to use force, **if necessary**.*
→ Opposite **unnecessary** adj

necessity /nəˈsesəti/ **noun** (plural **necessities**)
something that you need: *We took food and clothing and other necessities.*

neck /nek/ **noun**
A2 the part of the body between your head and your shoulders
→ See **The Body** on page C2

necklace /ˈnekləs/ **noun**
A2 a piece of jewellery that you wear around your neck: *a pearl necklace*
→ See picture at **jewellery**

need[1] /ni:d/ **verb**
1 A1 If you need something, you must have it, and if you need to do something, you must do it: *I need some new shoes.* ◦ *I **need to** ask you a few questions.*
2 don't need to do *something* A2 used in order to say that someone does not have to do something or should not do something: *You don't need to go.*
3 B1 If something needs doing or needs to be done, it should be done in order to be better: *Do these clothes need washing?*

need[2] /ni:d/ **noun**
1 something that is necessary to have or do: *There's an urgent **need for** fresh water.* ◦ *Is there any **need to** change the system?*
2 be in need of *something* to need something: *My car is in need of repair.*
3 no need If there is no need to do something or no need for something, it is not necessary or it is wrong: *There's no need to go to the shops – there's plenty of food here.* ◦ *I understand why she was angry, but there was no need to be so rude to him.*
4 needs the things you need in order to have a good life: *A home and food are basic needs.*

needle /ˈni:dl/ **noun**
1 a thin, pointed metal object with a small hole at one end for thread, used in sewing: *a needle and thread*
2 the thin metal part of a piece of medical equipment used to take blood out of the body, or to put drugs in

needle

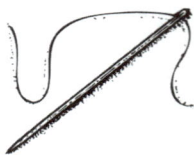

needless /ˈni:dləs/ **adj**
1 unnecessary: *needless suffering*
2 needless to say as you would expect: *Needless to say, I did all the work.*
• **needlessly** adv

needn't /ˈni:dᵊnt/
short form of need not: *You needn't have come.*

negative /ˈnegətɪv/ **adj**
1 A2 with the meaning 'no' or 'not': *We received a negative response to our request.*
2 B1 not hopeful or not interested: *She has a negative attitude to her work.*
3 A negative sentence or phrase is one that contains a word such as 'not', 'no', 'never', or 'nothing': *'I've never seen him in my life' is a negative sentence.* ◦ *'Don't' and 'do not' are negative forms of 'do'.*
4 A negative effect is bad and causes damage to something: *Terrorism has had a negative effect on tourism.*
5 A negative number is less than zero.

neglect[1] /nɪˈglekt/ **verb**
to not give enough attention to something or someone: *He neglects that poor dog.* ◦ *I'm afraid I've been neglecting the garden.*

neglect[2] /nɪˈglekt/ **noun** [no plural]
the fact of not giving enough attention to something or someone: *The children had suffered years of neglect.*

negotiate /nɪˈgəʊʃieɪt/ **verb** (**negotiating**, **negotiated**)
to try to make or change an agreement by talking about it: *We are negotiating for a new contract.*

neighbour UK (US **neighbor**) /ˈneɪbəʳ/ **noun**
1 A2 someone who lives very near you, especially in the next house: *Our **next-door neighbours** are always arguing.*
2 someone or something that is near or next to someone or something else: *Take five minutes to discuss this activity with your neighbour.*

neighbourhood UK (US **neighborhood**) /ˈneɪbəhʊd/ **noun**
B1 an area of a town or city that people live in: *Are there any good restaurants **in the neighbourhood**?*

neighbouring UK (US **neighboring**) /ˈneɪbᵊrɪŋ/ **adj**
near or next to somewhere: *neighbouring countries*

neither[1] /ˈnaɪðəʳ/, /ˈniːðəʳ/ **adv**
used to say that a negative fact is also true of someone or something else: *Jerry doesn't like it, and neither do I.* ◦ *She's not very tall and neither is her husband.*

neither[2] /ˈnaɪðəʳ/, /ˈniːðəʳ/ **pronoun, determiner**
not either of two people or things: *Neither child was hurt in the accident.* ◦ ***Neither of** us had ever been to London before.*

neither[3] /ˈnaɪðəʳ/, /ˈniːðəʳ/ **conjunction**
neither... nor used when a negative fact is true of two people or things: *Neither he nor his mother would talk to the police.*

nephew /ˈnefjuː/ **noun**
B1 the son of your brother or sister

nerve /nɜːv/ **noun** [no plural]
1 one of the very small parts in your body that carry messages between your brain and other parts of the body
2 the act of doing something that you know someone will not like: *I can't believe she **had the nerve** to talk to me after what happened!*

nerves /nɜːvz/ **plural noun**
1 the state of being nervous: *I always suffer from nerves before a match.*
2 **get on *someone's* nerves** to annoy someone: *If we spend too much time together, we get on each other's nerves.*

nervous /ˈnɜːvəs/ **adj**
1 B1 worried and anxious: *She's very **nervous about** her driving test.*
2 relating to the nerves in the body: *the nervous system*
• **nervously adv** *She waited nervously for her turn to speak.*

nest

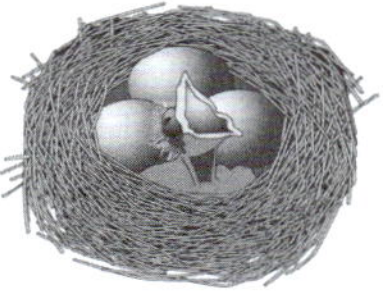

nest /nest/ **noun**
a home built by birds for their eggs

nets

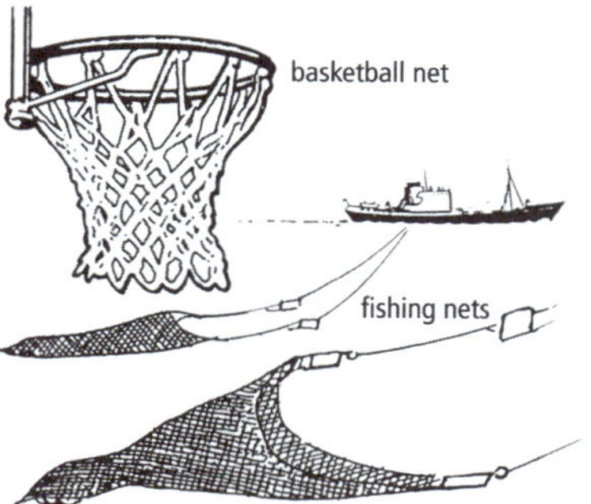

net /net/ **noun**
1 [no plural] material made of crossed threads with holes between them
2 B1 something made with a piece of net, for example for catching fish, or for sports: *a fishing net* ◦ *a basketball net*
3 **the Net** A2 short form of the Internet

netball /ˈnetbɔːl/ **noun** [no plural]
a game usually played by teams of women, where the players try to throw a ball through a high net

nettle /ˈnetl/ **noun**
a wild plant whose leaves hurt you if you touch them

network /ˈnetwɜːk/ **noun**
1 a system or group of connected parts: *a social network* ◦ *a network of tunnels*
2 a set of computers that are con-

a b c d e f g h i j k l m n o p q r s t u v w x y z

nected to each other: *All our offices are on the same network.*

neutral[1] /ˈnjuːtrᵊl/ **adj**
1 not supporting any side in an argument or fight: *He decided to remain neutral on the issue.*
2 Neutral colours are not strong or bright.

neutral[2] /ˈnjuːtrᵊl/ **noun** [no plural]
in driving, the position of the gears (= parts of a vehicle that control how fast the wheels turn) when they are not connected: *The car was* ***in neutral****.*

never /ˈnevəʳ/ **adv**
A1 not ever, not one time: *'Have you ever been to Australia?' 'No, never.'* ◦ *I've never thought about that before.*

nevertheless /ˌnevəðəˈles/ **adv**
despite that: *I knew a lot about the subject already, but her talk was interesting nevertheless.*

new /njuː/ **adj**
1 A1 different from before: *I need some new shoes.* ◦ *He starts his new job on Monday.*
2 A1 recently made: *Their house is quite new.*
3 A1 found or learned about a short time ago: *They have a new way of treating this illness.*
4 B1 If you are new, you arrived recently or do not know something well yet: *I'm* ***new to*** *the area.*

newcomer /ˈnjuːˌkʌməʳ/ **noun**
someone who has only recently arrived or started doing something: *He's a* ***newcomer to*** *the area.*

newly /ˈnjuːli/ **adv**
only a short time ago: *a newly married couple*

news /njuːz/ **noun** [no plural]
1 A2 new information: *Have you had any news about your job yet?*
2 the news B1 information on television, radio, and in newspapers about important things that have just happened: *the local/national news*

newsagent's /ˈnjuːzˌeɪdʒᵊnts/ **noun** UK
a shop that sells newspapers and magazines

newspaper /ˈnjuːsˌpeɪpəʳ/ **noun**
1 A1 large, folded sheets of paper that are printed with the news and sold every day or every week: *I read about his death* ***in the newspaper****.*
2 A2 [no plural] paper from a newspaper: *Wrap the mirror up in newspaper before you put it in the car.*

New Year /ˌnjuː ˈjɪəʳ/ **noun** (also **new year**)
the beginning of the year: *Happy New Year!*

New Year's Day /ˌnjuː jɪəz ˈdeɪ/ **noun**
1 January

New Year's Eve /ˌnjuː jɪəz ˈiːv/ **noun** [no plural]
31 December, the last day of the year: *Are you having a New Year's Eve party?*

next[1] /nekst/ **adj**
1 A1 coming after this one: *I'm leaving next week.* ◦ *She'll go to school next year.*
2 A2 nearest to now: *What time is the next train to London?*
3 A2 The next place is the one nearest to this place: *She only lives in the next village.*

next[2] /nekst/ **adv**
A2 immediately after: *Where shall we go next?*

next[3] /nekst/ **preposition**
next to *something/someone* A2 very close to something or someone, with nothing in between: *Come and sit next to me.*

next[4] /nekst/ **pronoun**
1 the person or thing that follows this person or thing: *Who's next to see the nurse?*
2 the weekend, week, etc. after next the weekend, week, etc. that follows the next one: *We're seeing Paul the Saturday after next.*

next door /ˌnekst ˈdɔːʳ/ **adj, adv**
in the next room, house, building, or other place: *What are your next-door neighbours like?* ◦ *He lives* ***next door to*** *the park.*

the NHS /ˌenertʃˈes/ **noun** [no plural]
abbreviation for National Health Service: the public health system in the UK

nibble /ˈnɪbl/ **verb** (**nibbling**, **nibbled**)
to eat something by taking very small bites: *We* ***nibbled on*** *crackers and cheese before dinner.*

nice /naɪs/ **adj**
1 A1 pleasant: *They have a very nice house.* ◦ *We'll go to the coast tomorrow if the weather's nice.* ◦ *It was* ***nice to*** *meet you.*
2 A1 kind and friendly: *He's a really nice person.* ◦ *She's always been very* ***nice to*** *me.*

nicely /ˈnaɪsli/ **adv**
1 well: *That table would fit nicely in the bedroom.*
2 in a pleasant way: *The room was nicely decorated.*

nickname /ˈnɪkneɪm/ **noun**
a name used informally instead of your real name: *His behaviour has earned him the nickname 'Mad Dog'.*
• **nickname** verb (**nicknaming**, **nicknamed**) *They nicknamed her 'The Iron Lady'.*

nicotine /ˈnɪkətiːn/ **noun** [no plural]
a poisonous chemical in tobacco

niece /niːs/ **noun**
B1 the daughter of your brother or sister

night /naɪt/ **noun**
1 A1 the time in every 24 hours when it is dark and people sleep: *I slept badly* ***last night****.* ◦ *It can get quite cold* ***at night****.*
2 A1 the period from the evening to the time when you go to sleep: *Are you doing anything* ***on*** *Friday* ***night****?*

nightclub /ˈnaɪtklʌb/ **noun**
B1 a place where you can dance and drink at night

nightlife /ˈnaɪtlaɪf/ **noun** [no plural]
B1 things to do at night, such as dancing and visiting bars: *Is the nightlife good around here?*

nightmare /ˈnaɪtmeəʳ/ **noun**
1 B1 something very bad that happened to you: *The trip was a nightmare.*
2 B1 a frightening dream

night school /ˈnaɪt ˌskuːl/ **noun** [no plural]
classes for adults that are taught in the evening

nil /nɪl/ **noun** [no plural] UK
In sports results, nil means 'zero': *Germany beat England three nil (= 3-0).*

nine /naɪn/
A1 the number 9

nineteen /ˌnaɪnˈtiːn/
A1 the number 19

nineteenth /ˌnaɪnˈtiːnθ/
19th written as a word

nineties /ˈnaɪntiz/ **plural noun**
1 the nineties the years from 1990 to 1999: *I moved to England* ***in the nineties.***
2 be in your nineties to be aged between 90 and 99: *She was* ***in her nineties*** *when she died.*

ninety /ˈnaɪnti/
A2 the number 90

ninth[1] /naɪnθ/
A2 9th written as a word

ninth[2] /naɪnθ/ **noun**
one of nine equal parts of something; 1/9

nip /nɪp/ **verb** (**nipping**, **nipped**)
1 UK informal to go somewhere quickly and for a short time: *I just nipped down the road to get a paper.*
2 to quickly bite someone

nipple /ˈnɪpl/ **noun**
the small, round area of darker skin in the centre of each breast in women, or on each side of the chest in men

no[1] /nəʊ/ **exclamation**
1 A1 something that you say in order to disagree, refuse something, or say that something is not true: *'Have you seen Louise?' 'No, I haven't.'* ◦ *'Can I come too?' 'No, I'm sorry.'* ◦ *'He's horrible.' 'No he isn't!'*
2 A2 something that you say to agree with something that is negative: *'He's not very clever, is he?' 'No, he isn't.'*
3 oh no! A2 something that you say when you are shocked and upset: *Oh no! I've lost my ring!*

no² /nəʊ/ **determiner**
1 A1 not any: *We have no money.*
2 A2 a word used to say that something is not allowed: *No smoking.*

no.
written abbreviation for number

nobody /ˈnəʊbədi/ **pronoun**
A2 no person: *There was nobody I could talk to.* ◦ *Nobody was listening.*

nod /nɒd/ **verb** (**nodding**, **nodded**)
to move your head up and down as a way of agreeing: *I asked Barbara if she liked him and she nodded.*
• **nod noun** *He **gave** a **nod** of approval.*
nod off phrasal verb informal
to start sleeping: *I nodded off after lunch.*

noise /nɔɪz/ **noun**
A1 a sound, especially a loud, bad sound: *Stop **making** so much **noise**!* ◦ *I had to shout above the noise of the party.*

noisy /ˈnɔɪzi/ **adj** (**noisier**, **noisiest**)
A2 Noisy people or things make a lot of noise: *noisy neighbours*
→ Opposite **quiet adj**
• **noisily adv**

none /nʌn/ **quantifier**
B1 not any: ***None of** my family smoke.* ◦ *He wanted some food but there was none left.*

nonsense /ˈnɒnsᵊns/ **noun** [no plural]
1 something silly and not true that someone has said or written: *She talks nonsense sometimes.* ◦ *It's nonsense to suggest they could have cheated.*
2 silly behaviour: *Please stop this childish nonsense!*

non-smoking /ˌnɒnˈsməʊkɪŋ/ **adj**
describes a place where people are not allowed to smoke: *Let's get a table in the non-smoking area.*

non-stop /ˌnɒnˈstɒp/ **adj**, **adv**
without stopping: *non-stop flights from Britain to the West Indies* ◦ *We talked non-stop the whole journey.*

noodles /ˈnuːdlz/ **plural noun**
thin pieces of pasta (= food made from flour and water)

noon /nuːn/ **noun** [no plural]
A2 twelve o'clock in the middle of the day: *The service will be held at noon.*

no one /ˈnəʊ ˌwʌn/ **pronoun**
A2 no person: *No one knows where he is.* ◦ *There was no one there.*

nor /nɔːʳ/ **adv**, **conjunction**
1 **neither... nor...** used after 'neither' and before the second thing in a negative sentence: *Strangely, neither James nor Emma saw what happened.*
2 used after something negative to say that the same thing is true for someone or something else: *'I don't like cats.' 'Nor do I.'* ◦ *She couldn't speak a word of Italian and nor could I.*

normal /ˈnɔːmᵊl/ **adj**
A2 usual and ordinary: *It's normal for couples to argue now and then.*

normally /ˈnɔːməli/ **adv**
1 B1 usually: *Normally, I start work around nine o'clock.*
2 in the ordinary way that you expect: *The car is working normally now.*

north, North /nɔːθ/ **noun** [no plural]
1 A2 the direction that is on your left when you face towards the rising sun: *Which way is north?*
2 **the north** A2 the part of an area that is farther towards the north than the rest: *She's from the north of England.*
• **north adj** A2 *the north bank of the river* ◦ *North America*
• **north adv** A2 *We drove north.*

northeast, Northeast /ˌnɔːθˈiːst/ **noun** [no plural]
1 B1 the direction between north and east
2 **the northeast** B1 the northeast part of a country
• **northeast, Northeast adj**, **adv**

northeastern, Northeastern /ˌnɔːθˈiːstən/ **adj**
in or from the northeast

northern, Northern /ˈnɔːðᵊn/ **adj**
in or from the north part of an area: *the northern counties*

the North Pole /ˌnɔːθ ˈpəʊl/ **noun** [no plural]
the point on the Earth's surface that is furthest north

northwest, Northwest /ˌnɔːθ ˈwest/ **noun** [no plural]
1 B1 the direction between north and west
2 the northwest B1 the northwest part of a country
• **northwest, Northwest adj, adv**

northwestern, Northwestern /ˌnɔːθˈwestən/ **adj**
in or from the northwest

nose /nəʊz/ **noun**
A1 the part of your face that you breathe through and smell with
→ See **The Body** on page C2

nostril /ˈnɒstrᵊl/ **noun**
one of the two holes at the end of your nose
→ See **The Body** on page C2

not /nɒt/ **adv**
1 A1 used to give something the opposite meaning: *I'm not interested.* ◦ *It's not mine.* ◦ *It's for you, not Daniel.*
2 A2 used after verbs such as 'be afraid', 'hope', or 'suspect' in short negative replies: *'Is he coming with us?' 'I hope not.'* ◦ *'Have you finished yet?' 'I'm afraid not.'*
3 or not A2 used to express the possibility that something might not happen: *Are you going to the party or not?* ◦ *I don't know if she's coming or not.*

note¹ /nəʊt/ **noun**
1 A1 a short letter: *He left a note on her desk.*
2 A2 (also **notes**) words that you write down to help you remember something: *She studied her notes before the exam.* ◦ *Let me* ***make a note of*** *(= write) your phone number.*
3 a single musical sound
4 B1 UK (US **bill**) a piece of paper money: *a ten-pound note*

note² /nəʊt/ **verb** (**noting**, **noted**)
B1 to notice something: *I noted her absence.*
note down *something* **phrasal verb**
to write something so that you do not forget it: *I noted down the telephone number for the police.*

notebook /ˈnəʊtbʊk/ **noun**
1 A2 a book with empty pages that you can write in
2 a small computer that can be carried around and used anywhere

notepad /ˈnəʊtpæd/ **noun**
a set of pieces of paper that are joined together at one edge and used for writing on

nothing /ˈnʌθɪŋ/ **pronoun**
1 A2 not anything: *I've had nothing to eat since breakfast.* ◦ *He said he did nothing wrong.*
2 B1 not something important or valuable: *She was crying about nothing.*
3 for nothing without a successful result: *I've come all this way for nothing.*
4 have nothing to do with *someone/something* to have no connection with someone or something: *He made the decision – I had nothing to do with it.*
5 be/have nothing to do with *someone* If you say that something is or has nothing to do with someone, you mean that they have no good reason to know about it or be involved with it: *I wish he wouldn't give advice on my marriage – it has nothing to do with him.*

notice¹ /ˈnəʊtɪs/ **verb** (**noticing**, **noticed**)
to see something and be aware of it: *I* ***noticed that*** *he was alone.* ◦ *No one noticed my new haircut.*

notice² /ˈnəʊtɪs/ **noun**
1 a sign giving information about something: *The notice said that the pool was closed for repairs.*
2 [no plural] attention: *I didn't* ***take*** *any* ***notice of*** *(= give attention to) his advice.*
3 [no plural] a warning that something will happen: *The next time you visit, can you* ***give*** *me more* ***notice****?*

noticeable /ˈnəʊtɪsəbl/ **adj**
easy to see or be aware of: *There has been a noticeable improvement in his work.*
• **noticeably adv** *As summer*

a b c d e f g h i j k l m **n** o p q r s t u v w x y z

approaches, the days get noticeably longer.

noticeboard /ˈnəʊtɪsbɔːd/ **noun** UK (US **bulletin board**)
B1 a board on a wall where you put pieces of paper telling people about things: *I saw the ad **on the noticeboard**.*
→ See **Classroom** on page C4

notorious /nəʊˈtɔːriəs/ **adj**
famous for something bad: *a notorious criminal* ◦ *She was **notorious for** her bad temper.*
• **notoriously** **adv**

nought /nɔːt/ **noun** UK
the number 0

noun /naʊn/ **noun**
A2 a word that refers to a person, place, object, event, substance, idea, feeling, or quality. For example the words 'teacher', 'book', and 'beauty' are nouns.

novel /ˈnɒvəl/ **noun**
B1 a book that tells a story about people and things that are not real: *Have you read any good novels lately?*

novelist /ˈnɒvəlɪst/ **noun**
a person who writes novels

November /nəʊˈvembər/ **noun**
A1 the eleventh month of the year

now[1] /naʊ/ **adv**
1 A1 at this time: *I'm going now.* ◦ *What is Eva doing now?* ◦ *I don't want to wait – I want it now!*
2 A2 immediately: *We're going home now.*
3 used when you start to tell someone something: *Now, I have been to Glasgow before.* ◦ ***Now then**, would anyone else like to ask a question?*
4 used to show the length of time that something has been happening, from the time it began until the present: *I've lived in Rio for two years now.*
5 **now and then** If something happens now and then, it happens sometimes but not very often: *I love chocolate, but I only eat it now and then.*

now[2] /naʊ/ **conjunction** (also **now that**)
as a result of a new situation: *Now that I've got a car I can visit her more often.*

nowadays /ˈnaʊədeɪz/ **adv**
B1 at the present time, especially when compared to the past: *Everything seems more expensive nowadays.*

nowhere /ˈnəʊweər/ **adv**
B1 not anywhere: *There was **nowhere to** sit.* ◦ *We had **nowhere else** to go.*

nuclear /ˈnjuːkliər/ **adj**
1 relating to the energy that is made when the nucleus (= central part) of an atom is divided: *nuclear weapons* ◦ *a nuclear power plant*
2 relating to the nucleus (= central part) of an atom: *nuclear physics*

nucleus /ˈnjuːkliəs/ **noun** (plural **nuclei** /ˈnjuːkliaɪ/)
the central part of an atom or cell

nude /njuːd/ **adj**
not wearing any clothes: *Both children were **in the nude**.*

nudge /nʌdʒ/ **verb** (**nudging**, **nudged**)
to gently push someone or something: *She nudged me towards the door.*
• **nudge** **noun** *I **gave** him a **nudge**.*

nuisance /ˈnjuːsəns/ **noun**
a person, thing, or situation that annoys you or causes problems for you: *Not being able to use my computer is a real nuisance.*

numb /nʌm/ **adj**
If a part of your body is numb, you cannot feel it: *My fingers and toes were numb with cold.*

number[1] /ˈnʌmbər/ **noun**
1 A1 a symbol or word used in a counting system: *Think of a number between 1 and 100.*
2 A1 a group of numbers that represents something: *What is your phone number?*
3 B1 an amount: *We contacted a large number of people.*
4 **a number of *something*** many: *There have been a number of problems.*

number² /ˈnʌmbəʳ/ **verb**
to give something a number: *I numbered the pages.*

number plate /ˈnʌmbə ˌpleɪt/ **noun**
UK (US **license plate**)
a sign with numbers and letters on the front and back of a vehicle
→ See **Car** on page C3

numerous /ˈnjuːmᵊrəs/ **adj** formal
many: *He has written numerous articles.*

nun /nʌn/ **noun**
a member of a group of religious women who live away from other people

nurse¹ /nɜːs/ **noun**
A2 someone whose job is looking after people who are ill and hurt

nurse² /nɜːs/ **verb** (**nursing**, **nursed**)
to look after a person or animal that is ill

nursery /ˈnɜːsᵊri/ **noun** (plural **nurseries**)
1 a place where babies and young children are looked after without their parents
2 a place where plants are grown and sold

nursery rhyme /ˈnɜːsᵊri ˌraɪm/ **noun**
a short poem or song for young children

nursery school /ˈnɜːsᵊri ˌskuːl/ **noun**
a school for very young children

nut /nʌt/ **noun**
1 the dry fruit of some trees that grows in a hard shell, and can often be eaten: *a Brazil nut*
2 a piece of metal with a hole in it that you screw onto a bolt (= metal pin) to hold pieces of wood or metal together

nutritious /njuːˈtrɪʃəs/ **adj**
Nutritious food contains things that your body needs to stay healthy: *a nutritious meal*

nylon /ˈnaɪlɒn/ **noun** [no plural]
a strong material that is not natural, which is used to make things like clothes and ropes: *nylon stockings*

a b c d e f g h i j k l m n o p q r s t u v w x y z

a b c d e f g h i j k l m n o p q r s t u v w x y z

Oo

O, o /əʊ/
the fifteenth letter of the alphabet

oak /əʊk/ **noun**
a large tree found in northern countries, or the wood of this tree

OAP /ˌəʊeɪˈpiː/ **noun** UK
abbreviation for old-age pensioner: a person who gets money from the government because they are too old to work

oar /ɔːʳ/ **noun**
a long pole with a flat end that you use to move a boat through water

oasis /əʊˈeɪsɪs/ **noun** (plural **oases** /əʊˈeɪsiːz/)
a place in the desert where there is water and where plants grow

oath /əʊθ/ **noun**
a formal promise

oats /əʊts/ **plural noun**
grain that people eat or feed to animals

obedience /əʊˈbiːdiəns/ **noun** [no plural]
the condition of being willing to do what someone tells you to do: *He demanded complete obedience from his soldiers.*

obedient /əʊˈbiːdiənt/ **adj**
willing to do what people tell you to do: *an obedient child*
→ Opposite **disobedient**
• **obediently adv** *The dog sat obediently by his owner.*

obese /əʊˈbiːs/ **adj**
very fat: *Obese people are more likely to suffer heart attacks.*

obey /əʊˈbeɪ/ **verb**
to do what someone tells you to do: *If you do not obey the law, you will be arrested.*
→ Opposite **disobey verb**

object[1] /ˈɒbdʒɪkt/ **noun**
1 B1 a thing that you can see or touch but that is not alive: *I could see a bright, shiny object in the sky.*
2 the object of *something* the purpose of something: *The object of the game is to score more points than the other team.*
3 B1 in grammar, the person or thing that is affected by the action of a verb

object[2] /əbˈdʒekt/ **verb**
to say that you do not agree with a plan: *Carlos has **objected to** the proposal.*

objection /əbˈdʒekʃᵊn/ **noun**
a reason why you do not like or agree with a plan: *Our main **objection to** the new factory is that it's noisy.*

objective[1] /əbˈdʒektɪv/ **noun**
something that you are trying to do: *His main objective was to increase profits.*

objective[2] /əbˈdʒektɪv/ **adj**
influenced only by facts and not by feelings: *I can't be objective when I judge my daughter's work.*

obligation /ˌɒblɪˈgeɪʃᵊn/ **noun**
something that you have to do because it is your duty: *Parents have an **obligation to** make sure their children receive a good education.*

oblige /əˈblaɪdʒ/ **verb** (**obliging**, **obliged**)
be obliged to do *something* to have to do something: *It's my mother's party so I'm obliged to attend.*

obliged /əˈblaɪdʒd/ **adj**
feel obliged to do *something* to think that you must do something: *They helped us so I feel obliged to do the same for them.*

oblivious /əˈblɪviəs/ **adj**
not knowing anything about something that is happening: *She seemed completely **oblivious to** what was happening around her.*

observant /əbˈzɜːvᵊnt/ **adj**
good or quick at noticing things: *He's very observant.*

observation /ˌɒbzəˈveɪʃᵊn/ **noun** [no plural]
the act of watching someone or something carefully: *The doctor wants to keep him **under observation** for a week.*

observe /əbˈzɜːv/ **verb** (**observing**, **observed**)
to watch someone or something carefully: *Children learn by observing adults.*

obsessed /əbˈsest/ **adj**
be obsessed with *someone/something* to think about someone or something all the time: *He is obsessed with money.*

obsession /əbˈseʃᵊn/ **noun**
someone or something that you think about all the time: *They have an **obsession with** making money.*

obstacle /ˈɒbstəkl/ **noun**
something that makes it difficult for you to go somewhere or do something: *Their refusal to agree is the main **obstacle to** peace.*

obstinate /ˈɒbstinət/ **adj**
not willing to change your ideas or plans, although you are wrong

obstruct /əbˈstrʌkt/ **verb**
1 to be in a place that stops someone or something from moving: *The parked car was obstructing the traffic.*
2 to try to stop something from happening: *He was accused of obstructing a police investigation.*

obstruction /əbˈstrʌkʃᵊn/ **noun**
something that stops someone or something from moving: *Your car's causing an obstruction.*

obtain /əbˈteɪn/ **verb** formal
to get something: *He obtained a law degree from Brown University.*

obvious /ˈɒbviəs/ **adj**
B1 easy to understand or see: ***It's obvious** that he doesn't like her.*

obviously /ˈɒbviəsli/ **adv**
B1 in a way that is easy to understand or see: *They're obviously in love.* ◦ *Obviously, we want to start as soon as possible.*

occasion /əˈkeɪʒᵊn/ **noun**
1 B1 an important event: *a special occasion* ◦ *She bought a new dress for the occasion.*
2 a time when something happens: *We met on several occasions to discuss the issue.*
3 on occasion(s) sometimes, but not often: *I only drink alcohol on occasion.*

occasional /əˈkeɪʒᵊnᵊl/ **adj**
not happening often: *He still plays the occasional game of football.*
• **occasionally adv** *They only meet occasionally.*

occupation /ˌɒkjəˈpeɪʃᵊn/ **noun**
A2 formal your job: *You need to put your name, address, and occupation on the form.*

occupy /ˈɒkjəpaɪ/ **verb** (**occupying**, **occupied**)
1 to fill a place or period of time: *His book collection occupies most of the room.* ◦ *The baby seems to occupy all our time.*
2 to live or work in a room or building: *They occupy the second floor of the building.*
3 to keep someone busy or interested: *The games **kept** the kids **occupied** for hours.*

occur /əˈkɜːʳ/ **verb** (**occurring**, **occurred**)
1 formal to happen, often without being planned: *According to the police, the shooting occurred at 12.30 a.m.*
2 to exist or be present: *The disease mainly **occurs in** women over 40.*
occur to *someone* phrasal verb to suddenly think of something: ***It occurred to** me that he might be lying.*

ocean /ˈəʊʃᵊn/ **noun**
B1 one of the five main areas of sea: *the Pacific Ocean*

o'clock /əˈklɒk/ **adv**
one, two, three, etc. o'clock A1 used after the numbers one to twelve to mean exactly that hour when you tell the time: *We got home at ten o'clock.*

October /ɒkˈtəʊbəʳ/ **noun**
A1 the tenth month of the year

octopus /ˈɒktəpəs/ **noun**
a sea creature with eight long arms

octopus

odd /ɒd/ **adj**
1 strange or unusual: *There is*

something odd about her. ◦ It's a bit odd that he didn't come.
2 being one of a pair when the other of the pair is missing: *an odd sock*
3 not happening often or regularly: *He does* ***odd jobs*** *for extra cash. ◦ She writes in odd hours here and there.*

odd number /ˌɒd ˈnʌmbəʳ/ **noun**
a number that does not produce a whole number when it is divided by two
→ Opposite **even number** noun

odds /ɒdz/ **plural noun**
the chance of something happening: *What are the odds of winning the top prize?*
• **odds and ends** informal a group of different objects that have little value

of strong /ɒv/ weak /əv/ **preposition**
1 A1 belonging to or relating to someone or something: *She is a friend of my cousin. ◦ I like the colour of her hair.*
2 A1 used after words that show an amount: *a bag of apples ◦ both of us*
3 A1 used with numbers, ages, and dates: *a boy of six ◦ the 14th of February 1995*
4 A1 containing: *a glass of milk*
5 A2 showing position or direction: *the front of the queue ◦ a small town north of Edinburgh*
6 A2 showing someone or something: *a map of the city ◦ a photo of my boyfriend*
7 A2 used when comparing related things: *He's the best-looking of the three brothers.*
8 B1 showing a reason or cause: *He died of cancer.*
9 used after an adjective when judging someone's behaviour: *It was very nice of you to think of us.*

off¹ /ɒf/ **adv, preposition**
1 A2 not touching or connected to something: *Keep off the grass! ◦ A button came off my coat.*
2 A2 not operating or being used: *Make sure you switch your computer off.*
3 A2 not at work: *I had six months off when my son was born.*
4 B1 away from a place or position: *He ran off to find his friend.*
5 B1 If a price has a certain amount of money off, it costs that much less than the usual price: *There's 40% off this week on all winter coats.*
6 near to a building or place: *an island off the coast of Brazil*

off² /ɒf/ **adj**
1 A2 not at work: *He's off today – I think he's ill.*
2 If food or drink is off, it is not now fresh and good to eat or drink: *This milk smells off.*

offence /əˈfens/ **noun** UK (US **offense**)
1 [no plural] an act of upsetting or insulting someone: *I hope my remark didn't cause offence.*
2 a crime: *He* ***committed*** *several serious* ***offences****.*

offend /əˈfend/ **verb**
to make someone upset or angry: *I was deeply offended by her comments.*

offender /əˈfendəʳ/ **noun**
someone who has committed a crime: *young offenders*

offensive /əˈfensɪv/ **adj**
likely to make people angry or upset: *an offensive remark*

offer¹ /ˈɒfəʳ/ **verb**
1 A2 to say that you will do something for someone: *He* ***offered to*** *get me a cab.*
2 B1 to ask someone if they would like something: *They offered me a job.*
3 B1 to give or provide something: *to offer advice ◦ Did he offer any explanation for his behaviour?*
4 to say that you will pay a particular amount of money: *I offered him £500 for the car.*

offer² /ˈɒfəʳ/ **noun**
1 A2 an act of asking someone if they would like something: *an offer of help ◦ a job offer*
2 an amount of money that you say you will pay for something: *They have* ***made*** *an* ***offer*** *on the house.*
3 on offer UK B1 at a cheaper price than usual: *Are these jeans still on offer?*

office /ˈɒfɪs/ **noun**
1 A2 a room or building where people

work: *an office worker* ◦ *I never get to the office before nine.*
→ See **The Office** on page C12
2 A2 a room or building where you can get information, tickets, or a particular service: *a ticket office* ◦ *the tourist office*

officer /ˈɒfɪsəʳ/ **noun**
1 B1 someone who works for a government department: *a customs officer*
2 B1 someone who is a member of the police: *a* ***police officer***
3 someone with an important job in the army, navy, etc.: *an* ***army officer***

official[1] /əˈfɪʃəl/ **adj**
approved by the government or someone in power: *the official language of Egypt* ◦ *an official document*
• **officially** adv

official[2] /əˈfɪʃəl/ **noun**
someone who has an important position in an organization, such as the government: *a senior official*

off-license /ˌɒfˈlaɪsəns/ **noun** UK
a shop that sells alcoholic drink

often /ˈɒfən/, /ˈɒftən/ **adv**
1 A1 many times or regularly: *I often see her there.* ◦ ***How often*** *(= How many times) do you go to the gym?*
2 If something often happens or is often true, it is normal for it to happen or it is usually true: *Brothers and sisters often argue.* ◦ *Headaches are often caused by stress.*

oh /əʊ/ **exclamation**
1 A1 said when you are surprised, pleased, disappointed, etc.: *Oh, no! I don't believe it!* ◦ *'I don't think I can come.' 'Oh, that's a shame.'*
2 A1 used to introduce an idea that you have just thought of, or something that you have just remembered: *Oh, and don't forget to lock the door.*
3 used before you say something, often before replying to what someone has said: *'Ian is leaving now.' 'Oh, I didn't realize that.'*

oil /ɔɪl/ **noun** [no plural]
1 A2 a thick liquid made from plants or animals that is used in cooking: *vegetable oil*
2 B1 a thick liquid that comes from under the Earth's surface and is used as a fuel: *an oil company* ◦ *an oil well*

ointment /ˈɔɪntmənt/ **noun**
a smooth, thick substance that is put on painful skin

okay[1] (also **OK**) /əʊˈkeɪ/ **exclamation** informal
1 A1 used when agreeing to do something or when allowing someone to do something: *'Let's meet this afternoon.' 'Okay.'* ◦ *'Can I use the car?' 'Okay.'*
2 A2 used to check that someone understands or agrees to something: *I'll see you at six o'clock, okay?*
3 A2 used as a way of showing that you are going to take action, start speaking, or start something new: *OK, if you're ready we'll start.* ◦ *Okay, let's go.*

okay[2] (also **OK**) /əʊˈkeɪ/ **adj, adv** informal
1 A1 safe or healthy: *Is your grandmother okay now?*
2 A2 good enough: *Is your food okay?*
3 A2 allowed: *Is it okay if I leave early today?*
4 A2 in a satisfactory way: *Did you sleep okay?*

old /əʊld/ **adj**
1 A1 having lived or existed for a long time: *an old man* ◦ *an old house* ◦ *We're all* ***getting older.***
2 A1 having been used or owned for a long time: *You might get dirty, so wear some old clothes.*
3 A1 used to describe or ask about someone's age: *How old are you?* ◦ *She'll be four* ***years old*** *in March.*
4 A2 used before or in the past: *I think the old system was better in many ways.*
5 A2 an old friend is one you have known and liked for a long time: *She's one of my oldest friends.*

old-fashioned /ˌəʊldˈfæʃənd/ **adj**
B1 not modern: *old-fashioned clothes*

olive /ˈɒlɪv/ **noun**
B1 a small green or black fruit that is eaten or used to produce oil

olive oil /ˌɒlɪv ˈɔɪl/ **noun** [no plural]
oil made from olives, used for cooking or on salads

the Olympic Games /əˈlɪmpɪk ˌɡeɪmz/ **plural noun** (also **the Olympics**)
an international sports competition that happens every four years

omelette /ˈɒmlət/ **noun**
A2 a food made with eggs that have been mixed and fried: *a cheese omelette*

omit /əʊˈmɪt/ **verb** (**omitting**, **omitted**)
to not include someone or something: *He was **omitted from** the team because of his behaviour.*

on[1] /ɒn/ **preposition**
1 A1 on a surface of something: *I put the book on that shelf.* ◦ *He stood on my foot.*
2 A1 covering, touching, attached to, or hanging from something: *You've got blood on your shirt.* ◦ *Which finger do you wear your ring on?*
3 A1 used to show the date or day when something happens: *He's due to arrive on 14 February.* ◦ *I'm working on my birthday.*
4 A2 used to refer to a place when giving directions: *Take the first turning on the right.* ◦ *Our house is the first on the left after the post office.*
5 A2 in a particular place: *the diagram on page 22* ◦ *I met her on a ship.*
6 A2 being shown on television: *What's on television tonight?*
7 A2 used to show some methods of travelling: *Did you go over on the ferry?* ◦ *Sam loves travelling on buses.*
8 A2 used to show what money or time is used for: *She refuses to spend more than £20 on a pair of shoes.* ◦ *I've wasted too much time on this already.*
9 B1 about: *a book on pregnancy*
10 B1 next to or along the side of: *The post office is on Bateman Street.* ◦ *Cambridge is on the River Cam.*
11 B1 using something: *I spoke to Dad on the phone.* ◦ *I was working on my computer.*

on[2] /ɒn/ **adv**
1 A2 If you have something on, you are wearing it: *She's got a black coat on.* ◦ *Why don't you **put** your new dress **on**?*
2 B1 into a bus, train, plane, etc.: *Amy got on in Stamford.*
3 used to show that an action or event continues: *The tradition lives on.*
4 working or being used: *The heating has been on all day.*
5 happening or planned: *I've got a lot on at the moment.* ◦ *What's on at the cinema?*
• **on and off** If something happens on and off during a period of time, it happens sometimes: *They've been seeing each other on and off since May.*

once[1] /wʌns/ **adv**
1 A2 one time: *It only snowed once or twice this year.* ◦ *I go swimming **once a week** (= one time every week).*
2 B1 in the past, but not now: *This house once belonged to my grandfather.*
3 at once B1 immediately: *I knew at once that I would like it here.*
4 at once at the same time: *They all started talking at once.*
5 once more B1 one more time: *If you say that once more, I'm going to leave.*
6 once upon a time B1 used at the beginning of a children's story to mean that something happened a long time ago
7 once again B1 again: *I'll explain it once again.*
8 for once used to mean that something is happening that does not usually happen: *For once, I think I have good news for him.*

once[2] /wʌns/ **conjunction**
as soon as: *Once I find somewhere to live, I'll send you my address.*

one[1] /wʌn/
A1 the number 1

one[2] /wʌn/ **pronoun**
1 A2 one person or thing in a group that has already been talked about: *I've just made some cakes. Do you want one?* ◦ *Chris is **the one** with glasses.*
2 formal any person in general: *One should respect one's parents.*

3 **one by one** separately, one after the other: *They entered the room one by one.*
4 **one after another** (also **one after the other**) first one, then another, then another, and so on: *One after another, they left the room.* ◦ *She ate the chocolates one after the other until the box was finished.*

one³ /wʌn/ **determiner**
1 (A2) one person or thing in a group: ***One of*** *our daughters has just got married.*
2 (A2) at a particular time in the past: *I first met him one day in the park.*
3 used to refer to a time in the future that is not yet decided: *We should have a drink together one evening.*
4 **one or two** (B1) a few: *I'd like to make one or two suggestions.*
5 used when saying there is no other person or thing: *He's the one person who never forgets my birthday.*
6 a single thing: *I think we should paint the bedroom all one color.*

one another /ˌwʌn əˈnʌðəʳ/ **pronoun**
(B1) used to show that each person in a group of two or more people does something to the others: *The children are always arguing with one another.*

oneself /wʌnˈself/ **pronoun** formal
the form of the pronoun 'one' when it refers to the person speaking or people in general: *How can one protect oneself and one's family?*

one-way /ˌwʌnˈweɪ/ **adj**
If a road is one-way, you can only drive on it in one direction: *a one-way street*

onion /ˈʌnjən/ **noun**
(A2) a round vegetable with layers that has a strong taste and smell
→ See **Fruit and Vegetables** on page C8

online /ˌɒnˈlaɪn/ **adj, adv**
(A2) connected to and shared by a system of computers, especially the Internet: *online services* ◦ *to **go online** (= start using the Internet)* ◦ *Most newspapers are now available online.*

only¹ /ˈəʊnli/ **adv**
1 (A1) not more than a particular size or amount: *It'll only take a few minutes.* ◦ *She's only fifteen.*
2 (A2) not anyone or anything else: *The offer is available to UK residents only.*
3 (B1) used to mean that something happened a very short time ago: *She's **only just** got here.*
4 (B1) used to say that something is not important, or that you did not mean to upset someone: *Don't worry – it's only a scratch.* ◦ *I was only joking.*
5 (B1) not in any other place: *These birds are only found in New Zealand.*
6 **if only** used to express a wish for something that is impossible or unlikely to happen: *If only I knew the answer!*
7 **I only hope/wish** used to emphasize what you are hoping or wishing for: *I only hope you know what you're doing.* ◦ *I only wish that I had more time.*
8 **not only... (but) also** used to say that more than one thing is true: *Not only did he turn up late, he also forgot his books.*

only² /ˈəʊnli/ **adj**
(A1) used to mean that there are no others: *This could be our only chance.* ◦ *You're the only person here I know.*

only³ /ˈəʊnli/ **conjunction**
but: *I would pay for it myself, only I don't have the money.*

onto (also **on to**) /ˈɒntuː/ **preposition**
1 (B1) used to show movement into or on a particular place: *I stepped onto the platform.* ◦ *Can you get back onto the path?*
2 used to show that you are starting to talk about a different subject: *How did we get onto this subject?*

onward /ˈɒnwəd/ **adv** (also **onwards**)
1 beginning at a time and continuing after it: *I'll be at home from nine o'clock onwards.*
2 If you move onwards, you continue to go forwards.

oops /uːps/ **exclamation**
something you say when you do something slightly wrong: *Oops! I've spilled my coffee.*

ooze /uːz/ **verb** (**oozing**, **oozed**)
1 If a liquid oozes from something, it

comes out slowly: *Blood was oozing out of the wound.*
2 informal to show a lot of a quality: *He oozes charm.*

open

Windows are open.

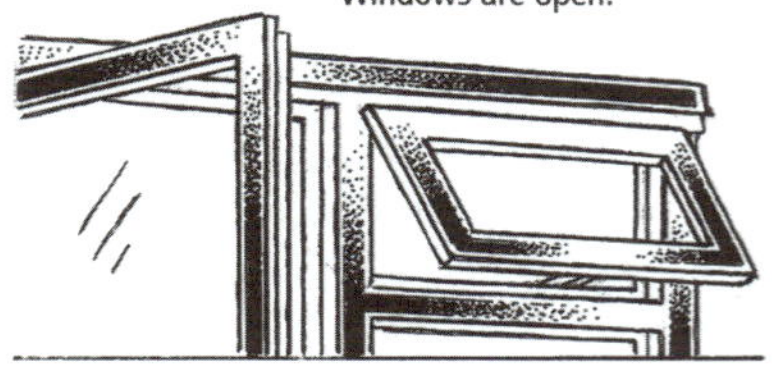

The book is open.

open¹ /ˈəʊpᵊn/ **adj**
1 A2 not closed or fastened: *an open door* ◦ *Is there an open bottle of wine?*
2 A1 A shop or business is open during the time it can do business: *Most shops are open on Sundays.*
3 B1 An open area of land has no buildings on it or near it: *large open spaces*

> **Common mistake: open and close**
>
> Be careful not to confuse the adjective and verb forms of these words. The adjectives are **open** and **closed**.
> *Is the supermarket open on Sunday?*
> *The museum is closed today.*
> The verbs are **open** and **close**.
> *The supermarket opens at 8 a.m.*
> *The museum closes at 5 p.m. today.*

open² /ˈəʊpᵊn/ **verb**
1 A1 If you open something, you make it change to a position that is not closed: *Could you open the window?* ◦ *Open your eyes.*
2 A1 If something opens, it changes to a position that is not closed: *The gate won't open, so we can't get in.*
3 A2 to remove part of a container or parcel so that you can see or use what it contains: *Come on, open your present!* ◦ *I can't open this bottle.*
4 A2 If a shop or office opens at a particular time of day, it starts to do business at that time: *What time does the bank open?*
5 B1 to make a computer document or program ready to be read or used: *First, open the file called Statistics.*
6 If a business or activity opens, or if you open it, it starts officially for the first time: *That restaurant's new – it only opened last month.* ◦ *The new hospital will be opened by the mayor.*
open (*something*) up **phrasal verb**
to start a new shop or business: *New bars are opening up everywhere.*

opener /ˈəʊpənəʳ/ **noun**
bottle, can, etc. opener a piece of kitchen equipment used to open bottles, cans, etc.

opening /ˈəʊpənɪŋ/ **noun**
1 a hole or space that something or someone can pass through: *We found an opening in the fence and climbed through.*
2 a ceremony at the beginning of an event or activity: *The official **opening of** the new school will take place next month.*
3 the beginning of something: *The opening of the novel is amazing.*

openly /ˈəʊpᵊnli/ **adv**
without hiding any of your thoughts or feelings: *He **talks openly** about his feelings.*

open return /ˌəʊpᵊn rɪˈtɜːn/ **noun**
a ticket that lets you travel to a place and come back when you like

opera /ˈɒpᵊrə/ **noun**
A2 a musical play in which most of the words are sung

operate /ˈɒpᵊreɪt/ **verb** (**operating**, **operated**)
1 B1 to cut someone's body and remove or repair part of it: *Did they have to **operate on** him?*
2 If an organization or business operates, it works: *Our company is operating under very difficult conditions.*
3 If a machine operates, it works, and if you operate it, you make it work: *You have to be trained to operate the machinery.*

operation /ˌɒpəʳ'eɪʃən/ **noun**
1 B1 the process of cutting someone's body to remove or repair part of it: *a heart operation* ◦ *My son is going to* ***have an operation****.*
2 an organization or business: *a large commercial operation*

operator /'ɒpəreɪtəʳ/ **noun**
1 someone who helps to connect people on a telephone system
2 someone whose job is to control a machine or vehicle: *a computer operator*
3 a company that does a particular type of business: *a tour operator*

opinion /ə'pɪnjən/ **noun**
1 B1 a thought or belief about something or someone: *What's your* ***opinion on*** *the matter?* ◦ ***In my opinion*** *(= I think) he's the best football player in this country.*
2 [no plural] the thoughts or beliefs that a group of people have: *The government will have to listen to* ***public opinion****.*

opponent /ə'pəʊnənt/ **noun**
someone who you compete against in a game or competition: *He beat his opponent six games to two.*

opportunity /ˌɒpə'tjuːnəti/ **noun** (plural **opportunities**)
1 B1 a chance to do something good: *If you* ***get the opportunity*** *to go there, it is a wonderful city.*
2 **take the/this opportunity to do** ***something*** to use an occasion to do or say something: *I'd like to take this opportunity to thank all of you.*

oppose /ə'pəʊz/ **verb** (**opposing**, **opposed**)
to disagree with a plan or activity and to try to stop it: *The committee opposed a proposal to allow women to join the club.*

opposed /ə'pəʊzd/ **adj**
be opposed to ***something*** to disagree with a plan or activity: *We're not opposed to tax increases.*

opposite[1] /'ɒpəzɪt/ **adj**
1 B1 in a position facing someone or something but on the other side: *We live on opposite sides of the city.*
2 completely different: *My attempt to calm him down had the opposite effect.*

opposite[2] /'ɒpəzɪt/ **adv, preposition**
A2 in a position facing something or someone but on the other side: *The couple sat down opposite her.* ◦ *Is there a bakery opposite your house?*

opposite[3] /'ɒpəzɪt/ **noun**
B1 someone or something that is completely different from another person or thing: *He's* ***the exact opposite of*** *my father.*

opposition /ˌɒpə'zɪʃən/ **noun** [no plural]
strong disagreement: *There is a lot of* ***opposition to*** *the new taxes.*

opt /ɒpt/ **verb**
opt for ***something*****; opt to do** ***something*** to choose something or to decide to do something: *Most people opt to have the operation.*

optician /ɒp'tɪʃən/ **noun**
someone whose job is to make glasses

optimist /'ɒptɪmɪst/ **noun**
someone who always thinks that good things will happen
→ Opposite **pessimist noun**

optimistic /ˌɒptɪ'mɪstɪk/ **adj**
always thinking that good things will happen: *We're* ***optimistic about*** *our chances of success.*
→ Opposite **pessimistic adj**

option /'ɒpʃən/ **noun**
B1 a choice: *The menu doesn't* ***have*** *many* ***options****.* ◦ *You always have the* ***option of*** *not attending.*

optional /'ɒpʃənəl/ **adj**
If something is optional, you can decide to have or do it but it is not necessary: *You must take English and science, but history is optional.*

or strong /ɔːʳ/ weak /əʳ/ **conjunction**
1 A1 used between possibilities, or before the last of many possibilities: *Is the baby a boy or a girl?* ◦ *You can have beer or wine.*
2 A2 used after a negative verb to mean not one thing and also not another: *Tim doesn't eat meat or fish.*
3 B1 used to give someone a warning

or advice: *You should be careful, or you'll have an accident.*
4 used to change or correct something you have said: *He finished the work, or most of it, anyway.*

oral /ˈɔːrəl/ **adj**
1 spoken: *an oral examination*
2 relating to the mouth: *oral medicine*

orange[1] /ˈɒrɪndʒ/ **adj**
A1 being a colour that is a mixture of red and yellow: *a deep orange sunset*

orange[2] /ˈɒrɪndʒ/ **noun**
1 A1 a round, sweet fruit with a thick skin and a centre that has many parts: *orange juice*
→ See **Fruit and Vegetables** on page C8
2 A2 a colour that is a mixture of red and yellow
→ See **Colours** on page C6

orbit /ˈɔːbɪt/ **noun**
the circular journey that a spacecraft or planet makes around the sun, the moon, or another planet: *the Earth's orbit*
• **orbit verb** *The moon orbits the Earth.*

orchard /ˈɔːtʃəd/ **noun**
a piece of land where there are fruit trees

orchestra /ˈɔːkɪstrə/ **noun**
B1 a large group of musicians who play different instruments together

order[1] /ˈɔːdər/ **noun**
1 A2 a request for food and drinks in a restaurant: *Has the waiter **taken your order**?*
2 B1 the arrangement of a group of people or things in a list from first to last: *The names are **in alphabetical order**.* ◦ *We put the tasks **in order of** importance.* ◦ *Please keep the books **in order** (= arranged correctly).*
3 something that someone tells you that you must do: *You must **obey orders** at all times.*
4 [no plural] the state of everything being tidy and in its correct place: *I like to have my desk **in order**.*
5 out of order B1 If a machine is out of order, it is not working: *The coffee machine is out of order.*
6 in order to do *something* B1 so that you can do something: *She worked all summer in order to save some money.*

order[2] /ˈɔːdər/ **verb**
1 A2 to ask for food or other things: *Have you ordered any drinks?* ◦ *We ordered new lights for the kitchen.*
2 to tell someone that they must do something: *He **ordered** them **to** leave.*
3 to arrange a group of people or things in a list from first to last: *Have you ordered the pages correctly?*

ordinary /ˈɔːdənəri/ **adj**
1 B1 not special or different in any way: *an ordinary life* ◦ *ordinary people* ◦ *I had a very ordinary childhood.*
2 out of the ordinary different from usual: *Their relationship was a little out of the ordinary.*

organ /ˈɔːgən/ **noun**
1 a part of an animal or plant that has a special purpose: *internal organs*
2 a large musical instrument like a piano that is played in churches: *a church organ*

organic /ɔːˈgænɪk/ **adj**
not using chemicals when keeping animals or growing plants for food: *organic vegetables*

organism /ˈɔːgənɪzəm/ **noun**
a living thing, often a very small one

organization /ˌɔːgənaɪˈzeɪʃən/ **noun**
1 B1 a group of people who work together for the same purpose: *a voluntary organization*
2 B1 [no plural] the way that something is planned: *Who was responsible for the organization of the conference?*

organize /ˈɔːgənaɪz/ **verb**
(**organizing**, **organized**)
B1 to plan or arrange something: *She was busy organizing the event.*

organized /ˈɔːgənaɪzd/ **adj**
1 An organized person plans things well.
→ Opposite **disorganized adj**
2 involving a group of people who plan to do something together: *organized crime*
3 planned or arranged: *We're going on an organized tour.*

origin /ˈɒrɪdʒɪn/ **noun**
1 the cause of something, or where something comes from: *the origin of the universe*
2 the country, race, or social class of a person's family: *She's* ***of*** *Irish* ***origin.***

original[1] /əˈrɪdʒənəl/ **adj**
1 B1 interesting and different from others: *Her essay was full of original ideas.*
2 B1 being the first or existing at the beginning: *Do you still have the original document?*
3 produced by the artist and not a copy: *an original drawing*

original[2] /əˈrɪdʒənəl/ **noun**
something that is in the form in which it was created, and has not been copied or changed: *If the painting is an original, it will be very valuable.*

originally /əˈrɪdʒənəli/ **adv**
at the beginning: *I originally planned to stay for a week but in the end stayed a month.*

ornament /ˈɔːnəmənt/ **noun**
an object that is used as a decoration in a home or garden
→ See **The Living Room** on page C11

orphan /ˈɔːfən/ **noun**
a child whose parents are dead

ostrich /ˈɒstrɪtʃ/ **noun**
a very large bird from Africa that cannot fly but can run very fast

ostrich

other[1] /ˈʌðər/ **adj, determiner**
1 A1 different from a thing or person that you have talked about: *Ask me some other time, when I'm not so busy.*
2 A2 used to talk about the remaining members of a group or items in a set: *I've found one earring – do you know where* ***the other one*** *is?* ◦ *Anna sat down to watch the other dancers.*
3 B1 more, not this or these: *I don't like chocolate – do you have* ***any other*** *desserts?* ◦ *I don't think he's funny, but other people do.*
4 **the other day, week, etc.** B1 a day or week in the recent past: *I asked Carlos about it just the other day.*
5 **the other side/end (of *something*)** the opposite side or end of something: *Put the chair at the other end of the desk.*
6 **the other way round/around** happening in the opposite way: *I thought the older people would be slower than the young people, but it was the other way round.*

other[2] /ˈʌðər/ **pronoun**
1 A2 a thing or person that is part of this set: *Hold the racket in one hand and the ball in the other.*
2 **others** B1 people in general, not including yourself: *You shouldn't expect others to do your work for you.*
3 **others** more people or things of the same type: *This is broken – do you have any others?* ◦ *Where are the others (= the other people)?*

> **Common mistake: other**
>
> Remember that **other** is used before a plural noun.
>
> *The other students were already there.*
>
> **Others** is used on its own.
>
> *Where are the others?*

otherwise[1] /ˈʌðəwaɪz/ **adv**
1 except for what you have just said: *She hurt her arm in the accident, but otherwise she was fine.*
2 different from what has just been said: *I'll meet you there at six o'clock unless I hear otherwise.*

otherwise[2] /ˈʌðəwaɪz/ **conjunction**
B1 used when saying what will happen if someone does not do something: *You'd better phone home, otherwise your parents will start to worry.*

ouch /aʊtʃ/ **exclamation**
something you say when you have a sudden pain: *Ouch! That hurt!*

ought /ɔːt/ **verb**
1 **ought to do *something*** B1 used to say or ask what someone should do: *You ought to see a doctor.*
2 **ought to be/do *something*** B1 used to say that you expect something to

be true or that you expect something to happen: *She ought to be home by now.*

ounce /aʊns/ **noun** (written abbreviation **oz**)
a unit for measuring weight, equal to 28.35 grams

our /aʊəʳ/ **determiner**
A1 belonging to us: *Alice is our youngest daughter.*

ours /aʊəz/ **pronoun**
A2 the thing or things that belong to us: *That's their problem – not ours.*

ourselves /ˌaʊəˈselvz/ **pronoun**
1 A2 used to show that the person who is speaking and other people are affected by an action: *We've promised ourselves a holiday abroad this year.*
2 by ourselves A2 alone or without anyone else's help: *We could invite some friends or we could go by ourselves.*

out /aʊt/ **adj, adv**
1 B1 used to show movement away from the inside of somewhere: *He dropped the bag and all the apples fell out.*
2 A2 used to refer to a period of time when someone goes away from home for a social activity: *He's asked me out to the cinema next week.*
3 A2 not in the place where you usually live or work: *I went round to see her but she was out.*
4 B1 ready to buy or see: *When is the new Spielberg movie out?*
5 B1 able to be seen: *The stars are out tonight.*
6 B1 to the point where something is removed or disappears: *The stain won't come out.*
7 A fire or light that is out is not burning or shining: *Bring some more wood, the fire's out.*

outbreak /ˈaʊtbreɪk/ **noun**
a time when something unpleasant suddenly starts, such as a war or disease: *an outbreak of flu*

outdoor /ˌaʊtˈdɔːʳ/ **adj**
B1 happening or used outside and not in a building: *an outdoor swimming pool* ◦ *outdoor activities*
→ Opposite **indoor adj**

outdoors /ˌaʊtˈdɔːz/ **adv**
B1 not inside a building: *If it's warm this evening, we could eat outdoors.*
→ Opposite **indoors adv**

outer /ˈaʊtəʳ/ **adj**
on the edge or surface of something: *Remove the outer layers of the onion.*
→ Opposite **inner adj**

outfit /ˈaʊtfɪt/ **noun**
all the clothes that you wear at the same time, usually special clothes: *a cowboy outfit*

outgrow /ˌaʊtˈgrəʊ/ **verb** (**outgrew**, **outgrown**)
to grow too big for something: *He's already outgrown these shoes.*

outing /ˈaʊtɪŋ/ **noun**
a short trip taken by a group of people, usually to enjoy themselves

outline /ˈaʊtlaɪn/ **noun**
the shape made by the outside edge of something

out of /aʊt əv/ **preposition**
1 A2 no longer in a particular place or area: *He's out of the country until next month.*
2 B1 used to show movement away from the inside of a place or container: *A pen fell out of her bag.* ◦ *She stepped out of the car.*
3 B1 used to show what something is made from: *The dress is made out of silk.*
4 B1 from among an amount or number: *Nine out of ten people said they liked the product.* ◦ *No one got 20 out of 20 in the test.*
5 out of work B1 not having a job: *I've been out of work for six months.*
6 be out of *something* to have no more of something left: *We're nearly out of petrol.*

out-of-date /ˌaʊtəvˈdeɪt/ **adj**
B1 old and no longer useful or correct: *an out-of-date road map*
→ Opposite **up-to-date adj**

outrageous /aʊtˈreɪdʒəs/ **adj**
shocking or very unusual: *That's an outrageous thing to say!* ◦ *outrageous behaviour*

outside[1] /ˌaʊtˈsaɪd/ **preposition**
1 A2 near a building or room but not in it: *She waited outside the room for almost two hours.*
→ Opposite **inside** **adv**
2 A2 not in: *an apartment just outside Boston*

outside[2] /ˌaʊtˈsaɪd/ **adv**
A1 not inside a building: *It's cold outside today.*

outside[3] /ˌaʊtˈsaɪd/ **noun**
the outside the outer part or surface of something: *The outside of the house is very attractive.*
→ Opposite **inside** **noun**

outside[4] /ˌaʊtsaɪd/ **adj**
not in a building: *an outside light*

the outskirts /ˈaʊtskɜːts/ **plural noun**
the outer area of a city or town

outstanding /ˌaʊtˈstændɪŋ/ **adj**
excellent and much better than most: *He was an outstanding football player.*

outward /ˈaʊtwəd/ **adj**
that you can see: *He was very ill but there were no outward signs of it.*

oval /ˈəʊvᵊl/ **adj**
in the shape of an egg
→ See picture at **shape**
• **oval** **noun** an oval shape

oven /ˈʌvᵊn/ **noun**
B1 a piece of kitchen equipment that is used for cooking food: *an electric oven*
→ See **The Kitchen** on page C10

over[1] /ˈəʊvəʳ/ **adv**, **preposition**
1 A2 covering someone or something: *I put the blanket over her.*
2 A2 more than an amount, number, or age: *Suitable for children aged five and over.*
3 B1 above or higher than something: *A huge plane flew over our heads.*
4 B1 from one side of something to the other side: *I climbed over the wall.*
5 B1 during a particular period of time: *I was in Seattle over the summer.*
6 B1 on the other side of: *The post office is over the bridge.*
7 **over here/there** B1 in this or that place: *Put your bags down over there.*
8 **over and over (again)** happening or done many times: *I read the article over and over until it made sense.*
9 describes the way an object moves or is moved so that a different part of it is facing up: *She turned another page over.*
10 down from a higher to a lower position: *The little boy fell over and started to cry.*

over[2] /ˈəʊvəʳ/ **adj**
B1 finished: *The exams will be over next week.*

over- /əʊvəʳ/ **prefix**
too much: *The children were over-excited (= too excited).*

overall /ˈəʊvᵊrɔːl/ **adj**
considering everything or everyone: *The overall cost of the flight was $900.*
• **overall** /ˌəʊvᵊrˈɔːl/ **adv** *Overall it has been a good year.*

overalls /ˈəʊvᵊrɔːlz/ **plural noun** US (UK **dungarees**)
trousers with a part that covers your chest and straps that go over your shoulders

overcome /ˌəʊvəˈkʌm/ **verb**
to deal with and control a problem or feeling: *Eventually she managed to overcome her fear of dogs.*

overflow /ˌəʊvəˈfləʊ/ **verb**
If a container or a place overflows, the thing that is inside it starts coming out because it is too full: *The bath overflowed, and the floor's all wet.*

overhead /ˌəʊvəˈhed/ **adj**, **adv**
above your head, usually in the sky: *A bird flew overhead.* ◦ *overhead lights*

overhear /ˌəʊvəˈhɪəʳ/ **verb** (**overheard**)
to hear what someone is saying to someone else: *I overheard him telling her he was leaving.*

overlook /ˌəʊvəˈlʊk/ **verb**
1 to have a view of something from above: *Our hotel room had a balcony overlooking the sea.*
2 to not notice or consider something: *Two important facts have been overlooked in this case.*

a b c d e f g h i j k l m n **o** p q r s t u v w x y z

overnight /ˌəʊvəˈnaɪt/ **adv**
1 B1 during the night: *We stayed overnight at my grandmother's house.*
2 very quickly or suddenly: *Change does not happen overnight.*

overseas /ˌəʊvəˈsiːz/ **adj**
from another country: *an overseas student*
• **overseas adv** *He worked overseas.*

oversleep /ˌəʊvəˈsliːp/ **verb**
(**overslept**)
to sleep longer than you wanted to: *Sorry I'm late – I overslept.*

overtake /ˌəʊvəˈteɪk/ **verb**
(**overtaking**, **overtook**, **overtaken**)
to go past a car or person that is going in the same direction: *Never overtake on a bend.*

overtime /ˈəʊvətaɪm/ **noun** [no plural]
extra time that you work after your usual working hours: *I* ***worked*** *a lot of* ***overtime*** *this week.*

overweight /ˌəʊvəˈweɪt/ **adj**
fat: *He's still a few pounds overweight.*

owe /əʊ/ **verb** (**owing**, **owed**)
1 B1 to have to pay money back to someone who gave you money in the past: *You still owe me money.* ◦ *He* ***owes*** *about £5,000* ***to*** *the bank.*
2 owe *someone* an apology, explanation, favour, etc. to have to give something to someone because they deserve it: *I think I owe you an apology.*

owing to /əʊɪŋ tuː/ **preposition**
because of: *The trip has been cancelled owing to the weather.*

owl /aʊl/ **noun**
a bird that has large eyes and hunts small animals at night

owl

own[1] /əʊn/
adj, pronoun, determiner
1 belonging to a particular person: *Each student has his or her own dictionary.* ◦ *Petra makes all her own clothes.*
2 (all) on your own alone: *Jessica lives on her own.*
3 (all) on your own without any help: *I cooked dinner all on my own.*

own[2] /əʊn/ **verb**
to have something that belongs to you: *He owns a lot of land.*

owner /əʊnəʳ/ **noun**
B1 someone who owns something: *car owners*

oxygen /ˈɒksɪdʒən/ **noun** [no plural]
a gas in the air that people and animals need to breathe

oz
written abbreviation for ounce: a unit for measuring weight

P p

P, p /piː/
the sixteenth letter of the alphabet

p
1 written abbreviation for page: *See p27.*
2 abbreviation for pence or penny (= UK unit of money): *This packet of crisps costs 60p.* ◦ *a 10p coin*

pace /peɪs/ **noun** [no plural]
how fast someone walks or runs: *We started to walk at a much faster pace.*

pacifier /ˈpæsɪfaɪəʳ/ **noun** US (UK **dummy**)
a small rubber object that you put in a baby's mouth to stop it from crying

pack[1] /pæk/ **verb**
1 A2 to put your things into bags or boxes when you are going on holiday or leaving the place where you live: *I've got to go home and pack.* ◦ *She was **packing her bags**.*
→ Opposite **unpack** verb
2 If people pack a place, a lot of them go there: *Thousands of fans packed the stadium.*
pack *something* in **phrasal verb** informal
to stop doing something: *He has packed in his job.*
pack (*something*) up **phrasal verb**
to put all your things together when you have finished doing something: *I'm about to pack my things up and go home.*

pack[2] /pæk/ **noun**
1 US a small box or paper container with a lot of things of the same kind in it: *a **pack of** gum*
2 a bag that you carry on your back
3 a group of animals that live together, especially dogs: *a pack of dogs*
4 UK (US **deck**) a set of cards used for playing games

package /ˈpækɪdʒ/ **noun**
1 something that is covered in paper so that it can be sent by post: *He was carrying a package under his arm.*
2 a related group of things that are offered together as a single unit: *This ski package includes hotel, flights, and four days of skiing.*

packages

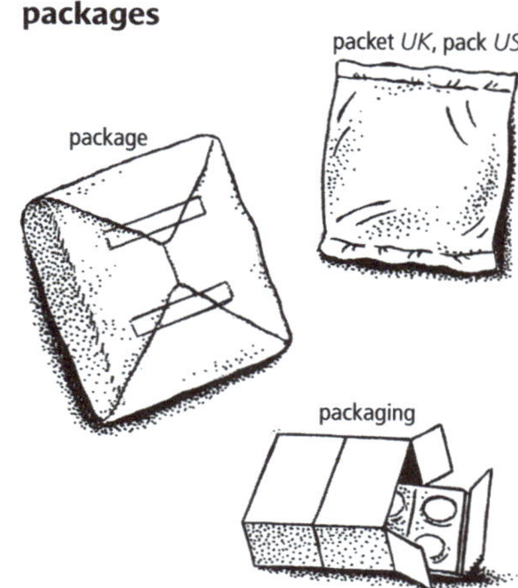

package tour /ˈpækɪdʒ ˌtʊəʳ/ **noun** (also **package holiday**)
a holiday that is arranged for you by a travel company and which costs a fixed price that includes travel, hotels, and sometimes meals: *We went on a package tour to Spain.*

packaging /ˈpækɪdʒɪŋ/ **noun** [no plural]
the paper, box, plastic, etc., that something is put in so that it can be sold or sent somewhere

packed /pækt/ **adj**
A packed place is full of people: *The hall was packed.*

packet /ˈpækɪt/ **noun** UK
B1 a small box or paper container with a lot of things of the same kind in it: *a **packet of** cigarettes*

packing /ˈpækɪŋ/ **noun** [no plural]
the act of putting things into bags or boxes so that you can take them somewhere: *I've got to **do** my **packing** because I'm leaving tomorrow.*

pad /pæd/ **noun**
1 pieces of paper that have been attached together at one edge: *There's a pad and pencil by the phone.*
2 a small piece of something soft that is used to protect something: *I wear knee pads when I go skating.*

padded /ˈpædɪd/ **adj**
Padded clothes are covered or filled with something soft, often so that they are warm: *a padded jacket*

paddle¹ /ˈpædl/ **noun**
1 a short pole with one flat end that you use to make a small boat move through the water
2 UK the activity of walking in water that is not deep: *The children* ***went for a paddle****.*

paddle² /ˈpædl/ **verb** (**paddling**, **paddled**)
1 to move a small boat through water with a paddle
2 UK to walk in water that is not deep

padlock /ˈpædlɒk/ **noun**
a metal lock with a U-shaped part that you use for fastening bicycles, doors, etc.
• **padlock** verb

page /peɪdʒ/ **noun**
1 A1 a piece of paper in a book, magazine, etc., or one side of a piece of paper: *The article is on page 36.* ◦ *I've only read 50 pages so far.*
2 A2 (also **web page**) one part of a website (= area of information on the Internet) that you can see or print separately

paid /peɪd/
past tense and past participle of pay

pail /peɪl/ **noun** mainly US (UK usually **bucket**)
a container with an open top and a handle, used for carrying liquids

pain /peɪn/ **noun**
1 A2 a bad feeling in a part of your body when you are ill or hurt: *stomach pains* ◦ *Are you* ***in pain****?* ◦ *I felt a sharp pain in my foot.*
2 [no plural] sadness: *I can't describe the pain I suffered when he died.*
3 be a pain (in the neck) informal to be annoying: *My brother can be a real pain in the neck sometimes.*

painful /ˈpeɪnfəl/ **adj**
1 B1 causing pain: *My hand is really painful where I hit it.*
2 making you feel sad or upset: *a painful memory*

painkiller /ˈpeɪnˌkɪləʳ/ **noun**
a drug that stops pain

paint¹ /peɪnt/ **noun**
A1 a coloured liquid that you put on a surface to decorate it: *Have you chosen the paint for your bedroom?*

paint² /peɪnt/ **verb**
1 A1 to make a picture of something or someone using paint: *These pictures were all painted by local artists.*
2 A2 to cover a surface with paint: *We've painted the kitchen yellow.*

paintbrush /ˈpeɪntbrʌʃ/ **noun**
a brush that is used for painting
→ See picture at **brush** noun

painter /ˈpeɪntəʳ/ **noun**
1 A2 someone who paints pictures
2 someone whose job is to paint walls and doors, etc.

painting /ˈpeɪntɪŋ/ **noun**
1 A2 a picture that someone has painted
2 A2 [no plural] the activity of painting pictures or painting surfaces

pair /peəʳ/ **noun**
1 A1 two people who are doing something together: *For the next exercise, you'll need to work* ***in pairs****.*
2 A2 two things that look the same and that are used together: *a pair of socks/shoes*
3 A2 something that is made of two parts that are joined together: *a pair of scissors* ◦ *a pair of jeans*

pajamas /pəˈdʒɑːməz/ **plural noun**
the US spelling of pyjamas

pal /pæl/ **noun** informal
a friend: *He's an old pal of mine.*

palace /ˈpælɪs/ **noun**
B1 a large house where a king or queen lives: *Buckingham Palace*

pale /peɪl/ **adj**
1 pale blue, green, etc. A2 light blue, green, etc.: *a pale yellow dress*
2 If your face is pale, it has less colour

pair

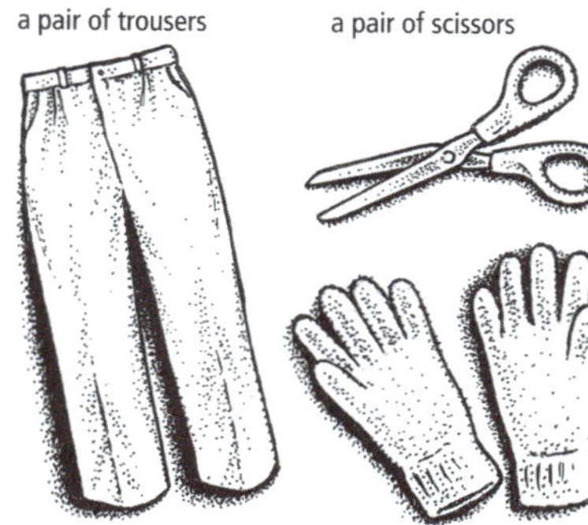

than usual because you are ill: *You're looking a bit pale – are you all right?*

palm /pɑːm/ **noun**
1 the inside surface of your hand
→ See **The Body** on page C2
2 a palm tree

palm tree /ˈpɑːm ˌtriː/ **noun**
a tall tree with long leaves at the top that grows in hot countries

pan /pæn/ **noun**
B1 a metal container with a handle that is used for cooking food in

pancake /ˈpænkeɪk/ **noun**
a thin, flat cake that you cook in a pan

panda /ˈpændə/ **noun**
a large, black and white animal that lives in forests in China

panda

pane /peɪn/ **noun**
a flat piece of glass in a window or door

panel /ˈpænᵊl/ **noun**
1 a flat piece of wood, metal, etc. that is the surface of a door, wall, etc.
2 a group of people who are chosen to talk about something or make a decision about something: *a panel of experts*

panic¹ /ˈpænɪk/ **noun**
a sudden, strong feeling of fear that makes you stop thinking clearly and do silly things: *He was* ***in a panic*** *about his exams.*

panic² /ˈpænɪk/ **verb** (**panicking**, **panicked**)
to suddenly feel very afraid so that you stop thinking clearly and do silly things: *Don't panic – we've got plenty of time.*

pant /pænt/ **verb**
to breathe quickly and loudly because you have been exercising

panties /ˈpæntiz/ **plural noun** US (UK **knickers**)
a piece of clothing for women that covers the bottom

pantomime /ˈpæntəmaɪm/ **noun**
a funny play for children that is performed in the UK around Christmas

pants /pænts/ **plural noun**
1 B1 UK (US **underpants**) a piece of clothing for women that covers the bottom
2 US (UK **trousers**) a piece of clothing that covers the legs and has a separate part for each leg
→ See **Clothes** on page C5

pantyhose /ˈpæntihəʊz/ **plural noun** US (UK **tights**)
a piece of women's clothing made of very thin material that covers the legs and bottom
→ See **Clothes** on page C5

paper /ˈpeɪpəʳ/ **noun**
1 A1 [no plural] thin, flat material used for writing on: *Have you got a piece of paper?*
2 A2 UK a part of an examination: *Candidates must answer two questions from each paper.*
3 B1 a newspaper: *I buy a paper every morning.*

paperback /ˈpeɪpəbæk/ **noun**
a book that has a soft paper cover

paper clips

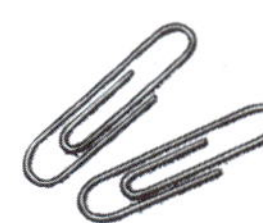

paper clip /ˈpeɪpə ˌklɪp/ **noun**
a small piece of

a b c d e f g h i j k l m n o p q r s t u v w x y z

metal used to hold pieces of paper together

parachute /ˈpærəʃuːt/ **noun** a large piece of cloth that is attached to your body with strings and helps you to drop safely from a plane

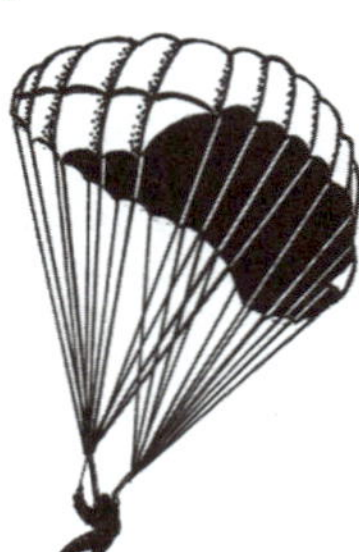

parachute

parade /pəˈreɪd/ **noun** an event where lines of people walk through a public place to celebrate a special day: *a victory parade*

paradise /ˈpærədaɪs/ **noun** [no plural]
1 in some religions, a place where good people go after they die
2 a perfect place or situation: *a tropical paradise*

paragraph /ˈpærəɡrɑːf/ **noun**
B1 a group of sentences that are together and start on a new line

parallel /ˈpærəlel/ **adj**
If two or more lines are parallel, the distance between them is the same along all their length: *The streets are parallel.*

paralyse (**paralysing**, **paralysed**) UK (US **paralyze**) /ˈpærᵊlaɪz/ **verb**
to make someone unable to move all or part of their body: *He was paralysed from the waist down in the accident.*

paramedic /ˌpærəˈmedɪk/ **noun**
someone who is not a doctor or nurse but who is trained to help people who are injured or very sick, until they get to hospital

parcel /ˈpɑːsᵊl/ **noun** mainly UK
B1 something that is covered in paper so that it can be sent by post

parcel

pardon /ˈpɑːdᵊn/ **exclamation**
1 A2 (US usually **pardon me**) a polite way of asking someone to say again what they have just said: *'You'll need an umbrella.' 'Pardon?' 'I said you'll need an umbrella.'*
2 **pardon me** used to say 'sorry' after you have done something rude, for example after burping (= letting air from your stomach out of your mouth)

parent /ˈpeərᵊnt/ **noun**
A1 your mother or father: *Her parents live in Oxford.*

> **Common mistake: parents or relations/relatives?**
>
> Your **parents** are only your mother and father. The other people in your family are **relations** or **relatives.**
>
> *We spent the holidays visiting all our relatives.*
>
> ~~*We spent the holidays visiting all our parents.*~~

parentheses /pəˈrenθəsiːz/ **plural noun**
mainly US (UK usually **brackets**) two curved lines ( ) used around extra information in a sentence: *The age of each student is listed* ***in parentheses.***

park[1] /pɑːk/ **noun**
A1 a large area of grass, often in a town, where people can walk and enjoy themselves: *We went for a walk in the park.*

park[2] /pɑːk/ **verb**
A2 to leave a car in a place for a period of time: *You can park outside the school.*

parking /ˈpɑːkɪŋ/ **noun** [no plural]
B1 leaving a car in a place for a period of time: *free parking*

parking lot /ˈpɑːkɪŋ ˌlɒt/ **noun** US (UK **car park**)
an area of ground where you can leave your car for a short time

parking meter /ˈpɑːkɪŋ ˌmiːtəʳ/ **noun**
a machine at the side of the road that you put money into so that you can leave your vehicle on that road

parliament /ˈpɑːləmənt/ **noun**
in some countries, a group of people

who make the laws for the country: *the Russian parliament*

parrot /ˈpærət/ **noun**
B1 a brightly coloured bird that can copy what people say

parsley /ˈpɑːsli/ **noun** [no plural]
a plant that you add to food to give it flavour

part[1] /pɑːt/ **noun**
1 A1 one of the things that, with other things, makes the whole of something: ***Part of*** *this form seems to be missing.* ◦ *That's only part of the problem.* ◦ *You're part of the family.*
2 part of *something* A2 some but not all of a thing: *Kate spent part of the day shopping.*
3 B1 a person in a movie or play: *He* ***plays*** *the* ***part*** *of the father.*
4 take part (in *something*) B1 to do an activity with other people: *She doesn't usually take part in any of the class activities.*
5 a piece of a machine or vehicle: *aircraft parts*
6 have/play a part in *something* to be one of the people or things that are involved in an event or situation: *We can all play a part in making our city a better place to live.*

part[2] /pɑːt/ **verb**
part with *something* **phrasal verb**
to give something to someone else, often when you do not want to: *It is so hard getting Simon to part with his money.*

partial /ˈpɑːʃəl/ **adj**
not complete: *He made a partial recovery.*

partially /ˈpɑːʃəli/ **adv**
not completely: *It was partially cooked.*

participant /pɑːˈtɪsɪpənt/ **noun**
someone who does an activity with other people: *All participants finishing the race will receive a medal.*

participate /pɑːˈtɪsɪpeɪt/ **verb**
(**participating**, **participated**)
to do an activity with other people: *She rarely* ***participates in*** *any of the discussions.*

participation /pɑːˌtɪsɪˈpeɪʃən/ **noun**
[no plural]
the act of doing an activity with other people: *Both shows encourage audience participation.*

participle /pɑːˈtɪsɪpl/ **noun**
in grammar, the form of a verb that usually ends with '-ed' or '-ing' and is used in some verb tenses

particle /ˈpɑːtɪkl/ **noun**
a very small piece of something: *particles of dust*

particular /pəˈtɪkjələr/ **adj**
1 used to talk about one thing or person and not others: *Is there any particular restaurant you'd like to go to?* ◦ *'Why did you ask?' 'No particular reason.'*
2 special: *'Was anything important said at the meeting?' 'Nothing of particular interest.'*
3 in particular B1 especially: *Are you looking for anything in particular?*

particularly /pəˈtɪkjələli/ **adv**
B1 especially: *She didn't seem particularly interested.* ◦ *'Was the food good?' 'Not particularly.'*

partly /ˈpɑːtli/ **adv**
B1 to some degree but not completely: *The house is partly owned by her father.*

partner /ˈpɑːtnər/ **noun**
1 A2 someone that you are dancing or playing a sport or game with
2 B1 someone that you are married to or having a sexual relationship with: *Are partners invited to the office dinner?*
3 someone who owns a business with another person: *He's a* ***partner in*** *a law firm.*

partnership /ˈpɑːtnəʃɪp/ **noun**
a situation in which two people or organizations work together to achieve something: *a* ***business partnership***

part of speech /ˌpɑːt əv ˈspiːtʃ/ **noun**
one of the grammatical groups into which words are divided, such as noun, verb, and adjective

a b c d e f g h i j k l m n o p q r s t u v w x y z

part-time /ˌpɑːtˈtaɪm/ **adj**, **adv**
B1 working or studying only for part of the day or the week: *a part-time job*

party /ˈpɑːti/ **noun** (plural **parties**)
1 A1 an event where people come together to enjoy themselves by talking, eating, drinking, and dancing: *a birthday party* ◦ *We're* ***having*** *a* ***party*** *to celebrate the occasion.*
2 B1 an organization that has the same political beliefs and tries to win elections: *a political party*
3 a group of people who are working or travelling together: *a party of tourists*

pass[1] /pɑːs/ **verb**
1 A2 to succeed at a test or an exam: *I passed my driving test the first time.*
2 B1 to go past something or someone: *She passed me this morning in the street.* ◦ *Cars kept passing us on the motorway.*
3 B1 to go in a particular direction: *Another plane* ***passed over*** *our heads.* ◦ *We* ***pass through*** *your village on the way home.*
4 B1 to give something to someone: *Could you pass the salt, please?*
5 B1 If a period of time passes, it happens: *Four years have passed since that day.*
6 **pass (the) time** to spend time doing something: *We played a few games to pass the time.*
7 **pass a law, measure, etc.** to officially approve something and make it into a law or rule: *The government passed a law to restrict the sale of guns.*
8 in sports, to throw or kick a ball to someone else: *Edwards* ***passes to*** *Brinkworth.*
pass *something* around/round **phrasal verb**
to offer something to each person in a group of people: *Could you pass these sandwiches around, please?*
pass away **phrasal verb**
to die: *She passed away peacefully in her sleep.*
pass *something* on **phrasal verb**
1 B1 to tell someone something that someone else has told you: *Did you pass on my message to him?*
2 B1 to give something to someone else: *Will you pass the book on to Lara when you've finished with it?*
pass out **phrasal verb**
to become unconscious: *I don't remember any more because I passed out then.*

pass[2] /pɑːs/ **noun**
1 B1 an official paper that allows you to do something: *You need a pass to get into the building.*
2 a successful result in a test or a course: *A pass is above 60%.*
3 in sports, when you throw or kick a ball to someone else

passage /ˈpæsɪdʒ/ **noun**
1 a long, thin space that connects one place to another: *There's a passage to the side of the house, leading to the garden.*
2 a short part of a book or speech: *She read a passage from the novel.*

passenger /ˈpæsəndʒər/ **noun**
A2 someone who is travelling in a car, plane, etc., but not controlling it: *a front-seat passenger* ◦ *a passenger seat/train*

passion /ˈpæʃən/ **noun**
1 [no plural] a strong, sexual feeling for someone: *She saw the passion in his eyes.*
2 a very strong feeling about a subject: *She spoke with passion about the injustice.*

passionate /ˈpæʃənət/ **adj**
1 having a strong, sexual feeling for someone: *They had a passionate love affair.*
2 showing a strong feeling about a subject: *She was a passionate speaker.*
• **passionately** **adv**

passive /ˈpæsɪv/ **adj**
1 B1 In grammar, a passive verb or sentence is one in which the subject does not do the action. For example 'It was written by a child' is a passive sentence.
2 letting things happen to you and not taking action: *He's very passive in the relationship.*

the passive /ˈpæsɪv/ **noun** [no plural]
B1 in grammar, the passive form of a verb

passport /ˈpɑːspɔːt/ **noun**
A2 a small book with your photograph that you need to enter a country: *a British passport*

passport control /ˈpɑːspɔːt kən ˌtrəʊl/ **noun** [no plural]
the place where your passport is officially checked when you enter or leave a country

password /ˈpɑːswɜːd/ **noun**
B1 a secret word that allows you to do something, especially to use your computer: *Type in your password.*

past[1] /pɑːst/ **adj**
1 B1 having happened or existed before now: *past relationships* ◦ *I know this from past experience.*
2 B1 used to refer to a period of time in the past that lasts until the present: *It's been raining for the past three days.*

past[2] /pɑːst/ **noun**
1 the past B1 the time before the present and all the things that happened then: ***In the past*** *people would bathe once a month.*
2 the past (also **the past tense**) A2 in grammar, the form of a verb that is used to show what happened in the past
3 ***someone's*** **past** B1 all of the things that someone has done in their life: *I knew nothing about his past.*

past[3] /pɑːst/ **adv, preposition**
1 A2 further than: *I live on Station Road, just past the Post Office.*
2 A2 up to and farther than someone or something: *Three boys went past us on mountain bikes.* ◦ *I've just seen the bus go past.*
3 A1 mainly UK used to say 'after' the hour when you are saying what time it is: *It's five past three.*
4 above a particular age or farther than a particular point: *She's past the age where she needs a babysitter.*

pasta /ˈpæstə/ **noun** [no plural]
A2 a food that is made from flour and water, and is made in many different shapes: *Spaghetti is my favourite pasta.*
→ See **Food** on page C7

paste[1] /peɪst/ **noun** [no plural]
a wet, sticky substance that is used to stick things together: *wallpaper paste*

paste[2] /peɪst/ **verb** (**pasting**, **pasted**)
to stick a piece of paper to another piece of paper: *He had pasted the pictures into a book.*

past participle /ˌpɑːst ˈpɑːtɪsɪpl/ **noun**
the form of a verb that usually ends with '-ed'. For example 'walked' is the past participle of 'walk'.

the past perfect /ˌpɑːst ˈpɜːfɪkt/ **noun**
in grammar, the form of a verb that is used to show that an action was already finished when another action happened. The sentence 'I had never been to Australia' is in the past perfect.

pastry /ˈpeɪstri/ **noun**
1 [no plural] a food made of flour, fat, and water that you cook and use for covering or containing other food
2 (plural **pastries**) a small cake

pat[1] /pæt/ **verb** (**patting**, **patted**)
to touch a person or animal with a flat hand in a gentle, friendly way: *She stopped to pat the dog.*

pat[2] /pæt/ **noun**
a gentle, friendly touch with a flat hand

patch /pætʃ/ **noun**
1 a small area that is different from the area around it: *There are icy patches on the road.*
2 a piece of material that you use to cover a hole in your clothes or in other material
3 a bad/rough patch a difficult time: *Their marriage is going through a bad patch.*

paternal /pəˈtɜːnəl/ **adj**
1 like a father: *paternal affection*
2 A paternal relation is part of your father's family: *He was my paternal grandfather.*
→ Opposite **maternal** **adj**

path /pɑːθ/ **noun**
A2 a long, thin area of ground for

a b c d e f g h i j k l m n o **p** q r s t u v w x y z

people to walk on: *There's a path through the forest.* ◦ *a garden path*

pathetic /pəˈθetɪk/ **adj** informal
bad and showing that you have not tried or are not brave: *He made a rather pathetic attempt to apologize.*

patience /ˈpeɪʃᵊns/ **noun** [no plural]
the ability to stay calm and not get upset, especially when something takes a long time: *You need patience when you are dealing with young children.* ◦ *Finally, I **lost** my **patience** and shouted at her.*

patient¹ /ˈpeɪʃᵊnt/ **adj**
B1 able to stay calm and not get upset, especially when something takes a long time: *You need to be **patient with** children.*
• **patiently adv**
→ Opposite **impatient adj**

patient² /ˈpeɪʃᵊnt/ **noun**
B1 someone who is being treated by a doctor, nurse, etc.: *a cancer patient*

patio /ˈpætiəʊ/ **noun**
an area outside a house with a hard floor, where people can sit to eat and relax: *In the summer we have breakfast **on the patio**.*

patriotic /ˌpætriˈɒtɪk/ **adj**
showing that you love your country and think it is very good: *a patriotic song*

patrol¹ /pəˈtrəʊl/ **noun**
the act of looking for trouble or danger around an area or building: *We passed a group of soldiers **on patrol**.*

patrol² /pəˈtrəʊl/ **verb** (**patrolling**, **patrolled**)
to look for trouble or danger in an area or around a building: *Police patrol the streets night and day.*

pattern /ˈpætᵊn/ **noun**
1 B1 a design of lines, shapes, colours, etc.: *The shirt has a pattern on it.*
2 a particular way that something is often done or repeated: *behaviour patterns*
3 a drawing, shape, or set of instructions that helps you to make something: *a dress pattern*

pause /pɔːz/ **verb** (**pausing**, **paused**)
1 B1 to stop doing something for a short time: *She **paused for** a moment and looked around her.*
2 to make a CD, DVD, etc. stop for a short time by pressing a button: *Can you pause the movie there, please?*
• **pause noun** a short time during which you stop doing something before starting again: *There was a short pause before he spoke.*

pavement /ˈpeɪvmənt/ **noun**
1 B1 UK (US **sidewalk**) a path by the side of a road that people walk on
2 US the hard surface of a road

paw /pɔː/ **noun**
the foot of an animal, such as a cat or a dog

paw

pay¹ /peɪ/ **verb** (**paying**, **paid**)
1 A1 to give money to someone because you are buying something from them: *Helen **paid for** the tickets.*
2 B1 to give someone money for the work that they do: *She **gets paid** twice a month.* ◦ *We **paid** them $600 **for** the work.*
3 pay attention B1 to look at or listen to someone or something carefully: *I missed what she was saying because I wasn't paying attention.*

> **Common mistake: pay for something**
>
> Remember that when **pay** means give money to buy something, it is usually followed by the preposition **for**.
>
> *Rachel paid for the meal.*
> ~~*Rachel paid the meal.*~~

pay *someone/something* back phrasal verb
B1 to pay someone the money that you owe them: *Has he paid you back the money he owes you?*

pay off phrasal verb
If something you have done pays off, it is successful: *All her hard work paid off and she passed the exam.*

pay *something* off phrasal verb
to pay all of the money that you owe: *I'm planning to pay off my bank loan in five years.*

pay[2] /peɪ/ **noun** [no plural]
B1 the money that you get for working: *a pay rise*

payment /ˈpeɪmənt/ **noun**
1 [no plural] the act of paying: *They will accept payment by credit card.*
2 the amount of money that is paid: *monthly payments*

payphone /ˈpeɪˌfəʊn/ **noun**
a telephone in a public place that you pay to use

PC /ˌpiːˈsiː/ **noun**
A2 a personal computer (= a computer for one person to use)

PE /ˌpiːˈiː/ **noun** [no plural]
abbreviation for physical education: classes at school where children do exercise and play sport

pea /piː/ **noun**
B1 a small, round, green seed that people eat as a vegetable

peace /piːs/ **noun** [no plural]
1 B1 a situation in which there is quiet and calm: *After a busy day, all I want is* ***peace and quiet****.*
2 a situation in which there is no war, violence, or arguing: *There seems little hope for world peace.*

peaceful /ˈpiːsfᵊl/ **adj**
1 B1 quiet and calm: *The park was quiet and peaceful.*
2 without violence: *a peaceful protest*
• **peacefully adv** *He died peacefully at home.*

peach /piːtʃ/ **noun**
B1 a soft, sweet, round fruit with red and yellow skin

peak /piːk/ **noun**
1 B1 the top of a mountain: *snow-covered peaks*
2 the highest level or value of something: *House prices have probably* ***reached*** *their* ***peak****.* ◦ *peak travel times*

peanut /ˈpiːnʌt/ **noun**
B1 an oval-shaped nut with a soft, brown shell
→ See **Food** on page C7

peanut butter /ˌpiːnʌt ˈbʌtəʳ/ **noun** [no plural]
a soft brown food made from peanuts

peak

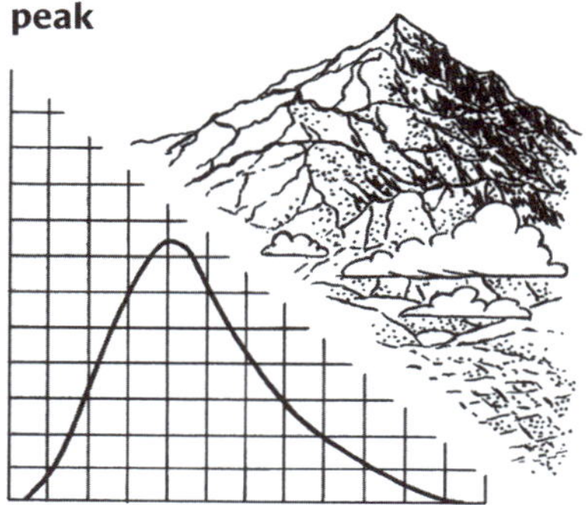

that is often eaten on bread: *a peanut butter sandwich*

pear /peəʳ/ **noun**
A2 an oval-shaped, green or yellow fruit

pear

pearl /pɜːl/ **noun**
a hard, white, round object that is made inside the shell of a sea creature and that is used to make jewellery: *a string of pearls*

pebble /ˈpebl/ **noun**
a small stone

peck /pek/ **verb**
If a bird pecks something, it quickly bites it: *chickens* ***pecking at*** *corn*

peculiar /pɪˈkjuːliəʳ/ **adj**
strange, often in a bad way: *The wine had a peculiar smell.*

pedal /ˈpedᵊl/ **noun**
a part of a machine that you press with your foot: *bicycle pedals*

pedestrian /pɪˈdestriən/ **noun**
B1 a person who is walking

peel[1] /piːl/ **verb**
B1 to take off the skin of fruit or vegetables: *Peel and chop the onions.*

peel[2] /piːl/ **noun** [no plural]
the skin of fruit or vegetables

peep[1] /piːp/ **verb**
to quickly look at something, often when you do not want other people to see you: *She peeped at them through the fence.*

peep² /piːp/ **noun** [no plural]
a quick look: *She* ***took a peep*** *at herself in the mirror.*

peer /pɪəʳ/ **verb**
to look carefully or with difficulty: *She peered at me over her glasses.*

peg /peg/ **noun**
1 an object on a wall or door that you hang things on
2 (also **clothes peg**) UK a short piece of wood or plastic that is used to hold clothes on a rope while they dry

pen /pen/ **noun**
A1 a long, thin object that you use to write or draw in ink
→ See **The Classroom** on page C4

penalty /ˈpenᵊlti/ **noun** (plural **penalties**)
1 a punishment for doing something that is against a law or rule: *There's a £50 penalty for late cancellation of tickets.*
2 in sports, an advantage given to a team when the other team has broken a rule: *They won a penalty in the first five minutes of the game.*

pence /pens/ **noun** UK
A2 plural of penny; p

> **Common mistake: pence, pennies, or p?**
>
> **Pence** is the usual plural of penny (UK) and is used to talk about amounts of money. In informal UK English you can also say **p**.
>
> *Can you lend me 50 pence?*
> *Can you lend me 50p?*
>
> The plural form **pennies** is only used to talk about the coins as objects.
>
> *He found some pennies in his pocket.*

pencil /ˈpensᵊl/ **noun**
A1 a long, thin wooden object with a black or coloured point that you write or draw with
→ See **The Classroom** on page C4

pencil sharpener /ˈpensᵊl ˌʃɑːpᵊnəʳ/ **noun**
a tool that you use to make pencils sharp
→ See **The Classroom** on page C4

penfriend /ˈpenfrend/ **noun**
A2 someone that you write to regularly but have never met: *When I was young I had a penfriend in Jamaica.*

penguin /ˈpeŋgwɪn/ **noun**
B1 a large, black and white sea bird that swims and cannot fly

penicillin /ˌpenɪˈsɪlɪn/ **noun** [no plural]
a type of medicine that kills bacteria and is used to treat illness

penis /ˈpiːnɪs/ **noun**
the part of a man's or male animal's body that is used for having sex

penny /ˈpeni/ **noun** (plural **pence**, **pennies**)
B1 a coin with a value of 1/100 of a pound (= UK unit of money); p: *There are 100 pence in a pound.*

pension /ˈpenʃᵊn/ **noun**
money that is given to a person who has stopped working because he or she is old or ill

pensioner /ˈpenʃᵊnəʳ/ **noun** UK
someone who receives a pension

people /ˈpiːpl/ **noun**
A1 more than one person: *Our company employs over 400 people.*

pepper /ˈpepəʳ/ **noun**
1 A2 [no plural] a powder that is made from seeds, used to give food a slightly spicy flavour: *salt and pepper*
2 B1 a green, red, or yellow vegetable
→ See **Fruit and Vegetables** on page C8

per strong /pɜːʳ/ weak /pəʳ/ **preposition**
A2 for each: *The hotel room costs $60 per night.*

percent /pəˈsent/ **adj, adv**
B1 out of every 100, shown by the symbol %: *a 40 percent increase in prices*

percentage /pəˈsentɪdʒ/ **noun**
an amount of something, shown as a number out of 100: *The* ***percentage of*** *women who work has increased.*

perch /pɜːtʃ/ **verb**
to sit near the edge of something: *The children* ***perched on*** *the edges of their seats.*

perfect /ˈpɜːfɪkt/ **adj**
1 A2 without fault, or the best possible: *a perfect day* ◦ *He was* ***the perfect*** *father.*

2 exactly right for someone or something: *You'd be **perfect for** the job.*

perfection /pəˈfekʃən/ **noun** [no plural]
a state of having no mistakes, faults, or damage: *We ask the children to do their best but we don't expect perfection.*

perfectly /ˈpɜːfɪktli/ **adv**
1 B1 in a perfect way: *The jacket fits perfectly.*
2 very: *I made my feelings perfectly clear.*

perform /pəˈfɔːm/ **verb**
1 B1 to act, sing, dance, or play music for other people to enjoy: *The orchestra will perform music by Mozart.*
2 formal to do a job or a piece of work: *Surgeons performed the operation in less than two hours.*
3 to succeed or not succeed: *Neither company has performed well this year.*

performance /pəˈfɔːməns/ **noun**
1 B1 acting, singing, dancing, or playing music for other people to enjoy: *a performance of Shakespeare's Hamlet*
2 [no plural] how successful someone or something is: *The company's performance was poor for the first two years.*

performer /pəˈfɔːməʳ/ **noun**
B1 someone who acts, sings, dances, or plays music for other people to enjoy

perfume /ˈpɜːfjuːm/ **noun**
A2 a liquid with a nice smell that you put on your skin

perhaps /pəˈhæps/ **adv**
A2 possibly: *Perhaps I'll go to the gym after work.* ◦ *Perhaps Ben will come.*

period /ˈpɪəriəd/ **noun**
1 B1 a length of time: *a 24-hour period* ◦ *a period of four months*
2 B1 in a school, one of the parts of the day when a subject is taught: *We have six periods of science a week.*
3 US (UK **full stop**) a mark (.) used at the end of a sentence, or to show that the letters before it are an abbreviation

permanent /ˈpɜːmənənt/ **adj**
B1 continuing always or for a long time: *She found a permanent job.*
• **permanently adv**

permission /pəˈmɪʃən/ **noun** [no plural]
B1 the act of allowing someone to do something: *I had to **get permission** to use the car.* ◦ *He took the car **without permission**.*

permit¹ /pəˈmɪt/ **verb** (**permitting**, **permitted**) formal
B1 to allow something: *Photography is not permitted inside the museum.*

permit² /ˈpɜːmɪt/ **noun**
a paper that allows you to do something: *a work permit*

person /ˈpɜːsən/ **noun** (plural **people**)
1 A1 a human being: *You're the only person I know here.*
2 **in person** If you do something in person, you go somewhere to do it yourself: *You have to collect the document in person.*

personal /ˈpɜːsənəl/ **adj**
1 B1 belonging to a particular person: *Please take all personal belongings with you when you leave the train.*
2 B1 connected with relationships and feelings and the private parts of someone's life: *He's got a few personal problems at the moment.*
3 B1 designed for or used by one person: *a personal computer*

personality /ˌpɜːsənˈæləti/ **noun** (plural **personalities**)
1 the qualities that make one person different from another: *She's got a lovely, warm personality.*
2 a famous person: *He is a well-known TV personality.*

personally /ˈpɜːsənəli/ **adv**
1 done by you and not someone else: *I'd like to personally apologize for the delay.*
2 B1 used when you are saying your opinion: *Personally, I don't like the man.*

personnel /ˌpɜːsənˈel/ **plural noun**
the people who work for an organization: *military personnel*

perspective /pəˈspektɪv/ **noun**
the way you think about something: *Being unemployed has made me see things* ***from a*** *different* ***perspective****.*

persuade /pəˈsweɪd/ **verb**
(**persuading**, **persuaded**)
1 B1 to make someone agree to do something by talking to them a lot about it: *We managed to* ***persuade*** *him* ***to*** *come with us.*
2 to make someone believe that something is true: *You won't be able to persuade him that you're innocent.*

pessimist /ˈpesɪmɪst/ **noun**
someone who always believes that bad things will happen: *Don't be such a pessimist!*
→ Opposite **optimist noun**

pessimistic /ˌpesɪˈmɪstɪk/ **adj**
always believing that bad things will happen: *He was feeling* ***pessimistic about*** *the future.*
→ Opposite **optimistic adj**

pest /pest/ **noun**
1 an animal that causes damage to plants, food, etc.: *Most farmers think foxes are pests.*
2 informal an annoying person

pet /pet/ **noun**
A1 an animal that someone keeps in their home: *my pet rabbit*

petal /ˈpetəl/ **noun**
one of the coloured parts on the outside of a flower: *rose petals*

petition /pəˈtɪʃən/ **noun**
a paper with a lot of people's names on it, that asks someone in authority to do something: *Will you sign this* ***petition against*** *the war?*

petrol /ˈpetrəl/ **noun** [no plural] UK (US **gas**)
A2 a liquid fuel used in cars

petrol station /ˈpetrəl ˌsteɪʃən/ **noun** UK (US **gas station**)
A2 a place where you can buy petrol

pharmacy /ˈfɑːməsi/ **noun** (plural **pharmacies**)
B1 a shop that prepares and sells medicines

phase /feɪz/ **noun**
a stage or period that is part of a longer period: *The first phase of the project has been completed.*

PhD /ˌpiːeɪtʃˈdiː/ **noun**
the highest college or university qualification: *a PhD course* ◦ *Maria has a* ***PhD in*** *mathematics.*

philosopher /fɪˈlɒsəfər/ **noun**
someone who studies or writes about the meaning of life

philosophy /fɪˈlɒsəfi/ **noun** [no plural]
the study or writing of ideas about the meaning of life

phone[1] /fəʊn/ **noun** (also **telephone**)
1 A1 a piece of equipment that is used to talk to someone who is in another place: *Would someone please* ***answer the phone****?* ◦ *I could hear the* ***phone ringing****.*
2 on the phone using the phone: *She's been on the phone all night.*

phone[2] /fəʊn/ **verb** (**phoning**, **phoned**)
A1 to speak to someone by telephone: *I tried to phone her last night, but she was out.* ◦ *I'm going to* ***phone for*** *a taxi.*

phone book /ˈfəʊn ˌbʊk/ **noun**
a book that has the telephone numbers of people who live in an area

phone box /ˈfəʊn ˌbɒks/ **noun** UK
a small structure containing a public telephone

phone call /ˈfəʊn ˌkɔːl/ **noun**
an act of using the telephone: *I've got to* ***make a phone call****.*

phone-in /ˈfəʊnɪn/ **noun** UK (US **call-in**)
a television or radio programme in which the public can ask questions or give opinions over the telephone

phone number /ˈfəʊn ˌnʌmbər/ **noun**
the number of a particular telephone

phonetic /fəʊˈnetɪk/ **adj**
relating to the sounds you make when you speak: *phonetic symbols*

photo /ˈfəʊtəʊ/ **noun**
A1 a picture made with a camera: *I* ***took a photo of*** *Jack lying on the beach.*

photocopier /ˈfəʊtəʊˌkɒpiəʳ/ **noun**
a machine that makes copies of papers with writing on them by photographing them
→ See **The Office** on page C12

photocopy /ˈfəʊtəʊˌkɒpi/ **noun**
(plural **photocopies**)
B1 a copy of a paper made with a photocopier: *I* ***made*** *a* ***photocopy*** *of my letter before sending it.*
• **photocopy** verb (**photocopying**, **photocopied**)

photograph¹ /ˈfəʊtəgrɑːf/ **noun**
A2 a picture made with a camera: *He* ***took a photograph of*** *the children.*

photograph² /ˈfəʊtəgrɑːf/ **verb**
to take a photograph of someone or something: *They were photographed leaving a nightclub together.*

photographer /fəˈtɒgrəfəʳ/ **noun**
A2 someone whose job is to take photographs

photography /fəˈtɒgrəfi/ **noun** [no plural]
A2 the activity or job of taking photographs

phrasal verb /ˌfreɪzəl ˈvɜːb/ **noun**
B1 a verb that has two or three words. For example, 'look up' and 'carry on' are phrasal verbs.
→ See **Phrasal Verbs** on page C13

phrase /freɪz/ **noun**
B1 a group of words that are often used together and have a particular meaning

physical /ˈfɪzɪkəl/ **adj**
1 relating to the body: *physical strength*
2 relating to real things that you can see and touch: *a physical object*

physical education /ˌfɪzɪkəl edjʊˈkeɪʃən/ **noun** [no plural]
classes at school where children do exercise and play sport

physically /ˈfɪzɪkəli/ **adv**
in a way that relates to the body: *He is physically fit.*

physicist /ˈfɪzɪsɪst/ **noun**
someone who studies physics

physics /ˈfɪzɪks/ **noun** [no plural]
A2 the scientific study of natural forces, such as energy, heat, light, etc.

piano

piano /piˈænəʊ/ **noun**
A2 a big, wooden musical instrument with black and white bars that make sounds when you press them

pick¹ /pɪk/ **verb**
1 B1 to choose something or someone: *He was picked for the school football team.*
2 B1 If you pick flowers, fruit, etc., you take them off a tree or out of the ground: *I picked some apples this morning.*
pick on ***someone*** **phrasal verb**
to treat one person badly in a group of people: *He just started picking on me for no reason.*
pick ***something/someone*** **up phrasal verb**
1 A2 to lift something or someone by using your hands: *He picked his coat up off the floor.*
2 A2 to go somewhere in order to get someone or something: *Can you pick me up from the airport?*
pick ***something*** **up phrasal verb**
A2 to learn a new skill or language by practising it, not by studying it: *When you live in a country you soon pick up the language.*

pick² /pɪk/ **noun** [no plural]
take your pick to choose what you want: *We've got tea, coffee, or hot chocolate – take your pick.*

pickpocket /ˈpɪkˌpɒkɪt/ **noun**
someone who steals things from people's pockets

picnic /ˈpɪknɪk/ **noun**
A1 food that you take from your home to eat outside: *We're going to **have a picnic** down by the lake.*

picture¹ /ˈpɪktʃəʳ/ **noun**
1 A1 a drawing, painting, or photograph of something or someone: *She's got pictures of pop stars all over her bedroom.* ◦ *Did you **take** many **pictures** (= photograph many things) while you were in Sydney?*
→ See **The Living Room** on page C11
2 B1 mainly US a movie: *It won an Oscar for best picture.*
3 an idea of what something is like: *After watching the news, I have a clearer **picture of** what is happening.*

picture² /ˈpɪktʃəʳ/ **verb** (**picturing**, **pictured**)
to imagine something in a particular way: *The house was very different from how I'd pictured it.*

pie /paɪ/ **noun**
B1 a type of food made with meat, vegetables, or fruit that is covered in pastry and baked: *an apple pie*

pie

piece /piːs/ **noun**
1 A2 an amount of something, or a part of something: *a **piece of** paper* ◦ *She cut the cake into eight pieces.*
2 A2 one of a particular type of thing: *a piece of equipment* ◦ *It's a beautiful piece of furniture.*
3 B1 a single amount of a particular type of thing: *I have an interesting piece of information for you.*
4 something that has been created by an artist, musician, or writer: *a beautiful **piece of** music*
5 **fall to pieces** to break into smaller parts: *These shoes are falling to pieces.*

pier /pɪəʳ/ **noun**
a long structure that is built from the land out over the sea and that sometimes has restaurants, etc. on it: *We went for a walk along the pier.*

pierce /pɪəs/ **verb** (**piercing**, **pierced**)
to make a hole in something using a sharp point: *I had my ears pierced.*

pig /pɪg/ **noun**
1 A1 a large pink farm animal that is kept for its meat
2 informal someone who is very unpleasant, or someone who eats a lot

pigeon /ˈpɪdʒən/ **noun**
a grey bird that often lives on buildings in towns

pile¹ /paɪl/ **noun**
1 B1 a lot of something in the shape of a small hill, or a number of things on top of each other: *There was a big **pile of** sand in the garden.* ◦ *The clothes were arranged **in piles** on the floor.*
2 **a pile of/piles of *something*** informal a lot of something: *He has piles of money.*

pile

pile² /paɪl/ **verb** (**piling**, **piled**)
pile up **phrasal verb**
If something unpleasant piles up, you get more and more of it: *My work's really starting to pile up.*
pile *something* up **phrasal verb**
to make a lot of things into a pile by putting them on top of each other: *Just pile those books up over there.*

pilgrim /ˈpɪlgrɪm/ **noun**
someone who travels to a place that is important in their religion

pill /pɪl/ **noun**
B1 a small, hard piece of medicine that you swallow: *a vitamin pill*

pillar /ˈpɪləʳ/ **noun**
a tall structure made of stone, wood, etc. that supports something above it: *The new bridge will be supported by 100 concrete pillars.*

a b c d e f g h i j k l m n o **p** q r s t u v w x y z

pillow

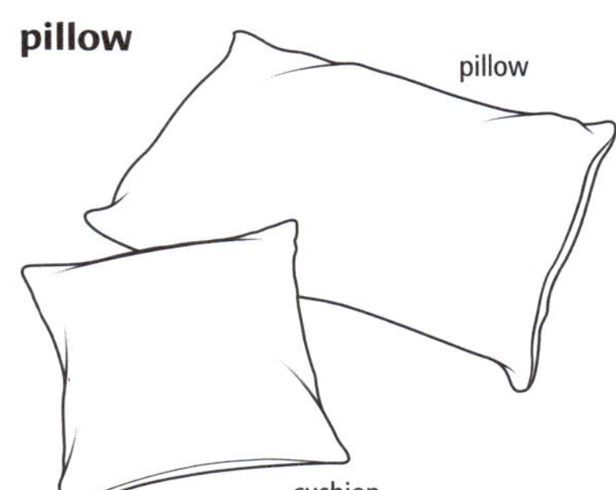

pillow /ˈpɪləʊ/ **noun**
A2 a soft object that you put your head on in bed

pilot /ˈpaɪlət/ **noun**
A2 someone who flies a plane

pimple /ˈpɪmpl/ **noun**
a small red mark on your skin

pin[1] /pɪn/ **noun**
B1 a thin piece of metal with a sharp point used to fasten pieces of cloth together or to fasten an object to cloth

pin[2] /pɪn/ **verb** (**pinning**, **pinned**)
B1 to fasten something with a pin: *She had a red ribbon* ***pinned to*** *her collar.*

PIN /pɪn/ **noun**
abbreviation for personal identification number: a number that no one else knows that allows you to use a plastic card to pay for things or get money from a bank

pinch[1] /pɪnʃ/ **verb**
1 to press someone's skin between your thumb and finger, sometimes causing pain: *One of the other children had pinched her and she was crying.*
2 mainly UK informal to steal something small: *Who's pinched my pen?*

pinch[2] /pɪnʃ/ **noun**
a very small amount of something: *a pinch of salt*
→ See **Quantities** on page C14

pine /paɪn/ **noun** (also **pine tree**)
a tall tree with long, thin leaves shaped like needles

pineapple /ˈpaɪnæpl/ **noun**
B1 a large fruit with leaves sticking out of the top that is sweet and yellow inside

pineapple

Ping-Pong /ˈpɪŋ pɒŋ/ **noun** [no plural] trademark (also **table tennis**)
a game in which two or four people hit a small ball over a low net on a large table

pink[1] /pɪŋk/ **adj**
A2 being a pale red colour: *pretty, pink flowers*

pink[2] **noun**
A2 the colour pink
→ See **Colours** on page C6

pint /paɪnt/ **noun**
1 a unit for measuring liquid, equal to 0.568 litres in the UK and 0.473 litres in the US
2 UK informal a pint of beer

pioneer /ˌpaɪəˈnɪəʳ/ **noun**
someone who is one of the first people to do something: *He was one of the pioneers of modern science.*

pip /pɪp/ **noun** UK
a small seed inside fruit such as apples and oranges

pipe /paɪp/ **noun**
1 B1 a long tube that liquid or gas can move through: *a water pipe*
2 a tube with a bowl-shaped part at one end, used to smoke tobacco: *He smokes a pipe.*

pirate /ˈpaɪərət/ **noun**
B1 someone who attacks ships and steals from them

pit /pɪt/ **noun**
1 a large hole that has been dug in the ground
2 US (UK **stone**) a large, hard seed that grows inside some types of fruits and vegetables
3 a place where coal is dug out from under the ground

pitch /pɪtʃ/ **noun**
1 UK an area of ground where a sport is played: *a football pitch*
2 [no plural] how high or low a sound is

a b c d e f g h i j k l m n o p q r s t u v w x y z

a b c d e f g h i j k l m n o p q r s t u v w x y z

pitcher /ˈpɪtʃəʳ/ **noun** US (UK **jug**)
a container with a handle used for pouring out liquids: *a pitcher of water*

pity¹ /ˈpɪti/ **noun**
1 **it's a pity...** A2 used to say that something is disappointing: *It's a pity you're not staying longer.*
2 [no plural] a feeling of sadness for someone who has problems: *She looked at me with pity in her eyes.*
3 **take pity on *someone*** to help someone who is in a difficult situation because you feel sad for them: *I finally took pity on Ben and told him the truth.*

pity² /ˈpɪti/ **verb** (**pitying**, **pitied**)
to feel sorry for someone: *I pity her because she is lonely.*

pizza /ˈpiːtsə/ **noun**
A1 a flat, round piece of bread covered with tomato, cheese, etc. and cooked in an oven
→ See **Food** on page C7

place¹ /pleɪs/ **noun**
1 A1 a position, building, town, area, etc.: *His leg's broken in two places.* ◦ *Edinburgh is a nice place to live.* ◦ *What a stupid place to park!*
2 A2 informal someone's home: *They've just bought a place in Spain.*
3 **take place** B1 to happen: *The meeting will take place next week.*
4 **in first, second, etc. place** B1 If you are in first, second, etc. place in a race or competition, that is your position: *He finished in fifth place.*
5 B1 the seat where you sit in a theatre, a classroom, a train, etc.: *The children collected their prizes and then went back to their places.*
6 B1 UK an opportunity to study at a college, to join a team, etc.: *She got a **place at** Oxford.* ◦ *He got a **place in** the team.*
7 **in place of *something*** instead of something: *Try adding fruit to your breakfast cereal in place of sugar.*
8 **all over the place** in many different places: *There was blood all over the place.*
9 **take *someone*'s place** to do something instead of someone else: *If I can't go to the show tonight, you can take my place.*
10 **in the first place** at the start of a situation: *Why did you invite her in the first place?*

place² /pleɪs/ **verb** (**placing**, **placed**)
1 to put something somewhere carefully: *She placed a dish in front of me.*
2 to cause someone to be in a situation: *One stupid action has placed us all at risk.*

plain¹ /pleɪn/ **adj**
1 B1 simple and not complicated: *plain food*
2 B1 not mixed with other colours: *a plain blue carpet*
3 obvious and clear: *It's **plain that** she is not happy here.*

plain² /pleɪn/ **noun**
a large area of flat land

plainly /ˈpleɪnli/ **adv**
1 in a simple way that is not complicated: *She was plainly dressed.*
2 in a clear and obvious way: *This is plainly wrong.*

plait /plæt/ **noun** UK (US **braid**)
a single piece of hair made by twisting three thinner pieces over and under each other: *She wore her hair **in plaits**.*
→ See **Hair** on page C9

plan¹ /plæn/ **noun**
1 A2 something that you are going to do: *What are your **plans for** the weekend?* ◦ *The plan is to meet at the hotel.*
2 a drawing that shows how something appears from above: *a street plan*

plan² /plæn/ **verb** (**planning**, **planned**)
A2 to decide what you are going to do or how you are going to do something: *We're just planning our holidays.* ◦ *I'd **planned** the meeting **for** Friday.* ◦ *She **plans to** go to college next year.*

plane /pleɪn/ **noun**
A1 a vehicle that flies and has an engine and wings: *What time does her plane get in (= arrive)?*

planet /ˈplænɪt/ **noun**
B1 a large, round object in space that moves around the sun or another star

planning /ˈplænɪŋ/ **noun** [no plural]
1 the activity of thinking about and deciding how you are going to do

plane

something: *The wedding took months of careful planning.*
2 control over which buildings are built in an area: *the* ***planning department*** *of the local council*

plant¹ /plɑːnt/ **noun**
A1 a living thing that grows in the soil or water and has leaves and roots: *Have you* ***watered the plants****?* ◦ *tomato plants*

plant² /plɑːnt/ **verb**
B1 to put seeds or plants in the ground so that they will grow: *We planted some trees in the garden.*

plaster /ˈplɑːstəʳ/ **noun**
1 [no plural] a substance that is spread on walls in order to make them smooth
2 UK a thin piece of material that you stick to the skin to cover a small cut

plastic /ˈplæstɪk/ **noun** [no plural]
A2 a light substance that can be made into different shapes when it is soft and has many uses: *Most children's toys are made of plastic.*
• **plastic adj** A2 *plastic bags*

plate /pleɪt/ **noun**
A1 a flat, round object that is used for putting food on: *a dinner plate* ◦ *a* ***plate of*** *biscuits*

platform /ˈplætfɔːm/ **noun**
1 A2 the area in a railway station where you get on and off the train: *The train for Belfast will depart from platform 12.*
2 a high part of a floor for a person to stand on: *The speakers all stood on a platform.*

play¹ /pleɪ/ **verb**
1 A1 When you play a sport or game, you compete or are involved in it: *Sam plays tennis every weekend.* ◦ *We often used to play cards.*
2 A1 When children play, they enjoy themselves with toys and games: *She likes to play with her dolls.*
3 A2 to make music with a musical instrument: *Tim was playing the piano.*
4 A2 to make a CD, DVD, etc. produce sounds or pictures: *Can you play that song again?*
5 B1 to be a character in a movie or play: *Who played Darth Vader in Star Wars?*
6 B1 to compete against a person or team in a game: *Who are Brazil playing in the final?*
7 play a joke/trick on *someone* to make someone believe something that is not true as a joke: *The class played a trick on the teacher.*

play² /pleɪ/ **noun**
1 A2 a story that is written for actors to perform, usually in a theatre: *We saw a play at the theatre.*
2 [no plural] things that people, especially children, do to enjoy themselves: *a play area*

player /ˈpleɪəʳ/ **noun**
1 A1 someone who plays a sport or game: *tennis players*
2 A2 someone who plays a musical instrument: *a trumpet player*
3 A2 a machine that produces sound or pictures: *an MP3 player* ◦ *a DVD player*

playful /ˈpleɪfəl/ **adj**
funny and not serious: *a playful remark*

playground /ˈpleɪɡraʊnd/ **noun**
A2 an area of land where children can play, especially at a school

playing card /ˈpleɪɪŋ ˌkɑːd/ **noun**
one of a set of 52 small pieces of stiff paper with numbers and pictures on, used for playing games

playing field /ˈpleɪɪŋ ˌfiːld/ **noun**
an area of land used for sports such as football

pleasant /ˈplezənt/ **adj**
A2 good or enjoyable: *pleasant weather* ◦ *We had a very pleasant evening.*
• **pleasantly adv** B1 *I was pleasantly surprised.*

please¹ /pliːz/ **exclamation**
1 A1 something that you say to be polite when you are asking for something: *Could I have a coffee, please?* ◦ *Please may I use your telephone?*
2 yes, please A1 used to accept something politely: *'Would you like a drink?' 'Oh yes, please.'*

please² /pliːz/ **verb** (**pleasing**, **pleased**)
B1 to make someone happy: *I only got married to please my parents.*

pleased /pliːzd/ **adj**
1 A2 happy about something: *I'm **pleased to** be back home.* ◦ *I'm really **pleased with** her work.* ◦ *I wasn't very **pleased about** having to pay for dinner.*
2 pleased to meet you A2 a polite thing to say to someone you are meeting for the first time

pleasure /ˈpleʒəʳ/ **noun**
1 B1 [no plural] a feeling of happiness or enjoyment: *The children **give** her a lot of **pleasure**.*
2 B1 an enjoyable activity: *Food is one of life's great pleasures.*

plenty /ˈplenti/ **quantifier**
B1 a lot of something, more than you need: *Don't bring any food – we've got plenty.* ◦ *There's **plenty of** room here.*

pliers /ˈplaɪəz/ **plural noun**
a tool for holding or pulling small things like nails or for cutting wire: *a pair of pliers*

plot¹ /plɒt/ **noun**
1 the things that happen in a story: *I don't like movies with complicated plots.*
2 a plan to do something bad: *There was a **plot to** blow up the embassy.*
3 a piece of land: *a building plot*

plot² /plɒt/ **verb** (**plotting**, **plotted**)
to plan to do something bad: *They plotted to bring down the government.*

plough UK (US **plow**) /plaʊ/ **noun**
a large tool used by farmers to turn over the soil before planting crops

pluck /plʌk/ **verb**
1 to quickly pull something or someone from the place where they are: *He plucked a £50 note out of his wallet.*
2 pluck your eyebrows to pull hairs out of your eyebrows (= lines of hair above your eyes) to make them look tidy

plugs

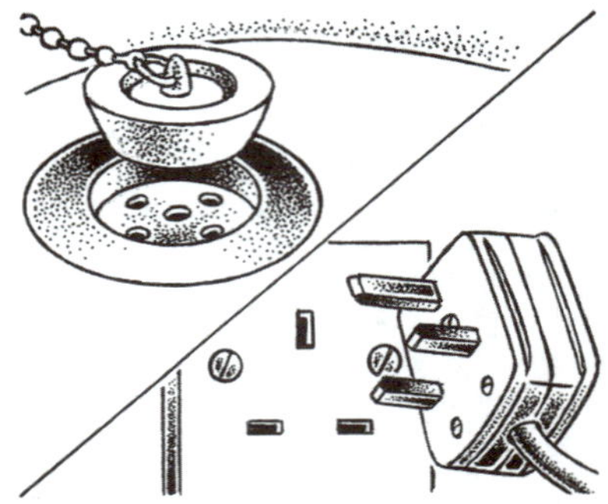

plug¹ /plʌg/ **noun**
1 B1 an object with metal parts that stick out of its end, used to connect electrical equipment to an electricity supply: *I need to change the plug on my hairdryer.*
2 B1 something you put in a hole to block it: *a bath plug*

plug² /plʌg/ **verb** (**plugging**, **plugged**)
to block a hole
plug *something* in **phrasal verb**
to connect a piece of electrical equipment to an electricity supply: *Could you plug the iron in for me?*

plum /plʌm/ **noun**
a soft, round fruit with red or yellow skin and a stone in the middle

plumber /ˈplʌməʳ/ **noun**
someone whose job is to repair or connect water pipes and toilets and baths

plumbing /ˈplʌmɪŋ/ **noun** [no plural]
the water pipes in a building

plunge /plʌndʒ/ **verb** (**plunging**, **plunged**)
to fall or move down very quickly and with force: *He plunged into the water.*

plural /ˈplʊərəl/ **noun**
A2 a word or part of a word that shows you are talking about more than one person or thing. For

example, 'babies' is the plural of 'baby'.
• **plural** adj A2 *'Cattle' and 'trousers' are plural nouns.*

plus /plʌs/ **preposition**
1 A2 added to: *Five plus three is eight.*
2 B1 and also: *She won their latest CD plus two tickets to their concert.*

p.m. /ˌpiːˈem/
A1 in the afternoon or evening: *Opening hours: 9 a.m. – 6 p.m.*

pneumonia /njuːˈməʊniə/ **noun** [no plural]
a serious illness in which your lungs fill with liquid and it is difficult to breathe

pocket /ˈpɒkɪt/ **noun**
1 A2 a part of a piece of clothing that you can put things in: *My wallet was in my coat pocket.*
2 B1 a container or bag that is attached to something: *Faye put her keys in a pocket in her bag.*

pocket

pocket money /ˈpɒkɪt ˌmʌni/ **noun** [no plural]
B1 an amount of money that parents give to a child each week

pod /pɒd/ **noun**
the long, flat part of some plants that has seeds in it: *a pea pod*

poem /ˈpəʊɪm/ **noun**
B1 a piece of writing, especially one that has short lines and uses words that sound the same: *love poems*

poet /ˈpəʊɪt/ **noun**
B1 someone who writes poems

poetic /pəʊˈetɪk/ **adj**
relating to poetry: *poetic language*

poetry /ˈpəʊɪtri/ **noun** [no plural]
B1 poems in general

point[1] /pɔɪnt/ **noun**
1 B1 an opinion, idea, or fact that someone says or writes: *He* ***made*** *some interesting* ***points*** *about the election.* ◦ *He explained his point by drawing a diagram.*
2 B1 a unit used for showing who is winning in a game: *Arsenal are five points ahead.*
3 an opinion or fact that should be considered seriously: *'She's always complaining that the office is cold.' 'Well, she's* ***got a point*** *(= that is true).'* ◦ *'How are we going to get there if there are no trains?' 'That's a good point.'*
4 a quality that someone has: *I know she's bossy, but she has lots of* ***good points*** *too.*
5 the thin, sharp end of something: *the point of a needle*
6 a particular place: *This is the point where the pipes enter the building.*
7 a particular time in an event or process: *At this point in the day, I'm too tired to think.*
8 the reason for or purpose of something: *What's the* ***point of*** *studying if you can't get a job afterwards?*
9 **the point** the most important part of what has been said or written: *Come on,* ***get to the point****!*
10 **up to a point** partly: *What he says is true up to a point.*
11 (also **decimal point**) the mark (.) that is used to separate the two parts of a decimal: *One mile equals one point six (= 1.6) kilometres.*
12 one of the marks on a compass: *the points of the compass*
13 **be on the point of doing *something*** to be going to do something very soon: *Amy was on the point of crying.*

Common mistake: point

A **point** (.) is used to separate a whole number from a fraction (= number less than 1).
Normal body temperature is 36.9° Celsius.
A **comma** (,) is used to divide large numbers into groups of three so that they are easier to read.
28,071,973

point[2] /pɔɪnt/ **verb**
1 A2 to show where someone or something is by holding your finger or a thin object towards it: *She* ***pointed to*** *a bird in the tree.*
2 B1 to hold something so that it

a b c d e f g h i j k l m n o p q r s t u v w x y z

faces towards someone or something: *She **pointed** her gun **at** them.*
3 B1 to face towards a particular direction: *The road sign points left.*
point *something* out **phrasal verb**
to tell someone a fact: *If he makes a mistake, I point it out immediately.*

pointed /ˈpɔɪntɪd/ **adj**
A pointed object has a thin, sharp end: *He has a pointed chin.*

pointless /ˈpɔɪntləs/ **adj**
Something that is pointless has no purpose: *It would be **pointless to** argue with him.*
• **pointlessly** **adv**

point of view /ˌpɔɪnt əv ˈvjuː/ **noun** (plural **points of view**)
1 an opinion: *I can see (= understand) his point of view.*
2 a way of thinking about a situation: *From a medical point of view, it is an important discovery.*

poison[1] /ˈpɔɪzᵊn/ **noun**
a substance that makes you ill or kills you if you eat or drink it

poison[2] /ˈpɔɪzᵊn/ **verb**
1 to try to kill someone by giving them a dangerous substance to drink or eat: *He tried to poison his wife.*
2 to put a dangerous substance in something: *Someone had poisoned his drink.*

poisonous /ˈpɔɪzᵊnəs/ **adj**
containing poison: *poisonous gas*

poke /pəʊk/ **verb** (**poking**, **poked**)
to quickly push your finger or other pointed object into someone or something: *Nell kept poking me in the arm.*

poker /ˈpəʊkəʳ/ **noun** [no plural]
a game played with cards in which people try to win money from each other

polar /ˈpəʊləʳ/ **adj**
relating to the North or South Pole

polar bear /ˌpəʊlə ˈbeəʳ/ **noun**
a large, white bear that lives in the Arctic

pole /pəʊl/ **noun**
1 a long, thin stick made of wood or metal, used to hold something up: *tent poles*
2 **the North/South Pole** the part of the Earth that is farthest north or south

police /pəˈliːs/ **noun**
A2 the organization that makes people obey the law and that protects people against crime: *I heard a shot and decided to **call the police**.* ◦ *A 30-year-old man is being interviewed by police.*

policeman /pəˈliːsmən/ **noun** (plural **policemen**)
A2 a man who is a member of the police

police officer /pəˈliːs ˌɒfɪsəʳ/ **noun**
A2 someone who is a member of the police

police station /pəˈliːs ˌsteɪʃᵊn/ **noun**
A2 the office of the police

policewoman /pəˈliːsˌwʊmən/ **noun** (plural **policewomen**)
A2 a woman who is a member of the police

policy /ˈpɒləsi/ **noun** (plural **policies**)
a set of ideas or a plan that has been agreed by a government, business, etc.: *the government's economic policies* ◦ *It is company policy to help staff progress in their careers.*

polish[1] /ˈpɒlɪʃ/ **noun** [no plural]
a substance that you rub on something in order to make it shine

polish[2] /ˈpɒlɪʃ/ **verb**
to rub something with a cloth in order to make it shine: *I polished my shoes.*

polite /pəˈlaɪt/ **adj**
A2 behaving in a way that is not rude and shows that you think about other people: *She was too polite to point out my mistake.*
• **politely** **adv** B1 *He thanked them politely.*
• **politeness** **noun** *We were impressed by their politeness.*

political /pəˈlɪtɪkᵊl/ **adj**
B1 relating to or involved in politics: *There are two main political parties in my country.*

politician /ˌpɒlɪˈtɪʃᵊn/ **noun**
B1 someone who works in politics,

especially a member of the government: *a distinguished politician*

politics /ˈpɒlətɪks/ **noun** [no plural]
1 B1 ideas and activities relating to how a country or area is governed: *He has little interest in politics.*
2 B1 a job in politics: *She's planning to retire from politics next year.*

poll /pəʊl/ **noun**
the process of asking people questions to discover what they think about a subject: *the results of an opinion poll*

pollen /ˈpɒlən/ **noun** [no plural]
a powder made by flowers, which is carried by insects and makes other flowers produce seeds

pollute /pəˈluːt/ **verb** (**polluting**, **polluted**)
to make water, air, soil, etc. dirty or harmful: *We need a fuel that won't pollute the environment.*
• **polluted** **adj** *The beaches were **polluted with** oil.*

pollution /pəˈluːʃən/ **noun** [no plural]
B1 damage caused to water, air, etc. by bad substances or waste

pond /pɒnd/ **noun**
a small area of water

pony /ˈpəʊni/ **noun** (plural **ponies**)
a small horse

ponytail /ˈpəʊniteɪl/ **noun**
hair tied at the back of your head

ponytail

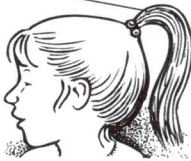

pool /puːl/ **noun**
1 A2 an area of water that has been made for people to swim in: *The hotel has two outdoor pools.*
2 B1 [no plural] a game in which you use a long stick to hit balls into holes around the edge of a table: *We **played pool** all evening.*
3 a small area of water or other liquid on a surface: *a pool of blood*

poor /pɔːʳ/ **adj**
1 A1 having little money: *He comes from a very poor family.* ◦ *Modern fertilizers are too expensive for poorer countries to afford.* ◦ *health care for the poor*
2 A2 used to show that you are sad for someone: *That cold sounds terrible, you poor thing!*
3 of bad quality: *It was a poor performance.* ◦ *Last year's exam results were poor.* ◦ *a poor harvest*
4 not having much skill at a particular activity: *Sam's a poor swimmer.*

poorly /ˈpɔːli/ **adv**
badly: *They were poorly educated.*

pop[1] /pɒp/ **verb** (**popping**, **popped**)
1 to make a short sound like a small explosion: *The music played and champagne corks popped.*
2 UK informal to go to a particular place: *I'll pop into the supermarket on my way home.*
pop up **phrasal verb**
informal to suddenly appear or happen: *A message just popped up on my screen.*

pop[2] /pɒp/ **noun**
1 A2 [no plural] (also **pop music**) modern music with a strong beat that is popular with young people
2 a short sound like a small explosion

popcorn /ˈpɒpkɔːn/ **noun** [no plural]
yellow seeds of grain that break open, get bigger, and turn white when you cook them

Pope /pəʊp/ **noun**
the leader of the Roman Catholic Church

popular /ˈpɒpjələʳ/ **adj**
1 A2 liked by many people: *a list of the most popular boys' names*
→ Opposite **unpopular** **adj**
2 for or involving ordinary people: *popular culture*

popularity /ˌpɒpjəˈlærəti/ **noun** [no plural]
the quality of being liked by many people

population /ˌpɒpjəˈleɪʃən/ **noun**
1 B1 the number of people living in a particular area: *What's the **population of** Brazil?*
2 all the people living in a particular area, or all the people or animals of a

a b c d e f g h i j k l m n o **p** q r s t u v w x y z

particular type: *The deer population has increased in the northeast.*

porch /pɔːtʃ/ **noun**
a covered area in front of the entrance to a house

pork /pɔːk/ **noun** [no plural]
B1 meat from a pig

port /pɔːt/ **noun**
B1 a town or an area of a town next to water where ships arrive and leave from: *the Belgian port of Zeebrugge*

portable /ˈpɔːtəbl/ **adj**
able to be carried: *a portable computer*

portion /ˈpɔːʃᵊn/ **noun**
1 the amount of food given to one person in a restaurant: *The portions in the restaurant were very small.*
2 a part of something: *A* ***portion of*** *their profits go to charity.*

portrait /ˈpɔːtrɪt/ **noun**
a painting, drawing, or photograph of someone: *a portrait of the princess*

posh /pɒʃ/ **adj**
1 expensive and for rich people: *a posh hotel*
2 UK from a high social class: *She has a posh voice.*

position /pəˈzɪʃᵊn/ **noun**
1 B1 the way someone is sitting, standing, or lying: *What position do you sleep in?*
2 B1 the situation that someone is in: *She's* ***in*** *a very difficult* ***position****.*
3 B1 the place where someone or something is: *I'm trying to find our position on the map.*
4 B1 the part that someone plays in a game such as football: *I didn't know you played hockey – what* ***position*** *do you* ***play****?*
5 a job: *He has applied for a senior position.*
6 your level of importance in a company or society: *the position of women in society*
7 **in first, second, third, etc. position** in first, second, third, etc. place in a race or other competition: *She finished the race in third position.*

positive /ˈpɒzətɪv/ **adj**
1 B1 feeling happy and confident about life or a particular situation: *She has a very positive attitude.*
2 certain that something is true: *'Are you sure you saw him?' 'Absolutely positive.'*

positively /ˈpɒzətɪvli/ **adv**
in a good way that makes you feel happier: *Most children respond positively to encouragement.*

possess /pəˈzes/ **verb** formal
to have or own something: *Certainly, he possesses the skills for the job.*

possession /pəˈzeʃᵊn/ **noun**
something that you own: *personal possessions*

possessive /pəˈzesɪv/ **adj**
B1 In grammar, a possessive word or form of a word shows who or what something belongs to, for example, the words 'my' and 'mine'.

possibility /ˌpɒsəˈbɪləti/ **noun** (plural **possibilities**)
1 B1 a chance that something may happen or be true: *Is there any* ***possibility of*** *changing this ticket?* ◦ *There's a* ***possibility that*** *Harvey might come.*
2 something that you can choose to do: *Have you considered the* ***possibility of*** *flying?*

> **Common mistake: possibility, occasion, or opportunity?**
>
> A **possibility** is a chance that something may happen or be true. **Possibility** cannot be followed by an infinitive.
> *Is there a possibility of finding a cure for AIDS?*
> ~~*Is there a possibility to find a cure for AIDS?*~~
> An **occasion** is an event, or a time when something happens. **Occasion** does not mean 'chance' or 'opportunity'.
> *Birthdays are always special occasions.*
> An **opportunity** is a possibility of doing something, or a situation that gives you the possibility of doing something.
> *The trip to Paris gave me an opportunity to speak French.*
> *Students had the opportunity to ask questions during the lecture.*
> *I have more opportunity to travel than my parents did.*
> ~~*I have more possibility to travel than my parents did.*~~

possible /ˈpɒsəbl/ **adj**
1 A1 If something is possible, it can happen or be done: *Is it **possible to** speak to the manager, please?* ◦ *I'll send it today, **if possible**.*
→ Opposite **impossible** adj
2 as much, quickly, soon, etc. as possible A2 as much, quickly, soon, etc. as something can happen or be done: *Call me as soon as possible after you arrive.*
3 B1 If something is possible, it might or might not exist or be true: *It's **possible that** the ring was stolen.* ◦ *That's one possible solution to the problem.*

possibly /ˈpɒsəbli/ **adv**
1 A2 used when something is not certain: *Someone, possibly Tom, had left the window open.*
2 B1 used in polite questions: *Could I possibly borrow your computer?*
3 used with 'can' or 'could' for emphasis: *We'll do everything we possibly can to help.*

post[1] /pəʊst/ **noun**
1 A2 [no plural] UK (US **mail**) letters, parcels, etc. that you send or get: *Has the post arrived yet?*
2 A2 [no plural] UK (US **mail**) the system for sending letters, parcels, etc.: *I'm sending the documents **by post**.*
3 formal a job: *a teaching post*
4 a long piece of wood or metal fixed into the ground at one end: *I found the dog tied to a post.*

post[2] /pəʊst/ **verb** UK (US **mail**)
1 A2 to send a letter or parcel by post: *Did you post my letter?*
2 B1 to leave a message on a website: *I posted a question about Mexican food.*

postage /ˈpəʊstɪdʒ/ **noun** [no plural]
money that you pay to send a letter or parcel: *first-class postage*

post box /ˈpəʊst ˌbɒks/ **noun** UK (US **mailbox**)
a large, metal container in a public place where you can post letters

postcard /ˈpəʊstkɑːd/ **noun**
A2 a card with a picture on one side that you send without an envelope

postcode /ˈpəʊstkəʊd/ **noun** UK
a group of letters and numbers that comes at the end of someone's address in the UK

poster /ˈpəʊstəʳ/ **noun**
A2 a large, printed picture or notice that you put on a wall

postman /ˈpəʊstmən/ **noun** (plural **postmen**) UK (US **mailman**)
B1 a man who takes and brings letters and parcels as a job

post office /ˈpəʊst ˌɒfɪs/ **noun**
A2 a place where you can buy stamps and send letters and parcels

postpone /pəʊstˈpəʊn/ **verb**
B1 to arrange for something to happen at a later time: *The trip has been **postponed until** next week.*

pot /pɒt/ **noun**
B1 a round container, usually used for keeping things or cooking: *a flower pot* ◦ *a pot of coffee* ◦ *There's plenty of space in the kitchen for all your **pots and pans**.*

potato /pəˈteɪtəʊ/ **noun** (plural **potatoes**)
A1 a round, white vegetable that grows in the ground
→ See **Fruit and Vegetables** on page C8

potential[1] /pəˈtenʃəl/ **adj**
possible: *A few **potential buyers** have been found.*

potential[2] /pəˈtenʃəl/ **noun**
[no plural] qualities that allow someone or something to develop or succeed: *She has a lot of potential as a writer.*

potentially /pəˈtenʃəli/ **adv**
possibly: *a potentially fatal disease* ◦ *This crisis is potentially very serious.*

pottery /ˈpɒtəri/ **noun** [no plural]
1 plates, bowls, etc. that are made from clay
2 the activity of making plates, bowls, etc. from clay

poultry /ˈpəʊltri/ **noun** [no plural]
chickens and other birds that people keep for meat and eggs

pound /paʊnd/ **noun**
1 A2 the unit of money used in the UK; £: *a hundred pounds/£100*
2 (written abbreviation **lb**) a unit for measuring weight, equal to 453.6 grams or

a b c d e f g h i j k l m n o p q r s t u v w x y z

16 ounces: *a pound of potatoes* ◦ *The baby weighed just four pounds when she was born.*

pour /pɔːʳ/ verb
1 B1 to make a liquid flow from or into a container: *I* ***poured*** *the milk* ***into*** *a jug.*
2 B1 to rain a lot: *We can't go out in this weather – it's pouring!*

pour

poverty /ˈpɒvəti/ noun [no plural]
the state of being very poor: *They live* ***in poverty****.*

powder /ˈpaʊdəʳ/ noun [no plural]
B1 a dry substance made of many small, loose grains: *curry powder*
• **powdered** adj in the form of a powder: *powdered milk/sugar*

power /paʊəʳ/ noun
1 B1 [no plural] energy, usually electricity, that is used to make light, heat, etc.: *nuclear power*
2 [no plural] control over people and things that happen: *He likes to have* ***power over*** *people.*
3 [no plural] political control in a country: *This government has been* ***in power*** *too long.*

powerful /ˈpaʊəfᵊl/ adj
1 B1 able to control or influence people or things that happen: *My mother was a powerful influence on me.*
2 B1 very strong: *a powerful weapon*
• **powerfully** adv

power station /ˈpaʊə ˌsteɪʃᵊn/ noun (US **power plant**)
a place where electricity is produced

practical /ˈpræktɪkᵊl/ adj
1 relating to real situations: *They can offer practical help.*
2 able to be done successfully: *The plan is simply not practical.*
3 Someone who is practical is good at planning things: *She has a lot of interesting ideas, but she's not very practical.*
4 good at repairing and making things

practically /ˈpræktɪkᵊli/ adv
almost: *We see her practically every day.*

practice /ˈpræktɪs/ noun
1 A2 [no plural] the act of doing an activity again and again to get better at it: *We need a bit more practice before the concert.*
2 the things people do or how they do them: *business practices* ◦ *the illegal practice of copying CDs*
3 **be out of practice** to not do something well because you have not done it recently: *I didn't play very well today – I'm out of practice.*
4 **in practice** used to say what really happens rather than what people think happens: *In practice, the new laws have had little effect.*

> Common mistake: **practice or practise?**
>
> In British English, **practice** is used for the noun, and **practise** for the verb.
>
> *He needs more practice before he can sail on his own.*
>
> In US English, **practice** is used for the noun and the verb.

practise /ˈpræktɪs/ verb (**practising**, **practised**)
A1 to do something again and again in order to get better at it: *They're* ***practising for*** *tomorrow's concert.*

praise[1] /preɪz/ verb (**praising**, **praised**)
to say that someone or something is very good: *He praised the team's performance.*

praise[2] /preɪz/ noun [no plural]
words that you say to show that you think someone or something is very good: *They deserve* ***praise for*** *their achievements.*

prawn /prɔːn/ noun
a small sea animal that you can eat. Prawns are pink when cooked.

pray /preɪ/ verb
A2 to speak to a god in order to show your feelings or to ask for something: *Let us* ***pray for*** *all the sick children.*

prayer /preəʳ/ **noun**
1 B1 the words you say to a god: *Let's **say a prayer for** him.*
2 [no plural] the act of saying words to a god: *They stood in silent prayer.*

pre- /priː-/ **prefix**
before (a time or an event): *a pre-lunch drink* ◦ *to preheat the oven*

preach /priːtʃ/ **verb**
to talk to a group of people about a religious subject, usually in a church

preacher /ˈpriːtʃəʳ/ **noun**
someone who speaks about religious subjects in public, especially in a church

precaution /prɪˈkɔːʃən/ **noun**
something that you do to stop bad things happening in the future: *They called the doctor **as a precaution**.* ◦ *He **took** the **precaution** of locking the door.*

precious /ˈpreʃəs/ **adj**
1 very important to you: *His books are his most precious possessions.*
2 very valuable: *a precious metal*

precise /prɪˈsaɪs/ **adj**
1 exact and accurate: *Her instructions were very precise.*
2 to be precise used to give exact details about something: *We met in 2004 – on October 11th to be precise.*

precisely /prɪˈsaɪsli/ **adv**
1 exactly: *He arrived at six o'clock precisely.*
2 used to emphasize what you are saying: *'You look tired – you should go home.' 'I'm going to do precisely that.'*

predict /prɪˈdɪkt/ **verb**
B1 to say what you think will happen in the future: *Companies are predicting massive profits.*

predictable /prɪˈdɪktəbl / **adj**
happening or behaving in a way that you expect; not unusual or interesting: *The results were predictable.*

prediction /prɪˈdɪkʃən/ **noun**
a statement of what you think will happen in the future: *I wouldn't like to **make** any **predictions about** the result of this match.*

prefer /prɪˈfɜːʳ/ **verb** (**preferring**, **preferred**)
1 A2 to like someone or something more than another person or thing: *I **prefer** dogs **to** cats.* ◦ *She prefers watching tennis to playing.*
2 would prefer A2 used to say what you want or ask someone what they want: *I'd **prefer to** eat alone.* ◦ *Would you prefer red or white wine?*

preferable /ˈprefərəbl/ **adj**
better or more suitable: *Buying a house is **preferable to** paying rent.*

preferably /ˈprefərəbli/ **adv**
if possible: *Serve the pudding with ice cream, preferably vanilla.*

preference /ˈprefərəns/ **noun**
a greater desire for someone or something than another person or thing: *personal preferences* ◦ *We have white and red wine. Do you **have a preference**?*

prefix /ˈpriːfɪks/ **noun**
a group of letters that you add to the beginning of a word to make another word. In the word 'unimportant', 'un-' is a prefix.

pregnancy /ˈpregnənsi/ **noun** (plural **pregnancies**)
the state of being pregnant: *a healthy pregnancy*

pregnant /ˈpregnənt/ **adj**
B1 A pregnant woman has a baby growing inside her body: *She's five months pregnant.*

prejudice /ˈpredʒədɪs/ **noun**
a strong dislike of a group of people because they are a different race, sex, religion, etc.: *racial prejudice*

prejudiced /ˈpredʒədɪst/ **adj**
not liking a group of people or treating them badly because they are a different race, sex, religion, etc.: *I think my boss is **prejudiced against** women.*

preparation /ˌprepərˈeɪʃən/ **noun**
1 B1 [no plural] the things that you do to prepare for something: *Did you **do** much **preparation for** your interview?*
2 preparations plans or arrangements that you make to prepare for some-

a b c d e f g h i j k l m n o p q r s t u v w x y z

thing: *We're **making preparations for** the trip.*

prepare /prɪˈpeəʳ/ **verb** (**preparing**, **prepared**)
1 A2 to get someone or something ready for something in the future: *I haven't prepared my speech yet.* ◦ *We're preparing the students for their end-of-year exams.*
2 A2 to make food ready to be eaten: *I prepared lunch for the kids.*
3 prepare *yourself* B1 to make yourself ready to deal with a difficult situation: ***Prepare yourself for** a shock.*

prepared /prɪˈpeəd/ **adj**
1 B1 ready for a situation: *I wasn't **prepared for** the cold.*
2 be prepared to do *something* to be willing to do something: *You must be prepared to work hard.*

preposition /ˌprepəˈzɪʃən/ **noun**
B1 a word or group of words that is used before a noun or pronoun to show place, direction, time, etc. For example 'on' in 'Your keys are on the table' is a preposition.

prescription /prɪˈskrɪpʃən/ **noun**
B1 a piece of paper on which a doctor writes what medicine an ill person needs: *a doctor's prescription*

presence /ˈprezəns/ **noun** [no plural]
the fact of someone or something being in a place: *Your presence at the meeting would be appreciated.* ◦ *She signed the document **in the presence of** two witnesses.*

present¹ /ˈprezənt/ **adj**
1 be present B1 to be in a particular place: *The whole family was present at the funeral.*
2 happening or existing now: *What is your present occupation?*

present² /ˈprezənt/ **noun**
1 A2 something that you give to someone, usually on a special day: *a birthday present*
2 the present B1 the period of time that is happening now: *Let's talk about the present, not the past.*
3 the present (also **the present tense**) A1 in grammar, the form of a verb that is used to show what happens or exists now
4 at present B1 now: *At present she's working in Baltimore.*

present

present³ /prɪˈzent/ **verb**
to give something to someone, often at a formal ceremony: *They **presented** her **with** a medal.*

presentation /ˌprezənˈteɪʃən/ **noun**
1 B1 a talk giving information about something: *She **gave** an interesting **presentation** on the city.*
2 a formal ceremony at which you give someone something: *a presentation ceremony*
3 [no plural] the way you show something to people: *Presentation is important if you want people to buy your products.*

presenter /prɪˈzentəʳ/ **noun** UK (US **host**)
someone who introduces a radio or television programme: *a news presenter*

present participle /ˌprezənt ˈpɑːtɪsɪpl/ **noun**
the form of a verb that ends with '-ing'

the present perfect /ˌprezənt ˈpɜːfɪkt/ **noun**
in grammar, the form of a verb that is used to show things that have happened in a period of time up to now. The sentence 'I have never been to Australia' is in the present perfect.

preserve /prɪˈzɜːv/ **verb** (**preserving**, **preserved**)
to keep something the same or stop it from being destroyed: *to preserve the rainforest*

presidency /ˈprezɪdənsi/ **noun** (plural **presidencies**)
1 the period when someone is president: *His presidency lasted four years.*
2 the presidency the job of being president: *He **won** the **presidency**.*

president /ˈprezɪdᵊnt/ **noun**
1 B1 the highest political position in some countries, usually the leader of the government: *the president of the United States*
2 the person in charge of a company or organization

presidential /ˌprezɪˈdenʃᵊl/ **adj**
relating to the president of a country: *a presidential candidate*

press[1] /pres/ **verb**
B1 to push something firmly: *Press the button to start the machine.* ◦ *He pressed his face against the window.*

press[2] /pres/ **noun**
the press newspapers and magazines, or the people who write them: *the national press*

pressure /ˈpreʃəʳ/ **noun**
1 [no plural] the act of trying to make someone else do something by arguing or persuading: *public/political pressure* ◦ *Teachers are* ***under pressure*** *to work longer hours.*
2 difficult situations that make you feel worried or unhappy: *the pressures of work*
3 [no plural] the force that you produce when you push something

presume /prɪˈzjuːm/ **verb**
to think that something is probably true, although you are not certain: *I presume you've done your homework.*

pretend /prɪˈtend/ **verb**
to behave as if something is true when it is not: *I can't* ***pretend that*** *I like him.* ◦ *Were you just* ***pretending to*** *be interested?*

pretty[1] /ˈprɪti/ **adv** informal
B1 quite, but not very: *The traffic was pretty bad.* ◦ *I'm pretty sure they'll accept the invitation.*

pretty[2] /ˈprɪti/ **adj** (**prettier**, **prettiest**)
A2 nice to look at, attractive: *Your daughter is very pretty.* ◦ *a pretty little garden*

prevent /prɪˈvent/ **verb**
B1 to stop something happening or to stop someone doing something: *to prevent crime* ◦ *Visitors were* ***prevented from*** *entering the building.*

prevention /prɪˈvenʃᵊn/ **noun** [no plural]
the act of stopping something happening or stopping someone doing something: *crime prevention* ◦ *the prevention of diseases*

previous /ˈpriːviəs/ **adj**
B1 existing or happening before this one: *the previous day/year* ◦ *his previous marriage*
• **previously adv** B1 before: *He previously worked as a teacher.*

prey /preɪ/ **noun** [no plural]
an animal that is hunted and killed by another animal

price /praɪs/ **noun**
A2 the amount of money that you pay to buy something: *high/low prices* ◦ *The* ***price of*** *fuel has gone up again.*

priceless /ˈpraɪsləs/ **adj**
very valuable: *a priceless antique/painting*

pride /praɪd/ **noun** [no plural]
1 a feeling of satisfaction at your achievements or the achievements of your family or friends: *She felt a great sense of pride as she watched him accept the award.*
2 the respect that you feel for yourself: *She has too much pride to accept any help.*

priest /priːst/ **noun**
B1 someone who performs religious duties and ceremonies

primary /ˈpraɪmᵊri/ **adj**
most important: *Her primary responsibility is to train new employees.*

primary school /ˈpraɪmᵊri ˌskuːl/ **noun** (also US **elementary school**)
B1 a school for children aged 5 to 11

prime minister /ˌpraɪm ˈmɪnɪstəʳ/ **noun**
the leader of an elected government in some countries

primitive /ˈprɪmɪtɪv/ **adj**
relating to a time long ago when people lived in a simple way without machines or a writing system: *primitive man*

prince /prɪns/ **noun**
1 B1 the son of a king or queen, or

one of their close male relatives: *Prince Edward*
2 the male ruler of a small country

princess /prɪnˈses/ **noun**
1 B1 the daughter of a king or queen, or one of their close female relatives
2 B1 the wife of a prince

principal[1] /ˈprɪnsɪpᵊl/ **adj**
B1 main, or most important: *Her principal reason for moving is to be nearer to her mother.*
• **principally** **adv** *The magazine is aimed principally at women.*

principal[2] /ˈprɪnsɪpᵊl/ **noun**
the person in charge of a school or college

principle /ˈprɪnsɪpl/ **noun**
1 a belief about how you should behave: *He must be punished – it's a matter of principle.*
2 **on principle** If you refuse to do something on principle, you refuse to do it because you think it is wrong: *She doesn't wear fur on principle.*

print[1] /prɪnt/ **verb**
1 A2 to make writing or images on paper or other material with a machine: *The instructions are printed on the side of the box.*
2 to make books, newspapers, magazines, etc., usually in large quantities, using machines: *Fifty thousand copies of the book have been printed.*

print[2] /prɪnt/ **noun**
1 [no plural] words, letters, or numbers that are made on paper by a machine: *The print is so small in this book that I can hardly read it.*
2 a mark that is left on a surface where someone has walked: *The dog left prints all over the kitchen floor.*

printer /ˈprɪntəʳ/ **noun**
1 A2 a machine that is connected to a computer which makes writing or images on paper: *a laser printer*
2 a person or company that prints books, newspapers, magazines, etc.

priority /praɪˈɒrəti/ **noun** (plural **priorities**)
something that is very important and that must be dealt with before other things: *My **first priority** is to find somewhere to live.*

prison /ˈprɪzᵊn/ **noun**
B1 a place where criminals are kept as a punishment: *He's spent most of his life **in prison**.*

prisoner /ˈprɪzᵊnəʳ/ **noun**
B1 someone who is being kept in prison as a punishment

privacy /ˈprɪvəsi/ **noun** [no plural]
the right to be alone and do things without other people seeing or hearing you: *I hate sharing a bedroom – I never get any privacy.*

private /ˈpraɪvət/ **adj**
1 B1 only for one person or group and not for everyone: *You can't park here – this is private property.*
2 controlled by or paid for by a person or company and not by the government: *Charles went to a private school.*
3 B1 If information or an emotion is private, you do not want other people to know about it: *This is a private matter – it doesn't concern you.*
4 **in private** If you do something in private, you do it where other people cannot see or hear you: *I need to talk to you in private.*

privilege /ˈprɪvᵊlɪdʒ/ **noun**
an advantage that only one person or group has, usually because of their position or because they are rich

prize /praɪz/ **noun**
A2 something valuable that is given to someone who wins a competition: *to win a prize* ◦ *first/second prize*

pro /prəʊ/ **noun**
the pros and cons the advantages and disadvantages of something: *We discussed the pros and cons of buying a bigger house.*

probable /ˈprɒbəbl/ **adj**
likely to be true or to happen: *The probable cause of death was heart failure.*

probably /ˈprɒbəbli/ **adv**
A2 used to mean that something is very likely: *I'll probably be home by midnight.*

problem /ˈprɒbləm/ **noun**
1 A1 a situation that causes difficulties: *health problems* ◦ *I'm **having problems with** my computer.* ◦ *Drugs have become a serious problem in the area.*
2 no problem informal A2 something that you say to mean you can or will do what someone has asked you to do: *'Can you get me to the airport by 11.30?' 'No problem.'*
3 no problem informal A2 something that you say when someone has thanked you for something: *'Thanks for taking me home.' 'No problem.'*
4 have a problem with *something/someone* informal to not like something or someone: *She can smoke in here – I don't have a problem with that.*

procedure /prəˈsiːdʒəʳ/ **noun**
the official or usual way of doing something: *You must **follow** the correct **procedure**.*

proceed /prəʊˈsiːd/ **verb** formal
to continue as planned: *His lawyers decided not to **proceed with** the case.*

process /ˈprəʊses/ **noun**
1 a series of actions that you take in order to do something: *Buying a house can be a long and complicated process.*
2 a series of changes that happen naturally: *the process of growing old*

procession /prəˈseʃᵊn/ **noun**
a line of people or cars that moves forward slowly as part of a ceremony or public event: *a funeral procession*

produce¹ /prəˈdjuːs/ **verb**
(**producing**, **produced**)
1 B1 to make or grow something: *The factory produces about 900 cars a year.*
2 to cause a particular result: *Nuts produce an allergic reaction in some people.*
3 to control how a movie, play, programme, or musical recording is made: *He produced some of the most famous shows on Broadway.*

produce² /ˈprɒdjuːs/ **noun** [no plural]
food that is grown or made in large quantities to be sold: *dairy produce*

producer /prəˈdjuːsəʳ/ **noun**
1 a company, country, or person that makes things or grows food: *Australia is one of the world's main producers of wool.*
2 someone who controls how a movie, programme, play, or musical recording is made: *a movie/record producer*

product /ˈprɒdʌkt/ **noun**
B1 something that someone makes or grows so that they can sell it: *We have a new range of skin-care products.*

production /prəˈdʌkʃᵊn/ **noun**
1 [no plural] the process of making or growing something: *Sand is used in the production of glass.*
2 [no plural] the amount of something that is made or grown: *We need to increase production by 20%.*
3 a performance or series of performances of a play or show: *a school production of 'Romeo and Juliet'*
4 [no plural] the control of how a movie, programme, play, or musical recording is made: *She wants a career in TV production.*

productive /prəˈdʌktɪv/ **adj**
1 having a good or useful result: *We had a very productive meeting and sorted out a lot of problems.*
2 producing a large amount: *a productive worker*

profession /prəˈfeʃᵊn/ **noun**
1 B1 a type of work that needs special training or education: *He's a teacher **by profession** (= he trained to be a teacher).*
2 the people who do a type of work, considered as a group: *The medical profession is worried about the new drug.*

professional¹ /prəˈfeʃᵊnᵊl/ **adj**
1 B1 Someone is professional if they get money for a sport or activity that most people do as a hobby: *a professional athlete/musician*
→ Opposite **amateur adj**
2 B1 showing skill and careful attention: *a professional attitude*
3 relating to a job that needs special training or education: *You should get some professional advice about your finances.*

• **professionally** **adv** *He's good enough at football to play professionally.*

professional² /prəˈfeʃənəl/ **noun** someone who gets money for doing a sport or activity that most other people do as a hobby: *a golf professional*

professor /prəˈfesəʳ/ **noun** B1 the highest rank of teacher in a British university, or a teacher in an American university or college: *a professor of history at Oxford*

profile /ˈprəʊfaɪl/ **noun**
1 a short description of a person, organization, etc., giving the main details about them: *He's updated his profile on the website.*
2 a side view of someone's face or head: *The picture shows him **in profile**.*

profit /ˈprɒfɪt/ **noun** money that you get from selling something for more than it cost you to buy or produce: *a profit of $4.5 million* ◦ *It's very hard for a new business to **make a profit** in its first year.*

profitable /ˈprɒfɪtəbl/ **adj** making a profit: *a profitable business*

program¹ /ˈprəʊgræm/ **noun**
1 A2 a set of instructions that you put into a computer to make it do something: *to write a computer program*
2 US spelling of programme

program² /ˈprəʊgræm/ **verb** (**programming**, **programmed**) If you program a computer, you give it a set of instructions to do something.

programme UK (US **program**) /ˈprəʊgræm/ **noun**
1 A2 a show on television or radio: *a TV programme*
2 a thin book that you buy at a concert, sports event, etc.
3 a plan of events or activities with a particular purpose: *The school offers an exciting programme of social events.*

programmer /ˈprəʊgræməʳ/ **noun** someone who writes computer programs as a job

progress¹ /ˈprəʊgres/ **noun** [no plural]
1 B1 development and improvement of skills, knowledge, etc.: *technological progress* ◦ *He has **made** good **progress** in French this year.*
2 movement towards a place
3 **in progress** happening or being done now: *Quiet please – exams in progress.*

progress² /prəˈgres/ **verb**
1 to improve: *Technology has progressed rapidly in the last 100 years.*
2 to continue gradually: *I began to feel more relaxed as the evening progressed.*

prohibit /prəʊˈhɪbɪt/ **verb** formal to say by law that you must not do something: *Smoking is prohibited on most international flights.*

project /ˈprɒdʒekt/ **noun**
1 A2 a piece of school work that involves detailed study of a subject: *We're **doing** a class **project on** the environment.*
2 a planned piece of work that has a particular purpose: *The new building project will cost $45 million.*

projector /prəʊˈdʒektəʳ/ **noun** a machine that shows movies, pictures, or words on a screen or a wall

prominent /ˈprɒmɪnənt/ **adj**
1 important or famous: *a prominent businessman*
2 very easy to see or notice: *a prominent nose*
• **prominently** **adv**

promise¹ /ˈprɒmɪs/ **verb** (**promising**, **promised**)
1 B1 to say that you will certainly do something or that something will certainly happen: *She **promised to** write to me every week.* ◦ *Paul **promised** me **that** he'd cook dinner tonight.*
2 B1 to say that you will certainly give something to someone: *Her parents have promised her a new car if she passes her exams.*

Common mistake: promise

When you use the expression **promise someone something**, no preposition is needed after the verb.

He promised his mum that he would clean his room.

~~*He promised to his mum that he would clean his room.*~~

promise² /ˈprɒmɪs/ **noun**
B1 a statement that you will certainly do something: *I'm not sure I can do it so I won't* ***make*** *any* ***promises***. ◦ *I've said I'll take her swimming and I don't want to* ***break*** *my* ***promise*** *(= not do what I said I would).*

promote /prəˈməʊt/ **verb** (**promoting**, **promoted**)
1 B1 to give someone a more important job in the same organization: *She's just been* ***promoted to*** *manager.*
2 to advertise something: *The band are promoting their new album.*

promotion /prəˈməʊʃən/ **noun**
1 activities that advertise something: *a sales promotion*
2 a move to a more important job in the same organization: *She was* ***given a promotion*** *in her first year with the company.*

prompt /prɒmpt/ **adj**
done or acting quickly and without waiting: *a prompt reply*
• **promptly** **adv**

pronoun /ˈprəʊnaʊn/ **noun**
B1 a word that is used instead of a noun which has usually already been talked about. For example, the words 'she', 'it', and 'mine' are pronouns.

pronounce /prəˈnaʊns/ **verb** (**pronouncing**, **pronounced**)
B1 to make the sound or sounds of a letter or word: *How do you pronounce his name?*

pronunciation /prəˌnʌnsiˈeɪʃən/ **noun**
B1 the way words are pronounced: *There are two different pronunciations of this word.*

proof /pru:f/ **noun** [no plural]
a fact or a piece of information that shows something exists or is true: *She showed us her passport as* ***proof of*** *her identity.* ◦ *My landlord has asked for* ***proof that*** *I'm employed.*

proper /ˈprɒpəʳ/ **adj**
1 B1 correct or suitable: *Please put those books back in the proper place.*
2 B1 real and satisfactory: *You should eat some proper food instead of just sweets.*

properly /ˈprɒpəli/ **adv**
B1 correctly, or in a satisfactory way: *If she doesn't behave properly, she will have to leave.*

property /ˈprɒpəti/ **noun**
1 B1 [no plural] objects that belong to someone: *The police recovered a large amount of stolen property.*
2 (plural **properties**) a building or area of land: *Private property – no parking.*

prophet /ˈprɒfɪt/ **noun**
someone sent by God to tell people what to do, or to say what will happen in the future

proportion /prəˈpɔːʃən/ **noun**
a part of a total number or amount: *Children make up a large* ***proportion of*** *the world's population.*

proposal /prəˈpəʊzəl/ **noun**
1 a suggestion for a plan: *a* ***proposal to*** *raise taxes*
2 an act of asking someone to marry you

propose /prəˈpəʊz/ **verb** (**proposing**, **proposed**)
1 to suggest a plan or action: *I* ***propose that*** *we delay our decision until we have more information.*
2 to ask someone to marry you: *He* ***proposed to*** *me on my birthday.*
3 **propose to do *something*** to intend to do something: *They propose to cross the desert by car.*

prosecute /ˈprɒsɪkjuːt/ **verb**
to accuse someone of a crime in a court of law: *No one has been* ***prosecuted for*** *the murders.*

prospect /ˈprɒspekt/ **noun**
1 the possibility that something good might happen in the future: *Is there any* ***prospect of*** *the weather improving?*
2 ***someone's*** **prospects** the possibility of being successful: *The course will improve his* ***career prospects***.

protect /prəˈtekt/ **verb**
B1 to keep someone or something safe from something dangerous or bad: *It's important to* ***protect*** *your skin* ***from*** *the sun.*
• **protection** /prəˈtekʃən/ **noun** [no plural] an act of keeping someone or

something safe from something dangerous or bad: *This coat doesn't provide any* ***protection against*** *the rain.*

protected /prəˈtektɪd/ **adj**
protected animals, plants, and land are kept safe by laws that stop people from harming or damaging them: *Tigers are a protected species.*

protective /prəˈtektɪv/ **adj**
giving protection: *protective clothing*

protein /ˈprəʊtiːn/ **noun**
a substance found in foods such as meat and milk that is necessary for the body to grow and be strong

protest[1] /ˈprəʊtest/ **noun**
an act of showing that you strongly disagree with something, often by standing somewhere and shouting, carrying signs, etc.: *There was a* ***protest against*** *the war.*

protest[2] /prəˈtest/ **verb**
to show that you disagree with something by standing somewhere, shouting, carrying signs, etc.: *They're on strike to* ***protest against*** *job losses.*

Protestant /ˈprɒtɪstᵊnt/ **noun**
a member of one of the Christian Churches that separated from the Roman Catholic Church during the 16th century
• **Protestant adj**

protester /prəˈtestəʳ/ **noun**
someone who shows that they disagree with something by standing somewhere, shouting, carrying signs, etc.

proud /praʊd/ **adj**
1 B1 feeling very pleased about something you own or something you have done: *She was so* ***proud of*** *her son.* ◦ *I'm very* ***proud to*** *be involved in this project.*
2 feeling that you are more important than you really are: *She's too proud to admit she is wrong.*
• **proudly adv**

prove /pruːv/ **verb** (**proving**, **proved**)
1 B1 to show that something is true: *Can you* ***prove that*** *you weren't there?* ◦ *He's desperately trying to prove his innocence.*
2 to show a particular result or quality after a period of time: *The operation proved a success.*

proverb /ˈprɒvɜːb/ **noun**
a famous phrase or sentence that gives you advice: *an ancient Chinese proverb*

provide /prəʊˈvaɪd/ **verb** (**providing**, **provided**)
B1 to give something to someone: *It's a new scheme to* ***provide*** *schools* ***with*** *free computers.*

provided /prəˈvaɪdɪd/ **conjunction** (also **providing** /prəˈvaɪdɪŋ/)
only if: *He's welcome to come,* ***provided that*** *he behaves himself.*

provider /prəˈvaɪdəʳ/ **noun**
a person or company that gives or sells someone something that they need: *an Internet service provider*

province /ˈprɒvɪns/ **noun**
one of the large areas into which some countries are divided: *the Canadian province of Alberta*

provoke /prəˈvəʊk/ **verb** (**provoking**, **provoked**)
to cause a strong and usually angry reaction: *Her statement provoked an angry response.*

psychiatrist /saɪˈkaɪətrɪst/ **noun**
a doctor who treats people who have a mental illness

psychological /ˌsaɪkəˈlɒdʒɪkᵊl/ **adj**
relating to the human mind and feelings: *psychological problems*
• **psychologically adv** *Are you psychologically prepared for your new job?*

psychologist /saɪˈkɒlədʒɪst/ **noun**
someone who studies the human mind and feelings

psychology /saɪˈkɒlədʒi/ **noun** [no plural]
the study of the human mind and feelings: *He's studying psychology at college.*

pub /pʌb/ **noun**
A2 a place where you can get drinks such as beer and usually food

public[1] /ˈpʌblɪk/ **adj**
1 public parks, toilets, transport, etc.

B1 parks, toilets, transport, etc. that are for everyone to use: *Smoking should be banned in public places.*
2 public health, support, etc. the health, support, etc. of all ordinary people: *Public opinion has turned against him.*
• **publicly** **adv** *The company publicly apologized for the accident.*

public² /ˈpʌblɪk/ **noun**
1 the (general) public B1 all ordinary people: *a member of the public* ◦ *The public has a right to know about this.*
2 in public where everyone can see you: *He shouldn't behave like that in public.*

publication /ˌpʌblɪˈkeɪʃᵊn/ **noun**
1 a book, newspaper, etc. in which information or stories are published: *Our latest publication is a magazine for teachers.*
2 [no plural] the act of making information or stories available to people in a printed form: *The book will be ready for publication in September.*

public holiday /ˌpʌblɪk ˈhɒlɪdeɪ/ **noun**
a day when most people in a particular country do not have to go to work or school: *New Year's Day is a public holiday in many countries.*

publicity /pʌbˈlɪsəti/ **noun** [no plural]
advertising or information about someone or something in the newspaper, on television, etc.: *a publicity campaign*

public school /ˌpʌblɪk ˈskuːl/ **noun**
1 in the UK, a school that you pay to go to
2 (UK **state school**) in the US, a school that is free to go to because the government provides the money for it

public transport /ˌpʌblɪk ˈtræns pɔːt/ **noun** [no plural] UK (US **public transportation** /ˌpʌblɪk ˌtrænspɔːˈteɪʃᵊn/)
B1 a system of vehicles such as buses and trains that everyone can use

publish /ˈpʌblɪʃ/ **verb**
1 B1 to prepare and print a book, newspaper, magazine, article, etc. so that people can buy it: *This book is published by Cambridge.*
2 B1 to make information available to the public

publisher /ˈpʌblɪʃəʳ/ **noun**
a company or person who prepares and prints books, newspapers, magazines, etc.

pudding /ˈpʊdɪŋ/ **noun** UK
sweet food that is usually eaten as the last part of a meal: *We've got apple pie for pudding.*

puddle /ˈpʌdl/ **noun**
a pool of liquid on the ground, usually from rain

puff¹ /pʌf/ **verb**
to breathe fast and with difficulty, usually because you have been running

puff² /pʌf/ **noun**
a small amount of smoke, gas, powder, etc.: *a puff of smoke*

pull

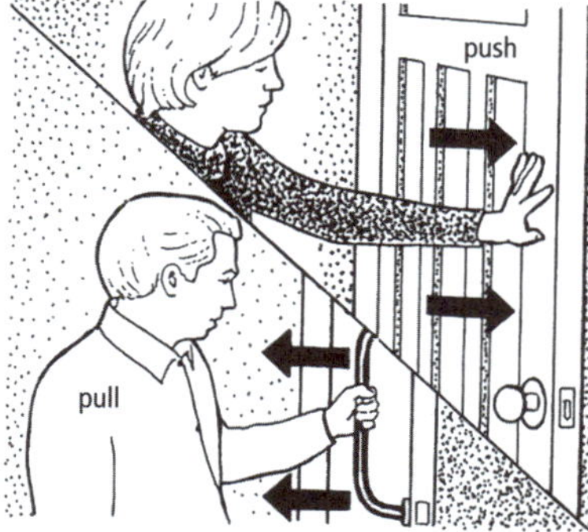

pull /pʊl/ **verb**
1 A2 to take hold of something and move it somewhere: *He* ***pulled off*** *his boots.* ◦ *She bent down and* ***pulled up*** *her socks.*
2 pull ***something*** **off, out, up, etc.** B1 to take hold of something and use physical effort to remove it from somewhere: *He pulled off his sweater.* ◦ *I pulled the plug out.*
3 pull ***yourself*** **along, up, etc.** to take hold of something and use effort to move your body: *She pulled herself up the stairs, holding onto the rail.*

a b c d e f g h i j k l m n o **p** q r s t u v w x y z

pullover /ˈpʊləʊvəʳ/ **noun**
B1 a warm piece of clothing that covers the top of your body and is pulled on over your head

pulse /pʌls/ **noun**
the regular movement of blood through your body when your heart is beating: *My* ***pulse rate*** *is 70.*

pump

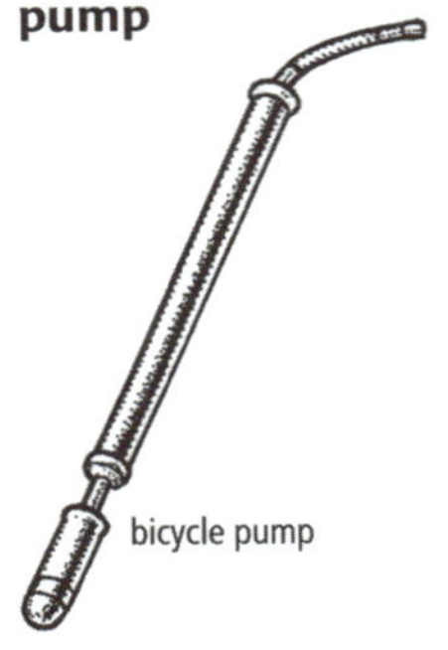
bicycle pump

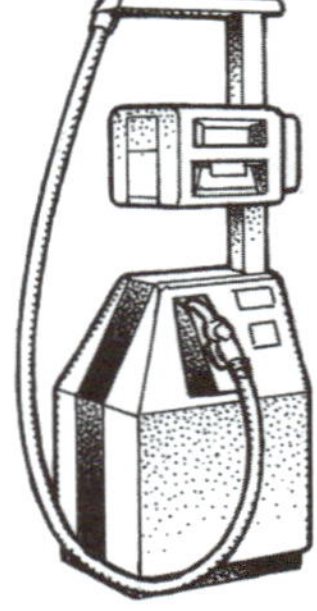
petrol pump *UK*, gas pump *US*

pump¹ /pʌmp/ **noun**
B1 a piece of equipment that forces liquid or gas to move somewhere: *a gas pump* ◦ *a water pump*

pump² /pʌmp/ **verb**
to force liquid or gas to move somewhere: *Your heart pumps blood around your body.*
pump *something* up **phrasal verb**
to fill something with air using a pump: *You should pump your tyres up.*

pumpkin /ˈpʌmpkɪn/ **noun**
a large, round vegetable with thick, orange skin

pumpkin

punch¹ /pʌntʃ/ **verb**
1 to hit someone or something with your fist (= closed hand): *He punched me twice in the stomach.*
2 **punch a hole in *something*** to make a hole in something with a special piece of equipment

punch² /pʌntʃ/ **noun**
an act of hitting someone or something with your fist (= closed hand): *a punch on the nose*

punctual /ˈpʌŋktʃuəl/ **adj**
arriving at the right time and not late
• **punctually** **adv**

punctuation /ˌpʌŋktʃuˈeɪʃᵊn/ **noun**
[no plural]
B1 the use of punctuation marks in writing so that people can see when a sentence begins and ends, that something is a question, etc.

puncture /ˈpʌŋktʃəʳ/ **noun**
1 a small hole made by a sharp object
2 UK a hole in a tyre that makes the air come out

punish /ˈpʌnɪʃ/ **verb**
B1 to make someone suffer because they have done something bad: *They must be severely* ***punished for*** *these crimes.*

punishment /ˈpʌnɪʃmənt/ **noun**
an act of punishing someone: *He had to stay in his bedroom as a punishment for fighting.*

pupil /ˈpjuːpᵊl/ **noun**
1 A2 a student at school: *The school has 1,100 pupils aged 11 to 18.*
→ See **The Classroom** on page C4
2 the black, round part in the centre of your eye

puppet /ˈpʌpɪt/ **noun**
a toy in the shape of a person or animal that you can move with strings or by putting your hand inside: *a glove puppet*

puppet

puppy /ˈpʌpi/ **noun** (plural **puppies**)
B1 a young dog

purchase¹ /ˈpɜːtʃəs/ **verb** (**purchasing**, **purchased**) formal
to buy something: *Tickets must be purchased two weeks in advance.*

purchase² /ˈpɜːtʃəs/ **noun** formal
1 the act of buying something: *the illegal purchase of guns*
2 something that you buy

pure /pjʊəʳ/ **adj**
1 B1 A pure substance is not mixed with anything else: *pure gold*
2 B1 clean and healthy: *pure air/water*
3 complete or only: *Getting the job was pure luck.*

purely /pjʊəli/ **adv**
only: *She married him purely for his money.*

purple[1] /ˈpɜːpl/ **adj**
A2 being a colour that is a mixture of red and blue

purple[2] /ˈpɜːpl/ **noun**
A2 the colour purple
→ See **Colours** on page C6

purpose /ˈpɜːpəs/ **noun**
1 B1 why you do something or why something exists: *The main* ***purpose of*** *the meeting is to discuss the future of the company.*
2 on purpose B1 If you do something bad on purpose, you wanted or planned to do it: *I didn't do it on purpose, it was an accident.*

purr /pɜːʳ/ **verb**
If a cat purrs, it makes a soft sound in its throat to show pleasure.

purse /pɜːs/ **noun**
1 A2 UK a small container for money, usually used by a woman: *a leather purse*
2 mainly US (mainly UK **handbag**) a bag carried by a woman with her money, keys, etc. inside

pursue /pəˈsjuː/ **verb** (**pursuing**, **pursued**)
to try to do something over a period of time: *She decided to pursue a career in television.*

push[1] /pʊʃ/ **verb**
1 A2 to move someone or something by pressing them with your hands or body: *He* ***pushed*** *me* ***out*** *of the door.* ◦ *Someone* ***pushed*** *him* ***into*** *the river.*
→ See picture at **pull**
2 B1 to press something: *If you push this button, your seat will go back.*
3 B1 to move somewhere by moving someone or something away from you: *She* ***pushed through*** *the crowd.*
4 push *someone* to do *something* to try hard to make someone do something: *My parents have always pushed me to do well in school.*
5 push *yourself* to work very hard in order to achieve something: *She really pushed herself to pass her exams.*

push[2] /pʊʃ/ **noun**
B1 an act of moving someone or something by pressing them with your hands or body: *She* ***gave*** *him a little* ***push*** *towards the door.*

pushchair /ˈpʊʃtʃeəʳ/ **noun** UK (US **stroller**)
a chair on wheels that is used to move small children

put /pʊt/ **verb** (**putting**, **put**)
1 A1 to move something to a place or position: *Where have you put the keys?* ◦ *She put her bag on the floor.* ◦ *He put his arm around her.*
2 A2 to write something: *Please put your name on the list.*
3 to cause someone or something to be in a particular condition or situation: *This puts me in a very difficult position.* ◦ *What's put you in such a bad mood?*

put *something* away **phrasal verb**
B1 to put something in the place where you usually keep it: *She folded the towels and put them away.*

put *something* back **phrasal verb**
B1 to put something where it was before it was moved: *I put the book back on the shelf.*

put *something* down **phrasal verb**
B1 to put something that you are holding onto the floor or onto another surface: *You can put your suitcase down in the hall.*

put *somebody* down **phrasal verb**
B1 to write someone's name on a list or document, usually in order to arrange for them to do something: *I've* ***put*** *you* ***down for*** *the trip next week.*

put *something* off **phrasal verb**
B1 to decide to do something at a later time: *I must talk to her about this. I can't put it off any longer.*

put *something* on **phrasal verb**
1 A2 to put clothes or shoes onto your body: *You'd better put your coat on – it's cold outside.*

2 A2 to put make-up or cream onto your skin: *I always put on my make-up before I go to work.*
3 A2 to put a CD, DVD, etc. into a machine so that you can hear or see it: *Do you mind if I put some music on?*
4 B1 to make a piece of equipment work by pressing a switch: *Can you put the light on?*
5 B1 If someone puts on weight, they become heavier: *She put on eight pounds in a month.*

put *something* out **phrasal verb**
B1 to make something that is burning stop burning: *to put out a fire*

put *someone* through **phrasal verb**
B1 to connect someone using a telephone to the person they want to speak to: *Can you put me through to customer services, please?*

put *something* up **phrasal verb**
1 B1 to raise something, or to fix something in a raised position: *I put my hand up to ask the teacher a question.* ◦ *They put a few pictures up on the wall.*
2 B1 to increase the price or value of something: *I see they've put up the price of fuel again.*

put up with *someone/something* **phrasal verb**
to accept something that is bad although you do not like it: *I don't know how you put up with him.*

puzzle /ˈpʌzl/ **noun**
1 A2 a game or activity in which you have to put pieces together or answer questions using skill: *a jigsaw puzzle*
2 a situation that is very difficult to understand: *Scientists have been trying to **solve** this **puzzle** for years.*

puzzled /ˈpʌzld/ **adj**
confused because you do not understand something: *He had a puzzled look on his face.*

pyjamas UK (US **pajamas**) /pɪˈdʒɑːməz/ **noun**
a shirt and trousers that you wear in bed

pyjamas

pyramid /ˈpɪrəmɪd/ **noun**
a shape with a square base and four triangular sides that meet to form a point at the top
→ See picture at **shape**

Qq

Q, q /kjuː/
the seventeenth letter of the alphabet

quack /kwæk/ **noun**
the sound made by a duck (= water bird)
• **quack verb**

quaint /kweɪnt/ **adj**
attractive and different in an old-fashioned way: *a quaint little village*

qualification /ˌkwɒlɪfɪˈkeɪʃᵊn/ **noun** UK
B1 an exam you have passed or a course of study you have completed: *medical qualifications* ◦ *What qualifications do you need to be a nanny?*

qualified /ˈkwɒlɪfaɪd/ **adj**
1 B1 having passed exams or courses: *a newly qualified teacher*
2 having the skills, qualities or experience that you need in order to do something: *I'm not really* ***qualified to*** *give advice on the subject.*

qualify /ˈkwɒlɪfaɪ/ **verb** (**qualifying**, **qualified**)
1 If you qualify for something, you are allowed to do it: *To* ***qualify for*** *the competition, you must be over 18.*
2 to succeed in getting into a competition: *Nigeria were the first team to* ***qualify for*** *the World Cup.*
3 to pass the exams that allow you to do a particular job: *She hopes to* ***qualify as*** *a lawyer.*

quality /ˈkwɒləti/ **noun**
1 B1 [no plural] how good or bad something is: *good/high quality* ◦ *The air quality in this area is terrible.*
2 B1 [no plural] the fact of being very good or well made: *I was impressed by the quality of her work.*
3 (plural **qualities**) part of the character of someone or something: *Anthony has leadership qualities.*

quantity /ˈkwɒntəti/ **noun** (plural **quantities**)
B1 the amount or number of something: *A vast quantity of information is available on the Internet.*

quarrel¹ /ˈkwɒrᵊl/ **noun**
an argument: *She walked out after* ***having a quarrel*** *with her boss.*

quarrel² /ˈkwɒrᵊl/ **verb** (**quarrelling**, **quarrelled**)
to have an argument with someone: *She'd been* ***quarrelling with*** *her mother all morning.*

quarry /ˈkwɒri/ **noun** (plural **quarries**)
a place where stone is dug out of a large hole in the ground: *a marble quarry*

quarter /ˈkwɔːtəʳ/ **noun**
1 A2 (also US **fourth**) one of four equal parts of something; 1/4: *I waited a quarter of an hour for her.*
2 A1 a period of 15 minutes before or after the hour: *It's* ***quarter to*** *three (= 2.45).* ◦ *We're leaving at* ***quarter past*** *six (= 6.15).*

quarter

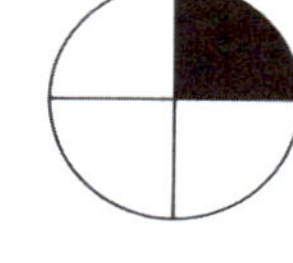

quarter-final /ˌkwɔːtəˈfaɪnᵊl/ **noun**
the part of a competition when eight people or teams are left and four will continue: *She was knocked out of the competition* ***in the quarter-finals.***

queen /kwiːn/ **noun**
1 A2 a female ruler in some countries: *Queen Elizabeth II*
2 A2 the wife of a king
3 a playing card that has a picture of a queen on it: *the queen of hearts*

query /ˈkwɪəri/ **noun** (plural **queries**)
a question: *I have a query about the last exercise.*

question¹ /ˈkwestʃən/ **noun**
1 A1 a sentence or phrase that asks you for information: *Is it OK if I* ***ask*** *you a few* ***questions****?* ◦ *He refused to* ***answer*** *my* ***question.***
2 A2 in an exam, a problem that tests a person's knowledge or ability: ***Answer*** *as many* ***questions*** *as you can.*
3 [no plural] doubt: *There is* ***no question*** *that the fire was an accident.*
4 a situation or problem that needs to be dealt with or considered: *Your article* ***raises*** *the* ***question*** *of human rights.*

a b c d e f g h i j k l m n o p q r s t u v w x y z

Common mistake: ask a question

Remember to use the verb **ask** with **question**.

We weren't allowed to ask any questions.

~~*We weren't allowed to make any questions.*~~

question² /ˈkwestʃən/ **verb**
1 to ask someone questions: *Detectives are* ***questioning*** *the boy* ***about*** *the murder.*
2 to show or feel doubt about something: *I'm just* ***questioning whether*** *we need the extra staff.*

question mark /ˈkwestʃən ˌmɑːk/ **noun**
B1 a mark (?) used at the end of a question

queue /kjuː/ **noun** UK (US **line**)
B1 a row of people waiting for something, one behind the other: *Are you* ***in the queue****?*
• **queue (up)** **verb** UK (US **line up**) to stand in a row in order to wait for something: *They're queueing up to get tickets.*

queue

quick /kwɪk/ **adj**
A1 doing something fast or taking only a short time: *I tried to catch him but he was too quick for me.*

quickly /ˈkwɪkli/ **adv**
A2 fast or in a short time: *I quickly shut the door.*

quid /kwɪd/ **noun** (plural **quid**) UK informal
a pound (= UK unit of money): *Could you lend me twenty quid (= £20)?*

quiet¹ /kwaɪət/ **adj**
1 A2 making little or no noise: *Can you* ***be quiet****, please? We're trying to work.*
2 A2 lacking noise or activity: *I fancy a quiet night in tonight.*
3 B1 If someone is quiet, they talk very little: *He was a shy, quiet man.*

quiet² /kwaɪət/ **noun** [no plural]
a state in which there is little or no noise: *She needs a bit of* ***peace and quiet****.*

quietly /ˈkwaɪətli/ **adv**
1 B1 making little or no noise: *'Don't worry,' she said quietly.*
2 B1 doing something without much noise or activity: *He sat quietly, waiting for her to come home.*

quilt /kwɪlt/ **noun**
a cover for a bed that is filled with feathers or other warm material

quit /kwɪt/ **verb** (**quitting**, **quit**)
1 B1 to leave your job: *She recently quit her job to spend more time with her family.*
2 B1 to stop doing something: *I put on weight after I quit smoking.*

quite /kwaɪt/ **adv**
1 A2 UK a little or a lot but not completely: *I'm quite tired, but I'm happy to walk a little further.*
2 **quite a bit, a few, a lot, etc.** A2 a large amount or number: *There are quite a few letters for you here.*
3 B1 completely: *The two situations are quite different.*
4 **not quite** almost but not completely: *The colours almost match but not quite.*

Common mistake: quiet or quite?

Be careful! These two words look very similar, but they are spelled differently and have completely different meanings.

Quiet means 'making little or no noise'.

The house was very quiet without the children around.

Quite means 'a little or a lot'.

It's quite cold today.

quiz /kwɪz/ **noun** (plural **quizzes**)
A2 a game in which you answer questions: *a television quiz show*

quotation /kwəʊˈteɪʃən/ **noun**
a sentence or phrase that is taken out of a book, poem, or play: *a quotation from Shakespeare*

quote /kwəʊt/ **verb** (**quoting**, **quoted**)
1 to repeat what someone has said or written: *I was* ***quoting from*** *Marx.*
2 to say how much a piece of work will cost before you do it

R r

R, r /ɑːʳ/
the eighteenth letter of the alphabet

rabbi /ˈræbaɪ/ **noun**
a leader and teacher in the Jewish religion

rabbit /ˈræbɪt/ **noun**
A2 a small animal with fur and long ears that lives in a hole in the ground

race¹ /reɪs/ **noun**
1 A2 a competition in which people run, ride, drive, etc. against each other in order to see who is the fastest: *a horse race*
2 one of the groups that people are divided into, having the same colour skin or hair and other things that are the same: *people of many different races*

race² /reɪs/ **verb** (**racing**, **raced**)
1 B1 to compete in a race: *I'll race you to the end of the road!*
2 to move somewhere very quickly: *I raced over to see what was the matter.*
3 to take someone somewhere very quickly: *Ambulances raced the injured to a nearby hospital.*

racial /ˈreɪʃəl/ **adj**
relating to people's race: *a racial minority*

racing /ˈreɪsɪŋ/ **noun** [no plural]
the activity or sport in which people, animals, or vehicles race against each other: *motor racing*

racism /ˈreɪsɪzəm/ **noun** [no plural]
the belief that other races of people are not as good as your own

racist /ˈreɪsɪst/ **noun**
someone who believes that other races of people are not as good as their own
• **racist adj** *a racist attack*

rack /ræk/ **noun**
a type of shelf that you can put things on or hang things from: *a luggage rack*

racket /ˈrækɪt/ **noun**
1 A2 a piece of equipment that you use to hit a ball in sports such as tennis
2 informal a loud noise: *The neighbours were **making** such **a racket**.*

racket

radar /ˈreɪdɑːʳ/ **noun** [no plural]
a system that uses radio waves to find out the position of something you cannot see

radiation /ˌreɪdiˈeɪʃən/ **noun** [no plural]
a dangerous form of energy that comes from certain substances: *high **levels of radiation***

radiator /ˈreɪdieɪtəʳ/ **noun**
1 a metal piece of equipment that is filled with hot water and is used to heat a room
2 a part of a car that makes the engine cool

radio /ˈreɪdiəʊ/ **noun**
1 A1 a piece of equipment used for listening to radio broadcasts: *a car radio*
2 the radio A1 the programmes that you hear when you listen to the radio: *We heard him speaking **on the radio** this morning.*
3 B1 [no plural] a system of sending and getting sound through the air: *local radio*

radioactive /ˌreɪdiəʊˈæktɪv/ **adj**
giving off radiation (= a harmful form of energy): *radioactive waste*

rag /ræg/ **noun**
a piece of old cloth that you use to clean things

rage /reɪdʒ/ **noun**
strong anger that you cannot control: *a jealous rage*

raid¹ /reɪd/ **noun**
a sudden attack on a place by soldiers: *an air raid*

raid² /reɪd/ **verb**
If soldiers raid a place, they suddenly attack it.

rail /reɪl/ **noun**
1 a bar on the wall that you hang things on: *a curtain rail*
2 B1 [no plural] trains as a method of transport: *rail travel*

a b c d e f g h i j k l m n o p q r s t u v w x y z

rail

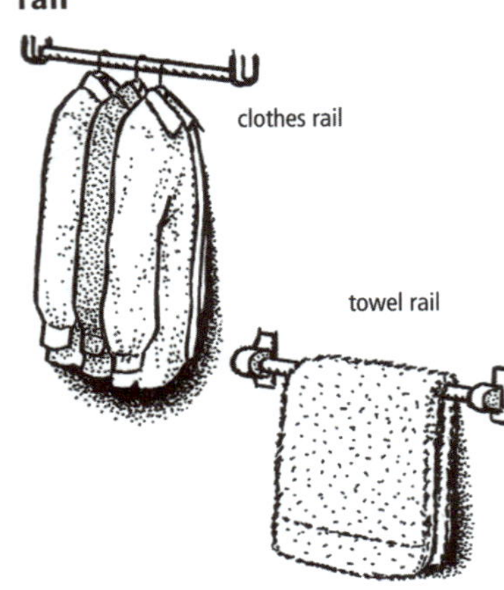

railing /ˈreɪlɪŋ/ **noun**
a fence made from posts and bars: *an iron railing*

railway /ˈreɪlweɪ/ **noun** UK (US **railroad** /ˈreɪlrəʊd/)
1 A2 the metal tracks that trains travel on: *Repairs are being carried out on the railway.*
2 the systems and organizations connected with trains: *He worked on the railways all his life.* ◦ *a railway worker*

rain[1] /reɪn/ **noun** [no plural]
A1 water that falls from the sky in small drops: *heavy rain*

rain[2] /reɪn/ **verb**
it rains A1 If it rains, water falls from the sky in small drops: *It was raining all weekend.*

rainbow /ˈreɪnbəʊ/ **noun**
a half circle with colours that sometimes appears in the sky when the sun shines through rain

raincoat /ˈreɪnkəʊt/ **noun**
A2 a coat that you wear when it is raining

raindrop /ˈreɪndrɒp/ **noun**
a single drop of rain

rainforest /ˈreɪnˌfɒrɪst/ **noun**
B1 a forest with a lot of tall trees where it rains a lot: *a tropical rainforest*

rainy /ˈreɪni/ **adj** (**rainier**, **rainiest**)
B1 raining a lot: *a rainy afternoon*

raise /reɪz/ **verb** (**raising**, **raised**)
1 B1 to lift something to a higher position: *She raised her hand.*
2 B1 to make an amount or level go up: *They have raised taxes.*
3 to look after a child until he or she has become an adult
4 to collect money from people in order to do a particular thing: *They held a sale to raise money for charity.*
5 raise a question, subject, etc. to start talking about a subject that you want other people to consider: *I'm going to **raise** the issue **with** Sally at the meeting.*

raisin /ˈreɪzᵊn/ **noun**
a dried grape (= small, round fruit)

rally /ˈræli/ **noun** (plural **rallies**)
1 a large public meeting in support of something: *an election/campaign rally*
2 a car or motorcycle race: *a rally driver*

ran /ræn/
past tense of run

ranch /rɑːnʃ/ **noun**
a large farm where animals are kept: *a cattle ranch*

random /ˈrændəm/ **adj**
by chance: *Winners will be chosen **at random**.*

rang /ræŋ/
past tense of ring[2]

range /reɪndʒ/ **noun**
1 B1 a group of different things of the same general type: *We discussed a wide range of subjects.*
2 the amount or number between a particular set of limits: *The product is aimed at young people in the 18-25 age range.*
3 [no plural] the distance from which things can be seen, heard, or reached: *He was shot **at** close **range** (= from very near).*
4 a line of hills or mountains

rank /ræŋk/ **noun**
a position in society or in an organization, for example the army: *He holds the rank of general.*

ransom /ˈrænsᵊm/ **noun**
the money that is demanded for the

return of someone who is being kept as a prisoner

rap /ræp/ **noun** [no plural]
A2 a type of music in which the words are spoken and there is a strong beat: *a rap artist*

rape /reɪp/ **verb**
to force someone to have sex when they do not want to: *She was pulled from the car and raped.*
• **rape noun** *He was accused of rape.*

rapid /ˈræpɪd/ **adj**
happening or moving very quickly: *rapid change*
• **rapidly adv**

rare /reəʳ/ **adj**
B1 very unusual: *a rare disease* ◦ *It's very* ***rare to*** *see these birds.*

rarely /ˈreəli/ **adv**
B1 not often: *I rarely see her these days.*

rash¹ /ræʃ/ **noun**
a group of small, red spots on the skin: *an itchy rash*

rash² /ræʃ/ **adj**
done suddenly and without thinking carefully: *It was a rash decision.*

raspberry /ˈrɑːzbᵊri/ **noun** (plural **raspberries**)
a small, soft, red fruit that grows on bushes

rat /ræt/ **noun**
A2 an animal that looks like a large mouse and has a long tail: *Rats carry disease.*

rat

rate /reɪt/ **noun**
1 how often something happens, or how many people something happens to: *the birth rate* ◦ *the rate of unemployment*
2 a fixed amount of money given for something: *rates of pay*
3 the speed at which something happens: *the rate of progress*

rather /ˈrɑːðəʳ/ **adv**
1 B1 slightly: *I find her books rather dull.*
2 rather than B1 instead of: *He saw his music as a hobby rather than a career.*
3 would rather B1 If you would rather do something, you would prefer to do that thing: *I'd much rather go out for a meal than stay at home and watch TV.*
4 used to change something you have just said and make it more correct: *The music, or rather noise, from the party upstairs went on all night.*

ration¹ /ˈræʃᵊn/ **noun**
the amount of something that you are allowed to have when there is little of it: *a food/petrol ration*

ration² /ˈræʃᵊn/ **verb**
to give people only a small amount of something because there is little of it: *They may have to start rationing water.*

rational /ˈræʃᵊnᵊl/ **adj**
based on facts and not affected by someone's emotions or imagination: *a rational decision*

rattle /ˈrætl/ **verb** (**rattling**, **rattled**)
to keep making a noise by knocking against something: *The wind blew hard, rattling the doors and windows.*

raw /rɔː/ **adj**
1 B1 not cooked: *raw meat/vegetables*
2 in the natural state and not changed: *Oil is an important* ***raw material.***

ray /reɪ/ **noun**
a narrow beam of light, heat, or energy: *the rays of the sun*

razor /ˈreɪzəʳ/ **noun**
a piece of equipment with a sharp blade used for removing hair from the face, legs, etc.

razor

razor blade /ˈreɪzə ˌbleɪd/ **noun**
a very thin, sharp blade that you put in a razor

Rd
written abbreviation for road: *17 Jay Rd*

a b c d e f g h i j k l m n o p q r s t u v w x y z

re- /riː-/ **prefix**
used to add the meaning 'do again', especially to verbs: *remarry* ◦ *reattach*

reach[1] /riːtʃ/ **verb**
1 B1 to arrive somewhere: *We won't reach Miami till five or six o'clock.*
2 to stretch your arm and hand to touch or take something: *She **reached for** a cigarette.* ◦ *He **reached out** and grabbed her arm.*
3 can reach (*something*) to be able to touch or take something with your hand: *Could you get that book down for me – I can't reach.*
4 reach a decision, agreement, conclusion, etc. to make a decision, agreement, conclusion, etc. about something: *She reached the conclusion that she couldn't help him.*
5 to get to a particular level, situation, etc.: *The temperature could reach 30°C today.* ◦ *He's reached the age of 95.*
6 to speak to someone on the telephone: *You can reach him at home.*

reach[2] /riːtʃ/ **noun** [no plural]
1 out of reach too far away for someone to take hold of: *I keep the medicines up here, out of the childrens' reach.*
2 be within reach to be close enough for someone to take hold of: *The gun lay within reach.*
3 the distance that can be travelled, especially easily: *We live **within easy reach** of the station.*

react /riˈækt/ **verb**
to say, do, or feel something because of something else that has been said or done: *He **reacted** angrily **to** her comments.*

reaction /riˈækʃᵊn/ **noun**
1 something you say, feel, or do because of something that has happened: *What was his **reaction to** the news?*
2 reactions the ability to move quickly when something suddenly happens: *Drivers need to have quick reactions.*
3 an unpleasant feeling or illness caused by something you have eaten or used on your body: *Some people **have a** bad **reaction to** this drug.*

read /riːd/ **verb** (**read** /red/)
1 A1 to look at words and understand what they mean: *What was the last book you read?* ◦ *I've been **reading about** Marilyn Monroe.*
2 A2 to look at words that are written and say them aloud for other people to listen to: *Do you want me to **read** it **to** you?*
read *something* out **phrasal verb**
to read something and say the words so that other people can hear: *He read out the names of all the winners.*
read *something* over/through **phrasal verb**
to read something from the beginning to the end, especially to find mistakes: *I read over my essay to check for errors.*

reader /ˈriːdəʳ/ **noun**
1 B1 someone who reads: *She's a slow reader.*
2 B1 a book containing a simple story for people who are learning to read or learning a language: *There are readers at different levels.*

readily /ˈredɪli/ **adv**
1 quickly and easily: *Information is readily available on the Internet.*
2 willingly and without stopping to think: *He readily agreed to help.*

reading /ˈriːdɪŋ/ **noun** [no plural]
A1 the activity or skill of getting information from books, newspapers, etc.: *I **did** a lot of **reading** on holiday.*

ready /ˈredi/ **adj**
1 A1 prepared for doing something: *Are you **ready to** go yet?* ◦ *We're going at eight, so you've got an hour to **get ready**.*
2 A2 prepared and available to be eaten, drunk, used, etc.: *Is dinner ready?*

real /rɪəl/ **adj**
1 A2 existing and not imagined: *He's not real you know, he's just a character in a book.* ◦ *Romance is never like that **in real life**.*
2 A2 not false: *real leather*
3 B1 true and not pretended: *Is that your real name?*
4 being the most important or the main thing: *The real problem is money.*

5 used to emphasize a noun: *She was a real help.*

real estate /ˈrɪəl ɪˌsteɪt/ **noun** [no plural] US
land or buildings: *We're going to buy a piece of real estate.* ◦ *a real estate agent*

realistic /ˌrɪəˈlɪstɪk/ **adj**
1 B1 showing things and people as they really are, or making them seem to be real: *The scene in the movie where they find a dinosaur is very realistic.*
2 accepting the true facts of a situation: *Let's be realistic – we're not going to finish this by Friday.*

reality /riˈæləti/ **noun** [no plural]
the way things or situations really are and not the way you would like them to be: *Listening to music is my escape from reality.* ◦ *He may seem charming but* ***in reality*** *he's quite nasty.*

realize /ˈrɪəlaɪz/ **verb** (**realizing**, **realized**)
B1 to notice or understand something that you did not notice or understand before: *I suddenly realized I'd met him before.*

really /ˈrɪəli/ **adv**
1 A1 very or very much: *She's really nice.* ◦ *I really want to go.*
2 B1 used when you are saying what is true about a situation: *She tried to hide what she was really thinking.*
3 A2 used to give particular importance to a verb: *You really shouldn't worry.*
4 **really?** A2 used when you are surprised at what someone has just said: *'Apparently, he's leaving.' 'Really?'*
5 **not really** B1 used for replying that something is not true in a way that is less strong than just 'no': *'Did you like him?' 'Not really.'*

rear[1] /rɪər/ **noun**
the rear the back part of something: *the rear of the train*
• **rear adj** *a rear window*

rear[2] /rɪər/ **verb**
If you rear children or young animals, you look after them until they are adults.

reason /ˈriːzən/ **noun**
1 A2 the facts about why something happens or why someone does something: *Is there any particular* ***reason why*** *he doesn't want to come?* ◦ *He left without* ***giving a reason****.* ◦ *That was the* ***reason for*** *telling her.*
2 something that makes it right for you to do something: *I think we have* ***reason to*** *be concerned.*

> **Common mistake: reason**
>
> Be careful to choose the correct preposition.
>
> *That was the main* ***reason for*** *the trip.*
>
> ~~*That was the main reason of the trip.*~~

reasonable /ˈriːzənəbl/ **adj**
1 B1 big enough or large enough in number, although not very big or not many: *There were a reasonable number of people there.*
2 B1 not expensive: *reasonable prices*
3 B1 good enough but not the best: *The service in the restaurant is reasonable.*
4 fair and showing good judgment: *It's not reasonable to expect people to work those hours.*
5 based on facts that can be explained: *There must be a* ***reasonable explanation*** *for all of this.*

reasonably /ˈriːzənəbli/ **adv**
1 in a fair way, showing good judgment: *Why can't we discuss this reasonably, like adults?*
2 **reasonably good, well, etc.** good, well, etc. enough but not very good or very well: *I did reasonably well at school but not as well as my sister.*
3 **reasonably priced** B1 available at a good price: *reasonably priced meals*

reassure /ˌriːəˈʃʊər/ **verb** (**reassuring**, **reassured**)
to say something to stop someone from worrying: *He reassured me that I would be paid soon.*

rebel[1] /ˈrebəl/ **noun**
someone who does not like authority and refuses to obey rules

rebel[2] /rɪˈbel/ **verb** (**rebelling**, **rebelled**)
to refuse to obey rules: *She* ***rebelled against*** *her family.*

rebellion /rɪˈbeliən/ **noun**
an act of fighting against the government of a country

rebuild /ˌriːˈbɪld/ **verb** (**rebuilt**)
B1 to build something again after it has been damaged: *The cathedral was rebuilt after the fire.*

receipt /rɪˈsiːt/ **noun**
A2 a piece of paper that proves that you have received goods or money: *Could I have a receipt?*

receive /rɪˈsiːv/ **verb** (**receiving**, **received**)

> **Common mistake: receive**
>
> Learners often spell **receive** wrong. Remember that the **e** comes before the **i**.

A2 to get something that someone has given or sent to you: *Occasionally, he **receives** letters **from** fans.*

recent /ˈriːsᵊnt/ **adj**
B1 happening or starting from a short time ago: *a recent photo* ◦ *In recent years, sales have decreased.*

recently /ˈriːsəntli/ **adv**
B1 not long ago: *Have you seen any good movies recently?*

reception /rɪˈsepʃᵊn/ **noun**
1 B1 the place in a hotel or office building where people go when they arrive: *Ask for me at reception.*
2 a formal party to celebrate a special event or to welcome someone: *a wedding reception*

receptionist /rɪˈsepʃᵊnɪst/ **noun**
A2 someone who works in a hotel or office and answers the telephone and deals with visitors when they arrive: *a **hotel receptionist***

recipe /ˈresɪpi/ **noun**
B1 a list of foods and a set of instructions telling you how to cook something: *a recipe for carrot cake*

reckless /ˈrekləs/ **adj**
doing something dangerous and not caring about what might happen: *reckless driving*
• **recklessly** **adv**

reckon /ˈrekᵊn/ **verb**
1 to think that something is probably true: *I reckon he likes her.*
2 to guess that a particular number is correct: *His fortune is **reckoned at** $5 million.*

recognition /ˌrekəgˈnɪʃᵊn/ **noun**
1 the act of accepting that something is true or real: *There is a growing **recognition of** the size of the problem.*
2 [no plural] the act of remembering something or someone because you have seen them before: *I waved at her, but she showed no sign of recognition.*

recognize /ˈrekəgnaɪz/ **verb** (**recognizing**, **recognized**)
1 B1 to know someone or something because you have seen them before: *I recognized her from her picture.*
2 to accept that something is true or real: *Smoking is **recognized as** a leading cause of lung cancer.*

recommend /ˌrekəˈmend/ **verb**

> **Common mistake: recommend**
>
> Learners often spell **recommend** wrong. Remember that there is one **c** and two **m**'s.

1 B1 to say that someone or something is good or suitable for a particular purpose: *Can you recommend a good wine to go with this dish?*
2 to advise someone that something should be done: *The report **recommends that** tourists avoid the region.*

recommendation /ˌrekəmenˈdeɪʃᵊn/ **noun**
a suggestion that someone or something is good or suitable for a particular purpose: *I bought this book **on** Andy's **recommendation**.*

record[1] /ˈrekɔːd/ **noun**
1 B1 the best, biggest, longest, tallest, etc.: *He **holds the** world **record** for 100 metres.*
2 B1 a song or music which has been recorded and which is available for the public to buy: *My favourite Beatles record is 'Love Me Do'.*
3 information that is written on paper or stored on computer so that it can be used in the future: *medical records* ◦ *My teacher **keeps** a **record of** my absences.*
4 A person's or company's record is

their behaviour or achievements: *Of all airlines they have the best safety record.*

record² /rɪˈkɔːd/ **verb**
1 A2 to store sounds or pictures using electronic equipment, a camera, etc. so that you can listen to them or see them again: *They have just recorded a new album.* ◦ *I recorded that programme for you.*
2 to write down information or store it on a computer so that it can be used in the future: *He recorded details of their conversation in his diary.*

record-breaking /ˈrekɔːdˌbreɪkɪŋ/ **adj**
better, bigger, longer, etc. than anything else before: *record-breaking sales of the new DVD*

recorder /rɪˈkɔːdəʳ/ **noun**
1 a machine for storing sounds or pictures: *a video recorder*
2 a long, thin instrument that you play by blowing into it

recording /rɪˈkɔːdɪŋ/ **noun**
B1 sounds or moving pictures that have been recorded, or the process of recording: *a new system of digital recording*

recover /rɪˈkʌvəʳ/ **verb**
B1 to become healthy again after being ill or hurt: *It takes a long time to* ***recover from*** *surgery.*

recovery /rɪˈkʌvəri/ **noun** [no plural]
the process of feeling better again after being ill or hurt: *She only had the operation last month but she's* ***made a*** *good* ***recovery****.*

recreation /ˌrekriˈeɪʃən/ **noun**
activities that you do for enjoyment when you are not working: *Shopping seems to be her only form of recreation.*
• **recreational adj**

recruit¹ /rɪˈkruːt/ **verb**
to try to persuade someone to join an organization
• **recruitment noun** [no plural] the act of persuading someone to join an organization: *graduate recruitment*

recruit² /rɪˈkruːt/ **noun**
someone who has recently joined an organization: *a new recruit*

rectangle /ˈrektæŋgl/ **noun**
a shape with four 90° angles and four sides, with opposite sides of equal length and two sides longer than the other two
→ See picture at **shape**
• **rectangular** /rekˈtæŋgjələʳ/ **adj** shaped like a rectangle: *a rectangular room*

recycle /ˌriːˈsaɪkl/ **verb** (**recycling**, **recycled**)
B1 to use paper, glass, plastic, etc. again and not throw it away: *We recycle all our newspapers and bottles.*
• **recycling noun** [no plural] B1 *Our office has* ***recycling bins*** *(= containers for material to be recycled).*

red¹ /red/ **adj** (**redder**, **reddest**)
1 A1 being the same colour as blood: *a red shirt*
2 A2 describes hair that is an orange-brown colour: *Both children have red hair.*
→ See **Hair** on page C9
3 red wine A2 Red wine is made from black grapes: *a bottle of red wine*
4 go red If someone goes red, their face becomes red because they are embarrassed or angry: *He kissed her on the cheek and she went bright red.*

red² /red/ **noun**
A2 the colour of blood
→ See **Colours** on page C6

reduce /rɪˈdjuːs/ **verb** (**reducing**, **reduced**)
B1 to make something less: *Prices have been reduced by almost 50 percent.*

reduction /rɪˈdʌkʃən/ **noun**
the act of making something less or smaller: *price reductions*

redundant /rɪˈdʌndənt/ **adj** UK
not working because your employer has told you there is not enough work: *Eight thousand people have been* ***made redundant*** *this year.*

refer /rɪˈfɜːʳ/ **verb** (**referring**, **referred**)
refer to *someone/something* **phrasal verb**
1 to talk or write about someone or something: *She didn't once refer to her son.*

a b c d e f g h i j k l m n o p q r s t u v w x y z

a b c d e f g h i j k l m n o p q r s t u v w x y z

2 If writing or information refers to someone or something, it relates to that person or thing: *The sales figures refer to UK sales only.*

referee /ˌrefᵊrˈiː/ **noun**
someone who makes sure that players follow the rules during a sports game
→ See **Sports 2** on page C16

reference /ˈrefᵊrᵊns/ **noun**
1 something you say or write about someone or something: *In his book he* ***makes*** *several* ***references to*** *his time in France.*
2 [no plural] the act of looking at something to get information: *Please keep this handout for* ***future reference*** *(= to look at in the future).*
3 a letter that is written by someone who knows you, to say if you are suitable for a job or course

reference book /ˈrefᵊrᵊns ˌbʊk/ **noun**
a book, such as a dictionary, that you look at to find information

reflect /rɪˈflekt/ **verb**
1 to show or be a sign of something: *The statistics reflect a change in people's spending habits.*
2 If a surface such as a mirror or water reflects something, you can see the image of that thing in the mirror, water, etc.: *He saw himself* ***reflected in*** *the shop window.*
3 to think in a serious and careful way: *In prison, he had plenty of time to* ***reflect on*** *his crimes.*

reflection /rɪˈflekʃᵊn/ **noun**
1 the image of something in a mirror, on a shiny surface, etc.: *I saw my reflection in the window.*
2 a reflection of *something* something that is a sign or result of a particular situation: *His poor performance is a reflection of his lack of training.*

reform¹ /rɪˈfɔːm/ **noun**
the process of making changes to improve a system, organization, or law: *political reform*

reform² /rɪˈfɔːm/ **verb**
to change a system, organization, or law in order to improve it: *Efforts have been made to reform the education system.*

refreshed /rɪˈfreʃt/ **adj**
feeling less tired: *I felt refreshed after a good night's sleep.*

refreshing /rɪˈfreʃɪŋ/ **adj**
1 different and interesting: *It's refreshing to see a movie that's so original.*
2 making you feel less hot or tired: *a refreshing shower*

refreshments /rɪˈfreʃmənts/ **plural noun**
B1 food and drinks that are given at a meeting, on a journey, etc.

refrigerator /rɪˈfrɪdʒᵊreɪtəʳ/ **noun**
a large container that uses electricity to keep food cold
→ See **The Kitchen** on page C10

refuge /ˈrefjuːdʒ/ **noun**
a place where you are protected from danger: *a refuge for homeless people*

refugee /ˌrefjʊˈdʒiː/ **noun**
someone who has been forced to leave their country, especially because of a war: *a refugee camp*

refund¹ /ˈriːfʌnd/ **noun**
B1 an amount of money that is given back to you, especially because you are not happy with something you have bought: *The holiday company gave us a* ***full refund****.*

refund² /ˌriːˈfʌnd/ **verb**
to give back money that someone has paid to you: *Your deposit cannot be refunded.*

refusal /rɪˈfjuːzᵊl/ **noun**
an act of saying you will not do or accept something: *I was surprised by his* ***refusal to*** *admit his mistake.*

refuse¹ /rɪˈfjuːz/ **verb** (**refusing**, **refused**)
B1 to say that you will not do or accept something: *I asked him to leave but he refused.* ◦ *Cathy* ***refuses to*** *admit that she was wrong.*

refuse² /ˈrefjuːs/ **noun** [no plural] formal
things that no one needs that have been thrown away: *a pile of refuse*

regain /rɪˈgeɪn/ **verb**
to get something back again: *The army has* ***regained control*** *of the city.*

regard¹ /rɪˈgɑːd/ **verb**
to think of someone or something in a particular way: *She is generally* ***regarded as*** *one of the greatest singers this century.*

regard² /rɪˈgɑːd/ **noun** [no plural]
1 respect or admiration for someone or something: *I* ***have*** *the greatest* ***regard for*** *her.*
2 in/with regard to *something* formal relating to something: *I am writing with regard to your letter of June 24.*

regarding /rɪˈgɑːdɪŋ/ **preposition** formal
B1 about or relating to: *I am writing to you regarding your application dated 29 April.*

regardless /rɪˈgɑːdləs/ **adv**
regardless of *something* despite something: *She'll make a decision regardless of what we think.*

regards /rɪˈgɑːdz/ **plural noun**
B1 friendly greetings: ***Give my regards*** *to your mother when you see her.*

regiment /ˈredʒɪmənt/ **noun**
a large group of soldiers

region /ˈriːdʒᵊn/ **noun**
B1 a particular area in a country or the world: *the polar regions*

regional /ˈriːdʒᵊnᵊl/ **adj**
relating to a particular area in a country or the world: *a regional accent*

register¹ /ˈredʒɪstəʳ/ **noun**
an official list of names: *the class register*

register² /ˈredʒɪstəʳ/ **verb**
1 B1 to put information about someone or something, especially a name, on an official list: *Students need to* ***register for*** *the course by April.*
2 to show an amount on an instrument that measures something: *The earthquake registered 7.3 on the Richter scale.*

registration /ˌredʒɪˈstreɪʃᵊn/ **noun** [no plural]
B1 the act of recording a name or information on an official list

registration number /ˌredʒɪˈstreɪʃᵊn ˌnʌmbəʳ/ **noun** (US **license plate number**)
the official set of numbers and letters shown on the front and back of a vehicle: *Police are looking for a car with the registration number Z17 EMW.*

regret¹ /rɪˈgret/ **verb** (**regretting, regretted**)
1 B1 to feel sorry about a situation, especially something that you wish you had not done: *If you don't tell her the truth you'll regret it later.* ◦ *I really regret leaving school so young.*
2 formal used to say that you are sorry that you have to tell someone about a situation: *We* ***regret that*** *we cannot supply this information.*

regret² /rɪˈgret/ **noun**
a feeling of sadness about a situation, especially something that you wish you had not done: *We married very young but I've* ***no regrets****.*

regular /ˈregjələʳ/ **adj**
1 B1 happening or doing something often, especially at the same time every week, year, etc.: *a regular visitor to Brussels*
2 repeated with the same amount of time or space between one thing and the next: *a regular pulse* ◦ *Plant the trees at regular intervals.*
3 B1 following the usual rules or patterns in grammar: *'Talk' is a regular verb but 'go' is not.*
→ Opposite **irregular adj**
4 B1 informal being a standard size: *a burger and regular fries*
5 US usual or normal: *I couldn't see my regular dentist.*
• **regularity** /ˌregjəˈlærəti/ **noun** [no plural] the fact that something happens again and again

regularly /ˈregjələli/ **adv**
1 B1 often: *Accidents occur regularly on this stretch of the road.*
2 B1 at the same time each day, week, month, etc.: *They meet regularly – usually once a week.*

regulation /ˌregjəˈleɪʃᵊn/ **noun**
an official rule that controls how something is done: *building regulations*

a b c d e f g h i j k l m n o p q r s t u v w x y z

rehearsal /rɪˈhɜːsəl/ **noun**
a time when people practise a play, dance, etc. in order to prepare for a performance

rehearse /rɪˈhɜːs/ **verb** (**rehearsing**, **rehearsed**)
to practise a play, dance, etc. in order to prepare for a performance

reign¹ /reɪn/ **noun**
a period of time when a king or queen rules a country: *the reign of Henry VIII*

reign² /reɪn/ **verb**
to be the king or queen of a country: *Queen Victoria reigned for 64 years.*

reindeer /ˈreɪndɪəʳ/ **noun** (plural **reindeer**)
a type of deer with large horns that lives in northern parts of Europe, Asia, and America

reject /rɪˈdʒekt/ **verb**
1 to refuse to accept or agree with something: *The United States government rejected the proposal.*
2 to refuse to accept someone for a job, course, etc.

rejection /rɪˈdʒekʃən/ **noun**
1 the act of refusing to accept or agree with something: *Their* ***rejection of*** *the peace plan is very disappointing.*
2 a letter that says you have not been successful in getting a job, a place at a university, etc.: *I've sent off ten applications but I've only had rejections so far.*

relate /rɪˈleɪt/ **verb** (**relating**, **related**)
relate to *someone/something* **phrasal verb**
to be connected to someone or something: *Please provide all information relating to the claim.*

related /rɪˈleɪtɪd/ **adj**
1 If two or more people are related, they belong to the same family: *Did you know that I'm* ***related to*** *Jackie?*
2 connected: *We discussed unemployment and related issues.* ◦ *There's been an increase in crimes* ***related to*** *drugs.*

relation /rɪˈleɪʃən/ **noun**
1 B1 someone who belongs to the same family as you
2 relations the way in which two people or groups of people feel and behave towards each other: *Britain has good* ***relations with*** *Canada.*
3 in relation to *something* compared with something: *Prices are too high in relation to salaries.*
4 in relation to *something* about or relating to something: *I'd like to ask you something in relation to what you said earlier.*

relationship /rɪˈleɪʃənʃɪp/ **noun**
1 B1 the way two people feel and behave towards each other: *He has a very good* ***relationship with*** *his older sister.*
2 B1 a sexual or romantic friendship: *I don't feel ready for a relationship at the moment.*
3 the way in which two things are connected: *the relationship between sunburn and skin cancer*

relative /ˈrelətɪv/ **noun**
B1 someone in your family: *a party for friends and relatives*

relatively /ˈrelətɪvli/ **adv**
quite, when compared with other things or people: *Students will find the course relatively easy.*

relax /rɪˈlæks/ **verb**
B1 to become happy and comfortable because nothing is worrying you, or to make someone do this: *I find it difficult to relax.*

relaxation /ˌriːlækˈseɪʃən/ **noun** [no plural]
B1 the feeling of being relaxed: *He listens to music* ***for relaxation.***

relaxed /rɪˈlækst/ **adj**
1 B1 feeling happy and comfortable because nothing is worrying you: *She seemed relaxed and in control of the situation.*
2 B1 A relaxed situation or place is comfortable and informal: *There was a very* ***relaxed atmosphere*** *at the party.*

relaxing /rɪˈlæksɪŋ/ **adj**
B1 making you feel relaxed: *a relaxing bath*

release[1] /rɪˈliːs/ **verb** (**releasing**, **released**)
1 to allow a prisoner to be free: *Six hostages were released before noon.*
2 to make a record or movie ready for people to buy or see: *The album is due to be released in time for Christmas.*

release[2] /rɪˈliːs/ **noun**
1 permission to leave prison: *After his release from jail, Jackson found it difficult to find work.*
2 a new movie or music that is available for the public to buy: *Have you heard the band's latest release?*

relevant /ˈreləvᵊnt/ **adj**
related to or useful for what is happening or being talked about: *The website has all the* ***relevant information****.*

reliable /rɪˈlaɪəbl/ **adj**
B1 able to be trusted or believed: *a reliable car* ◦ *reliable information*
→ Opposite **unreliable adj**

relief /rɪˈliːf/ **noun** [no plural]
the good feeling that you have when something bad stops or does not happen: *It was such a relief when the exams were over.*

relieve /rɪˈliːv/ **verb** (**relieving**, **relieved**)
to make pain or a bad feeling less bad: *Breathing exercises can help to relieve stress.*

relieved /rɪˈliːvd/ **adj**
feeling happy because something bad did not happen: *I'm just* ***relieved that*** *she's safe and well.*

religion /rɪˈlɪdʒᵊn/ **noun**
B1 the belief in a god or gods, or a particular system of belief in a god or gods: *the Christian religion*

religious /rɪˈlɪdʒəs/ **adj**
1 relating to religion: *religious paintings*
2 having a strong belief in a religion: *He's a very religious man.*

reluctant /rɪˈlʌktᵊnt/ **adj**
not wanting to do something: *I'm* ***reluctant to*** *spend all that money.*
• **reluctance noun** [no plural]
• **reluctantly adv**

rely /rɪˈlaɪ/ **verb** (**relying**, **relied**)
rely on *someone/something* phrasal verb
1 to need someone or something: *Families rely more on their cars than before.*
2 to trust someone or something: *I know I can rely on you to help me.*

remain /rɪˈmeɪn/ **verb**
1 B1 to continue to be in the same state: *Despite the chaos around him, he remained calm.*
2 to continue to exist when everything or everyone else has gone: *Only a few hundred of these animals remain today.*
3 formal to stay in the same place: *The doctor ordered him to* ***remain in*** *bed for a few days.*

remaining /rɪˈmeɪnɪŋ/ **adj**
continuing to exist when everything or everyone else has gone or been done: *Mix in half the butter and keep the remaining 50 grams for later.*

remains /rɪˈmeɪnz/ **plural noun**
the parts of something that exist when other parts of it have gone: *the remains of a Buddhist temple*

remark[1] /rɪˈmɑːk/ **noun**
something that you say: *He* ***made a remark*** *about her clothes.*

remark[2] /rɪˈmɑːk/ **verb**
to say something: *He* ***remarked that*** *she was looking thin.*

remarkable /rɪˈmɑːkəbl/ **adj**
very unusual in a way that you admire: *He has a remarkable memory.*

remarkably /rɪˈmɑːkəbli/ **adv**
in a way that makes you feel surprised: *She is remarkably young-looking for 50.*

remedy /ˈremədi/ **noun** (plural **remedies**)
1 something that makes you better when you are ill: *a flu remedy*
2 something that stops a problem: *So what is the* ***remedy for*** *the traffic problem?*

remember /rɪˈmembəʳ/ **verb**
1 A1 to keep something in your mind, or bring it back into your mind: *I can't remember his name.* ◦ *I don't remember signing a contract.* ◦ *I suddenly **remembered that** it was her birthday.*
2 remember to do *something* A2 to not forget to do something: *Remember to take your passport.*

remind /rɪˈmaɪnd/ **verb**
B1 to make someone remember something, or remember to do something: *Every time we meet he **reminds** me **about** the money he lent me.* ◦ *Will you **remind** me **to** buy some eggs?*

> **Common mistake: remind or remember?**
>
> If you **remember** a fact or something from the past, you keep it in your mind, or bring it back into your mind.
> *I can't remember the name of the film.*
> *Did you remember to bring your passport?*
> When you **remind** someone to do something, you make them remember it.
> *Can you remind me to phone Anna tomorrow?*
> ~~*Can you remember me to phone Anna tomorrow?*~~

remind *someone* of *something/someone* **phrasal verb**
B1 to make someone think of something or someone else: *This song reminds me of our trip to Spain.*

remote /rɪˈməʊt/ **adj**
far away: *a remote mountain village*

remote control /rɪˌməʊt kənˈtrəʊl/ **noun**
1 B1 (also **remote**) a piece of equipment that is used to control something such as a television from a distance
2 [no plural] the use of radio waves to control something such as a television from a distance

remote control

remotely /rɪˈməʊtli/ **adv**
not remotely interested, surprised, etc. not at all interested, surprised, etc.: *I'm not remotely interested in football.*

removal /rɪˈmuːvəl/ **noun** [no plural]
the act of taking something out of something: *stain removal*

remove /rɪˈmuːv/ **verb** (**removing**, **removed**)
1 B1 to take something away: *An operation was needed to **remove** the bullets **from** his chest.*
2 to take something off: *She removed her jacket and hung it on a chair.*

rent[1] /rent/ **verb**
1 A2 to pay money to live in a building that someone else owns: *He rents an apartment.*
2 A2 US (UK **hire**) to pay money to use something for a short time: *We could rent a car for the weekend.*
3 B1 (also **rent out**) to allow someone to pay you money to live in your building: *He has a cottage which he rents to tourists.*

> **Common mistake: rent and hire**
>
> In British English you **rent** something for a long time.
> *I rent a two-bedroom flat.*
> In British English you **hire** something for a short time.
> *We hired a car for the weekend.*
> In American English the word **rent** is used in both situations.
> *I rent a two-bedroom apartment.*
> *We rented a car for the weekend.*

rent[2] /rent/ **noun**
A2 the amount of money that you pay to live in a building that someone else owns

rep /rep/ **noun** informal
someone whose job is to sell things for a company: *the company's UK **sales rep***

repaid /ˌriːˈpeɪd/
past tense and past participle of repay

repair[1] /rɪˈpeəʳ/ **verb**
A2 to fix something that is broken or damaged: *I must **get** my bike **repaired**.*

a b c d e f g h i j k l m n o p q **r** s t u v w x y z

repair² /rɪˈpeəʳ/ **noun**
B1 something that you do to fix something that is broken or damaged: *The repairs cost me £150.*

repay /ˌriːˈpeɪ/ **verb** (**repaying**, **repaid**)
to pay back money that you have borrowed: *to repay a loan*

repeat /rɪˈpiːt/ **verb**
A2 to say or do something more than once: *He repeated the number.* ◦ *The test must be repeated several times.*

repeated /rɪˈpiːtɪd/ **adj**
done or happening more than once: *He has refused repeated requests to be interviewed.*
• **repeatedly adv** *The victim was stabbed repeatedly with a knife.*

repetition /ˌrepɪˈtɪʃᵊn/ **noun**
the act of saying or doing something more than once: *We don't want a repetition of last year's disaster.*

replace /rɪˈpleɪs/ **verb** (**replacing**, **replaced**)
1 B1 to get something new because the one you had before has been lost or damaged: *We'll have to replace this carpet soon.*
2 B1 to start using another thing or person instead of the one that you are using now: *We're thinking of* ***replacing*** *our old TV.*
3 to start to be used instead of the thing or person that is being used now: *This system will replace the old one.*

replacement /rɪˈpleɪsmənt/ **noun**
a new thing or person in place of something or someone that was there before: *It's not going to be easy to find a replacement for you.*

replay /ˈriːpleɪ/ **noun** UK
a game of sport that is played again

reply¹ /rɪˈplaɪ/ **verb** (**replying**, **replied**)
B1 to answer: *'I don't understand,' she replied.* ◦ *He didn't* ***reply to*** *my email.*

reply² /rɪˈplaɪ/ **noun** (plural **replies**)
B1 an answer: *Have you had a* ***reply to*** *your letter?*

report¹ /rɪˈpɔːt/ **noun**
1 B1 a description of an event or situation: *a police report*
2 UK a written statement by a teacher about a child's progress at school for their parents

report² /rɪˈpɔːt/ **verb**
1 B1 to describe something that has just happened, especially on television, radio, or in a newspaper: *She* ***reported that*** *the situation had changed dramatically.*
2 B1 to tell someone in authority that something has happened, especially an accident or crime: *He reported the accident immediately.*

reported speech /rɪˌpɔːtɪd ˈspiːtʃ/ **noun** [no plural]
speech or writing that is used to report what someone has said, but not using exactly the same words: *The sentence 'He told me that he would like to go' is an example of reported speech.*

reporter /rɪˈpɔːtəʳ/ **noun**
B1 someone whose job is to discover information about news events and describe them on television, radio, or in a newspaper

represent /ˌreprɪˈzent/ **verb**
1 to officially speak for someone else because they have asked you to: *The union represents over 200 employees.*
2 to be a sign or symbol of something: *The crosses on the map represent churches.*

representative /ˌreprɪˈzentətɪv/ **noun**
someone who speaks or does something officially for another person

reproduce /ˌriːprəˈdjuːs/ **verb** (**reproducing**, **reproduced**)
1 to make a copy of something
2 formal If people, animals, or plants reproduce, they produce babies or young animals or plants.

reproduction /ˌriːprəˈdʌkʃᵊn/ **noun**
1 [no plural] the process of producing babies or young animals and plants
2 a copy of something, especially a painting

reptile /ˈreptaɪl/ **noun**
an animal whose body is covered with scales (= pieces of hard skin), and

a b c d e f g h i j k l m n o p q r s t u v w x y z

whose blood changes temperature, for example a snake

republic /rɪˈpʌblɪk/ **noun**
a country with no king or queen but with an elected government: *France is a republic.*

reputation /ˌrepjəˈteɪʃᵊn/ **noun**
the opinion that people have about someone or something: *Both hotels have a good reputation.*

request¹ /rɪˈkwest/ **noun**
B1 the act of asking for something: *His doctor* ***made*** *an urgent* ***request for*** *a copy of the report.*

request² /rɪˈkwest/ **verb**
B1 to ask for something: *We have requested two more computers.*

require /rɪˈkwaɪəʳ/ **verb** (**requiring**, **required**)
B1 to need something: *The job requires a high level of concentration.*

requirement /rɪˈkwaɪəmənt/ **noun**
something that is needed: *college entrance requirements*

rescue¹ /ˈreskjuː/ **verb** (**rescuing**, **rescued**)
B1 to save someone or something from a dangerous situation: *Fifty passengers had to be rescued from a sinking ship.*

rescue² /ˈreskjuː/ **noun**
B1 the act of saving someone or something from a dangerous situation: *a rescue attempt*

research¹ /rɪˈsɜːtʃ/ **noun** [no plural]
B1 the study of a subject in order to discover new information: *She does research into language development.*

research² /rɪˈsɜːtʃ/ **verb**
to study a subject in order to discover new information about it
• **researcher** **noun**

resemblance /rɪˈzembləns/ **noun**
the way in which two people or things appear similar: *There's a striking* ***resemblance between*** *Diane and her mother.*

resemble /rɪˈzembl/ **verb** (**resembling**, **resembled**)
to look like or be like someone or something: *She resembles her father.*

resent /rɪˈzent/ **verb**
to feel angry and upset about an unfair situation: *I resent having to work late.*

resentment /rɪˈzentmənt/ **noun** [no plural]
a feeling of anger about an unfair situation

reservation /ˌrezəˈveɪʃᵊn/ **noun**
B1 an arrangement that you make to have a seat on a plane, a room in a hotel, etc.: *I'd like to* ***make a reservation*** *for Friday evening.*

reserve¹ /rɪˈzɜːv/ **verb** (**reserving**, **reserved**)
1 B1 to arrange to have a seat on a plane, a room in a hotel, etc.: *I'd like to reserve two seats on the 9.15 to Glasgow.*
2 B1 to not allow people to use something because it is only for a particular person or for a particular purpose: *This space is reserved for ambulances.*

reserve² /rɪˈzɜːv/ **noun**
1 an amount of something that you keep until it is needed: *emergency cash reserves*
2 **in reserve** ready to be used if needed: *I always keep a little money in reserve.*
3 an area of land where animals and plants are protected: *We visited a nature reserve in Kenya.*

residence /ˈrezɪdᵊns/ **noun** formal
a building where someone lives: *the Queen's official residence*

resident /ˈrezɪdᵊnt/ **noun**
someone who lives in a particular place: *We have had complaints from local residents.*

residential /ˌrezɪˈdenʃᵊl/ **adj**
A residential area has only houses and not offices or factories.

resign /rɪˈzaɪn/ **verb**
to officially tell your employer that you are leaving your job: *Mr Aitken has* ***resigned from*** *the company.*

resign *yourself* to *something* phrasal verb
to make yourself accept something bad because you cannot change it: *He resigned himself to living alone.*

resignation /ˌrezɪɡˈneɪʃᵊn/ noun
1 the act of telling your employer that you are leaving your job: *a letter of resignation* ◦ *I **handed in my resignation** yesterday.*
2 [no plural] the act of accepting something bad because you cannot change it

resist /rɪˈzɪst/ verb
1 to stop yourself from doing something that you want to do: *I can't resist eating chocolate.*
2 to refuse to accept something and try to stop it from happening: *The President is resisting calls for him to resign.*
3 to fight against someone or something that is attacking you: *British troops resisted the attack for two days.*

resistance /rɪˈzɪstᵊns/ noun [no plural]
the act of disagreeing with a plan or idea and refusing to accept it: *resistance to political change*

resolution /ˌrezᵊlˈuːʃᵊn/ noun
a promise to yourself to do something: *My **New Year's resolution** is to do more exercise.*

resort /rɪˈzɔːt/ noun
B1 a place where many people go for a holiday: *a ski resort*

resource /rɪˈzɔːs/ noun
something that a country, person, or organization has that they can use: ***financial/natural resources***

respect[1] /rɪˈspekt/ noun
1 B1 [no plural] polite behaviour to someone, especially because they are older or more important than you: *You should show more **respect for** your parents.*
2 B1 [no plural] a feeling of admiration that you have for someone because of their knowledge, skill, or achievements: *She's an excellent teacher and I have the greatest **respect for** her.*
3 **in this respect/many respects** in a particular way, or in many ways: *The school has changed in many respects.*

respect[2] /rɪˈspekt/ verb
1 B1 to admire someone because they know a lot or have done good things, etc.: *I **respect** him **for** his honesty.*
2 If you respect someone's rights, customs, wishes, etc., you accept that they are important: *The agreement will respect the rights of both countries.*
• **respected** adj *He's a **highly respected** doctor.*

respectable /rɪˈspektəbl/ adj
behaving well, in a way that most people think is right: *a respectable family*

respond /rɪˈspɒnd/ verb
to answer someone or react to something: *How quickly did the police **respond to** the call?*

response /rɪˈspɒns/ noun
an answer or reaction to something that has been said or done: *I'm writing **in response to** your letter of May 14.*

responsibility /rɪˌspɒnsəˈbɪləti/ noun (plural **responsibilities**)
something that it is your job or duty to do: *It is your **responsibility to** make sure that the work is done on time.*

responsible /rɪˈspɒnsəbl/ adj
1 B1 having to do something as your duty: *I'm **responsible for** organizing the conferences.*
2 having caused something to happen, especially something bad: *Who was **responsible for** the accident?*
3 showing good judgment and able to be trusted: *He's hard-working and responsible.*
4 A responsible job is important because you have to make decisions that affect other people: *It's a very responsible job, being a teacher.*

rest[1] /rest/ noun
1 **the rest** A2 the part of something that remains: *Do you want to spend **the rest of** your life with him?*
2 A2 a period of time when you relax or sleep: *Why don't you **have a rest**?*

rest[2] /rest/ verb
1 B1 to relax or sleep because you are tired: *Pete's resting after his long drive.*

a b c d e f g h i j k l m n o p q r s t u v w x y z

a b c d e f g h i j k l m n o p q r s t u v w x y z

2 to put something on or against a surface: *She rested her head on his shoulder.*

restaurant /ˈrestərɒnt/ **noun**
A1 a place where you can buy and eat a meal: *an Italian restaurant*

restless /ˈrestləs/ **adj**
not able to be still or relax because you are bored or nervous: *The audience was getting restless.*

restore /rɪˈstɔːʳ/ **verb** (**restoring**, **restored**)
1 to make something good exist again: *We hope to restore peace in the region.*
2 to repair something old: *to restore antiques*

restrain /rɪˈstreɪn/ **verb**
to stop someone doing something, sometimes by using force: *He became violent and had to be physically restrained.*

restrict /rɪˈstrɪkt/ **verb**
to limit something: *They've brought in new laws to restrict the sale of cigarettes.* ◦ *I* ***restrict*** *myself* ***to*** *two glasses of wine most evenings.*

restriction /rɪˈstrɪkʃᵊn/ **noun**
a rule or law that limits what people can do: *parking restrictions*

restroom /ˈrestruːm/ **noun** US
a room with toilets that is in a public place

result¹ /rɪˈzʌlt/ **noun**
1 **B1** something that happens or exists because something else has happened: *Most accidents are* ***the result of*** *human error.*
2 **B1** information that you get from something such as an exam, a scientific experiment, or a medical test: *I finished my exams yesterday, but I won't* ***get the results*** *until August.*
3 **B1** the score or number of votes at the end of a competition or election: *The election results will be known by Sunday.* ◦ *What was the result of this afternoon's game?*

result² /rɪˈzʌlt/ **verb**
result in ***something*** **phrasal verb**
to be the reason something happens: *The improvements in training resulted in better performance.*

resume /rɪˈzjuːm/ **verb** formal
If an activity resumes, or if you resume it, it starts again: *The talks are due to resume today.*

résumé /ˈrezəmeɪ/ **noun** US (UK **CV**)
a document that describes your education and work experience

retain /rɪˈteɪn/ **verb**
to continue to keep something: *The local authority will* ***retain control*** *of the school.*

retire /rɪˈtaɪəʳ/ **verb** (**retiring**, **retired**)
B1 to leave your job and stop working because you are old: *She* ***retired from*** *the company in 1990.*
• **retired** **adj** *Both my parents are retired.*

retirement /rɪˈtaɪəmənt/ **noun** [no plural]
1 the period of your life after you have stopped working: *We wish you a long and happy retirement.*
2 the time when you leave your job and stop working, usually because you are old: *What is the normal* ***retirement age*** *in this country?*

retreat /rɪˈtriːt/ **verb**
When soldiers retreat, they move away from the enemy, especially to avoid fighting: *The army was forced to retreat.*

return¹ /rɪˈtɜːn/ **verb**
1 **A2** to go or come back to a place where you were before: *She* ***returned to*** *America in 1954.*
2 **A2** to give, send, or put something back where it came from: *I have to return the book by Friday.*
3 **return to *something*** to start doing an activity again or talking about something again: *I returned to work three months after Susie was born.*
4 to happen again or start to exist again: *You need to go to the doctor if the pain returns.*

return² /rɪˈtɜːn/ **noun**
1 **B1** [no plural] the act of going or coming back to a place where you were before: ***On*** *his* ***return*** *to Sydney, he started up a business.*

2 B1 UK (US **round-trip ticket**) a ticket that lets you travel to a place and back again
3 B1 [no plural] a key on a computer keyboard that is used to make the computer accept information: *Type in the password and **press return**.*
4 in return in exchange for something or as a reaction to something: *I'd like to give them something **in return for** everything they've done for us.*

reunion /ˌriːˈjuːniən/ **noun**
an occasion when people who have not met each other for a long time meet again: *We're having a **family reunion** next week.*

reuse /ˌriːˈjuːz/ **verb**
to use something again: *Businesses are finding new ways to reuse materials.*

reveal /rɪˈviːl/ **verb**
to tell someone a piece of secret information: *It was revealed in the papers that the couple intend to marry.*

revenge /rɪˈvendʒ/ **noun** [no plural]
something that you do to punish someone who has done something bad to you: *He was shot **in revenge** for the murder.*

reverse /rɪˈvɜːs/ **verb** (**reversing**, **reversed**)
1 to drive backwards: *I reversed into a parking space.*
2 to change a situation or change the order of things so that it becomes the opposite: *It is unlikely that the judge will reverse his decision.*
3 reverse the charges to make a telephone call that is paid for by the person receiving it

review[1] /rɪˈvjuː/ **noun**
B1 a piece of writing in a newspaper that gives an opinion about a new book, movie, etc.: *a book review*

review[2] /rɪˈvjuː/ **verb**
1 to give your opinion about a book, movie, television show, etc.: *He reviews movies for the Times.*
2 US (UK **revise**) to study a subject again before you take a test

revise /rɪˈvaɪz/ **verb** (**revising**, **revised**)
1 B1 UK (US **review**) to study a subject again before you take a test
2 to change something so that it is more accurate: *a revised edition of the book*

revision /rɪˈvɪʒᵊn/ **noun** [no plural] UK
B1 the work of studying a subject again before taking a test

revive /rɪˈvaɪv/ **verb** (**reviving**, **revived**)
to become conscious again or make someone conscious again: *A police officer tried to revive her.*

revolt /rɪˈvəʊlt/ **noun**
an act of trying to change a government, often using violence

revolting /rɪˈvəʊltɪŋ/ **adj**
very unpleasant: *The food was revolting.*

revolution /ˌrevᵊlˈuːʃᵊn/ **noun**
1 a change in the way a country is governed, usually to a different political system and often using violence: *the French Revolution*
2 a very important change in the way that people do things: *This discovery caused a **revolution in** medicine.*

revolutionary /ˌrevᵊlˈuːʃᵊnᵊri/ **adj**
1 completely different from what was done before: *a revolutionary new medical treatment*
2 relating to a political revolution: *a revolutionary movement*

revolve /rɪˈvɒlv/ **verb** (**revolving**, **revolved**)
to move in a circle around a central point: *A fan was revolving slowly.*

revolver /rɪˈvɒlvəʳ/ **noun**
a small gun

reward[1] /rɪˈwɔːd/ **noun**
1 B1 something good that you get because you have done something good: *There'll be a **reward for** whoever finishes first.*
2 B1 money given to someone for helping to find something or for helping the police: *The police offered a **reward for** any information about the robbery.*

a b c d e f g h i j k l m n o p q r s t u v w x y z

reward² /rɪˈwɔːd/ **verb**
to give a reward to someone: *She was **rewarded for** her bravery.*

rewrite /ˌriːˈraɪt/ **verb** (**rewrote**, **rewritten**)
to write something again in order to improve it: *I had to rewrite my essay.*

rheumatism /ˈruːmətɪzəm/ **noun** [no plural]
a disease in which there is pain in the joints (= parts of the body where bones connect)

rhino /ˈraɪnəʊ/ **noun**
short form of rhinoceros

rhinoceros /raɪˈnɒsərəs/ **noun**
a large animal from Africa or Asia that has thick skin and one or two horns on its nose

rhyme¹ /raɪm/ **verb** (**rhyming**, **rhymed**)
If a word rhymes with another word, the end part of the words sound the same: *'Moon' rhymes with 'June'.*

rhyme² /raɪm/ **noun**
1 a short poem that has words that rhyme at the end of each line
2 a word that rhymes with another word

rhythm /ˈrɪðəm/ **noun**
a regular, repeating pattern of sound: *You need a sense of rhythm to be a good dancer.*
• **rhythmically** **adv**

rib /rɪb/ **noun**
one of the curved bones in the chest

ribbon /ˈrɪbən/ **noun**
a long, thin piece of cloth that is used for decoration

rice /raɪs/ **noun** [no plural]
A1 small grains from a plant that are cooked and eaten
→ See **Food** on page C7

rich /rɪtʃ/ **adj**
1 A2 A rich person has a lot of money.
→ Opposite **poor** **adj**
2 Rich food has a lot of butter, cream, or eggs in it: *a rich sauce*
3 containing a lot of something that is important or valuable: *Oranges are **rich in** vitamin C.*

rid /rɪd/ **adj**
1 **get rid of *something*** B1 to throw something away: *We must get rid of some of those old books.*
2 **get rid of *something*** to end something unpleasant: *I can't get rid of this headache.*

ridden /ˈrɪdən/
the past participle of ride

riddle /ˈrɪdl/ **noun**
a strange and difficult question that has a clever and often funny answer

ride¹ /raɪd/ **verb** (**riding**, **rode**, **ridden**)
A1 to travel by sitting on a horse, bicycle, or motorcycle and controlling it: *I ride my bike to work.*

ride² /raɪd/ **noun**
1 B1 a journey in a car or train: *Can I give you a ride to the station?*
2 B1 a journey riding a bicycle, motorcycle, or horse: *He's gone out for a **ride on** his bicycle.*
3 B1 a machine at a fair that moves people up and down, around in circles, etc. as they sit in it: *She wanted me to go on a ride with her.*

rider /ˈraɪdəʳ/ **noun**
B1 someone who rides a horse, bicycle, or motorcycle
→ See **Sports 1** on page C15

ridiculous /rɪˈdɪkjələs/ **adj**
very silly: *It was a ridiculous suggestion.*

riding /ˈraɪdɪŋ/ **noun** [no plural]
the sport or activity of riding horses: *She **goes riding** every Saturday.*

rifle /ˈraɪfl/ **noun**
a long gun that you hold against your shoulder when you shoot

right¹ /raɪt/ **adj**
1 A1 correct or true: *He only got half the answers right.* ◦ *You're **right about** Alison – she's incredible!* ◦ *'You came here in 1989, didn't you?' '**That's right**.'*
2 A2 on or towards the side of your body that is to the east when you are facing north: *your right hand*
3 B1 suitable or best in a particular situation: *I'm not sure she's the right person for the job.*
4 fair or morally acceptable: *It isn't*

right to lie. ◦ *Someone had to tell him – I think you did the right thing.*

right² /raɪt/ **adv**
1 A2 to the right side: *Turn right after the bridge.*
2 A2 used at the beginning of a sentence to get someone's attention or to show you have understood someone: *Right, whose turn is it to tidy up?*
3 B1 exactly in a place or time: *He's right here with me.*
4 **right away/now** B1 immediately: *Do you want to start right away?* ◦ *I'm busy right now.*
5 correctly: *Nothing was going right.*
6 all the way: *Did you read it right through to the end?*

right³ /raɪt/ **noun**
1 A2 [no plural] the right side of your body, or the direction towards this side: *You'll find her in the second room* ***on the right***.
2 something that the law allows you to do: *the* ***right to*** *vote*
3 [no plural] morally good behaviour: *She knows the difference between right and wrong.*

right⁴ /raɪt/ **exclamation**
A2 informal used to express agreement with someone: *'Johnny, you climb up first.' 'Right!'*

right-hand /ˌraɪtˈhænd/ **adj**
A2 on the right of something: *On* ***the right-hand side*** *you'll see a sign.*

right-handed /ˌraɪtˈhændɪd/ **adj**
using your right hand to do most things

rigid /ˈrɪdʒɪd/ **adj**
1 not able to change or be changed easily: *I found the rules a little too rigid.*
2 not able to bend or move easily: *a rigid structure*

rim /rɪm/ **noun**
the edge of something round: *the rim of a cup*

rind /raɪnd/ **noun**
the thick skin of fruits such as oranges and lemons and other foods, for example cheese

ring¹ /rɪŋ/ **noun**
1 A2 a round piece of jewellery that you wear on your finger: *a wedding ring*
→ See picture at **jewellery**
2 **give *someone* a ring** A2 to telephone someone
3 something that is the shape of a circle: *The children sat in a ring around the teacher.*
4 the sound a bell makes: *The ring of the doorbell woke him up.*
5 an area with seats around it where people perform or compete: *a boxing ring*

ring² /rɪŋ/ **verb** (**rang**, **rung**)
1 A2 UK to telephone someone: *Have you rung your mother?*
2 B1 If something rings, it makes the sound of a bell, and if you ring a bell, you cause it to make a sound: *The phone's ringing.*
ring (*someone*) back **phrasal verb** UK
B1 to telephone someone a second time, or to telephone someone who rang you earlier: *I'm a bit busy – can I ring you back later?*
ring (*someone*) up **phrasal verb**
B1 to telephone someone: *Ring Paul up and ask what he's doing tonight.*

ringtone /ˈrɪŋtəʊn/ **noun**
the sound that a mobile phone makes

rinse /rɪns/ **verb** (**rinsing**, **rinsed**)
to wash something in clean water in order to remove dirt or soap: *Rinse the beans with cold water.*

riot /raɪət/ **noun**
angry, violent behaviour by a crowd of people: *a race riot*

rip /rɪp/ **verb** (**ripping**, **ripped**)
to tear quickly and suddenly: *She ripped her dress getting off her bike.* ◦ *He ripped open the parcel.*

ripe /raɪp/ **adj**
developed enough and ready to be eaten: *ripe bananas*

rip-off /ˈrɪpɒf/ **noun** informal
something that costs far too much money: *The drinks here are a complete rip-off.*

rise¹ /raɪz/ **verb** (**rising**, **rose**, **risen**)
1 B1 to move up: *The balloon rose slowly into the air.*
2 B1 When the sun or moon rises, it

appears in the sky: *The sun rises in the East.*

3 to get bigger in level: *Prices* ***rose by*** *ten percent.*

4 to stand, especially after sitting: *He rose from his seat.*

> **Common mistake: rise or raise?**
>
> Be careful not to confuse these two verbs.
> **Rise** means 'to increase or move up'. This verb cannot be followed by an object.
>
> *The price of petrol is rising.*
>
> ~~*The price of petrol is raising.*~~
>
> **Raise** means 'to lift something to a higher position or to increase an amount or level'. This verb must always be followed by an object.
>
> *The government has raised the price of petrol.*
>
> ~~*The government has rised the price of petrol.*~~

rise[2] /raɪz/ **noun**
an increase in the level of something: *a tax rise*

risk[1] /rɪsk/ **noun**
1 the possibility of something bad happening: *the risk of heart disease*
2 take a risk to do something although something bad might happen because of it
3 at risk being in a situation where something bad is likely to happen: *All houses within 100 yards of the sea are* ***at risk of*** *flooding*

risk[2] /rɪsk/ **verb**
1 If you risk something bad, you do something although that bad thing might happen: *I'd like to help you, but I can't risk losing my job.*
2 to put something or yourself in danger: *He risked his life to save me.*

risky /ˈrɪski/ **adj**
dangerous because something bad might happen: *It's risky to buy a car without some good advice.*

rival /ˈraɪvᵊl/ **noun**
someone or something that is competing against another person or thing: *political rivals*
• **rivalry noun** a situation in which two people or things are competing against each other: *There is intense* ***rivalry between*** *the two teams.*

river /ˈrɪvəʳ/ **noun**
A1 a long, natural area of water that flows across the land: *the River Thames*

road /rəʊd/ **noun**
1 A1 a long, hard surface built for vehicles to drive on: *Be careful when you cross the road.* ◦ *The journey takes about three hours* ***by road*** *(= in a car, bus, etc.).*
2 Road A1 used in the name of a road as part of an address: *142 Park Road*

roar[1] /rɔːʳ/ **verb**
to make a loud, deep sound: *She* ***roared with laughter.***

roar[2] /rɔːʳ/ **noun**
a loud, deep sound: *a lion's roar*

roast /rəʊst/ **verb**
A2 If you roast food, you cook it in an oven or over a fire: *Roast the lamb in a hot oven for 35 minutes.*
→ See picture at **cook**
• **roast adj** A2 *roast beef*

rob /rɒb/ **verb** (**robbing**, **robbed**)
B1 to steal from someone or somewhere, often using violence: *to rob a bank*

robber /ˈrɒbəʳ/ **noun**
someone who steals: *a bank robber*

robbery /ˈrɒbᵊri/ **noun** (plural **robberies**)
the crime of stealing from someone or somewhere: *a bank robbery*

robe /rəʊb/ **noun**
a long, loose piece of clothing, covering most of the body

robot /ˈrəʊbɒt/ **noun**
a machine controlled by a computer that can move and do other things that people can do

rock[1] /rɒk/ **noun**
1 B1 [no plural] the hard, natural substance that forms part of the Earth's surface
2 B1 a large piece of rock or stone: *Huge waves crashed against the rocks.*
3 A2 [no plural] loud, modern music with a strong beat, often played with electric guitars and drums: *a rock band*

rock[2] /rɒk/ **verb**
to move backwards and forwards or

from side to side, or to make someone or something do this: *She rocked backwards and forwards in her chair.* ◦ *He gently rocked the baby to sleep.*

rocket /ˈrɒkɪt/ **noun**
a tube-shaped vehicle for travelling in space

rocky /ˈrɒki/ **adj** (**rockier**, **rockiest**)
with lots of rocks: *a rocky beach*

rod /rɒd/ **noun**
a thin, straight pole: *a fishing rod*

rode /rəʊd/
past tense and past participle of ride

role /rəʊl/ **noun**
1 B1 a part in a play or movie: *In his latest movie, he* ***plays the role of*** *a violent gangster.*
2 the job someone or something has in a particular situation: *Schools* ***play*** *an important* ***role in*** *society.*

role play /ˈrəʊl ˌpleɪ/ **noun**
an activity in which people pretend to be someone else, especially as part of learning a new skill: *a role-play activity*

roll[1] /rəʊl/ **verb**
1 to move somewhere by turning in a circular direction, or to make something move this way: *The ball rolled through the goalkeeper's legs.* ◦ *She rolled over onto her side.*
2 to turn something around itself to make the shape of a ball or tube: *to roll a cigarette*
3 to move somewhere smoothly: *Tears* ***rolled down*** *her face.*

roll[2] /rəʊl/ **noun**
1 something that has been turned around itself into a round shape like a tube: *a roll of toilet paper*
2 B1 a small loaf of bread for one person
→ See **Food** on page C7

Rollerblades /ˈrəʊləbleɪdz/ **plural noun** trademark
boots with a single line of wheels on the bottom, used for moving across the ground
• **rollerblading** **noun** [no plural] *People* ***go rollerblading*** *in Central Park.*
→ See **Sports 1** on page C15

roller skate /ˈrəʊlə ˌskeɪt/ **noun**
a boot with wheels on the bottom, used for moving across the ground
• **roller skating** **noun** [no plural]

romance /rəʊˈmæns/ **noun**
1 B1 an exciting relationship of love between two people, often a short one: *They had a brief romance.*
2 a story about love

romantic /rəʊˈmæntɪk/ **adj**
1 B1 relating to exciting feelings of love: *a romantic dinner for two*
2 B1 relating to a story about love: *a romantic movie*

roof

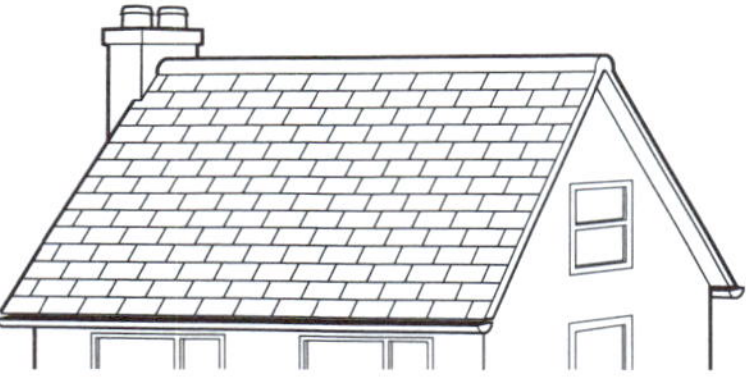

roof /ruːf/ **noun**
A2 the surface that covers the top of a building or vehicle: *He climbed onto the roof.*

room /ruːm/, /rʊm/ **noun**
1 A1 a part of the inside of a building, that is separated from other parts by walls, floors, and ceilings: *a hotel room*
2 B1 [no plural] space for things to fit into: *Is there enough* ***room for*** *all of us in your car?*

roommate /ˈruːmmeɪt/ **noun**
1 someone who you share a room with: *He was my roommate while we were at college.*
2 US someone who you share your home with

root /ruːt/ **plural noun**
1 the part of a plant that grows under the ground
2 **roots** where someone or something originally comes from: *He lives in London but his roots are in Ireland.*

rope /rəʊp/ **noun**
very thick, strong string

rose[1] /rəʊz/
past tense and past participle of rise

a b c d e f g h i j k l m n o p q r s t u v w x y z

rose² /rəʊz/ **noun**
B1 a flower with a pleasant smell and thorns (= sharp points on the stem)

rose

rot /rɒt/ **verb** (**rotting**, **rotted**)
to become bad and soft because of being dead or old: *The fruit had been left to rot on the trees.*

rotate /rəʊˈteɪt/ **verb** (**rotating**, **rotated**)
to turn in a circular direction, or to make something turn in a circular direction: *The handle rotates freely.*
• **rotation** /rəʊˈteɪʃən/ **noun** *the rotation of the Earth*

rotten /ˈrɒtən/ **adj**
1 old and bad: *rotten eggs*
2 informal very bad: *rotten weather*

rough /rʌf/ **adj**
1 B1 A rough surface is not smooth: *rough hands*
2 B1 not completely accurate but close: *Can you give me a rough idea of the cost?*
3 dangerous or violent: *Hockey can be a rough game.*
4 If the sea or weather is rough, there is a lot of strong wind and sometimes rain: *The boat sank in rough seas.*
5 difficult or unpleasant: *She's having a rough time at work.*

roughly /ˈrʌfli/ **adv**
1 close to a particular number, although not exactly that number: *There's been an increase of roughly 30% since last year.*
2 with force or violence: *He pushed us roughly out of the door.*

round¹ /raʊnd/ **adj**
A2 in the shape of a circle or ball: *a round table* ◦ *round eyes*
→ See picture at **flat** adj

round² /raʊnd/ **adv, preposition** (also **around**)
1 A2 to someone's home: *Wendy's coming round this afternoon.*
2 A2 on all sides of something: *We sat round the table.*
3 B1 in a circular movement: *This switch makes the wheels go round.*
4 B1 from one place or person to another: *Could you pass these forms round, please?*
5 B1 to the opposite direction: *She looked round.*
6 B1 to or in different parts of a place: *He showed me round the flat.*
7 near an area: *Do you live round here?*
8 **round and round** moving in a circle without stopping: *We drove round and round trying to find the hotel.*

roundabout /ˈraʊndəˌbaʊt/ **noun** UK (US **traffic circle**)
A2 a circular place where roads meet and where cars drive around until they arrive at the road that they want to turn into

round trip /ˌraʊnd ˈtrɪp/ **noun**
a journey from one place to another and back to where you started: *I have a round trip of 45 miles to get to work.*

round-trip ticket /ˌraʊndtrɪp ˈtɪkɪt/ **noun** US (UK **return**)
a ticket that lets you travel to a place and back again

route /ruːt/ **noun**
B1 the roads you follow to get from one place to another place

routine /ruːˈtiːn/ **noun**
B1 the things that you do every day at the same time: *a daily routine*

row¹ /rəʊ/ **noun**
1 B1 a straight line of people or things: *a **row of** trees*
2 B1 a line of seats: *I was sitting **in the front row**.*
3 **in a row** one after another without a break: *He's just won the race for the fifth year in a row.*

row² /rəʊ/ **verb**
to move a boat or move someone in a boat through the water using oars (= poles with flat ends)

• **rowing** **noun** [no plural]

row³ /raʊ/ **noun** UK
a loud, angry argument: *The couple next door are always* ***having rows****.*

rowing boat /ˈrəʊɪŋ ˌbəʊt/ **noun** (US **rowboat** /ˈrəʊbəʊt/)
a small boat that is moved by pulling oars (= poles with flat ends) through the water

royal /ˈrɔɪəl/ **adj**
relating to a queen or king and their family: *the British royal family*

royalty /ˈrɔɪəlti/ **noun** [no plural]
the people in the royal family

rub /rʌb/ **verb** (**rubbing**, **rubbed**)
to press your hand or a cloth on a surface and move it backwards and forwards: *He rubbed himself dry with a towel.* ◦ *Rub the stain with a damp cloth.*
rub ***something*** **out** **phrasal verb** UK
to remove writing from something by rubbing it with a piece of rubber or a cloth

rubber /ˈrʌbəʳ/ **noun**
1 [no plural] a strong material that bends easily and is used to make tyres, boots, etc.
2 A2 UK (US **eraser**) a small object that is used to remove pencil marks from paper
→ See **Classroom** on page C4

rubber band /ˌrʌbə ˈbænd/ **noun**
a thin circle of rubber used to hold things together

rubbish /ˈrʌbɪʃ/ **noun** [no plural] UK
1 B1 things that you throw away because you do not want them: *Our rubbish gets collected on Thursdays.*
2 informal something that is of bad quality: *There's so much rubbish on TV.*

rubbish bin /ˈrʌbɪʃ ˌbɪn/ **noun**
a container that is used to put waste in

ruby /ˈruːbi/ **noun** (plural **rubies**)
a valuable bright red stone that is used in jewellery

rucksack /ˈrʌksæk/ **noun** UK
a bag that you carry on your back

rude /ruːd/ **adj**
1 B1 behaving in a way that is not polite and upsets other people: *a rude remark* ◦ *He was very* ***rude to*** *me.* ◦ *It would be rude to leave without saying goodbye.*
→ Opposite **polite** **adj**
2 Rude words or jokes relate to sex or going to the toilet.
• **rudely** **adv**
• **rudeness** **noun** [no plural]

rug /rʌg/ **noun**
B1 a soft piece of material used to cover the floor: *The dog was lying on the rug in front of the fire.*

rug

rugby /ˈrʌgbi/ **noun** [no plural]
A2 a sport played by two teams with an oval ball and H-shaped goals
→ See **Sports 2** on page C16

ruin¹ /ˈruːɪn/ **verb**
to spoil or destroy something: *They were late and the dinner was ruined.*

ruin² /ˈruːɪn/ **noun**
B1 the broken parts that are left from an old building or town: *Thousand of tourists wander around these ancient ruins every year.*

rule¹ /ruːl/ **noun**
1 B1 an official statement about what you must or must not do: *You can't smoke at school. It's* ***against the rules*** *(= not allowed).*
2 B1 a basic idea that explains how a system, such as a language or science, works: *the rules of grammar*
3 the usual way something is: *I visit my parents once a week* ***as a rule****.*

rule² /ruːl/ **verb** (**ruling**, **ruled**)
to be in control of somewhere, usually a country: *They were ruled for many years by a dictator.*

ruler /ˈruːləʳ/ **noun**
1 the leader of a country
2 A2 a flat, straight stick that is used to measure things
→ See **The Classroom** on page C4

a b c d e f g h i j k l m n o p q r s t u v w x y z

rum /rʌm/ **noun**
a strong, alcoholic drink made from sugar

rumble /ˈrʌmbl/ **verb** (**rumbling**, **rumbled**)
to make a deep, long sound: *The smell of cooking made his stomach rumble.*

rumour UK (US **rumor**) /ˈruːməʳ/ **noun**
a fact that a lot of people are talking about although they do not know if it is true: *I **heard a rumour** that you were leaving.*

run[1] /rʌn/ **verb** (**running**, **ran**, **run**)
1 (A1) to move on your feet at a faster speed than walking: *He can run very fast.* ◦ *I run about three miles every morning.*
2 (B1) to organize or control something: *She ran her own restaurant for five years.*
3 If a piece of equipment is running, it is switched on and working: *The engine is running more smoothly now.*
4 If trains or buses are running, they are available to travel on: *The buses only run until 11 p.m.*
5 If liquid runs somewhere, it flows: *Tears ran down her face.*
run away **phrasal verb**
to secretly leave a place because you are unhappy there: *He ran away from home as a child.*
run out **phrasal verb**
1 (B1) to use all of something so that there is none left: *I've nearly **run out of** money.*
2 (B1) If a supply of something runs out, all of it has been used or it is completely finished: *The milk has run out.*
run *someone/something* over **phrasal verb**
to hit someone or something with a car, bus, etc. and hurt or kill them: *He was run over by a bus as he crossed the road.*

run[2] /rʌn/ **noun**
1 (B1) the act of moving on your feet at a speed faster than walking as a sport: *to go for a run*
2 in cricket or baseball, a single point: *to score a run*

rung /rʌŋ/
the past participle of ring[2]

runner /ˈrʌnəʳ/ **noun**
(A2) someone who runs: *a long-distance runner*

running /ˈrʌnɪŋ/ **noun** [no plural]
(A2) the sport of moving on your feet at a speed faster than walking: *I **go running** three times a week.*
→ See **Sports 1** on page C15

runway /ˈrʌnweɪ/ **noun**
a long piece of ground that planes use to land on or to start flying from

rural /ˈrʊərᵊl/ **adj**
relating to the countryside and not to towns: *a rural area*

rush[1] /rʌʃ/ **verb**
to hurry or move quickly somewhere: *We had to rush to catch the bus.*

rush[2] /rʌʃ/ **noun** [no plural]
a situation in which you have to hurry or move somewhere quickly: *I'm sorry I can't talk now – I'm **in a rush**.*

rush hour /ˈrʌʃ ˌaʊəʳ/ **noun** [no plural]
the time when roads and trains are very busy because a lot of people are travelling to or from work: *I hate driving during the rush hour.*

rust /rʌst/ **noun** [no plural]
a dark orange substance that you get on metal when it is wet
• **rust** **verb**

rusty /ˈrʌsti/ **adj** (**rustier**, **rustiest**)
Rusty metal has rust on its surface: *rusty nails*

Ss

S, s /es/
the nineteenth letter of the alphabet

sachet /ˈsæʃeɪ/ **noun** UK (US **packet**)
a small paper bag containing a small amount of something: *a sachet of sugar*

sack¹ /sæk/ **noun**

1 a large, strong bag used to carry or keep things
2 get the sack UK When someone gets the sack, they are told to leave their job: *He got the sack from his last job.*

sack² /sæk/ **verb** UK
to tell someone to leave their job: *He was sacked for being late.*

sacred /ˈseɪkrɪd/ **adj**
relating to a religion or considered to be holy: *sacred music*

sacrifice¹ /ˈsækrɪfaɪs/ **noun**
1 something good that you must stop having in order to achieve something: *Sometimes you have to **make sacrifices** to succeed.*
2 an animal that is killed and offered to a god in a religious ceremony

sacrifice² /ˈsækrɪfaɪs/ **verb** (**sacrificing**, **sacrificed**)
1 to stop having something good in order to achieve something: *There are thousands of men ready to **sacrifice** their lives **for** their country.*
2 to kill an animal and offer it to a god in a religious ceremony

sad /sæd/ **adj** (**sadder**, **saddest**)
1 A1 unhappy: *I was very sad when our cat died.* ◦ *a sad book*
2 UK informal boring or not fashionable: *I cleaned the house on Saturday night, which is a bit sad.*
• **sadness** **noun** [no plural]

saddle /ˈsædl/ **noun**

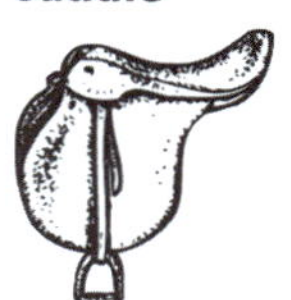

1 a leather seat that you put on a horse so that you can ride it
2 a seat on a bicycle or motorcycle

sadly /ˈsædli/ **adv**
1 in a sad way: *She shook her head sadly.*
2 used to say that you are sorry something is true: *Sadly, the marriage ended.*

safari /səˈfɑːri/ **noun**
a journey, usually to Africa, to see wild animals

safe¹ /seɪf/ **adj**
1 A2 not dangerous: *a safe driver* ◦ *Air travel is generally quite safe.*
2 B1 not hurt or in danger: *She said that all the hostages were safe.*
• **safely** **adv** B1 *Drive safely!*

safe² /seɪf/ **noun**
a strong metal box with locks where you keep money, jewellery, etc.

safety /ˈseɪfti/ **noun** [no plural]
a state of being safe from harm or danger: *road safety*

safety belt /ˈseɪfti ˌbelt/ **noun**
a strap that you fasten across your body when travelling in a car or plane: *Please **fasten** your **safety belt**.*

sag /sæg/ **verb** (**sagging**, **sagged**)
to sink or bend down: *Our mattress sags in the middle.*

said /sed/
past tense and past participle of say

sail¹ /seɪl/ **verb**
1 B1 to control or travel in a boat or a ship that has an engine or sails: *We sailed to Barbados.* ◦ *She sails her own boat.*
2 When a boat or a ship sails, it travels on the water: *The boat **sailed along** the coast.*

sail² /seɪl/ **noun**
a large piece of material that is fixed to a pole on a boat to catch the wind and make the boat move

sailing /ˈseɪlɪŋ/ **noun** [no plural]
A2 a sport using boats with sails: *We're **going sailing** next weekend.*

sailor /ˈseɪləʳ/ **noun**
B1 someone who sails ships or boats as their job or as a sport

saint /seɪnt/ **noun**
a dead person who lived their life in a holy way

sake /seɪk/ **noun**
1 for the sake of *someone* in order to help or please someone: *He asked her to stay for the sake of the children.*
2 for goodness sake! something you say when you are angry about something: *For goodness sake, come here!*

salad /ˈsæləd/ **noun**
A2 a cold mixture of vegetables that have not been cooked

salad

salary /ˈsælᵊri/ **noun** (plural **salaries**)
B1 the money that you get, usually every month, for working

sale /seɪl/ **noun**
1 the act of selling something: *The sale of alcohol is now banned.*
2 A2 a time when a shop sells things for less money than usual: *I bought this dress **in the sale**.*
3 for sale A2 available to buy: *Is this painting for sale?*
4 on sale UK A2 available to buy in a shop, on the Internet, etc.: *The video and book are now on sale.*
5 sales the number of items sold: *Our sales have doubled this year.*

salesclerk /ˈseɪlzklɑːk/ **noun** US (UK **shop assistant**)
someone whose job is selling things in a shop

salesman, saleswoman /ˈseɪlzmən/, /ˈseɪlzˌwʊmən/ **noun** (plural **salesmen**, **saleswomen**)
B1 a man or woman whose job is selling things

salmon /ˈsæmən/ **noun** (plural **salmon**)
B1 a large, silver fish, or the pink meat of this fish

salon /ˈsælɒn/ **noun**
a shop where you can have your hair cut or have your appearance improved: *a **hair salon***

salt /sɔːlt/, /sɒlt/ **noun** [no plural]
A1 a white substance used to add flavour to food: *salt and pepper*

salty /ˈsɔːlti/, /ˈsɒlti/ **adj** (**saltier**, **saltiest**)
tasting of or containing salt: *Is the soup too salty?*

salute[1] /səˈluːt/ **noun**
a sign of respect to someone of a higher rank in a military organization, often made by putting the right hand at the side of the head

salute[2] /səˈluːt/ **verb** (**saluting**, **saluted**)
to give a salute to someone of a higher rank in a military organization

same[1] /seɪm/ **adj**
1 the same A1 exactly alike: *He's **the same** age **as** me.* ◦ *We work at the same speed.*
2 the same A1 not another different person, thing or situation: *My brother and I sleep in the same room.*
3 at the same time B1 If two things happen at the same time, they happen together: *We arrived at the same time.*

same[2] /seɪm/ **pronoun**
1 the same A2 exactly like: *People say I look **just the same as** my sister.* ◦ *He looks **exactly the same as** he did ten years ago.*
2 the same B1 not another different thing or situation: *I'd do the same if I was in your situation.*

same[3] /seɪm/ **adv**
the same in the same way: *We treat all our children the same.*

sample /ˈsɑːmpl/ **noun**
a small amount of something that shows you what it is like: *She brought in some samples of her work.* ◦ *The doctor took a blood sample.*

sand /sænd/ **noun** [no plural]
B1 a substance that is found on beaches, which is made from very small grains of rock

sandal /ˈsændəl/ **noun**
B1 a light shoe with straps that you wear in warm weather
→ See **Clothes** on page C5

sandwich /ˈsænwɪdʒ/ **noun**
A1 two slices of bread with meat, cheese, etc. between them: *a cheese sandwich*

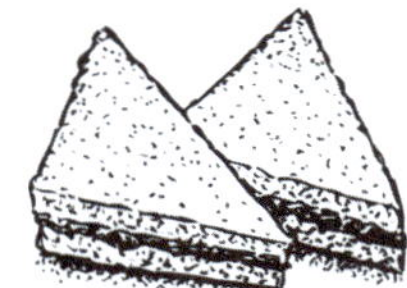
sandwiches

sandy /ˈsændi/ **adj** (**sandier**, **sandiest**)
B1 covered with sand: *a sandy beach*

sane /seɪn/ **adj**
having a healthy mind
→ Opposite **insane** **adj**

sang /sæŋ/
past tense and past participle of sing

sank /sæŋk/
past tense and past participle of sink

sarcasm /ˈsɑːkæzəm/ **noun** [no plural]
a way of using words that are the opposite of what you mean to be unpleasant to someone or show them that you are angry

sarcastic /sɑːˈkæstɪk/ **adj**
using sarcasm: *Are you being sarcastic?*

sat /sæt/
past tense and past participle of sit

satellite /ˈsætəlaɪt/ **noun**
a piece of equipment that is sent into space around the Earth to get and send signals: *a weather satellite*

satellite dish /ˈsætəlaɪt ˌdɪʃ/ **noun**
a round piece of equipment that is used for receiving television or radio signals

satin /ˈsætɪn/ **noun** [no plural]
a smooth, shiny cloth

satisfaction /ˌsætɪsˈfækʃən/ **noun** [no plural]
a good feeling because you have done something well: *job satisfaction*

satisfactory /ˌsætɪsˈfæktəri/ **adj**
good enough: *We hope to find a satisfactory solution to the problem.*
→ Opposite **unsatisfactory** **adj**

satisfied /ˈsætɪsfaɪd/ **adj**
B1 pleased because you have got what you wanted: *Are you* ***satisfied with*** *the new arrangement?*
→ Opposite **dissatisfied** **adj**

satisfy /ˈsætɪsfaɪ/ **verb** (**satisfying**, **satisfied**)
to please someone by giving them what they want: *They sell 31 flavours of ice cream – enough to satisfy everyone!*

Saturday /ˈsætədeɪ/ **noun**
A1 the day of the week after Friday and before Sunday

sauce /sɔːs/ **noun**
A2 a liquid that you put on food to add flavour: *pasta with tomato sauce*

saucepan /ˈsɔːspən/ **noun**
B1 a metal pan with a long handle and a lid, that is used to cook food in
→ See **The Kitchen** on page C10

saucer /ˈsɔːsəʳ/ **noun**
B1 a small plate that you put under a cup
→ See picture at **cup**

sauna /ˈsɔːnə/ **noun**
a room that is hot and filled with steam where people sit to relax or feel healthy

sausage /ˈsɒsɪdʒ/ **noun**
A2 a mixture of meat and spices pressed into a long tube

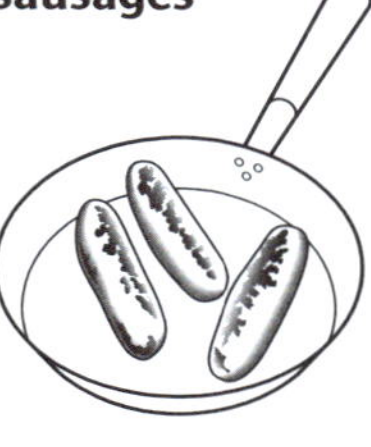
sausages

save /seɪv/ **verb** (**saving**, **saved**)
1 A2 (also **save up**) to keep money so that you can buy something with it in the future: *We've* ***saved*** *almost $900* ***for*** *our wedding.*
2 A2 to keep something to use in the future: *I've* ***saved*** *some food* ***for*** *you.*
3 **save files, work, etc.** A2 to store work or information on a computer
4 B1 to stop someone or something

a b c d e f g h i j k l m n o p q r s t u v w x y z

from being killed or destroyed: *He was badly injured, but the doctors saved his life.*
5 save money, space, time, etc. B1 to reduce the amount of money, space, time, etc. that you have to use: *You'll save time by doing it yourself.*
6 save a goal to stop a player from scoring a goal

savings /ˈseɪvɪŋz/ **plural noun**
money that you have saved, usually in a bank: *a savings account*

saw¹ /sɔː/
past tense and past participle of see

saw² /sɔː/ **noun**
a tool with a sharp edge that you use to cut wood or other hard material

saxophone /ˈsæksəfəʊn/ **noun**
a metal musical instrument that you play by blowing into it and pressing keys

say /seɪ/ **verb** (**saying**, **said**)
1 A1 to speak words: *'I'd like to go home,' she said.* ◦ *How do you say this word?*
2 B1 to tell someone about a fact or opinion: *He **said that** he was leaving.*
3 B1 to give information in writing, numbers, or signs: *My watch says one o'clock.*
4 B1 to think or believe: *People **say that** he's over 100.*

Common mistake: say or tell?

Say can refer to any type of speech.
'Good night,' she said.
She said she was unhappy.
Jim said to meet him here.
Tell is used to report that someone has given information or an order. The verb **tell** is always followed by the person that the information or order is given to.
Simon told me about his new job.
Say is never followed by the person that the information or order is given to.
He told us to stay here.
~~*He said us to stay here.*~~

saying /ˈseɪɪŋ/ **noun**
a famous phrase that people use to give advice about life

scale /skeɪl/ **noun**
1 the size or level of something: *We don't yet know the scale of the problem.*
2 the set of numbers, amounts, etc. used to measure or compare the level of something: ***On a scale of** 1-10, I would give him a 9.*
3 US (UK **scales**) a piece of equipment for measuring weight: *a bathroom scale*
→ See **The Bathroom** on page C1
→ See **The Kitchen** on page C10
4 how the size of things on a map, model, etc. relates to the same things in real life: *a map with a scale of one centimetre per ten kilometres*
5 a series of musical notes that is always played in order and that goes up from the first note
6 one of the flat pieces of hard material that covers the skin of fish and snakes

scales /skeɪlz/ **plural noun** UK (US **scale**)
a piece of equipment for measuring weight: *kitchen scales*
→ See **The Bathroom** on page C1
→ See **Kitchen** on page C10

scalp /skælp/ **noun**
the skin on the top of your head under your hair

scan /skæn/ **verb** (**scanning**, **scanned**)
1 to examine something with a machine that can see inside an object or body: *Airports use X-ray machines to scan luggage for weapons.*
2 to use a machine that copies words or pictures from paper into a computer: *I scanned the photos into my computer.*
3 to read something quickly in order to understand the main meaning or to find a particular piece of information: *I scanned the travel brochures looking for a cheap holiday.*

scandal /ˈskændəl/ **noun**
something that shocks people because they think it is very bad: *a sex scandal*

scanner /ˈskænəʳ/ **noun**
a piece of equipment that copies words or pictures from paper into a computer

scar /skɑːʳ/ **noun**
a permanent mark left on the body from a cut or other injury
• **scar verb** (**scarring**, **scarred**) to cause

a scar: *He was **scarred for life** by the accident.*

scarce /skeəs/ **adj**
rare, existing only in small amounts: *scarce resources*

scarcely /ˈskeəsli/ **adv**
only just: *They had scarcely finished eating when the doorbell rang.*

scare[1] /skeəʳ/ **verb** (**scaring**, **scared**)
to frighten a person or animal: *Sudden loud noises scare me.*

scare[2] /skeəʳ/ **noun**
1 a sudden feeling of fear or worry: *The earthquake **gave** us **a scare**.*
2 a situation that worries or frightens people: *a health scare*

scared /skeəd/ **adj**
B1 frightened or worried: *Robert's **scared of** heights.*

scarf /skɑːf/ **noun** (plural **scarves** /skɑːvz/)
A2 a piece of cloth that you wear around your neck or head to keep warm or for decoration
→ See **Clothes** on page C5

scary /ˈskeəri/ **adj** informal
B1 frightening: *a scary story*

scatter /ˈskætəʳ/ **verb**
1 to throw a lot of small objects over an area: *He scattered some flower seeds in the garden.*
2 to suddenly move away in different directions: *The crowd scattered at the sound of shots being fired.*

scene /siːn/ **noun**
1 B1 a short part of a movie, play, or book in which things happen in one place: *a love scene*
2 a view or picture of a place, event, or activity: *scenes of horror*
3 a place where a bad thing has happened: *the scene of the crime*

scenery /ˈsiːnəri/ **noun** [no plural]
1 B1 the attractive, natural things that you see in the countryside
2 the large pictures of buildings, countryside, etc. used in a theatre

scent /sent/ **noun**
1 a nice smell: *the sweet scent of orange blossoms*
2 a nice smelling liquid that people put on their skin

schedule /ˈʃedjuːl/ **noun**
a plan that tells you when things will happen: *Will the work be completed **on schedule** (= at the expected time)?*

scheduled /ˈʃedjuːld/ **adj**
1 planned to happen at a particular time or on a particular date: *The play will start half an hour later than the scheduled time.*
2 travelling at a regular time each day or week: *a **scheduled flight***

scheme[1] /skiːm/ **noun** UK
an official plan or system: *a savings scheme*

scheme[2] /skiːm/ **verb** (**scheming**, **schemed**)
to make a secret plan

scholar /ˈskɒləʳ/ **noun**
someone who has studied a subject and knows a lot about it: *a legal scholar*

scholarship /ˈskɒləʃɪp/ **noun**
an amount of money given to a person by an organization to pay for their education

school /skuːl/ **noun**
1 A1 a place where children go to learn things: *I ride my bike to school.*
2 A2 [no plural] the time that you spend at school: *I like school.* ◦ *I started school when I was five.*
3 a dance, language, riding, etc. school A2 a place where you can study a particular subject: *She goes to a riding school every Saturday.*
4 US informal any college or university

schoolchild /ˈskuːltʃaɪld/ **noun** (plural **schoolchildren**)
A2 a child who goes to school: *The bus was full of schoolchildren.*

schoolteacher /ˈskuːlˌtiːtʃəʳ/ **noun**
someone who teaches children in a school

science /saɪəns/ **noun**
1 A2 [no plural] the study of the structure of natural things and the way that they behave
2 B1 a particular type of science:

Chemistry, physics, and biology are all sciences.

science fiction /ˌsaɪəns ˈfɪkʃən/ **noun** [no plural] (also **sci-fi** /ˈsaɪfaɪ/) **B1** stories about life in the future or in other parts of the universe

scientific /ˌsaɪənˈtɪfɪk/ **adj** **B1** relating to science: *scientific experiments*
• **scientifically** **adv** *The theory has not been scientifically proven.*

scientist /ˈsaɪəntɪst/ **noun** **B1** someone who studies science or works in science

scissors /ˈsɪzəz/ **plural noun** **A2** a tool for cutting paper, hair, etc. that you hold in your hand and that has two blades: *a pair of scissors*

scissors

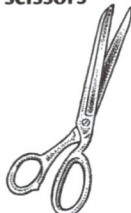

scold /skəʊld/ **verb** to speak angrily to someone, especially a child, because they have done something wrong: *His mother **scolded** him **for** breaking a vase.*

scoop /skuːp/ **verb** to remove something from a container using a spoon, your curved hands, etc.: *She scooped the ice cream into the dishes.*

scooter /ˈskuːtəʳ/ **noun**
1 **A2** a small motorcycle
2 a child's vehicle that has two wheels fixed to the ends of a long board and a long handle

score¹ /skɔːʳ/ **noun** **B1** the number of points someone gets in a game or test: *a high/low score* ◦ *What's the score?*

score² /skɔːʳ/ **verb** (**scoring**, **scored**) **B1** to get points in a game or test: *He scored just before half-time to put Liverpool 2-1 ahead.*

scorn /skɔːn/ **noun** [no plural] formal the belief that something is stupid

scowl /skaʊl/ **verb** to look at someone angrily: *He **scowled at** me from behind his paper.*
• **scowl** **noun**

scramble /ˈskræmbl/ **verb** (**scrambling**, **scrambled**) to move or climb quickly but with difficulty, often using your hands: *We scrambled up the hill.*

scrambled eggs /ˌskræmbld ˈegz/ **plural noun** a dish of eggs that are mixed together then cooked: *a plate of scrambled eggs*

scrap /skræp/ **noun** a small piece or amount of something: *He wrote his phone number on **a scrap of** paper.*

scrape /skreɪp/ **verb** (**scraping**, **scraped**)
1 to damage the surface of something by rubbing it against something rough: *Jamie fell over and scraped his knee.*
2 to remove something from a surface using a sharp edge: *I had to scrape the ice off the car.*

scratch¹ /skrætʃ/ **verb**
1 to rub your skin with your nails: *My skin was so itchy, I had to scratch it.*
2 to make a slight cut or long, thin mark with a sharp object: *The car was scratched.*
3 to rub a hard surface with a sharp object, often making a noise: *The dog is **scratching at** the door – he wants to be let in.*

scratch² /skrætʃ/ **noun**
1 a slight cut or a long, thin mark made with a sharp object: *I've got all these scratches on my arm from the cat.*
2 **from scratch** from the beginning: *We didn't have any furniture of our own so we had to start from scratch.*

scream¹ /skriːm/ **verb** **B1** to make a loud, high noise with your voice because you are afraid or hurt: *Someone was screaming in the street.*

scream² /skriːm/ **noun** **B1** an act of screaming: *We heard screams coming from their apartment.*

screech /skriːtʃ/ **verb** to make an unpleasant, high, loud sound: *A car came screeching around the corner.*

screen

screen /skri:n/ **noun**
1 A2 the part of a television or computer that shows images or writing: *I spend most of my day working in front of a computer screen.*
2 A2 a large, flat surface where a film or an image is shown
3 movies: *She first appeared* ***on screen*** *in 1965.*

screw¹ /skru:/ **noun**
a small, pointed piece of metal that you turn round and round to fix things together

screw² /skru:/ **verb**
1 to fasten something with a screw: *You need to screw the cabinet to the wall.*
2 to fasten something by turning it round until it is tight

screwdriver /ˈskru:ˌdraɪvəʳ/ **noun**
a tool for turning screws

scribble /ˈskrɪbl/ **verb** (**scribbling**, **scribbled**)
to write or draw something quickly and without care: *She scribbled some notes in her book.*

scroll /skrəʊl/ **verb**
to move text or an image on a computer screen so that you can look at the part that you want

scrub /skrʌb/ **verb** (**scrubbing**, **scrubbed**)
to clean something by rubbing it hard with a brush: *She scrubbed the floor.*

sculpture /ˈskʌlptʃəʳ/ **noun**
B1 a piece of art that is made from stone, wood, clay, etc.: *a wooden sculpture*

sea /si:/ **noun**
1 A1 a large area of salt water: *I'd like to live by the sea.* ◦ *We went swimming in the sea.*
2 a particular area of salt water: *the Black Sea*

seafood /ˈsi:fu:d/ **noun** [no plural]
animals from the sea that are eaten as food

seagull /ˈsi:gʌl/ **noun**
a grey and white bird that lives near the sea

seagull

seal¹ /si:l/ **noun**
an animal with smooth fur that eats fish and lives near the sea

seal

seal² /si:l/ **verb**
to close an entrance or container so that air or liquid cannot enter or leave it: *She sealed the bottle.*

sea level /ˈsi: ˌlevəl/ **noun** [no plural]
the level of the sea's surface, used to measure the height of an area of land: *The town is 500 feet above sea level.*

seam /si:m/ **noun**
a line of sewing where two pieces of cloth have been joined together

search¹ /sɜ:tʃ/ **verb**
1 B1 to try to find someone or something: *He* ***searched*** *in his pockets* ***for*** *some change.*
2 B1 to use a computer to find information, especially on the Internet: *I searched the Internet to find cheap flights to Barcelona.*
3 If the police search a place or a person, they look to see if they are hiding anything illegal, such as drugs: *Police are still* ***searching*** *the forest* ***for*** *the missing girl.*

a b c d e f g h i j k l m n o p q r s t u v w x y z

search² /sɜːtʃ/ **noun**
1 B1 an attempt to find someone or something: *Police are continuing their **search for** the missing girl.*
2 B1 the act of looking for information with a computer, especially using the Internet: *We **did** a **search for** hotels in the city.*
3 the process of trying to find an answer to a problem: *the search for happiness*

the seashore /ˈsiːʃɔːʳ/ **noun** [no plural]
the area of land along the edge of the sea

seasick /ˈsiːsɪk/ **adj**
feeling ill because of the way a boat is moving

seaside /ˈsiːsaɪd/ **adj**
B1 next to the sea: *a seaside town*

the seaside /ˈsiːsaɪd/ **noun**
B1 an area or town next to the sea: *We had a picnic **at the seaside**.*

season /ˈsiːzᵊn/ **noun**
1 B1 one of the four periods of the year; winter, spring, summer, or autumn
2 B1 a period of the year when a particular thing happens: *the holiday season*
3 **in season** if vegetables or fruit are in season, they are available and ready to eat: *Fruit is cheaper when it's in season.*

seat¹ /siːt/ **noun**
A2 something that you sit on: *Please, **have/take a seat** (= sit down).*

seat² /siːt/ **verb**
be seated to be sitting: *The director was seated on his right.*

seat belt /ˈsiːt ˌbelt/ **noun**
a strap that you fasten across your body when travelling in a car or plane
→ See **Car** on page C3

seaweed /ˈsiːwiːd/ **noun** [no plural]
a plant that grows in the sea

second¹ /ˈsekᵊnd/ **adj**
1 A1 being the one after the first: *This is my second piece of cake.*
2 B1 used to show that only one thing is better, bigger, etc. than the thing mentioned: *St. Petersburg is Russia's second city.*
3 another: *Accept the invitation – you won't get a **second chance**.*

second² /ˈsekᵊnd/ **pronoun**
B1 the one after the first: *You're second on the list.*

second³ /ˈsekᵊnd/ **adv**
B1 after one other person or thing in order or importance: *She didn't win, but she came second.*

second⁴ /ˈsekᵊnd/ **noun**
1 A2 one of the 60 parts a minute is divided into
2 B1 informal a very short period of time: *I'll be back in just a second.*

secondary school /ˈsekᵊndᵊri ˌskuːl/ **noun** mainly UK
B1 a school for students aged between 11 and 18

second-class /ˌsekənd'klɑːs/ **adj**
relating to the less expensive quality or service: *a second-class ticket*

second-hand /ˌsekᵊndˈhænd/ **adj, adv**
B1 If something is second-hand, someone else had it or used it before you: *second-hand books*

secret¹ /ˈsiːkrət/ **adj**
B1 If something is secret, other people are not allowed to know about it: *a secret meeting ◦ I'll tell you, but you must **keep it secret**.*
• **secretly** **adv** B1 *He secretly taped their conversation.*

secret² /ˈsiːkrət/ **noun**
1 B1 something that you tell no one about or only a few people: *I'm having a party for him but it's a secret. ◦ Can you **keep a secret**?*
2 the best way of achieving something: *What's **the secret of** your success?*
3 **in secret** without telling other people: *For years they met in secret.*

secretary /ˈsekrətᵊri/ **noun** (plural **secretaries**)
1 A2 someone who works in an office, typing letters, answering the telephone, etc.
2 an official who is in charge of a

large department of the government: *the Secretary of State*

section /ˈsekʃᵊn/ **noun**
B1 one of the parts that something is divided into: *a non-smoking section in a restaurant* ◦ *the business section of a newspaper*

secure /sɪˈkjʊəʳ/ **adj**
1 not likely to fail or be lost: *a secure job*
2 safe from danger: *I don't feel that the house is secure.*
3 firmly fastened and not likely to fall: *Check that all windows and doors are secure.*
4 confident about yourself and the situation that you are in: *Children need to feel secure in order to do well.*

security /sɪˈkjʊərəti/ **noun** [no plural]
1 B1 the things that are done to keep someone or something safe: *airport security*
2 B1 protection from something failing or being lost: *job security*

see /siː/ **verb** (**seeing**, **saw**, **seen**)
1 A1 to notice people and things with your eyes: *Have you seen Jo?* ◦ *Turn the light on so I can see.*
2 A1 to meet or visit someone: *I'm seeing Peter tonight.*
3 A2 to watch a movie, television programme, etc.: *Did you see that documentary last night?*
4 B1 to understand something: *I see what you mean.* ◦ *I don't see why I should go.*
5 B1 to find out information: *I'll just see what time the train gets in.*
6 to imagine or think about something or someone in a particular way: *She didn't **see** herself **as** brave.*
7 **see you!** informal A1 used for saying goodbye
8 **see you later, soon, tomorrow, etc.** A1 used for saying goodbye to someone you are going to meet again later, soon, tomorrow, etc.: *I'll see you later!*
9 **I'll/we'll see** used to say that you will make a decision about something later: *'Dad, can I have a guitar?' 'We'll see.'*

seed /siːd/ **noun**
a small round thing that a new plant can grow from

seek /siːk/ **verb** (**sought**)
to try to find or get something: *I am seeking advice on the matter.*

seem /siːm/ **verb**
1 B1 to appear to be: *She seemed happy.* ◦ *It **seemed like** a good idea at the time.* ◦ *There doesn't **seem to be** any real solution.*
2 **it seems...** used to say that something appears to exist or be true: *It seems that the banks close early here.* ◦ *It seems to me that she's in the wrong job.*

seen /siːn/
the past participle of see

seize /siːz/ **verb** (**seizing**, **seized**)
1 to take hold of something quickly and firmly: *She seized my arm and pulled me towards her.*
2 **seize a chance/opportunity** to do something quickly in order to use an opportunity: *You need to seize every opportunity.*

seldom /ˈseldəm/ **adv**
not often: *We seldom go out in the evenings.*

select /sɪˈlekt/ **verb**
B1 to choose someone or something: *We've selected three candidates.*

selection /sɪˈlekʃᵊn/ **noun**
a group of people or things that has been chosen: *We have a wide selection of furniture.*

self /self/ **noun** (plural **selves** /selvz/)
your character: *Lucy didn't seem her usual cheerful self today.*

self-confident /ˌselfˈkɒnfɪdᵊnt/ **adj**
feeling sure about yourself and your abilities
• **self-confidence** **noun** [no plural]

self-control /ˌselfkənˈtrəʊl/ **noun** [no plural]
the ability to control your emotions, especially when you are angry or upset

self-defence UK (US **self-defense**) /ˌselfdɪˈfens/ **noun** [no plural]
actions you take to protect yourself

from someone who is attacking you: *He used the gun **in self-defence**.*

self-employed /ˌselfɪmˈplɔɪd/ **adj**
working for yourself and not for a company or other organization: *He is a self-employed builder.*

selfish /ˈselfɪʃ/ **adj**
B1 caring only about yourself and not other people
• **selfishly** **adv**
• **selfishness** **noun** [no plural]

self-service /ˌselfˈsɜːvɪs/ **adj**
B1 A self-service restaurant or shop is one in which you get food or things yourself.

sell /sel/ **verb** (**sold**)
1 A2 to give something to someone who gives you money for it: *He **sold** his guitar **for** £50.* ◦ *I **sold** my bike **to** Claire.*
2 A2 to offer something for people to buy: *Excuse me, do you sell newspapers?*
sell out **phrasal verb**
to sell all of one thing in a shop: *They'd **sold out of** bread when I got there.*

seller /ˈseləʳ/ **noun**
B1 someone who sells something: *a flower seller*

Sellotape /ˈseləʊteɪp/ **noun** [no plural]
UK trademark
clear, thin material with glue on it, used to stick things together, especially paper
→ See **The Classroom** on page C4

semester /sɪˈmestəʳ/ **noun** mainly US
one of two time periods that a school or college year can be divided into

semicircle /ˈsemɪˌsɜːkl/ **noun**
half a circle

semicolon /ˌsemɪˈkəʊlɒn/ **noun**
a mark (;) used to separate parts of a sentence

semi-detached /ˌsemidɪˈtætʃt/ **adj** UK
A semi-detached house is joined to another similar house on one side: *They live in a semi-detached house.*

semifinal /ˌsemɪˈfaɪnᵊl/ **noun**
one of the two games in a sports competition that are played to decide who will play in the final game

semicircle

the Senate /ˈsenɪt/ **noun**
a part of a government in some countries

senator /ˈsenətəʳ/ **noun**
someone who has been elected to the Senate

send /send/ **verb** (**sent**)
1 A1 to arrange for something to go or be taken somewhere, especially by post: *I sent him a letter last week.*
2 to make someone go somewhere: *I sent him into the house to fetch some glasses.*
send *something* back **phrasal verb**
B1 to return something to the person who sent it to you, especially because it is damaged or not suitable: *I had to send the shirt back because it didn't fit me.*
send *something* off **phrasal verb**
to send a letter, document, or parcel by post: *Have you sent off your application form yet?*

senior /ˈsiːniəʳ/ **adj**
1 having a more important job or position than someone else: *a senior executive*
→ Opposite **junior** **adj**
2 older: *senior students*
→ Opposite **junior** **adj**

senior citizen /ˌsiːniə ˈsɪtɪzᵊn/ **noun**
an older person, especially one who no longer works: *Entry is free for senior citizens.*

sensation /senˈseɪʃᵊn/ **noun**
1 a physical feeling, or the ability to physically feel things: *a burning sensa-*

tion ◦ *Three months after the accident she still has no sensation in her foot.*
2 a lot of excitement and interest: *Their affair* ***caused a sensation****.*
3 a strange feeling or idea that you cannot explain: *I had the odd* ***sensation that*** *someone was following me.*

sense[1] /sens/ **noun**
1 B1 [no plural] the ability to make good decisions and do things that will not make problems: *He had the* ***good sense*** *to book a seat in advance.*
2 B1 [no plural] a feeling or understanding about yourself or about a situation: *Living in the countryside gave us a great sense of freedom.*
3 **a sense of humour** UK B1 the ability to understand funny things and to be funny yourself
4 the ability to do something: *a* ***sense of*** *direction* ◦ *good business sense*
5 one of the five natural abilities of sight, hearing, touch, smell, and taste: *I have a very poor* ***sense of*** *smell.*
6 the meaning of a word, phrase, or sentence
7 **make sense** to have a meaning or reason that you can understand: *He's written me this note but it doesn't make any sense.*
8 **make sense** to be a good thing to do: *It makes sense to buy now while prices are low.*

sense[2] /sens/ **verb** (**sensing**, **sensed**)
to understand what someone is thinking or feeling without being told about it: *I* ***sensed that*** *you weren't happy.*

sensible /ˈsensɪbl/ **adj**
B1 showing the ability to make good decisions and do things that will not make problems: *That seems a sensible decision.* ◦ *Wouldn't it be more* ***sensible to*** *leave before the traffic gets bad?*
• **sensibly adv** *She eats sensibly.*

sensitive /ˈsensɪtɪv/ **adj**
1 able to understand what people are feeling and behave in a way that does not upset them: *I want a man who's kind and sensitive.*
2 often upset by the things people say or do: *She's very* ***sensitive about*** *her weight.*
3 able to react very quickly and easily: *He has a very sensitive nose.*
4 A sensitive subject or situation needs to be dealt with carefully in order to avoid upsetting people: *Religion is a sensitive issue.*

Common mistake: sensitive or sensible?

Remember that **sensible** does not mean 'easily upset' or 'able to understand what people are feeling'. The word you need to express that is **sensitive**.

Don't criticize her too much. She's very sensitive.

sent /sent/
past tense and past participle of send

sentence[1] /ˈsentəns/ **noun**
1 A1 a group of words, usually containing a verb, that expresses a complete idea: *I wasn't able to complete my sentence.*
2 a punishment that a judge gives to someone who has committed a crime: *He got a three-year jail sentence.*

sentence[2] /ˈsentəns/ **verb** (**sentencing**, **sentenced**)
to give a punishment to someone who has committed a crime: *He was sentenced to six years in prison.*

sentimental /ˌsentɪˈmentəl/ **adj**
showing feelings such as sympathy, love, etc., especially in a silly way: *a sentimental song*

separate[1] /ˈsepərət/ **adj**
1 B1 not joined or touching anything else: *I try to keep meat* ***separate from*** *other food.*
2 B1 different: *Use a separate sheet of paper for the next exercise.*
3 not related: *I try to keep my work and my private life separate.*
• **separately adv**

separate[2] /ˈsepəreɪt/ **verb** (**separating**, **separated**)
1 to divide into parts, or to make something divide into parts: *I* ***separated*** *the class* ***into*** *three groups.*
2 to move apart, or to make people move apart: *I shall separate you two if you don't stop talking!*
3 to start to live in a different place from your husband or wife because

a b c d e f g h i j k l m n o p q r s t u v w x y z

the relationship has ended: *My parents separated when I was four.*

separation /ˌsepəˈreɪʃən/ **noun**
1 [no plural] the fact of people or things being separate: *a long period of separation*
2 an agreement between two people who are married to stop living together: *She wanted a separation from her husband.*

September /sepˈtembəʳ/ **noun**
A1 the ninth month of the year

sequence /ˈsiːkwəns/ **noun**
a group of related events or things that have a particular order: *We still don't know the sequence of events that led to his death.*

sergeant /ˈsɑːdʒənt/ **noun**
1 an officer of low rank in the police
2 a soldier of middle rank in the army or air force

serial /ˈsɪəriəl/ **noun**
a story that is told in separate parts over a period of time

series /ˈsɪəriːz/ **noun** (plural **series**)
1 many things or events of the same type that come one after the other: *a series of lectures*
2 B1 a group of television or radio programmes that have the same main characters or deal with the same subject: *'Friends' is my favourite series.*

serious /ˈsɪəriəs/ **adj**
1 B1 A serious problem or situation is bad and makes people worry: *a serious accident/illness* ◦ *This is a serious matter.*
2 B1 thinking or speaking honestly about something and not joking: *Are you **serious about** changing your job?*
3 B1 A serious person is quiet and does not laugh often: *a serious child*
4 important and needing your complete attention: *That's an interesting job offer – I'm going to give it some serious consideration.*
• **seriousness** **noun** [no plural]

seriously /ˈsɪəriəsli/ **adv**
1 B1 in a serious way: *Smoking can seriously damage your health.*
2 **take *someone/something* seriously** to believe that someone or something is important and that you should give attention to them: *The police have to take any terrorist threat seriously.*

sermon /ˈsɜːmən/ **noun**
a religious speech given by a priest in church: *to **give** a **sermon***

servant /ˈsɜːvənt/ **noun**
someone who works and lives in someone else's house, especially in the past

serve /sɜːv/ **verb** (**serving**, **served**)
1 A2 to give someone food or drink, especially in a restaurant or bar: *Are you still serving?*
2 B1 to help customers and sell things to them in a shop: *Are you being served?*
3 to do work that helps society: *to serve in the army*
4 to be useful as something: *The spare bedroom also **serves as** a study.*
5 to be in prison for a period of time

server /ˈsɜːvəʳ/ **noun**
B1 a computer that stores and manages programs and information used by other computers: *an Internet server*

service /ˈsɜːvɪs/ **noun**
1 B1 [no plural] the work that people who work in shops, restaurants, hotels, etc. do to help customers: *The food was good, but the service was awful.*
2 B1 a system that supplies something that people need: *financial services* ◦ *They **provide** a free bus **service** from the station.*
3 [no plural] the time you spend working for an organization: *He retired last week after 25 years' service.*
4 [no plural] extra money that is added to your bill in a restaurant to pay the waiters: *Does the bill include service?*
5 a religious ceremony: *Not many people **attended** the funeral **service**.*

service station /ˈsɜːvɪs ˌsteɪʃən/ **noun**
a petrol station

serviette /ˌsɜːviˈet/ **noun** UK
a piece of cloth or paper used while you are eating to keep your clothes clean and to clean your mouth and hands

session /ˈseʃᵊn/ **noun**
B1 a period during which you do one activity: *We're having a training session this afternoon.*

set[1] /set/ **verb** (**setting**, **set**)
1 B1 to arrange a time when something will happen: *The next meeting is **set for** 6 February.*
2 B1 to make a piece of equipment ready to be used: *He set the alarm for 7 a.m.*
3 B1 When the sun sets, it moves down in the sky so that it cannot be seen.
4 B1 If a book, play, or movie is set in a place or period of time, the story happens there or at that time: *It's a historical adventure set in India in the 1940s.*
5 **set *someone* free** to allow someone to leave prison
6 **set fire to *something*** to make something start burning
7 **set the table** to put plates, knives, forks, etc. on the table before you have a meal
8 If a liquid substance sets, it becomes solid.
9 UK If you set work or an exam at a school or college, you ask the students to do it: *Mr Harley forgot to set us any maths homework.*
set off **phrasal verb**
B1 to start a journey: *What time are you setting off tomorrow morning?*
set out **phrasal verb**
B1 to start a journey: *We had to set out early.*
set *something* up **phrasal verb**
B1 to start a company or organization: *He set up his own company.*

set[2] /set/ **noun**
1 A2 a group of things which belong together: *a set of instructions* ◦ *a set of keys*
2 B1 a television or radio: *a TV set*

settle /ˈsetl/ **verb** (**settling**, **settled**)
1 If you settle an argument, you stop the problem and stop arguing.
2 to start living somewhere that you are going to live for a long time: *Finally he settled in Vienna.*
3 to decide or arrange something: *Right, that's settled. We're going to Spain.*
4 to relax into a comfortable position: *She settled herself into the chair.*
5 **settle a bill** to pay the money that you owe: *I've got some bills to settle.*
settle down **phrasal verb**
1 to start living in a place where you will stay for a long time, usually with a person you love: *Do you think he'll ever settle down and have a family?*
2 to become familiar with a place and to feel happy and confident in it: *She quickly **settled down in** her new job.*
settle in **phrasal verb**
to begin to feel relaxed and happy in a new home or job: *Are you settling in OK?*

settlement /ˈsetlmənt/ **noun**
1 an official agreement that finishes an argument: *a **peace settlement***
2 a town or village that people build to live in after arriving from somewhere else: *a Jewish settlement*

seven /ˈsevᵊn/
A1 the number 7

seventeen /ˌsevᵊnˈtiːn/
A1 the number 17

seventeenth /ˌsevᵊnˈtiːnθ/
17th written as a word

seventh[1] /ˈsevᵊnθ/
A2 7th written as a word

seventh[2] /ˈsevᵊnθ/ **noun**
one of seven equal parts of something; 1/7

seventies /ˈsevᵊntiz/ **plural noun**
1 **the seventies** the years from 1970 to 1979: *He wrote the book **in the seventies**.*
2 **be in your seventies** to be aged between 70 and 79: *He's **in his seventies**.*

seventy /ˈsevᵊnti/
A2 the number 70
• **seventieth** 70th written as a word

several /ˈsevᵊrᵊl/ **pronoun, determiner**
A2 some, but not a lot: *Several people have complained about the scheme.*

a b c d e f g h i j k l m n o p q r s t u v w x y z

severe /sɪˈvɪər/ **adj**
1 very bad: *a severe headache* ◦ *severe weather conditions*
2 not kind or gentle: *a severe punishment*
• **severely** **adv** *He was severely injured.*

sew /səʊ/ **verb** (**sewed**, **sewn**)
B1 to join things together with a needle and thread: *I need to sew a button on my shirt.*

sewing /ˈsəʊɪŋ/ **noun** [no plural]
the activity of joining pieces of cloth together with a needle and thread

sewing machine /ˈsəʊɪŋ məˌʃiːn/ **noun**
a machine that joins pieces of cloth together with a needle and thread

sex /seks/ **noun** [no plural]
1 B1 sexual activity between people
2 B1 whether a person or animal is male or female: *Do you know what sex the baby is?*

sexual /ˈsekʃʊəl/ **adj**
relating to sex: *sexual organs* ◦ *sexual equality*
• **sexually** **adv**

shade

shade shadow

shade¹ /ʃeɪd/ **noun**
1 B1 [no plural] an area where there is no light from the sun and it is darker: *I'd prefer to sit **in the shade**.*
2 a colour, especially when saying how dark or light it is: *a pale/dark **shade of** grey*

shade² /ʃeɪd/ **verb** (**shading**, **shaded**)
to cover something in order to protect it from the sun: *He shaded his eyes with his hand.*

shadow /ˈʃædəʊ/ **noun**
B1 a dark area made by something that is stopping the light: *Our dog chases his own shadow.*
→ See picture at **shade** **noun**

shady /ˈʃeɪdi/ **adj** (**shadier**, **shadiest**)
A shady place is protected from the sun and is darker and cooler: *We found a shady spot to sit in.*

shake /ʃeɪk/ **verb** (**shaking**, **shook**, **shaken**)

shake

1 B1 to make quick, short movements from side to side or up and down, or to make something or someone do this: *Shake the bottle.*
2 If you are shaking, your body makes quick short movements because you are frightened or nervous: *He was shaking with nerves.*
3 **shake hands** B1 to hold someone's hand and move it up and down when you meet them for the first time: *The two leaders smiled and shook hands.*
4 **shake your head** to move your head from side to side to mean 'no'

shaken
the past participle of shake

shall strong /ʃæl/ weak /ʃəl/ **verb**
1 **shall I/we...?** A2 used to make an offer or suggestion: *Shall I cook dinner tonight?*
2 **shall I/we...?** A2 used to ask someone what to do: *Who shall I ask?*
3 **I/we shall...** B1 used to say what you are going to do in the future: *I shall talk to her tomorrow.*

shallow /ˈʃæləʊ/ **adj**
1 not deep: *shallow water*
→ Opposite **deep** **adj**
2 not showing any interest in serious ideas

shame /ʃeɪm/ **noun**
1 **a shame** A2 something you say about something that disappoints you: *What a shame that Joe couldn't come.*

a b c d e f g h i j k l m n o p q r s t u v w x y z

2 [no plural] a bad feeling about something wrong that you have done

shampoo /ʃæmˈpuː/ **noun**
A2 a liquid substance that you use to wash your hair
• **shampoo verb**

shan't /ʃɑːnt/ mainly UK
short form of shall not: *I was invited to the party, but I shan't be going.*

shapes

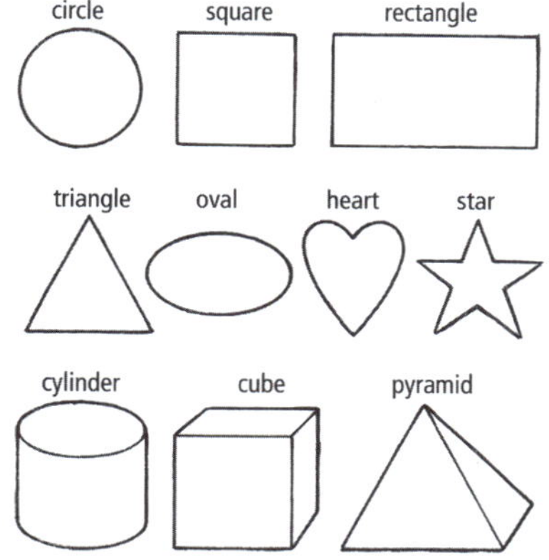

shape /ʃeɪp/ **noun**
1 B1 the physical form of something made by the line around its outer edge: *a circular shape* ◦ *I like the shape of the jacket.*
2 in good, bad, etc. shape in good, bad, etc. health or condition: *She runs every day so she's in great shape.*

-shaped /ʃeɪpt/ **suffix**
used after nouns to mean 'having a particular shape': *a heart-shaped cake*

share[1] /ʃeəʳ/ **verb** (**sharing**, **shared**)
1 A2 to have or use something at the same time as someone else: *She* ***shares*** *a house* ***with*** *Paul.*
2 A2 to divide something between two or more people: *We shared a pizza and a bottle of wine.*
3 B1 If two or more people or things share a feeling, quality, or experience, they both or all have the same feeling, quality or experience: *I don't share your views.*

share[2] /ʃeəʳ/ **noun**
1 one of the equal parts that the value of a company is divided into when it is owned by a group of people: *We own shares in a number of companies.*
2 a part of something that has been divided: *When am I going to get my share of the money?*

shark /ʃɑːk/ **noun**
B1 a large fish with very sharp teeth

shark

sharp /ʃɑːp/ **adj**
1 B1 having a very thin edge or point that can cut things: *a sharp knife* ◦ *sharp teeth*
2 sudden and very large: *a sharp rise in house prices*
3 quick to notice and understand things: *a sharp mind*

sharpen /ˈʃɑːpᵊn/ **verb**
to make something sharper: *to sharpen a knife*

sharply /ˈʃɑːpli/ **adv**
quickly and suddenly: *Prices have risen sharply this week.*

shatter /ˈʃætəʳ/ **verb**
to break into very small pieces: *The windscreen shattered.*

shave /ʃeɪv/ **verb** (**shaving**, **shaved**)
B1 to cut hair off your face or body: *He shaves every day.*

shave

shaver /ˈʃeɪvəʳ/ **noun**
a piece of electrical equipment used to cut hair off the head or body
→ See **The Bathroom** on page C1

shaving foam /ˈʃeɪvɪŋ ˌfəʊm/ **noun** [no plural]
a substance that you put on your face to make the skin soft before shaving

she strong /ʃiː/ weak /ʃi/ **pronoun**
A1 used when talking about a woman who has already been talked about:

'When is Ruth coming?' 'She'll be here soon.'

shed[1] /ʃed/ **noun**
a small building used to keep things such as tools: *a garden shed*

shed[2] /ʃed/ **verb** (**shedding**, **shed**)
shed leaves, skin, hair, etc. to lose something because it falls off: *A lot of trees shed their leaves in the autumn.*

she'd /ʃi:d/
1 short form of she had: *By the time I got there, she'd fallen asleep.*
2 short form of she would: *She knew that she'd be late.*

sheep /ʃi:p/ **noun**
(plural **sheep**)
(A1) a farm animal whose skin is covered with wool: *a flock of sheep*

sheep

sheer /ʃɪəʳ/ **adj**
1 used to say that a feeling or quality is very strong: *a look of sheer delight* ◦ *sheer determination*
2 very steep: *a sheer cliff face*

sheet

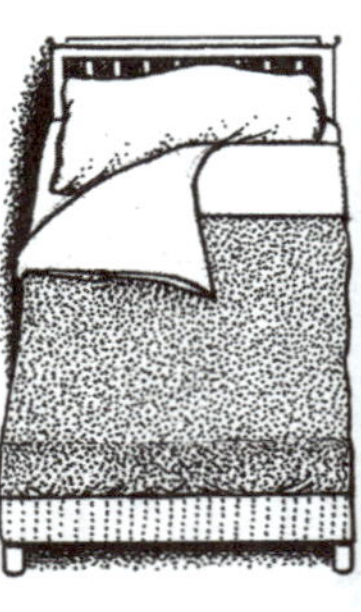

sheets on a bed

sheets of paper

sheet /ʃi:t/ **noun**
1 (B1) a large piece of cloth on a bed that you lie on or under
2 **a sheet of paper, glass, metal, etc.** (A2) a flat piece of paper, glass, etc.

shelf /ʃelf/ **noun** (plural **shelves** /ʃelvz/)
(A2) a board used to put things on, often attached to a wall: *kitchen shelves*

shell /ʃel/ **noun**
the hard outer covering of some creatures and of eggs, nuts, or seeds: *a snail's shell*

shells

she'll /ʃi:l/
short form of she will: *She'll be away until Tuesday.*

shellfish /ˈʃelfɪʃ/
noun [no plural]
sea creatures that live in shells and are eaten as food

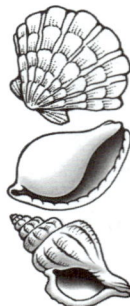

shelter[1] /ˈʃeltəʳ/
noun
1 a place that protects you from bad weather or danger: *a bomb shelter*
2 [no plural] protection from bad weather or danger: *We* ***took shelter*** *from the rain in a doorway.*

shelter[2] /ˈʃeltəʳ/ **verb**
to go under a cover or inside a building to be protected from bad weather or danger: *We sheltered from the rain under a tree.*

shepherd /ˈʃepəd/ **noun**
someone whose job is to look after sheep

sheriff /ˈʃerɪf/ **noun**
an elected law officer in the US

she's /ʃi:z/
1 short form of she is: *She's very nice.*
2 short form of she has: *She's been working very hard.*

shield[1] /ʃi:ld/ **noun**
a large, flat object that soldiers hold in front of their bodies to protect themselves

shield[2] /ʃi:ld/ **verb**
to protect someone or something from something bad: *She* ***shielded*** *her eyes* ***from*** *the sun.*

shift /ʃɪft/ **noun**
1 a change in something: *There has been a* ***shift in*** *public opinion on this matter.*
2 a period of work in a place such as a factory or hospital: *a night shift*

shin /ʃɪn/ **noun**
the front part of a leg between the knee and the foot
→ See **The Body** on page C2

shine /ʃaɪn/ **verb** (**shining**, **shone**)
1 B1 to make bright light: *The sun was shining brightly through the window.*
2 to point a light somewhere: *The car's headlights shone right into my eyes.*
3 If a surface shines, it reflects light: *Her hair really shines.*

shiny /ˈʃaɪni/ **adj** (**shinier**, **shiniest**)
B1 A shiny surface is bright because it reflects light: *shiny, black shoes*

ship /ʃɪp/ **noun**
A2 a large boat that carries people or things by sea

shirt /ʃɜːt/ **noun**
A1 a piece of clothing worn on the top part of the body, fastened with buttons down the front
→ See **Clothes** on page C5

shiver /ˈʃɪvəʳ/ **verb**
to shake because you are cold or frightened: *She **shivered with** cold.*
• **shiver noun**

shock[1] /ʃɒk/ **noun**
1 B1 a big, unpleasant surprise: *Her death **came as a** terrible **shock** to him.*
2 (also **electric shock**) a sudden, painful feeling that you get when electricity flows through your body

shock[2] /ʃɒk/ **verb**
to surprise and upset someone: *Many people were shocked by the violent scenes in the movie.*

shocking /ˈʃɒkɪŋ/ **adj**
B1 very bad and making you feel upset: *shocking news*

shoe /ʃuː/ **noun**
A1 a strong covering for the foot, often made of leather: *a pair of shoes*
→ See **Clothes** on page C5

shoelace /ˈʃuːleɪs/ **noun**
a long, thin piece of material used to fasten shoes

shone /ʃɒn/
past tense and past participle of shine

shook /ʃʊk/
past tense of shake

shoot[1] /ʃuːt/ **verb** (**shot**)
1 B1 to hurt or kill a person or animal by firing a bullet from a gun: *He was **shot dead** in the incident.*
2 B1 to fire a bullet from a gun: *Don't shoot!*
3 B1 to try to score points in some sports by hitting, kicking, or throwing the ball towards the goal: *He shot from the middle of the field and managed to score.*
4 to move somewhere very quickly: *She shot out of the room.*

shoot[2] /ʃuːt/ **noun**
a new branch or stem growing on a plant: *bamboo shoots*

shooting /ˈʃuːtɪŋ/ **noun**
1 an occasion when someone is injured or killed by a bullet from a gun: *There have been several shootings in the capital this week.*
2 [no plural] the sport of firing bullets from guns, sometimes to kill animals

shop[1] /ʃɒp/ **noun** (also US **store**)
A1 a building or part of a building where you can buy things: *a shoe shop*

shop[2] /ʃɒp/ **verb** (**shopping**, **shopped**)
B1 to buy things in shops: *I'm **shopping for** baby clothes.*

shop assistant /ˈʃɒp əˌsɪstᵊnt/ **noun** UK (US **sales clerk**)
A2 someone whose job is selling things in a shop

shoplifting /ˈʃɒpˌlɪftɪŋ/ **noun** [no plural]
the act of taking things from a shop without paying for them: *He was arrested for shoplifting.*
• **shoplifter noun**

shopping /ˈʃɒpɪŋ/ **noun** [no plural]
1 A1 the activity of going to shops and buying things: *I love shopping.* ◦ *I usually **go shopping** on Saturday.*
2 A2 the things that you buy from a shop or shops: *Can you help me unpack the shopping?*

shopping centre /ˈʃɒpɪŋ ˌsentəʳ/ **noun** UK
a place where lots of shops have been built close together

shore /ʃɔːʳ/ **noun**
B1 the area of land along the edge of the sea or a lake

a b c d e f g h i j k l m n o p q r s t u v w x y z

a b c d e f g h i j k l m n o p q r **s** t u v w x y z

short /ʃɔːt/ **adj**
1 A1 having a small distance from one end to the other: *short, brown hair* ◦ *short legs*
→ Opposite **long** **adj**
2 A1 continuing for a small amount of time: *a short visit*
→ Opposite **long** **adj**
3 A1 A short person is not as tall as most people.
→ Opposite **tall** **adj**
4 A2 A short book or other piece of writing has not many pages or words: *It's a very short book – you'll read it in an hour.*
5 used to refer to a shorter form of a name or word: *Her name's Jo – it's* ***short for*** *Josephine.*

shortage /ˈʃɔːtɪdʒ/ **noun**
a situation in which there is not enough of something that is needed: *food shortages*

shortcut /ˈʃɔːtkʌt/ **noun**
1 a quicker way of getting somewhere or doing something: *I* ***took a shortcut*** *through the car park.*
2 a quick way to start or use a computer program

shorten /ˈʃɔːtᵊn/ **verb**
to become shorter or to make something shorter: *Smoking shortens your life.*

shortly /ˈʃɔːtli/ **adv**
1 B1 not long: *I got home at midnight and Jane arrived shortly afterwards.*
2 soon: *Our plans for next year will be announced shortly.*

shorts /ʃɔːts/ **plural noun**
1 A2 a very short pair of trousers that stop above the knees: *cycling shorts*
2 US men's underwear to wear under trousers
→ See **Clothes** on page C5

Common mistake: shorts

Shorts is a plural word.
These shorts are too big for me.

short-term /ˌʃɔːtˈtɜːm/ **adj**
continuing only a short time into the future: *a short-term weather forecast*

shot¹ /ʃɒt/
past tense and past participle of shoot

shot² /ʃɒt/ **noun**
1 the act of firing a bullet from a gun: *Three* ***shots*** *were* ***fired****.*
2 an attempt to score a point in sports such as football: *Good shot!*

should strong /ʃʊd/ weak /ʃəd/ **verb**
1 A2 used to say or ask what is the correct or best thing to do: *He should go to the doctor.* ◦ *Should I apologize to her?*
2 B1 used to say that you think something is true or that you think something will happen: *She should be feeling better by now.* ◦ *The letter should arrive by Friday.*
3 **why should/shouldn't…?** used to ask or give the reason for something, especially when you are surprised or angry about it: *Why shouldn't I get a new car if I want one?*

shoulder /ˈʃəʊldəʳ/ **noun**
B1 where your arm joins your body next to your neck: *He put his arm around my shoulder.*

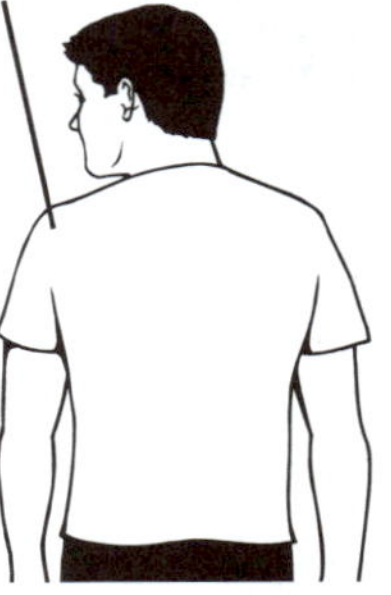

shouldn't /ˈʃʊdᵊnt/
short form of should not: *I shouldn't have said that.*

shout¹ /ʃaʊt/ **verb**
A2 to say something very loudly: *'Look out!' she shouted.* ◦ *I was angry and I* ***shouted at*** *him.*

shout² /ʃaʊt/ **noun**
B1 a loud cry of anger, excitement, or fear: *He was woken by a loud shout.*

show¹ /ʃəʊ/ **verb** (**showed**, **shown**)
1 A1 to let someone look at something: *Show me your photos.*
2 B1 to teach someone how to do something by explaining it or by doing it yourself: *She* ***showed*** *me* ***how*** *to use the new computer system.* ◦ *Have you* ***shown*** *him* ***what to do****?*
3 B1 to take someone to or round a

place: *She showed me round the factory.*
4 B1 to give information in a book, on a website, on a piece of equipment, etc.: *On this map, cities are* ***shown in*** *grey.*
5 to prove that something is true: *Sales figures showed a significant increase last month.*
6 to express a feeling so that other people are able to notice it: *If she was upset, she certainly didn't show it.*
show off phrasal verb
to try to make people think you are clever or rich: *Stop showing off!*
show up phrasal verb
B1 informal to arrive somewhere: *I invited him for eight, but he didn't show up until nine-thirty.*

show[2] /ʃəʊ/ **noun**
1 A2 a television or radio programme or a theatre performance: *He's got his own show on Channel 5.*
2 a time at which a group of similar things are brought together for the public to see: *a fashion show* ◦ *a flower show*

shower[1] /ʃaʊəʳ/ **noun**
1 A1 an act of washing your whole body while standing under a flow of water: *I* ***had a shower*** *and got dressed.*
2 A1 a piece of bathroom equipment that you stand under to wash your whole body: *He's* ***in the shower****.*
→ See **The Bathroom** on page C1
3 B1 a short period of rain

shower[2] /ʃaʊəʳ/ **verb**
to wash standing under a shower: *I shower every morning.*

shown /ʃəʊn/
past participle of show

shrank /ʃræŋk/
past tense of shrink

shred /ʃred/ **noun**
a very small piece that has been torn from something: *She tore the letter* ***to shreds****.*

shrimp /ʃrɪmp/ **noun** (plural **shrimp**)
a small sea animal that you can eat. A shrimp is smaller than a prawn.

shrine /ʃraɪn/ **noun**
a holy place where people go to pray

shrink /ʃrɪŋk/ **verb** (**shrank**, **shrunk**)
to become smaller, or to make something smaller: *My shirt shrank in the wash.*

shrub /ʃrʌb/ **noun**
a large plant that is smaller than a tree

shrug /ʃrʌg/ **verb** (**shrugging**, **shrugged**)
to move your shoulders up and down to show that you do not care about something or that you do not know something: *He just shrugged his shoulders.*
• **shrug** noun

shrunk /ʃrʌŋk/
past participle of shrink

shudder /ˈʃʌdəʳ/ **verb**
to shake, usually because you are thinking of something bad: *She* ***shuddered with*** *horror.*
• **shudder** noun

shut[1] /ʃʌt/ **verb** (**shutting**, **shut**)
1 A2 to close something, or to become closed: *Shut the door.* ◦ *He lay back and shut his eyes.* ◦ *The door shut with a bang.*
2 A2 When a shop, restaurant, etc. shuts, it stops serving customers and does not allow people to enter: *The museum shuts at four o'clock.*
shut (*something*) down phrasal verb
B1 If a computer or machine shuts down or someone shuts it down, it stops operating: *Make sure you shut down your computer before you go.*
shut up phrasal verb informal
to stop talking: *Just shut up and get on with your work!*

shut[2] /ʃʌt/ **adj**
1 B1 closed: *We had to keep the windows shut because of the fire next door.*
2 B1 When a shop, restaurant, etc. is shut, it is not serving customers: *The banks are shut now.*

shutter /ˈʃʌtəʳ/ **noun**
a wooden or metal cover on the outside of a window

a b c d e f g h i j k l m n o p q r s t u v w x y z

a b c d e f g h i j k l m n o p q r s t u v w x y z

shy /ʃaɪ/ **adj**
B1 not confident, especially about meeting new people: *He was too shy to say anything to her.*

sick /sɪk/ **adj**
1 A2 ill: *He was off work sick for most of last week.*
2 feel sick A2 to feel that the food or drink in your stomach will soon come up through your mouth
3 be sick B1 If you are sick, food and drink comes up from your stomach and out of your mouth: *The baby was sick all down his shirt.*
4 be sick of *something* informal to be bored with or angry about something: *I'm sick of people telling me how to run my life.*

sickness /ˈsɪknəs/ **noun** [no plural]
1 illness or poor health
2 the feeling that the food or drink in your stomach will come up through your mouth: *travel sickness*

side /saɪd/ **noun**
1 A2 one of the two parts that something would divide into if you drew a line down the middle: *Which side of the bed do you sleep on?*
2 A2 a flat, outer surface of an object, especially one that is not its top, bottom, front, or back: *The side of the car was badly scratched.*
3 A2 one edge of something: *A square has four sides.*
4 B1 the area next to something: *There were trees growing by the side of the road.*
5 either of the two surfaces of a thin, flat object such as a piece of paper or a coin: *Write on both sides of the paper.*
6 one of the people or groups who are arguing, fighting, or competing: *Whose **side** is he **on**?*
7 one of the two areas of your body from under your arms to the tops of your legs: *She lay on her side.*
8 [no plural] part of a situation that can be considered or dealt with separately: *She looks after the financial side of things.*
9 [no plural] a part of someone's character: *She has a very practical side.*
10 from side to side If something moves from side to side, it moves from left to right and back again repeatedly: *He shook his head from side to side.*
11 side by side If two things or people are side by side, they are next to each other: *We sat side by side on the sofa.*

sidewalk /ˈsaɪdwɔːk/ **noun** US (UK **pavement**)
a path with a hard surface by the side of a road that people walk on

sideways /ˈsaɪdweɪz/ **adv**
in a direction to the left or right, not forwards or backwards: *He glanced sideways.*

sigh /saɪ/ **verb**
to make a noise when you breathe out, often because you are sad: *He sighed deeply and sat down.*
• **sigh noun** *a sigh of relief*

sight /saɪt/ **noun**
1 B1 [no plural] the ability to use your eyes to see: *Doctors managed to save his sight.*
2 the act of seeing someone or something: *The sight of so much blood shocked him.*
3 something that you see, especially something interesting: *the sights and sounds of the market*
4 used to talk about the area that it is possible for you to see: *I **caught sight of** (= suddenly saw) Tony in the crowd.* ◦ *She kept **out of sight** (= hidden) behind a tree.*
5 the sights B1 the beautiful or interesting places in a city or country: *He took me around New York and showed me the sights.*
6 at first sight the time when you first see or hear about something or someone: *It may, at first sight, seem a surprising choice.*

sightseeing /ˈsaɪtsiːɪŋ/ **noun** [no plural]
A2 the activity of visiting interesting or beautiful places: *a sightseeing tour of London*
• **sightseer** /ˈsaɪtˌsiːə^r/ **noun** a person who goes sightseeing

sign¹ /saɪn/ **noun**
1 A2 a symbol or message in a public place that gives information or instructions: *a road sign* ◦ *a 'no-smoking' sign*
2 B1 something that shows that something is happening: *Flowers are the first* ***sign of*** *Spring.* ◦ *It's a* ***sign that*** *things are improving.*
3 B1 a movement you make to give someone information or tell them what to do
4 a symbol that has a particular meaning: *a pound sign*

sign² /saɪn/ **verb**
B1 to write your name on something to show that you wrote, painted, or created it or to show that you agree to it: *He signs his letters 'James D. Nelson.'*
sign up **phrasal verb**
B1 to arrange to do an organized activity: *I've* ***signed up for*** *evening classes at the local college.*

signal¹ /ˈsɪgnᵊl/ **noun**
1 a movement, light, or sound that gives information, or tells people what to do: *Don't move until I give the signal.*
2 a series of electrical waves that are sent to a radio, television, mobile phone, etc.: *My phone doesn't work here – there's no signal.*

signal² /ˈsɪgnᵊl/ **verb** (**signalling**, **signalled**)
to make a movement that gives information or tells people what to do: *He* ***signalled for*** *them to be quiet.*

signature /ˈsɪgnətʃəʳ/ **noun**
B1 your name written in your own way, which is difficult for someone else to copy

significance /sɪgˈnɪfɪkᵊns/ **noun** [no plural]
the importance or meaning of something: *I still don't understand* ***the significance of*** *his remark.*

significant /sɪgˈnɪfɪkᵊnt/ **adj**
important or large: *These measures will save a significant amount of money.*
• **significantly** **adv** *Prices have risen significantly (= a lot).*

signpost /ˈsaɪnpəʊst/ **noun**
B1 a sign by the side of the road that gives information

signpost

silence /ˈsaɪləns/ **noun**
1 B1 [no plural] a lack of sound: *The three men ate* ***in silence.***
2 a period of time in which there is complete quiet or no speaking: *There were long silences during the discussion.*

silent /ˈsaɪlənt/ **adj**
1 B1 without any sound: *The building was dark and silent.*
2 without talking: *She said a silent goodbye to her old house.*
• **silently** **adv** *The snow fell silently all around them.*

silk /sɪlk/ **noun** [no plural]
B1 a type of cloth that is light and smooth: *a silk dress*

silky /ˈsɪlki/ **adj** (**silkier**, **silkiest**)
soft and smooth, like silk: *a cat with silky grey fur*

silly /ˈsɪli/ **adj** (**sillier**, **silliest**)
1 B1 stupid: *Do I look silly in this hat?* ◦ *It's silly to spend money on something you don't need.*
2 B1 small and not important: *She gets upset over silly things.*

silver¹ /ˈsɪlvəʳ/ **noun** [no plural]
A2 a valuable, shiny, grey-white metal used to make jewellery: *silver and gold*

silver² /ˈsɪlvəʳ/ **adj**
1 A2 made of silver: *a silver necklace*
2 A2 being the colour of silver: *a silver sports car*

similar /ˈsɪmɪləʳ/ **adj**
B1 Something that is similar to something else has many things the same, although it is not exactly the same: *The two houses are remarkably similar.*

similarity /ˌsɪmɪˈlærəti/ **noun** (plural **similarities**)
the fact of two things or people being

similar, or a way in which they are similar: *There are a number of **similarities between** the two systems.*
→ Opposite **difference** noun

simmer /ˈsɪməʳ/ **noun**
to cook something so that it is very hot, but does not boil, or to be cooked in this way: *The soup needs to simmer for another hour.*

simple /ˈsɪmpl/ **adj**
1 A2 not difficult to do or to understand: *It's very simple to use.*
2 B1 not complicated: *a simple life* ◦ *a simple dress (= without decoration)*
3 used to describe the one important fact, truth, etc.: *We didn't go swimming for the simple reason that the water was too cold.*

simplicity /sɪmˈplɪsəti/ **noun** [no plural]
the quality of being simple

simplify /ˈsɪmplɪfaɪ/ **verb** (**simplifying**, **simplified**)
to make something easier to do or understand: *We need to simplify the instructions.*

simply /ˈsɪmpli/ **adv**
1 in a way that is not complicated or difficult to understand: *He explained it as simply as he could.*
2 used to emphasize what you are saying: *We simply don't have the time.*
3 only: *A lot of people miss this opportunity simply because they don't know about it.*

sin /sɪn/ **noun**
something that is against the rules of a religion: *the sin of pride*

since[1] /sɪns/ **adv, preposition**
A2 from a time in the past until a later time or until now: *They've been waiting since March.* ◦ *The factory had been closed since the explosion.*

> **Common mistake: since or for?**
>
> When you talk about the beginning of a period of time, use **since**.
>
> *I have lived here since 2006.*
>
> When you talk about a length of time, use **for**.
>
> *I have lived here for five years.*
>
> ~~*I have lived here since five years.*~~

since[2] /sɪns/ **conjunction**
1 B1 from a time in the past until a later time or until now: *I've known Tom since he was seven.*
2 B1 because: *Since we had a few minutes to wait, we had a coffee.*

sincere /sɪnˈsɪəʳ/ **adj**
honest and saying what you really feel or believe: *He seems to be sincere.*

sincerely /sɪnˈsɪəli/ **adv**
1 in a sincere way: *I sincerely hope that this never happens again.*
2 Yours sincerely formal B1 used at the end of formal letters where you know the name of the person you are writing to

sing /sɪŋ/ **verb** (**sang**, **sung**)
A1 to make musical sounds with your voice: *They all sang 'Happy Birthday' to him.*

singer /ˈsɪŋəʳ/ **noun**
A2 someone who sings: *a jazz singer*

singing /ˈsɪŋɪŋ/ **noun** [no plural]
A2 the activity of singing: *a singing teacher*

single[1] /ˈsɪŋgl/ **adj**
1 A2 not married: *He's young and single.*
2 A2 for only one person: *a single bed*
3 B1 looking after your children alone: *a single mother*
4 B1 used to make the word 'every' stronger: *I call him **every single** day.* ◦ *He could hear every single word.*
5 only one: *There was a single light in the corner of the room.*

single[2] /ˈsɪŋgl/ **noun** UK
B1 a ticket for a journey that is from one place to another but not back again: *Could I have a single to London?*

singular /ˈsɪŋgjələʳ/ **adj**
A2 The singular form of a word is used to talk about one person or thing: *'Woman' is the singular form of 'women'.*

the singular /ˈsɪŋgjələʳ/ **noun**
A2 the form of a word for one person or thing and no more

sink[1] /sɪŋk/ **verb** (**sank**, **sunk**)
1 B1 to go down or make something go down under the surface of water

a b c d e f g h i j k l m n o p q r **s** t u v w x y z

and not come back up: *The Titanic sank after hitting an iceberg.*
→ See picture at **float**
2 B1 to go down, or make something go down, into something soft: *My feet keep sinking into the sand.*

sink² /sɪŋk/ **noun**
A2 a bowl that is fixed to the wall in a kitchen or bathroom that you wash dishes, your hands, etc. in
→ See **The Bathroom** on page C1

sip /sɪp/ **verb** (**sipping**, **sipped**)
to drink, taking only a small amount at a time: *She sipped her champagne.*
• **sip** **noun** *He* ***took a sip of*** *his coffee.*

sir /sɜːʳ/ **noun**
1 B1 (also **Sir**) You call a man 'sir' when you are speaking to him politely: *Excuse me, sir, is this seat taken?*
2 **Dear Sir** a way of beginning a formal letter to a man whose name you do not know
3 **Sir** a title used in the UK before the name of a man who has been officially respected or who has a high social rank: *Sir Cliff Richard*

siren /ˈsaɪərən/ **noun**
a piece of equipment that makes a loud sound as a warning: *a police siren*

sister /ˈsɪstəʳ/ **noun**
A1 a girl or woman who has the same parents as you: *an older/younger sister*

sister-in-law /ˈsɪstəʳɪnlɔː/ **noun** (plural **sisters-in-law**)
the woman married to someone's brother, or the sister of someone's husband or wife: *She and her sister-in-law are good friends.*

sit /sɪt/ **verb** (**sitting**, **sat**)
1 A1 to be in a position with the weight of your body on your bottom and the top part of your body up, for example, on a chair: *Emma was* ***sitting on*** *a stool.* ◦ *The children* ***sat at*** *the table by the window.*
2 A2 (also **sit down**) to move your body into a sitting position after you have been standing: *She sat down on the grass.*
sit up **phrasal verb**
to move your body to a sitting position after you have been lying down: *I sat up and opened my eyes.*

site /saɪt/ **noun**
1 A2 short form of website (= an area on the Internet where information about a particular subject, organization, etc. can be found)
2 B1 an area that is used for something or where something happens: *a building site*
3 the place where something important happened in the past: *the site of a battle*

sitting room /ˈsɪtɪŋ ˌruːm/ **noun** UK
A2 the room in a house where people sit to relax and, for example, watch television

situated /ˈsɪtjueɪtɪd/ **adj** formal
be situated in, on, by, etc. B1 to be in a particular place: *a hotel situated by Lake Garda*

situation /ˌsɪtjuˈeɪʃən/ **noun**
B1 the set of things that are happening at a particular time and place: *the current political situation* ◦ *He's* ***in a*** *difficult* ***situation.***

six /sɪks/
A1 the number 6

sixteen /ˌsɪkˈstiːn/
A1 the number 16

sixteenth /ˌsɪkˈstiːnθ/
16th written as a word

sixth¹ /sɪksθ/
A2 6th written as a word

sixth² /sɪksθ/ **noun**
one of six equal parts of something; 1/6

sixth form /ˈsɪksθ ˌfɔːm/ **noun**
in the UK, the part of a school for students between the ages of 16 and 18

sixties /ˈsɪkstiz/ **plural noun**
1 **the sixties** the years from 1960 to 1969: *The Beatles became famous* ***in the sixties.***
2 **be in your sixties** to be aged between 60 and 69: *Many people retire* ***in their sixties.***

sixty /ˈsɪksti/
A2 the number 60
• **sixtieth** 60th written as a word

a b c d e f g h i j k l m n o p q r **s** t u v w x y z

size /saɪz/ **noun**
1 A2 how big or small something is: *It's an area about the size of Florida.* ◦ *The size of some of those trees is incredible.*
2 A2 one of the different measurements in which things, for example clothes, food, etc. are made: *What **size** shoes do you **take**?*

skate[1] /skeɪt/ **noun**
1 A2 (also **roller skate**) a boot with wheels on the bottom, used for moving across the ground: *a pair of skates*
2 A2 (also **ice skate**) a boot with a metal part on the bottom, used for moving across ice
→ See **Sports 1** on page C15

skate[2] /skeɪt/ **verb** (**skating**, **skated**)
B1 to move using skates
• **skater noun**
• **skating noun** [no plural]

skateboard /ˈskeɪtbɔːd/ **noun**
A2 a board with wheels on the bottom, which you stand on and move forward by pushing one foot on the ground
• **skateboarding noun** [no plural] A2 *a skateboarding park*
→ See **Sports 1** on page C15

skeleton /ˈskelɪtᵊn/ **noun**
the structure made of all the bones in the body of a person or animal: *the skeleton of a dog*

sketch[1] /sketʃ/ **noun**
a simple picture that you draw quickly: *He did a quick **sketch of** the cat.*

sketch[2] /sketʃ/ **verb**
to draw a sketch: *I sketched a map for him on a scrap of paper.*

ski[1] /skiː/ **noun** (plural **skis**)
B1 one of a pair of long, thin things that you wear on the bottom of boots to move over snow

ski[2] /skiː/ **verb**
B1 to move over snow wearing skis
• **skiing noun** [no plural] A2 *I'd like to **go skiing** in Switzerland.*
→ See **Sports 1** on page C15

skid /skɪd/ **verb** (**skidding**, **skidded**)
If a vehicle skids, it slides along a surface and you cannot control it: *The car skidded on ice and hit a tree.*

skilful UK (US **skillful**) /ˈskɪlfᵊl/ **adj**
good at doing something: *a skilful artist*
• **skilfully** UK (US **skillfully**) **adv**

skill /skɪl/ **noun**
B1 the ability to do an activity or job well, especially because you have done it many times: *You need good communication skills to be a teacher.*

skilled /skɪld/ **adj**
having the abilities needed to do an activity or job well: *a highly skilled (= very skilled) photographer* ◦ *He is **skilled in** dealing with the media.*

skin /skɪn/ **noun**
1 B1 the outer layer of a person or animal's body: *dark skin*
2 the outer layer of a fruit or vegetable: *a banana skin*

skinny /ˈskɪni/ **adj** (**skinnier**, **skinniest**)
too thin

skip /skɪp/ **verb** (**skipping**, **skipped**)
1 to move forward, jumping quickly from one foot to the other: *She watched her daughter skipping down the street.*
2 to jump over a rope while you or two other people move it over and then under your body again and again: *I skip for ten minutes every day to keep fit.*
3 to not do something that you usually do: *I think I'll skip lunch today.*

skirt /skɜːt/ **noun**
A1 a piece of women's clothing that hangs from the waist and has no legs
→ See **Clothes** on page C5

ski slope /ˈskiː ˌsləʊp/ **noun**
an area of land on a hill or mountain where people can ski

skull /skʌl/ **noun**
the bones in your head

sky /skaɪ/ **noun** (plural **skies**)
A2 the area above the Earth where you can see clouds, the sun, the moon, etc.: *a beautiful, blue sky*

skyscraper /ˈskaɪˌskreɪpəʳ/ **noun**
a very tall building

slab /slæb/ **noun**
a thick, flat piece of something, especially stone: *a slab of concrete*

slack /slæk/ **adj**
loose or not tight: *Suddenly the rope became slack.*
→ Opposite **tight** adj

slam /slæm/ **verb** (**slamming**, **slammed**)
to close with great force, or to make something close with great force: *Kate heard the front door slam.*

slang /slæŋ/ **noun** [no plural]
informal language

slant[1] /slɑːnt/ **verb**
to slope in a particular direction: *Pale sunlight* ***slanted through*** *the curtain.*

slant[2] /slɑːnt/ **noun**
a position that is sloping: *The road is* ***on a slant****.*

slap[1] /slæp/ **verb** (**slapping**, **slapped**)
to hit someone with the flat, inside part of your hand: *She slapped him across the face.*

slap[2] /slæp/ **noun**
a hit with the flat, inside part of your hand

slaughter[1] /ˈslɔːtəʳ/ **verb**
1 to kill an animal for meat
2 to kill a lot of people in a cruel way

slaughter[2] /ˈslɔːtəʳ/ **noun** [no plural]
a situation in which a lot of people or animals are killed in a cruel way

slave[1] /sleɪv/ **noun**
someone who is owned by someone else and has to work for them: *He treats his mother like a slave.*

slave[2] /sleɪv/ **verb** (**slaving**, **slaved**)
informal
to work very hard: *Giorgio was* ***slaving away at*** *his homework.*

slavery /ˈsleɪvᵊri/ **noun** [no plural]
the practice of having slaves

sledge /sledʒ/ **noun** UK (US **sled** /sled/)
a vehicle that is used for travelling on snow

sleep[1] /sliːp/ **verb** (**slept**)
A1 to be in the state of rest when your eyes are closed, your body is not active, and your mind is unconscious: *We had to sleep in the car that night.* ◦ *Did you sleep well?*
sleep in **phrasal verb**
to sleep longer in the morning than you usually do

sleep[2] /sliːp/ **noun**
1 B1 [no plural] the state you are in when you are sleeping, or a period of time when you are sleeping: *You need to go home and* ***get some sleep****.* ◦ *It took me ages to* ***get to sleep*** *(= to succeed in sleeping).*
2 B1 a period of sleeping: *Why don't you* ***have*** *a little* ***sleep****?*
3 **go to sleep** B1 to begin to sleep: *Babies often go to sleep after a feed.*

sleeping bag /ˈsliːpɪŋ ˌbæg/ **noun**
a long bag made of thick material that you sleep inside

sleepless /ˈsliːpləs/ **adj**
sleepless night a night when you are not able to sleep

sleepy /ˈsliːpi/ **adj** (**sleepier**, **sleepiest**)
B1 feeling tired and wanting to go to sleep: *The heat had made me sleepy.*

sleet /sliːt/ **noun** [no plural]
a mixture of snow and rain
• **sleet** **verb** ***It was sleeting*** *when I looked outside.*

sleeve /sliːv/ **noun**
B1 the part of a jacket, shirt, etc. that covers your arm: *He rolled up his sleeves to do the dishes.*
→ See picture at **jacket**
• **have *something* up your sleeve**
informal to have a secret plan

slender /ˈslendəʳ/ **adj**
thin in an attractive way

slept /slept/
past tense and past participle of sleep

slice[1] /slaɪs/ **noun**
A2 a flat piece of food that has been cut from a larger piece: *a slice of bread/cake*
→ See **Quantities** on page C14

slice[2] /slaɪs/ **verb** (**slicing**, **sliced**) (also **slice up**)
to cut food into flat pieces: *Could you slice the tomatoes?*

a b c d e f g h i j k l m n o p q r s t u v w x y z

a b c d e f g h i j k l m n o p q r **s** t u v w x y z

slide[1] /slaɪd/ **verb** (**sliding**, **slid**)
to move smoothly over a surface: *He likes sliding on the ice.*

slide[2] /slaɪd/ **noun**
1 a small piece of film that you shine light through in order to see a photograph
2 a large object that children climb and slide down as a game

slight /slaɪt/ **adj**
small and not important: *slight differences in colour*

slightly /ˈslaɪtli/ **adv**
a little: *I find it slightly worrying.*

slim[1] /slɪm/ **adj** (**slimmer**, **slimmest**)
A1 Someone who is slim is thin in an attractive way.

slim[2] /slɪm/ **verb** (**slimming**, **slimmed**) UK
to eat less in order to become thinner

slime /slaɪm/ **noun** [no plural]
a thick, sticky liquid that is unpleasant to touch

slimy /ˈslaɪmi/ **adj** (**slimier**, **slimiest**)
covered in slime

sling /slɪŋ/ **noun**
a piece of cloth that you wear around your neck and put your arm into when it is hurt

slip[1] /slɪp/ **verb** (**slipping**, **slipped**)
1 B1 to slide by accident and fall or almost fall: *She slipped on the ice and broke her ankle.*
2 to slide out of the correct position: *The photo had slipped from the frame.*
3 to go somewhere quietly or quickly: *I'll slip out of the room if I get bored.*
slip up **phrasal verb**
to make a mistake

slip[2] /slɪp/ **noun**
1 a small piece of paper: *He wrote the number on a slip of paper.*
2 a small mistake
• **a slip of the tongue** a mistake made by using the wrong word

slipper /ˈslɪpə^r/ **noun**
a soft, comfortable shoe that you wear in the house

slippery /ˈslɪp^{ə}ri/ **adj**
smooth and wet and difficult to hold or walk on: *Be careful – the floor is slippery.*

slit[1] /slɪt/ **noun**
a long, thin cut or hole in something

slit[2] /slɪt/ **verb** (**slitting**, **slit**)
to make a long, thin cut in something: *She slit her wrists.*

slogan /ˈsləʊgən/ **noun**
a short phrase that is easy to remember and is used to make people notice something: *an advertising slogan*

slope[1] /sləʊp/ **noun**
a surface or piece of land that is high at one end and low at the other: *There's a* ***steep slope*** *to climb before we're at the top.*

slope[2] /sləʊp/ **verb** (**sloping**, **sloped**)
to be high at one end and low at the other: *The field* ***slopes down*** *to the river.*

slot /slɒt/ **noun**
a long, thin hole that you put something into, especially money

slot machine /ˈslɒt məˌʃiːn/ **noun**
a machine that you put money into in order to try to win more money

slow[1] /sləʊ/ **adj**
1 A1 moving, happening, or doing something without much speed: *He's a very slow reader.*
→ Opposite **fast** **adj**
2 If a clock is slow, it shows a time that is earlier than the correct time.
→ Opposite **fast** **adj**

slow[2] /sləʊ/ **verb**
slow (*something*) down **phrasal verb**
to become slower or to make something become slower: *Slow down, Claire, you're walking too fast!*

slowly /ˈsləʊli/ **adv**
A2 at a slow speed: *Could you speak more slowly, please?*

slug /slʌg/ **noun**
a small, soft creature with no legs that moves slowly and eats plants
→ See picture at **snail**

slum /slʌm/ **noun**
a poor and crowded area of a city: *He grew up in the slums of Mexico City.*

slump /slʌmp/ **verb**
1 If a price, value, or amount slumps, it goes down suddenly: *Sales have slumped by 50%.*
2 to fall or sit down suddenly because you feel tired or weak: *She slumped back in her chair, exhausted.*

smack /smæk/ **verb**
to hit someone with the flat, inside part of your hand

small /smɔːl/ **adj**
1 A1 little in size or amount: *We teach the children in small groups.*
→ Opposite **big** adj, **large** adj
2 A1 A small child is very young: *a woman with three small children*
3 A2 not important or serious: *a small mistake*

smart /smɑːt/ **adj**
1 B1 If you look smart or your clothes are smart, you look clean and tidy: *I need to look smart for my interview.*
2 B1 clever: *Rachel's one of the smartest kids in the class.*
3 fashionable and expensive: *a smart, new restaurant*

smash /smæʃ/ **verb**
to break into a lot of pieces with a loud noise, or to make something do this: *Someone had smashed the shop window.*

smear[1] /smɪəʳ/ **verb**
to spread a thick liquid or sticky substance over something: *His shirt was* ***smeared with*** *paint.*

smear[2] /smɪəʳ/ **noun**
a dirty mark: *There was a smear of oil on his cheek.*

smell[1] /smel/ **verb** (**smelled**, **smelt**)
1 B1 to have a particular quality that people notice by using their nose: *That soup smells delicious – what's in it?* ◦ *This coffee* ***smells like*** *soap.*
2 B1 to notice something by using your nose: *I think I can smell something burning.*
3 B1 to have a bad smell: *Your running shoes really smell!*
4 to have the ability to notice or discover that a substance is present by using your nose: *Humans can't smell as well as dogs can.*

smell[2] /smel/ **noun**
1 B1 the quality that something has which you notice by using your nose: *The* ***smell of*** *roses filled the room.*
2 [no plural] the ability to notice smells: *Smoking can affect your* ***sense of smell****.*
3 a bad smell: *I wish I could get rid of that smell in the bathroom.*

smelly /ˈsmeli/ **adj** (**smellier**, **smelliest**)
having a bad smell: *smelly feet*

smelt /smelt/
past tense and past participle of smell

smile[1] /smaɪl/ **verb** (**smiling**, **smiled**)
B1 to make the corners of your mouth go up so that you look happy or friendly: *She* ***smiled at*** *me.*

smile[2] /smaɪl/ **noun**
B1 an expression on your face that makes the corners of your mouth go up so that you look happy or friendly: *He* ***gave*** *me a big* ***smile*** *and wished me good luck.*

smog /smɒg/ **noun** [no plural]
air pollution in a city that is a mixture of smoke, gases, and chemicals

smoke[1] /sməʊk/ **noun** [no plural]
B1 the grey or black gas that is made when something burns

smoke[2] /sməʊk/ **verb** (**smoking**, **smoked**)
1 A1 to breathe smoke into your mouth from a cigarette: *Do you mind if I smoke?*
2 to make or send out smoke: *smoking chimneys*

smoker /ˈsməʊkəʳ/ **noun**
someone who often smokes cigarettes

smoking /ˈsməʊkɪŋ/ **noun** [no plural]
A1 the activity of smoking cigarettes

smooth /smuːð/ **adj**
1 B1 having a regular surface that has no holes or lumps in it: *soft, smooth skin*
→ Opposite **rough** adj
2 A substance that is smooth has no lumps in it: *Mix the butter and sugar together until smooth.*
3 happening without any sudden

movements: *The plane made a smooth landing.*

smoothly /ˈsmuːðli/ **adv**
go smoothly to happen without any problems: *Everything was going smoothly until Darren arrived.*

smother /ˈsmʌðəʳ/ **verb**
to kill someone by covering their face with something so that they cannot breathe

smoulder UK (US **smolder**) /ˈsməʊldəʳ/ **verb**
to burn slowly, producing smoke but no flames: *The fire was still smouldering the next morning.*

smudge[1] /smʌdʒ/ **noun**
a dirty mark: *a smudge of ink*

smudge[2] /smʌdʒ/ **verb** (**smudging**, **smudged**)
to make something dirty by touching it: *Be careful you don't smudge the drawing.*

smuggle /ˈsmʌgl/ **verb** (**smuggling**, **smuggled**)
to take something into or out of a place in an illegal or secret way: *He was arrested for smuggling drugs.*
• **smuggler noun** *drug smugglers*

snack /snæk/ **noun**
A2 a small amount of food

snack bar /ˈsnæk ˌbɑːʳ/ **noun**
a place where you can buy a small meal such as a sandwich

snag /snæg/ **noun** informal
a problem

snail /sneɪl/ **noun**
a small creature with a long, soft body and a round shell

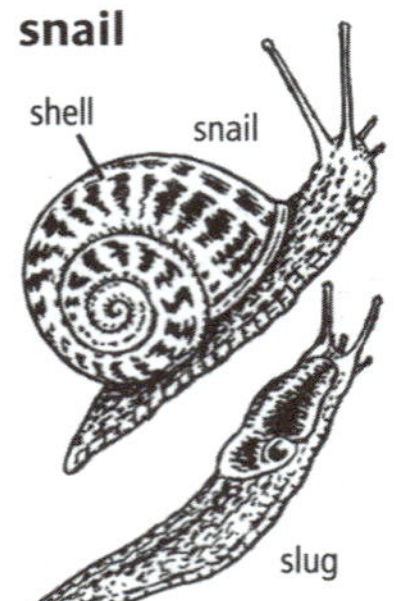

snake /sneɪk/ **noun**
A2 a long, thin creature with no legs that slides along the ground

snap[1] /snæp/ **verb** (**snapping**, **snapped**)
1 If something long and thin snaps, it breaks making a short, loud sound, and if you snap it, you break it, making a short, loud sound: *The twigs snapped as we walked on them.*
2 to say something suddenly in an angry way: *I was* ***snapping at*** *the children because I was tired.*
3 If an animal snaps, it tries to bite someone.

snap[2] /snæp/ **noun**
1 a sudden, short, loud sound like something breaking: *I heard a snap as I sat on the pencil.*
2 UK informal a photograph: *holiday snaps*

snarl /snɑːl/ **verb**
1 to speak angrily: *'Go away!' he snarled.*
2 If an animal snarls, it shows its teeth and makes an angry sound.

snatch /snætʃ/ **verb**
to take something or someone quickly and suddenly: *Bill snatched the phone from my hand.*

sneak /sniːk/ **verb**
to go somewhere quietly because you do not want anyone to hear you: *I sneaked into his bedroom while he was asleep.*

sneaker /ˈsniːkəʳ/ **noun** US (UK **trainer**)
a soft sports shoe

sneeze /sniːz/ **verb** (**sneezing**, **sneezed**)
When you sneeze, air suddenly comes out through your nose and mouth: *He had a cold and was sneezing a lot.*
• **sneeze noun**

sniff /snɪf/ **verb**
1 to breathe air in through your nose in a way that makes a noise: *Sam had a cold and she kept sniffing.*
2 to breathe air in through your nose in order to smell something: *She sniffed the flowers.*
• **sniff noun**

snob /snɒb/ **noun**
someone who thinks they are better than other people

snooker /ˈsnuːkəʳ/ **noun** [no plural]
a game in which two people use long sticks to hit coloured balls into holes at the edge of a table

snooze /snuːz/ **verb** (**snoozing**, **snoozed**) informal
to sleep for a short time, especially during the day: *Grandad was snoozing in his chair.*
• **snooze noun** [no plural] informal *Why don't you **have a snooze**?*

snore /snɔːʳ/ **verb** (**snoring**, **snored**)
to breathe in a very noisy way while you are sleeping
• **snore noun**

snorkel /ˈsnɔːkəl/ **noun**
a tube that you use to breathe when you are swimming underwater

snow[1] /snəʊ/ **noun** [no plural]
A1 soft white pieces of frozen water that fall from the sky when the weather is cold: *Children were playing in the snow.*

snow[2] /snəʊ/ **verb**
it snows A2 If it snows, snow falls from the sky: *It snowed all day.*

snowball /ˈsnəʊbɔːl/ **noun**
a ball made from snow that children throw at each other

snowboard /ˈsnəʊbɔːd/ **noun**
B1 a large board that you stand on to move over snow
→ See **Sports 1** on page C15

snowboarding /ˈsnəʊbɔːdɪŋ/ **noun** [no plural]
A2 a sport in which you stand on a large board and move over snow
→ See **Sports 1** on page C15

snowflake /ˈsnəʊfleɪk/ **noun**
a small piece of snow that falls from the sky

snowman /ˈsnəʊmæn/ **noun** (plural **snowmen**)
something that looks like a person and is made from snow

snowplough UK (US **snowplow**) /ˈsnəʊplaʊ/ **noun**
a vehicle used for removing snow from roads and railways

snowy /ˈsnəʊi/ **adj** (**snowier**, **snowiest**)
snowing or covered with snow: *a cold, snowy day*

so[1] /səʊ/ **adv**
1 A2 used before an adjective or adverb to make that adjective or adverb stronger: *I was so tired when I got home.* ◦ *I love her so much.* ◦ *I was so upset that I couldn't speak.*
2 A2 used to give a short answer to a question to avoid repeating a phrase: *'Is Ben coming to the party?' 'I hope so.'*
3 A2 used at the beginning of a sentence to connect it with something that was said or happened previously: *So, here we are again.*
4 and so on A2 used after a list of things to show that you could add other similar things: *She plays a lot of tennis and squash and so on.*
5 or so B1 used after a number or amount to show that it is not exact: *'How many people were at the party?' 'Fifty or so, I guess.'*
6 So (what)? used to say that you do not think something is important, especially in a rude way: *'She might tell Emily.' 'So what?'*
7 so did we, so have I, so is mine, etc. B1 used to say that someone else also does something or that the same thing is true about someone or something else: *She likes golf and so do I.*

so[2] /səʊ/ **conjunction**
1 A2 used to say that something is the reason why something else happens: *I was tired so I went to bed.* ◦ *Greg had some money so he bought a bike.*
2 so (that) B1 in order to make something happen or be possible: *He put his glasses on so that he could see the television better.*

soak /səʊk/ **verb**
1 to put something in a liquid for a period of time: *Soak the bread in the milk.*
2 to make something very wet: *The rain soaked my clothes.*

soaking /ˈsəʊkɪŋ/ **adj**
completely wet: *The dog was **soaking wet**.*

a b c d e f g h i j k l m n o p q r s t u v w x y z

a b c d e f g h i j k l m n o p q r s t u v w x y z

soap /səʊp/ **noun**
1 A2 [no plural] a substance that you use for washing: *a bar of soap*
→ See **The Bathroom** on page C1
2 B1 (also **soap opera**) a television programme about the lives of a group of people that is shown regularly

soar /sɔːʳ/ **verb**
1 to go up to a high level very quickly: *House prices have soared.*
2 to move quickly and smoothly in the sky: *The birds were soaring high above.*

sob /sɒb/ **verb** (**sobbing**, **sobbed**)
to cry in a noisy way
• **sob noun**

sober /ˈsəʊbəʳ/ **adj**
Someone who is sober is not drunk.

so-called /ˌsəʊˈkɔːld/ **adj**
used to show that you think a word that is used to describe someone or something is wrong: *My so-called friend has stolen my girlfriend.*

soccer /ˈsɒkəʳ/ **noun** [no plural] (also UK **football**)
a game in which two teams kick a ball and try to score goals

sociable /ˈsəʊʃəbl/ **adj**
B1 Someone who is sociable likes being with people and meeting new people.

social /ˈsəʊʃəl/ **adj**
1 B1 relating to the things you do with other people for enjoyment when you are not working: *I have a very busy* ***social life****.*
2 relating to society and the way people live: *social problems*

socialize /ˈsəʊʃəlaɪz/ **verb** (**socializing**, **socialized**)
to spend time enjoying yourself with other people: *Students can* ***socialize with*** *teachers at the café.*

social networking /ˌsəʊʃəl ˈnetwɜːkɪŋ/ **noun** [no plural]
B1 the activity of communicating with other people who have similar interests using a website that provides this service: *a social networking site*

social worker /ˈsəʊʃəl ˌwɜːkəʳ/ **noun**
someone whose job is to help people who have problems because they are poor, old, have difficulties with their family, etc.

society /səˈsaɪəti/ **noun**
1 B1 [no plural] a large group of people who live in the same country or area and have the same laws, traditions, etc.: *Unemployment is a problem for society.*
2 (plural **societies**) an organization for people who have the same interest: *the London Zoological Society*

sock /sɒk/ **noun**
A2 something that you wear on your foot inside your shoe: *a pair of black socks*
→ See **Clothes** on page C5

socket /ˈsɒkɪt/ **noun**
the place on a wall where you connect electrical equipment to the electricity supply

soda /ˈsəʊdə/ **noun**
1 [no plural] (also **soda water**) water with bubbles in it that you mix with other drinks
2 (also **soda pop**) US a sweet drink with bubbles: *a can of soda*

sofa

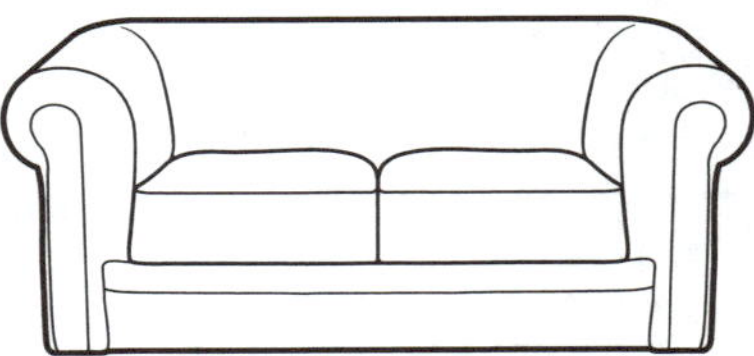

sofa /ˈsəʊfə/ **noun**
A2 a large, comfortable seat for more than one person

soft /sɒft/ **adj**
1 A2 not hard, and easy to press: *a soft cushion* ◦ *Cook the onion until it's soft.*
→ Opposite **hard adj**
2 A2 smooth and pleasant to touch: *soft hair/skin*
→ Opposite **rough adj**
3 B1 A soft sound is very quiet: *He spoke in a soft voice.*

4 B1 A soft colour or light is not bright: *soft yellow paint*
→ Opposite **bright** **adj**
5 too kind: *You're too soft to be a teacher.*
• **softness** **noun** [no plural]

soft drink /ˌsɒft ˈdrɪŋk/ **noun**
A2 a cold, sweet drink that does not have alcohol in it

soften /ˈsɒfᵊn/ **verb**
to become softer or to make something become softer: *Heat the butter until it softens.*

softly /ˈsɒftli/ **adv**
B1 in a quiet or gentle way: *'Are you OK?' she asked softly.*

software /ˈsɒftweəʳ/ **noun** [no plural]
A2 programs that you use to make a computer do different things: *educational software*

soil /sɔɪl/ **noun** [no plural]
the top layer of earth that plants grow in

solar /ˈsəʊləʳ/ **adj**
relating to the sun: *solar power*

sold /səʊld/
past tense and past participle of sell

soldier /ˈsəʊldʒəʳ/ **noun**
B1 a person in an army

sole[1] /səʊl/ **adj**
only: *the sole survivor*

sole[2] /səʊl/ **noun**
the bottom part of your foot that you walk on

solely /ˈsəʊlli/ **adv**
only, and not involving anyone or anything else: *I bought it solely for that purpose.*

solemn /ˈsɒləm/ **adj**
serious or sad: *solemn music*

solicitor /səˈlɪsɪtəʳ/ **noun**
in the UK, a lawyer who gives legal advice and help

solid[1] /ˈsɒlɪd/ **adj**
1 hard and firm without holes or spaces, and not liquid or gas: *solid ground* ◦ *solid food*
2 strong and not easily broken or damaged: *solid furniture*

solid[2] /ˈsɒlɪd/ **noun**
a substance or object that is not a liquid or a gas

solo[1] /ˈsəʊləʊ/ **adj**, **adv**
done alone by one person only: *a **solo performance*** ◦ *to fly solo*

solo[2] /ˈsəʊləʊ/ **noun**
a piece of music for one person or one instrument: *a trumpet solo*

solution /səˈluːʃᵊn/ **noun**
B1 the way to stop a problem: *There's no easy **solution to** this problem.*

solve /sɒlv/ **verb** (**solving**, **solved**)
B1 to find the answer to something or to stop a problem: *We have solved the problem.* ◦ *Police are still no nearer to solving the crime.*

some strong /sʌm/ weak /sᵊm/ **pronoun**, **determiner**
1 A1 used to mean an amount of something without saying exactly how much or how many: *You'll need a pair of scissors and some glue.* ◦ *I can't eat all this, would you like some?* ◦ *Could I have some more paper?*
2 A1 used to mean a part of a larger amount or number of something and not all of it: *Some people don't like this.* ◦ ***Some of** the children were frightened.*
3 a large amount or number of something: *It will be **some time** before we meet again.*

Common mistake: some or any?

Be careful not to confuse these two words. **Any** is used in questions and negative sentences.

Have you got any friends in America?
I haven't got any money.

Some is used in positive sentences.

I've got some friends in America.

Sometimes **some** is used in questions, especially when the speaker thinks that the answer will be 'yes'.

Have you got some money I could borrow?

The same rules are true for 'something/anything' and 'someone/anyone'.

I didn't see anyone I knew.
I saw someone I knew at the party.

somebody /ˈsʌmbədi/ **pronoun**
A2 another word for someone

somehow /ˈsʌmhaʊ/ **adv**
1 B1 in a way that you do not know or do not understand: *Don't worry, we'll fix it somehow.* ◦ *Somehow they managed to get in.*
2 for a reason that is not clear: *It was my birthday, but somehow I felt sad.*

someone /ˈsʌmwʌn/ **pronoun** (also **somebody**)
1 A2 used to mean a person when you do not know who they are or when it is not important who they are: *There's someone at the door.* ◦ *Will someone please answer the phone?*
2 someone else a different person: *Sorry, I thought you were talking to someone else.*

someplace /ˈsʌmpleɪs/ **adv** mainly US
another word for somewhere: *They live someplace in the South.*

something /ˈsʌmθɪŋ/ **pronoun**
1 A1 used to mean a thing when you do not know what it is or when it is not important what it is: *As soon as I walked in, I noticed that something was missing.* ◦ *We know about the problem and we're trying to do something about it.* ◦ *There's* ***something else*** *(= another thing) I wanted to tell you.*
2 or something (like that) A2 used to show that what you have just said is only an example or that you are not certain about it: *Why don't you go to a movie or something?*

sometime /ˈsʌmtaɪm/ **adv**
used to mean a time when you do not know exactly what it is or when it is not important what it is: *We'll arrange it for sometime before June.* ◦ *You must come over and visit sometime.*

sometimes /ˈsʌmtaɪmz/ **adv**
A1 on some occasions but not always or often: *He does cook sometimes, but not very often.* ◦ *Sometimes I feel so lonely.*

somewhat /ˈsʌmwɒt/ **adv**
rather: *We were somewhat disappointed with the food.*

somewhere /ˈsʌmweəʳ/ **adv**
A2 used to mean a place when you do not know exactly where it is, or when it is not important exactly where it is: *They had difficulties finding somewhere to live.* ◦ *He comes from somewhere near London.* ◦ *Can you think of* ***somewhere else*** *(= a different place) we could go?*

son /sʌn/ **noun**
A1 someone's male child: *They have two sons.*

song /sɒŋ/ **noun**
A2 words that go with a short piece of music: *a love song* ◦ *to sing a song*

son-in-law /ˈsʌnɪnlɔː/ **noun** (plural **sons-in-law**)
the husband of someone's daughter: *Our daughter and son-in-law live close to us.*

soon /suːn/ **adv**
1 A2 after a short period of time: *I've got to leave quite soon.* ◦ *It's too soon to make a decision.*
2 as soon as B1 at the same time or a very short time after: *They want it as soon as possible.*
3 sooner or later used to say that you do not know exactly when something will happen, but you are sure that it will happen: *Sooner or later they'll realize it's not going to work.*

soot /sʊt/ **noun** [no plural]
a black powder made when coal, wood, etc. is burnt

soothe /suːð/ **verb** (**soothing**, **soothed**)
1 to make something feel less painful: *I had a long, hot bath to soothe my aching muscles.*
2 to make someone feel calm or less worried: *to soothe a crying baby*

soothing **adj**
making you feel calm or in less pain: *soothing music*

sore /sɔːʳ/ **adj**
B1 painful, especially when touched: *a sore throat* ◦ *Her eyes were red and sore.*

sorry /ˈsɒri/ **adj**
1 (I'm) sorry A1 something that you say to be polite when you have done something wrong: *Sorry I'm late.* ◦ *Oh, I'm sorry. I didn't see you there.*
2 A2 used to show that you are sad

about a person or situation: *I was* ***sorry to hear*** *about your accident.*
3 feel sorry for *someone* B1 to feel sympathy for someone because they are in a difficult situation: *I feel so sorry for the children.*
4 sorry? mainly UK used as a polite way to say that you did not hear what someone has just said: *Sorry? What was that?*
5 used to say that you wish something in the past had been different: *I'm sorry that I ever met him.*
6 used to politely disagree or refuse to do something: *I'm sorry, I don't agree with you.*

sort[1] /sɔːt/ **noun**
1 A2 a type of something: *We both like the same* ***sort of*** *music.* ◦ *What sort of shoes does she wear?*
2 all sorts of A2 many different types of something
3 that sort of thing B1 used to show that what you have just said is only an example from a larger group of things: *They sell souvenirs, postcards, that sort of thing.*
4 sort of used to describe something approximately: *It's a sort of pale orange colour.*

sort[2] /sɔːt/ **verb**
to put things into different groups or types or into an order: *The names are sorted alphabetically.*
sort *something* out **phrasal verb**
1 to organize or arrange things that are untidy: *I must sort out my drawers.*
2 to do something that stops a problem: *Have you sorted out your schedule yet?*

sought /sɔːt/
past tense and past participle of seek

soul /səʊl/ **noun**
1 the part of a person that is not their body, which some people believe continues to exist after they die
2 a soul used instead of 'anyone' in order to emphasize what you are saying: *I didn't see a soul when I went out.*
3 A2 a type of popular music that expresses deep feelings, originally performed by African Americans

sound[1] /saʊnd/ **noun**
A2 something that you hear: *I could* ***hear*** *the* ***sounds*** *of the city through the open window.* ◦ *She stood completely still, not* ***making a sound.***

sound[2] /saʊnd/ **verb**
1 sound good, interesting, strange, etc. A2 to seem good, interesting, strange, etc. from what you have heard or read: *Your job sounds really interesting.*
2 sound like/as if/as though B1 to seem like something, from what you have heard or read: *That sounds like a really good idea.* ◦ *It sounds like you've got a sore throat.*
3 sound angry, happy, rude, etc. to seem angry, happy, rude, etc. when you speak: *You don't sound too sure about it.*

sound[3] /saʊnd/ **adj**
good or safe and able to be trusted: *sound advice*

sound[4] /saʊnd/ **adv**
sound asleep in a deep sleep

soundly /ˈsaʊndli/ **adv**
sleep soundly to sleep well

soundtrack /ˈsaʊndtræk/ **noun**
the music used in a movie

soup /suːp/ **noun** [no plural]
A1 a hot, liquid food, made from vegetables, meat, or fish: *chicken soup*
→ See **Food** on page C7

sour /saʊəʳ/ **adj**
B1 having a sharp taste like a lemon, and not sweet: *These plums are a bit sour.*

source /sɔːs/ **noun**
where something comes from: *Oranges are a good* ***source of*** *vitamin C.*

south, South /saʊθ/ **noun** [no plural]
1 A2 the direction that is on your right when you face towards the rising sun: *The stadium is to the south of the city.*
2 the south A2 the part of an area that is farther towards the south than the rest: *She's from the south of England.*
• **south adj** A2 *the south side of the house* ◦ *South America*

• **south** **adv** A2 *We drove south.*

southeast, Southeast /ˌsaʊθˈiːst/ **noun** [no plural]
1 B1 the direction between south and east
2 the southeast B1 the southeast part of a country
• **southeast** **adj**, **adv**

southeastern, Southeastern /ˌsaʊθˈiːstən/ **adj**
in or from the southeast

southern, Southern /ˈsʌðən/ **adj**
in or from the south part of an area: *the southern half of the country*

the South Pole /ˌsaʊθ ˈpəʊl/ **noun** [no plural]
the point on the Earth's surface that is furthest south

southwest, Southwest /ˌsaʊθ ˈwest/ **noun** [no plural]
1 B1 the direction between south and west
2 the southwest B1 the southwest part of a country
• **southwest** **adj**, **adv**

southwestern, Southwestern /ˌsaʊθˈwestən/ **adj**
in or from the southwest

souvenir /ˌsuːvᵊnˈɪəʳ/ **noun**
B1 something that you buy or keep to remember a special time or holiday: *I kept the ticket as a* ***souvenir of*** *my trip.*

sow /səʊ/ **verb** (**sowed**, **sown**)
to put seeds into the ground

space /speɪs/ **noun**
1 A2 an empty area that is free to be used: *a parking space* ◦ *We need more open spaces for children to play in.* ◦ *There wasn't enough* ***space for*** *everyone.*
2 B1 [no plural] the area outside the Earth: *space travel*

spacecraft /ˈspeɪskrɑːft/ **noun** (plural **spacecraft**)
a vehicle that can travel outside the Earth and into space

spaceman /ˈspeɪsmæn/ **noun** (plural **spacemen**)
a man who travels into space

spaceship /ˈspeɪsʃɪp/ **noun**
a vehicle used for travel in space

spade /speɪd/ **noun**
a tool with a long handle and a flat metal part at one end used for digging

spades /speɪdz/ **plural noun**
one of the four suits (= groups) of playing cards: *the ten of spades*

spaghetti /spəˈgeti/ **noun** [no plural]
long, thin pieces of pasta

spam /spæm/ **noun** [no plural]
emails that you do not want, usually advertisements

span /spæn/ **noun**
the period of time that something exists or happens: *an average life span of seventy years*
• **span** **verb** (**spanning**, **spanned**) to continue for a particular amount of time: *Her acting career spanned almost forty years.*

spanner /ˈspænəʳ/ **noun** UK
a tool with a round end that is used to turn nuts and bolts (= metal objects used to fasten things together)

spare¹ /speəʳ/ **adj**
1 B1 If something is spare, it is extra and not being used: *a spare bedroom* ◦ *spare cash*
2 spare time A2 time when you are not working: *I enjoy gardening* ***in my spare time****.*

spare² /speəʳ/ **verb** (**sparing**, **spared**)
to give time or money to someone: *I have to go soon, but I can spare a few minutes.*

spark /spɑːk/ **noun**
a very small, bright piece of burning material: *The fire was caused by a spark from a cigarette.*

sparkle /ˈspɑːkl/ **verb** (**sparkling**, **sparkled**)
to shine brightly because of reflected light: *The water sparkled in the sun.*

sparkling /ˈspɑːklɪŋ/ **adj**
sparkling water/wine B1 water or wine with bubbles in it: *Would you like still or sparkling water?*

spat /spæt/
past tense and past participle of spit

speak /spiːk/ **verb** (**speaking**, **spoke**, **spoken**)
1 A1 to say something using your voice: *She speaks very quietly.* ◦ *There was complete silence – nobody spoke.*
2 speak to *someone* A1 UK (US **speak with someone**) to talk to someone: *Could I speak to Mr Davis, please?*
3 speak English, French, German, etc. A1 to be able to say things in English, French, German, etc.: *Do you speak English?*

Common mistake: speak or talk?
Remember that you **speak** a language. You do not 'talk' it.
She speaks French.
~~*She talks French.*~~

speak up **phrasal verb**
to say something in a louder voice so that people can hear you: *Could you speak up a bit? I can't hear you.*

speaker /ˈspiːkəʳ/ **noun**
1 A2 the part of a radio, CD player, etc., that the sound comes out of
→ See **The Living Room** on page C11
2 B1 someone who makes a speech to a group of people: *a guest speaker*
3 B1 someone who can speak a particular language: *He's a fluent Russian speaker.*

spear /spɪəʳ/ **noun**
a long weapon with a sharp point at one end used for hunting

special /ˈspeʃəl/ **adj**
1 A2 better or more important than usual things: *I'm cooking something special for her birthday.*
2 special attention/treatment treatment that is better than usual
3 B1 different from normal things, or used for one purpose: *You need to use a special kind of paint.*
4 special offer B1 a price that is lower than usual: *There's a **special offer on** sunglasses this week.*

specialist /ˈspeʃəlɪst/ **noun**
someone who has a lot of knowledge, or skill in a particular subject: *a software specialist* ◦ *He's **a specialist in** childhood illnesses.*

specialize /ˈspeʃəlaɪz/ **verb** (**specializing**, **specialized**)
to spend most of your time studying one subject or doing one type of business: *She works for a company **specializing in** business law.*

specially /ˈspeʃəli/ **adv**
B1 for one purpose: *I made this **specially for** you.*

species /ˈspiːʃiːz/ **noun** (plural **species**)
a group of plants or animals that are the same in some way: *a rare species of bird*

specific /spəˈsɪfɪk/ **adj**
1 particular and not general: *I asked you for a specific reason.* ◦ *Could we arrange a specific time to meet?*
2 exact or containing details: *Could you **be** more **specific about** the problem?*

specifically /spəˈsɪfɪkəli/ **adv**
1 for one reason, purpose, etc.: *They're designed **specifically for** children.*
2 exactly or in detail: *I specifically told them that I don't eat meat.*

specify /ˈspesɪfaɪ/ **verb** (**specifying**, **specified**)
to say or describe something in an exact way: *They didn't specify what colour they wanted.*

specimen /ˈspesəmɪn/ **noun**
an animal, plant, etc. used as an example of its type, especially for scientific study: *This is one of the museum's finest specimens.*

speck /spek/ **noun**
a very small amount of something: *a **speck of** dirt*

spectacular /spekˈtækjələʳ/ **adj**
B1 very good or exciting: *a spectacular view*
• **spectacularly** **adv** *a spectacularly beautiful country*

spectator /spekˈteɪtəʳ/ **noun**
someone who watches an event, sport, etc.: *They won 4-0 in front of 40,000 cheering spectators.*

a b c d e f g h i j k l m n o p q r s t u v w x y z

sped /sped/
past tense and past participle of speed

speech /spiːtʃ/ **noun**
1 B1 [no plural] someone's ability to talk, or an example of someone talking: *His speech was very slow and difficult to understand.*
2 a formal talk that someone gives to a group of people: *I had to* ***make a speech*** *at my brother's wedding.*

speed[1] /spiːd/ **noun**
B1 how fast something moves or happens: *He was travelling* ***at a speed of*** *90 mph.*

speed[2] /spiːd/ **verb** (**sped**)
1 to move somewhere or happen very fast: *The three men jumped into a car and sped away.*
2 **be speeding** to be driving faster than you are allowed to
speed up **phrasal verb**
to move or happen faster: *Can you try to speed up a bit please?*

speed limit /ˈspiːd ˌlɪmɪt/ **noun**
the fastest speed that a car is allowed to travel on a particular road: *I never* ***break*** *the* ***speed limit.***

spell[1] /spel/ **verb** (**spelled**, **spelt**)
A2 to write or tell someone the letters that are used to make a word: *How do you spell that?*

spell[2] /spel/ **noun**
1 a period of time: *a short spell in Australia*
2 magic words that are supposed to make a person or thing change shape, disappear, etc.: *The witch* ***cast a spell*** *over him and he turned into a frog.*

spelling /ˈspelɪŋ/ **noun**
1 A2 the letters that are used to write a word: *There are two possible spellings of this word.* ◦ *spelling mistakes*
2 [no plural] someone's ability to spell words: *My spelling is terrible.*

spend /spend/ **verb** (**spent**)
1 A2 to use money to buy or pay for something: *She* ***spends*** *a lot* ***on*** *clothes.* ◦ *How much did you spend?*
2 A2 to use time doing something or being somewhere: *He spent 18 months working on the project.* ◦ *He's planning to* ***spend*** *some* ***time*** *at home with his family.*

spice /spaɪs/ **noun**
B1 a substance made from a plant, which is used to give a special taste to food: *herbs and spices*

spicy /ˈspaɪsi/ **adj** (**spicier**, **spiciest**)
B1 containing strong flavours from spice: *spicy food*

spider /ˈspaɪdəʳ/ **noun**
B1 a creature with eight long legs that catches insects in a web (= structure like a net)

spike /spaɪk/ **noun**
a long, thin piece of metal, wood, etc. with a sharp point at one end
• **spiky** **adj** (**spikier**, **spikiest**) covered with spikes or having that appearance: *spiky hair*
→ See **Hair** on page C9

spill /spɪl/ **verb** (**spilled**, **spilt**)
B1 to pour liquid somewhere where you do not want it, by accident: *I spilt wine all over the carpet.*

spin /spɪn/ **verb** (**spinning**, **spun**)
1 If something spins or you spin something, it turns around and around quickly: *The car* ***spun across*** *the road.*
2 to make thread by twisting together cotton, wool, etc.

spinach /ˈspɪnɪtʃ/ **noun** [no plural]
B1 a vegetable with large, dark green leaves

spine /spaɪn/ **noun**
a long line of bones in a person's or animal's back

spiral /ˈspaɪərəl/ **noun**
a shape made by a curve turning around and around a central point: *a spiral staircase*

spiral

spire /spaɪəʳ/ **noun**
a tall, pointed tower on the top of a building such as a church

spirit /ˈspɪrɪt/ **noun**
1 the way people think and feel about something: *a* ***spirit of*** *adventure*
2 the part of a person that is not their

body, which some people believe continues to exist after they die
3 a strong alcoholic drink, such as whisky
4 in good, high, low, etc. spirits feeling good, excited, unhappy, etc.: *The whole class was in good spirits.*

spiritual /ˈspɪrɪtʃuəl/ **adj**
relating to deep feelings and beliefs, especially religious beliefs: *a spiritual leader*

spit /spɪt/ **verb** (**spitting**, **spat**)
to force out the liquid in your mouth: *He took a mouthful of coffee and then **spat** it **out**.*

spite /spaɪt/ **noun**
1 in spite of *something* B1 although something exists or happens: *In spite of a bad storm, the plane landed safely.*
2 [no plural] a feeling of anger towards someone that makes you want to upset them: *He hid my new jacket **out of spite**.*

spiteful /ˈspaɪtfᵊl/ **adj**
said or done to upset someone: *That was a very spiteful thing to do.*

splash[1] /splæʃ/ **verb**
1 If a liquid splashes or you splash a liquid, drops of it fall on something: *She splashed some cold water on her face.*
2 to move in water so that drops of it go in all directions: *The children splashed about in the puddles.*

splash[2] /splæʃ/ **noun**
1 a drop of liquid that has fallen on something, or the mark made by it: *There were several small splashes of paint on the carpet.*
2 the sound of something falling into or moving in water

splendid /ˈsplendɪd/ **adj**
very good or very beautiful: *a splendid idea* ◦ *a splendid view*

splinter /ˈsplɪntəʳ/ **noun**
a small, sharp piece of wood, glass, etc., that has broken from a large piece: *I've got a splinter in my finger.*

split /splɪt/ **verb** (**splitting**, **split**)
1 If something splits or if you split it, it tears so that there is a long, thin hole in it: *He split his trousers when he bent over.*
2 to share something by dividing it into smaller parts: *The cost of the wedding will be **split between** the two families.*
split up **phrasal verb**
B1 If two people split up, they end their relationship: *She **split up with** her boyfriend.*

spoil /spɔɪl/ **verb**
1 B1 to stop something from being enjoyable or successful: *The picnic was spoiled by the bad weather.*
2 If you spoil a child, you let them have anything they want, usually making them badly behaved.

spoilt /spɔɪlt/ **adj** UK
badly behaved because you are always given what you want or allowed to do what you want: *He was behaving like a **spoilt child**.*

spoke /spəʊk/
past tense of speak

spoken /ˈspəʊkᵊn/
past participle of speak

spokesman /ˈspəʊksmən/ **noun** (plural **spokesmen**)
a man who is chosen to speak officially for a group or organization

spokesperson /ˈspəʊksˌpɜːsᵊn/ **noun** (plural **spokespeople**)
someone who is chosen to speak officially for a group or organization

spokeswoman /ˈspəʊksˌwʊmən/ **noun** (plural **spokeswomen**)
a woman who is chosen to speak officially for a group or organization

sponge /spʌndʒ/ **noun**
a soft substance full of small holes, which is used for washing things

sponge

sponsor[1] /ˈspɒnsəʳ/ **noun**
a person or organization that gives money to support an activity, event, etc.: *The organizers of the event are looking for new sponsors.*

sponsor² /ˈspɒnsəʳ/ **verb**
to give money to support an activity, event, etc.: *The festival was sponsored by a software company.*

spoon /spuːn/ **noun**
A2 an object with a handle and a round, curved part at one end, used for eating and serving food: *knives, forks, and spoons*

spoonful /ˈspuːnfʊl/ **noun**
the amount of something that can be held on a spoon: *Add a* ***spoonful of*** *sugar.*

sport /spɔːt/ **noun**
1 A1 a game or activity that people do to keep healthy or for enjoyment, often competing against each other: *winter sports* ◦ *team sports*
2 A1 [no plural] UK (US **sports**) all types of physical activity that people do to keep healthy or for enjoyment: *She used to do a lot of sport when she was younger.*
→ See **Sports 1 & 2** on page C15 & 16

sports car /ˈspɔːts ˌkɑːʳ/ **noun**
a fast car, often with only two seats and an open roof

sports centre /ˈspɔːts ˌsentəʳ/ **noun**
A2 a building with places where you can play different sports

sportsman /ˈspɔːtsmən/ **noun**
a man who is good at sport

sporty /ˈspɔːti/ **adj** (**sportier**, **sportiest**)
good at sport

spot¹ /spɒt/ **noun**
1 B1 a small, round mark that is a different colour to the surface it is on: *a blue shirt with white spots*
2 UK a small, red mark on your skin: *He suffered with spots as a teenager.*
3 a place: *We found a good spot to sit and have our picnic.*

spot² /spɒt/ **verb** (**spotting**, **spotted**)
to see or notice something or someone: *She soon spotted the mistake.*

spotless /ˈspɒtləs/ **adj**
very clean: *Her house is spotless.*

sprain /spreɪn/ **verb**
to hurt part of your body by twisting it: *I slipped on the ice and sprained my ankle.*

sprang /spræŋ/
past tense of spring

spray¹ /spreɪ/ **noun**
liquid in a container that forces it out in small drops: *hair spray*

spray² /spreɪ/ **verb**
to force liquid out of a container in many small drops: *She sprayed a little perfume on her wrists.*

spread /spred/ **verb** (**spread**)
1 to arrange something so that it covers a large area: *He* ***spread*** *the cards* ***out*** *on the table.*
2 to affect a larger number of people: *The virus is spread by rats.*
3 to move a soft substance across a surface so that it covers it: *He* ***spread*** *a thin layer of glue* ***on*** *the paper.*
4 to tell information to a lot of people: *News of his death spread quickly.*

spring¹ /sprɪŋ/ **noun**
1 A2 the season of the year between winter and summer, when the weather becomes warmer and plants start to grow again
2 a piece of metal which curves round and round: *bed springs*
3 a place where water comes out of the ground: *hot springs*

spring² /sprɪŋ/ **verb** (**sprang**, **sprung**)
to jump or move somewhere suddenly: *The cat sprang onto the sofa.*

sprinkle /ˈsprɪŋkl/ **verb** (**sprinkling**, **sprinkled**)
to gently drop small pieces of something over a surface: *Sprinkle the cake with sugar before serving.*

sprinkle

sprung /sprʌŋ/
past participle of spring

spun /spʌn/
past tense of spin

spy¹ /spaɪ/ **noun** (plural **spies**)
B1 someone who secretly tries to find information about a person, country, etc.

spy[2] /spaɪ/ **verb** (**spying**, **spied**)
to see someone or something, often from a long way away: *I spied him on the dance floor.*
spy on *someone* **phrasal verb**
to secretly watch someone: *He spied on her through the keyhole.*

squad /skwɒd/ **noun**
1 a group of people who have special skills to deal with particular problems: *a police drugs squad*
2 a sports team: *the England rugby squad*

square[1] /skweəʳ/ **noun**
1 A2 a shape with four equal sides and four 90° angles
→ See picture at **shape**
2 A2 an open area with buildings around it, often in the centre of a town: *Trafalgar Square*

square[2] /skweəʳ/ **adj**
A2 having the shape of a square: *a square room*

squash[1] /skwɒʃ/ **noun** [no plural]
a sport in which two people hit a small rubber ball against the four walls of a room

squash[2] /skwɒʃ/ **verb**
to press something into a flat shape: *I stepped on a spider and squashed it.*

squeak /skwiːk/ **verb**
to make a short, high sound: *His shoes squeaked loudly as he walked.*
• **squeak** **noun**

squeal /skwiːl/ **verb**
to make a loud, high sound, often because of fear or excitement: *She* ***squealed with*** *delight.*
• **squeal** **noun** *squeals of laughter*

squeeze /skwiːz/ **verb** (**squeezing**, **squeezed**)
to press something firmly: *She squeezed his hand and said goodbye.*

squid /skwɪd/ **noun** (plural **squid**)
a sea creature with a long body and ten long arms

squirrel /ˈskwɪrəl/ **noun**
a small animal with a big tail that climbs trees and eats nuts

squirrel

St
1 written abbreviation for street: *Oxford St*
2 written abbreviation for saint: *St Patrick*

stab /stæb/ **verb** (**stabbing**, **stabbed**)
to push a knife into someone: *He was stabbed several times in the chest.*

stable[1] /ˈsteɪbl/ **adj**
1 not likely to change or end suddenly: *a stable relationship*
2 fixed or safe and not likely to move: *Be careful! That chair isn't very stable.*

stable[2] /ˈsteɪbl/ **noun**
a building where horses are kept

stack[1] /stæk/ **noun**
a tidy pile of things: *a* ***stack of*** *books*

stack[2] /stæk/ **verb**
to put things in a tidy pile: *Can you help me stack these chairs?*

stadium /ˈsteɪdiəm/ **noun**
A2 a large, open area with seats around it, used for playing and watching sports: *a football stadium*

staff /stɑːf/ **noun** [no plural]
A2 the people who work for an organization: *The company has a staff of over 500 employees.*

stage /steɪdʒ/ **noun**
1 A2 the raised area in a theatre where actors perform: *He's* ***on stage*** *for most of the play.*
2 a period of development, or a particular time in a process: *an early stage in his career* ◦ *Our project is in its final stages.*

stagger /ˈstægəʳ/ **verb**
to walk as if you might fall

stain[1] /steɪn/ **noun**
a dirty mark on something that is difficult to remove: *a blood stain* ◦ *a stain on the carpet*

stain[2] /steɪn/ **verb**
to leave a dirty mark on something that is difficult to remove, or to become dirty in this way: *That wine I spilt has stained my shirt.*

staircase /ˈsteəkeɪs/ **noun**
a set of stairs and the structure around them: *a spiral staircase*

stairs /steəz/ **noun**
A2 a set of steps from one level in a

building to another: *to go up/down the stairs*

stale /steɪl/ **adj**
old and not fresh: *stale bread*

stalk /stɔːk/ **noun**
the main stem of a plant

stall /stɔːl/ **noun**
B1 a small shop with an open front or a table from which things are sold: *a market stall*

stall

stamp¹ /stæmp/ **noun**
1 A2 a small piece of paper that you buy and stick onto a letter before you post it
2 a tool for putting a special ink mark on something, or the mark made by it: *a stamp in a passport*

stamp² /stæmp/ **verb**
1 to make a mark on something with a tool that you put ink on and press down: *She stamped the date on the invoice.*
2 to put your foot down on the ground hard and quickly, often to show anger: *'No!' she shouted, stamping her foot.*

stand¹ /stænd/ **verb** (**stood**)
1 A2 to be in a vertical position on your feet: *We'd been standing for hours.* ◦ *He's standing over there, next to Karen.*
2 A2 (also **stand up**) to rise to a vertical position on your feet from sitting or lying down: *I get dizzy if I stand up too quickly.* ◦ *Please stand when the bride arrives.*
3 to be in or to put something in a particular place or position: *The tower stands in the middle of a field.* ◦ *She stood the umbrella by the door.*
4 can't stand *someone/something* informal B1 to hate someone or something: *I can't stand him.* ◦ *She can't stand doing housework.*
stand for *something* **phrasal verb**
If a letter stands for a word, it is used to mean it: *UFO stands for 'unidentified flying object'.*
stand out **phrasal verb**
1 to be very easy to see or notice: *The bright blue letters really stand out.*
2 to be much better than other similar things or people: *One candidate* ***stood out from*** *the rest.*
stand up for *something/someone* **phrasal verb**
to defend or support a particular idea or a person who is being criticized or attacked: *We should all stand up for our rights.*

stand² /stænd/ **noun**
1 a small shop with an open front or a table from which things are sold: *Visit our stand at the trade fair.*
2 UK a structure in a sports ground where people can stand or sit to watch an event

standard¹ /ˈstændəd/ **noun**
1 a level of quality, especially a level that is good enough: *a high standard of service* ◦ *low safety standards* ◦ *His work was below standard (= not good enough).*
2 a level of behaviour, especially a level that is good enough: *high moral standards*
3 standard of living how much money and comfort someone has: *a low/high standard of living*

standard² /ˈstændəd/ **adj**
usual and not special: *standard practice*

standby /ˈstændbaɪ/ **noun**
be on standby to be ready to do something or to be used if needed: *I left the TV on standby.*

stank /stæŋk/
past tense of stink

staple /ˈsteɪpl/ **noun**
a small piece of wire that you put through pieces of paper to join them together

stapler /ˈsteɪpləʳ/ **noun**
a piece of equipment used for putting staples through paper

star¹ /stɑːʳ/ **noun**
1 A2 a ball of burning gases that you

stars

see as a small point of light in the sky at night
2 A2 a famous singer, actor, sports person, etc.: *a pop star*
3 A2 a shape that has five or more points

star² /stɑːʳ/ **verb** (**starring**, **starred**)
B1 to be the main person in a movie, play, etc.: *a movie starring Julia Roberts*

stare /steəʳ/ **verb** (**staring**, **stared**)
to look at someone or something for a long time and not move your eyes: *Sean was* ***staring at*** *me.*
• **stare noun**

start¹ /stɑːt/ **verb**
1 A1 to begin doing something: *Maria started to laugh.* ◦ *We start work at nine o'clock.*
2 B1 to begin to happen or to make something begin to happen: *The fire started in the kitchen.*
start (*something*) off phrasal verb
B1 to begin by doing something, or to make something begin by doing something: *I'd like to start off by thanking you all for coming.*

start² /stɑːt/ **noun**
B1 the beginning of something: *Our teacher checks who is in class at the start of each day.* ◦ *Ivan has been involved* ***from the start****.*

starter /ˈstɑːtəʳ/ **noun** UK (US **appetizer**)
something that you eat as the first part of a meal: *We had soup as a starter.*

startle /ˈstɑːtl/ **verb** (**startling**, **startled**)
to suddenly surprise or frighten someone: *The sound startled me.*

starve /stɑːv/ **verb** (**starving**, **starved**)
to become ill or die because you do not have enough food: *Many people* ***starved to death*** *in those days.*
• **starvation** /stɑːˈveɪʃᵊn/ **noun** [no plural] *Children were dying of starvation.*

starving /ˈstɑːvɪŋ/ **adj**
1 dying because there is not enough food: *starving people*
2 informal very hungry: *I'm absolutely starving.*

state¹ /steɪt/ **noun**
1 the condition that something or someone is in: *the state of the economy* ◦ *The building is in a terrible state.*
2 (also **State**) one of the parts that some countries such as the US are divided into: *Alaska is the largest state in the US.*
3 the state the government of a country: *financial help from the state*

state² /steɪt/ **verb** (**stating**, **stated**)
to officially say or write something: *Two medical reports stated that he was mentally ill.*

statement /ˈsteɪtmənt/ **noun**
something that someone says or writes officially: *The government is expected to* ***make a statement*** *later.*

station /ˈsteɪʃᵊn/ **noun**
1 A1 a place where trains stop so that you can get on or off them: *Dad met me at the station.*
2 B1 a company that shows or sends out television or radio programmes: *a classical music station*

stationery /ˈsteɪʃᵊnᵊri/ **noun** [no plural]
things that you use for writing, such as pens and paper

statistics /stəˈtɪstɪks/ **noun** [no plural]
the subject that involves collecting and studying numbers to show information

a b c d e f g h i j k l m n o p q r s t u v w x y z

statue

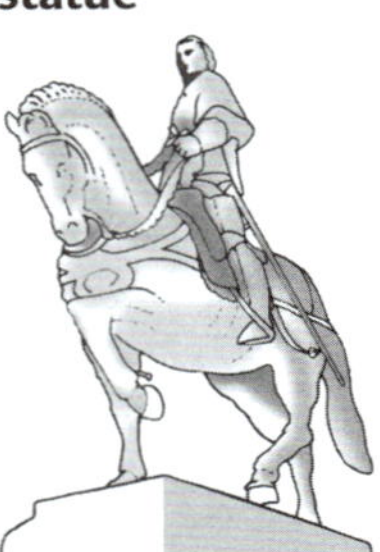

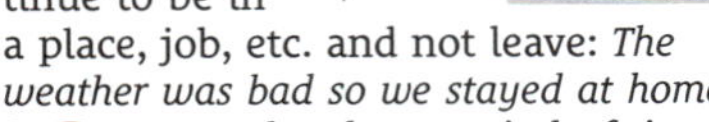

statue /ˈstætʃuː/ **noun**
(B1) a model that looks like a person or animal, usually made from stone or metal

stay¹ /steɪ/ **verb**
1 (A1) to continue to be in a place, job, etc. and not leave: *The weather was bad so we stayed at home.*
2 (A2) to spend a short period of time in a place: *We* ***stayed in*** *a hotel.*
3 (B1) to continue to be in a particular state: *The supermarket stays open late.*
stay behind **phrasal verb**
(B1) to not leave a place when other people leave it: *He stayed behind after class to speak to the teacher.*
stay in **phrasal verb**
(B1) to stay in your home: *Let's stay in tonight and watch a movie.*
stay out **phrasal verb**
to not come home at night, or to go home late: *Our cat usually stays out at night.* ◦ *My mum won't let me* ***stay out late****.*

stay² /steɪ/ **noun**
(B1) a period of time that you spend in a place: *Did you enjoy your stay in Tokyo?*

steady /ˈstedi/ **adj** (**steadier**, **steadiest**)
1 happening at a gradual, regular rate: *a steady improvement*
2 still and not shaking: *You need steady hands to be a dentist.*
3 not changing: *She drove at a steady speed.*
• **steadily** **adv**

steak /steɪk/ **noun**
(A2) a thick, flat piece of meat or fish

steal /stiːl/ **verb** (**stole**, **stolen**)
(A2) to secretly take something that belongs to someone else: *Burglars broke in and stole a computer.*

steam /stiːm/ **noun** [no plural]
the gas that water makes when you heat it

steel /stiːl/ **noun** [no plural]
a very strong metal made from iron, used for making knives, machines, etc.

steam

steep /stiːp/ **adj**
(B1) A steep slope, hill, etc. goes up or down very quickly: *The hill was too steep to cycle up.*
• **steeply** **adv**

steer /stɪəʳ/ **verb**
to control the direction of a car, boat, etc.: *I tried to steer the boat away from the bank.*

steering wheel /ˈstɪərɪŋ ˌwiːl/ **noun**
a wheel that you turn to control the direction of a vehicle
→ See **Car** on page C3

stem /stem/ **noun**
the long, thin part of a plant that the leaves and flowers grow on

step¹ /step/ **noun**
1 (B1) one of the movements you make with your feet when you walk: *She* ***took*** *a few* ***steps*** *forward.*
2 (B1) one of the surfaces that you walk on when you go up or down stairs
3 one of the things that you do to achieve something: *This meeting is the first step towards a peace agreement.*

step² /step/ **verb** (**stepping**, **stepped**)
1 (B1) to move somewhere by lifting your foot and putting it down in a different place: *She stepped carefully over the dog.*
2 (B1) to put your foot on or in something: *I accidentally stepped on her foot.*

stepfather /ˈstepˌfɑːðəʳ/ **noun**
the man who has married your mother but is not your father

stepmother /ˈstepˌmʌðəʳ/ **noun**
the woman who has married your father but is not your mother

stereo /ˈsteriəʊ/ **noun**
a piece of equipment for playing

music that has two speakers (= parts where sound comes out): *a car stereo*
→ See **The Living Room** on page C11

sterling /ˈstɜːlɪŋ/ **noun** [no plural]
British money

stern /stɜːn/ **adj**
very serious and not friendly or funny: *a stern face*

stew /stjuː/ **noun**
food made of vegetables and meat cooked together in liquid: *beef stew*

steward /ˈstjuːəd/ **noun**
a man who looks after people on a plane, boat, or train: *an air steward*

stewardess /ˈstjuːədes/ **noun**
a woman who looks after people on a plane, boat, or train: *air stewardess*

stick[1] /stɪk/ **verb** (**stuck**)
1 B1 to become joined to something else or to make something become joined to something else, usually with a substance like glue: *Annie stuck a picture of her boyfriend on the wall.*
2 informal to put something somewhere: *Just stick your bag under the table.*
3 If you stick something sharp somewhere, you push it into something: *She stuck the needle into his arm.*
4 to become fixed in one position and not be able to move: *This drawer has stuck – I can't open it.*
stick out phrasal verb
to go past the surface or edge of something: *Paul's ears stick out a little.*
stick *something* out phrasal verb
to make part of your body come forward from the rest of your body: *The little boy stuck his tongue out.*
stick together phrasal verb
If people stick together, they support and help each other: *it's important for all of us to stick together in situations like this.*
stick up phrasal verb
to point up above a surface and not lie flat: *I can't go out with my hair sticking up like this.*

stick[2] /stɪk/ **noun**
1 B1 a long, thin piece of wood
2 walking, hockey, etc. stick B1 a long, thin piece of wood that you use when you are walking, playing hockey, etc.

sticky /ˈstɪki/ **adj** (**stickier, stickiest**)
B1 made of or covered with a substance that can stick to other things: *sticky fingers* ◦ *sticky tape*

stiff /stɪf/ **adj**
1 hard and difficult to bend: *stiff material*
2 A door, drawer, etc. that is stiff does not move as easily as it should.

still[1] /stɪl/ **adv**
1 A2 used to say that something is continuing to happen now: *He's still here if you want to speak to him.* ◦ *Do you still play basketball?*
2 used to say that something continues to be possible: *We could still catch the train if we leave now.*
3 B1 used to show that you did not expect something to happen: *He didn't do much work but still came top.*
4 still better, worse, etc./better, worse, etc. still even better, worse, etc.: *I'm worried that his car has broken down or, worse still, that he's had an accident.*

still[2] /stɪl/ **adj**
1 stand, stay, sit, etc. still B1 to stand, stay, sit, etc. without moving: *Sit still so I can brush your hair.*
2 B1 UK A still drink does not have any bubbles in it: *Would you like still or sparkling water?*

sting[1] /stɪŋ/ **verb** (**stung**)
If an insect, plant, etc. stings you, it causes pain by putting poison into your skin: *He was stung by a wasp.*

sting[2] /stɪŋ/ **noun**
painful skin that you get when an insect, plant, etc. puts poison into your skin: *a wasp/bee sting*

stink[1] /stɪŋk/ **verb** (**stank, stunk**)
to smell very bad: *The kitchen **stinks of** fish.*

stink[2] /stɪŋk/ **noun**
a very bad smell

stir /stɜːʳ/ **verb** (**stirring, stirred**)
1 B1 to mix food or liquid by moving a spoon round and round in it: *Stir the mixture until it is smooth.*

2 to move slightly: *The baby stirred in its sleep.*

stitch /stɪtʃ/ **noun**
a short line of thread that is sewn through a piece of material

stock[1] /stɒk/ **noun**
1 [no plural] all the things that you can buy in a shop: *We're expecting some new stock in this afternoon.*
2 be in stock/out of stock to be available or not available in a shop
3 an amount of something that is ready to be used: *stocks of weapons*
4 the value of a company, or a share in its value: *to buy or sell stock*

stock[2] /stɒk/ **verb**
to have something for people to buy: *They stock a wide range of books and magazines.*

stocking /ˈstɒkɪŋ/ **noun**
a very thin piece of clothing that covers a woman's foot and leg: *a pair of stockings*
→ See **Clothes** on page C5

stole /stəʊl/
past tense of steal

stolen /ˈstəʊlən/
past participle of steal

stomach /ˈstʌmək/ **noun**
1 A2 the part of your body where food is digested
2 the front part of your body just below your chest
→ See **The Body** on page C2

stomach ache /ˈstʌmək ˌeɪk/ **noun**
A2 pain in your stomach

stone /stəʊn/ **noun**
1 B1 [no plural] a hard, natural substance that is found in the ground: *a stone wall*
2 B1 a small rock or piece of rock
3 B1 a hard, valuable substance that is often used in jewellery: *precious stones*
4 (plural **stone**) UK a unit for measuring weight, equal to 6.35 kilograms or 14 pounds
5 the hard seed that is at the centre of some fruits: *a cherry stone*

stood /stʊd/
past tense and past participle of stand

stool /stuːl/ **noun**
a seat that does not have a back or arms

stool

stoop /stuːp/ **verb**
to bend the top half of your body forward and down: *He stooped to pick up the letter.*

stop[1] /stɒp/ **verb** (**stopping**, **stopped**)
1 A1 to finish doing something: *Stop laughing – it's not funny.* ◦ *He started to say something and then stopped.*
2 A2 If a bus, train, etc. stops at a particular place, it lets people get on and off: *Does this train stop at Cambridge?*
3 A2 to stop a journey or an activity for a short time: *We stopped at a café for lunch.*
4 B1 to not move any more, or make someone or something not move any more: *A car stopped outside the house.*
5 B1 to not continue to operate, or to make something not continue to operate: *My watch has stopped.*
6 B1 to prevent something from happening or prevent someone from doing something: *Doctors are trying to stop the disease from spreading.*
7 to make something end: *We must find a way to stop the war.*

Common mistake: stop doing something or stop to do something?

Stop doing something means 'not continue with an activity'.
Suddenly, everyone stopped talking.
~~*Suddenly, everyone stopped to talk.*~~
Stop to do something means 'stop one activity so that you can do something else'.
We stopped to look at the map.

stop[2] /stɒp/ **noun**
1 A1 a place where a bus or train stops so that people can get on or off: *We need to get off **at** the next **stop**.*
2 B1 the act of stopping an activity or journey, or a period of time when you stop: *We made a stop to get petrol.*

3 put a stop to *something* to end something bad: *We must put a stop to the violence.*

store[1] /stɔːʳ/ **noun**
1 B1 US a shop: *a men's clothing store*
2 an amount of something that you are keeping to use later: *a store of grain*

store[2] /stɔːʳ/ **verb** (**storing**, **stored**)
1 to put something somewhere and not use it until you need it: *We have a lot of old clothes stored in the attic.*
2 to keep information on a computer: *All the data is stored on disks.*

storey UK (US **story**) /ˈstɔːri/ **noun**
a level of a building: *a three-storey house*

storm /stɔːm/ **noun**
A2 very bad weather with a lot of rain, snow, wind, etc.: *a snow/thunder storm*

stormy /ˈstɔːmi/ **adj** (**stormier**, **stormiest**)
If it is stormy, the weather is bad with a lot of wind and rain: *a stormy night*

story /ˈstɔːri/ **noun** (plural **stories**)
1 A2 a description of a series of real or imaginary events that people read for enjoyment: *a horror story* ◦ *She **reads stories** to the children every night.*
2 US (UK **storey**) a level of a building: *a three-story house*

straight[1] /streɪt/ **adj**
1 A2 not curved or bent: *a straight road* ◦ *straight hair*
→ See **Hair** on page C9
2 in a position that is level or vertical: *That shelf's not straight.*
3 honest: *a straight answer*

straight[2] /streɪt/ **adv**
1 A2 in a straight line: *It's straight ahead.*
2 B1 without pausing or delaying: *I went straight back to sleep.*
3 straight away B1 now: *Go there straight away.*
4 sit up/stand up straight to sit or stand with your body vertical

straighten /ˈstreɪtᵊn/ **verb**
to become straight or to make something straight

strain[1] /streɪn/ **noun**
1 the feeling of being worried and nervous about something: *The strain of looking after four children was too much for her.*
2 pressure put on something by a bad situation or by too much weight or force: *Their arguments were putting a strain on their marriage.*

strain[2] /streɪn/ **verb**
1 to try hard to do something, usually to see or hear something: *I had to strain to hear the music.*
2 to hurt part of your body by using it too much: *I think I've strained a muscle.*

strait /streɪt/ **noun**
a narrow area of sea that connects two large areas of sea: *the straits of Florida*

strand /strænd/ **noun**
a thin piece of hair, thread, rope, etc.: *She tucked a strand of hair behind her ear.*

stranded /ˈstrændɪd/ **adj**
not able to leave a place: *We were stranded at the airport for ten hours.*

strange /streɪndʒ/ **adj**
1 A2 unusual or not expected: *It's strange that she hasn't called.* ◦ *What a strange-looking dog.*
2 B1 A strange person or place is one that you are not familiar with: *I've never been here before, so it's all strange to me.*
• **strangely adv** *She's been behaving very strangely recently.*

stranger /ˈstreɪndʒəʳ/ **noun**
B1 someone you have never met before

strangle /ˈstræŋgl/ **verb** (**strangling**, **strangled**)
to kill someone by pressing their throat

strap /stræp/ **noun**
a thin piece of material used to fasten two things together or to carry something: *a watch strap* ◦ *I want a bag with a shoulder strap.*

a b c d e f g h i j k l m n o p q r s t u v w x y z

a b c d e f g h i j k l m n o p q r s t u v w x y z

• **strap** verb (**strapping**, **strapped**) to fasten something using a strap

strategy /ˈstrætədʒi/ **noun** (plural **strategies**)
a plan that you use to do something: *a sales strategy*

straw /strɔː/ **noun**
1 [no plural] the long, dried stems of plants, often given to animals: *a straw hat*
2 a thin plastic or paper tube that you use for drinking through

strawberry /ˈstrɔːbəri/ **noun** (plural **strawberries**)
B1 a small, red fruit with small, brown seeds on its surface

stray /streɪ/ **adj**
A stray animal is lost or has no home: *a stray dog*

streak /striːk/ **noun**
a thin line or mark: *She has a streak of white hair.*

stream /striːm/ **noun**
1 B1 a small river
2 a stream of *something* a line of people or cars moving in the same direction: *a constant stream of traffic*

street /striːt/ **noun**
1 A1 a road in a town or city that has houses or other buildings: *We live on the same street.*
2 Street A1 used in the name of a street as part of an address: *221B Baker Street*

streetcar /ˈstriːtkɑːʳ/ **noun** US (UK **tram**)
an electric vehicle for carrying passengers, mostly in cities, that moves along metal lines in the road

street light /ˈstriːt ˌlaɪt/ **noun**
a light on a tall post next to a street
→ See picture at **light** noun

strength /streŋθ/ **noun**
1 [no plural] the quality of being strong: *A good boxer needs skill as well as strength.*
2 [no plural] the power that an organization, country, etc. has: *economic strength*
3 a good quality or ability: *We all have our strengths and weaknesses.*

strengthen /ˈstreŋθən/ **verb**
to become stronger or make something become stronger: *These exercises strengthen the leg muscles.*

stress¹ /stres/ **noun**
1 B1 feelings of worry caused by difficult situations such as problems at work: *work-related stress* ◦ *She's been **under** a lot of **stress** recently.*
2 [no plural] a greater force you use to say one part of a word or sentence: *In the word 'blanket', the **stress** is **on** the first syllable.*

stress² /stres/ **verb**
1 to show that something is important: *I stressed that this was our policy.*
2 to say one part of a word more strongly than the rest: *In the word 'engine', you stress the first syllable.*

stressed /strest/ **adj**
B1 worried and not able to relax: *She's really stressed about her exams.*

stressful /ˈstresfʊl/ **adj**
B1 making someone worry a lot: *a stressful job*

stretch /stretʃ/ **verb**
1 to become longer or wider, or to pull something so that it becomes longer or wider: *Don't pull my sweater – you'll stretch it.*
2 to make your body or part of your body straighter and longer: *Stretch your arms above your head.*
3 to cover a large area: *The fields stretched away into the distance.*

stretcher /ˈstretʃəʳ/ **noun**
a flat structure covered with cloth that is used to carry someone who is hurt

stretcher

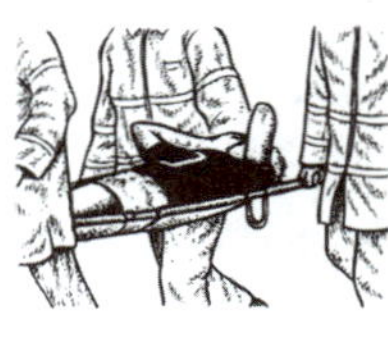

strict /strɪkt/ **adj**
1 B1 A strict person makes sure that children or people working for them behave well and does not allow them to break any rules: *a strict teacher* ◦ *My parents were very **strict with** us.*
2 If a rule, law, etc. is strict, it must be

obeyed: *She gave me strict instructions to be there by ten.*
3 always behaving in a particular way because of your beliefs: *She's a strict vegetarian.*

strictly /ˈstrɪktli/ **adv**
1 exactly or correctly: *That's not strictly true.*
2 done for a particular person or purpose: *Her visit is strictly business.*
3 used to emphasize that something is not allowed: *The use of cameras is strictly forbidden.*

strike[1] /straɪk/ **verb** (**striking**, **struck**)
1 B1 formal to hit someone or something: *Two climbers were struck by falling rocks.* ◦ *His car went out of control and struck a tree.*
2 If a thought or idea strikes you, you suddenly think of it: ***It struck me that*** *I'd forgotten to order the champagne.*
3 If a group of workers strike, they stop working for a period of time to try to force their employer to give them more money or to improve their working situation: *Bus drivers are threatening to strike.*
4 If a clock strikes, a bell rings to show what the time is.

strike[2] /straɪk/ **noun**
B1 a period of time when a group of workers stop working, to try to force their employer to give them more money or to improve their working situation: *Teachers are planning to* ***go on strike*** *next month.*

string /strɪŋ/ **noun**
1 very thin rope used for tying things: *a ball of string*
2 a piece of wire that is part of a musical instrument: *guitar strings*

strip[1] /strɪp/ **verb** (**stripping**, **stripped**)
to remove all your clothes, or to remove all someone else's clothes: *She was stripped and searched by the guards.*

strip[2] /strɪp/ **noun**
a long, thin piece of something: *a strip of paper*

stripe /straɪp/ **noun**
B1 a long, straight area of colour: *His shirt was white with blue stripes.*

striped /straɪpt/ **adj**
with a pattern of stripes: *a striped shirt*

stroke[1] /strəʊk/ **verb** (**stroking**, **stroked**)
to gently move your hand over a surface: *She stroked the dog.*

stroke[2] /strəʊk/ **noun**
1 a serious medical condition in the brain that makes you suddenly unable to move part of your body
2 a movement that you make against something with your hand, a pen, brush, etc.: *a brush stroke*
3 a style of swimming
• **a stroke of luck** something good that happens to you by chance

stroll /strəʊl/ **verb**
to walk somewhere in a slow and relaxed way: *They strolled along the beach.*
• **stroll noun** *Shall we* ***go for a stroll*** *around the garden?*

stroller /ˈstrəʊləʳ/ **noun** US (UK **push-chair**)
a chair on wheels that is used to move small children

strong /strɒŋ/ **adj**
1 A2 A strong person or animal is physically powerful: *Are you strong enough to lift this table on your own?*
→ Opposite **weak adj**
2 B1 A strong object does not break easily or can support heavy things: *a strong box*
3 B1 If a taste, smell, etc. is strong, it is very easy to notice: *There's a strong smell of burning.*
4 B1 produced using a lot of power: *a strong kick* ◦ *Her voice was clear and strong.*
5 B1 Strong relationships last for a long time, and are not easily spoiled: *During the crisis their marriage remained strong.*
6 of a good quality or level and likely to be successful: *a strong team* ◦ *a strong economy*
7 A strong feeling, belief, or opinion

a b c d e f g h i j k l m n o p q r s t u v w x y z

is felt in a very deep and serious way: *a strong sense of pride*
8 If someone is strong, they are confident and able to deal with problems well: *All my aunts were strong women.*

strongly /ˈstrɒŋli/ **adv**
very much or in a very serious way: *He is strongly opposed to violence of any sort.*

struck /strʌk/
past tense and past participle of strike

structure /ˈstrʌktʃəʳ/ **noun**
1 the way that parts of something are arranged or put together: *a cell's structure* ◦ *grammatical structure*
2 a building or something that has been built

struggle[1] /ˈstrʌgl/ **verb** (**struggling**, **struggled**)
1 to try very hard to do something difficult: *He's **struggling to** pay off his debts.*
2 to fight someone when they are holding you: *She struggled but couldn't break free.*

struggle[2] /ˈstrʌgl/ **noun**
1 the act of trying very hard to do something difficult: *It was a real **struggle to** stay awake.*
2 a fight between people

stubborn /ˈstʌbən/ **adj**
never changing your ideas, plans, etc. even when you should
• **stubbornly** **adv**

stuck[1] /stʌk/
past tense and past participle of stick

stuck[2] /stʌk/ **adj**
1 not able to move anywhere: *We were stuck at the airport for twelve hours.*
2 not able to continue reading, answering questions, etc. because something is too difficult: *I keep getting stuck on difficult words.*

student /ˈstjuːdənt/ **noun**
A1 someone who is studying at a school or university: *a law student*
→ See **The Classroom** on page C4

studies /ˈstʌdiz/ **plural noun**
A2 the work that you do while you are at a college or university: *I'm enjoying my studies a lot more this year.*

studio /ˈstjuːdiəʊ/ **noun**
1 B1 a room where television or radio programmes or musical recordings are made
2 B1 a company that makes movies or a place where movies are made: *a major movie studio*
3 a room where an artist or photographer works

study[1] /ˈstʌdi/ **verb** (**studying**, **studied**)
1 A1 to learn about a subject, usually at school or university: *I studied biology before going into medicine.*
2 to look at something very carefully: *He studied his face in the mirror.*
3 to examine a subject in detail in order to discover new information: *Researchers have been **studying how** babies learn to speak.*

study[2] /ˈstʌdi/ **noun**
1 [no plural] the activity of learning about a subject, usually in school or at a college or university: *the study of English literature*
2 B1 (plural **studies**) a room in a house where you can read, write, etc.
3 (plural **studies**) a piece of work that examines a subject in detail in order to find new information: *For years, studies have shown the link between smoking and cancer.*

stuff[1] /stʌf/ **noun** [no plural] informal
B1 used to mean a substance or a group of things or ideas, etc. without saying exactly what they are: *There's some sticky stuff on the carpet.* ◦ *Can I leave my stuff at your house?*

stuff[2] /stʌf/ **verb**
1 to quickly push something into a small space: *He stuffed the papers into his briefcase and left.*
2 to completely fill a container with something: *an envelope stuffed with money*

stuffing /ˈstʌfɪŋ/ **noun** [no plural]
1 a substance that is used to fill a hollow object: *a toy bear's stuffing*
2 a type of food made from pieces of bread, vegetables, and spices that is cooked inside a large piece of meat: *turkey stuffing*

stuffy /ˈstʌfi/ **adj** (**stuffier**, **stuffiest**)
hot, with no clean air: *a stuffy room*

stumble /ˈstʌmbl/ **verb** (**stumbling**, **stumbled**)
to step badly and almost fall over: *Rachel stumbled on the rocks.*

stung /stʌŋ/
past tense and past participle of sting

stunk /stʌŋk/
past participle of stink

stunt /stʌnt/ **noun**
1 an exciting and dangerous action that is usually done by a skilled person for a movie: *Tom Cruise* ***did*** *his own* ***stunts*** *for Mission Impossible 2.*
2 something that is done to get people's attention: *Their marriage was a* ***publicity stunt****.*

stupid /ˈstjuːpɪd/ **adj**
B1 very silly or not clever: *That's a stupid thing to say.* ◦ *Don't be stupid!*
• **stupidly** **adv** *I stupidly left my key inside the room.*

stupidity /stjuːˈpɪdəti/ **noun** [no plural]
behaviour that is very silly or shows you do not think about your actions: *I can't believe the stupidity of these people!*

sturdy /ˈstɜːdi/ **adj** (**sturdier**, **sturdiest**)
very strong and solid: *sturdy walking boots*

stutter /ˈstʌtəʳ/ **verb**
to repeat the first sound of a word many times when you talk, usually because you have a speech problem: *'C-c-can we g-go now?' she stuttered.*
• **stutter** **noun**

style /staɪl/ **noun**
1 B1 a way of doing something that is typical of a particular person, group, place, or period: *a* ***style of*** *painting*
2 B1 a way of designing hair, clothes, furniture, etc.: *She's had her hair cut in a really nice style.*

stylish /ˈstaɪlɪʃ/ **adj**
B1 fashionable and attractive

subject /ˈsʌbdʒɪkt/ **noun**
1 A1 an area of knowledge studied at school or university: *Chemistry is my favourite subject.*
2 B1 what someone is writing or talking about: *The subject of the programme was mental health.*
3 B1 in grammar, the person or thing that does the action described by a verb. In the sentence 'Bob phoned me yesterday', 'Bob' is the subject.
4 someone who is from a particular country: *a British subject*

submarine /ˌsʌbmᵊrˈiːn/ **noun**
a boat that travels under water

substance /ˈsʌbstᵊns/ **noun**
a solid, liquid, or gas: *a dangerous substance*

substitute /ˈsʌbstɪtjuːt/ **verb**
to use someone or something instead of another person or thing: *You can* ***substitute*** *pasta* ***for*** *the rice in this recipe.*

subtitles /ˈsʌbˌtaɪtlz/ **plural noun**
words shown at the bottom of a cinema or television screen to explain what is being said: *It's a French film with English subtitles.*

subtle /ˈsʌtl/ **adj**
not obvious or easy to notice: *a subtle change*

subtract /səbˈtrækt/ **verb**
to take one number away from another number: *You need to* ***subtract*** *25%* ***from*** *the final figure.*
• **subtraction** /səbˈtrækʃᵊn/ **noun**

suburb /ˈsʌbɜːb/ **noun**
an area where people live outside the centre of a city: *a suburb of New York*
• **suburban** /səˈbɜːbᵊn/ **adj** *a suburban area*

subway /ˈsʌbweɪ/ **noun**
1 US (UK **underground**) a system of trains that is built under a city: *a subway station*
2 UK a tunnel that goes below a busy road for people who are crossing on foot

succeed /səkˈsiːd/ **verb**
B1 to do something good that you have been trying to do: *He finally* ***succeeded in*** *passing his exams.*
→ Opposite **fail** **verb**
→ See note on page 396

a b c d e f g h i j k l m n o p q r **s** t u v w x y z

Common mistake: succeed

Remember that **succeed** is often followed by the preposition **in + doing something**. It is not used with 'to do something'.

Two prisoners succeeded in escaping.

~~*Two prisoners succeeded to escape.*~~

success /sək'ses/ **noun**
1 B1 [no plural] the fact of achieving something good that you have been trying to do: *Her success is due to hard work.*
→ Opposite **failure** **noun**
2 B1 something that has a good result or that is very popular: *His first movie was a great success.*
→ Opposite **failure** **noun**

successful /sək'sesfᵊl/ **adj**
1 B1 having a good result: *The operation was successful.*
2 very popular: *a successful book*
3 having achieved a lot or made a lot of money through your work: *a successful businesswoman*
• **successfully** **adv**

such /sʌtʃ/ **pronoun, determiner**
1 A2 used to make an opinion stronger: *She's such a nice person.* ◦ *It's such a shame that he's leaving.*
2 like the person or thing you were just talking about: *It's difficult to know how to treat such cases.*
3 **such as** A2 for example: *She can't eat dairy products, such as milk and cheese.*

suck /sʌk/ **verb**
to have something in your mouth and use your tongue, lips, etc. to pull on it: *I was sucking a sweet.* ◦ *Martha still sucks her thumb.*

sudden /'sʌdᵊn/ **adj**
1 done or happening quickly and not expected: *a sudden change* ◦ *His sudden death was a shock to us all.*
2 **all of a sudden** quickly and in a way that was not expected: *All of a sudden she got up and walked out.*

suddenly /'sʌdᵊnli/ **adv**
B1 quickly and when not expected: *I suddenly realized who she was.*

sue /suː/ **verb** (**suing**, **sued**)
to take legal action against someone and try to get money from them because they have harmed you: *She's threatening to **sue** the firm **for** age discrimination.*

suede /sweɪd/ **noun** [no plural]
leather that has a slightly rough surface

suffer /'sʌfəʳ/ **verb**
1 ***suffer from something*** B1 to have an illness: *She suffers from depression.*
2 to feel pain or sadness and worry: *I can't bear to see animals suffering.*
3 to experience something bad: *Many people in this country have suffered discrimination.*

suffering /'sʌfərɪŋ/ **noun** [no plural]
a feeling of pain or sadness and worry: *human suffering*

sufficient /sə'fɪʃᵊnt/ **adj**
enough: *She didn't have sufficient time to answer all the questions.*

suffix /'sʌfɪks/ **noun**
a group of letters that you add to the end of a word to make another word. In the word 'slowly', '-ly' is a suffix.

sugar /'ʃʊgəʳ/ **noun** [no plural]
A1 a very sweet substance used to give flavour to food and drinks: *coffee with milk and sugar*

suggest /sə'dʒest/ **verb**
1 B1 to say an idea or plan for someone else to consider: *I **suggest that** we park the car here.* ◦ *He suggested having the meeting at his house.*
2 B1 to say that someone or something is suitable for something: *Can you suggest a good hotel?*

suggestion /sə'dʒestʃᵊn/ **noun**
B1 an idea or plan that someone suggests: *Philip **made** a few **suggestions**.*

suicide /'suːɪsaɪd/ **noun**
the act of deliberately killing yourself: *He **committed suicide** after a long period of depression.*

suit[1] /suːt/ **noun**
1 A2 a jacket and trousers or a jacket and skirt that are made from the same material: *She wore a dark blue suit.*
2 one of the four types of card in a set of playing cards, each having a different shape printed on it: *The four*

suits in a pack of cards are hearts, spades, clubs, and diamonds.

suit² /suːt/ **verb**
1 to make someone look more attractive: *Green really suits you.*
2 to be acceptable or right for someone: *It would suit me better if we left a bit earlier.*

suitable /ˈsuːtəbl/ **adj**
B1 acceptable or right for someone or something: *What is a suitable time to call?* ◦ *This movie is* ***suitable for*** *children.*
→ Opposite **unsuitable adj**
• **suitably adv** *He was suitably dressed for an interview.*

suitcase /ˈsuːtkeɪs/ **noun**
A2 a rectangular case with a handle that you use for carrying clothes when you are travelling
→ See picture at **luggage**

sulk /sʌlk/ **verb**
to look unhappy and not speak to anyone because you are angry about something: *He's upstairs sulking in his bedroom.*
• **sulky adj** (**sulkier**, **sulkiest**) often sulking: *a sulky teenager*

sum¹ /sʌm/ **noun**
1 B1 an amount of money: *a large* ***sum of*** *money*
2 UK a simple mathematical calculation such as adding two numbers together: *Kids these days can't* ***do sums*** *without a calculator.*

sum² /sʌm/ **verb** (**summing**, **summed**)
sum (*something/someone*) up phrasal verb
to describe the most important facts or details of something: *The situation can be* ***summed up as*** *unacceptable.*

summary /ˈsʌmᵊri/ **noun** (plural **summaries**)
a short description that gives the main facts or ideas about something: *He* ***gave*** *a brief* ***summary of*** *what happened.*

summer /ˈsʌməʳ/ **noun**
A1 the warmest season of the year, between spring and autumn: *We usually go away* ***in the summer.***

summit /ˈsʌmɪt/ **noun**
the top of a mountain: *We hope to* ***reach the summit*** *before night.*

summon /ˈsʌmən/ **verb** formal
to officially order someone to come to a place: *He was summoned to a meeting.*

sun /sʌn/ **noun** [no plural]
1 the sun the large, bright star that shines in the sky during the day and gives light and heat to the Earth
2 A1 the light and heat that comes from the sun: *I can't sit* ***in the sun*** *for too long.*

sunbathe /ˈsʌnbeɪð/ **verb** (**sunbathing**, **sunbathed**)
B1 to sit or lie in the sun so that your skin becomes darker
• **sunbathing noun** [no plural]

sunburn /ˈsʌnbɜːn/ **noun** [no plural]
painful, red skin that you get from being in the sun too long
• **sunburnt adj** (also **sunburned**) *I got sunburnt when I fell asleep in the sun.*

Sunday /ˈsʌndeɪ/ **noun**
A1 the day of the week after Saturday and before Monday

sung /sʌŋ/
the past participle of sing

sunglasses /ˈsʌnˌglɑːsɪz/ **plural noun**
A2 dark glasses that you wear to protect your eyes from the sun
→ See **Clothes** on page C5

sunk /sʌŋk/
past participle of sink

sunlight /ˈsʌnlaɪt/ **noun** [no plural]
the light from the sun

sunny /ˈsʌni/ **adj** (**sunnier**, **sunniest**)
A2 bright because of light from the sun: *a lovely sunny day*

sunrise /ˈsʌnraɪz/ **noun**
B1 the time when the sun appears in the morning and the sky becomes light

sunscreen /ˈsʌnˌskriːn/ **noun**
a substance that protects your skin in the sun

sunset /ˈsʌnset/ **noun**
B1 the time when the sun disappears

in the evening and the sky becomes dark

sunshine /ˈsʌnʃaɪn/ **noun** [no plural]
B1 the light from the sun: *Let's sit over there in the sunshine.*

suntan /ˈsʌntæn/ **noun** (also **tan**)
darkened skin you get from being in the sun: *suntan oil*
• **suntanned adj** (also **tanned**)

super /ˈsuːpəʳ/ **adj, adv** informal
very good: *We had a super time.*

superb /suːˈpɜːb/ **adj**
excellent: *a superb restaurant*

superior /suːˈpɪəriəʳ/ **adj**
better than other things: *This car is far* ***superior to*** *the others.*
→ Opposite **inferior adj**

superlative /suːˈpɜːlətɪv/ **noun**
A2 the form of an adjective or adverb that is used to show that someone or something has more of a particular quality than anyone or anything else. For example 'best' is the superlative of 'good' and 'slowest' is the superlative of 'slow'.

supermarket /ˈsuːpəˌmɑːkɪt/ **noun**
A1 a large shop that sells food, drink, things for the home, etc.

supernatural /ˌsuːpəˈnætʃərəl/ **adj**
Supernatural events cannot be explained by science: *People thought that cats had supernatural powers.*

superstition /ˌsuːpəˈstɪʃən/ **noun**
a belief that particular actions or objects are lucky or unlucky

supervise /ˈsuːpəvaɪz/ **verb** (**supervising**, **supervised**)
to watch a person or activity and make certain that everything is done correctly, safely, etc.: *Students must be supervised by a teacher at all times.*
• **supervisor noun** someone who supervises

supervision /ˌsuːpəˈvɪʒən/ **noun** [no plural]
the act of watching a person or activity to make certain that everything is done correctly or safely: *He needs constant supervision.*

supper /ˈsʌpəʳ/ **noun**
A2 a meal that you eat in the evening: *What are we having* ***for supper****?*

supply¹ /səˈplaɪ/ **verb** (**supplying**, **supplied**)
to give things that people want or need, often over a long period of time: *This lake* ***supplies*** *the whole town* ***with*** *water.*

supply² /səˈplaɪ/ **noun** (plural **supplies**)
an amount of something that is ready to be used: *a supply of water* ◦ *food supplies*

support¹ /səˈpɔːt/ **verb**
1 B1 to help someone, often when they are having problems: *My family has always supported me in my career.*
2 B1 to take care of someone by paying for their food, clothes, etc.: *He has four children to support.*
3 B1 UK to like a particular sports team and want them to win: *Who do you support?*
4 to agree with an idea, group, or person: *Do you support their views on nuclear weapons?*
5 to hold the weight of someone or something: *Is this ladder strong enough to support me?*
6 to give encouragement or money to someone or something because you want them to succeed: *I think it's important to support local businesses.*

support² /səˈpɔːt/ **noun** [no plural]
1 B1 help or encouragement given to someone when they are having problems: *You* ***have*** *my* ***full support*** *if you decide to apply for the job.*
2 B1 the money someone needs in order to buy food and clothes and pay for somewhere to live: *He is dependent on his father for support.*
3 agreement with an idea, group or person: *Is there much public* ***support for*** *the death penalty?*

supporter /səˈpɔːtəʳ/ **noun** UK
1 B1 someone who likes a particular sports team and wants them to win: *English football supporters*
2 someone who supports a particular

idea, group, or person: *The new law has few supporters.*

suppose /sə'pəʊz/ **verb** (**supposing**, **supposed**)
1 A2 to think that something is probably true: *I suppose he feels angry with her.*
2 I suppose (so) B1 used to show agreement to something when you do not really want to: *I suppose you're right.* ◦ *'Can I come with you?' 'I suppose so.'*
3 be supposed to do *something* B1 to be expected to do something, especially when this does not happen: *He was supposed to be here by nine.*
4 be supposed to be *something* to be expected to be something, especially because of a rule, agreement, etc.: *The children are supposed to be at school by 8 a.m.*
5 be supposed to be *something* to be considered by many people to be something: *The scenery is supposed to be fantastic.*

sure[1] /ʃɔːʳ/ **adj**
1 A2 certain: *I'm **sure that** he won't mind.* ◦ *I'm quite **sure about** the second answer.*
→ Opposite **unsure** adj
2 make sure (that) A2 to take action so that you are certain that something happens, is true, etc.: *Make sure that you close all the windows before you leave.*
3 for sure B1 without any doubts: *I think he's from Korea but don't know for sure.*
4 be sure of *something* to be confident that something is true: *He'll win this year, I'm sure of it.*
5 be sure of *yourself* to be confident of your own abilities, qualities, etc.: *She seems a bit more sure of herself since she got a job.*

sure[2] /ʃɔːʳ/ **adv**
A2 used to show agreement: *'Do you want to come swimming with us?' 'Sure.'*

surely /'ʃɔːli/ **adv**
used to show surprise that something has happened or is going to happen: *You surely didn't tell him, did you?*

surf /sɜːf/ **verb**
1 B1 to ride on a wave in the sea using a special board
2 surf the Internet/Net/Web A2 to look at information on the Internet by moving from one page to another
• **surfer** **noun** someone who surfs
• **surfing** **noun** [no plural] *Let's **go surfing** this afternoon.*

surface /'sɜːfɪs/ **noun**
1 the top or outside part of something: *the Earth's surface* ◦ *The sun was reflected on the surface of the water.*
2 [no plural] what someone or something seems to be like when you do not know much about them: *On the surface, he seemed very pleasant.*

surfboard /'sɜːfbɔːd/ **noun**
a long piece of wood or plastic that you use to ride on waves in the sea

surgeon /'sɜːdʒᵊn/ **noun**
a doctor who cuts people's bodies and removes or repairs part of them

surgeon

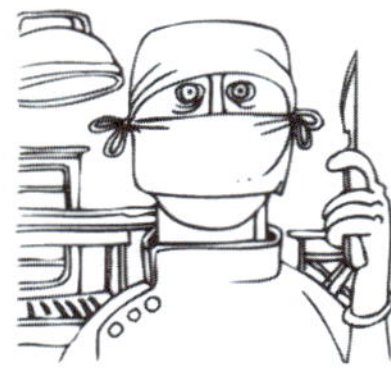

surgery /'sɜːdʒᵊri/ **noun**
1 [no plural] medical treatment in which a doctor cuts your body open and repairs or removes something: *She has **had surgery** for the problem.* ◦ *heart surgery*
2 (plural **surgeries**) UK a place where doctors or other medical workers treat people: *What time does the surgery open?*

surname /'sɜːneɪm/ **noun**
A2 the name that you and people in your family all have: *His surname is Walker.*

surprise[1] /sə'praɪz/ **noun**
1 A2 something that you did not expect to happen: *I didn't know that my parents were coming – it was a lovely surprise.* ◦ *a surprise party*
2 [no plural] the feeling that you get when something happens that you did

not expect: *He agreed to everything, much **to** my **surprise**.*

surprise² /səˈpraɪz/ **verb** (**surprising**, **surprised**)
B1 to make someone feel surprise: *I didn't tell her I was coming home early – I thought I'd surprise her.*

surprised /səˈpraɪzd/ **adj**
A2 feeling surprise because something has happened that you did not expect: *I'm **surprised to** see you here.* ◦ *She wasn't **surprised at** his decision.*

surprising /səˈpraɪzɪŋ/ **adj**
B1 not expected and making someone feel surprised: *That was a surprising decision.*

surprisingly /səˈpraɪzɪŋli/ **adv**
B1 used to say that something is surprising: *a surprisingly good meal*

surrender /sᵊrˈendəʳ/ **verb**
to stop fighting because you know the other side will win: *Rebel troops are refusing to surrender.*
• **surrender noun** [no plural]

surround /səˈraʊnd/ **verb**
B1 to be or go everywhere around something or someone: *The house is surrounded by a large garden.* ◦ *The police have surrounded the building.*

surrounding /səˈraʊndɪŋ/ **adj**
in a position around something: *the surrounding countryside*

surroundings /səˈraʊndɪŋz/ **plural noun**
the place where someone or something is and the things that are in it: *Have you got used to your new surroundings?*

survey /ˈsɜːveɪ/ **noun**
an examination of people's opinions or behaviour done by asking people questions: *A recent **survey showed** that 58% of people do not exercise enough.*

survival /səˈvaɪvᵊl/ **noun** [no plural]
the state of continuing to live, especially after a dangerous situation: *Flood victims had to fight for survival.*

survive /səˈvaɪv/ **verb** (**surviving**, **survived**)
to continue to live after almost dying because of an accident, illness, etc.: *No one survived the plane crash.*

survivor /səˈvaɪvəʳ/ **noun**
someone who continues to live after almost dying because of an accident, illness, etc.: *Rescuers have given up hope of finding any more survivors.*

suspect¹ /ˈsʌspekt/ **noun**
someone who may have done a crime: *He's a suspect in the murder case.*

suspect² /səˈspekt/ **verb**
1 to think that someone may have done a crime or done something else bad: *He was **suspected of** drug dealing.*
2 to think that something is probably true: *They **suspected that** he was lying.*

suspend /səˈspend/ **verb**
1 to stop something happening for a short time: *The match was suspended because of bad weather.*
2 to hang something from somewhere: *A light bulb was **suspended from** the ceiling.*

suspense /səˈspens/ **noun** [no plural]
the feeling of excitement that you have when you are waiting for something to happen: *What's your answer then? Don't **keep** me **in suspense**.*

suspicion /səˈspɪʃᵊn/ **noun**
1 a belief that someone has done something wrong: *They were arrested **on suspicion of** drug dealing.*
2 an idea that something may be true: *I had a **suspicion that** he might like her.*

suspicious /səˈspɪʃəs/ **adj**
1 making you feel that something is wrong or that something bad is happening: *suspicious behaviour*
2 not trusting someone: *Many of them remain **suspicious of** journalists.*
• **suspiciously adv** *His shoes were suspiciously clean (= the fact that they were clean made me suspicious).*

swallow /ˈswɒləʊ/ **verb**
to move your throat in order to make food or drink go down: *These tablets are too big to swallow.*

swam /swæm/
the past tense of swim

a b c d e f g h i j k l m n o p q r s t u v w x y z

swamp /swɒmp/ **noun**
an area of very wet, soft land

swan /swɒn/ **noun**
a large, white bird with a long neck that lives on lakes and rivers

swan

swap /swɒp/ **verb** (**swapping**, **swapped**)
to give something to someone and get something from them in return: *Would you mind if Dave* ***swapped*** *places* ***with*** *you for a bit?*
• **swap noun** *We'll* ***do a swap****.*

sway /sweɪ/ **verb**
to move slowly from one side to the other: *The trees swayed gently in the wind.*

swear /sweəʳ/ **verb** (**swore**, **sworn**)
1 to use rude language about sex, the body, etc.: *He was sent home because he* ***swore at*** *the teacher.*
2 to promise: *I swear I won't tell anyone.*

swear word /ˈsweə ˌwɜːd/ **noun**
a rude word about sex, the body, etc.

sweat /swet/ **verb**
to make liquid through your skin because you are hot: *I'd been running and I was sweating.*
• **sweat noun** [no plural] the liquid that is on your skin when you are hot: *The sweat was running down his face.*

sweater /ˈswetəʳ/ **noun**
A2 a warm piece of clothing that covers the top of your body and is pulled on over your head
→ See **Clothes** on page C5

sweatshirt /ˈswetʃɜːt/ **noun**
B1 a piece of clothing made of soft cotton that covers the top of your body
→ See **Clothes** on page C5

sweaty /ˈsweti/ **adj** (**sweatier**, **sweatiest**)
covered in sweat: *He was hot and sweaty from working in the garden.*

sweep /swiːp/ **verb** (**swept**)
1 to clean the floor using a brush: *She's just swept the floor.*
2 to push or carry something with force: *Many trees were swept away in the flood.*

sweet[1] /swiːt/ **adj**
1 A1 with a taste like sugar: *The sauce was too sweet.*
2 A2 attractive, often because of being small: *Look at that sweet little puppy!*
3 B1 kind: *It was really sweet of you to come.*

sweet[2] /swiːt/ **noun** UK (US **candy**)
A2 a small piece of sweet food, often made of sugar or chocolate: *Sweets are bad for your teeth.*

sweetcorn /ˈswiːtkɔːn/ **noun** [no plural] UK
the sweet, yellow seeds of maize (= a plant) which are eaten as a vegetable
→ See **Fruit and Vegetables** on page C8

swell /swel/ **verb** (**swelled**, **swollen**)
to get bigger: *One side of his face had swollen up where he'd been stung.*

swelling /ˈswelɪŋ/ **noun**
a part of your body that has become bigger because of illness or injury: *The doctor gave me drugs to reduce the swelling in my ankle.*

swept /swept/
past tense and past participle of sweep

swerve /swɜːv/ **verb** (**swerving**, **swerved**)
to change direction suddenly, especially when you are driving a car: *He swerved to avoid a cyclist and hit another car.*

swift /swɪft/ **adj**
happening or moving quickly: *a swift response*
• **swiftly adv**

swim[1] /swɪm/ **verb** (**swimming**, **swam**, **swum**)
A1 to move through water by moving your body: *I learnt to swim when I was about five years old.*
• **swimming noun** [no plural] A2 *I usually* ***go swimming*** *about twice a week.*

a b c d e f g h i j k l m n o p q r s t u v w x y z

→ See **Sports 1** on page C15
• **swimmer** **noun** B1 *I'm not a very strong swimmer.*

swim[2] /swɪm/ **noun**
A2 a time when you swim: *I* ***went for a swim*** *before breakfast.*

swimming costume /ˈswɪmɪŋ ˌkɒstjuːm/ **noun** UK (US **swimsuit**)
A2 a piece of clothing that you wear for swimming

swimming pool /ˈswɪmɪŋ ˌpuːl/ **noun**
A1 an area of water that has been made for people to swim in

swimming trunks /ˈswɪmɪŋ ˌtrʌŋks/ **plural noun**
a piece of clothing that boys and men wear for swimming
→ See **Clothes** on page C5

swimsuit /ˈswɪmsuːt/ **noun**
a piece of clothing that girls and women wear to go swimming

swing[1] /swɪŋ/ **verb** (**swinging**, **swung**)
to move smoothly backwards and forwards, or to make something do this: *She swings her arms when she walks.*

swing[2] /swɪŋ/ **noun**
a chair hanging on two ropes that children sit on and swing backwards and forwards

switch[1] /swɪtʃ/ **verb**
to change from one thing to another: *He's just switched jobs.*
switch (*something*) off **phrasal verb**
B1 to turn off a light, television, etc. by using a switch: *Have you switched the computer off?*
switch (*something*) on **phrasal verb**
B1 to turn on a light, television, etc. by using a switch: *Could you switch on the light?*

switch[2] /swɪtʃ/ **noun**
1 B1 a small object that you push up or down with your finger to turn something electrical on or off
2 a change: *There has been a switch in policy.*

swollen[1] /ˈswəʊlən/
the past participle of swell

swollen[2] /ˈswəʊlən/ **adj**
bigger than usual: *a swollen wrist* ◦ *swollen rivers*

sword /sɔːd/ **noun**
a weapon with a long, metal blade and a handle, used especially in the past

swore /swɔːr/
the past tense of swear

sworn /swɔːn/
the past participle of swear

swum /swʌm/
the past participle of swim

swung /swʌŋ/
past tense and past participle of swing

syllable /ˈsɪləbl/ **noun**
a word or part of a word that has one vowel sound: *'But' has one syllable and 'apple' has two syllables.*

syllabus /ˈsɪləbəs/ **noun**
a list of the subjects that are included in a course of study

symbol /ˈsɪmbəl/ **noun**
a sign or object that is used to mean something: *A heart shape is the symbol of love.*

symbolic /sɪmˈbɒlɪk/ **adj**
representing something else: *The blue in the flag is symbolic of the ocean.*

sympathetic /ˌsɪmpəˈθetɪk/ **adj**
showing that you understand and care about someone's problems: *My boss is very* ***sympathetic about*** *my situation.*
• **sympathetically** **adv** *All requests for help will be treated sympathetically.*

Common mistake: sympathetic

Be careful not to use **sympathetic** when you simply want to say that someone is **nice, friendly**, or **kind**. Remember that if someone is **sympathetic**, they understand your problems.

sympathy /ˈsɪmpəθi/ **noun** [no plural]
an act of showing that you understand and care about someone's problems: *You have my sympathy – it's horrible having a bad cold.*

symptom /ˈsɪmptəm/ **noun**
a physical feeling or problem that shows that you have a particular illness: *A sleeping problem is often a* ***symptom of*** *some other illness.*

a b c d e f g h i j k l m n o p q r s t u v w x y z

synagogue /ˈsɪnəɡɒɡ/ **noun**
a building in which Jewish people pray

synonym /ˈsɪnənɪm/ **noun**
a word that means the same as another word

syringe /sɪˈrɪndʒ/ **noun**
a piece of medical equipment used to push liquid into or take liquid out of someone's body

syringe

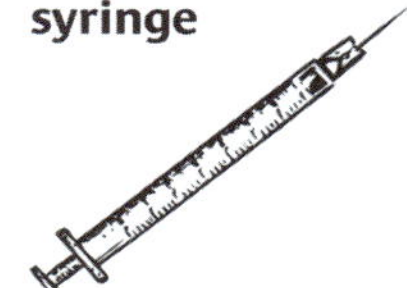

syrup /ˈsɪrəp/ **noun** [no plural]
a very sweet liquid made from sugar and water

system /ˈsɪstəm/ **noun**
1 (B1) a set of connected pieces of equipment that work together: *We have an alarm system at home.*
2 a way or method of doing things: *the American legal system* ◦ *the public transport system*

Tt

T, t /tiː/
the twentieth letter of the alphabet

table /ˈteɪbl/ **noun**

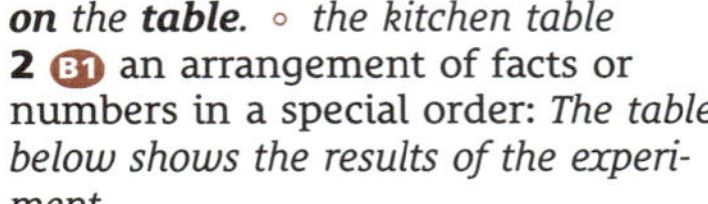

1 A1 a piece of furniture with four legs, used for eating off, putting things on, etc.: *The plates are **on the table**.* ◦ *the kitchen table*
2 B1 an arrangement of facts or numbers in a special order: *The table below shows the results of the experiment.*
3 lay/set the table B1 to put plates, knives, forks, etc. on the table to prepare for a meal: *Can you lay the table for me, please?*

tablecloth /ˈteɪblklɒθ/ **noun**
a piece of material that covers a table
→ See picture at **table**

tablet /ˈtæblət/ **noun**
B1 a small, round thing containing medicine that you swallow

tablets

table tennis /ˈteɪbl ˌtenɪs/ **noun** [no plural]
A2 a game in which two or four people hit a small ball over a low net on a large table

tabloid /ˈtæblɔɪd/ **noun**
a small newspaper with a lot of pictures and short, simple news stories

tackle[1] /ˈtækl/ **verb** (**tackling**, **tackled**)
1 to try to stop a problem: *We must find new ways to tackle crime.*
2 to try to get the ball from someone in a game like football

tackle[2] /ˈtækl/ **noun**
an attempt to get the ball from someone in a game like football

tact /tækt/ **noun** [no plural]
the ability to talk to people about difficult subjects without upsetting them

tactful /ˈtæktfəl/ **adj**
careful not to say or do anything that could upset someone

tactless /ˈtæktləs/ **adj**
not being careful about saying or doing something that could upset someone

tag /tæg/ **noun**
a small piece of paper or plastic with information on it that is fixed to something: *a price tag*

tail /teɪl/ **noun**
the long, narrow part that sticks out at the back of an animal's body: *The dog's pleased to see you – he's **wagging** his **tail**.*

take /teɪk/ **verb** (**taking**, **took**, **taken**)
1 A1 to get and carry something with you when you go somewhere: *I always **take** my umbrella **with** me.*
2 A1 to go somewhere with someone, often paying for them: *I'm **taking** my wife **to** Florence for the weekend.*
3 A2 to travel somewhere by using a bus, train, car, etc.: *Are you taking the train to Paris?*
4 A2 used to tell someone which road to go along in order to get somewhere: *Take the third turning on the left.*
5 A2 to do an exam or test: *When are you taking your driving test?*
6 A2 If something takes a particular amount of time, or a particular quality, you need that amount of time or that quality in order to be able to do it: *It's taken me three days to get here.*
7 A2 to swallow or use medicine: *Take two tablets, three times a day.*
8 B1 to remove something without asking someone: *Someone's taken my coat.*
9 B1 to get hold of something and move it: *He reached across and took the glass from her.*
10 B1 used with some nouns to say that someone performs an action: *I need to take a shower.* ◦ *Take a look at this.*
11 B1 to study a subject in order to do an exam: *He's taking chemistry and physics.*

12 B1 to wear a particular size of clothes: *I take a size 12.*
13 B1 to accept something: *So, are you going to take the job?*
14 take a picture, photograph, etc. A1 to photograph someone or something: *I took some great photos of the kids.*
15 take milk, sugar, etc. to usually have milk, sugar, etc. in your tea or coffee: *Do you take milk in your tea?*

take *something* away phrasal verb
1 to remove something: *A waiter came to take our plates away.*
2 B1 to remove one number from another number: *If you take 4 away from 12 you get 8.*
3 B1 UK to buy food in a restaurant to eat somewhere else: *Is that to eat here or take away?*

take *something* back phrasal verb
B1 to return something to the place where you got it

take *something* down phrasal verb
to remove something that is on a wall or something that is temporary: *I've taken the pictures down.*

take *something* off phrasal verb
A2 to remove something: *If you're hot, take your jacket off.*

take off phrasal verb
A2 If a plane takes off, it begins to fly.

take *someone* out phrasal verb
B1 to go somewhere with someone and pay for them: *Our boss took us out for a meal.*

take *something* out phrasal verb
B1 to remove something from somewhere: *He reached into his bag and took out a book.*

take (*something*) over phrasal verb
to get control of something: *They've recently been taken over by a larger company.*

take *something* up phrasal verb
1 B1 to start doing a particular job or activity: *I've taken up cycling.*
2 to fill an amount of space or time: *This desk takes up too much room.* ◦ *The children take up most of my time.*

takeaway /ˈteɪkəweɪ/ **noun** UK (US **takeout** /ˈteɪkaʊt/)
B1 a meal that you buy in a restaurant but eat at home

take-off /ˈteɪkɒf/ **noun**
the moment when a plane leaves the ground and begins to fly

tale /teɪl/ **noun**
a story, especially one that is not true: *My grandfather used to **tell** us **tales** of his time as a pilot during the war.*

talent /ˈtælənt/ **noun**
B1 a natural ability to do something: *She showed an early **talent for** drawing.*

talented /ˈtæləntɪd/ **adj**
B1 showing natural ability in a particular area: *a talented young musician*

talk[1] /tɔːk/ **verb**
A1 to say things to someone: *We were just **talking about** Simon's new girlfriend.* ◦ *I was just **talking to** Adam.*

> **Common mistake: talk about or talk of?**
> After **talk** we normally use **about**.
> *We talked about politics.*
> ~~*We talked of politics.*~~

talk[2] /tɔːk/ **noun**
1 B1 a conversation about a particular subject: *I **had a** long **talk with** Chris about going to university.*
2 a speech to a group of people about a particular subject: *She **gave a talk about** road safety at the school.*

talkative /ˈtɔːkətɪv/ **adj**
A talkative person talks a lot.

talk show /ˈtɔːk ˌʃəʊ/ **noun** mainly US (UK usually **chat show**)
a television or radio programme where people are asked questions about themselves: *I saw her on a talk show last week.*

tall /tɔːl/ **adj**
1 A1 being higher than most other people or things: *He's tall and thin.* ◦ *It's one of the tallest buildings in the city.*
→ Opposite **short** adj
2 A2 used to describe or ask how high

someone or something is: *How tall is she?* ◦ *He's almost two metres tall.*

the Talmud /ˈtælmʊd/ **noun**
the collection of Jewish laws and traditions relating to religious and social matters

tame¹ /teɪm/ **adj**
If an animal is tame, it is not wild and not frightened of people.

tame² /teɪm/ **verb** (**taming**, **tamed**)
to make a wild animal tame

tan /tæn/ **noun** (also **suntan**)
brown skin you get from being in the sun

tangled /ˈtæŋgld/ **adj** (also **tangled up**)
twisted together in an untidy way: *The wires are all tangled.*

tank /tæŋk/ **noun**
1 a large container for keeping liquid or gas: *a hot-water tank*
2 a large, strong military vehicle with a gun on it

tanker /ˈtæŋkəʳ/ **noun**
a ship or truck used to carry large amounts of liquid or gas: *an oil tanker*

tap¹ /tæp/ **noun** UK (US **faucet**)
B1 the part at the end of a pipe that controls the flow of water: *the cold/hot tap*

tap *UK*, **faucet** *US*

tap² /tæp/ **verb** (**tapping**, **tapped**)
to knock or touch something gently: *I **tapped** her **on** the back to get her attention.*

tape¹ /teɪp/ **noun**
1 a long, thin piece of plastic that is used to store sound, pictures, or information, or a plastic box containing it: *I've got the match **on tape**.*
2 [no plural] a thin piece of plastic that has glue on one side and is used for sticking things together: *sticky tape*

tape² /teɪp/ **verb** (**taping**, **taped**)
1 to record something onto tape: *Their conversations were taped by the police.*
2 to stick something somewhere using tape

tape measure /ˈteɪp ˌmeʒəʳ/ **noun**
a long, thin piece of cloth or metal used to measure lengths

tar /tɑːʳ/ **noun** [no plural]
a thick, black substance that is sticky when hot and is used to cover roads

target /ˈtɑːgɪt/ **noun**
1 something or someone that you attack, shoot at, try to hit, etc.: *It's very difficult to hit a moving target.*
2 something that you are trying to do: *I'm hoping to save £3,000 by June – that's my target.*

tart /tɑːt/ **noun**
an open pastry case with a sweet filling, often of fruit: *an apple tart*

tartan /ˈtɑːtᵊn/ **noun**
cloth with a pattern of different coloured squares and crossing lines

task /tɑːsk/ **noun**
a piece of work, especially something unpleasant: *I was given the task of tidying the shelves.*

taste¹ /teɪst/ **noun**
1 B1 the flavour of a particular food in your mouth: *a bitter taste* ◦ *It's got quite a strong taste.*
2 [no plural] the ability to feel different flavours in your mouth: *When you've got a cold you often lose your sense of taste.*
3 the particular things you like, such as styles of music, clothes, decoration, etc.: *I don't like his **taste in** music.*

taste² /teɪst/ **verb** (**tasting**, **tasted**)
1 taste funny, nice, sweet, etc. B1 If food tastes a particular way, it has that flavour: *This sauce tastes strange.*
2 B1 to put food or drink in your mouth to find out what its flavour is like: *I always taste food while I'm cooking it.*

tasty /ˈteɪsti/ **adj** (**tastiest**, **tastiest**)
B1 Food that is tasty has a good flavour and is nice to eat.

tattoo /tæt'uː/ **noun**
a picture on someone's skin that is put on using ink and a needle

tattoo

taught /tɔːt/
past tense and past participle of teach

tax /tæks/ **noun**
B1 money that you have to pay to the government from what you earn or when you buy things: *They're putting up the **tax on** cigarettes.*

taxi /'tæksi/ **noun**
A1 a car with a driver that you pay to take you somewhere: *I'll take a taxi to the airport.*

taxi rank /'tæksi ˌræŋk/ **noun** UK (US **taxi stand**)
a place where you can go to get a taxi

tea /tiː/ **noun**
1 A1 a hot drink that you make by pouring water onto dried leaves: *Would you like **a cup of tea** or coffee?*
2 B1 UK a small afternoon meal of cakes, biscuits, etc. and tea to drink: *They invited us for **afternoon tea**.*
3 UK the meal that you eat in the evening

teabag /'tiːbæg/ **noun**
a small paper bag with dried leaves inside, used for making tea

teach /tiːtʃ/ **verb** (**taught**)
1 A1 to give classes in a particular subject at a school, university, etc.: *He teaches history.*
2 A2 to show or explain to someone how to do something: *My dad **taught** me **to** drive.*
3 B1 If a situation teaches you something, it gives you new knowledge or helps you to understand something: *The experience **taught** him **to** be more careful.*

teacher /'tiːtʃəʳ/ **noun**
A1 someone whose job is to teach in a school, college, etc.: *a science teacher*
→ See **The Classroom** on page C4

teaching /'tiːtʃɪŋ/ **noun** [no plural]
B1 the job of being a teacher: *He decided to **go into teaching** (= become a teacher).*

team /tiːm/ **noun**
1 A2 a group of people who play a sport or game together: *a football team*
2 B1 a group of people who work together to do something: *a management team*

teapot /'tiːpɒt/ **noun**
a container used for making and serving tea

teapot

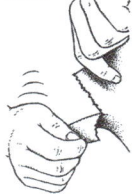

tear¹ /teəʳ/ **verb** (**tearing, tore, torn**)
1 B1 to pull paper, cloth, etc. into pieces, or to make a hole in it by accident: *The nail had **torn a hole in** my skirt.*
2 be torn between ***something*** **and** ***something*** to be unable to decide between two choices: *I'm torn between the apple pie and the tart.*

tear

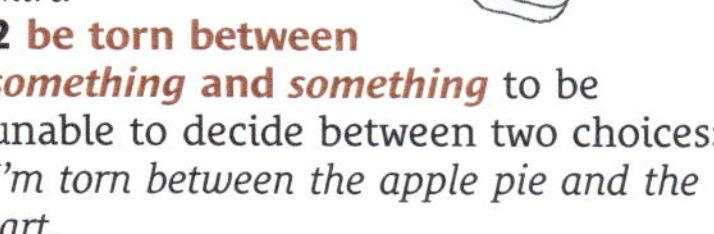

tear ***something*** **up** **phrasal verb**
to tear paper into a lot of small pieces: *He tore up her photograph.*

tear² /teəʳ/ **noun**
a hole in a piece of cloth, paper, etc. where it has been torn

tear³ /tɪəʳ/ **noun**
B1 a drop of water that comes from your eye when you cry: *I was **in tears** (= crying) by the end of the movie.* ◦ *She **burst into tears** (= started crying) when she heard the news.*

tease /tiːz/ **verb** (**teasing, teased**)
to laugh at someone or say bad things to them: *They were **teasing** Dara **about** her new haircut.*

teaspoon /'tiːspuːn/ **noun**
a small spoon that is used for mixing drinks and measuring small amounts of food

technical /'teknɪkəl/ **adj**
1 relating to the knowledge,

machines, or methods used in science and industry: *We're having a few technical problems.*
2 relating to practical skills and methods that are used in a particular activity: *As a dancer she had great technical skill.*

technician /tekˈnɪʃᵊn/ **noun**
someone whose job involves practical work with scientific or electrical equipment: *a computer technician*

technique /tekˈniːk/ **noun**
B1 a particular way of doing something: *It's a new technique for taking blood samples.*

technology /tekˈnɒlədʒi/ **noun** [no plural]
B1 knowledge, equipment, and methods that are used in science and industry: *computer technology*
• **technological** /ˌteknəˈlɒdʒɪkᵊl/ **adj** relating to, or involving technology: *technological developments*

teddy bear /ˈtedi ˌbeəʳ/ **noun**
a soft toy bear

tedious /ˈtiːdiəs/ **adj**
boring: *a tedious job*

teenage /ˈtiːneɪdʒ/ **adj**
B1 aged between 13 and 19, or suitable for people of that age: *a teenage daughter* ◦ *teenage magazines*

teenager /ˈtiːnˌeɪdʒəʳ/ **noun**
A2 someone who is between 13 and 19 years old

teens /tiːnz/ **noun** [plural]
be in your teens to be aged between 13 and 19: *Her youngest daughter is still **in her teens**.*

teeth /tiːθ/
plural of tooth

teeth

telephone[1] /ˈtelɪfəʊn/ **noun** (also **phone**)
A2 a piece of equipment that is used to talk to someone who is in another place: *The **telephone rang** and she hurried to pick it up.* ◦ *Could you **answer** the **telephone**?*
→ See **The Office** on page C12

telephone[2] /ˈtelɪfəʊn/ **verb** (**telephoning, telephoned**) (also **phone**) formal
A2 to speak to someone by telephone

telephone number /ˈtelɪfəʊn ˌnʌmbəʳ/ **noun** (also **phone number**)
the number of a particular telephone

telescope /ˈtelɪskəʊp/ **noun**
a piece of equipment, in the shape of a tube, that makes things which are far away look bigger

telescope

television /ˈtelɪvɪʒᵊn/ **noun**
1 A1 a piece of equipment with a screen on the front, used for watching programmes: *I switched the television on.*
2 A1 [no plural] the programmes that are shown on a television: *I mostly **watch television** in the evening.*
3 B1 [no plural] the system or business of making and broadcasting programmes for television: *a television company/network*

> **Common mistake: watch television**
> Be careful to choose the correct verb with **television**.
> *My children watch too much television.*
> ~~*My children look too much television.*~~

tell /tel/ **verb** (**told**)
1 A1 to say something to someone, usually giving them information: *He **told** me **about** his new school.*
2 **tell *someone* to do *something*** A2 to order someone to do something: *I told you to stay here.*
3 **can tell** to know something from what you hear, see, etc.: *You could tell that he was tired.*
tell *someone* off **phrasal verb**
to tell someone that they have done something wrong and that you are angry about it: *Darren **got told off** for talking in class.*

telly /ˈteli/ **noun** (plural **tellies**) UK informal
short form of television

temper /ˈtempəʳ/ **noun**
1 If a person has a temper, they

become angry very easily: *He's got a really **bad temper**.*
2 lose your temper (with *someone*) to suddenly become very angry: *I lost my temper with the children.*

temperature /ˈtemprətʃəʳ/ **noun**
1 A2 how hot or cold something is: *Last night the temperature dropped to below freezing.*
2 have a temperature A2 to be hotter than usual because you are ill

temple /ˈtempl/ **noun**
B1 a building where people in some religions go to pray: *a Buddhist temple*

temporary /ˈtempᵊrᵊri/ **adj**
B1 existing or happening for only a short time: *a temporary job*
• **temporarily** **adv**

tempt /tempt/ **verb**
to make someone want to have or do something that they should not: *Can I tempt you to go shopping?*

temptation /tempˈteɪʃᵊn/ **noun**
a feeling that you want to do or have something, although you know you should not

ten /ten/
A1 the number 10

tenant /ˈtenənt/ **noun**
someone who pays money to live in a room, house, etc.

tend /tend/ **verb**
tend to do *something* to often do a particular thing: *I tend to wear dark colours.*

tendency /ˈtendənsi/ **noun** (plural **tendencies**)
something that someone often does, or something that often happens: *She **has a tendency** to talk for too long.*

tender /ˈtendəʳ/ **adj**
1 kind and gentle: *a tender kiss*
2 Tender meat or vegetables are soft and easy to cut.
• **tenderly** **adv** *He kissed her tenderly on the cheek.*
• **tenderness** **noun** [no plural]

tennis /ˈtenɪs/ **noun** [no plural]
A1 a sport in which two or four people hit a small ball to each other over a net
→ See **Sports 2** on page C16

tense[1] /tens/ **adj**
1 nervous and not able to relax: *The students looked tense as they waited for their exam results.*
2 A tense situation makes you feel nervous.

tense[2] /tens/ **noun**
B1 in grammar, the form of a verb that shows the time at which an action happened. For example, 'I sing' is in the present tense and 'I sang' is in the past tense.

tension /ˈtenʃᵊn/ **noun**
1 a feeling of fear or anger between people or countries who do not trust each other: *There are increasing **tensions between** the two countries.*
2 [no plural] a feeling that you are nervous, worried, and not relaxed: *You could feel the tension in the room as we waited for our exam results.*

tent /tent/ **noun**
B1 a structure for sleeping in made of cloth fixed to metal poles: *It only took twenty minutes to **put the tent up** (= make it ready to use).*

tent

tenth[1] /tenθ/
10th written as a word

tenth[2] /tenθ/ **noun**
one of ten equal parts of something; 1/10; 0.1

term /tɜːm/ **noun**
1 A2 one of the periods of time that the school or university year is divided into: *We've got a test at the end of term.*
2 a word or phrase that is used to mean a particular thing: *a legal term*
3 a fixed period of time: *a prison term*
4 in the short/long term over a period of time that continues for a short way or a long way into the future: *In the short term we do not expect an improvement in sales.*

a b c d e f g h i j k l m n o p q r s t u v w x y z

a b c d e f g h i j k l m n o p q r s **t** u v w x y z

terminal /ˈtɜːmɪnəl/ **noun**
a building where you can get onto an plane, bus, or ship

terms /tɜːmz/ **plural noun**
1 the rules of an agreement
2 in... terms used to explain which part of a situation you mean: *In financial terms, the project was not a success.*
3 come to terms with *something* to accept a sad situation: *He still hasn't come to terms with his brother's death.*

terrace /ˈterɪs/ **noun**
1 a flat area outside a house, restaurant, etc. where you can sit
2 UK a row of houses that are joined together

terraced house /ˌterəst ˈhaʊs/ **noun** UK
one of a row of houses that are joined together

terrible /ˈterəbl/ **adj**
A2 very bad: *a terrible accident* ◦ *The weather was terrible.*

terribly /ˈterəbli/ **adv**
1 B1 very: *She was terribly upset.*
2 very badly: *I slept terribly last night.*

terrific /təˈrɪfɪk/ **adj**
B1 excellent: *I thought she looked terrific.*

terrified /ˈterəfaɪd/ **adj**
B1 very frightened: *I'm **terrified of** flying.*

terrify /ˈterəfaɪ/ **verb**
to make someone feel very frightened: *Snakes terrify me.*

terrifying /ˈterəˌfaɪɪŋ/ **adj**
very frightening: *It was a terrifying experience.*

territory /ˈterɪtəri/ **noun** (plural **territories**)
1 land that is owned or controlled by a particular country: *Canadian territory*
2 an area that an animal or person thinks belongs to them: *Cats like to protect their territory.*

terror /ˈterər/ **noun** [no plural]
a feeling of being very frightened

terrorism /ˈterərɪzəm/ **noun** [no plural]
the use of violence for political purposes, for example putting bombs in public places: *an act of terrorism*

terrorist /ˈterərɪst/ **noun**
someone who is involved in terrorism: *a terrorist attack*

test[1] /test/ **noun**
1 A1 a set of questions to find out how much someone knows or how well they can do something: *a driving test* ◦ *You have to **take a test**.*
2 B1 a short medical examination of part of your body or of something such as blood that is taken from your body: *a blood test* ◦ *The doctors have done some tests to try to find out what's wrong with her.*

test[2] /test/ **verb**
1 B1 to give someone a set of questions in order to find out how much they know or how well they can do something: *You'll be **tested on** all the subjects we've studied this term.*
2 to do a medical examination of part of someone's body: *I'm going to get my hearing tested.*

text[1] /tekst/ **noun**
1 A2 a message in writing sent from one mobile phone to another: *I sent her a text.*
2 B1 [no plural] the written words in a book, magazine, etc., not the pictures: *a page of text*
3 B1 a short piece of writing that you discuss in class: *Read the text on page 34.*

text[2] **verb**
A2 to send a text from a mobile phone: *Text me when you get there.*

textbook /ˈtekstbʊk/ **noun**
A2 a book about a particular subject, written for students: *a chemistry textbook*
→ See **The Classroom** on page C4

text message /ˈtekst ˌmesɪdʒ/ **noun**
a message in writing sent from one mobile phone to another

texture /ˈtekstʃər/ **noun**
the way that something feels when you touch it: *wood with a rough texture*

than strong /ðæn/ weak /ðᵊn/ **preposition, conjunction**
A1 used to compare two different things or amounts: *Sue's car is bigger than mine.* ◦ *It cost less than I expected.*

thank /θæŋk/ **verb**
A2 to tell someone that you are pleased about something they have given you or done for you: *I must **thank** her **for** her present.*

thanks /θæŋks/ **exclamation** informal
1 A1 used to tell someone that you are pleased about something they have given you or done for you: *Can you pass me the book? Thanks very much.* ◦ ***Thanks for** all your help.*
2 **no, thanks** A2 used to refuse someone's offer: *'Would you like a cup of coffee?' 'No, thanks.'*

thank you¹ /ˈθæŋk ˌjuː/ **exclamation**
1 A1 used to tell someone that you are pleased about something they have given you or done for you: ***Thank you** very much **for** the birthday card.* ◦ *'Here's the money I promised you.' 'Thank you.'*
2 **no, thank you** A2 used to refuse someone's offer: *'Would you like something to eat?' 'No, thank you.'*

thank you² /ˈθæŋk ˌjuː/ **noun**
B1 something that you say or do in order to show that you are grateful for something: *I'd like to say a big thank you to everyone for all their help.* ◦ *a thank-you letter*

that¹ strong /ðæt/ weak /ðət/ **conjunction**
1 A2 used after some verbs, nouns, and adjectives to start a new part of a sentence: *He said that he'd collect it later.*
2 B1 used instead of 'who' or 'which' in the middle of a sentence: *Have you eaten all the cake that I made yesterday?*

that² /ðæt/ **determiner** (plural **those**)
1 A1 used to mean something or someone that has already been talked about or seen: *Did you see that woman in the post office?* ◦ *How much are those shoes?*
2 A1 used to mean something or someone that is not near you: *Have you seen that man over there?*

that³ /ðæt/ **pronoun**
1 A1 used to mean something that has already been talked about or seen: *That looks heavy.*
2 A1 used to mean something that is not near you: *What's that in the corner?*
3 A2 used to make a connection with an earlier statement: *My train was cancelled. That's why I'm late.*
4 **that's it** used to say that something is correct: *You need to push the two pieces together. That's it.*

Common mistake: this/these or that/those?

Use **this** or **these** to talk about people and things that are close to the speaker.
This is my sister Sarah.
Do you like these earrings I'm wearing?
Use **that** or **those** to talk about people and things that are further away from the speaker.
That girl over there is called Sarah.
I liked those earrings you wore last night.

Common mistake: that's

Remember that **that's** is always written with an apostrophe.

thaw /θɔː/ **verb**
to become warmer and softer, or to change to liquid: *Allow the meat to thaw before cooking it.*

the weak /ðə/, /ði/ strong /ðiː/ **determiner**
1 A1 used before nouns to mean things or people that have already been talked about or are already known: *Can you pass the salt?* ◦ *I'll pick you up at the station.*
2 A1 used before nouns when only one of something exists: *the Eiffel Tower* ◦ *the world*
3 used before some adjectives to make them into nouns: *a home for the elderly*
4 used before numbers that refer to dates: *Thursday the 29th of April*

theatre UK (US **theater**) /ˈθɪətəʳ/ **noun**
A2 a building with a stage where

a b c d e f g h i j k l m n o p q r s t u v w x y z

people go to watch plays: *the Arts Theatre*

theft /θeft/ **noun**
the action or crime of stealing something: *car theft*

their /ðeəʳ/ **determiner**
A1 belonging to or relating to them: *It was their problem, not mine.*

theirs /ðeəz/ **pronoun**
A2 the things that belong or relate to them: *I think she's a friend of theirs.*

them strong /ðem/ weak /ðəm/ **pronoun**
A1 the group of people, animals, or things that have already been talked about: *I'm looking for my keys – have you seen them?*

theme /θiːm/ **noun**
the subject of a book, movie, speech, etc.: *The theme of loss is present in most of his novels.*

theme park /ˈθiːm ˌpɑːk/ **noun**
a park with entertainments, such as machines to ride on, that is often based on one idea

themselves /ðəmˈselvz/ **pronoun**
1 A2 used to show that the people who do the action are also the people who are affected by it: *They're both old enough to look after themselves.*
2 (all) by themselves A2 alone or without anyone else's help: *The children arranged the party all by themselves.*
3 used to give more attention to the word 'them': *They've decided to run the club themselves.*

then /ðen/ **adv**
1 A1 at that time: *Call me tomorrow – I'll have time to speak then.*
2 A1 next, or after something has happened: *Let me finish, then we'll go.*
3 A2 so or because of that: *Have a rest now, then you won't be tired this evening.*

theory /ˈθɪəri/ **noun** (plural **theories**)
an idea or set of ideas that explains something: *Darwin's theory of evolution*

therapy /ˈθerəpi/ **noun** (plural **therapies**)
the work of treating mental or physical illness without using an operation: *He is **having therapy** to help him after his wife's death.*

there¹ strong /ðeəʳ/ weak /ðəʳ/ **pronoun**
there is, are, was, etc. A1 used to show that something exists or happens: *There are three schools in the town.* ◦ *Is there any milk?*

there² /ðeəʳ/ **adv**
1 A1 in or at a particular place: *We live in York because my wife works there.*
2 A1 used when you are pointing at something in order to make someone look somewhere: *Put them in that box there.*
3 A2 used when you are giving something to someone: *There's some money for your ticket.* ◦ *'Can I have a pen?' '**There you are.**'*

therefore /ˈðeəfɔːʳ/ **adv**
B1 for that reason: *There has been an accident on the road and people are therefore asked to avoid it.*

thermometer /θəˈmɒmɪtəʳ/ **noun**
a piece of equipment that shows how hot or cold something is

thermometer

these /ðiːz/ **pronoun, determiner**
A1 plural of this

thesis /ˈθiːsɪs/ **noun** (plural **theses** /ˈθiːsiːz/)
a long piece of writing that you do as part of an advanced university course: *I'm writing my thesis on Spanish literature.*

they /ðeɪ/ **pronoun**
1 A1 used as the subject of the verb when meaning a group of people, animals, or things that have already been talked about: *I saw Kate and Nick yesterday – they came over for dinner.*
2 B1 used to refer to a person when you want to avoid saying 'he' or 'she' or when you do not know if the

person is male or female: *If anybody comes, they can wait in the hall.*
3 people in general: *They say that money can't buy happiness.*

they'd /ðeɪd/
1 short form of they had: *They'd just left when I arrived.*
2 they would: *They'd like to take us out to dinner.*

they'll /ðeɪl/
short form of they will: *They'll be in Scotland next week.*

they're /ðeəʳ/
short form of they are: *They're both from Washington.*

they've /ðeɪv/
short form of they have: *They've got three children – two girls and a boy.*

thick /θɪk/ **adj**
1 B1 Something that is thick is larger than usual between its opposite sides: *a thick layer of snow*
→ Opposite **thin** adj

thick

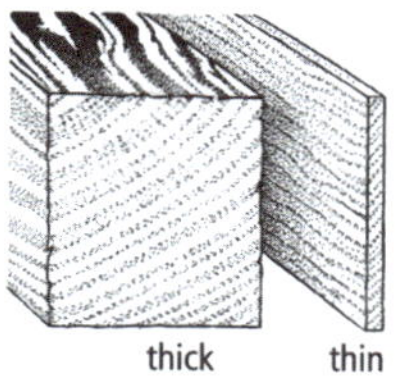

2 **10 cm, 2 m, etc. thick** being 10 cm, 2 m, etc. thick: *a piece of wood 2 cm thick*
3 B1 growing very close together and in large amounts: *thick, dark hair*
4 Thick smoke, cloud, or fog is difficult to see through: *Thick, black smoke was pouring out of the chimney.*
5 UK informal not intelligent

thief /θi:f/ **noun** (plural **thieves** /θi:vz/)
B1 someone who steals things: *a car thief*

thigh /θaɪ/ **noun**
the top part of your leg above your knee
→ See **The Body** on page C2

thin /θɪn/ **adj** (**thinner, thinnest**)
1 A2 Something that is thin is smaller than usual between its opposite sides: *a thin slice of meat*
→ Opposite **thick** adj
2 A2 A thin person or animal has very little fat on their body.
3 A thin substance or liquid has a lot of water in it: *thin soup*

thing /θɪŋ/ **noun**
1 A1 used to mean an object without saying its name: *I need to get a few things in town.*
2 A2 a fact or characteristic of someone or something: *The best thing about the holiday was the food.*
3 **a thing** B1 used instead of 'anything' in order to emphasize what you are saying: *I haven't got a thing to wear.*
4 used to refer to an idea or comment: *I just want to forget the whole thing.*
5 used to refer to an activity or event: *Meeting Nina was the best thing that's ever happened to me.*
6 **thing to do/say** something that is done or said: *What a silly thing to do.*

things /θɪŋz/ **plural noun**
1 A1 the objects that you own: *I'll just get my things and then I'll be ready.*
2 B1 what is happening, especially in your life: *How are things with you?*

think /θɪŋk/ **verb** (**thought**)
1 A1 to believe that something is true, or to expect that something will happen, although you are not sure: *I think we've met before.* ◦ *Do you think it's going to rain?*
2 A1 to have an opinion about some-

Common mistake: think about or think of?

Think about someone/something means to have thoughts in your mind about a person or thing, or to consider them.
I was thinking about my mother.
I thought about the question before answering.
~~*I thought the question before answering.*~~

Think of/about something/someone also means to have an opinion about something or someone.
What do you think of/about the colour?
~~*What do you think the colour?*~~

Think of doing something means to consider the possibility of doing something.
We are thinking of having a party.
~~*We are thinking to have a party.*~~

thing or someone: *What did you **think of** the show?*
3 B1 to use the brain to plan something, solve a problem, understand a situation, etc.: *He thought for a few seconds before answering.*
think about/of *someone/something* **phrasal verb**
1 A2 to consider doing something: *I'm thinking of moving to Sydney.*
2 B1 to remember someone or something: *I was just thinking about you when you phoned.*
think *something* over **phrasal verb**
to consider an idea or plan carefully before making a decision: *I'll think it over and give you an answer next week.*
think *something* through **phrasal verb**
to carefully consider the possible results of doing something: *It sounds like a good idea, but we need to think it through.*

third[1] /θɜːd/
A2 3rd written as a word

third[2] /θɜːd/ **noun**
one of three equal parts of something; 1/3

thirst /θɜːst/ **noun** [no plural]
the feeling that you want to drink something

thirsty /ˈθɜːsti/ **adj** (**thirstier, thirstiest**)
A2 wanting or needing a drink: *I felt really hot and thirsty after my run.*

thirteen /θɜːˈtiːn/
A1 the number 13

thirteenth /θɜːˈtiːnθ/
13th written as a word

thirties /ˈθɜːtiz/ **plural noun**
1 the thirties the years from 1930 to 1939: *Our house was built **in the thirties**.*
2 be in your thirties to be aged between 30 and 39: *My brother is **in his thirties**.*

thirty /ˈθɜːti/
A2 the number 30
• **thirtieth** 30th written as a word

this[1] /ðɪs/ **determiner**
1 A1 used to mean something that you have already talked about: *Most people don't agree with this decision.*
2 A1 used to mean something or someone that is near you or that you are pointing to: *How much does this DVD cost?*
3 A1 used to mean the present week, month, year, etc. or the one that comes next: *I'll see you this evening.*

this[2] /ðɪs/ **pronoun**
1 A2 used to mean something that you have already talked about: *When did this happen?*
2 A2 used to mean something or someone that is near you or that you are pointing to: *This is my girlfriend, Beth.*
3 A2 used to refer to something that is happening or something that you are doing: *This is how you prepare the fish.*

thorough /ˈθʌrə/ **adj**
careful and covering every detail: *She wrote a very thorough report on the matter.*

thoroughly /ˈθʌrəli/ **adv**
1 very carefully: *Wash the fruit thoroughly.*
2 very, or very much: *We thoroughly enjoyed ourselves.*

those /ðəʊz/ **pronoun, determiner**
A1 plural of that: *These apples look much nicer than those.* ◦ *I want those shoes.*

though[1] /ðəʊ/ **conjunction**
1 B1 used before a fact or opinion that makes the other part of the sentence surprising: *And though she's quite small, she's very strong.* ◦ *Nina didn't phone, **even though** she said she would.*
2 but: *They're coming next week, though I don't know when.*

though[2] /ðəʊ/ **adv**
used especially at the end of a sentence to add a fact or opinion to what you have just said: *Okay, I'll come. I'm not staying late though.*

thought[1] /θɔːt/
past tense and past participle of think

thought[2] /θɔːt/ **noun**
1 B1 an idea or opinion: *The thought*

of seeing her again filled him with happiness.
2 [no plural] the activity of thinking: *You'll need to **give** the matter some **thought**.*

thoughtful /ˈθɔːtfᵊl/ **adj**
kind and always thinking about how you can help other people: *Thank you for the card – it was very **thoughtful of** you.* ◦ *She's a very thoughtful person.*

thousand /ˈθaʊzᵊnd/
1 A2 the number 1,000: *There were over **a thousand** people in the audience.* ◦ *There are **one thousand** grams in a kilogram.*
2 thousands informal a lot: ***Thousands of** homes were destroyed by the storm.*

thousandth¹ /ˈθaʊzᵊndθ/
1000th written as a word

thousandth² /ˈθaʊzᵊndθ/ **noun**
one of a thousand equal parts of something; 1/1000; .001: *a thousandth of a second*

thread /θred/ **noun**
a long, thin piece of cotton, wool, etc. that is used for sewing: *a needle and thread*

threat /θret/ **noun**
a statement that you will harm or punish someone if that person does not not do what you want: *a death threat*

threaten /ˈθretᵊn/ **verb**
to tell someone that you will do something bad to them if they do not do what you want: *He **threatened to** report her to the police.*

three /θriː/
A1 the number 3

threw /θruː/
past tense of throw

thrill /θrɪl/ **noun**
a strong feeling of excitement and pleasure: *It was a big thrill meeting the stars of the show.*

thrilled /θrɪld/ **adj**
very excited and pleased: *She was thrilled with your present.*

thriller /ˈθrɪləʳ/ **noun**
B1 a book or movie with an exciting story, often about crime

thrilling /ˈθrɪlɪŋ/ **adj**
very exciting: *It was a thrilling game.*

throat /θrəʊt/ **noun**
1 B1 the back part of your mouth and the part inside your neck: *a sore throat*
2 the front of your neck: *He grabbed her round the throat.*
→ See **The Body** on page C2

throne /θrəʊn/ **noun**
the special chair that a king or queen sits on

through /θruː/ **preposition**
1 A2 from one end or side of something to the other: *The River Seine flows through Paris.*
2 B1 from the start to the end of something: *He worked through the night.*
3 B1 because of someone or something, or with someone's help: *She got the job through hard work.*
4 US (UK **to**) from one time until another time: *The store is open Monday through Friday.*

throughout /θruˈaʊt/ **adv, preposition**
1 in every part of a place: *The same laws apply throughout much of Europe.*
2 during the whole of a period of time: *He yawned throughout the performance.*

throw

throw /θrəʊ/ **verb** (**threw**, **thrown**)
A2 to make something move through the air by pushing it out of your hand: *Amy **threw** the ball **to** the dog.*
throw *something* away phrasal verb
B1 to get rid of something that you

a b c d e f g h i j k l m n o p q r s t u v w x y z

do not want any more: *He read the magazine and then threw it away.*

thud /θʌd/ **noun**
the sound that is made when something heavy falls: *There was a thud as he fell on the floor.*

thug /θʌg/ **noun**
a bad person who behaves violently

thumb /θʌm/ **noun**
B1 the short, thick finger on the side of your hand
→ See **The Body** on page C2

thumbtack /ˈθʌmtæk/ **noun** US (UK **drawing pin**)
a pin with a wide, flat top, used for fastening pieces of paper to a wall

thump /θʌmp/ **verb** UK
to hit someone with your fist (= closed hand)

thunder /ˈθʌndəʳ/ **noun** [no plural]
B1 the loud noise in the sky that you hear during a storm: *thunder and lightning*

thunderstorm /ˈθʌndəstɔːm/ **noun**
A2 a storm that has thunder (= loud noise) and lightning (= sudden flashes of light in the sky)

Thursday /ˈθɜːzdeɪ/ **noun**
A1 the day of the week after Wednesday and before Friday

thus /ðʌs/ **adv** formal
1 used to say what happened as a result: *The guard fell asleep, thus allowing the prisoner to escape.*
2 in this way: *They limit the number of people allowed into the forest, thus preventing damage to the trails.*

tick¹ /tɪk/ **noun**
1 the sound that a clock or watch makes every second
2 B1 UK (US **check**) a mark (✓) that shows something is correct or has been done

tick² /tɪk/ **verb**
1 If a clock or watch ticks, it makes a sound every second.
2 B1 UK to put a mark (✓) by something to show that it is correct or has been done

ticket /ˈtɪkɪt/ **noun**

ticket

1 A1 a small piece of paper that shows you have paid to do something, for example travel on a bus, watch a movie, etc.: *a lottery ticket* ◦ *plane tickets* ◦ *a* ***ticket machine*** *(= where you can buy tickets)*
2 an official notice that says you must pay a fine because you have parked in an illegal place, driven too fast, etc.: *I* ***got*** *a* ***ticket for*** *speeding.*

ticket office /ˈtɪkɪt ˌɒfɪs/ **noun**
a place where you can buy a ticket

tickle /ˈtɪkl/ **verb** (**tickling**, **tickled**)
to touch someone lightly with your fingers, in order to make them laugh

tide /taɪd/ **noun**
the regular rise and fall in the level of the sea: *high/low tide*

tidy¹ /ˈtaɪdi/ **adj** (**tidier**, **tidiest**)
A2 having everything in the right place and arranged in good order: *Her room was clean and tidy.*

tidy² /ˈtaɪdi/ **verb** (**tidying**, **tidied**) (also **tidy up**) UK
A2 to make a place tidy: *I'm tidying up before our guests arrive.*

tie

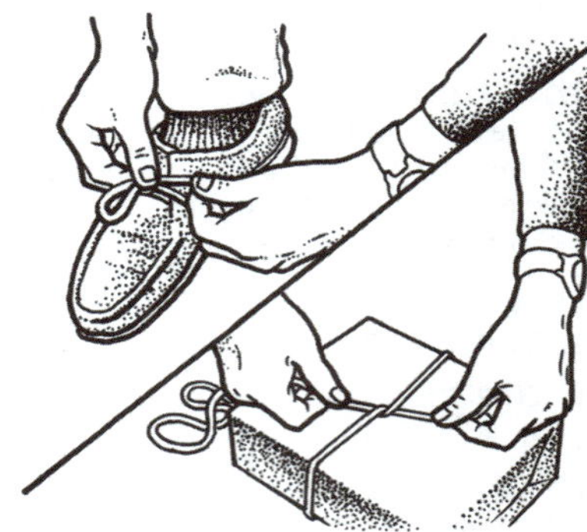

tie¹ /taɪ/ **verb** (**tying**, **tied**)
1 B1 to fasten something with string, rope, etc.: *She gave me a pretty box tied with a red ribbon.* ◦ *The dog was tied to a tree.*

a b c d e f g h i j k l m n o p q r s t u v w x y z

2 B1 to make a knot in a piece of string, rope, etc.: *She tied the scarf.*
→ Opposite **untie** verb

tie *something* up phrasal verb
to fasten something together using string, rope, etc.

tie² /taɪ/ **noun**
A2 a long, thin piece of cloth that a man wears around his neck with a shirt
→ See **Clothes** on page C5

tiger /ˈtaɪɡəʳ/ **noun**
B1 a large wild cat that has yellow fur with black lines on it

tight /taɪt/ **adj**
1 B1 fitting your body very closely: *a tight skirt*
→ Opposite **loose** adj
2 firm and difficult to move: *Make sure the knot is tight.*
3 strongly controlled and obeying all rules completely: *They kept tight control of the budget.*
• **tightly** adv

tighten /ˈtaɪtᵊn/ **verb**
to become tighter or to make something become tighter: *His hand tightened around her arm.*

tights /taɪts/ **plural noun**
a piece of women's clothing made of very thin material that fits tightly over the legs and bottom
→ See **Clothes** on page C5

tile /taɪl/ **noun**
one of the flat, square pieces that are used for covering roofs, floors, or walls
• **tile** verb (**tiling**, **tiled**) *a tiled kitchen*

till¹ /tɪl/ **preposition**, **conjunction**
A2 until: *The supermarket is open till midnight.*

till² /tɪl/ **noun** UK
a machine that holds the money in a shop

tilt /tɪlt/ **verb**
to move into a position where one end or side is higher than the other: *He tilted backwards on his chair.*

time¹ /taɪm/ **noun**
1 A1 a particular point in the day or night: *What time is it?* ◦ *What time do you leave for school in the mornings?*
2 A2 [no plural] Time is what we measure in minutes, hours, days, etc.: *He wants to **spend** more **time** with his family.*
3 A2 a period of minutes, hours, years, etc.: *I lived in Switzerland for a long time.*
4 A2 an occasion when something happens: *How many times have you been to Germany?*
5 all the time A2 very often: *It happens all the time.*
6 have time A2 to have enough time to do something: *I never have time to eat breakfast.*
7 it's time for/to do *something* B1 used to say that something should happen or be done now: *It's time to get up.*
8 on time B1 not early or late: *I got to school on time.*
9 in time B1 early or at the right time: *We arrived **in time to** catch the train.*
10 at the same time B1 If two things happen at the same time, they happen together: *We arrived at the same time.*
11 in a day's, two months', etc. time B1 a week, two months, etc. from now: *I have to go to the doctor again in a month's time.*
12 three, nine, etc. times B1 used to say how much bigger, better, etc. one thing is than another thing: *Ben earns three times more than me.*
13 in no time very soon: *We'll be home in no time.*
14 at times sometimes: *At times, I wish I didn't have to go to school.*
15 from time to time sometimes, but not often: *I still see my ex-boyfriend from time to time.*
• **take your time** to do something without hurrying

time² /taɪm/ **verb** (**timing**, **timed**)
to measure how long it takes for something to happen: *It's a good idea to time yourself on the exercises.*

times /taɪmz/ **preposition**
used to say that one number is multi-

plied by another number: *Two times three is six.*

timetable /ˈtaɪmˌteɪbl/ **noun**
1 A2 a list of dates and times that shows when things will happen
2 B1 mainly UK (US usually **schedule**) a list of times when buses, trains, etc. arrive and leave
3 B1 mainly UK (US usually **schedule**) a list of the times and days of lessons at a school, college, etc.
→ See **The Classroom** on page C4

timid /ˈtɪmɪd/ **adj**
shy and easily frightened: *a timid little boy*
• **timidly adv**

tin /tɪn/ **noun** UK
1 B1 (US **can**) a metal container in which food is sold: *a tin of soup*
→ See picture at **container**
2 a metal container with a lid that you keep food or other substances in: *a biscuit tin*

tinned /tɪnd/ **adj** UK (US **canned**)
Tinned food is sold in metal containers.

tin opener /ˈtɪn ˌəʊpənəʳ/ **noun** UK (US **can opener**)
a piece of kitchen equipment for opening metal food containers
→ See **The Kitchen** on page C10

tiny /ˈtaɪni/ **adj** (**tinier**, **tiniest**)
B1 very small: *a tiny baby*

tip¹ /tɪp/ **noun**
1 the end of something long and narrow: *the tips of your fingers*
2 B1 a piece of useful advice: *gardening tips*
3 B1 an extra amount of money that you give to someone such as a driver to thank him or her for a service: *We left a big tip because the waiter was so friendly.*

tip² /tɪp/ **verb** (**tipping**, **tipped**)
1 to move so that one side is higher than the other side: *The table tipped and all the drinks fell on the floor.*
2 to make the contents of a container fall out by turning the container over: *She tipped the contents of her purse onto the table.*
3 to give an extra amount of money to someone such as a driver to thank him or her for a service

tiptoe¹ /ˈtɪptəʊ/ **noun**
on tiptoe standing on your toes

tiptoe² /ˈtɪptəʊ/ **verb** (**tiptoeing**, **tiptoed**)
to walk quietly on your toes

tire /taɪəʳ/ **noun** US (UK **tyre**)
a thick, round piece of rubber filled with air that fits around a wheel
→ See **Car** on page C3

tired /taɪəd/ **adj**
1 A1 feeling that you want to rest or sleep: *I'm too tired to go out tonight.* ◦ *He was **tired out** (= very tired) by the end of the day.*
2 tired of doing *something* B1 bored or angry about something that has happened too often: *I'm tired of listening to her problems.*
• **tiredness noun** [no plural]

tiring /ˈtaɪərɪŋ/ **adj**
B1 making you feel tired: *a long and tiring day*

tissue /ˈtɪʃuː/ **noun**
1 B1 a soft piece of paper that you use for cleaning your nose
2 the material that animals and plants are made of: *human brain tissue*

title /ˈtaɪtl/ **noun**
1 B1 the name of a book, movie, etc.
2 a word such as 'Lord', 'Dr', etc. that is used before someone's name

to¹ /tə/
1 A1 used with a verb to make the infinitive: *I want to learn Spanish.*
2 A2 used to give the reason for doing something: *I'm just going out to get some milk.*

to² strong /tuː/ weak /tʊ/, /tə/ **preposition**
1 A1 in the direction of somewhere: *I ran to the door.*
2 A2 used to show who gets something: *Could you give these keys to Pete?*
3 from... to... A2 used to give information about periods of time and distances: *The museum is open from Monday to Saturday.* ◦ *The bus goes from London to Cambridge.*

4 A1 used to say 'before' the hour when you are saying what time it is: *It's five to three.*
5 B1 used to say who is treated in a particular way or who or what is affected by something: *She was very kind to us.*

toad /təʊd/ **noun**
a small, brown animal with long back legs for swimming and jumping

toast /təʊst/ **noun** [no plural]
A2 bread that has been heated to make it brown: *a slice of toast*

toaster /ˈtəʊstəʳ/ **noun**
a machine that heats bread so that it becomes brown
→ See **The Kitchen** on page C10

tobacco /təˈbækəʊ/ **noun** [no plural]
dried leaves that are inside cigarettes

today /təˈdeɪ/ **noun** [no plural], **adv**
1 A1 this day, or on this day: *It's Jack's birthday today.* ◦ *Today is Friday.*
2 A1 the period of time that is happening now or in this period of time: *More young people smoke today than in the past.*

toddler /ˈtɒdləʳ/ **noun**
a child who has just learned to walk

toe /təʊ/ **noun**
A2 one of the five separate parts at the end of your foot
→ See **The Body** on page C2

toenail /ˈtəʊneɪl/ **noun**
one of the hard, flat parts on top of the end of your toes: *I need to* ***cut*** *my* ***toenails****.*

toffee /ˈtɒfi/ **noun**
a sticky, brown sweet

together /təˈgeðəʳ/ **adv**
1 A1 with each other: *They live together.*
2 in the same place or close to each other: *We all sat together.*
3 B1 at the same time: *We can deal with both problems together.*

toilet /ˈtɔɪlət/ **noun**
1 A1 a bowl that you sit on or stand near when you get rid of waste substances from your body
→ See **The Bathroom** on page C1
2 A2 UK (US **bathroom**) a room with a toilet in it
3 **go to the toilet** A2 to use the toilet: *I need to go to the toilet.*

toilet paper /ˈtɔɪlət ˌpeɪpəʳ/ **noun** [no plural]
paper used for cleaning your body after you have used the toilet
→ See **The Bathroom** on page C1

told /təʊld/
past tense and past participle of tell

tolerate /ˈtɒlᵊreɪt/ **verb**
to accept or allow something although you do not like it: *We will not tolerate racism of any sort.*

tomato /təˈmɑːtəʊ/ **noun** (plural **tomatoes**)
A1 a soft, round, red fruit eaten in salads or as a vegetable
→ See **Fruit and Vegetables** on page C8

tomb /tuːm/ **noun**
a place where a dead person is buried

tombstone /ˈtuːmstəʊn/ **noun**
a stone that shows the name of a dead person who is buried under it

tomorrow /təˈmɒrəʊ/ **noun** [no plural], **adv**
1 A1 the day after today or on the day after today: *It's my birthday tomorrow.*
2 A1 the future, or in the future: *the children of tomorrow*

ton /tʌn/ **noun** (plural **tons**, **ton**)
a unit for measuring weight, equal to 1016 kilograms in the UK and 907 kilograms in the US

tone /təʊn/ **noun**
the quality of a sound, especially of someone's voice: *I knew by her* ***tone of voice*** *that she was serious.*

tongue /tʌŋ/ **noun**
B1 the soft thing inside your mouth that you use for tasting and speaking

tonight /təˈnaɪt/ **noun** [no plural], **adv**
A1 the night of this day, or during the night of this day: *What are you doing tonight?*

a b c d e f g h i j k l m n o p q r s t u v w x y z

tonne /tʌn/ **noun** (plural **tonnes**, **tonne**) UK
a metric ton (= unit for measuring weight, equal to 1000 kilograms)

too /tuː/ **adv**
1 too small, heavy, much, etc. A1 used before adjectives and adverbs to mean 'more than is allowed, necessary, possible, etc.': *It's too late.* ◦ *The movie was too long.*
2 A1 also: *Do you know Jason too?*
3 not too A2 used before adjectives and adverbs to mean 'not very': *I didn't play too well today.*

took /tʊk/
past tense of take

tool /tuːl/ **noun**
a piece of equipment that you use with your hands in order to help you do something

tooth /tuːθ/ **noun** (plural **teeth**)
A1 one of the hard, white things in your mouth that you use for biting: *You should* ***brush*** *your* ***teeth*** *twice a day.*

toothache /ˈtuːθeɪk/ **noun** [no plural]
A2 a pain in one of your teeth

toothbrush /ˈtuːθbrʌʃ/ **noun**
A2 a small brush that you use to clean your teeth

toothbrush

toothpaste /ˈtuːθpeɪst/ **noun** [no plural]
B1 a substance that you use to clean your teeth
→ See **The Bathroom** on page C1

top¹ /tɒp/ **noun**
1 A2 the highest part of something: *They were waiting for him* ***at the top of*** *the stairs.*
2 the lid or cover of a container, pen, etc.: *Put the top back on the bottle.*
3 B1 a piece of women's clothing worn on the upper part of the body

top² /tɒp/ **adj**
1 B1 the best, most important, or most successful: *He's one of the country's top athletes.*
2 B1 at the highest part of something: *I can't reach the top shelf.*

topic /ˈtɒpɪk/ **noun**
B1 a subject that you talk or write about

the Torah /ˈtɔːrə/ **noun**
the first five books of the Jewish bible, or all of the Jewish law and tradition

torch /tɔːtʃ/ **noun**
1 UK (US **flashlight**) a small electric light that you hold in your hand
2 a long stick with material that burns tied to the top of it

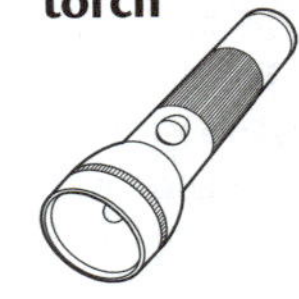

tore /tɔːʳ/
past tense of tear

torn /tɔːn/
past participle of tear

tornado /tɔːˈneɪdəʊ/ **noun** (plural **tornadoes**)
an extremely strong wind that blows in a circle

torrent /ˈtɒrᵊnt/ **noun**
a torrent of *something* a lot of something bad: *a torrent of abuse*

torrential /təˈrenʃᵊl/ **adj**
Torrential rain is very heavy rain.

tortoise /ˈtɔːtəs/ **noun**
a slow animal with a thick, hard shell

torture¹ /ˈtɔːtʃəʳ/ **verb** (**torturing**, **tortured**)
to cause someone pain, often in order to make them tell you something

torture² /ˈtɔːtʃəʳ/ **noun**
1 an act of causing someone pain
2 a very unpleasant experience: *I had to listen to her for hours – it was torture!*

toss /tɒs/ **verb**
to throw something somewhere carelessly: *He read the letter quickly, then tossed it into the bin.*

total¹ /ˈtəʊtəl/ **adj**
1 B1 including everything: *The total cost of the work was $800.*
2 extreme or complete: *The whole evening was a total disaster.*

total² /ˈtəʊtəl/ **noun**
B1 the amount you get when you add several smaller amounts together: *The total came to £762.*

totally /ˈtəʊtəli/ **adv**
B1 completely: *They look totally different.*

touch¹ /tʌtʃ/ **verb**
1 B1 to put your hand on something: *You can look at them but please don't touch them.*
2 If two things touch, they are so close to each other that there is no space between them: *These two wires must not touch.*
3 to feel pleased because someone has been kind to you: *I was deeply touched by her letter.*

touch² /tʌtʃ/ **noun**
1 the act of putting your hand on something: *I felt the touch of his hand on my face.*
2 [no plural] the ability to feel things by putting your hand on them: *It was cold **to the touch** (= when I touched it).*
3 get in touch B1 to contact someone: *I've been trying to **get in touch with** her.*
4 keep in touch B1 to often speak to someone or write to them
5 lose touch to stop speaking with someone or writing to them: *We've lost touch over the years.*

tough /tʌf/ **adj**
1 difficult: *Starting a new job can be tough.*
2 not easily damaged, cut, etc.: *Children's shoes have to be tough.*
3 strong and not afraid of violence: *a tough guy*
4 describes food that is difficult to cut or eat: *This steak is very tough.*

tour¹ /tʊəʳ/ **noun**
A2 a visit to and around a place, area, or country: *a tour of Europe*

tour² /tʊəʳ/ **verb**
B1 to travel around a place for pleasure: *to tour the States*

tour guide /ˈtʊə ˌgaɪd/ **noun**
A2 someone whose job is to show visitors a place or area: *Our tour guide explained the church's history.*

tourism /ˈtʊərɪzəm/ **noun** [no plural]
B1 the business of providing services for tourists

tourist /ˈtʊərɪst/ **noun**
A2 someone who visits a place for pleasure and does not live there

tournament /ˈtʊənəmənt/ **noun**
B1 a competition: *a tennis tournament*

tow /təʊ/ **verb**
to pull a car, boat, etc.: *His car was **towed away** by the police.*

towards /təˈwɔːdz/ **preposition** mainly UK (US usually **toward**)
1 B1 in the direction of someone or something: *She stood up and walked towards him.*
2 near to a time or place: *Your seats are towards the back of the theatre.*

towel /taʊəl/ **noun**
A2 a soft piece of cloth or paper that you use for drying yourself: *a bath towel*
→ See **The Bathroom** on page C1

tower /taʊəʳ/ **noun**
B1 a very tall, narrow building, or part of a building: *a church tower*

town /taʊn/ **noun**
1 A1 a place where people live and work that is larger than a village: *It's a small town in the north of England.*
2 A2 the central area of a town where the shops are: *I usually go into town on a Saturday.* ◦ *Let's meet in town.*

town hall /ˌtaʊn ˈhɔːl/ **noun**
a large building where a town's local government is based

toxic /ˈtɒksɪk/ **adj**
poisonous: *toxic chemicals*

toy /tɔɪ/ **noun**
A2 an object for children to play with: *a toy car*

trace¹ /treɪs/ **verb** (**tracing**, **traced**)
to find someone or something that

was lost: *Police are trying to trace the missing woman.*

trace² /treɪs/ **noun**
proof that someone or something was in a place: *There was no trace of her anywhere.*

track¹ /træk/ **noun**
1 B1 a narrow path or road: *We followed a dirt track off the main road.*
2 B1 a path, often circular, used for races: *a race track*
3 the long metal lines that a train travels along
4 a mark or line of marks left on the ground or on another surface by an animal, person, or vehicle that has moved over it: *The hunters followed the tracks of the deer.*
5 one song or piece of music on a CD, record, etc.
6 lose track to not know what is happening to someone or something any more: *I've lost track of how much we've spent.*

track² /træk/ **verb**
to follow a person or animal: *Scientists are tracking the wildlife in the valley.*

tracksuit /ˈtræksuːt/ **noun** UK
B1 loose, comfortable clothes, usually trousers and a top, especially worn for exercising

tractor /ˈtræktər/ **noun**
a strong vehicle with large back wheels, used on farms for pulling things

trade¹ /treɪd/ **noun**
1 B1 [no plural] the buying and selling of large numbers of things, especially between countries: *a trade agreement*
2 a type of business: *the tourist trade*
3 someone's job: *He's a builder **by trade**.*

trade² /treɪd/ **verb** (**trading**, **traded**)
to buy and sell things, especially between countries: *Do you **trade with** Asia?*

trade union /ˌtreɪd ˈjuːnjən/ **noun**
(also **union**) an organization that represents people who do a particular job

tradition /trəˈdɪʃən/ **noun**
a custom or way of behaving that has continued for a long time in a group of people: *There is a great tradition of dance in St Petersburg.*

traditional /trəˈdɪʃənəl/ **adj**
B1 following the customs or ways of behaving that have continued in a group of people for a long time: *traditional farming methods*
• **traditionally adv**

traffic /ˈtræfɪk/ **noun** [no plural]
A2 the cars, trucks, etc. using a road: *Sorry we're late – we got stuck in traffic.*

traffic jam /ˈtræfɪk ˌdʒæm/ **noun**
B1 a line of cars, trucks, etc. that are moving slowly

traffic light /ˈtræfɪk ˌlaɪt/ **noun**
A2 a set of red, green, and yellow lights that is used to stop and start traffic
→ See picture at **light noun**

traffic warden /ˈtræfɪk ˌwɔːdən/ **noun** UK
someone whose job is to make sure people do not leave their cars in places where it is not allowed

tragedy /ˈtrædʒədi/ **noun** (plural **tragedies**)
something very sad that happens, usually involving death: *the tragedy of their daughter's death*

tragic /ˈtrædʒɪk/ **adj**
very sad, often involving death: *a tragic accident*
• **tragically adv**

trail /treɪl/ **noun**
1 a line of marks that someone or something leaves behind as they move: *a trail of muddy footprints*
2 a path through the countryside: *a nature trail*

trailer /ˈtreɪlər/ **noun**
a container with wheels that can be pulled by a car or a truck

train¹ /treɪn/ **noun**
A1 a long, thin vehicle that travels along metal tracks and carries people or goods: *We could go **by train**.*

train² /treɪn/ **verb**
1 B1 to practise a sport or exercise in order to prepare for a competition
2 to learn the skills you need to do a job: *He **trained as** a lawyer in Vienna.*
3 to teach someone how to do something, usually a skill that is needed for a job: *We **train** all our staff **in** first aid.*

trainer /ˈtreɪnəʳ/ **noun**
1 A2 UK a soft sports shoe: *a pair of trainers*
→ See **Clothes** on page C5
2 B1 someone who trains people: *a fitness trainer*

training /ˈtreɪnɪŋ/ **noun** [no plural]
1 B1 the process of learning a skill: *computer training*
2 B1 the process of preparing for a sport or competition: *weight training*

traitor /ˈtreɪtəʳ/ **noun**
someone who does something that harms their country, especially by helping its enemies

tram /træm/ **noun** UK (US **streetcar**)
A2 an electric vehicle for carrying passengers, mostly in cities, that moves along metal lines in the road

tramp /træmp/ **noun**
someone who has no home, job, or money and who lives outside

trample /ˈtræmpl/ **verb** (**trampling**, **trampled**)
to walk on something, usually damaging it: *She shouted at the boys for **trampling on** her flowers.*

transfer /trænsˈfɜːʳ/ **verb** (**transferring**, **transferred**)
B1 to move someone or something from one place to another: *She was **transferred to** a different hospital.*
• **transfer** /ˈtrænsfɜːʳ/ **noun** *I'm hoping for a **transfer to** the Brussels office.*

transform /trænsˈfɔːm/ **verb**
to change something completely, usually to improve it: *You have transformed this house!*
• **transformation** /ˌtrænsfəˈmeɪʃᵊn/ **noun** a complete change

transitive /ˈtrænsətɪv/ **adj**
A transitive verb always has an object. In the sentence 'I'll make a drink', 'make' is a transitive verb.

translate /trænzˈleɪt/ **verb** (**translating**, **translated**)
B1 to change words from one language to another: *We were asked to translate a list of sentences.*
• **translator** **noun** *a Japanese translator*

translation /trænzˈleɪʃᵊn/ **noun**
B1 something that has been changed from one language to another

transparent /trænˈspærᵊnt/ **adj**
If a substance or material is transparent, you can see through it: *transparent plastic*

transport¹ /ˈtrænspɔːt/ **noun** [no plural]
1 B1 mainly UK (US **transportation** /ˌtrænspɔːˈteɪʃᵊn/) a vehicle or system of vehicles, such as buses, trains, planes, etc., for getting from one place to another: *I rely on **public transport**.*
2 the act of moving people or things from one place to another: *the transport of live animals*

transport² /trænˈspɔːt/ **verb**
to move people or things from one place to another

trap¹ /træp/ **noun**
a piece of equipment for catching animals: *a mouse trap*

trap² /træp/ **verb** (**trapping**, **trapped**)
1 If someone or something is trapped, they cannot escape from a place or situation: *The car turned over, trapping the driver underneath.*
2 to catch an animal using a trap

trash /træʃ/ **noun** [no plural]
1 US (UK **rubbish**) things that you throw away because you do not want them: *a trash can (= a container for trash)*
2 informal something that is of bad quality: *Why are you reading that trash?*

travel¹ /ˈtrævᵊl/ **verb** (**travelling**, **travelled**)
1 A1 to make a journey: *I spent a year travelling around Asia.*
2 B1 If light, sound, or news travels, it moves from one place to another: *News of the accident travelled fast.*

travel² /ˈtrævᵊl/ **noun** [no plural]
B1 the activity of travelling: *space travel*

> **Common mistake: travel, journey, or trip?**
>
> The noun **travel** is a general word that means the activity of travelling.
>
> *Air travel has become much cheaper.*
>
> Use **journey** to talk about when you travel from one place to another.
>
> *He fell asleep during the train journey.*
> *Did you have a good journey?*
> ~~*Did you have a good travel?*~~
>
> A **trip** is a journey in which you visit a place for a short time and come back again.
>
> *a business trip*
> *a three-day trip to Spain*

travel agency /ˈtrævᵊl ˌeɪdʒᵊnsi/ **noun** (plural **travel agencies**) (also **travel agent's**)
a shop that makes travel arrangements for people

travel agent /ˈtrævᵊl ˌeɪdʒᵊnt/ **noun**
B1 someone whose job is making travel arrangements for people

traveller /ˈtrævᵊləʳ/ **noun**
B1 someone who is travelling

traveller's cheque /ˈtrævᵊləz ˌtʃek/ **noun** UK
a special piece of paper that you exchange for the money of another country

tray /treɪ/ **noun**
a flat object with higher edges, used for carrying food and drinks

tread /tred/ **verb** (**trod**, **trodden**) UK
to put your foot on something: *I* ***trod on*** *a piece of broken glass.*

treason /ˈtriːzᵊn/ **noun** [no plural]
the crime of doing something that harms your country, especially by helping its enemies

treasure /ˈtreʒəʳ/ **noun** [no plural]
a collection of gold, silver, jewellery, and valuable objects: *buried treasure*

treat¹ /triːt/ **verb**
1 to behave towards someone in a particular way: *He treats her really badly.* ◦ *They* ***treat*** *her* ***like*** *one of their own children.*
2 to give medical care to someone who is ill or hurt: *He's being* ***treated for*** *cancer at a hospital in Manchester.*

treat² /triːt/ **noun**
something special that you buy or do for someone else: *a birthday treat* ◦ *As a special treat I'm taking him out for dinner.*

treatment /ˈtriːtmənt/ **noun**
1 something that you do to try to cure an illness or injury: *She's receiving treatment for a lung infection.*
2 [no plural] the way you behave towards someone: *There have been complaints about the treatment of prisoners.*

treaty /ˈtriːti/ **noun** (plural **treaties**)
a written agreement between two or more countries: *a peace treaty*

tree

tree /triː/ **noun**
A1 a tall plant with a thick stem that has branches coming from it and leaves

tremble /ˈtrembl/ **verb** (**trembling**, **trembled**)
to shake slightly, especially because you are frightened or cold

tremendous /trɪˈmendəs/ **adj**
1 very good: *I think she's doing a tremendous job.*
2 very large, great, strong, etc.: *a tremendous amount of money*
• **tremendously** **adv** very much

trend /trend/ **noun**
B1 a general development or change in a situation: *I'm not familiar with the latest* ***trends in*** *teaching.*

trendy /ˈtrendi/ **adj** (**trendier**, **trendiest**) informal
fashionable at the moment: *She has some trendy new glasses.*

trial /traɪəl/ **noun**
1 a legal process to decide if someone has done a crime: *The two men are now* ***on trial for*** *attempted murder.*
2 a test of something new to find out if it is safe, works correctly, etc.: *The drug is currently undergoing trials.*

triangle /ˈtraɪæŋgl/ **noun**
a flat shape with three sides
→ See picture at **shape**
• **triangular** /traɪˈæŋgjələʳ/ **adj** shaped like a triangle

tribe /traɪb/ **noun**
a group of people who live together, usually in areas far away from cities, and who still have a traditional way of life: *Native American tribes*
• **tribal** **adj** relating to a tribe

tribute /ˈtrɪbjuːt/ **noun**
something that you do or say to show that you respect and admire someone: *The concert was organized as* ***a tribute to*** *the singer who died last year.*

trick[1] /trɪk/ **noun**
1 (B1) something you do to deceive someone, or to make someone look stupid: *I wasn't really ill – it was just a trick.*
2 (B1) something that is done to entertain people and that seems to be magic: *a card trick*

trick[2] /trɪk/ **verb**
to deceive someone: *They tricked him into signing the papers.*

trickle /ˈtrɪkl/ **verb** (**trickling**, **trickled**)
If liquid trickles somewhere, it flows slowly and in a thin line: *The sweat trickled down her back.*
• **trickle** **noun** *a trickle of blood*

tricky /ˈtrɪki/ **adj** (**trickier**, **trickiest**)
difficult: *a tricky question*

tried
past tense and past participle of try

trigger /ˈtrɪgəʳ/ **noun**
the part of a gun that you pull when you shoot

trillion /ˈtrɪljən/
the number 1,000,000,000,000

trim /trɪm/ **verb** (**trimming**, **trimmed**)
to cut a small amount from something: *I've had my hair trimmed.*

trip[1] /trɪp/ **noun**
(A2) a journey in which you visit a place for a short time and come back again: *a business trip*

trip[2] /trɪp/ **verb** (**tripping**, **tripped**)
to fall because you hit your foot on something when you are moving: *She* ***tripped over*** *the cat.*

triple[1] /ˈtrɪpl/ **adj**
having three parts of the same type, or happening three times: *a triple world champion*

triple[2] /ˈtrɪpl/ **verb**
to increase three times in size or amount, or to make something do this: *Sales have tripled in the past five years.*

triumph /ˈtraɪəmf/ **noun**
an important success: *Barcelona's 2-0 triumph over Manchester United*

trivial /ˈtrɪviəl/ **adj**
small and not important: *a trivial problem*

trod /trɒd/
the past tense of tread

trodden /ˈtrɒdᵊn/
the past participle of tread

trolleys

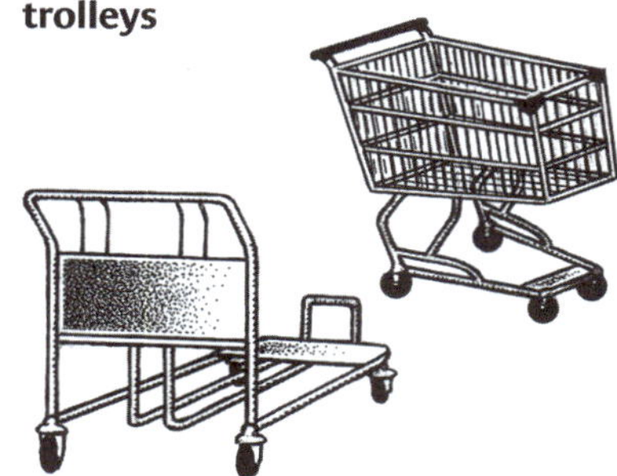

trolley /ˈtrɒli/ **noun** UK (US **cart**)
a metal structure on wheels that is used for carrying things: *a luggage trolley*

a b c d e f g h i j k l m n o p q r s t u v w x y z

troops /tru:ps/ **plural noun**
soldiers: *UN troops*

trophy /ˈtrəʊfi/ **noun** (plural **trophies**)
a prize, such as a silver cup, that you get for winning a competition

tropical /ˈtrɒpɪkəl/ **adj**
from or in the hottest parts of the world: *a tropical climate*

the tropics /ˈtrɒpɪks/ **plural noun**
the hottest parts of the world

trot /trɒt/ **verb** (**trotting**, **trotted**)
to walk with quick, short steps: *The little boy trotted along behind his father.*

trouble¹ /ˈtrʌbl/ **noun**
1 B1 problems: *We had trouble finding somewhere to park.*
2 the trouble with *someone/something* used to say what is wrong with someone or something: *The trouble with white is that it gets dirty quickly.*
3 [no plural] a problem with a machine or part of your body: *back trouble* ◦ *car trouble*
4 B1 [no plural] a situation in which you have done something wrong and will be punished: *They **got into trouble** with the police.*

> **Common mistake: trouble or problem?**
>
> **Problem** means 'a situation that causes difficulties and that needs to be dealt with'. You can talk about **a problem** or **problems.**
> *Tell me what the problem is.*
> *There's a problem with the engine.*
> *He's having a few problems at work.*
> **Trouble** means 'problems, difficulties, or worries' and is used to talk about problems in a more general way. **Trouble** is almost always uncountable so do not use **a** before it.
> *We had some trouble while we were on holiday.*
> *He helped me when I was in trouble.*
> *I had trouble with the car last night.*
> ~~*I had a trouble with the car last night.*~~

trouble² /ˈtrʌbl/ **verb** (**troubling**, **troubled**)
1 to make someone worry: *The situation has been troubling me for a while.*
2 formal used to ask someone politely to help you: *I'm sorry to trouble you, but could you tell me how to get to the station?*

trousers /ˈtraʊzəz/ **plural noun** (US **pants**)
A1 a piece of clothing that covers the legs and has a separate part for each leg: *a pair of trousers*

trousers

> **Common mistake: trousers**
>
> **Trousers** is a plural word.
> *These trousers are too big for me.*

truck /trʌk/ **noun** (also UK **lorry**)
B1 a large road vehicle for carrying things from place to place
→ See picture at **vehicle**

true /tru:/ **adj**
1 A2 based on facts and not imagined: *a true story* ◦ *Is it true that Martin and Sue are getting married?*
2 B1 real: *true love*
3 come true B1 If a dream or hope comes true, it really happens.

truly /ˈtru:li/ **adv**
used to say that something is sincere or honest: *I truly believe that he is innocent.*

trumpet /ˈtrʌmpɪt/ **noun**
B1 a metal musical instrument that you play by blowing into it

trumpet

trunk /trʌŋk/ **noun**
1 the thick stem of a tree that the branches grow from
→ See picture at **tree**
2 the long nose of an elephant

trunks /trʌŋks/ **plural noun** (also **swimming trunks**)
a piece of clothing that boys and men wear for swimming
→ See **Clothes** on page C5

trust¹ /trʌst/ **verb**
1 B1 to believe that someone is good

and honest and will not harm you: *My sister warned me not to trust him.*
2 trust *someone* to do *something* to be sure that someone will do the right thing: *I trust them to make the right decision.*

trust² /trʌst/ **noun** [no plural]
the belief that you can trust someone or something: *a marriage based on love and trust*

truth /truːθ/ **noun**
the truth B1 the real facts about a situation: *Do you think he was **telling the truth**?*

truthful /ˈtruːθfəl/ **adj**
honest and not containing or telling any lies: *a truthful answer*
• **truthfully** **adv**
• **truthfulness** **noun** [no plural]

try¹ /traɪ/ **verb** (**trying**, **tried**)
1 A2 to attempt to do something: *I tried to open the window but couldn't.*
2 B1 to do, test, taste, etc. something to discover if it works or if you like it: *I tried that recipe you gave me.*
try *something* on **phrasal verb**
A2 to put on a piece of clothing to see if it fits you: *Could I try this dress on, please?*

try² /traɪ/ **noun** (plural **tries**)
an attempt to do something

T-shirt /ˈtiːʃɜːt/ **noun**
A1 a piece of cotton clothing for the top part of the body with short sleeves and no collar

T-shirt

tub /tʌb/ **noun**
a small, plastic container with a lid, used for keeping food: *a tub of ice cream*
→ See picture at **container**

tube /tjuːb/ **noun**
1 a pipe made of glass, plastic, metal, etc., especially for liquids or gases to flow through
2 B1 a long, thin container for a soft substance that you press to get the substance out: *a tube of toothpaste*
→ See picture at **container**
3 the Tube B1 the system of railways under the ground in London

tuck /tʌk/ **verb**
to push a loose piece of clothing or material somewhere to make it tidy: *Tuck your shirt in.*

Tuesday /ˈtjuːzdeɪ/ **noun**
A1 the day of the week after Monday and before Wednesday

tug /tʌg/ **verb** (**tugging**, **tugged**)
to pull something suddenly and strongly: *Tom **tugged at** his mother's arm.*

tumble /ˈtʌmbl/ **verb** (**tumbling**, **tumbled**)
to suddenly fall: *He **tumbled down** the stairs.*

tummy /ˈtʌmi/ **noun** (plural **tummies**)
informal
stomach

tuna /ˈtjuːnə/ **noun** (plural **tuna**)
B1 a large sea fish, or the meat from this fish

tune /tjuːn/ **noun**
B1 a series of musical notes that are nice to listen to: *He was humming a tune.*

tunnel /ˈtʌnəl/ **noun**
B1 a long passage under the ground or through a mountain: *The train went into the tunnel.*

tunnel

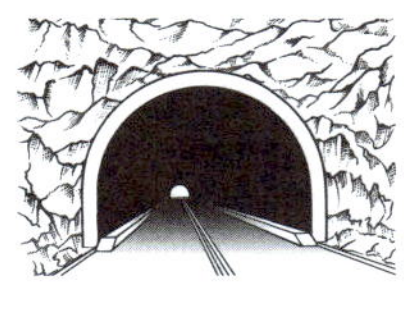

turkey /ˈtɜːki/ **noun**
B1 a bird that looks like a large chicken

turn¹ /tɜːn/ **verb**
1 A2 to change direction when you are moving, or to make a car do this: *Turn left at the traffic lights.* ◦ *I turned the car into the drive.*
2 B1 to move your body so that you are facing a different direction: *Ricky turned and saw Sue standing in the doorway.*
3 B1 to move a page in a book or magazine in order to see the next one: *I offered to turn the pages for the pianist.* ◦ ***Turn to** page 35.*

4 to move around a central point in a circle, or to make something do this: *Turn the steering wheel as quickly as you can.*
5 turn blue, cold, etc. to become blue, cold, etc.: *The sky turned black and it started to rain.*
turn *something* down phrasal verb
1 B1 to reduce the level of sound or heat that a machine produces: *Could you turn the radio down, please?*
2 to refuse an offer or request: *They did offer me the job, but I turned it down.*
turn (*someone/something*) into *someone/something* phrasal verb
B1 to change and become someone or something different, or to make someone or something do this: *The countryside is turning into a desert.* ◦ *They want to turn the offices into apartments.*
turn *something* off phrasal verb
A2 to move the switch on a machine, light, etc. so that it stops working: *How do you turn the computer off?*
turn *something* on phrasal verb
A2 to move the switch on a machine, light, etc. so that it starts working: *Ben turned the TV on.*
turn out phrasal verb
to happen in a particular way or to have a particular result, especially an unexpected one: *How did the recipe turn out?*
turn up phrasal verb informal
to arrive: *Fred turned up late again.*
turn *something* up phrasal verb
B1 to increase the level of sound or heat that a machine produces: *Could you turn the heating up please?*

turn² /tɜːn/ noun
1 B1 the time when you can or must do something, usually before or after someone else: *It's your **turn to** clean the flat.*
2 a change in the direction in which you are moving or facing: *a right/left turn*
3 a bend or corner in a road, river, etc.: *Take the next turn on the right.*
4 in turn one after another: *He spoke to the three boys in turn.*

turning /ˈtɜːnɪŋ/ noun UK
B1 a corner where one road meets another: *Take the second turning on the left.*

turtle /ˈtɜːtl/ noun
an animal with four legs and a hard shell that lives mainly in water

tusk /tʌsk/ noun
one of the two long, pointed teeth that come out of the mouth of some animals

tutor /ˈtjuːtəʳ/ noun
someone who teaches one person or a very small group of people: *a private tutor*

TV /ˌtiːˈviː/ noun
A1 television: *What's **on TV** tonight?*

tweezers /ˈtwiːzəz/ plural noun
a small tool with two narrow pieces of metal joined at one end, used for picking up very small things

tweezers

twelfth¹ /twelfθ/
12th written as a word

twelfth² /twelfθ/ noun
one of twelve equal parts of something; 1/12

twelve /twelv/
A1 the number 12

twenties /ˈtwentiz/ plural noun
1 the twenties the years from 1920 to 1929: *She was born **in the twenties**.*
2 be in your twenties to be aged between 20 and 29: *I think he's **in his twenties**.*

twenty /ˈtwenti/
A1 the number 20
• **twentieth** 20th written as a word

twice /twaɪs/ adv
A2 two times: *I've been there twice.*

twig /twɪg/ noun
a small, thin branch on a tree

twin /twɪn/ noun
B1 one of two children who are born to the same mother at the same time

a b c d e f g h i j k l m n o p q r s t u v w x y z

twinkle /ˈtwɪŋkl/ **verb** (**twinkling**, **twinkled**)
If light twinkles, it shines and seems to be quickly flashing on and off: *The lights of the town twinkled in the distance.*

twin room /ˌtwɪn ˈruːm/ **noun**
a room in a hotel that has two small beds, each for one person

twist[1] /twɪst/ **verb**
1 to turn something around: *You're twisting my arm.*
2 to bend and turn something many times and change its shape: *The wheels of the bike had been twisted in the accident.*
3 If a road, river, etc. twists, it has a lot of bends in it.

twist[2] /twɪst/ **noun**
1 the act of twisting something
2 a bend in a river, road, etc.

twitch /twɪtʃ/ **verb**
If a part of your body twitches, it suddenly makes a slight movement: *His face twitched nervously.*
• **twitch noun**

two /tuː/
A1 the number 2

tying /ˈtaɪɪŋ/
the present participle of tie

type[1] /taɪp/ **noun**
A2 a group of people or things that have similar qualities: *They sell over 20 different types of cheese.* ◦ *Illnesses of this type are very common in children.*

type[2] /taɪp/ **verb** (**typing**, **typed**)
B1 to write something using a keyboard
• **typing noun** [no plural]

typical /ˈtɪpɪkəl/ **adj**
B1 having all the qualities you expect a particular person, object, place, etc. to have: *typical German food* ◦ *This style of painting is* ***typical of*** *Monet.*

typically /ˈtɪpɪkəli/ **adv**
1 B1 used for saying what usually happens: *Schools in the area typically start at 8.30.*
2 used for saying that something is typical of a person, thing, place, etc.: *His reply was typically frank.*

tyre UK (US **tire**) /taɪəʳ/ **noun**
A2 a thick, round piece of rubber filled with air that fits around a wheel: *My bike's got a* ***flat tyre*** *(= tyre with no air in it).*
→ See **Car** on page C3

Uu

U, u /juː/
the twenty-first letter of the alphabet

ugly /ˈʌgli/ **adj** (**uglier**, **ugliest**)
B1 bad to look at: *an ugly city*

ultimate /ˈʌltɪmət/ **adj**
better, worse, or greater than all similar things: *Climbing Mount Everest is the ultimate challenge.*

umbrella /ʌmˈbrelə/ **noun**
A2 a thing that you hold above your head to keep yourself dry when it is raining

umbrella

umpire /ˈʌmpaɪər/ **noun**
someone whose job is to watch a sports game and make sure that the players obey the rules: *a tennis umpire*

the UN /ˌjuːˈen/ **noun**
abbreviation for the United Nations

unable /ʌnˈeɪbl/ **adj**
be unable to do *something* B1 to not be able to do something: *Some days he is unable to get out of bed.*

unanimous /juːˈnænɪməs/ **adj**
agreed by everyone: *The jury was unanimous in finding him guilty.*

unattractive /ˌʌnəˈtræktɪv/ **adj**
bad to look at: *I felt old and unattractive.*

unaware /ˌʌnəˈweər/ **adj**
not knowing about something: *He seems totally **unaware of** the problem.*

unbearable /ʌnˈbeərəbl/ **adj**
very painful or unpleasant: *The heat was almost unbearable.*
• **unbearably** **adv**

unbelievable /ˌʌnbɪˈliːvəbl/ **adj**
B1 extremely bad or good and making you feel surprised: *It's unbelievable how lucky she's been.*

uncertain /ʌnˈsɜːtən/ **adj**
not sure or not able to decide about something: *We're a bit **uncertain about** what we're doing this weekend.*

uncle /ˈʌŋkl/ **noun**
A2 the brother of someone's mother or father, or the husband of someone's aunt: *My uncle taught me how to fish.*

unclear /ʌnˈklɪər/ **adj**
not easy to understand: *It is unclear how many people have lost their homes in the disaster.*

uncomfortable /ʌnˈkʌmftəbl/ **adj**
1 B1 not making you feel comfortable and pleasant: *These shoes are really uncomfortable.*
2 slightly embarrassed, or making you feel slightly embarrassed: *an uncomfortable silence*
• **uncomfortably** **adv** *It was uncomfortably hot in the room.*

uncommon /ʌnˈkɒmən/ **adj**
unusual: *It's not uncommon for people to get sick when they travel (= it often happens).*

unconscious /ʌnˈkɒnʃəs/ **adj**
in a state as though you are sleeping, for example because you have been hit on the head: *She was **knocked unconscious**.*

uncontrollable /ˌʌnkənˈtrəʊləbl/ **adj**
unable to be controlled: *uncontrollable anger*

uncountable noun /ʌnˌkaʊntəbəl ˈnaʊn/ **noun**
B1 a noun that does not have a plural form and cannot be used with 'a' or 'one': *'Music' is an uncountable noun.*

uncover /ʌnˈkʌvər/ **verb**
to discover something that had been secret or hidden: *The inspectors uncovered evidence of corruption.*

undeniable /ˌʌndɪˈnaɪəbl/ **adj**
certainly true: *an undeniable fact*

under /ˈʌndər/ **preposition**
1 A1 below something: *She pushed her bag under the table.*
2 A2 less than a number, amount, or age: *You can buy the whole system for just under $2,000.*

under- /ʌndər-/ **prefix**
1 not enough: *undercooked potatoes*

2 below: *underwear*

underage /ˌʌndərˈeɪdʒ/ **adj**
younger than the legal age when you are allowed to do something: *underage drinking*

undergo /ˌʌndəˈɡəʊ/ **verb** (**underwent**, **undergone**)
to experience something, especially a change or medical treatment: *He is undergoing surgery for a heart problem.*

undergraduate /ˌʌndəˈɡrædʒuət/ **noun**
a student who is studying for their first university degree (= qualification)

underground¹ /ˌʌndəˈɡraʊnd/ **adj**, **adv**
under the surface of the ground: *an animal that lives underground*

underground² /ˈʌndəɡraʊnd/ **noun** UK (US **subway**)
A2 a system of trains that is built under a city: *the London Underground*

underline /ˌʌndəˈlaɪn/ **verb**
1 B1 to draw a line under a word or words: *All the technical words have been underlined in red.*
2 to emphasize the importance or truth of something: *The report underlines the need for more teachers in schools.*

underneath /ˌʌndəˈniːθ/ **adv**, **preposition**
under something: *I found her shoes underneath the bed.*

underpants /ˈʌndəpænts/ **plural noun**
B1 a piece of clothing for men that covers the bottom
→ See **Clothes** on page C5

understand /ˌʌndəˈstænd/ **verb** (**understood**)
1 A1 to know the meaning of something that someone says: *She didn't understand so I explained it again.*
2 A2 to know why or how something happens or works: *We still don't fully understand how the brain works.*
3 B1 to know how someone feels or why they behave in a particular way: *I don't understand James sometimes.*

understandable /ˌʌndəˈstændəbl/ **adj**
An understandable feeling or action is one that you would expect in the situation: *It's understandable that he's angry.*

understanding¹ /ˌʌndəˈstændɪŋ/ **noun** [no plural]
1 knowledge about a subject, situation, etc.: *We now have a better understanding of this disease.*
2 sympathy: *Thank you for your understanding.*

understanding² /ˌʌndəˈstændɪŋ/ **adj**
showing sympathy for someone's problems: *Fortunately, my girlfriend is very understanding.*

understood /ˌʌndəˈstʊd/
past tense and past participle of understand

underwater /ˌʌndəˈwɔːtəʳ/ **adj**, **adv**
under the surface of water: *an underwater camera*

underwear /ˈʌndəweəʳ/ **noun** [no plural]
B1 the clothes that you wear next to your skin, under your other clothes

underwent /ˌʌndəˈwent/
past tense of undergo

undid /ʌnˈdɪd/
past tense of undo

undo /ʌnˈduː/ **verb** (**undoing**, **undid**, **undone**)
to open something that is fastened: *I undid my coat.*

undone /ʌnˈdʌn/ **adj**
not fastened or tied: *Her coat was undone.*

undoubtedly /ʌnˈdaʊtɪdli/ **adv**
used to say that something is true: *She is undoubtedly good at her job.*

undress /ʌnˈdres/ **verb**
B1 to remove your clothes or someone else's clothes: *I **got undressed** and went to bed.*

uneasy /ʌnˈiːzi/ **adj**
worried because you think something bad might happen: *I feel a bit **uneasy about** her travelling alone.*

a b c d e f g h i j k l m n o p q r s t u v w x y z

unemployed /ˌʌnɪmˈplɔɪd/ **adj**
B1 not having a job: *I've been unemployed for six months.*

unemployment /ˌʌnɪmˈplɔɪmənt/ **noun** [no plural]
1 the fact of being unemployed: *unemployment benefit (= paid to people who are unemployed)*
2 B1 the number of people who are unemployed: *a rise in unemployment*

uneven /ʌnˈiːvᵊn/ **adj**
not level or smooth: *an uneven floor*
• **unevenly adv**

unexpected /ˌʌnɪkˈspektɪd/ **adj**
B1 Something that is unexpected surprises you because you did not know it was going to happen: *His death was completely unexpected.*
• **unexpectedly adv**

unfair /ʌnˈfeəʳ/ **adj**
B1 not treating people in an equal way: *an unfair system*
• **unfairly adv**

unfashionable /ʌnˈfæʃᵊnəbl/ **adj**
not fashionable at a particular time

unfasten /ʌnˈfɑːsᵊn/ **verb**
to open something that is closed or fixed together: *to unfasten a seat belt*

unfit /ʌnˈfɪt/ **adj**
1 B1 UK not healthy because you do too little exercise
2 not suitable or good enough: *The food was judged* ***unfit for*** *human consumption.*

unforgettable /ˌʌnfəˈgetəbl/ **adj**
B1 Something that is unforgettable is so good, interesting, etc. that you remember it for a long time: *Seeing Niagara Falls was an* ***unforgettable experience****.*

unfortunate /ʌnˈfɔːtʃᵊnət/ **adj**
bad and causing problems: *an unfortunate mistake*

unfortunately /ʌnˈfɔːtʃənətli/ **adv**
A2 used to say that you wish something was not true or that something had not happened: *I'd love to come, but unfortunately I have to work.*

unfriendly /ʌnˈfrendli/ **adj**
B1 not friendly

unfurnished /ʌnˈfɜːnɪʃt/ **adj**
If a room, apartment, etc. is unfurnished, there is no furniture in it.

ungrateful /ʌnˈgreɪtfᵊl/ **adj**
not thanking someone who has done something good for you

unhappy /ʌnˈhæpi/ **adj**
(**unhappier**, **unhappiest**)
1 A2 sad: *an unhappy childhood*
2 B1 not satisfied: *Giorgio was* ***unhappy with*** *his test results.*
• **unhappiness noun** [no plural]

unhealthy /ʌnˈhelθi/ **adj**
(**unhealthier**, **unhealthiest**)
1 B1 likely to damage your health: *Eating too much is unhealthy.*
2 looking ill: *She looks pale and unhealthy.*

uniform /ˈjuːnɪfɔːm/ **noun**
A2 a special set of clothes that are worn by people who do a particular job or children at school: *a school uniform* ◦ *a nurse's uniform*

unimportant /ˌʌnɪmˈpɔːtᵊnt/ **adj**
B1 not important

uninhabited /ˌʌnɪnˈhæbɪtɪd/ **adj**
If a place is uninhabited, no one lives there: *an uninhabited island*

uninterested /ʌnˈɪntrəstɪd/ **adj**
B1 not interested: *He's completely* ***uninterested in*** *politics.*

uninteresting /ʌnˈɪntrəstɪŋ/ **adj**
B1 not interesting: *His later work is uninteresting in comparison with his first novel.*

union /ˈjuːnjən/ **noun**
1 B1 (also **trade union**) an organization that represents people who do a particular job: *a teachers' union*
2 two or more countries, groups, etc. that join together to make one country, group, etc.

unique /juːˈniːk/ **adj**
1 different from everyone and everything else: *Everyone's fingerprints are unique.*
2 unusual and special: *a unique opportunity*

unit /ˈjuːnɪt/ **noun**
1 a measure used to express an

amount or quantity: *The kilogram is a **unit of** weight.*
2 B1 a single, complete thing that is part of a larger thing: *a French course-book with ten units*

unite /juːˈnaɪt/ **verb** (**uniting**, **united**)
to join together as a group, or to make people join together as a group: *We need a leader who can unite the party.*

the United Nations /juːˌnaɪtɪd ˈneɪʃənz/ **noun**
an international organization that tries to stop world problems in a peaceful way

universal /ˌjuːnɪˈvɜːsəl/ **adj**
relating to everyone in the world, or to everyone in a particular group: *Kittens and puppies have an almost universal appeal.*
• **universally** **adv** *It's a style of music that is universally popular.*

the universe /ˈjuːnɪvɜːs/ **noun**
B1 everything that exists, including stars, space, etc.

university /ˌjuːnɪˈvɜːsəti/ **noun** (plural **universities**)
A1 a place where students study at a high level to get a degree (= type of qualification): *Cambridge University*

unkind /ʌnˈkaɪnd/ **adj**
B1 slightly cruel: *an unkind remark*

unknown /ʌnˈnəʊn/ **adj**
1 B1 not known: *The cause of his death is still unknown.*
2 not famous: *an unknown actor*

unleaded /ʌnˈledɪd/ **adj**
Unleaded fuel does not contain lead (= a metal).

unless /ənˈles/ **conjunction**
B1 except if: *I won't call you unless there are any problems.*

unlike /ʌnˈlaɪk/ **preposition**
different from someone or something

unlikely /ʌnˈlaɪkli/ **adj** (**unlikelier**, **unlikeliest**)
B1 not expected to happen: *It's **unlikely that** I'll be able to come to the party.*

unload /ʌnˈləʊd/ **verb**
to remove things from a vehicle: *Can you help me unload the car?*

unlock /ʌnˈlɒk/ **verb**
to open something that is locked using a key

unlucky /ʌnˈlʌki/ **adj** (**unluckier**, **unluckiest**)
B1 having or causing bad luck: *Some people think it's unlucky to walk under ladders.*

unmarried /ʌnˈmærid/ **adj**
not married

unmistakable /ˌʌnmɪˈsteɪkəbl/ **adj**
Something that is unmistakable is very obvious and cannot be confused with anything else: *an unmistakable look of disappointment*

unnatural /ʌnˈnætʃərəl/ **adj**
not normal or right: *an unnatural interest in death*

unnecessary /ʌnˈnesəsəri/ **adj**
B1 not needed: *Don't make any unnecessary car journeys in this weather.*

unofficial /ˌʌnəˈfɪʃəl/ **adj**
not said or done by the government or someone in authority: *The President made an unofficial visit to Paris (= not representing the government).*
• **unofficially** **adv**

unpack /ʌnˈpæk/ **verb**
B1 to take things out of a bag, box, etc.: *Bella unpacked her suitcase.*

unpack

unpleasant /ʌnˈplezənt/ **adj**
B1 not enjoyable or pleasant: *an unpleasant experience*

unplug /ʌnˈplʌg/ **verb** (**unplugging**, **unplugged**)
to stop a piece of electrical equipment being connected to an electricity supply by pulling its plug out of the wall

a b c d e f g h i j k l m n o p q r s t u v w x y z

unpopular /ʌnˈpɒpjələʳ/ **adj** disliked by most people: *an unpopular idea*

unpredictable /ˌʌnprɪˈdɪktəbl/ **adj** changing so much that you do not know what will happen next: *unpredictable weather conditions*

unreasonable /ʌnˈriːzᵊnəbl/ **adj** not fair: *unreasonable demands*

unreliable /ˌʌnrɪˈlaɪəbl/ **adj** not able to be trusted or depended on: *The trains were noisy, dirty, and unreliable.*

unsafe /ʌnˈseɪf/ **adj** dangerous: *The building is unsafe.*

unsatisfactory /ʌnˌsætɪsˈfæktᵊri/ **adj** not good enough to be acceptable: *Many school buildings are in an unsatisfactory condition.*

unsuccessful /ˌʌnsəkˈsesfᵊl/ **adj** not achieving what was wanted or planned: *an unsuccessful attempt*
• **unsuccessfully adv**

unsuitable /ʌnˈsuːtəbl/ **adj** not acceptable or right for someone or something: *My parents considered the programme unsuitable for children.*

unsure /ʌnˈʃʊəʳ/ **adj** not certain or having doubts: *I'm a bit **unsure about** what to do.*

unsympathetic /ˌʌnsɪmpəˈθetɪk/ **adj** showing that you do not understand or care about someone's problems: *I told him I'd got a cold but he was completely unsympathetic.*

untidy /ʌnˈtaɪdi/ **adj** B1 not tidy: *an untidy room* ◦ *She's really untidy at home.*

untie /ʌnˈtaɪ/ **verb** (**untying**, **untied**) to open a knot or something that has been tied with a knot: *I untied my shoelaces and kicked off my shoes.*

until /ᵊnˈtɪl/ **preposition, conjunction** (also **till**)
1 A1 continuing to happen before a particular time or event and then stopping: *The show will be on until the end of the month.* ◦ *We walked until it got dark.*
2 A2 as far as: *Carry on until the traffic lights and then turn right.*
3 not until B1 not before a particular time or event: *It doesn't open until seven.*

untie

untrue /ʌnˈtruː/ **adj** false

unusual /ʌnˈjuːʒuəl/ **adj** A2 different and not ordinary, often in a way that is interesting: *an unusual name*

unwanted /ʌnˈwɒntɪd/ **adj** not wanted or needed: *unwanted advice*

unwelcome /ʌnˈwelkəm/ **adj** not wanted: *an unwelcome visitor*

unwell /ʌnˈwel/ **adj** ill: *I was feeling unwell.*

unwilling /ʌnˈwɪlɪŋ/ **adj** not wanting to do something: *A lot of people are unwilling to accept change.*

unwind /ʌnˈwaɪnd/ **verb** (**unwound**) informal to relax, especially after working: *Music helps me to unwind.*

unwise /ʌnˈwaɪz/ **adj** stupid and likely to cause problems: *an unwise decision*
• **unwisely adv**

unwrap /ʌnˈræp/ **verb** (**unwrapping**, **unwrapped**) to remove the paper, cloth, etc. that is covering something: *She carefully unwrapped the present.*

up[1] /ʌp/ **adv, preposition**
1 A2 towards or in a higher place: *He ran up the stairs.* ◦ *She looked up and smiled at me.*
2 A1 vertical or as straight as possible: *He stood up.* ◦ *She sat up.*

3 to a greater degree, amount, volume, etc.: *Can you turn up the heat?*
4 used to say that someone completes an action or uses all of something: *I used up all my money.* ◦ *Eat up the rest of your dinner.*
5 up the road, street, etc. A2 along or further along the street, road, etc.: *They live just up the road.*
6 go, walk, etc. up to *someone/something* B1 to walk directly towards someone or something until you are next to them: *He came straight up to me and introduced himself.*
7 up to 10, 20, etc. B1 any amount under 10, 20, etc.: *We can invite up to 65 people.*
8 up to/till/until B1 until a particular time: *You can call me up till midnight.*
9 be up to *someone* B1 If an action or decision is up to someone, they are responsible for doing or making it: *I can't decide. It's up to you.*
10 be up to *something* informal B1 to be doing or planning something bad: *What are you two up to?*

up² /ʌp/ **adj**
B1 not in bed: *Is she up yet?*

upbringing /ˈʌpˌbrɪŋɪŋ/ **noun** [no plural]
the way that your parents look after you and the things that they teach you when you are growing up: *She had a very strict upbringing.*

update¹ /ʌpˈdeɪt/ **verb** (**updating**, **updated**)
B1 to add new information: *We've just updated our website.*

update² /ˈʌpdeɪt/ **noun**
a new form of something that existed at an earlier time: *a software update*

upgrade /ʌpˈgreɪd/ **verb** (**upgrading**, **upgraded**)
to get something that is newer and better: *We have upgraded our computer.*
• **upgrade** /ˈʌpgreɪd/ **noun**

uphill /ʌpˈhɪl/ **adv**
towards the top of a hill: *We'd walked half a mile uphill.*

upload /ʌpˈləʊd/ **verb**
B1 to copy computer information, usually from a small computer to the Internet

upon /əˈpɒn/ **preposition** formal
on

upper /ˈʌpəʳ/ **adj**
B1 at a higher position: *an upper floor* ◦ *the upper lip*

upright /ˈʌpraɪt/ **adj**
straight up or vertical: *Please return your seat to an upright position.*

upset¹ /ʌpˈset/ **adj**
A2 sad or worried because something bad has happened: *They'd had an argument and she was still **upset about** it.*

upset² /ʌpˈset/ **verb** (**upsetting**, **upset**)
1 to make someone feel sad or worried: *The phone call had clearly upset her.*
2 to cause problems for something: *If I arrived later, would that upset your plans?*

upsetting /ʌpˈsetɪŋ/ **adj**
making you sad or worried: *I found the programme very upsetting.*

upside down /ˌʌpsaɪd ˈdaʊn/ **adv**
turned so that the part that is usually at the top is now at the bottom: ***Turn** the jar **upside down** and shake it.*

upside down

upstairs /ʌpˈsteəz/ **adv**
A2 on or to a higher level of a building: *He ran upstairs to answer the phone.*
• **upstairs adj** B1 *an upstairs bedroom*

up-to-date /ˌʌptəˈdeɪt/ **adj**
B1 modern, and using the most recent technology or knowledge

upwards /ˈʌpwədz/ **adv** mainly UK (US **upward**)
towards a higher place or level: *House*

prices have started moving upwards again.

urban /ˈɜːbᵊn/ **adj**
belonging or relating to a town: *urban areas*

urge[1] /ɜːdʒ/ **verb** (**urging**, **urged**)
urge *someone* to do *something* to try to persuade someone to do something: *His parents urged him to go to university.*

urge[2] /ɜːdʒ/ **noun**
a strong wish or need: *I felt a powerful urge to slap him.*

urgent /ˈɜːdʒᵊnt/ **adj**
B1 very important and needing you to take action immediately: *an urgent message*
• **urgently** **adv** B1 *I need to speak to you urgently.*

us strong /ʌs/ weak /əs/ **pronoun**
A1 used after a verb or preposition to mean the person who is speaking or writing and one or more other people: *She gave us all a present.*

use[1] /juːz/ **verb** (**using**, **used**)
1 A1 If you use something, you do something with it for a particular purpose: *Can I use your pen?* ◦ *She **uses** her car **for** work.*
2 B1 to take an amount from a supply of something: *These light bulbs use less electricity.*
use *something* up **phrasal verb**
to finish an amount of something: *Someone's used up all the milk.*

use[2] /juːs/ **noun**
1 A2 [no plural] the act of using something, or the state of something being used: *Guests have free use of the hotel swimming pool.*
2 B1 a purpose for which something is used: *Can you **find a use for** this box?*
3 B1 one of the meanings of a word, or the way that a particular word is used: *Can you list all the uses of the word 'point'?*
4 **be no use** used to say that trying to do something has no effect: *It was no use talking to him – he wouldn't listen.*

used /juːst/ **adj**
be used to *something*/doing *something* B1 If you are used to something, you have done it or had it many times before: *He's used to working long hours.* **get used to *something*/doing *something*** B1 to become familiar with something or someone: *You'll soon get used to getting up early.*

used to /ˈjuːst tuː/ **modal verb**
used to do/be *something* B1 If something used to happen, it happened often or existed in the past but it does not happen now: *I used to go out every night when I was a student.* ◦ *Monica used to live in Glasgow.*

> **Common mistake: used to and be used to**
>
> **Used to + verb** is for talking about a situation or regular activity in the past.
>
> *My dad used to smoke when he was younger.*
> *I used to live in Italy, but now I live in England.*
>
> When you make **used to + verb** into a question or negative using the verb **do**, the correct form is **use to**.
>
> *My dad didn't use to smoke.*
> *Where did you use to live?*
> ~~*Where did you used to live?*~~
>
> The expression **be used to something/doing something** is for talking about something that you have done or experienced a lot before.
>
> *I don't mind the heat. I'm used to hot weather.*
> *He's not used to working long hours.*
> ~~*He's not use to working long hours.*~~

useful /ˈjuːsfᵊl/ **adj**
A2 helping you to do or get something: *useful information*

useless /ˈjuːsləs/ **adj**
B1 If something is useless, it does not work well or it has no effect: *This umbrella's useless – there's a big hole in it.*

user /ˈjuːzər/ **noun**
B1 someone who uses a product, machine, or service: *a new service for Internet users*

usual /ˈjuːʒuəl/ **adj**
1 B1 normal and happening most often: *I went to bed at my usual time.* ◦ *This winter has been much colder than usual.*

→ Opposite **unusual** adj
2 as usual A2 in the way that happens most of the time: *As usual, Nick was the last to arrive.*

usually /ˈjuːʒəli/ **adv**
A2 in the way that most often happens: *I usually get home at about six o'clock.*

utensil /juːˈtensᵊl/ **noun**
a tool that you use for doing jobs in the house, especially cooking: *wooden cooking utensils*
→ See **Kitchen** on page C10

utter /ˈʌtəʳ/ **adj**
complete: *She dismissed the article as utter nonsense.*

utterly /ˈʌtəli/ **adv**
completely: *It's utterly ridiculous.*

a b c d e f g h i j k l m n o p q r s t u v w x y z

Vv

V, v /viː/
the twenty-second letter of the alphabet

v UK (US **vs**) /viː/ **preposition**
abbreviation for versus: used to say that one team or person is competing against another: *Germany v France*

vacancy /ˈveɪkənsi/ **noun** (plural **vacancies**)
1 a room that is not being used in a hotel: *Do you have any vacancies?*
2 a job that is free for someone to do: *Tell me if you hear of any vacancies for secretaries.*

vacant /ˈveɪkənt/ **adj**
1 Somewhere that is vacant is not being used: *a vacant building*
2 A vacant job is free for someone to do.

vacation /vəˈkeɪʃən/ **noun** US (UK **holiday**)
a period of time when you are not at home but are staying somewhere else for enjoyment: *We're **taking a vacation** in Florida.*

vaccinate /ˈvæksɪneɪt/ **verb** (**vaccinating**, **vaccinated**)
to give someone a substance to stop them from getting a disease: *Have you been **vaccinated against** the disease?*
• **vaccination** /ˌvæksɪˈneɪʃən/ **noun**

vacuum /ˈvækjuːm/ **verb**
to clean somewhere using a vacuum cleaner

vacuum cleaner /ˈvækjuːm ˌkliːnər/ **noun**
an electric machine that cleans floors by sucking up dirt

vagina /vəˈdʒaɪnə/ **noun**
the part of a woman's body that connects her outer sex organs to the place where a baby grows

vague /veɪɡ/ **adj**
not clear or certain: *I have a vague idea of where the hotel is.*
• **vaguely** **adv** *I vaguely (= slightly) remember meeting her.*

vain /veɪn/ **adj**
too interested in your own appearance and thinking you are very attractive

valid /ˈvælɪd/ **adj**
A valid ticket or document is legally acceptable: *The ticket is valid for three months.*
→ Opposite **invalid** adj

valley /ˈvæli/ **noun**
B1 an area of low land between hills or mountains

valuable /ˈvæljuəbl/ **adj**
1 B1 Valuable objects could be sold for a lot of money: *valuable paintings*
2 Valuable information, help, advice, etc. is very helpful.

value[1] /ˈvæljuː/ **noun**
1 B1 how much money something could be sold for: *Cars quickly go down in value.*
2 B1 [no plural] how useful or important something is: *a document of great historical value*
3 **good value** B1 If something is good value, it is of good quality or you think the amount of money you spent on it was right: *The meal was very good value.*

value[2] /ˈvæljuː/ **verb** (**valuing**, **valued**)
1 If you value something or someone, they are very important to you: *I always value his opinion.*
2 to judge how much money something could be sold for: *The ring was **valued at** $1,000.*

valve /vælv/ **noun**
something that opens and closes to control the flow of liquid or gas

vampire /ˈvæmpaɪər/ **noun**
in stories, a dead person who bites people's necks and drinks their blood

van /væn/ **noun**
B1 a vehicle that is used for carrying things but that is smaller than a truck
→ See picture at **vehicle**

vandal /ˈvændəl/ **noun**
someone who damages things in public places: *Vandals had smashed the shop window.*

vandalism /ˈvændəlɪzəm/ **noun** [no plural]
the crime of damaging things in public places

vanilla /vəˈnɪlə/ **noun** [no plural]
a substance that is used to give flavour to some sweet foods: *vanilla ice cream*

vanish /ˈvænɪʃ/ **verb**
to disappear suddenly: *The sun vanished behind the trees.*

vanity /ˈvænəti/ **noun** [no plural]
too much pride in your appearance or achievements

vapour /ˈveɪpər/ **noun** [no plural] UK
many small drops of liquid in the air that look like a cloud

varied /ˈveərid/ **adj**
having many different types of things: *a long and varied career*

variety /vəˈraɪəti/ **noun**
1 B1 [no plural] a lot of different activities, situations, people, etc.: *I need more variety in my life.*
2 a variety of *something/someone* A2 many different types of things or people: *Ben has done a variety of jobs.*
3 (plural **varieties**) a different type of something: *a new variety of potato*

various /ˈveəriəs/ **adj**
A2 many different: *They have offices in various parts of the country.*

varnish[1] /ˈvɑːnɪʃ/ **noun**
a clear liquid that you paint onto wood to protect it

varnish[2] /ˈvɑːnɪʃ/ **verb**
to put varnish on a surface

vary /ˈveəri/ **verb** (**varying**, **varied**)
If things of the same type vary, they are different from each other: *Car prices vary greatly across Europe.*

vase /vɑːz/ **noun**
B1 a container that you put flowers in

vase

vast /vɑːst/ **adj**
very big: *a vast amount of money*

veg /vedʒ/ **noun**
(plural **veg**) UK informal short form of vegetables: ***fruit and veg***

vegetable /ˈvedʒtəbl/ **noun**
A1 a plant that you eat, for example a potato, onion, etc.
→ See **Fruit and Vegetables** on page C8

vegetarian /ˌvedʒɪˈteəriən/ **noun**
B1 someone who does not eat meat or fish

vehicles

vehicle /ˈviːɪkl/ **noun** formal
B1 something such as a car or bus that takes people from one place to another

veil /veɪl/ **noun**
a thin piece of material that covers a woman's face

vein /veɪn/ **noun**
one of the tubes in your body that carries blood to your heart
• **in the same vein** in the same style of speaking or writing

velvet /ˈvelvɪt/ **noun** [no plural]
cloth that has a thick, soft surface on one side: *a black velvet jacket*

ventilate /ˈventɪleɪt/ **verb** (**ventilating**, **ventilated**)
to let air come into and go out of a room or building
• **ventilation** /ˌventɪˈleɪʃən/ **noun** [no plural] *a ventilation system*

venue /ˈvenjuː/ **noun**
a place where a sports game, musical performance, etc. happens

verb /vɜːb/ **noun**
A2 a word or group of words that refers to an action, state, or experience. For example, the words 'arrive', 'make', 'be', and 'feel' are verbs.

verdict /ˈvɜːdɪkt/ **noun**
a decision in a court of law saying if someone has done a crime: *a guilty verdict*

verse /vɜːs/ **noun**
1 one of the parts that a song or

poem is divided into: *I only know the first verse.*
2 [no plural] words that are in the form of poetry: *The story was told in verse.*

version /ˈvɜːʃᵊn/ **noun**
one form of something that has many forms: *I saw the original version of the movie.*

versus /ˈvɜːsəs/ **preposition**
used to say that one team or person is competing against another: *Tomorrow's game is Newcastle versus Arsenal.*

vertical /ˈvɜːtɪkᵊl/ **adj**
pointing straight up from a surface: *a vertical line*
→ See picture at **horizontal**

very /ˈveri/ **adv**
1 A1 used to make an adjective or adverb stronger: *She was very pleased.* ◦ *Thank you very much.*
2 not very good, tall, happy, etc. A1 not good, happy, etc.: *The movie wasn't very good.*

vest /vest/ **noun** UK
1 a piece of underwear that you wear under a shirt
2 US (UK **waistcoat**) a piece of clothing with buttons at the front and no sleeves
→ See **Clothes** on page C5

vet /vet/ **noun**
B1 someone whose job is to give medical care to animals that are ill

via /ˈvaɪə/ **preposition**
1 B1 going through or stopping at a place on the way to another place: *The train to Utrecht goes via Amsterdam.*
2 B1 using a particular machine, system, or person to send or receive something: *Reports are coming in via satellite.*

vibrate /vaɪˈbreɪt/ **verb** (**vibrating**, **vibrated**)
to shake with small, quick movements: *The music was so loud that the floor was vibrating.*
• **vibration** /vaɪˈbreɪʃᵊn/ **noun**

vicar /ˈvɪkəʳ/ **noun**
a priest in some Christian churches

vice /vaɪs/ **noun**
something bad that someone often does: *Smoking is his only vice.*

vice president /ˌvaɪs ˈprezɪdᵊnt/ **noun**
the person who is a rank lower than the president of a country

vicious /ˈvɪʃəs/ **adj**
violent and dangerous: *a vicious attack on a child*

victim /ˈvɪktɪm/ **noun**
someone who has been hurt or killed: *victims of crime* ◦ *flood victims*

victory /ˈvɪktᵊri/ **noun** (plural **victories**)
an act of winning a fight or competition: *Phoenix managed a 135-114* ***victory over*** *Denver.*

video /ˈvɪdiəʊ/ **noun**
A2 a recording of a movie, TV programme, etc. that you can watch on a television or computer: *You can get the movie* ***on video.***

video game /ˈvɪdiəʊ ˌɡeɪm/ **noun**
A2 a game in which you make pictures move on a screen

view /vjuː/ **noun**
1 A2 the things that you can see from a place: *There was a lovely view of the lake from the bedroom window.*
2 B1 your opinion: *We have different* ***views on*** *education.* ◦ ***In*** *her* ***view*** *this is wrong.*
3 [no plural] how well you can see something from a place: *We had a great view of the procession.*

viewer /ˈvjuːəʳ/ **noun**
someone who watches a television programme

vigorous /ˈvɪɡᵊrəs/ **adj**
showing or needing a lot of physical energy: *vigorous exercise*
• **vigorously** **adv** *He nodded his head vigorously.*

villa /ˈvɪlə/ **noun**
a large house, especially one used for holidays in a warm country

village /ˈvɪlɪdʒ/ **noun**
A1 a place where people live in the countryside which is smaller than a town: *She lives in a small village outside Oxford.*

villain /ˈvɪlən/ **noun**
a bad person in a movie, book, etc.

vine /vaɪn/ **noun**
a plant that grapes (= small fruit used for making wine) grow on

vinegar /ˈvɪnɪgəʳ/ **noun** [no plural]
a sour liquid that is used in cooking, often made from wine

vineyard /ˈvɪnjəd/ **noun**
an area of land where someone grows grapes (= small, green or purple fruit) for making wine

violence /ˈvaɪələns/ **noun** [no plural]
an act of hurting or killing someone else: *A number of people were killed in the violence.*

violent /ˈvaɪələnt/ **adj**
1 involving violence: *I don't like violent movies (= movies that show violence).*
2 likely to hurt or kill someone else: *a violent criminal*
3 sudden and causing damage: *a violent storm*
• **violently** **adv**

violin /ˌvaɪəˈlɪn/ **noun**
A2 a wooden musical instrument that you hold against your neck and play by moving a stick across strings

violin

VIP /ˌviːaɪˈpiː/ **noun**
abbreviation for very important person: someone who is famous or powerful and is treated in a special way

virtual /ˈvɜːtʃuəl/ **adj**
1 almost a particular thing or quality: *They played the game in virtual silence.*
2 using computer images and sounds to make you think something is real: *an online virtual museum*

virtually /ˈvɜːtʃuəli/ **adv**
almost: *They're virtually the same.*

virtue /ˈvɜːtjuː/ **noun**
1 a useful quality: *The great* ***virtue of*** *having a small car is that you can park it easily.*
2 a good quality that someone has: *Patience is not among his virtues.*

virus /ˈvaɪrəs/ **noun**
1 a very small thing that causes illnesses, or an illness that it causes
2 B1 a program that is secretly put onto a computer in order to destroy the information that is stored on it

visa /ˈviːzə/ **noun**
B1 an official mark in your passport (= book showing where you come from) that allows you to enter or leave a particular country

visible /ˈvɪzəbl/ **adj**
able to be seen: *The fire was visible from five kilometres away.*
→ Opposite **invisible** **adj**

vision /ˈvɪʒən/ **noun**
1 an idea or image in your mind of what something could be like in the future: *a vision of a better society*
2 [no plural] the ability to see: *He has poor vision in his left eye.*

visit[1] /ˈvɪzɪt/ **verb**
1 A1 to go somewhere to see someone or a place: *Did you visit St Petersburg while you were in Russia?* ◦ *We have friends coming to visit this weekend.*
2 A2 to look at a website: *Visit our website!*

visit[2] /ˈvɪzɪt/ **noun**
B1 an occasion when you go to see a place or a person: *the President's visit to Hong Kong*

visitor /ˈvɪzɪtəʳ/ **noun**
A2 someone who visits a person, place, or website: *The museum attracts large numbers of visitors.*

visual /ˈvɪʒuəl/ **adj**
relating to seeing: *I have a strong visual imagination.*

vital /ˈvaɪtəl/ **adj**
necessary: *Tourism is* ***vital to*** *the country's economy.*

vitamin /ˈvɪtəmɪn/ **noun**
one of a group of natural substances in food that you need to be healthy: *Oranges are full of vitamin C.*

vivid /ˈvɪvɪd/ **adj**
1 Vivid descriptions or memories produce strong, clear images in your

mind: *He gave a very vivid description of life in Caracas.*
2 A vivid colour is very bright.
• **vividly** **adv** *I vividly remember my first day at work.*

vocabulary /vəʊˈkæbjələri/ **noun** (plural **vocabularies**)
A2 words: *Reading helps to widen your vocabulary.* ◦ *Computing has its own specialist vocabulary.*

voice /vɔɪs/ **noun**
B1 the sounds that you make when you speak or sing: *I could hear voices in the next room.* ◦ *Jessie has a beautiful singing voice.*

voice mail /ˈvɔɪs ˌmeɪl/ **noun** [no plural]
an electronic telephone answering system

volcano /vɒlˈkeɪnəʊ/ **noun** (plural **volcanoes**, **volcanos**)
a mountain with a large hole at the top, which sometimes explodes
• **volcanic** /vɒlˈkænɪk/ **adj** *volcanic ash*

volcano

volleyball /ˈvɒlibɔːl/ **noun** [no plural]
A2 a game in which two teams use their hands to hit a ball over a net

volleyball

volt /vəʊlt/ **noun**
a unit for measuring the force of an electric current

volume /ˈvɒljuːm/ **noun**
1 **B1** [no plural] the level of sound made by a television, radio, etc.: *Could you turn the volume down?*
2 [no plural] the amount of space inside an object
3 a book, especially one of a set: *a new dictionary in two volumes*

voluntary /ˈvɒləntᵊri/ **adj**
Voluntary work is done without being paid and usually involves helping people: *She does voluntary work for the Red Cross.*
• **voluntarily** /ˌvɒlənˈteərᵊli/ **adv** *She left voluntarily.*

volunteer¹ /ˌvɒlənˈtɪəʳ/ **verb**
to offer to do something without being asked to do it: *Rob volunteered to look after the kids.*

volunteer² /ˌvɒlənˈtɪəʳ/ **noun**
someone who works without being paid, especially work that involves helping people: *a Red Cross volunteer*

vomit¹ /ˈvɒmɪt/ **verb**
If someone vomits, the food or liquid that was in their stomach comes up and out of their mouth.

vomit² /ˈvɒmɪt/ **noun** [no plural]
the food or liquid that comes from your mouth when you vomit

vote /vəʊt/ **verb** (**voting**, **voted**)
B1 to choose someone or something in an election or meeting by writing a cross on an official piece of paper or putting your hand up: *Who did you* ***vote for****?* ◦ *Staff have voted to accept the pay offer.*
• **vote** **noun** *He lost the election by twenty votes.*

voter /ˈvəʊtəʳ/ **noun**
someone who votes or who is officially allowed to vote

vowel /vaʊəl/ **noun**
B1 a speech sound that you make with your lips and teeth open, shown in English by the letters 'a', 'e', 'i', 'o', or 'u'

voyage /ˈvɔɪɪdʒ/ **noun**
a long journey, especially by ship or in space: *He was a young sailor* ***on*** *his first* ***voyage****.*

vulnerable /ˈvʌlnᵊrəbl/ **adj**
easy to hurt or attack: *The troops are in a vulnerable position.*

vulture /ˈvʌltʃəʳ/ **noun**
a large bird with no feathers on its head or neck that eats dead animals

Ww

W, w /ˈdʌbljuː/
the twenty-third letter of the alphabet

wade /weɪd/ **verb** (**wading**, **waded**)
to walk through water: *He waded across the river.*

wag /wæg/ **verb** (**wagging**, **wagged**)
If a dog wags its tail, it moves it from side to side.

wage /weɪdʒ/ **noun** (also **wages**)
B1 the amount of money a person regularly gets for their job: *weekly wages*

wail /weɪl/ **verb**
to cry loudly because you are very sad: *'I've lost my mummy,' she wailed.*

waist /weɪst/ **noun**
the part around the middle of your body where you wear a belt

waist

waistcoat /ˈweɪstkəʊt/ **noun** UK (US **vest**)
a piece of clothing with buttons at the front and no sleeves
→ See **Clothes** on page C5

wait¹ /weɪt/ **verb**
1 A1 to stay in a place until someone or something arrives: *I'm* ***waiting for*** *Guy.*
2 **can't wait** informal A2 used to say how excited you are about something that you are going to do: *I can't wait to see him.*
3 **wait a minute/moment** B1 said in order to interrupt someone, or to get their attention or when you have suddenly thought of something important: *Now, wait a moment – I don't agree with that.*
4 **keep *somebody* waiting** B1 to be late so that someone has to wait for you: *I'm sorry to have kept you waiting.*

> **Common mistake: wait or expect?**
> When you **wait**, you stay somewhere until a person or thing arrives or is ready.
> *I waited twenty minutes for the bus.*
> *She's waiting for her exam results.*
> When you **expect** something, you think that it will happen.
> *I'm expecting the bus to arrive in about five minutes.*
> *She expected to do well in the exam.*
> ~~*She waited to do well in the exam.*~~

wait² /weɪt/ **noun** [no plural]
the act of staying in a place until someone or something arrives or someone or something is ready for you: *We had a long wait at the airport.*

waiter /ˈweɪtəʳ/ **noun**
A1 a man who works in a restaurant, bringing food to customers

waiting room /ˈweɪtɪŋ ˌruːm/ **noun**
a room in which people wait for something, for example to see a doctor

waitress /ˈweɪtrəs/ **noun**
A1 a woman who works in a restaurant, bringing food to customers

wake /weɪk/ **verb** (**waking**, **woke**, **woken**) (also **wake up**)
A1 to stop sleeping or to make someone else stop sleeping: *I've only just woken up.* ◦ *Could you wake me up before you go?*

walk¹ /wɔːk/ **verb**
A1 to move forward by putting one foot in front of the other and then repeating the action: *She walks to school.* ◦ *We walked twenty miles.*

walk² /wɔːk/ **noun**
A2 a journey that you make by walking, often for enjoyment: *He took the dog for a walk.*

walking /ˈwɔːkɪŋ/ **noun** [no plural]
A2 the activity of going for a walk, especially for pleasure in the countryside: *We're* ***going walking*** *in Wales for a week.*

wall /wɔːl/ **noun**
1 A1 one of the sides of a room or building: *There were several large paintings on the wall.*
2 A1 a structure made of brick or

a b c d e f g h i j k l m n o p q r s t u v w x y z

stone that divides different areas: *a garden wall*

wallet /ˈwɒlɪt/ **noun**
A2 a small, flat container for paper money and credit cards (= plastic cards used for paying with), usually used by a man

wallpaper /ˈwɔːlˌpeɪpəʳ/ **noun** [no plural]
paper, usually with a pattern, that you decorate walls with
• **wallpaper verb**

walnut /ˈwɔːlnʌt/ **noun**
a nut that is in two halves inside a brown shell

wander /ˈwɒndəʳ/ **verb**
to walk slowly about a place without any purpose: *They wandered around the town.*

want /wɒnt/ **verb**
A1 to hope to have or do something: *He wants a new car.* ◦ *I don't* ***want to*** *talk about it.*

war /wɔːʳ/ **noun**
A2 fighting, using soldiers and weapons, between two or more countries, or two or more groups inside a country: *They've been* ***at war*** *for the past five years.*

ward /wɔːd/ **noun**
a room in a hospital: *the cancer ward*

warden /ˈwɔːdᵊn/ **noun** UK
someone who looks after a building or the people in it

wardrobe /ˈwɔːdrəʊb/ **noun** UK (US **closet**)
B1 a large cupboard for keeping clothes in

warehouse /ˈweəhaʊs/ **noun**
a large building for keeping things that are going to be sold

warfare /ˈwɔːfeəʳ/ **noun** [no plural]
fighting in a war, especially using a particular type of weapon: *chemical warfare*

warm¹ /wɔːm/ **adj**
1 A1 having a temperature between cool and hot: *It's nice and warm in here.* ◦ *Are you warm enough?*
2 A2 Warm clothes or covers keep your body warm: *a warm sweater*
3 B1 friendly: *a warm welcome*

warm² /wɔːm/ **verb**
to become warm or to make something become warm: *I'll warm the soup.*
warm up phrasal verb
to do gentle exercises before a sport: *They were warming up before the match.*
warm (*someone/something*) up phrasal verb
to become warmer or to make someone or something warmer: *A hot drink will warm you up.*

warmly /ˈwɔːmli/ **adv**
in a friendly way

warmth /wɔːmθ/ **noun** [no plural]
1 the heat that is made by something: *the warmth of the fire*
2 the quality of being friendly: *There was no warmth in his eyes.*

warn /wɔːn/ **verb**
B1 to tell someone that something bad may happen in the future: *I* ***warned*** *you* ***that*** *it would be cold.*

warning /ˈwɔːnɪŋ/ **noun**
B1 something that tells or shows you that something bad may happen: *All cigarette packets carry a warning.*

was strong /wɒz/ weak /wəz/ **verb**
the past tense of be, used with 'I', 'he', 'she', and 'it': *He was young.*

wash¹ /wɒʃ/ **verb**
1 A1 to make something clean using water and soap: *Dad was washing the dishes.*
2 A1 to clean part of your body with water and soap: *Have you washed your hands?*
wash (*something*) up phrasal verb UK
A2 to wash the dishes, pans, and other things you have used for cooking and eating a meal
wash up phrasal verb US
to wash your hands, especially before a meal

wash² /wɒʃ/ **noun**
1 a wash an act of washing a part of your body: *Have you* ***had a wash****?*
2 a wash mainly UK an act of washing

a b c d e f g h i j k l m n o p q r s t u v w x y z

something: *Could you **give** the car **a wash**?*
3 A2 clothes, sheets, etc. that are being washed together: *Your jeans are **in the wash**.*

washbasin /ˈwɒʃˌbeɪsᵊn/ **noun** UK
a bowl in a bathroom, used for washing your face or hands

washing /ˈwɒʃɪŋ/ **noun** [no plural]
things that are being washed, such as clothes, or the act of washing these: *I'm **doing** the **washing** this morning.*

washing machine /ˈwɒʃɪŋ məˌʃiːn/ **noun**
A2 a machine that washes clothes

washing-up /ˌwɒʃɪŋˈʌp/ **noun** [no plural] UK
A2 the activity of washing the dishes, pans, and other things you have used for cooking and eating a meal: *He offered to **do the washing-up**.* ◦ ***washing-up liquid** (= liquid soap for washing dishes)*

wasn't /ˈwɒzᵊnt/
short form of was not: *I wasn't hungry this morning.*

wasp /wɒsp/ **noun**
a flying insect with a thin, black and yellow body
→ See picture at **insect**

waste¹ /weɪst/ **noun**
1 B1 a bad use of something useful, such as time or money: *Meetings are **a waste of** time.* ◦ *They throw away loads of food – it's such a waste.*
2 [no plural] things that are not wanted: *household waste*

waste² /weɪst/ **verb** (**wasting**, **wasted**)
B1 to use too much of something or use something badly: *Why waste your money on things you don't need?*

waste³ /weɪst/ **adj**
B1 Waste material is no longer needed and can be got rid of: *waste paper*

waste-paper basket /ˌweɪstˈpeɪpə ˌbɑːskɪt/ **noun** UK (US **wastebasket** /ˈweɪstˌbɑːskɪt/)
a container that is used for paper that you want to get rid of

watch¹ /wɒtʃ/ **verb**
1 A1 to look at something for a period of time: *The kids are watching TV.* ◦ *I watched him as he arrived.*
2 to be careful about something: *She has to watch what she eats.*
watch out **phrasal verb**
used to tell someone to be careful: *Watch out! There's a car coming!*

watch² /wɒtʃ/ **noun**
1 A1 a small clock on a strap that you fasten round your arm
2 [no plural] an act of watching or giving attention to something or someone: *We're **keeping a** close **watch** on the situation.*

watch

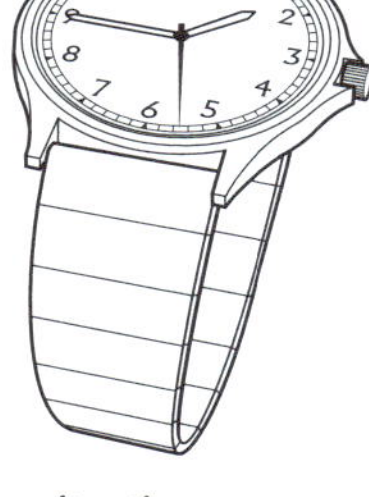

water¹ /ˈwɔːtəʳ/ **noun** [no plural]
A1 the clear liquid that falls from the sky as rain and that is in seas, lakes, and rivers: *hot/cold water* ◦ *a drink of water*

water² /ˈwɔːtəʳ/ **verb**
to pour water over plants

waterfall /ˈwɔːtəfɔːl/ **noun**
B1 a stream of water that falls from a high place, often to a pool below

watermelon /ˈwɔːtəˌmelən/ **noun**
a large, round, green fruit that is pink inside with a lot of black seeds

waterproof /ˈwɔːtəpruːf/ **adj**
Waterproof material or clothing does not let water through: *a waterproof sleeping bag*

watt /wɒt/ **noun**
a unit for measuring electrical power: *a 60 watt light bulb*

wave¹ /weɪv/ **verb** (**waving**, **waved**)
1 B1 to put your hand up and move it from side to side in order to attract someone's attention or to say goodbye: ***Wave goodbye** to Grandma.* ◦ *She **waved at** him.*
2 to move from side to side in the air

or make something move this way: *The long grass waved in the breeze.*

wave

a wave she's waving

wave² /weɪv/ **noun**

1 B1 a line of higher water that moves across the surface of the sea or a lake: *I could hear the waves crashing against the rocks.*

2 the act of waving your hand: *She **gave a** little **wave** as the train left.*

3 the pattern in which some types of energy, such as sound, light, and heat, are spread or carried: *radio waves*

wavy /ˈweɪvi/ **adj** (**wavier**, **waviest**) not straight but with slight curves: *wavy hair*

→ See **Hair** on page C9

wax /wæks/ **noun** [no plural] a solid substance that becomes soft when warm and melts easily, often used to make candles

way /weɪ/ **noun**

1 A2 how you do something: *I must **find a way** to help him.* ◦ *We looked at various **ways of** solving the problem.*

2 A2 the route you take to get from one place to another: *Is there another way out of here?* ◦ *I must buy a paper **on the way** home.*

3 B1 a particular choice, opinion, belief, or action, especially from among several possibilities: *I like the way you've had your hair done.*

4 B1 a direction something faces or travels in: *This bus is going the wrong way.*

5 B1 an amount of space or time: *We're **a long way** from home.* ◦ *The exams are still **a long way away/off**.*

6 **by the way** A2 used when you say something new or on a different subject: *Oh, by the way, my name's Julie.*

7 **way of life** B1 the way in which a person lives: *Stealing became a way of life for him.*

8 **no way!** informal B1 certainly not: *'Would you invite him to a party?' 'No way!'*

9 **be on her, my, its, etc. way** to be arriving soon: *Apparently she's on her way.*

10 **get in the way** to stop someone from doing or continuing with something: *Don't let your new friends get in the way of your studies.*

11 **give way** If something gives way, it falls because it is not strong enough to support the weight on top of it: *Suddenly the ground gave way under me.*

12 **in a way/in many ways** used to say that you think something is partly true: *In a way his behaviour is understandable.*

13 **make your way** to move somewhere, often with difficulty: *We made our way through the shop to the main entrance.*

14 **get/have your own way** to get what you want, although it upsets other people: *She always gets her own way in the end.*

WC /ˌdʌbljuːˈsiː/ **noun** UK a toilet, especially in a public place

we strong /wiː/ weak /wi/ **pronoun**

1 A1 used as the subject of the verb when the person speaking or writing is referring to themselves and one or more other people: *My wife and I both play golf and we love it.*

2 B1 used to refer to people generally: *The world in which we live today is very different.*

weak /wiːk/ **adj**

1 B1 not physically strong: *He felt too weak to sit up.*

2 B1 not good at something: *She reads well but she is **weak at** spelling.*

→ Opposite **strong** adj

3 likely to break and not able to support things: *a weak bridge*

4 A weak drink has little taste or contains little alcohol: *weak coffee*

5 not powerful, or not having a strong character: *a weak leader*
• **weakly** **adv**

weaken /ˈwiːkᵊn/ **verb**
to become less strong or powerful, or to make someone or something less strong or powerful: *Another war would weaken the economy.*

weakness /ˈwiːknəs/ **noun**
1 [no plural] a lack of strength or power: *Asking for help is not a sign of weakness.*
2 a part or quality of something or someone that is not good: *What are your weaknesses as a manager?*

wealth /welθ/ **noun** [no plural]
a large amount of money or property someone has

wealthy /ˈwelθi/ **adj** (**wealthier**, **wealthiest**)
rich: *a wealthy businessman*

weapon /ˈwepən/ **noun**
a gun, knife, or other object used to kill or hurt someone: *nuclear weapons*

wear /weəʳ/ **verb** (**wore**, **worn**)
1 A1 to have a piece of clothing, jewellery, etc. on your body: *I wear jeans a lot of the time.* ◦ *She wears glasses.*
2 to become thin and damaged after being used a lot, or to make this happen: *The carpet is already starting to wear in places.*
wear off **phrasal verb**
If a feeling or the effect of something wears off, it gradually stops: *The anaesthetic is starting to wear off.*
wear *someone* out **phrasal verb**
to make someone very tired: *All this walking is wearing me out.*
wear *something* out **phrasal verb**
B1 to use something so much that it is damaged and cannot be used any more: *He's already worn out two pairs of shoes this year.*

weather /ˈweðəʳ/ **noun** [no plural]
A1 the temperature or conditions outside, for example if it is hot, cold, sunny, etc.: *bad/good weather*

weather forecast /ˈweðə ˌfɔːkɑːst/ **noun**
B1 a description of what the weather will be like for the next few hours, days, etc.: *Have you heard the **weather forecast for** tomorrow?*

weave /wiːv/ **verb** (**weaving**, **wove**, **woven**)
to make cloth on a machine by crossing threads under and over each other

web /web/ **noun**
1 B1 a type of net made by a spider (= creature with eight legs) to catch insects: *a spider's web*
2 **the Web** A2 part of the Internet that consists of all the connected websites (= pages of text and pictures)

webcam /ˈwebkæm/ **noun**
B1 a camera that records moving pictures and sounds and allows these to be shown on the Internet as they happen

web page /ˈweb ˌpeɪdʒ/ **noun**
A2 a part of a website that can be read on a computer screen

website /ˈwebsaɪt/ **noun**
A1 an area on the Web where information about a particular subject, organization, etc. can be found

we'd /wiːd/
1 short form of we had: *By the time she arrived we'd eaten.*
2 we would: *We'd like two tickets, please.*

wedding /ˈwedɪŋ/ **noun**
B1 an official ceremony at which a man and woman get married: *We're going to a wedding on Saturday.*

Wednesday /ˈwenzdeɪ/ **noun**
A1 the day of the week after Tuesday and before Thursday

weed[1] /wiːd/ **noun**
a wild plant that you do not want in your garden

weed[2] /wiːd/ **verb**
to remove wild plants from a garden where they are not wanted

week /wiːk/ **noun**
1 A1 a period of seven days: *last week* ◦ *I've got three exams this week.*
2 A1 the five days from Monday to Friday when people usually go to work or school: *I don't go out much during the week.*

a b c d e f g h i j k l m n o p q r s t u v w x y z

weekday /ˈwiːkdeɪ/ **noun**
A2 one of the five days from Monday to Friday, when people usually go to work or school

weekend /ˌwiːkˈend/ **noun**
Saturday and Sunday, the two days in the week when many people do not work: *Are you doing anything this weekend?*

weekly /ˈwiːkli/ **adj, adv**
A2 happening once a week or every week: *a weekly newspaper*

weep /wiːp/ **verb** (**wept**)
to cry, usually because you are sad

weigh /weɪ/ **verb**
1 weigh 200 g, 75 kg, 10 stone, etc. B1 to have a weight of 200 g, 75 kg, 10 stone, etc.: *How much do you weigh?*
2 to measure how heavy someone or something is: *Can you weigh that piece of cheese for me?*

weight /weɪt/ **noun** [no plural]
1 B1 how heavy someone or something is: *He's about average height and weight.*
2 the quality of being heavy: *The shelf collapsed under the weight of the books.*
3 lose weight If someone loses weight, they become lighter and thinner: *You look thinner – have you lost weight?*
4 put on weight If someone puts on weight, they become heavier and fatter: *I put on a lot of weight when I lost my job.*

weird /wɪəd/ **adj**
very strange: *I had a really weird dream last night.*

welcome[1] /ˈwelkəm/ **exclamation**
1 A2 said to someone who has just arrived somewhere: *Welcome home!* ◦ ***Welcome to** the UK.*
2 you're welcome A2 said as a polite answer when someone thanks you for doing something: *'It was very kind of you to help.' 'You're welcome.'*
3 B1 If you are welcome, people are pleased that you are there: *You will always be welcome here.*
4 be welcome to do *something* B1 used to tell someone that they can certainly do something, if they want to: *Anyone who is interested is welcome to come.*

welcome[2] /ˈwelkəm/ **verb** (**welcoming, welcomed**)
1 B1 to say hello to someone who has arrived in a place: *Both families were there to welcome us.*
2 to be pleased about something and want it to happen: *The decision was welcomed by everybody.*

welcome[3] /ˈwelkəm/ **noun**
B1 the act of saying hello to someone who arrives somewhere: *He was **given** a warm **welcome** by his fans.*

welfare /ˈwelfeəʳ/ **noun** [no plural]
Someone's welfare is their health and happiness: *He is concerned about the welfare of young men in prison.*

well[1] /wel/ **adj** (**better, best**)
A1 healthy: *You look well!* ◦ *I'm not very well.*

well[2] /wel/ **adv**
1 A1 in a good way: *I thought they played well.* ◦ *He's **doing well** at school.*
2 A2 in a complete way or as much as possible: *I know him quite well.*
3 well done! A1 used to tell someone how pleased you are about their success: *'I passed my exams.' 'Well done!'*
4 as well A1 also: *Are you going to invite Steve as well?*
5 as well as *something* A1 in addition to something: *They have lived in the United States as well as Britain.*
6 oh well B1 used to say that a situation cannot be changed although it might be disappointing: *Oh well, you'll have plenty of other chances to find a job.*
7 all is well B1 everything is in a good or acceptable state: *I hope all is well with Zack.*
8 may/might as well used to say that it is better to do something, even though it is not a lot better: *It's not raining, so we might as well walk there.*

well[3] /wel/ **exclamation**
A1 something you say before you

start speaking: *'You'll go, won't you?' 'Well, I'm not sure.'*

well⁴ /wel/ **noun**
a deep hole in the ground from which you can get water, oil, or gas

we'll /wiːl/
short form of we will: *We'll be home on Friday.*

well behaved /ˌwel bɪˈheɪvd/ **adj**
behaving in a polite and quiet way: *The children are polite and well behaved.* ◦ *a well-behaved child*

well dressed /ˌwel ˈdrest/ **adj**
B1 wearing attractive, good quality clothes: *a well-dressed woman*

well known /ˌwel ˈnəʊn/ **adj**
A2 famous: *These pictures show her before she was well known.* ◦ *a well-known actor*

well off /ˌwel ˈɒf/ **adj**
having a lot of money: *Her parents are really well off.* ◦ *a well-off family*

well paid /ˌwel ˈpeɪd/ **adj**
earning a lot of money: *a well-paid job*

went /went/
past tense of go

wept /wept/
past tense and past participle of weep

were /wɜːʳ/
past tense of be, used with 'you', 'we', and 'they': *They were happy.*

we're /wɪəʳ/
short form of we are: *Hurry! We're late!*

weren't /wɜːnt/
short form of were not: *They weren't there.*

west, West /west/ **noun** [no plural]
1 A2 the direction that you face to see the sun go down: *Which way is west?*
2 the west A2 the part of an area that is farther toward the west than the rest: *The west of the state has a lot of farms.*
3 the West the countries of North America and western Europe
• **west adj** A2 *the west shore of the lake* ◦ *West Virginia*
• **west adv** A2 *We drove west.*

western, Western /ˈwestən/ **adj**
1 in or from the west part of an area: *western France*
2 related to the countries of North America and western Europe: *a Western diplomat*

wet /wet/ **adj** (**wetter**, **wettest**)
1 A2 covered in water or another liquid: *a wet towel*
2 A2 raining: *a wet and windy day*
3 B1 not dry yet: *wet paint*

we've /wiːv/
short form of we have: *We've bought a house.*

whale /weɪl/ **noun**
B1 a very large animal that looks like a fish and lives in the sea

whale

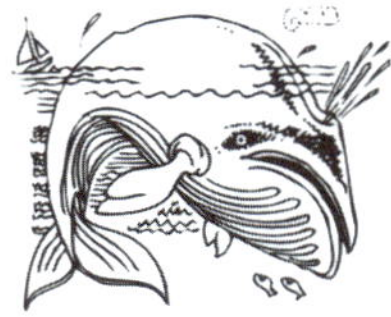

what /wɒt/ **pronoun, determiner**
1 A1 used to ask for information about something: *What's this?* ◦ *What time is it?*
2 A1 informal used when you have not heard what someone has said and you want them to repeat it: *'Do you want a drink Tom?' 'What?'*
3 B1 used to mean something without giving it a name: *I heard what he said.* ◦ *Do you know what I mean?*
4 informal used to ask what someone wants when they call you: *'Jenny?' 'Yes, what?'*
5 what about...? A2 used to suggest something: *What about asking Martin to help?*
6 what a/an... B1 used to give your opinion: *What an awful day!*
7 what if...? B1 used to ask about something that could happen in the

Common mistake: what

When you have not heard what someone has said and you want them to repeat it, you can say **what?**, but this is not polite. It is better to say **sorry?** or **pardon?**.
'It's ten o'clock.' 'Sorry/Pardon?' 'I said it's ten o'clock.'

future, especially something bad: *What if I miss the plane?*
8 what... for? used to ask about the reason or the purpose for something: *What are these tools for?* ◦ *What are you doing that for?*

whatever /wɒtˈevəʳ/ **adv, pronoun, determiner**
1 B1 anything or everything: *He eats whatever I put in front of him.*
2 used to say that what happens is not important because it does not change a situation: *Whatever happens I'll still love you.*

wheat /wiːt/ **noun** [no plural]
a plant whose grain is used for making flour, or the grain itself

wheel /wiːl/ **noun**
A2 a circular object fixed under a vehicle so that it moves smoothly over the ground: *My bike needs a new front wheel.*

wheelchair /ˈwiːltʃeəʳ/ **noun**
B1 a chair with wheels used by someone who cannot walk

when¹ /wen/ **adv**
A1 used to ask at what time something happened or will happen: *When's your birthday?* ◦ *When did he leave?*

when² /wen/ **conjunction**
A2 used to say at what time something happened or will happen: *I found it when I was cleaning out the cupboards.* ◦ *We'll go when you're ready.*

whenever /wenˈevəʳ/ **conjunction**
B1 every time or at any time: *You can go whenever you want.*

where¹ /weəʳ/ **adv**
A1 used to ask about the place or position of someone or something: *Where does she live?* ◦ *Where are my car keys?*

where² /weəʳ/ **conjunction**
A2 at, in, or to a place or position: *I know where to go.*

whereas /weərˈæz/ **conjunction**
used to compare things that are different: *You eat a big lunch, whereas I have a sandwich.*

wherever /weəˈrevəʳ/ **conjunction**
1 B1 in or to any place or every place: *You can sit wherever you like.*
2 wherever possible every time it is possible: *We try to use natural fabrics wherever possible.*

whether /ˈweðəʳ/ **conjunction**
1 B1 used to talk about a choice between two or more possibilities: *I didn't know* ***whether or not*** *to go.*
2 B1 if: *I wasn't sure whether you'd like it.*

which /wɪtʃ/ **pronoun, determiner**

> **Common mistake: which**
> Learners often spell **which** wrong. Remember that there is an **h** after the **w**.

1 A2 used to ask or talk about a choice between two or more things: *Which of these do you like best?* ◦ *Which way is it to the station?*
2 A2 used to show what thing is being talked about or written about: *These are principles which we all believe in.*
3 B1 used to give more information about something: *The book, which includes a map, gives you all the information you need about Venice.*

> **Common mistake: which or who?**
> Use **which** to refer to a thing.
> *The restaurant which is next to the pub is good.*
> ~~*The restaurant who is next to the pub is good.*~~
> Use **who** to refer to a person.
> *The boy who is wearing the red coat is called Paul.*
> ~~*The boy which is wearing the red coat is called Paul.*~~
> Sometimes it is possible to use 'that' or no word instead of **which** or **who**.
> *He's the man (that) I saw in the bar.*
> *This is the shirt (that) I bought yesterday.*

while¹ /ˈwaɪl/ **conjunction** (also UK formal **whilst**)
1 A2 during the time that: *I can't talk to anyone while I'm driving.*
2 B1 used to compare two different facts or situations: *Tom is very confident while Katy is shy and quiet.*

while² /ˈwaɪl/ **noun**
a while B1 a period of time: *I'm going out for a while.*

whimper /ˈwɪmpəʳ/ **verb**
to make quiet crying sounds because of fear or pain: *The dog was whimpering with pain.*

whine /waɪn/ **verb** (**whining**, **whined**)
to complain in an annoying way: *She's always whining about something.*

whip¹ /wɪp/ **noun**
a long piece of leather fixed to a handle and used to hit an animal or person

whip² /wɪp/ **verb** (**whipping**, **whipped**)
1 to hit a person or animal with a whip
2 to make a food such as cream more solid by mixing it hard with a kitchen tool

whirl /wɜːl/ **verb**
to move or make something move quickly round and round

whisker /ˈwɪskəʳ/ **noun**
one of the long, stiff hairs that grow around the mouths of animals such as cats

whisky /ˈwɪski/ **noun** (plural **whiskies**)
a strong alcoholic drink made from grain

whisper /ˈwɪspəʳ/ **verb**
to speak very quietly so that other people cannot hear: *She whispered something to the girl sitting next to her.*
• **whisper** noun

whisper

whistle¹ /ˈwɪsl/ **verb** (**whistling**, **whistled**)
to make a sound by breathing air out through a small hole made with your lips: *Someone whistled at her as she walked past.*

whistle² /ˈwɪsl/ **noun**
1 a small, simple instrument that makes a high sound when you blow through it: *The referee **blew** the **whistle** to end the game.*
2 the sound made by someone or something whistling

white¹ /waɪt/ **adj**
1 A1 being the colour of snow or milk: *a white T-shirt* ◦ *white walls*
2 A2 UK White coffee has milk or cream added to it: *Two coffees please, one black and one white.*
3 A2 White wine is a light yellow colour.
4 B1 Someone who is white has skin that is pale in colour.

white² /waɪt/ **noun**
1 A2 the colour of snow or milk
→ See **Colours** on page C6
2 the part of an egg that is white when it is cooked: *Mix the egg whites with the sugar.*

whiteboard /ˈwaɪtbɔːd/ **noun**
a large white board that teachers write on
→ See **The Classroom** on page C4

who /huː/ **pronoun**
1 A1 used to ask about someone's name or which person or group someone is talking about: *Who told you?* ◦ *Who's that?*
2 A2 used to show which person or group of people you are talking about: *That's the man who I saw in the bank.*
3 B1 used to give more information about someone: *My brother, who's only just seventeen, has already passed his driving test.*

who'd /huːd/
1 short form of who had: *I read about a man who'd sailed around the world.*
2 who would: *Who'd like to go?*

whoever /huːˈevəʳ/ **pronoun**
1 the person who: *Whoever broke the window will have to pay for it.*
2 used to ask who a person is when you are surprised: *Whoever could that be phoning at this time?*

whole¹ /həʊl/ **adj**
A2 complete, including every part: *She spent the whole afternoon studying.*

whole² /həʊl/ **noun**
1 **the whole of *something*** B1 all of something: *His behaviour affects the whole of the class.*

2 on the whole B1 generally: *On the whole we're very happy.*
3 as a whole when considered as a group and not in parts: *The population as a whole is getting healthier.*

who'll /huːl/
short form of who will: *Who'll be at your party?*

wholly /ˈhəʊlli/ **adv**
completely: *The news was wholly unexpected.*

whom /huːm/ **pronoun** formal
used instead of 'who' as the object of a verb or preposition: *I met a man with whom I used to work.*

who's /huːz/
1 short form of who is: *Who's your new friend?*
2 who has: *Who's been using my computer?*

whose /huːz/ **pronoun, determiner**
1 B1 used to ask who something belongs to or who someone or something is connected with: *Whose gloves are these?* ◦ *Whose car shall we use?*
2 B1 used for adding information about a person or thing just mentioned: *The story was about a man whose family came from Russia.* ◦ *It was an old house whose owner had died.*

why /waɪ/ **adv**
1 A1 used to ask or talk about the reasons for something: *Why didn't you call me?* ◦ *I wonder why he didn't come.*
2 why don't you...? A2 used to make a suggestion: *Why don't you come with us?* ◦ *Why don't you give it a try?*
3 why not? B1 used to agree with something that someone has suggested: *'Let's have an ice cream.' 'Yes, why not?'*

wicked /ˈwɪkɪd/ **adj**
1 very bad and morally wrong: *a wicked man*
2 very informal very good: *They sell some wicked clothes.*

wide[1] /waɪd/ **adj**
1 A2 measuring a long distance or longer than usual from one side to the other: *a wide road* ◦ *I have very wide feet.*
→ See picture at **narrow**
2 5 miles, 3 inches, etc. wide B1 having a distance of 5 miles, 3 inches, etc. from one side to the other: *The swimming pool is 15 feet wide.*
3 a wide range, selection, etc. B1 a lot of different types of thing: *They have a wide range of goods.*

wide[2] /waɪd/ **adv**
1 wide apart/open as far apart or open as possible: *The window was wide open.*
2 wide awake completely awake: *The baby is still wide awake.*

widely /waɪdli/ **adv**
including a lot of different places, people, subjects, etc.: *He has travelled widely in Europe.*

widen /ˈwaɪdᵊn/ **verb**
to become wider or make something become wider: *The road is being widened to two lanes.*

widespread /ˈwaɪdspred/ **adj**
affecting or including a lot of places, people, etc.: *This is a widespread problem.*

widow /ˈwɪdəʊ/ **noun**
a woman whose husband has died

widower /ˈwɪdəʊəʳ/ **noun**
a man whose wife has died

width /wɪtθ/ **noun**
the distance from one side of something to the other side: *a width of two metres*
→ See picture at **length noun** (1)

wife /waɪf/ **noun** (plural **wives** /waɪvz/)
A1 the woman that someone is married to

wig /wɪg/ **noun**
a covering of hair that you wear on your head

wild /waɪld/ **adj**
1 A2 A wild animal or plant lives or grows in its natural place and not where people live: *a wild dog* ◦ *wild flowers*
2 not controlled: *a wild party* ◦ *wild dancing*
3 be wild about *something* informal to

like something very much: *I'm not wild about jazz.*

wildlife /ˈwaɪldlaɪf/ **noun** [no plural]
B1 animals, birds, and plants in the place where they live

will[1] strong /wɪl/ weak /wəl/, /əl/ **verb**
1 A2 used to talk about what is going to happen in the future, especially things that you are certain about: *Claire will be five next month.* ◦ *I'll see him on Saturday.* ◦ *She'll have a great time.*
2 A1 used to talk about what someone or something is willing or able to do: *Ask Susie if she will take them.* ◦ *The car won't start.*
3 A2 used to ask someone to do something: *Will you give me her address?* ◦ *Will you give that to Tony when you see him, please?*

will[2] /wɪl/ **noun**
1 the power to control your thoughts and actions: *She has a very **strong will**.* ◦ *He lacks the **will to** win.*
2 what someone wants: *She was forced to marry him **against** her **will**.*
3 a piece of paper that says who will get your money, house, and things when you die: *She left me some money **in** her **will**.*

willing /ˈwɪlɪŋ/ **adj**
1 be willing to do *something* B1 to be happy to do something: *He's willing to lend us some money.*
2 wanting to do something: *He is a very willing assistant.*
→ Opposite **unwilling** **adj**
• **willingly** **adv** *She willingly agreed to help.*
• **willingness** **noun** [no plural]

win[1] /wɪn/ **verb** (**winning**, **won**)
1 A2 to get the most points in a competition or game: *Barcelona won the game 6-0.*
2 A2 to get a prize in a game or competition: *He won $500.* ◦ *She won a gold medal at the Olympics.*
3 B1 to get the most votes in an election: *Who do you think will win the election?*
4 to be successful in a war, fight, or argument: *This is a war that no one can win.*

> **Common mistake: win or beat?**
> You **win** a game or competition.
> *Who do you think will win the game?*
> You **beat** someone, or a team you are playing against.
> *We beat both teams.*
> ~~*We won both teams.*~~

win[2] /wɪn/ **noun**
success or victory in a game or competition: *The Jets have only had three wins this season.*

wind[1] /wɪnd/ **noun**
A1 a natural, fast movement of air: *The wind blew her hat off.*

wind[2] /waɪnd/ **verb** (**wound**)
1 to turn or twist something long and thin around something else several times: *She **wound** the rope **around** the tree.*
2 If a river, road, etc. winds somewhere, it bends a lot and is not straight: *The path winds along the edge of the bay.*

window /ˈwɪndəʊ/ **noun**

window

1 A1 a space in the wall of a building or car that has glass in it, used for letting light and air inside and for looking through: *Open the window if you're too hot.*
→ See **The Living Room** on page C11
2 B1 a separate area on a computer screen showing information, which you can move around

windscreen /ˈwɪndskriːn/ **noun** UK (US **windshield** /ˈwɪndʃiːld/)
B1 the window at the front end of a car, bus, etc.
→ See **Car** on page C3

windscreen wiper /ˈwɪndskriːn ˌwaɪpər/ **noun** UK (US **windshield wiper** /ˈwɪndʃiːld ˌwaɪpər/)
one of two long parts that move against a car's window to remove rain
→ See **Car** on page C3

windsurfing /ˈwɪndsɜːfɪŋ/ **noun** [no plural]
B1 a sport in which you sail across water by standing on a board and holding onto a large sail
• **windsurfer** noun

windy /ˈwɪndi/ **adj** (**windier**, **windiest**)
A2 with a lot of wind: *a windy day*

wine /waɪn/ **noun**
A1 an alcoholic drink that is made from the juice of grapes (= small, green or purple fruit): *a glass of wine*

wings

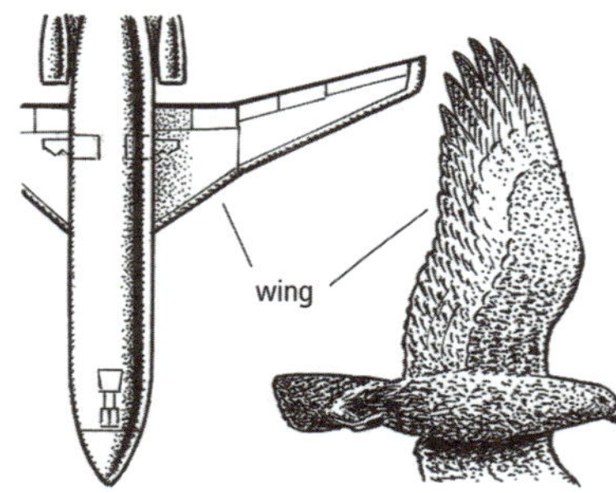

wing /wɪŋ/ **noun**
1 B1 one of the two parts that a bird or insect uses to fly
2 one of the two long, flat parts at the sides of a plane that make it stay in the sky

wink¹ /wɪŋk/ **verb**
to quickly close and then open one eye, in order to be friendly or to show that something is a joke: *She smiled and **winked at** me.*

wink

wink² /wɪŋk/ **noun**
an act of winking at someone: *He gave me a friendly wink.*

winner /ˈwɪnəʳ/ **noun**
A2 someone who wins a game, competition, or election: *the winners of the World Cup*

winter /ˈwɪntəʳ/ **noun**
A1 the coldest season of the year, between autumn and spring: *We went skiing last winter.*

wipe¹ /waɪp/ **verb** (**wiping**, **wiped**)
to clean or dry something by moving a cloth across it: *She wiped her hands on the towel.*

wipe

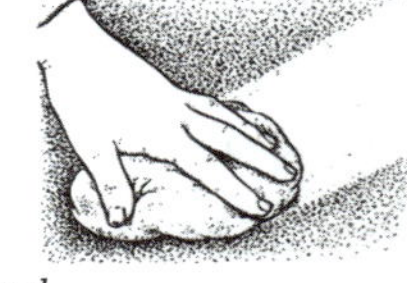

wipe² /waɪp/ **noun**
1 an act of cleaning or drying something with a cloth: *I'll **give** the table **a wipe**.*
2 a thin cloth or piece of paper used for cleaning: *baby wipes*

wire /waɪəʳ/ **noun**
1 thin, metal thread, used to fasten things or to make fences, cages, etc.
2 a long, thin piece of metal thread, usually covered in plastic, that carries electricity: *electrical wires*

wisdom /ˈwɪzdəm/ **noun** [no plural]
the ability to use your knowledge and experience to make good decisions

wise /waɪz/ **adj**
B1 having or showing the ability to make good judgments, based on a deep understanding and experience of life: *a wise leader* ◦ *I think we've made a wise choice.*
→ Opposite **unwise** adj
• **wisely** adv

wish¹ /wɪʃ/ **verb**
1 **wish (that)** B1 to want a situation that is different from the one that exists: *I wish that I didn't have to go to work.* ◦ *I **wish** he **would** leave.*
2 **wish *someone* luck, success, etc.** B1 to say that you hope someone will be lucky, successful, etc.: *I wished him luck for his test.*
3 **wish to do *something*** formal to want to do something: *I wish to speak to the manager.*

wish² /wɪʃ/ **noun**
1 what you want to do or what you

want to happen: *I **have no wish to** leave.*
2 best wishes A2 something you say or write at the end of a letter: *Best wishes, Pete*

wit /wɪt/ **noun** [no plural]
the ability to say things that are funny and clever

witch /wɪtʃ/ **noun**
in stories, a woman who has magical powers

witch

with /wɪð/ **preposition**
1 A1 used to say that people or things are in a place together or are doing something together: *Emma lives with her boyfriend.* ◦ *Hang your coat with the others.*
2 A1 having or including something: *a house with a swimming pool* ◦ *a woman with brown eyes*
3 A2 using something: *She hit him over the head with a tennis racket.*
4 B1 used to describe the way someone does something: *He plays with great enthusiasm.*
5 B1 used to say what fills, covers, etc. something: *a bucket filled with water* ◦ *shoes covered with mud*
6 because of something: *She was trembling with fear.*
7 relating to something or someone: *There's something wrong with the car.*

withdraw /wɪð'drɔː/ **verb** (**withdrew**, **withdrawn**)
1 to take money out of a bank account: *She withdrew $50.*
2 to remove something, especially because of an official decision: *He has threatened to withdraw his support.*

withdrawal /wɪð'drɔːəl/ **verb**
1 the act of taking money out of a bank account: *I'd like to make a cash withdrawal.*
2 the act of removing something, especially because of an official decision: *Despite the withdrawal of financial support, the festival went ahead.*

within /wɪ'ðɪn/ **preposition**
1 B1 before a particular period of time has finished: *The ambulance arrived within ten minutes.*
2 B1 less than a particular distance from something: *She was born within 20 miles of New York.*
3 inside an area, group, or system: *There's a pharmacy within the hospital building.*

without /wɪ'ðaʊt/ **preposition**
1 A2 not having, using, or doing something: *I did the test without any problems.* ◦ *I can't see without my glasses.*
2 A2 not with someone: *You can start the meeting without me.*

witness¹ /'wɪtnəs/ **noun**
someone who sees an accident or crime: *Police are appealing for witnesses to the shooting.*

witness² /'wɪtnəs/ **verb**
to see something happen, especially an accident or crime: *Did anyone witness the attack?*

witty /'wɪti/ **adj** (**wittier**, **wittiest**)
using words in a funny and clever way: *He was witty and charming.*

wives /waɪvz/
plural of wife

wizard /'wɪzəd/ **noun**
in stories, a man who has magical powers

wobble /'wɒbl/ **verb** (**wobbling**, **wobbled**)
If something wobbles, it moves from side to side, often because it is not on a flat surface: *The ladder started to wobble.*
• **wobbly adj** (**wobblier**, **wobbliest**) likely to wobble: *a wobbly chair*

woke /wəʊk/
past tense of wake

woken /'wəʊkən/
past participle of wake

wolf /wʊlf/ **noun** (plural **wolves** /wʊlvz/)
a wild animal like a large dog: *Wolves hunt in packs.*

woman /ˈwʊmən/ **noun** (plural **women** /ˈwɪmɪn/)
A1 an adult female person: *a 30-year-old woman*

womb /wuːm/ **noun**
the part inside a woman's body where a baby grows

won /wʌn/
past tense and past participle of win

wonder[1] /ˈwʌndəʳ/ **verb**
1 B1 to want to know something or to try to understand the reason for something: *I wonder what he's making for dinner.*
2 I/we wonder if… B1 used to politely ask someone for something or to suggest something: *I wonder if you could help me?*

wonder[2] /ˈwʌndəʳ/ **noun**
1 [no plural] surprise and admiration: *The boys gazed* ***in wonder*** *at the shiny, red Ferrari.*
2 no wonder used to say that you are not surprised about something: *No wonder she failed the test if she didn't do any work.*

wonderful /ˈwʌndəfᵊl/ **adj**

> **Common mistake: wonderful**
> Learners often spell **wonderful** wrong.
> Remember that there is only one **l**.

A2 very good: *We had a wonderful time in Spain.*
• **wonderfully** **adv**

won't /wəʊnt/
short form of will not: *I won't be home before midnight.*

wood /wʊd/ **noun**
1 A2 the hard material that trees are made of: *a piece of wood*
2 A2 (also **woods**) a large area of trees growing near each other: *We went for a walk in the woods.*

wooden /ˈwʊdᵊn/ **adj**
A2 made of wood: *a wooden chair*

wool /wʊl/ **noun** [no plural]
1 the soft, thick hair on a sheep
2 A2 thick thread or material that is made from the hair of a sheep: *a wool suit*

woollen UK (US **woolen**) /ˈwʊlən/ **adj**
made of wool: *woollen gloves*

word /wɜːd/ **noun**
1 A1 a group of letters or sounds that mean something: *'Hund' is the German word for 'dog'.*
2 have a word with *someone* to talk to someone for a short time: *I'll have a word with Ted and see if he wants to come.*
3 in other words used to explain what something means in a different way: *He said he's too busy. In other words, he isn't interested.*
4 word for word using the exact words that were originally used: *She repeated word for word what he had told her.*
5 not believe, understand, say, etc. a word B1 to not believe, understand, say, etc. anything: *I don't believe a word he says.*

wore /wɔːʳ/
past tense of wear

work[1] /wɜːk/ **verb**
1 A1 to do a job that you get money for: *Helen* ***works for*** *a computer company.* ◦ *He* ***works as*** *a waiter in an Italian restaurant.*
2 A2 If a machine or piece of equipment works, it is not broken: *The washing machine isn't working.*
3 B1 If something works, it is successful: *Her plan to get rid of me didn't work.*
work *something* out **phrasal verb**
to calculate an amount: *I'm trying to work out the total cost.*
work out **phrasal verb**
1 If a problem or difficult situation works out, it gradually becomes better: *Don't worry – everything will work out in the end.*
2 B1 to do exercises to make your body stronger

work[2] /wɜːk/ **noun**
1 A1 [no plural] something you do to get money: *Has she got any work yet?*
2 A1 [no plural] the place where you go to do your job: *He had an accident* ***at work***.
3 A2 [no plural] the activities that you

do at school, for your job, etc.: *Have you got a lot of work to do?*

4 A2 a painting, book, piece of music, etc.: *the complete works of Shakespeare*

5 B1 [no plural] the effort needed to do something: *Decorating that room was hard work.*

6 get/set to work to start doing something

> **Common mistake: work, job, or occupation?**
>
> **Work** is something you do to earn money. Remember that this noun is uncountable.
>
> *She enjoys her work in the hospital.*
>
> *He's looking for work.*
>
> ~~*He's looking for a work.*~~
>
> **Job** is used to talk about the particular work activity that you do.
>
> *He's looking for a job in computer programming.*
>
> *Teaching must be an interesting job.*
>
> ~~*Teaching must be an interesting work.*~~
>
> **Occupation** is a formal word that means the job that you do. It is often used on forms. See also: **career** and **profession**.

worker /ˈwɜːkəʳ/ **noun**

1 A2 someone who works for a company or organization but does not have a powerful position: *an office worker*

2 a quick, slow, good, etc. worker B1 someone who works quickly, slowly, well, etc.: *He's a slow worker, but he is very thorough.*

working /ˈwɜːkɪŋ/ **adj** [always before noun]

1 B1 relating to your job: *good working conditions*

2 a working man, woman, etc. someone who has a job: *a working mother*

3 a working knowledge of sth knowledge about something that is good enough to be useful: *She has a working knowledge of German and Russian.*

workman /ˈwɜːkmən/ **noun** (plural **workmen**)

a man who does a physical job such as building

workout /ˈwɜːkaʊt/ **noun**

B1 a series of exercises that you do to make your body strong and healthy: *I do a daily workout at the gym.*

worksheet /ˈwɜːkˌʃiːt/ **noun**

a piece of paper with questions and exercises for students

workshop /ˈwɜːkˌʃɒp/ **noun**

1 a place where people make or repair things

2 a meeting where people learn about something by discussing it and doing practical exercises

world /wɜːld/ **noun**

1 the world A1 the Earth and all the people, places, and things on it: *Everest is the highest mountain in the world.* ◦ *She's travelled all over the world.*

2 B1 the people and things that are involved in a particular activity or subject: *the world of politics*

3 your world A2 your life and experiences: *His whole world fell apart when she left.*

world-famous /ˌwɜːldˈfeɪməs/ **adj**

known by people everywhere in the world: *The Taj Mahal is a world-famous monument.*

worldwide /ˌwɜːldˈwaɪd/ **adj, adv**

in all parts of the world: *ten million copies have been sold worldwide.* ◦ *a worldwide success*

the World Wide Web /ˌwɜːld waɪd ˈweb/ **noun**

part of the Internet that consists of all the connected websites (= pages of text and pictures)

worm /wɜːm/ **noun**

a small creature with a long, thin, soft body and no legs

worn /wɔːn/

past participle of wear

worn out /ˌwɔːn ˈaʊt/ **adj**

1 very tired: *I was worn out after all that dancing.*

2 damaged after being used too much: *a worn-out carpet*

worried /ˈwʌrid/ **adj**

A2 unhappy because you are thinking about bad things that might happen: *She's really **worried about** her son.* ◦ *I'm **worried that** she'll tell Maria.*

a b c d e f g h i j k l m n o p q r s t u v w x y z

a b c d e f g h i j k l m n o p q r s t u v w x y z

worry[1] /ˈwʌri/ **verb** (**worrying**, **worried**)
1 A1 to think about problems or bad things that might happen: ***Don't worry*** *– she'll be all right.* ◦ *She's always **worrying about** something.*
2 to make someone feel anxious because of problems or unpleasant things that might happen: *It **worries** me **that** he hasn't called yet.*

> **Common mistake: worry about something or someone**
> Be careful to use the correct preposition after this verb.
> *They were worried about the weather.*
> ~~*They were worried for the weather.*~~

worry[2] /ˈwʌri/ **noun** (plural **worries**)
B1 a problem that makes you feel unhappy: *health worries*

worrying /ˈwʌriɪŋ/ **adj**
making you feel anxious: *It's a very worrying situation.*

worse[1] /wɜːs/ **adj**
1 A2 comparative of bad: more unpleasant, difficult, etc.: *The exam was **worse than** I expected.* ◦ *We'll have to stop the game if the rain **gets** any **worse**.*
2 B1 more ill: *The drugs aren't working – he just seems to be **getting worse**.*

worse[2] /wɜːs/ **adv**
B1 comparative of badly: *He was treated much worse than I was.*

worship /ˈwɜːʃɪp/ **verb** (**worshipping**, **worshipped**)
1 to show respect for a god by saying prayers
2 to love and respect someone very much: *She worshipped her mother.*
• **worship noun** [no plural] *a place of worship (= a religious building)*

worst[1] /wɜːst/ **adj**
A2 superlative of bad: the most unpleasant, difficult, etc.: *What's the worst job you've ever had?*

worst[2] /wɜːst/ **adv**
superlative of badly: *Roads in the north were the worst affected by the snow.*

worst[3] /wɜːst/ **noun**
the worst B1 the most unpleasant or difficult thing, person, or situation: *I've made some mistakes in the past, but this is definitely the worst.*

worth[1] /wɜːθ/ **adj**
1 be worth *something* B1 to have a particular value, especially in money: *Our house is worth about £60,000.*
2 be worth doing, seeing, trying, etc. B1 to be useful or enjoyable to do, see, try, etc.: *It's not as good as his last book but it's definitely worth reading.*
3 be worth it B1 to be useful or enjoyable despite needing a lot of effort: *It was a long climb up the mountain but the view was worth it.*

> **Common mistake: be worth doing something**
> When **worth** is followed by a verb, the verb is always in the **-ing** form.
> *Do you think it's worth asking Patrick first?*
> ~~*Do you think it's worth to ask Patrick first?*~~

worth[2] /wɜːθ/ **noun**
1 a month's, year's, etc. worth of *something* the amount of something that can be done or used in a month, year, etc.: *an hour's worth of free phone calls*
2 £20, $100, etc. worth of *something* the amount of something that you can buy for £20, $100, etc.: *I've put £2 worth of stamps on the letter.*

worthless /ˈwɜːθləs/ **adj**
having no value in money

worthwhile /ˌwɜːθˈwaɪl/ **adj**
useful and enjoyable, despite needing a lot of effort: *It's a difficult course but it's very worthwhile.*

worthy /ˈwɜːði/ **adj** (**worthier**, **worthiest**)
deserving respect or support: *a worthy cause*

would strong /wʊd/ weak /wəd/ **verb**
1 B1 used to say what might happen if something else happens: *What would you do if you lost your job?*
2 B1 used as the past form of 'will': *Lottie promised that she would help.* ◦ *The car wouldn't start this morning.*
3 B1 used to talk about a situation

that you can imagine happening: *It would be lovely to go to New York.*
4 would like/love *something* A1 used to say politely that you want something: *I'd (= I would) like a cup of coffee, please.*
5 would you...? used to politely ask someone something: *Would you like a drink?*

wouldn't /ˈwʊdᵊnt/
short form of would not: *She wouldn't let us watch TV.*

wound¹ /wuːnd/ **noun**
an injury

wound² /wuːnd/ **verb**
to hurt someone, especially with a knife or gun: *He was badly wounded in the attack.*
• **wounded adj** *a wounded bird*

wound³ /waʊnd/
past tense and past participle of wind³

wove /wəʊv/
past tense of weave²

woven /wəʊvᵊn/
past participle of weave²

wow /waʊ/ **exclamation** informal
A2 something that you say to show surprise, excitement, admiration, etc.: *Wow! Look at that car!*

wrap /ræp/ **verb** (**wrapping**, **wrapped**) (also **wrap up**)
B1 to cover something or someone with paper, cloth, etc.: *to wrap a present* ◦ *They wrapped him in a blanket.*
→ Opposite **unwrap verb**

wrapping paper /ˈræpɪŋ ˌpeɪpəʳ/ **noun** [no plural]
decorated paper that is used to cover presents: *a sheet of wrapping paper*

wreck /rek/ **verb**
to destroy something completely: *The explosion wrecked several cars.*

wreckage /ˈrekɪdʒ/ **noun** [no plural]
the parts that remain of a car, ship, or plane that has been destroyed: *Two survivors were pulled from the wreckage.*

wrench /rentʃ/ **verb**
to pull something violently away from a fixed position: *The phone had been wrenched off the wall.*

wrestle /ˈresl/ **verb** (**wrestling**, **wrestled**)
to fight with someone by holding them and trying to push them to the ground

wrestling /ˈreslɪŋ/ **noun** [no plural]
a sport in which two people fight and try to push each other to the ground
• **wrestler noun**

wriggle /ˈrɪgl/ **verb** (**wriggling**, **wriggled**)
to twist your body or move part of your body with short, quick movements: *She wriggled her toes in the warm sand.*

wring /rɪŋ/ **verb** (**wrung**) (also **wring out**)
to twist a cloth or piece of clothing with your hands to remove water from it: *He wrung out his socks and hung them up to dry.*

wrinkle /ˈrɪŋkl/ **noun**
a small line on your face that you get when you grow old
• **wrinkled adj** *a wrinkled face*

wrinkles

wrist /rɪst/ **noun**
the part of your body between your hand and your arm

write /raɪt/ **verb** (**writing**, **wrote**, **written**)

> **Common mistake: writing**
> Remember that the -ing form of **writing** has only one **t**.

1 A1 to make words, letters, or numbers on a surface using a pen or pencil: *Write your name at the top of the page.*
2 A2 to send someone a letter: *I wrote her a letter last week.*
3 B1 to create a book, story, article,

etc. or a piece of music: *He's writing a book on Russian literature.*
write *something* down **phrasal verb**
B1 to write something on a piece of paper so that you do not forget it: *Did you write Jo's phone number down?*

writer /ˈraɪtəʳ/ **noun**
B1 someone whose job is writing books, stories, articles, etc.

writing /ˈraɪtɪŋ/ **noun** [no plural]
1 A1 the skill or activity of producing words on a surface: *Speaking and writing are important parts of learning a language.*
2 A2 words that have been written or printed: *The writing was too small to read.*
3 B1 the way that someone writes: *You've got very neat writing.*
4 the activity or job of creating books, stories, or articles
5 **in writing** in the form of an official letter or document: *Please confirm your reservation in writing.*

written[1] /ˈrɪtᵊn/
past participle of write

written[2] /ˈrɪtᵊn/ **adj**
expressed in writing, or involving writing: *a written exam* ◦ *written instructions*

wrong[1] /rɒŋ/ **adj**
1 A1 not correct: *the wrong answer* ◦ *We're going the wrong way.*
2 **be wrong** A2 to think or say something that is not correct: *You were **wrong about** the party – it's today, not tomorrow.*
3 B1 If something is wrong, there is a problem: *What's wrong?* ◦ *There's something **wrong with** my computer.*
4 **get *something* wrong** B1 to produce an answer or result that is not correct, or to say or write something that is not correct: *I got most of the answers wrong.* ◦ *The newspapers got the story completely wrong.*
5 morally bad: *It's wrong to tell lies.*
6 not suitable: *I think she's **wrong for** this job.*

wrong[2] /rɒŋ/ **adv**
1 A2 in a way that is not correct: *He always says my name wrong.*
2 **go wrong** B1 to develop problems: *Something's gone wrong with my car.*

wrong[3] /rɒŋ/ **noun**
behaviour that is not morally right: *She's old enough to know the difference between right and wrong.*

wrongly /ˈrɒŋli/ **adv**
in a way that is not correct: *The letter was wrongly addressed.*

wrote /rəʊt/
past tense of write

wrung /rʌŋ/
past tense and past participle of wring

www /ˌdʌbljuːˌdʌbljuːˈdʌbljuː/ **noun**
abbreviation for World Wide Web: the part of the Internet that consists of all the connected websites

X, x /eks/
1 the twenty-fourth letter of the alphabet
2 used to show that an answer is wrong
3 used to mean a kiss at the end of a letter
4 used to mean an unknown person or thing

Xmas /ˈkrɪsməs/ **noun** informal
used as a short way of writing 'Christmas', mainly on signs or cards: *Happy Xmas!*

X-ray /ˈeksreɪ/ **noun**
a photograph that shows the inside of your body: *They **took an X-ray** of his leg.*
• **X-ray verb** to take a photograph that shows the inside of something

a b c d e f g h i j k l m n o p q r s t u v w x **y** z

Y y

Y, y /waɪ/
the twenty-fifth letter of the alphabet

yacht /jɒt/ noun
a large boat with sails used for pleasure or in races: *a luxury yacht*

yacht

yard /jɑːd/ noun (written abbreviation **yd**)
1 B1 a unit for measuring length, equal to 0.9144 metres or three feet
2 US (UK **garden**) an area of land in front of or behind a house

yawn /jɔːn/ **verb**
to take a deep breath with your mouth wide open, because you are tired or bored: *She yawned and looked at her watch.*
• **yawn** noun

yd
written abbreviation for yard: a unit for measuring length

yeah /jeə/ **exclamation** informal spoken
A2 yes: *Yeah, I agree.*

year /jɪəʳ/ **noun**
1 A1 a period of twelve months, or 365 or 366 days, especially from 1 January to 31 December: *He joined the company a year ago.*
2 be … years old A1 to be a particular age: *Her son is six years old.*
3 A2 the part of the year, in a school or university, during which courses are taught: *the school year* ◦ *I'm* ***in my second year*** *at Pisa University.*
4 years B1 a long time: *I haven't seen Linda for years.*

Common mistake: describing age

If you describe someone's age by saying 'Tom is eight years old', you always write the age as three separate words.
My son is eight years old.
You can use eight-year-old, etc. as an adjective. When you do this, the words are written together using hyphens.
I've got a twelve-year-old son.
You can also do the same with days, weeks, and months.
I've got a ten-week-old rabbit.
The baby is three months old.
a three-month-old baby

yearly /jɪəli/ **adj, adv**
happening once a year or every year: *a yearly fee*

yeast /jiːst/ **noun** [no plural]
a substance used to make bread rise and to make beer and wine

yell /jel/ **verb**
to shout something very loudly: *The policeman* ***yelled at*** *them to stop.*
• **yell** noun

yellow[1] /ˈjeləʊ/ **adj**
A1 being the same colour as a lemon or the sun: *a bright yellow tablecloth*

yellow[2] **noun**
A2 the colour yellow
→ See **Colours** on page C6

yes /jes/ **exclamation**
1 A1 used to agree with something, or to give a positive answer to something: *'Can I borrow your pencil?' 'Yes, of course.'* ◦ *'Coffee?' 'Yes, please.'*
2 A1 used as an answer when someone calls you: *'Jack!' 'Yes?'*
3 A2 used when you are disagreeing with a negative statement: *'I'm not a very good cook.' 'Yes, you are – you cook really well!'*

yesterday /ˈjestədeɪ/ **noun** [no plural], **adv** [no plural]
A1 the day before today: *I went to see the doctor yesterday.*

yet[1] /jet/ **adv**
1 A2 before now or before that time: *Have you read his book yet?* ◦ *'Has he called?' 'No, not yet.'*
2 A2 now or as early as this time: *I don't want to go home yet.*
3 the best, worst, etc. yet the best, worst, etc. until now: *That was my worst exam yet.*

yet[2] /jet/ **conjunction**
B1 used to connect two words, phrases, or clauses when the second part adds something surprising to the first part: *Her solution was simple yet*

effective. ◦ *The price of the house was low, yet no one wanted to buy it.*

yield /jiːld/ **verb**
1 to make or provide something: *to yield a profit*
2 yield to demands, pressure, etc. to be forced to do something

yoga /ˈjəʊgə/ **noun** [no plural]
B1 a set of exercises for the mind and body, based on the Hindu religion: *She does yoga three times a week.*

yogurt /ˈjɒgət/ **noun**
A2 a thick, liquid food with a slightly sour taste that is made from milk
→ See **Food** on page C7

yolk /jəʊk/ **noun**
the round, yellow part in the middle of an egg

you strong /juː/ weak /ju/, /jə/ **pronoun**
1 A1 used to mean the person or people you are talking to: *I love you.* ◦ *You said I could go with you.*
2 A2 people generally: *You learn to accept these things as you get older.*

you'd /juːd/
1 short form of you had: *You'd better go home now.*
2 you would: *I expect you'd like some lunch.*

you'll /juːl/
short form of you will: *I hope you'll come again.*

young[1] /jʌŋ/ **adj**
A1 having lived or existed for only a short time and not old: *young people*

young[2] /jʌŋ/ **noun** [no plural]
1 the young young people generally: *It's the sort of music that appeals mainly to the young.*
2 ***something's*** **young** an animal's babies

your strong /jɔːʳ/ weak /jəʳ/ **determiner**
1 A1 belonging or relating to the person or people you are talking to: *Can I borrow your pen?* ◦ *It's not your fault.*
2 B1 belonging or relating to people in general: *You never stop loving your children.*

you're /jɔːʳ/
short form of you are: *You're my best friend.*

yours /jɔːz/ **pronoun**
1 A2 the things that belong or relate to the person or people you are talking to: *Is this pen yours?*
2 Yours faithfully, sincerely, etc. B1 used just before your name at the end of a polite or formal letter

yourself /jɔːˈself/ **pronoun**
1 A2 used to show that it is you who is affected by an action: *Don't cut yourself with that sharp knife.*
2 used to give more attention to the word 'you': *Did you make the dress yourself?*
3 by yourself/yourselves A2 alone or without anyone else's help: *I'm amazed you managed to move those boxes all by yourself.*
4 used when both the subject and object of the verb are 'you', and 'you' is also being used to refer to people generally: *You tell yourself everything's all right but you know it's not really.*

youth /juːθ/ **noun** formal
1 a young man: *gangs of youths*
2 B1 young people generally: *the youth of today*
3 ***someone's*** **youth** the period of time when someone is young: *I was very shy* ***in*** *my* ***youth***.
4 [no plural] the quality of being young

youth club /ˈjuːθ ˌklʌb/ **noun**
a place where older children can go to play sports and do other social activities

youth hostel /ˈjuːθ ˌhɒstᵊl/ **noun**
a cheap, simple hotel, especially for young people who are travelling around

you've /juːv/
short form of you have: *If you've finished your work, you can go.*

a b c d e f g h i j k l m n o p q r s t u v w x y z

Zz

Z, z /zed/
the twenty-sixth and last letter of the alphabet

zebra /ˈzebrə/ **noun**
an animal like a horse with black and white lines

zero /ˈzɪərəʊ/
1 A2 the number 0
2 B1 [no plural] the temperature at which water freezes in degrees centigrade: *The temperature is ten degrees **below zero**.*

zigzag /ˈzɪgzæg/ **noun**
a line that changes direction from left to right and back again at sharp angles

zip[1] /zɪp/ **noun** UK (US **zipper**)
a thing for fastening clothes, bags, etc., consisting of two rows of very small parts that connect together: *Your zip's undone.*

zip[2] /zɪp/ **verb** (**zipping**, **zipped**) (also **zip up**)
to fasten something with a zip: *He zipped up his jacket.*

ZIP code /ˈzɪp ˌkəʊd/ **noun** US
a set of numbers that go after someone's address in the US

zipper /ˈzɪpər/ **noun** US
a zip

zone /zəʊn/ **noun**
B1 an area where a particular thing happens: *an earthquake zone (= where earthquakes happen often)*

zoo /zuː/ **noun**
A1 a place where wild animals are kept and people come to look at them

zucchini /zʊˈkiːni/ **noun** (plural **zucchini**, **zucchinis**) US (UK **courgette**)
a long, green vegetable that is white inside

Irregular Verbs

This list gives the infinitive form of the verb, its past tense, and then the past participle.

Infinitive	Past Tense	Past Participle
arise	arose	arisen
be	was/were	been
bear	bore	borne
beat	beat	beaten
become	became	become
begin	began	begun
bend	bent	bent
bet	bet	bet
bid	bid	bid
bind	bound	bound
bite	bit	bitten
bleed	bled	bled
blow	blew	blown
break	broke	broken
breed	bred	bred
bring	brought	brought
broadcast	broadcast	broadcast
build	built	built
burn	burnt, burned	burnt, burned
burst	burst	burst
buy	bought	bought
cast	cast	cast
catch	caught	caught
choose	chose	chosen
cling	clung	clung
come	came	come
cost	cost	cost
creep	crept	crept
cut	cut	cut
deal	dealt	dealt
dig	dug	dug
draw	drew	drawn
dream	dreamed, dreamt	dreamed, dreamt
drink	drank	drunk
drive	drove	driven
eat	ate	eaten

Infinitive	Past Tense	Past Participle
feed	fed	fed
fall	fell	fallen
feel	felt	felt
fight	fought	fought
find	found	found
flee	fled	fled
fling	flung	flung
fly	flew	flown
forbid	forbade	forbidden
forecast	forecast	forecast
foresee	foresaw	foreseen
forget	forgot	forgotten
forgive	forgave	forgiven
freeze	froze	frozen
get	got	got, *US* gotten
give	gave	given
go	went	gone
grind	ground	ground
grow	grew	grown
hang	hung	hung
have	had	had
hear	heard	heard
hide	hid	hidden
hit	hit	hit
hold	held	held
hurt	hurt	hurt
keep	kept	kept
kneel	knelt	knelt
know	knew	known
lay	laid	laid
lead	led	led
lean	leaned, leant	leaned, leant
leap	leapt	leapt
learn	learned, learnt	learned, learnt
leave	left	left
lend	lent	lent
let	let	let

Infinitive	Past Tense	Past Participle
lie	lay	lain
light	lit	lit
lose	lost	lost
make	made	made
mean	meant	meant
meet	met	met
mistake	mistook	mistaken
misunderstand	misunderstood	misunderstood
mow	mowed	mown
outgrow	outgrew	outgrown
overhear	overheard	overheard
oversleep	overslept	overslept
overtake	overtook	overtaken
pay	paid	paid
put	put	put
quit	quit	quit
read	read	read
rebuild	rebuilt	rebuilt
repay	repaid	repaid
rewind	rewound	rewound
ride	rode	ridden
ring	rang	rung
rise	rose	risen
run	ran	run
say	said	said
see	saw	seen
seek	sought	sought
sell	sold	sold
send	sent	sent
set	set	set
sew	sewed	sewn
shake	shook	shaken
shed	shed	shed
shine	shone	shone
shoot	shot	shot
show	showed	shown
shrink	shrank	shrunk
shut	shut	shut
sing	sang	sung
sink	sank	sunk
sit	sat	sat
sleep	slept	slept
slide	slid	slid
slit	slit	slit

Infinitive	Past Tense	Past Participle
smell	smelled, smelt	smelled, smelt
sow	sowed	sown
speak	spoke	spoken
speed	sped	sped
spell	spelled, spelt	spelled, spelt
spend	spent	spent
spill	spilled, spilt	spilled, spilt
spin	spun	spun
spit	spat	spat
split	split	split
spread	spread	spread
spring	sprang	sprung
stand	stood	stood
steal	stole	stolen
stick	stuck	stuck
sting	stung	stung
stink	stank	stunk
strike	struck	struck
swear	swore	sworn
sweep	swept	swept
swell	swelled	swollen
swim	swam	swum
swing	swung	swung
take	took	taken
teach	taught	taught
tear	tore	torn
tell	told	told
think	thought	thought
throw	threw	thrown
tread	trod	trodden
undergo	underwent	undergone
understand	understood	understood
undo	undid	undone
unwind	unwound	unwound
upset	upset	upset
wake	woke	woken
wear	wore	worn
weave	wove	woven
weep	wept	wept
win	won	won
wind	wound	wound
withdraw	withdrew	withdrawn
wring	wrung	wrung
write	wrote	written

Essential phrasal verbs

Phrasal verbs are verbs that have two or three words. For example, **look up** and **carry on** are phrasal verbs. In this section you will find the most important phrasal verbs. Try to learn them, starting with those marked A1, then A2, then B1.

add something **up** B1
to put two or more numbers together to get a total:
Have you added up all the figures?

base something **on** something B1
If you base something on facts or ideas, you use those facts or ideas to develop it:
This book is based on a true story.

believe in something B1
to be certain that something exists:
Do you believe in life after death?

belong to someone A2
If something belongs to you, you own it:
This necklace belonged to my grandmother.

belong to something B1
to be a member of an organization:
We belong to the same health club.

blow (something) **away** B1
If something blows away, or if the wind blows something away, that thing moves because the wind blows it:
The letter blew away and I had to run after it.

blow (something) **down** B1
If something blows down, or if the wind blows something down, that thing falls to the ground because the wind blows it:
The wind blew our fence down last night.

blow something **out** B1
to stop a flame burning by blowing on it:
Emma blew out the candle.

blow something **up** B1
to destroy something with a bomb:
Terrorists blew up an office building in the city.

book someone **in**/**book** someone **into** something B1
to arrange for someone to stay at a hotel:
She booked me into a hotel in the town centre.

break down B1
If a car or machine breaks down, it stops working:
My car broke down on the way to work.

break into something B1
to get into a building or car using force, usually to steal something:
Someone broke into the office and stole some computers.

break up
1 B1 to stop having a relationship:
He's just broken up with his girlfriend.
2 B1 **UK** When schools or colleges break up, the classes end and the holidays begin.

bring something **back** B1
to return from somewhere with something:
Look at what I brought back from my trip.

bring someone **up** B1
to take care of a child until he or she becomes an adult:
Her grandparents brought her up.

call (someone) **back** B1
to telephone someone a second time, or to telephone someone who telephoned you earlier

call for someone B1
to go to a place in order to get someone:
I'll call for you at eight.

call in B1
to visit a place or person for a short time, usually while you are going somewhere else:
I'll call in on my way home.

care for someone B1
to look after someone who is young, old, or ill:
The children are being cared for by a relative.

carry on B1
to continue doing something:
*We will **carry on with** the game unless it rains.*

carry something **out** B1
to do or complete something, especially something that you have said you would do or that you have been told to do:
The hospital is carrying out tests to find out what's wrong.

catch (someone/something) **up** B1
to reach the same level or quality as someone or something else:
*She's doing extra work to **catch up with** the rest of the class.*

check in B1
to show your ticket at an airport so they can tell you your seat number

check in/check into something B1
to say who you are when you arrive at a hotel so that you can be given a key for your room:
Please check in at the reception desk.

check out B1
to leave a hotel after paying

come along B1
to go somewhere with someone:
We're going to the zoo. Do you want to come along?

come back A2
to return to a place:
I've just come back from the dentist's.

come from something A1
to be born, got from, or made somewhere:
She comes from Poland. ○ *Milk comes from cows.*

come in A2
to enter a room or building:
Come in and have a cup of coffee.

come on B1
said to encourage someone to do something, especially to hurry or try harder:
Come on, the taxi's waiting.

come out
1 B1 If a book, movie, etc. comes out, it becomes available for people to buy or see:
When does their new album come out?
2 B1 If the sun, the moon, or a star comes out, it appears in the sky:
It's really warm when the sun comes out.

come round UK A2
to visit someone at their house:
You must come round for dinner some time.

complain of something B1
to tell other people that something is making you feel ill:
She's been complaining of a headache all day.

consist of something B1
to be made from something:
The dessert consisted of fruit and cream.

cut something **up** B1
to cut something into pieces:
*I **cut up** the meat **into** small pieces.*

deal with something B1
to do something to make a situation work or to solve a problem:
How will we deal with these problems?

depend on someone/something
1 B1 to need the help of someone or something:
Our economy depends on the car industry.
2 B1 to be affected by someone or something:
What you buy depends on how much you can spend.

eat out B1
to eat at a restaurant:
Let's eat out tonight.

end up B1
to finally be in a particular place or situation:
He ended up in prison.

fall down B1
to fall onto the ground:
The wall is in danger of falling down.

fall over B1
to fall to the ground:
She fell over and hurt her knee.

fill something **in/out** A2
to write all the information that is needed on a document:
Please fill out this form.

fill (something) **up** B1
to become full, or to make something become full:
The restaurant soon filled up with people.

find (something) **out** A2
to get information about something:
I must find out the train times.

get at something B1
to be able to reach or get something:
Put the cake on a high shelf where the kids can't get at it.

get back A2
to return to a place after you have been somewhere else:
We got back home late last night.

get something back B1
to be given something again that you had before:
Don't lend him money – you'll never get it back.

get in
1 B1 to succeed in entering a place, especially a building:
The thieves got in through the bathroom window.
2 B1 to arrive at a place at a particular time:
My train gets in at 9.45 p.m.
3 B1 to succeed in being chosen or elected:
He wanted to go to Cambridge University but he didn't get in.

get off (something) A2
to leave a bus, train, plane, or boat:
We should get off at the next stop.

get on **UK**
1 B1 If two or more people get on, they like each other and are friends:
Karen and Dianne don't get on.
2 B1 to manage or deal with a situation:
How are you getting on in your new flat?

get on (something) A2
to go onto a bus, train, plane, or boat:
I think we got on the wrong bus.

get out B1
to move out of a car:
I'll get out when you stop at the traffic lights.

get together B1
to meet in order to do something or spend time together:
Let's get together next week for a game of tennis.

get (someone) **up** A1
to wake up and get out of bed, or to make someone do this:
I had to get up at five o'clock this morning.

give something **away** B1
to give something to someone without asking for payment:
They're giving away a CD with this magazine.

give something **back** A2
to give something to the person who gave it to you:
Has she given you those books back yet?

give in
1 B1 to finally agree to do something that someone wants:
We will never give in to terrorists' demands.
2 B1 to accept that you have been defeated and agree to stop competing or fighting:
You'll never guess the answer – do you give in?

give something **in** B1
to give a piece of written work, etc. to someone to read:
Have you given that essay in yet?

give something **out** B1
to give something to a lot of people:
He gave out copies of the report.

give up something
1 B1 If you give up something bad, such as smoking, you stop doing it or having it:
I gave up smoking two years ago.
2 B1 to stop doing an activity or piece of work before you have completed it, usually because it is too difficult:
I've given up trying to help her.
3 B1 to stop doing a regular activity or job:
Are you going to give up work when you have your baby?

go away
1 B1 to leave a place:
Just go away and leave me alone.
2 B1 to leave your home in order to spend time in a different place:
We're going away for a few weeks in the summer.

go back B1
to return to a place where you were or where you have been before:
When are you going back to Paris?

go down
1 B1 to become lower in level:
Food prices have gone down recently.
2 B1 When the sun goes down, it moves down in the sky until it cannot be seen any more:
I sat and watched the sun go down.

go for something B1 to choose something:
I don't know whether to go for the fish or the steak.

go in A2 to enter a place:
I looked through the window but I didn't go in.

go off
1 B1 to leave a place and go somewhere else:
She went off with Laurie.
2 B1 If a light or machine goes off, it stops working:
The heating goes off at ten o'clock.

go on
1 B1 to last for a particular period of time:
The speech seemed to go on forever.
2 B1 to happen:
What's going on?

go out
1 A1 to leave a place in order to go somewhere else:
Are you going out tonight?
2 B1 If two people go out together, they have a romantic relationship with each other:
Tina is ***going out with*** *Peter.*
3 B1 If a light or something that is burning goes out, it stops producing light or heat:
I'm sorry – I let the fire go out.

go up B1
to become higher in level:
House prices keep going up.

grow up A2
to become older or an adult:
She grew up in Madrid.

hand something **in** B1
to give your finished work to a teacher:
Have you handed your history essay in yet?

hand something **out** B1
to give something to all the people in a group:
The teacher handed out worksheets to the class.

hang about/around *informal* B1
to spend time somewhere, usually doing little:
Teenagers hang around on street corners.

hang on *informal* B1
to wait for a short time:
Hang on – I'm coming.

hang out *informal* B1
to spend a lot of time in a place or with someone:
I've been ***hanging out with*** *my cousins.*

hang up B1
to finish talking on the telephone:
When I said who I was, she just hung up.

hang something **up** B1
to put something such as a coat somewhere where it can hang:
You can hang up your jacket over there.

have (got) something **on** B1
If you have clothes or shoes on, you are wearing them:
He's got a red shirt on.

hear from someone B1
to get a letter, telephone call, or other message from someone:
Have you heard from Helena recently?

hold on *informal* B1
to wait:
Hold on! I'll just check my diary.

hold something/someone **up** B1
to make something or someone slow or late:
Sorry I'm late. I got held up in traffic.

hurry up B1
to start moving or doing something more quickly:
Hurry up! We're going to be late.

join in (something) B1
to do an activity with other people:
We're playing cards. Would you like to join in?

keep someone **in** B1
to make a child stay inside, often as a punishment, or to make someone stay in hospital:
She kept the children in as it was so cold.

keep (someone/something) **off** something B1
to not go onto an area, or to stop someone or something from going onto an area:
Keep off the grass.

keep on doing something B1
to continue to do something, or to do something again and again:
She kept on asking me questions.

keep (someone/something) **out** B1
to not go into a place, or to stop someone or something from going into a place:
The building sign said 'Danger – Keep out'.

keep something **up** B1
to not allow something that is good, strong, etc. to become less good, strong, etc.:
Keep up the good work!

key something **in** B1
to put information into a computer using a keyboard:
Key in your name and password.

knock someone **down** **UK** B1
to hit someone with a car and hurt or kill them:
She was knocked down by a bus.

laugh at someone/something B1
to show that you think someone or something is stupid:
The other children laughed at him because of his strange clothes.

leave someone/something **behind** A2
to leave a place without taking someone or something with you:
We were in a hurry and I left my keys behind.

lie down A2
to move into a position in which your body is flat, usually in order to sleep or rest:
I'm not feeling well – I'm going to lie down.

look after someone/something A2
to take care of someone or something:
Could you look after the children while I'm out?

look around/round (something) B1
to visit a place and look at the things in it:
She spent the afternoon looking round the town.

look forward to something B1
to feel happy and excited about something that is going to happen:
I'm really looking forward to seeing him.

look out! B1
something you say when someone is in danger:
Look out – there's a car coming!

look something **up** B1
to look at a book or computer in order to find information:
I looked it up on the Internet.

move in B1
to begin living in a new home:
We're moving in next week.

move out B1
to stop living in a particular home:
He moved out when he was only 18.

pass something **on**
1 B1 to tell someone something that someone else has told you:
Did you pass on my message to him?
2 B1 to give something to someone else:
Will you pass the book on to Lara when you've finished with it?

pay someone/something **back** B1
to pay someone the money that you owe them:
Has he paid you back the money he owes you?

pick something/someone **up**
1 A2 to lift something or someone by using your hands:
He picked his coat up off the floor.
2 A2 to go somewhere in order to get someone or something:
Can you pick me up from the airport?

pick something **up** A2
to learn a new skill or language by practising it, not by studying it:
When you live in a country you soon pick up the language.

put something **away** B1
to put something in the place where you usually keep it:
She folded the towels and put them away.

put something **back** B1
to put something where it was before it was moved:
I put the book back on the shelf.

put something **down** B1
to put something that you are holding onto the floor or onto another surface:
You can put your suitcase down in the hall.

put someone **down** B1
to write someone's name on a list or document, usually in order to arrange for them to do something:
I've ***put*** *you* ***down for*** *the trip next week.*

put something **off** B1
to decide to do something at a later time:
I must talk to her about this. I can't put it off any longer.

put something **on**
1 A2 to put clothes or shoes onto your body:
You'd better put your coat on – it's cold outside.
2 A2 to put make-up or cream onto your skin:
I always put on my make-up before I go to work.
3 A2 to put a CD, DVD, etc. into a machine so that you can hear or see it:
Do you mind if I put some music on?
4 B1 to make a piece of equipment work by pressing a switch:
Can you put the light on?
5 B1 If someone puts on weight, they become heavier:
She put on eight pounds in a month.

put something **out** B1
to make something that is burning stop burning:
to put out a fire

put someone **through** B1
to connect someone using a telephone to the person they want to speak to:
Can you put me through to customer services, please?

put something **up**
1 B1 to raise something, or to fix something in a raised position:
I put my hand up to ask the teacher a question. ○ They put a few pictures up on the wall.
2 B1 to increase the price or value of something:
I see they've put up the price of fuel again.

remind someone **of** something/someone B1
to make someone think of something or someone else:
This song reminds me of our trip to Spain.

ring (someone) **back** **UK** B1
to telephone someone a second time, or to telephone someone who rang you earlier:
I'm a bit busy – can I ring you back later?

ring (someone) **up** B1
to telephone someone:
Ring Paul up and ask what he's doing tonight.

run out
1 B1 to use all of something so that there is none left:
*I've nearly **run out of** money.*
2 B1 If a supply of something runs out, all of it has been used or it is completely finished:
The milk has run out.

send something **back** B1
to return something to the person who sent it to you, especially because it is damaged or not suitable:
I had to send the shirt back because it didn't fit me.

set off B1
to start a journey:
What time are you setting off tomorrow morning?

set out B1
to start a journey:
We had to set out early.

set something **up** B1
to start a company or organization:
He set up his own company.

show up B1 *informal*
to arrive somewhere:
I invited him for eight, but he didn't show up until nine-thirty.

shut (something) **down** B1
If a computer or machine shuts down or someone shuts it down, it stops operating:
Make sure you shut down your computer before you go.

sign up B1
to arrange to do an organized activity:
*I've **signed up for** evening classes at the local college.*

split up B1
If two people split up, they end their relationship:
*She **split up with** her boyfriend.*

start (something) **off** B1
to begin by doing something, or to make something begin by doing something:
I'd like to start off by thanking you all for coming.

stay behind B1
to not leave a place when other people leave it:
He stayed behind after class to speak to the teacher.

stay in B1
to stay in your home:
Let's stay in tonight and watch a movie.

switch (something) **off** B1
to turn off a light, television, etc. by using a switch:
Have you switched the computer off?

switch (something) **on** B1
to turn on a light, television, etc. by using a switch:
Could you switch on the light?

take something **away**
1 **B1** **UK** to buy food in a restaurant to eat somewhere else:
Is that to eat here or take away?
2 **B1** to remove one number from another number:
If you take 4 away from 12 you get 8.

take something **back** **B1**
to return something to the place where you got it

take something **off** **A2**
to remove something:
If you're hot, take your jacket off.

take off **A2**
If a plane takes off, it begins to fly.

take someone **out** **B1**
to go somewhere with someone and pay for them:
Our boss took us out for a meal.

take something **out** **B1**
to remove something from somewhere:
He reached into his bag and took out a book.

take something **up** **B1**
to start doing a particular job or activity:
I've taken up cycling.

think about/ofsomeone/something
1 **A2** to consider doing something:
I'm thinking of moving to Sydney.
2 **B1** to remember someone or something:
I was just thinking about you when you phoned.

throw something **away** **B1**
to get rid of something that you do not want any more:
He read the magazine and then threw it away.

try something **on** **A2**
to put on a piece of clothing to see if it fits you:
Could I try this dress on, please?

turn something **down** **B1**
to reduce the level of sound or heat that a machine produces:
Could you turn the radio down, please?

turn (someone/something) **into** someone/something **B1**
to change and become someone or something different, or to make someone or something do this:
The countryside is turning into a desert. ◦ *They want to turn the offices into apartments.*

turn something **off** **A2**
to move the switch on a machine, light, etc. so that it stops working:
How do you turn the computer off?

turn something **on** **A2**
to move the switch on a machine, light, etc. so that it starts working:
Ben turned the TV on.

turn something **up** **B1**
to increase the level of sound or heat that a machine produces:
Could you turn the heating up, please?

wash (something) **up** **UK** **A2**
to wash the dishes, pans, and other things you have used for cooking and eating a meal

wear something **out** **B1**
to use something so much that it is damaged and cannot be used any more:
He's already worn out two pairs of shoes this year.

work out **B1**
to do exercises to make your body stronger

write something **down** **B1**
to write something on a piece of paper so that you do not forget it:
Did you write Jo's phone number down?

Countries, regions, and continents

This list shows the spellings and pronunciations of countries, regions, and continents. Each name is followed by its related adjective. Most of the time you can use the adjective to talk about a person who comes from each place. For example, a person from Brazil is a **Brazilian**. However, in some cases you must use a special word, which is shown after the adjective (for example, **Finn** is the word for a person from Finland). Sometimes the word shown ends in 'man'. This word can only be used to refer to a man; the word for a woman ends in 'woman' (for example **Frenchman**, **Frenchwoman**).

To talk about more than one person from a particular place, add 's', except for:
- words ending in 'ese' or 's', which remain the same (**Chinese**, **Swiss**);
- words ending in 'man' or 'woman', which change to 'men' and 'women' (**Irishman**, **Irishwoman** become **Irishmen**, **Irishwomen**).

This list is for reference only. Inclusion does not imply or suggest status as a sovereign nation.

Name	Adjective/Person
Afghanistan /æfˈgænɪstæn/	Afghan /ˈæfgæn/
Africa /ˈæfrɪkə/	African /ˈæfrɪkən/
Albania /ælˈbeɪniə/	Albanian /ælˈbeɪniən/
Algeria /ælˈdʒɪəriə/	Algerian /ælˈdʒɪəriən/
Central America /ˌsentrᵊl əˈmerɪkə/	Central American /ˌsentrᵊl əˈmerɪkən/
North America /ˌnɔːθ əˈmerɪkə/	North American /ˌnɔːθ əˈmerɪkən/
South America /ˌsaʊθ əˈmerɪkə/	South American /ˌsaʊθ əˈmerɪkən/
Andorra /ænˈdɔːrə/	Andorran /ænˈdɔːrən/
Angola /æŋˈgəʊlə/	Angolan /æŋˈgəʊlən/
Antarctica /ænˈtɑːktɪkə/	Antarctic /ænˈtɑːktɪk/
Antigua and Barbuda /ænˌtiːgə ᵊnd bɑːˈbjuːdə/	Antiguan /ænˈtiːgən/, Barbudan /bɑːˈbjuːdᵊn/
The Arctic /ˈɑːktɪk/	Arctic /ˈɑːktɪk/
Argentina /ˌɑːdʒᵊnˈtiːnə/	Argentine /ˈɑːdʒᵊntaɪn/, Argentinian /ˌɑːdʒᵊnˈtɪniən/
Armenia /ɑːˈmiːniə/	Armenian /ɑːˈmiːniən/
Asia /ˈeɪʒə/	Asian /ˈeɪʒᵊn/
Australasia /ɒstrəˈleɪʒə/	Australasian /ɒstrəˈleɪʒᵊn/
Australia /ɒsˈtreɪliə/	Australian /ɒsˈtreɪliən/
Austria /ˈɒstriə/	Austrian /ˈɒstriən/
Azerbaijan /ˌæzəbaɪˈdʒɑːn/	Azerbaijani /ˌæzəbaɪˈdʒɑːni/; *Person*: Azeri /əˈzeəri/
The Bahamas /bəˈhɑːməz/	Bahamian /bəˈheɪmiən/
Bahrain /bɑːˈreɪn/	Bahraini /bɑːˈreɪni/
Bangladesh /ˌbæŋgləˈdeʃ/	Bangladeshi /ˌbæŋgləˈdeʃi/
Barbados /bɑːˈbeɪdɒs/	Barbadian /bɑːˈbeɪdiən/
Belarus /ˌbeləˈruːs/	Belorussian /ˌbeləˈrʌʃᵊn/
Belgium /ˈbeldʒəm/	Belgian /ˈbeldʒən/
Belize /bəˈliːz/	Belizean /bəˈliːziən/
Benin /beˈniːn/	Beninese /ˌbenɪˈniːz/

Bhutan /buːˈtɑːn/	**Bhutanese** /ˌbuːtəˈniːz/
Bolivia /bəˈlɪviə/	**Bolivian** /bəˈlɪviən/
Bosnia-Herzegovina /ˌbɒzniəˌhɜːtsəˈgɒvɪnə/	**Bosnian** /ˈbɒzniən/
Botswana /bɒtˈswɑːnə/	**Botswanan** /bɒtˈswɑːnən/; *Person:* **Motswana** /mɒtˈswɑːnə/
Brazil /brəˈzɪl/	**Brazilian** /brəˈzɪliən/
Britain /ˈbrɪt^{ə}n/	**British** /ˈbrɪtɪʃ/; *Person:* **Briton** /ˈbrɪt^{ə}n/
Brunei /bruːˈnaɪ/	**Bruneian** /bruːˈnaɪən/
Bulgaria /bʌlˈgeəriə/	**Bulgarian** /bʌlˈgeəriən/
Burkina Faso /bɜːˌkiːnə ˈfæseʊ/	**Burkinabe** /bɜːˈkiːnəˌbeɪ/
Burma /ˈbɜːmə/	**Burmese** /bɜːˈmiːz/
Burundi /bʊˈrʊndi/	**Burundian** /bʊˈrʊndiən/
Cambodia /ˌkæmˈbəʊdiə/	**Cambodian** /ˌkæmˈbəʊdiən/
Cameroon /ˌkæməˈruːn/	**Cameroonian** /ˌkæməˈruːniən/
Canada /ˈkænədə/	**Canadian** /kəˈneɪdiən/
Cape Verde /ˌkeɪp ˈvɜːd/	**Cape Verdean** /ˌkeɪp ˈvɜːdiən/
The Caribbean /ˌkærɪˈbiːən/	**Caribbean** /ˌkærɪˈbiːən/
The Central African Republic /ˌsentr^{ə}l ˌæfrɪkən rɪˈpʌblɪk/	**Central African** /ˌsentr^{ə}l ˈæfrɪkən/
Chad /tʃæd/	**Chadian** /ˈtʃædiən/
Chile /ˈtʃɪli/	**Chilean** /ˈtʃɪliən/
China /ˈtʃaɪnə/	**Chinese** /tʃaɪˈniːz/
Colombia /kəˈlɒmbiə/	**Colombian** /kəˈlɒmbiən/
Comoros /ˈkɒmərəʊz/	**Comoran** /kəˈmɔːrən/
The Democratic Republic of Congo /ˌdeməˌkrætɪk rɪˌpʌblɪk əv ˈkɒŋgəʊ/	**Congolese** /ˌkɒŋgəˈliːz/
The Republic of Congo /rɪˌpʌblɪk əv ˈkɒŋgəʊ/	**Congolese** /ˌkɒŋgəˈliːz/
Costa Rica /ˌkɒstə ˈriːkə/	**Costa Rican** /ˌkɒstə ˈriːkən/
Côte d'Ivoire /ˌkəʊt diːˈvwɑː^{r}/	**Ivorian** /aɪˈvɔːriən/
Croatia /krəʊˈeɪʃə/	**Croatian** /krəʊˈeɪʃ^{ə}n/; *Person:* **Croat** /ˈkrəʊæt/
Cuba /ˈkjuːbə/	**Cuban** /ˈkjuːbən/
Cyprus /ˈsaɪprəs/	**Cypriot** /ˈsɪpriət/
The Czech Republic /ˌtʃek rɪˈpʌblɪk/	**Czech** /tʃek/
Denmark /ˈdenmɑːk/	**Danish** /ˈdeɪnɪʃ/; *Person:* **Dane** /deɪn/
Djibouti /dʒɪˈbuːti/	**Djiboutian** /dʒɪˈbuːtiən/
Dominica /dəˈmɪnɪkə/	**Dominican** /dəˈmɪnɪkən/
The Dominican Republic /dəˌmɪnɪkən rɪˈpʌblɪk/	**Dominican** /dəˈmɪnɪkən/
East Timor /ˌiːst ˈtiːmɔː^{r}/	**East Timorese** /ˌiːst ˌtiːmɔːˈriːz/
Ecuador /ˈekwədɔː^{r}/	**Ecuadorian** /ˌekwəˈdɔːriən/
Egypt /ˈiːdʒɪpt/	**Egyptian** /ɪˈdʒɪpʃ^{ə}n/
El Salvador /ˌel ˈsælvədɔː^{r}/	**Salvadoran** /ˌsælvəˈdɔːrən/
England /ˈɪŋglənd/	**English** /ˈɪŋglɪʃ/; *Person:* **Englishman** /ˈɪŋglɪʃmən/
Equatorial Guinea /ˌekwətɔːriəl ˈgɪni/	**Equatorial Guinean** /ˌekwətɔːriəl ˈgɪniən/

Eritrea /ˌerɪˈtreɪə/	**Eritrean** /ˌerɪˈtreɪən/
Estonia /esˈtəʊniə/	**Estonian** /esˈtəʊniən/
Ethiopia /ˌiːθiˈəʊpiə/	**Ethiopian** /ˌiːθiˈəʊpiən/
Europe /ˈjʊərəp/	**European** /ˌjʊərəˈpiːən/
Fiji /ˈfiːdʒiː/	**Fijian** /fɪˈdʒiːən/
Finland /ˈfɪnlənd/	**Finnish** /ˈfɪnɪʃ/; *Person:* Finn /fɪn/
France /frɑːns/	**French** /frentʃ/; *Person:* Frenchman /ˈfrentʃmən/
Gabon /gæbˈɒn/	**Gabonese** /ˌgæbəˈniːz/
Gambia /ˈgæmbiə/	**Gambian** /ˈgæmbiən/
Georgia /ˈdʒɔːdʒə/	**Georgian** /ˈdʒɔːdʒən/
Germany /ˈdʒɜːməni/	**German** /ˈdʒɜːmən/
Ghana /ˈgɑːnə/	**Ghanaian** /gɑːˈneɪən/
Great Britain /ˌgreɪt ˈbrɪt^{ə}n/	**British** /ˈbrɪtɪʃ/; *Person:* Briton /ˈbrɪt^{ə}n/
Greece /griːs/	**Greek** /griːk/
Greenland /ˈgriːnlənd/	**Greenland** /ˈgriːnlənd/; *Person:* Greenlander /ˈgriːnləndə^{r}/
Grenada /grəˈneɪdə/	**Grenadian** /grəˈneɪdiən/
Guatemala /ˌgwɑːtəˈmɑːlə/	**Guatemalan** /ˌgwɑːtəˈmɑːlən/
Guinea /ˈgɪni/	**Guinean** /ˈgɪniən/
Guinea-Bissau /ˌgɪnibɪˈsaʊ/	**Guinea-Bissauan** /ˌgɪnibɪˈsaʊən/
Guyana /gaɪˈænə/	**Guyanese** /ˌgaɪəˈniːz/
Haiti /ˈheɪti/	**Haitian** /ˈheɪʃ^{ə}n/
Honduras /hɒnˈdjʊərəs/	**Honduran** /hɒnˈdjʊərən/
Hungary /ˈhʌŋg^{ə}ri/	**Hungarian** /hʌŋˈgeəriən/
Iceland /ˈaɪslənd/	**Icelandic** /aɪsˈlændɪk/; *Person:* Icelander /ˈaɪsləndə^{r}/
India /ˈɪndiə/	**Indian** /ˈɪndiən/
Indonesia /ˌɪndəˈniːʒə/	**Indonesian** /ˌɪndəˈniːʒ^{ə}n/
Iran /ɪˈrɑːn/	**Iranian** /ɪˈreɪniən/
Iraq /ɪˈrɑːk/	**Iraqi** /ɪˈrɑːki/
Ireland /ˈaɪələnd/	**Irish** /ˈaɪrɪʃ/; *Person:* Irishman /ˈaɪrɪʃmən/
Israel /ˈɪzreɪl/	**Israeli** /ɪzˈreɪli/
Italy /ˈɪt^{ə}li/	**Italian** /ɪˈtæliən/
Jamaica /dʒəˈmeɪkə/	**Jamaican** /dʒəˈmeɪkən/
Japan /dʒəˈpæn/	**Japanese** /ˌdʒæp^{ə}nˈiːz/
Jordan /ˈdʒɔːd^{ə}n/	**Jordanian** /dʒɔːˈdeɪniən/
Kazakhstan /ˌkæzækˈstɑːn/	**Kazakh** /ˈkæzæk/
Kenya /ˈkenjə/	**Kenyan** /ˈkenjən/
Kiribati /ˌkɪrəˈbæs/	**Kiribati** /ˌkɪrəˈbæs/
North Korea /ˌnɔːθ kəˈriːə/	**North Korean** /ˌnɔːθ kəˈriːən/
South Korea /ˌsaʊθ kəˈriːə/	**South Korean** /ˌsaʊθ kəˈriːən/
Kuwait /kuːˈweɪt/	**Kuwaiti** /kuːˈweɪti/
Kyrgyzstan /ˌkɜːgɪˈstɑːn/	**Kyrgyz** /ˈkɜːgɪz/
Laos /laʊs/	**Laotian** /ˈlaʊʃ^{ə}n/
Latvia /ˈlætviə/	**Latvian** /ˈlætviən/
Lebanon /ˈlebənən/	**Lebanese** /ˌlebəˈniːz/

Lesotho /ləˈsuːtuː/	**Basotho** /bəˈsuːtuː/; ***Person:*** Mosotho /məˈsuːtuː/
Liberia /laɪˈbɪəriə/	**Liberian** /laɪˈbɪəriən/
Libya /ˈlɪbiə/	**Libyan** /ˈlɪbiən/
Liechtenstein /ˈlɪktᵊnstaɪn/	**Liechtenstein** /ˈlɪktᵊnstaɪn/; ***Person:*** **Liechtensteiner** /ˈlɪktᵊnstaɪnəʳ/
Lithuania /ˌlɪθjuˈeɪniə/	**Lithuanian** /ˌlɪθjuˈeɪniən/
Luxembourg /ˈlʌksᵊmbɜːg/	**Luxembourg** /ˈlʌksᵊmbɜːg/; ***Person:*** **Luxembourger** /ˈlʌksᵊmbɜːgəʳ/
The Former Yugoslav Republic of Macedonia /ˌfɔːmə ˌjuːgəslɑːv rɪˌpʌblɪk əv ˌmæsəˈdəʊniə/	**Macedonian** /ˌmæsəˈdəʊniən/
Madagascar /ˌmædəˈgæskəʳ/	**Malagasy** /ˌmæləˈgæsi/
Malawi /məˈlɑːwi/	**Malawian** /məˈlɑːwiən/
Malaysia /məˈleɪziə/	**Malaysian** /məˈleɪziən/
The Maldives /ˈmɔːldiːvz/	**Maldivian** /mɔːlˈdɪviən/
Mali /ˈmɑːli/	**Malian** /ˈmɑːliən/
Malta /ˈmɔːltə/	**Maltese** /mɔːlˈtiːz/
The Marshall Islands /ˈmɑːʃᵊl ˌaɪləndz/	**Marshallese** /ˌmɑːʃᵊlˈiːz/
Mauritania /ˌmɒrɪˈteɪniə/	**Mauritanian** /ˌmɒrɪˈteɪniən/
Mauritius /məˈrɪʃəs/	**Mauritian** /məˈrɪʃᵊn/
Mexico /ˈmeksɪkəʊ/	**Mexican** /ˈmeksɪkᵊn/
Micronesia /ˌmaɪkrəˈniːziə/	**Micronesian** /ˌmaɪkrəˈniːziən/
Moldova /mɒlˈdəʊvə/	**Moldovan** /mɒlˈdəʊvən/
Monaco /ˈmɒnəkəʊ/	**Monégasque** /mɒneɪˈgæsk/
Mongolia /mɒŋˈgəʊliə/	**Mongolian** /mɒŋˈgəʊliən/
Montenegro /ˌmɒntɪˈniːgrəʊ/	**Montenegrin** /ˌmɒntɪˈniːgrən/
Morocco /məˈrɒkəʊ/	**Moroccan** /məˈrɒkən/
Mozambique /ˌməʊzæmˈbiːk/	**Mozambican** /ˌməʊzæmˈbiːkən/
Myanmar /ˈmjænmɑːʳ/	**Burmese** /bɜːˈmiːz/
Namibia /nəˈmɪbiə/	**Namibian** /nəˈmɪbiən/
Nauru /nɑːˈuːruː/	**Nauruan** /nɑːuːˈruːən/
Nepal /nəˈpɔːl/	**Nepalese** /ˌnepᵊlˈiːz/
The Netherlands /ˈneðələndz/	**Dutch** /dʌtʃ/; ***Person:*** Dutchman /ˈdʌtʃmən/
New Zealand /ˌnjuː ˈziːlənd/	**New Zealand** /ˌnjuː ˈziːlənd/; ***Person:*** **New Zealander** /ˌnjuː ˈziːləndəʳ/
Nicaragua /ˌnɪkᵊrˈægjuə/	**Nicaraguan** /ˌnɪkᵊrˈægjuən/
Niger /niːˈʒeəʳ/	**Nigerien** /niːˈʒeəriən/
Nigeria /naɪˈdʒɪəriə/	**Nigerian** /naɪˈdʒɪəriən/
Northern Ireland /ˌnɔːðᵊn ˈaɪələnd/	**Northern Irish** /ˌnɔːðᵊn ˈaɪrɪʃ/; ***Person:*** **Northern Irishman** /ˌnɔːðᵊn ˈaɪrɪʃmən/
Norway /ˈnɔːweɪ/	**Norwegian** /nɔːˈwiːdʒᵊn/
Oman /əʊˈmɑːn/	**Omani** /əʊˈmɑːni/
Pakistan /ˌpɑːkɪˈstɑːn/	**Pakistani** /ˌpɑːkɪˈstɑːni/
Palau /pəˈlaʊ/	**Palauan** /pəˈlaʊən/
Palestine /ˈpæləstaɪn/	**Palestinian** /ˌpæləˈstɪniən/
Panama /ˈpænəmɑː/	**Panamanian** /ˌpænəˈmeɪniən/

Papua New Guinea /ˌpæpuə njuː ˈgɪni/	**Papua New Guinean** /ˌpæpuə njuː ˈgɪniən/
Paraguay /ˈpærəgwaɪ/	**Paraguayan** /ˌpærəˈgwaɪən/
Peru /pəˈruː/	**Peruvian** /pəˈruːviən/
The Philippines /ˈfɪlɪpiːnz/	**Philippine** /ˈfɪlɪpiːn/; *Person:* **Filipino** /ˌfɪlɪˈpiːnəʊ/, **Filipina** /ˌfɪlɪˈpiːnə/
Poland /ˈpəʊlənd/	**Polish** /ˈpəʊlɪʃ/; *Person:* **Pole** /pəʊl/
Portugal /ˈpɔːtʃəg^{ə}l/	**Portuguese** /ˌpɔːtʃəˈgiːz/
Qatar /ˈkʌtɑː^{r}/	**Qatari** /kʌˈtɑːri/
Romania /rʊˈmeɪniə/	**Romanian** /rʊˈmeɪniən/
Russia /ˈrʌʃə/	**Russian** /ˈrʌʃ^{ə}n/
Rwanda /ruˈændə/	**Rwandan** /ruˈændən/
St Kitts and Nevis /s^{ə}nt kɪts ^{ə}nd ˈniːvɪs /	**Kittsian** /ˈkɪtsiən/, **Nevisian** /niːˈvɪsiən/
St Lucia /s^{ə}nt ˈluːʃə/	**St Lucian** /s^{ə}nt ˈluːʃ^{ə}n/
St Vincent and the Grenadines /s^{ə}nt ˌvɪns^{ə}nt ^{ə}nd ðə ˌgrenəˈdiːnz/	**Vincentian** /vɪnˈsɪntiən/
Samoa /səˈməʊə/	**Samoan** /səˈməʊən/
San Marino /ˌsæn məˈriːnəʊ/	**Sanmarinese** /ˌsænmærɪˈniːz/
São Tomé and Príncipe /ˌsaʊ təˌmeɪ ^{ə}nd ˈprɪnsɪpeɪ/	**São Tomean** /ˌsaʊ təˈmeɪən/
Saudi Arabia /ˌsaʊdi əˈreɪbiə/	**Saudi** /ˈsaʊdi/
Scandinavia /ˌskændɪˈneɪviə/	**Scandinavian** /ˌskændɪˈneɪviən/
Scotland /ˈskɒtlənd/	**Scottish** /ˈskɒtɪʃ/; *Person:* **Scot** /skɒt/, **Scotsman** /ˈskɒtsmən/
Senegal /ˌsenɪˈgɔːl/	**Senegalese** /ˌsenɪgəˈliːz/
Serbia /ˈsɜːbiə/	**Serbian** /ˈsɜːbiən/; *Person:* **Serb** /sɜːb/
The Seychelles /seɪˈʃelz/	**Seychelles** /seɪˈʃelz/; *Person:* **Seychellois** /ˌseɪʃelˈwɑː/
Sierra Leone /siˌerə liˈəʊn/	**Sierra Leonean** /siˌerə liˈəʊniən/
Singapore /ˌsɪŋəˈpɔː^{r}/	**Singaporean** /ˌsɪŋəˈpɔːriən/
Slovakia /sləˈvækiə/	**Slovak** /ˈsləʊvæk/
Slovenia /sləˈviːniə/	**Slovenian** /sləˈviːniən/; *Person:* **Slovene** /ˈsləʊviːn/
The Solomon Islands /ˈsɒləmən ˌaɪləndz/	**Solomon Islander** /ˈsɒləmən ˌaɪləndə^{r}/
Somalia /səˈmɑːliə/	**Somali** /səˈmɑːli/
South Africa /ˌsaʊθ ˈæfrɪkə/	**South African** /ˌsaʊθ ˈæfrɪkən/
Spain /speɪn/	**Spanish** /ˈspænɪʃ/; *Person:* **Spaniard** /ˈspænjəd/
Sri Lanka /ˌsriː ˈlæŋkə/	**Sri Lankan** /ˌsriː ˈlæŋkən/
Sudan /suːˈdɑːn/	**Sudanese** /ˌsuːd^{ə}nˈiːz/
Suriname /ˌsʊərɪˈnæm/	**Surinamese** /ˌsʊərɪnæmˈiːz/
Swaziland /ˈswɑːzilænd/	**Swazi** /ˈswɑːzi/
Sweden /ˈswiːd^{ə}n/	**Swedish** /ˈswiːdɪʃ/; *Person:* **Swede** /swiːd/
Switzerland /ˈswɪtsələnd/	**Swiss** /swɪs/
Syria /ˈsɪriə/	**Syrian** /ˈsɪriən/

Taiwan /ˌtaɪˈwɑːn/
Taiwanese /ˌtaɪwəˈniːz/

Tajikistan /tɑːˌdʒiːkɪˈstɑːn/
Tajik /tɑːˈdʒiːk/

Tanzania /ˌtænzəˈniːə/
Tanzanian /ˌtænzəˈniːən/

Thailand /ˈtaɪlænd/
Thai /taɪ/

Tibet /tɪˈbet/
Tibetan /tɪˈbetᵊn/

Togo /ˈtəʊgəʊ/
Togolese /ˌtəʊgəˈliːz/

Tonga /ˈtɒŋə/
Tongan /ˈtɒŋᵊn/

Trinidad and Tobago /ˌtrɪnɪdæd ᵊnd təˈbeɪgəʊ/
Trinidadian /ˌtrɪnɪˈdædiən/

Tunisia /tjuːˈnɪziə/
Tunisian /tjuːˈnɪziən/

Turkey /ˈtɜːki/
Turkish /ˈtɜːkɪʃ/; ***Person:*** Turk /tɜːk/

Turkmenistan /tɜːkˌmenɪˈstɑːn/
Turkmen /ˈtɜːkmen/

Tuvalu /tuːˈvɑːluː/
Tuvaluan /ˌtuːvɑːˈluːən/

Uganda /juːˈgændə/
Ugandan /juːˈgændən/

Ukraine /juːˈkreɪn/
Ukrainian /juːˈkreɪniən/

The United Arab Emirates /juːˌnaɪtɪd ˌærəb ˈemɪrəts/
Emirati /emɪˈrɑːti/

The United Kingdom (UK) /juːˌnaɪtɪd ˈkɪŋdəm/
British /ˈbrɪtɪʃ/; ***Person:*** **Briton** /ˈbrɪtᵊn/

The United States of America (USA) /juːˌnaɪtɪd ˌsteɪts əv əˈmerɪkə/
American /əˈmerɪkən/

Uruguay /ˈjʊərəgwaɪ/
Uruguayan /ˌjʊərəˈgwaɪən/

Uzbekistan /ʊzˌbekɪˈstɑːn/
Uzbek /ˈʊzbek/

Vanuatu /ˌvænuˈɑːtuː/
Vanuatuan /ˌvænuɑːˈtuːən/

Vatican City /ˌvætɪkən ˈsɪti/
Vatican /ˈvætɪkən/

Venezuela /ˌvenɪˈzweɪlə/
Venezuelan /ˌvenɪˈzweɪlən/

Vietnam /ˌvjetˈnæm/
Vietnamese /ˌvjetnəˈmiːz/

Wales /weɪlz/
Welsh /welʃ/; ***Person:*** **Welshman** /ˈwelʃmən/

Western Sahara /ˌwestən səˈhɑːrə/
Sahrawian /sɑːˈrɑːwiən/

Yemen /ˈjemən/
Yemeni /ˈjeməni/

Zambia /ˈzæmbiə/
Zambian /ˈzæmbiən/

Zimbabwe /zɪmˈbɑːbweɪ/
Zimbabwean /zɪmˈbɑːbwiən/